VALUATION

**MEASURING AND
MANAGING THE
VALUE OF
COMPANIES**

D1428610

Founded in 1807, John Wiley & Sons is the oldest independent publishing company in the United States. With offices in North America, Europe, Australia, and Asia, Wiley is globally committed to developing and marketing print and electronic products and services for our customers' professional and personal knowledge and understanding.

The Wiley Finance series contains books written specifically for finance and investment professionals as well as sophisticated individual investors and their financial advisers. Book topics range from portfolio management to e-commerce, risk management, financial engineering, valuation, and financial instrument analysis, as well as much more.

For a list of available titles, please visit our Web site at www.WileyFinance.com.

VALUATION

MEASURING AND MANAGING THE VALUE OF COMPANIES

FOURTH EDITION

McKinsey & Company

Tim Koller
Marc Goedhart
David Wessels

JOHN WILEY & SONS, INC.

106 2671
07-1510
ECON

About the Authors

The authors are all current or former consultants of McKinsey & Company's corporate finance practice. Collectively they have more than 50 years of experience in consulting and financial education.

McKinsey & Company is a management-consulting firm that helps leading corporations and organizations make distinctive, lasting, and substantial improvements in their performance. Over the past seven decades, the firm's primary objective has remained constant: to serve as an organization's most trusted external advisor on critical issues facing senior management. With consultants deployed from over 80 offices in more than 40 countries, McKinsey advises companies on strategic, operational, organizational, financial, and technological issues. The firm has extensive experience in all major industry sectors and primary functional areas, as well as in-depth expertise in high-priority areas for today's business leaders.

Tim Koller is a partner in McKinsey's New York office. He leads the firm's Corporate Performance Center and is a member of the leadership group of the firm's global corporate finance practice. In his 20 years in consulting Tim has served clients in North America and Europe on corporate strategy and capital markets, M&A transactions, and value-based management. He leads the firm's research activities in valuation and capital markets. He was formerly with Stern Stewart & Company, and Mobil Corporation. He received his MBA from the University of Chicago.

Marc Goedhart is an associate principal in McKinsey's Amsterdam office and a member of the leadership group of the firm's corporate finance practice in Europe. Marc has served clients across Europe on portfolio restructuring, capital markets, and M&A transactions. He taught finance as an assistant professor at Erasmus University in Rotterdam, where he also earned a PhD in finance.

David Wessels is an adjunct professor of finance at the Wharton School of the University of Pennsylvania. Named by *BusinessWeek* as one of America's top business school instructors, he teaches courses on investment banking and corporate valuation at the MBA and Executive MBA levels. David is also a director in Wharton's executive education group, serving on the executive development faculties of several Fortune 500 companies. David, a former consultant with McKinsey, received his PhD from the University of California at Los Angeles.

Preface

The first edition of this book appeared in 1990, and we are encouraged that it continues to attract readers around the world. We believe that the book has succeeded because the approach it advocates is grounded in universal economic principles. While we continue to improve, update, and expand the text as our experience grows and as business and finance continue to evolve, the fundamental principles do not change.

The 15 years since that first edition appeared have been a truly remarkable period in business history, and managers and investors continue to face the opportunities and challenges that emerged from it. For us, the events of the Internet boom and its demise have only strengthened our conviction in the core principles of value creation. This may seem illogical, given that one of the things we learned was that for some companies, during some periods of time, the stock market may not be a reliable indicator of value. Paradoxically, this has only strengthened our conviction that managers attune themselves even more to the underlying value of their company and how it can create more value, because signals from the stock market may not always be reliable.

This book's message is simple: Companies thrive when they create real economic value for their shareholders. Companies create value by investing capital at rates of return that exceed their cost of capital. These principles apply across time and geography. This book explains the core principles, describes how companies can increase value by applying the principles, and demonstrates the practical ways to implement the principles.

We wrote this book for managers (and future managers) and investors who want their companies to create value. It is a how-to book. We hope that it is a book that you will use again and again. If we have done our job well, it will soon be full of underlining, margin notations, and highlighting. This is no coffee-table book.

WHY THIS BOOK

This book began life as a handbook for McKinsey consultants. This beginning is reflected in the nature of the book. While it draws on leading-edge academic thinking, its purpose is practical application. It aims to demystify the field of valuation and to clarify the linkages between strategy and finance.

We believe that clear thinking about valuation, and skill in using valuation to guide business decisions, are prerequisites for success. CEOs, business managers, and financial managers alike do not always understand value well enough. But they must understand it if they are to do their jobs well and fulfill their responsibilities.

In this book, we hope to lift the veil on valuation by explaining, step-by-step, how to do it well. We spell out valuation frameworks that we use in our consulting work, and we bring these frameworks to life with detailed case studies that highlight the practical judgments involved in developing and using valuations. Most important, we discuss how to use valuation to make good decisions about courses of action for a company.

This book will help business managers better understand how to:

- Decide among alternative business strategies by estimating the value of each strategic choice.
- Develop a corporate portfolio strategy, understanding which business units a corporate parent is best positioned to own, and which might perform better under someone else's ownership.
- Assess major transactions, including acquisitions, divestitures, and restructurings.
- Improve a company's performance management systems to better align an organization's various parts to create value.
- Design an effective capital structure to support the corporation's strategy and minimize the risk of financial distress.

INTELLECTUAL FOUNDATIONS

Valuation is an age-old methodology in finance. Its intellectual origins lie in the present value method of capital budgeting and in the valuation approach developed by Professors Merton Miller and Franco Modigliani (both Nobel laureates) in their 1961 *Journal of Business* article entitled "Dividend Policy, Growth and the Valuation of Shares." Our intellectual debt is primarily to them, but others have gone far to popularize their approach. In particular, Professor Alfred Rappaport (Northwestern University) and Joel

Stern (Stern Stewart & Co.) were among the first to extend the Miller-Modigliani enterprise valuation formula to real-world applications.

STRUCTURE OF THE BOOK

The book is organized in four parts. Part One provides the fundamental principles of value creation. Part Two is a step-by-step approach to valuing a company. Part Three applies value creation principles to managerial problems. Part Four deals with more complex valuation issues and special cases.

Part One provides an overview of value creation. Chapter 1 makes the case that managers should focus on long-term value creation, despite the capital market turmoil of the past several years. In Chapter 2 we develop a picture of what it means to be a value manager through a detailed case study based on the actual experiences of a CEO who needed to restructure his company and create a culture dedicated to managing for value. Chapter 3 summarizes the basic principles of value creation using both a simple case example and a rigorous derivation of these principles. Chapter 4 provides the empirical evidence supporting the discounted cash flow (DCF) view of valuation.

Part Two—Chapters 5 through 12—is a self-contained handbook for using discounted cash flow to value a company. A reader will learn how to analyze historical performance, forecast free cash flows, estimate the appropriate opportunity cost of capital, identify sources of value, and interpret results. As further guidance to the practitioner, we walk through the valuation of a company (Heineken) from an outside perspective, using publicly available information. We also show how to use multiples of comparable companies to supplement DCF valuation.

Part Three applies the value creation principles to the issues that managers face. Chapter 13 provides a framework for evaluating corporate performance, incorporating both short-term financial performance and indicators of a company's "health," or its ability to create value over the long term. Chapter 14 explains how to align a company's performance management process with value creation. Chapters 15 and 16 explore creating value through mergers, acquisitions, and divestitures. Chapter 17 will guide managers as they make capital structure decisions to create value. Finally, Chapter 18 examines ways companies can improve their communications with the financial markets.

Part Four—Chapters 19 through 25—is devoted to valuation in more complex situations. We explore the challenges of valuing high-growth companies, companies in emerging markets, multibusiness companies, cyclical companies, banks, and insurance companies. In addition, we show the way uncertainty and flexibility affect value and the application of option pricing theory and decision trees.

WHAT'S NEW ABOUT THE FOURTH EDITION

With the fourth edition, we continue to expand the practical application of finance to real business problems, reflecting the economic events of the past decade, new developments in academic finance, and the authors' own experiences. Most of the case examples and empirical analyses have been updated, and we have reflected changes in accounting rules. We have enhanced the global perspective in the book, with extensive examples and data from outside the United States, including discussions of both U.S. and international accounting standards, as well as a chapter dedicated to emerging markets.

We have substantially expanded or revised most chapters to add insights on practical applications. Among them:

- *Do Fundamentals Really Drive the Stock Market?* (Chapter 4), which describes the empirical evidence to support discounted cash flows, now includes a discussion of the emerging area of behavioral finance.
- *Frameworks for Valuation* (Chapter 5) has been expanded to provide a more detailed overview of the alternative DCF techniques, such as the adjusted present value (APV) method.
- *Forecasting Performance* (Chapter 8) now includes practical tips on building robust financial models.
- *Estimating the Cost of Capital* (Chapter 10) contains a new discussion on the market risk premium based on recent empirical work as well as alternative models to the Capital Asset Pricing Model (CAPM) and practical ways to estimate beta.
- *Calculating and Interpreting Results* (Chapter 11) includes a more detailed discussion of how to estimate the value of nonoperating assets and liabilities, such as unfunded pensions and stock options.
- *Creating Value through Mergers and Acquisitions* (Chapter 15) and *Creating Value through Divestitures* (Chapter 16) have added practical approaches to evaluating deals and estimating synergies.
- *Valuing Flexibility* (Chapter 20) incorporates a systematic approach to comparing option pricing and decision trees as a way to value flexibility.
- *Cross-Border Valuation* (Chapter 21) has been recast to account for the fact that most major European and Asian companies have adopted International Financial Reporting Standards.

In addition, the fourth edition has five new chapters, including:

- *Thinking about Return on Invested Capital and Growth* (Chapter 6) introduces return on capital and growth as the key drivers of value. This chapter helps executives forecast ROIC and growth by providing historical evidence on the long-term performance of companies.
- *Using Multiples for Valuation* (Chapter 12) explores how to use multiples to draw additional insights about valuation from comparable companies, keeping the focus on DCF valuation.
- *Performance Measurement* (Chapter 13) explores the complexities of measuring corporate performance, particularly the imperative to analyze a company's long-term health on par with its short-term financial performance.
- *Capital Structure* (Chapter 17) provides a practical perspective on the impact of capital structure on corporate value and explains how executives can use capital structure (including decisions about debt levels, dividends, and share repurchases) to support their corporate strategies.
- *Investor Communications* (Chapter 18) grounds investor communications in rigorous analysis of a company's value, its strategy story, and its current and potential investor base.

VALUATION SPREADSHEET

An Excel spreadsheet valuation model is available on a CD-ROM or via web download. This valuation model is similar to the model we use in practice. Practitioners will find the model easy to use in a variety of situations: mergers and acquisitions, valuing business units for restructuring or value-based management, or testing the implications of major strategic decisions on the value of your company. We accept no responsibility for any decisions based on your inputs to the model. If you would like to purchase the model on CD, ISBN 0-471-70217-X, please call (800) 225-5945, or visit www.WileyValuation.com to purchase the model via web download, ISBN 0-471-73389-X.

Acknowledgments

No book is solely the effort of its authors. This book is certainly no exception, especially since it grew out of the collective work of McKinsey's corporate finance practice and the experiences of its consultants throughout the world.

Most important, we would like to thank Tom Copeland and Jack Murrin, two of the coauthors on the first three editions of this book. We are deeply indebted to them for establishing the early success of this book, for mentoring the current authors, and for their hard work in providing the foundations that this edition builds on.

Ennius Bergsma also deserves our special thanks. Ennius initiated the development of McKinsey's corporate finance practice in the mid-1980s. He inspired the original internal McKinsey valuation handbook and mustered the support and sponsorship to turn that handbook into a real book for an external audience.

We would also like to acknowledge those who shaped our knowledge of valuation, corporate finance, and strategy. For their support and teachings, we thank Tony Bernardo, Bob Holthausen, Rob Kazanjian, Ofer Nemirovsky, Eduardo Schwartz, Jaap Spronk, Sunil Wahal, and Ivo Welch.

A number of colleagues worked closely with us on the fourth edition, providing support that was essential to the completion of this edition. André Annema, one of the longest serving members of our European corporate finance practice, led much of the analysis for three chapters: Do Fundamentals Really Drive the Stock Market? (Chapter 4) with assistance from Terence Nahar and Fredrik Gustavsson; Creating Value through Divestitures (Chapter 16); and Cross-Border Valuation (Chapter 21). Bin Jiang, with the support of Carrie Chen, conducted the analysis for Chapter 6, Thinking about Return on Invested Capital and Growth, using the Corporate Performance database that she has been developing for McKinsey, and which was inspired by Dick Foster. Nidhi Chadda assisted with Chapter 12, on Using Multiples for Valuation. Richard Dobbs co-wrote Chapter 13, Performance Measurement and Chapter 14, Performance Management, with support from Paul Todd, Vanessa Lau, and Joe Hughes. Werner Rehm co-wrote Chapter 15, Creating Value through Mergers and Acquisitions. Chapter 16, Creating Value through Divestitures, draws on work by Lee Dranikoff and Antoon Schneider. Régis Huc supported the analyses for Chapter 17, Capital Structure, which benefited from the credit rating models developed by Harry Markl and Michael Rudolf. Jean-Hugues Monier, Paul Adam, and Yuri Maslov provided support in the preparation of Chapter 18, Investor Communications. This chapter also draws on work by Kevin Coyne and Jonathan Witter. S. R. Rajan drove the work on Chapter 19, Valuing Multibusiness Companies. Marijn de Wit supported the case examples in Chapter 20, Valuing Flexibility. William Jones and Gustavo Wigman contributed to Chapter 22, Valuation in Emerging Markets, and Alexandre Amson and Fabienne Moimaux provided support for the analyses. Marco de Heer's dissertation formed the basis for Chapter 24, Valuing Cyclical Companies. Susan Nolen Foushee co-wrote Chapter 25, Valuing Financial Institutions. Meg Smoot, Yasser Salem, Martijn Olthof, and Neha Patel helped prepare the analysis and valuation of Heineken that appears throughout the book. Neha Patel and Yan Yang helped update the valuation model CD. We thank them all for their insights and hard work.

We would like to thank again all those who contributed to the first three editions. We owe a special debt to Dave Furer for help and late nights developing the original drafts of this book more than 15 years ago. The first three editions and this edition drew upon work, ideas, and analyses from Carlos Abad, Petri Allas, Buford Alexander, Pat Anslinger, Vladimir Antikarov, Ali Asghar, Bill Barnett, Dan Bergman, Olivier Berlage, Peter Bisson, the late Joel Bleeke, Steve Coley, Johan Depraetere, Mikel Dodd, Will Draper, Christian von Drathen, David Ernst, Bill Fallon, George Fenn, Russ Fradin, Gabriel Garcia, Alo Ghosh, Irina Grigorenko, Keiko Honda, Alice Hu, Mimi James, Chris Jones, Phil Keenan, Phil Kholos, David Krieger, Shyanjaw Kuo, Kurt Losert, Bill Lewis, Perry Moilinoff, Mike Murray, Juan Ocampo, John Patience, Bill Pursche, Frank Richter, David Rothschild, Silvia Stefini, Konrad Stiglbrunner, Ahmed Taha, Bill Trent, David Twiddy, Valerie Udale, Sandeep Vaswani, Kim Vogel, Jon Weiner, Jack Welch, David Willensky, Pieter de Wit, and David Wright.

For help in preparing the manuscript and coordinating the flow of paper, e-mails, and phone calls, we owe our thanks to our assistants, Kimberly Davenport, Lynette Murray, Eveline de Bruijn, and Denise de Jong.

We also extend thanks to the team at John Wiley & Sons, including Pamela van Giessen, Jennifer MacDonald, and Mary Daniello.

Of course, we could not have devoted the time and energy to this book without the support and encouragement of McKinsey's corporate finance practice leadership, in particular Richard Dobbs, Bernie Ferrari, Christian Caspar, and Jan Willem Breen. We are also indebted to Fred Gluck, a former managing director of McKinsey, who supported the creation of the corporate finance practice in the late 1980s and who played a vital role in creating a knowledge-building culture within McKinsey.

Stuart Flack, in addition to providing moral support based on his experience with other book projects, ensured that we received superior editorial support from McKinsey's external publishing team.

Joanne Mason, along with Richard Dobbs and Bill Javetski, planned and executed the launch of this book, helping us to get the word out, orchestrating articles, speeches, and meetings. When we thought our task complete with the writing of the manuscript, they gently reminded us otherwise and kept us going.

Dennis Swinford oversaw the production of the more than 300 exhibits in this book, a truly Herculean task given the variety of formats and technologies employed. We are grateful for his hard work and patience.

Bill Javetski was in many ways the fourth author of this book. He edited the entire manuscript, ensuring consistency of style and structure. Most important, he served as our coach, sounding board, and occasional arbiter, participating in every meeting and conference call among the authors, debating the structure of each chapter, and helping us find the best language to make it accessible to every reader. Karen Schenkenfelder provided careful editing and feedback throughout the process. Sue Catapano diligently checked important references.

The University Edition of this book includes end-of-chapter questions and an instructor's resource guide based on the material in this book. In addition, a professional workbook accompanies this book. We would like to thank Professor Jeffrey P. Lessard at the Rochester Institute of Technology for preparing the questions for the University Edition and for creating the *Valuation Workbook*. This workbook, originally developed by Bill Foote, is an important complement to the text for practitioners and students alike.

Finally, thank you to Melissa Koller, Monique Donders, Jennifer Wessels, and our children. Our wives and families are our true inspirations. This book would not have been possible without their encouragement, support, and sacrifice.

Contents

VALUATION

MEASURING AND MANAGING THE VALUE OF COMPANIES

Part One

Foundations of Value

1

Why Maximize Value?

Chief executives from North America to Europe and Asia may be forgiven if they appear perplexed as they try to figure out how to lead their companies following the tumultuous business evolution of the past decade. A 20-year bull market in equities that began in 1980 carried nearly every company on an upward spiral of wealth generation. Shareholders who reaped these rewards cheered CEOs even as executives built up lucrative stock option packages and in some cases attained rock-star celebrity status. By the time the Internet frenzy peaked at the end of the 1990s, even staunch traditionalists like Warren Buffett pondered whether the economy had entered a new era of prosperity unbounded by traditional constraints. Some economists took to questioning long-held tenets of competitive advantage, and "new economy" analysts asked, with the utmost seriousness, why a three-year-old-money-losing Internet purveyor of pet supplies *shouldn't* be worth more than a billion dollars.

The subsequent market crash left aftershocks that have yet to be sorted out as we prepare this book. The Internet, source of the dot-com fever, continues to change the way we shop, communicate, and manage; but its assault on the fundamental laws of economics has been brusquely turned back. The sky-high market capitalizations of many Internet companies proved to be simply unsustainable, and their plunge has left a generation of chastened investors in search of a new approach. A flurry of major corporate accounting scandals turned hero CEOs into villains, spawned government investigations and new regulations, and unleashed a new spirit of shareholder activism whose impact on corporate governance has yet to fully play out. For their part, U.S. business groups have begun to challenge the authority of regulators to impose new rules.

Ironically, one thing that did not change was the stock market's obsession with quarterly earnings. This focus continues to confront business leaders with the dilemma of often having to choose between short-term results and the long-term health of the companies they lead.

3

The good news? Amid this angst and uncertainty, executives and investors alike can draw reassurance from an important trend that has gained momentum even through years of the market's twists and turns. More and more investors, analysts, and investment bankers are turning to fundamental financial analysis and sophisticated discounted cash flow (DCF) models as the touchstone of corporate valuation.

This book explains how to value companies using the DCF approach and apply that information to make wiser business and investment decisions. With DCF, assumptions about a company's profits and cash flows years down the road determine a company's stock price. Using it, CEOs can focus on long-term value creation, confident that their stock's market price will eventually reflect their efforts. This is not a book for traders looking to profit from short-term movements in share prices. Nor is it intended for managers trying to manage their company's share price from quarter to quarter. It's purpose is to help managers looking to create lasting value in their companies.

Managers who focus on shareholder value create healthier companies, which in turn provide spillover benefits, such as stronger economies, higher living standards, and more employment opportunities. Our central message: Companies thrive when they create real economic value for their shareholders.

The movement underway to improve corporate governance will encourage companies to focus on long-term value creation. Managers and board members, therefore, should set long-term shareholder value creation as their primary objective. This book tells managers how, explaining specifically what it means to create sustainable value and how to measure value creation.

In the chapters that follow, we lay out the principles of value creation with examples and supporting empirical evidence. Companies create value by investing capital at rates of return that exceed their cost of capital. The more capital they can invest at attractive rates of return, the more value they will create, and as long as returns on capital exceed the cost of that capital, faster growth will create more value. Furthermore, value creation plans must always be grounded in realistic assessments of product market opportunities and the competitive environment. We also explore how value creation principles must be part of important decisions such as corporate strategy, mergers, acquisitions, divestitures, capital structure, and investor communications. We explain why value creation should be part of a company's culture and how it manages itself on a day-to-day basis. And we provide detailed explanations for measuring value.

These fundamental principles have been around for a long time, and the events of the recent past have only strengthened our conviction in them. This may seem counterintuitive, since we learned during the recent past that financial markets may not have been as efficient as we thought they were. At times, the stock market may not be a reliable indicator of a company's intrinsic value. Paradoxically, the fact that markets can deviate from intrinsic values means that managers have to be more attuned to the underlying value of their businesses and how their companies go about creating value, because they can't always rely on signals from the stock market.

Specifically, managers must not only have a theoretical understanding of value creation, but must be able to create tangible links between their strategies and value creation. This means, for example, focusing less on recent financial performance and more on what they are doing to create a "healthy" company that can create value over the longer term. It means having a thorough grounding in the economics of an industry and setting aspirations accordingly. Once they've mastered the economics of value creation, they need to be able to educate their internal and external constituents. They need to install performance management systems that encourage real value creation, not merely short-term accounting results. Finally, they need to educate their investors about how and when the company will create value.

These principles apply equally to mature manufacturing companies and high-growth technology companies. They apply to companies in all geographies. When managers, boards of directors, and investors forget these simple truths, the consequences can be destructive. Consider the rise and fall of business conglomerates in the 1970s, hostile takeovers in the United States in the 1980s, the collapse of Japan's bubble economy in the 1990s, the Southeast Asian crisis in 1998, the Internet bubble, and the corporate governance scandals of the late 1990s.

We begin this chapter by arguing that, from a long-term perspective, the stock market does indeed track the fundamental performance of companies and the economy. When deviations arise, they typically come from individual sectors and rarely last more than a couple of years. Deviations from fundamentals occur when companies, investors and bankers ignore the principles of economics or assume that they have changed.

MARKETS TRACK ECONOMIC FUNDAMENTALS

The U.S. stock market's behavior from 1980 through today has confused and frustrated investors and managers. For roughly 20 of those years, the market was quite bullish as the Standard & Poor's (S&P) 500 index rose from a level of 108 in January 1980 to 1,469 in December 1999. Including dividends, the nominal annual return to shareholders was 17 percent, or 13 percent after adjusting for inflation, more than double the 6½ percent average annual return that stocks have delivered over the past 100 years. By early 2000, many investors had come to expect consistently high returns from equity investing. Then the market abruptly fell, tumbling more than 30 percent over the next three years. Such a large run-up, followed by such a sharp decline, led many to question whether the stock market was anything more than a giant roulette table, essentially unconnected to the real world.

The stock market's performance, however, can be explained. More important, the explanation derives directly from the real economy, in terms of inflation, interest rates, growth in gross domestic product, and corporate profits. This relationship may not be perfect, but research shows that deviations from what we call a company's fundamental, or intrinsic, value based on financial performance and risk, tend to be short-lived and most often limited to certain industrial or service sectors.

The stock market's real surprise lies, not in the occurrence of spectacular share price bubbles, but rather in how closely the market has mirrored economic fundamentals throughout a century of technological revolutions, monetary changes, political and economic crises, and wars. And it is not just true for the U.S. stock market. We believe stock markets in the United States, Europe, and Asia correctly reflect these regions' different underlying economic prospects.

The Stock Market's Long-Term Returns

U.S. equities over the past 200 years have on average returned about 6½ percent annually, adjusted for inflation. Spectacular market bubbles, crashes, or scandals occasionally captivate public attention, as they did during the recent high-tech market frenzy, the accounting scandals of the late 1990s, the Black Monday crash in October 1987, the leveraged-buyout craze of the 1980s, and of course the great Wall Street crash of 1929. But against the backdrop of decade after decade of consistent stock returns, the effect of any of these single events pales. At a minimum, as Exhibit 1.1 shows, stock markets are far from chaotic and do not lead a life of their own.

That 6½ percent long-term real return on common stocks is no random number either. Its origins lie in the fundamental performance of companies and the returns investors have expected for taking on the risk of investing in companies. One way to understand this linkage is to examine the economy's underlying performance and its relationship to stocks. After adjusting for inflation, median price-to-earnings ratios (P/E) tend to revert to a normal level of about 15, suggesting that the typical investor's risk-return trade-offs haven't changed much over the past 100 years. Assuming that investor risk preferences have not changed, we can easily connect shareholders' long-term returns with the fundamental performance of companies. Over the past 70 years, real corporate profits have grown about 3 to 3.5 percent per year. If P/E ratios revert to a normal level over time, stock prices should also increase about 3 to 3.5 percent per year. In addition, corporate

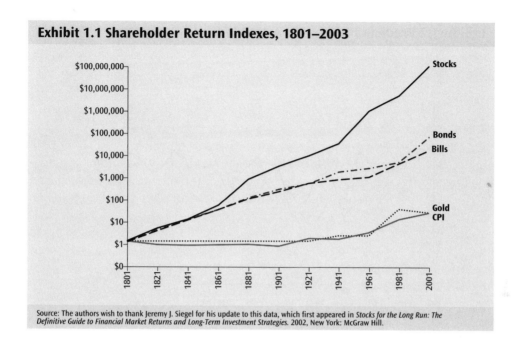

Exhibit 1.1 Shareholder Return Indexes, 1801–2003

Source: The authors wish to thank Jeremy J. Siegel for his update to this data, which first appeared in *Stocks for the Long Run: The Definitive Guide to Financial Market Returns and Long-Term Investment Strategies.* 2002, New York: McGraw Hill.

America, as a whole, typically reinvests about 50 percent of its profits every year to achieve this profit growth, leaving the other half to pay to shareholders as dividends and share repurchases. This translates to a cash yield to shareholders of about 3 to 3.5 percent at the long-term average P/E ratio of 15.[1] Adding the annual 3 to 3.5 percent increase in share prices to the cash yield of 3 to 3.5 percent results in total real shareholder returns of about 6½ percent per year.

The Link between Market Price Levels and Fundamentals

Now we need to look at the level of the stock market at different points in time and compare that with what one might expect, given the fundamental performance of companies and the economy. The results show that the overall market tracks our expected fundamental value closely over the past 40 years.

Using a discounted cash flow model, we estimated the intrinsic value for the median company in the U.S. stock market for each year from 1962 to 2003 (see Chapter 4 for more details). We used long-term trends to project

---

[1] The payout ratio is driven by a company's growth and its return on capital. The 50 percent payout ratio is based on a typical company earning a 12 percent return on equity and growing at 3.5 percent in real terms, or 5 to 6 percent including inflation. The cash yield of 3.5 percent equals the inverse of the price-earnings ratio times the payout ratio.

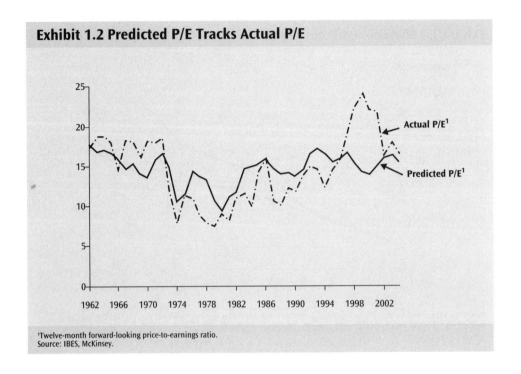

Exhibit 1.2 Predicted P/E Tracks Actual P/E

[1]Twelve-month forward-looking price-to-earnings ratio.
Source: IBES, McKinsey.

profit growth, the cost of equity, and returns on equity. We based inflation projections on the most recent year's inflation. To keep the scale constant, we expressed fundamental values in terms of P/E ratios.

Exhibit 1.2 compares our resulting intrinsic values with actual P/E ratios for the median company. As you can see, the P/E ratios associated with our estimates of intrinsic value track the actual P/E ratios, except for the late 1990s Internet bubble. The stock market follows a clear and simple economic logic over the long term; there is not much complexity or chaos in these patterns, despite what some have argued. We conducted similar tests—and found similar results—in the United Kingdom and broader European markets.

What Was behind the 20-Year Bull Market . . .

During the prolonged bull market in the United States from 1980 to 1999, many investors concluded that this period of growth meant that the stock market had somehow changed. From then on, they figured, companies would be valued permanently higher, and high returns would continue for a long time to come. Many investors and commentators simply extrapolated from the recent past, predicting ongoing high returns because they could perceive nothing that would stop them. Others developed reasoned arguments to back the same view. In 1999, two economists, James Glassman and Kevin Hassett, published a book titled *Dow 36,000: The New Strategy for Profiting from the Coming Rise in the Stock Market.*[2] Glassman and Hassett predicted that the Dow Jones Industrial Average would reach 36,000 sometime in the 2002 to 2004 period, after rising from 700 in 1980 to 11,000 in 1999. They argued that investors were beginning to realize that stocks were low risk, and were thus bidding up stock prices. Others argued that stocks were gaining broader acceptance and that higher demand for stocks would push up prices.

These investors and commentators had failed to understand the real factors behind the long bull market. In our analysis, we identified three elements that were responsible for nearly all the change in the broad market index. The first two, growth in earnings and declines in interest rates and inflation, were precisely the factors one would expect to influence share prices. The third was the temporary emergence of what we call *mega-capitalization* stocks associated with the Internet bubble of the late 1990s (see Exhibit 1.3).

Between 1980 and 1999, earnings per share for the S&P 500 rose from $15 to $56. If the forward P/E ratio had remained constant, earnings growth alone would have boosted the index by 302 points. This nominal annual growth in earnings of 6.9 percent equals 3.2 percent in real terms, close to the long-term average growth in real profits for the economy.

Simultaneously, U.S. interest rates and inflation fell dramatically. Long-term U.S. government bond yields peaked at nearly 15 percent in 1981 and then fell, more or less steadily, to 5.7 percent in 1999. The decline in inflation and interest rates drove P/E ratios back up to more typical levels. This occurred because during the high-inflation years, companies were unable to increase returns on capital commensurate with the rise in cost of capital, leading to extremely low P/E ratios.

We attribute much of the remaining increase to a lopsided distribution of value within the index. Between 1997 and 1999, a handful of companies, including Cisco, EMC, and General Electric, attained market capitalizations in the hundreds of billions of dollars, at very high P/E ratios. By 1999, the average P/E of these megacap stocks, representing the 30 largest companies in the index, was twice that of the other 470. Such a divergence in P/E ratios had no precedent in the prior 40 years and has not been definitively explained. As this gap emerged, the resulting increase in forward P/E ratios

[2] J. Glassman and K. Hassett, *Dow 36,000: The New Strategy for Profiting from the Coming Rise in the Stock Market* (New York: Times Books, 1999).

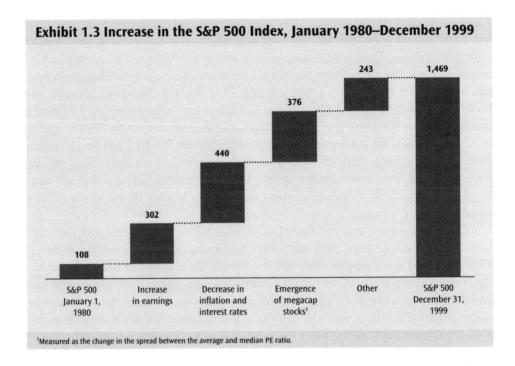

Exhibit 1.3 Increase in the S&P 500 Index, January 1980–December 1999

S&P 500 January 1, 1980	Increase in earnings	Decrease in inflation and interest rates	Emergence of megacap stocks[1]	Other	S&P 500 December 31, 1999
108	302	440	376	243	1,469

[1]Measured as the change in the spread between the average and median PE ratio.

accounted for an additional 376 points of the increase in the S&P 500 from 1980 to 1999.

. . . And the Bear Market That Followed

The same factors were at work as the index tumbled almost 40 percent between the end of 1999 and the end of 2002. Much of the decline was due to a reversal of the gap in P/Es between the megacap stocks and the rest of the market.

In 1999, investors should have realized that share prices could not continue increasing at 17 percent per year. Whereas they might count on corporate profits to continue increasing as the economy grew, interest rates and inflation had reached very low levels and were not likely to boost P/E ratios by declining further. Whether or not you believed that the valuations of the megacap stocks were valid, it would have been unreasonable to expect that they could continue to boost the overall market's P/E in the way they had previously.

Dissecting the causes of the 20-year bull market and the bear market that followed demonstrates something else, too: Periodic deviations from fundamental values do occur. Fortunately, these deviations tend to be concentrated in a small number of stocks, as shown by the behavior of the market in the late 1990s and early 2000s.

Stocks Behaving Badly

Consider the distribution of shareholder returns stretching from March 1997 through March 2000. In Exhibit 1.4, the bars represent the number of companies in the S&P 500 that increased, by a given amount, over the period. The light-gray bars represent companies in the Technology-Media-Telecommunications (TMT) sector. The dark-gray bars represent the megacap companies. The distribution is somewhat normal, but the TMT and megacap stocks are skewed to the right with the highest returns. The non-TMT stocks increased a median of 21 percent, whereas the megacap and TMT stocks increased a median of 62 percent.

The bear market that settled in between March 2000 and March 2003 was a reversal of the TMT bubble (see Exhibit 1.5). The majority of large decliners were the TMT and megacap companies. In fact, the median S&P 500 company declined only 8 percent from peak to trough, while the index itself, which is value weighted, to give more clout to the mostly highly valued companies, declined by almost 40 percent. Interestingly, fully 40 percent of the companies in the S&P 500 actually increased in value during the bear market.

Most of the companies in the S&P 500 index never went through the major gyrations of the TMT sectors. In other words, the U.S. stock market bubble of the late 1990s was for the most part a large sector bubble. Sector

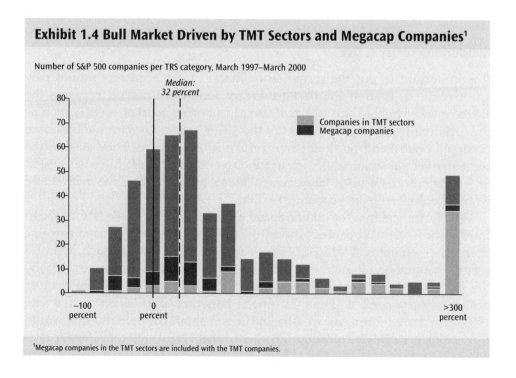

Exhibit 1.4 Bull Market Driven by TMT Sectors and Megacap Companies[1]

Number of S&P 500 companies per TRS category, March 1997–March 2000

Median: 32 percent

Companies in TMT sectors
Megacap companies

−100 percent   0 percent   >300 percent

[1] Megacap companies in the TMT sectors are included with the TMT companies.

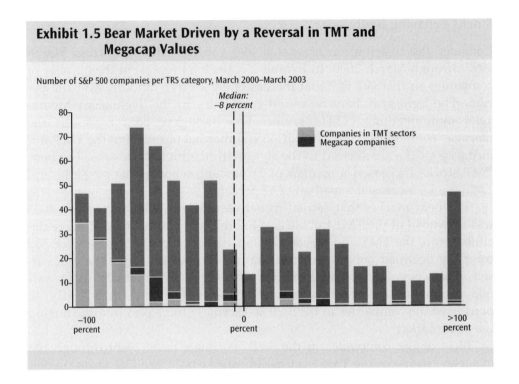

Exhibit 1.5 Bear Market Driven by a Reversal in TMT and Megacap Values

Number of S&P 500 companies per TRS category, March 2000–March 2003

Median: −8 percent

Companies in TMT sectors
Megacap companies

−100 percent

0 percent

>100 percent

bubbles occur frequently, but generally they are not large enough to distort a broad market index such as the S&P 500.

Maintaining Perspective

It is important to put the recent stock market bubble into its proper perspective. First, against the background of long-term market returns, the 1990s' market bubble was not as dramatic as other market events, such as the inflation-induced bear market of the 1970s. Second, sector bubbles have occurred before and no doubt will return in the future. They arise when some market players do not stick to fundamental economic rules because of greed, ignorance, or both. However, this does not mean that the market as a whole is detached from economic reality.

The European markets experienced a similar bubble in the late 1990s. In Europe, however, companies beyond the TMT sectors experienced extreme share price changes. Thus, the European bear market was much less of a sector phenomenon than it was in the United States. We are not certain why the European boom and bust was broader and flatter, but several factors probably influenced it. First, Europe's monetary unification in the late 1990s may have produced excessive optimism about the benefits that would flow from growth and productivity increases resulting from deeper economic integration. When the U.S. market turned down, the euphoria may have triggered an overly pessimistic response on the part of investors.

Another factor may have been that Europe's corporate incumbents stood more likely to capture benefits from the new economy than their United States counterparts, where small start-up companies were better financed. Finally, European investors may have bid up prices to match those of the U.S. market without fully grasping that U.S. stock prices were mainly driven by TMT stocks, a sector that has a far more modest role in Europe.

Cross-Country Comparisons

Differences in fundamental economic performance also explain variations in performance from country to country. A look at the 100-year real returns for the stock markets of 16 countries shows a range of returns from 2.5 percent per year in Belgium to 7.6 percent in Sweden, with most countries between 4.5 percent and 7.0 percent, as shown in Exhibit 1.6. Anecdotally, the countries with the lowest returns have been those that experienced the most economic upheaval, often with long periods of high inflation, civil strife, or defeat in war. The high returns in South Africa and Australia flowed from these countries' dependence on metals and mining, sectors that happened to earn high returns during this period. Also, most of these markets have relatively few companies listed on stock markets, compared with the United States and United Kingdom, so they may not be representative of the entire economy.

In addition to higher returns in the United States, P/E and market-to-book ratios have been significantly higher for the U.S. market when

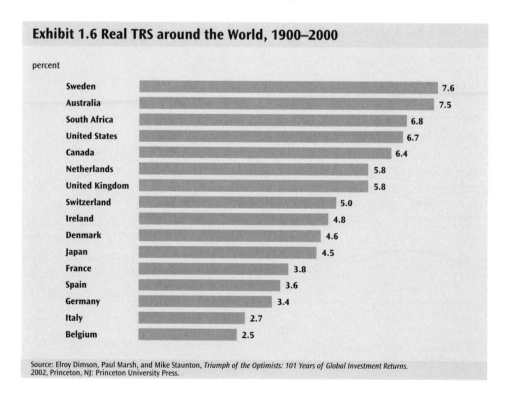

Exhibit 1.6 Real TRS around the World, 1900–2000

percent

Country	Percent
Sweden	7.6
Australia	7.5
South Africa	6.8
United States	6.7
Canada	6.4
Netherlands	5.8
United Kingdom	5.8
Switzerland	5.0
Ireland	4.8
Denmark	4.6
Japan	4.5
France	3.8
Spain	3.6
Germany	3.4
Italy	2.7
Belgium	2.5

Source: Elroy Dimson, Paul Marsh, and Mike Staunton, *Triumph of the Optimists: 101 Years of Global Investment Returns.* 2002, Princeton, NJ: Princeton University Press.

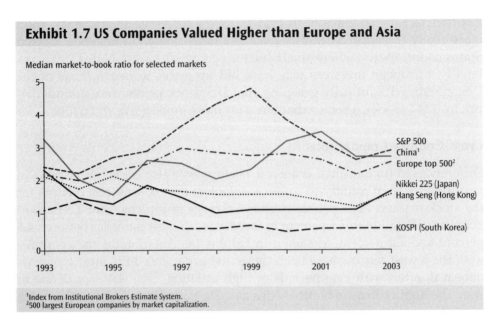

Exhibit 1.7 US Companies Valued Higher than Europe and Asia

Median market-to-book ratio for selected markets

[1] Index from Institutional Brokers Estimate System.
[2] 500 largest European companies by market capitalization.

compared with Europe and key Asian markets (see Exhibit 1.7). Although accounting rules, monetary conditions, and corporate governance have differed over time, performance differences can explain much of the difference in valuation, particularly in the case of return on capital. U.S. companies, for example, consistently earned higher returns on capital than companies in Europe and Asia (see Exhibit 1.8). We see this as further proof that economic fundamentals drive stock markets.

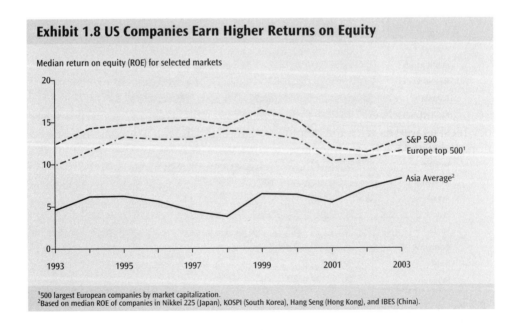

Exhibit 1.8 US Companies Earn Higher Returns on Equity

Median return on equity (ROE) for selected markets

[1] 500 largest European companies by market capitalization.
[2] Based on median ROE of companies in Nikkei 225 (Japan), KOSPI (South Korea), Hang Seng (Hong Kong), and IBES (China).

DEVIATIONS ASSOCIATED WITH SLOPPY ECONOMIC ANALYSIS

An implication emerges from the stock market's overall reflection of long-term economic fundamentals: Deviations are usually short-lived, focused on a particular segment of the economy, or both. Managers are therefore best off focusing their energy on long-term value creation and not worrying about the latest stock market trends. In fact, when managers and market participants take their eye off the fundamentals of long-term value creation, market bubbles can result. Two examples come to mind: the LBO bubble in the late 1980s and the Internet bubble a decade later.

The LBO Bubble

In the early 1980s the U.S. Federal Reserve wrestled inflation under control, the U.S. economy began to grow again, and companies and investors redis-covered the confidence to innovate. A market for corporate control emerged, in which companies and private investors (later grouped under the moniker of *corporate raiders*) demonstrated their ability to successfully undertake hos-tile takeovers of poorly performing companies. Once in control, the new owners would often improve operations, divest unrelated businesses, and then resell the newly made-over company for a substantial profit. Although large companies led many of the early hostile takeovers, the emergence of high-yield bond financing opened the door for smaller investors, known as *leveraged-buyout* (LBO) firms, to take a leading role in the hostile-takeover game.

The LBO firms' early successes attracted the attention of other investors, commercial bankers, and investment bankers. Every year, more LBO firms formed to go after deals, investment bankers scrambled to identify opportuni-ties, and lenders saw opportunities to earn lucrative fees. In 1981, 99 LBO deals took place in the United States; by 1988, the number was 381. Early on, LBO players grounded their deal activity in solid analysis and realistic eco-nomics. Yet as the number of participants in the hot market increased, disci-pline declined. The swelling ranks of LBO firms bid up prices for takeover prospects encouraged by investment bankers, who stood to reap large advi-sory fees, as well as with the help of commercial bankers, who were willing to support aggressive financing plans.

We have reviewed some financial projections that underpinned several high-profile LBO bankruptcies in the late 1980s. Many of these transactions were based on assumptions that the companies could achieve levels of perfor-mance, revenue growth, operating margins, and capital utilization never be-fore achieved in their industry. The buyers of these companies typically had no concrete plans for executing the financial performance necessary to meet their obligations. In many such transactions, the buyers simply assumed that they could resell pieces of the acquired companies for a higher price to some-one else.

Why wouldn't investors see through such shoddy analyses? In many of these failed transactions, bankers and loan committees felt great pressure to keep up with their peers and generate big up-front fees, so they approved highly questionable loans. In other cases, each participant assumed someone else had carefully done the homework. Buyers assumed that if they could get financing, the deal must be good. High-yield bond investors figured that the commercial bankers providing the senior debt must surely have worked their numbers properly. After all, the bankers selling the bonds had their reputations at stake, and the buyers had some capital in the game as well.

Whatever the assumption, however, the immutable laws of economics and value creation prevailed. Many deals went under. Since then, participants seem to have learned their lesson. Today, LBO deals are typically built on more moderate levels of debt and are mostly based on sound economics, though recent signs of too much capital chasing too few deals are troubling. LBO deals and high-yield debt continue to thrive and play an important role in corporate restructuring and value creation.

The Internet Bubble

A decade after the heyday of the LBO deal, the business world once again found itself consumed by a frenzy, this time around the development of the Internet. When Netscape Communications became a public company in 1995, the company saw its market capitalization soar to $6 billion on an annual revenue base of just $85 million, the financial world quickly became convinced that the Internet would change the world. That set off a race to create companies and take them public. Between 1995 and 2000, more than 4,700 companies went public in the United States and Europe, many with billion-dollar-plus market capitalizations. Such apparently easy wealth led individual investors to quickly invest in the stock market. The trend gave birth to a new kind of investing animal, the day trader, who specialized in trading stocks for the money that could be earned from short-term swings. As the bull market rolled on, many investors amassed impressive paper wealth before the excitement ended. The NASDAQ index, a proxy for technology stocks, increased from 2,010 in January 1997 to 5,047 at its peak in March 2000. It subsequently fell to 1,945 in December 2001.

During the mania of the Internet boom, some real substance fed the hype amid the rise in share values. Many of the companies born in this era, including Amazon.com, eBay, and Yahoo! have created and are likely to create substantial profits and economic value. But for every solid, innovative new business idea, there were dozens of companies that represented the triumph of hype over experience in terms of their ability to generate revenue or profit in either the short or long term.

As with the LBO era, many executives and investors either forgot or purposely threw out fundamental rules of economics in the rarified air of the Internet revolution. Consider the concept of *increasing returns to scale*, also known as "network effects" or "demand-side economies of scale." The idea enjoyed great popularity during the 1990s after Carl Shapiro and Hal Varian, professors at the University of California–Berkeley, described it in a book titled *Information Rules: A Strategic Guide to the Network Economy.*[3]

The basic idea is this: In certain situations, as companies get bigger, they can earn higher margins and return on capital because their product becomes more valuable with each customer who purchases it. In most industries, competition forces returns back to reasonable levels. But in so-called increasing-return industries, returns become high and stay there.

Take Microsoft's Office software, which provides word processing, spreadsheets, and graphics. It is important for customers to be able to share their work with others, so they are unwilling to purchase and use competing products. As the installed base gets bigger and bigger, it becomes even more attractive for customers to use Office for these tasks. Because of this advantage, Microsoft earns 75 percent margins and operating profits of $7 billion on this product, one of the most profitable products of all time.

As the Microsoft example illustrates, the concept of increasing returns to scale is sound economics. What was unsound during the Internet era was its application to almost every product and service related to the Internet. Shapiro and Varian describe the rare conditions that permit increasing returns to scale. In the case of Microsoft Office, a key driver is the desire for compatibility to share documents. But during the Internet bubble, the concept was misinterpreted to mean that merely getting big faster than your competitors in a given market would result in enormous profits. Some analysts applied the idea to mobile-phone service providers, even though customers can and do easily switch from provider to provider, forcing these providers to compete largely on price. The same logic seemed to apply to Internet grocery delivery services, even though the result of attracting more customers is that these services need more drivers, trucks, warehouses, and inventory.

The Internet bubble years were full of such intellectual shortcuts to justify absurd share prices for technology companies. The history of innovation has shown how difficult it is to earn monopoly-sized rents except in very limited circumstances. But that was no matter to the commentators who ignored those lessons. Those who questioned the new economics were branded as people who simply "didn't get it"—the new-economy equivalents of the defenders of Ptolemaic astronomy.

When the laws of economics prevailed, as they always do, competition reined in returns in most product areas. The Internet has revolutionized the

---

[3] C. Shapiro and H. Varian, *Information Rules: A Strategic Guide to the Network Economy* (Boston: Harvard Business School Press, 1999).

economy, as have other innovations, but it could not render obsolete the rules of economics and competition.

The Internet bubble shows what happens when managers, investors, and bankers ignore the fundamental principles of economics and the underlying history of value creation. It was also a classic example of herding behavior, as investors, managers, and commentators followed the crowd instead of relying on their own independent analysis. For example, many equity analysts could not justify the values of companies based on fundamentals, so they resorted to commenting only on relative values—how one company was valued relative to another—instead of dealing in absolute terms.

CHANGES IN CORPORATE GOVERNANCE AND SHAREHOLDER INFLUENCE

With share prices steadily rising for 20 years, shareholders accepted the oversized pay packages CEOs began to take home. Boards of directors reaped windfalls as well, so they were unlikely to ask hard questions about the value-creation priorities of senior management. But in the wake of corporate scandals and a market correction back to more historical levels, shareholders, regulators, and boards have become engaged in a struggle with executive management. The objective is to remake the corporate landscape in a way that restores the faith of battered shareholders and imposes greater discipline on management to focus on long-term value creation.

Some initial actions have been controversial. Reforms under the Sarbanes-Oxley legislation passed by the U.S. Congress create strict requirements for CEOs and CFOs to attest to the validity of their financial statements and to strengthen and document internal control processes. In Europe, many countries have also adopted corporate governance codes. In the Netherlands, the traditional corporate form (known as Structuur NV) was radically reformed in 2004. Under the old law, the supervisory boards of most major companies elected themselves, and shareholders had no say in the choice of directors. Soon shareholders will be able to elect the board members of the companies whose shares they own.

Shareholders, particularly large institutional investors, have become more activist in the companies they own, especially when they oppose the strategic direction management is taking. In 2003, shareholders voted down a proposed pay package for the CEO of one of the United Kingdom's largest companies. The following year, many large companies in the United States, including Boeing, Dell, the Walt Disney Company, Oracle, and Tenet Healthcare, separated the roles of chairman and chief executive officer, sometimes under shareholder pressure.

Board members are looking for ways to improve their oversight of companies. In a recent survey of 150 U.S. corporate directors, 72 percent supported separating the roles of CEO and chairman, an approach that has been standard practice at companies in the United Kingdom and Europe for many years.[4] In the same survey, board directors expressed support for the need to improve the accountability of the board and to reform executive compensation.

The crosscurrents of corporate scandals, newly active shareholders and board members, and regulatory reforms are not easy to read. But in the wake of the corporate excesses of the past decade, it is safe to say that there will be more pressure on CEOs to build long-term shareholder value.

FOCUSING ON VALUE LEADS TO HEALTHIER COMPANIES

Why should management's primary objective be long-term value creation? Companies dedicated to value creation are healthier and build stronger economies, higher living standards, and more opportunities for individuals.

There has long been vigorous debate on the importance of shareholder value relative to other measures such as employment, social responsibility, and the environment. The debate is often cast in terms of shareholder versus stakeholder. At least in ideology and legal frameworks, the United States and the United Kingdom have given the most weight to the idea that shareholders are the owners of the corporation, the board of directors is their representative and elected by them, and the objective function of the corporation is to maximize shareholder value.

In continental Europe, an explicitly broader view of the objectives of business organizations has long been more influential. In many cases, it is embedded in the governance structures of the corporate form of organization. In the Netherlands and Germany, the board of a large corporation has its fiduciary duties toward the corporation (e.g., in support of the continuity of the business in the interests of all its stakeholders), not only toward shareholders in the pursuit of value maximization. Similar philosophies lay at the foundation of corporate governance in other continental European countries.

Pursuing shareholder value does not mean that other stakeholders suffer. Consider employee stakeholders. A company that tries to fatten its profits by providing a shabby work environment, underpaying employees, and skimping on benefits will have trouble attracting and retaining high-quality employees. With today's increased labor mobility and more educated workforce, such a company would be less profitable. While it may feel good to treat people well, it is also good business.

When examining employment, we found that the United States and European companies that created the most shareholder value in the past 15 years have shown healthier employment growth. In Exhibit 1.9, companies with the highest total returns to shareholders (TRS) also had the largest

[4] R. Felton, "What Directors and Investors Want from Governance Reform," *McKinsey Quarterly,* 2 (2004): pp. 30–39.

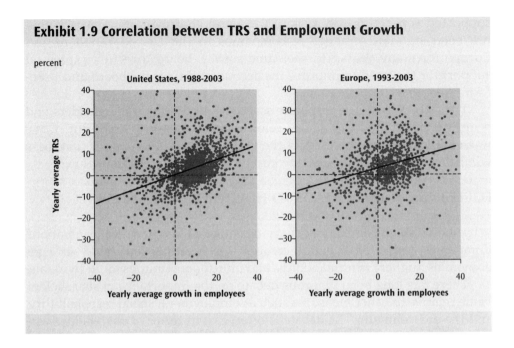

Exhibit 1.9 Correlation between TRS and Employment Growth

increases in employment. We also tested this link within individual sectors of the economy and found similar results.

Another often-expressed concern is that companies that emphasize creating value for shareholders are shortsighted. We disagree. For example, we found a strong positive correlation between shareholder returns and investments in research and development (R&D). As shown in Exhibit 1.10, com-

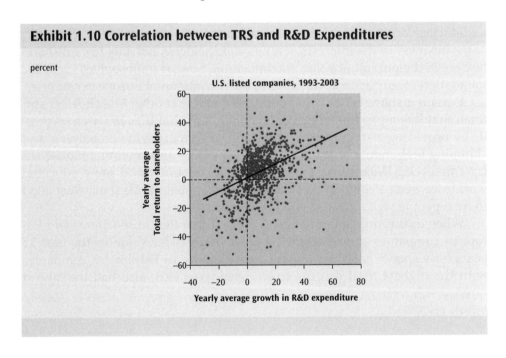

Exhibit 1.10 Correlation between TRS and R&D Expenditures

panies that earned the highest shareholder returns also invested the most in R&D. These results also hold within individual sectors in the economy.

CAUTIOUS OPTIMISM

Overall, capital markets reward companies that focus on long-term value creation, and these companies help the economy and other stakeholders. It is unfortunate but true, however, that managers are often under pressure to achieve short-term results at the expense of long-term value creation. Many succumb. In a recent survey of 401 executives, 55 percent of them said they would delay or cancel a value-creating project to avoid missing the consensus analysts' forecast for the current quarter's earnings.[5]

The pressure to show short-term results often occurs when companies start to mature and begin a transition from high to low growth. Investors clamor for high growth. Managers are tempted to find ways to keep profits growing in the short term while they try to stimulate longer-term growth. Usually, the short-term efforts make achieving long-term growth even more difficult, spawning a vicious cycle.

Perhaps no action was more disappointing and damaging than the wave of accounting fraud that managers resorted to in the late 1990s and early 2000s to improve the appearance of their short-term results. Eventually, fraudulent profits must be turned into real profits, so we wonder how these managers thought they would ultimately generate enough real earnings to cover the fraudulent ones.

Stock markets will always clamor for short-term results, just as coaches push athletes to achieve a higher level of performance. That pressure will always be there, and it is not all bad. It is up to managers to sort out the trade-offs between short-term earnings and long-term value creation and be courageous enough to act accordingly. Perhaps even more important, it is up to corporate boards to investigate sufficiently and be active enough to judge when managers are making the right trade-offs—and to protect them when they choose to build long-term value.

REVIEW QUESTIONS

1. Compare and contrast shareholder value maximization to stakeholder value maximization. Describe market forces that influence the ideological tension between shareholder and stakeholder. How does a shareholder define value?

[5] J. Graham, C. Harvey, and S. Rajgopal, "The Economic Implications of Corporate Financial Reporting" (*Journal of Accounting and Economics*, forthcoming).

2. How can a short-term orientation, which focuses on metrics such as ROI and EPS, negatively impact shareholder value?

3. Describe both the principal forces and the directions of the pressure placed on companies to generate shareholder value.

4. Why should equity holders have the greatest decision-making power in the firm?

5. Identify two examples where the capital markets misjudged corporate values. In your answer, emphasize the impact of executives maintaining a short-term focus stressing industry and company fundamentals versus a long-term focus of corporate valuation.

6. Has the role of the institutional investor influenced managerial decision making over the past 25 years?

7. Critique the following statement: "Companies that focus on shareholder value create healthier companies."

8. Describe the linkage between the long-run TRS of the market and key macroeconomic variables, such as GDP growth, inflation, interest rates, and return on capital.

9. Describe one of the fundamental performance factors that explains why U.S. companies are valued more highly that European or Asian companies.

2

The Value Manager

Managing for value creation requires managers to break with the perspective that many of their peers typically use. Value managers are a special breed: They focus on long-term cash flow rather than on quarter-to-quarter earnings. They judge businesses by returns above opportunity costs, not by size, prestige, and other emotional issues. Most important, they recognize that managing for value means instilling the philosophy of value creation throughout the organization.

To do so, value managers not only must set value as the company's overall strategic objective—that includes defining the portfolio of businesses, identifying major strategic initiatives, and determining value creation targets—but must ensure that the company's day-to-day processes are aligned with value creation. These processes include planning, performance management, compensation systems, and investor communications.

In this chapter, we describe how one manager transformed his company into such a value management organization, thereby boosting cash flow, earnings, and the recognition of shareholders. The case serves as an overview of and framework for the application of more detailed valuation approaches that we develop later.

PART 1: SITUATION

In 2004, EG Corporation (as we call it) had sales of about $10.7 billion (see Exhibit 2.1 on p. 24). The company had three major divisions: Consumerco, Foodco, and Woodco.

Consumerco manufactured consumer products, selling to groceries and drugstores throughout the United States. Consumerco had built strong brand names, and most of its product lines enjoyed a dominant market share.

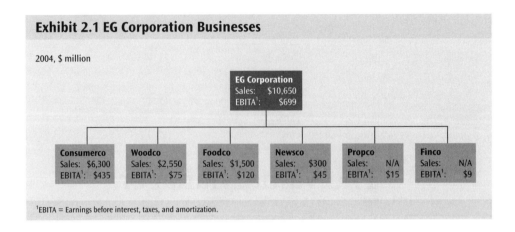

Exhibit 2.1 EG Corporation Businesses

2004, $ million

EG Corporation		
Sales:	$10,650
EBITA[1]:	$699

Consumerco	Woodco	Foodco	Newsco	Propco	Finco
Sales: $6,300	Sales: $2,550	Sales: $1,500	Sales: $300	Sales: N/A	Sales: N/A
EBITA[1]: $435	EBITA[1]: $75	EBITA[1]: $120	EBITA[1]: $45	EBITA[1]: $15	EBITA[1]: $9

[1]EBITA = Earnings before interest, taxes, and amortization.

Woodco was formed through the gradual acquisition of eight smaller companies, and was a midsize player in the furniture business. By 2005, EG's managers had begun to combine Woodco's companies into a single unit that they hoped would reduce operating costs and strengthen the company's ability to control the business.

Foodco operated a contract food business and a chain of fast-food restaurants. As of early 2005, Foodco was earning a profit, but faced formidable competition. Still, management believed that its operating approach and EG's Consumerco brand name (which Foodco used) would eventually establish Foodco as a major industry player. For that reason, Foodco's operations were under expansion.

EG also owned a few other small businesses: A property development company (Propco); a small consumer finance company (Finco); and several small newspapers (Newsco). These EG had acquired in the 1980s (though no one was still at the company who could explain why). All were profitable, though modestly so compared with EG's three main divisions.

For the previous five years, EG's overall financial performance had been mediocre. Earnings had not kept pace with inflation. Return on capital was less than 10 percent. The company had failed to deliver on growth and earnings commitments, and its stock price had lagged the market for several years.

Analysts bemoaned EG's lackluster performance, especially in view of the strength of the Consumerco brand. They were also disenchanted with the slow progress in building profits in other parts of the company. Some analysts ventured that EG would make a good breakup play. EG's board and senior management were frustrated because they couldn't convince the market that EG should be more highly valued.

In early 2005, Ralph Demsky became EG's chairman and CEO. For 10 years, Ralph had been president of Consumerco. Ralph was familiar with EG's worrisome corporate predicament and was equally convinced that the company could unleash great opportunities if it just focused its attention on creating value. That, in fact, was why he was tapped to lead EG upon the retirement of the previous chairman and CEO.

PART 2: RALPH AS CORPORATE STRATEGIST

During his first week on the job, Ralph began to assess the value creation opportunities at EG. He knew that quick action was necessary if he wanted to convince the market that EG could be worth more than its current market value. His first step was to create a task force that included EG's chief financial officer, the heads of the major businesses, and himself, as chairman. The team met twice a week to review progress and had an eight-week deadline to reach some conclusions.

Ralph had considered using a small team, perhaps consisting of himself, the chief financial officer, and several financial analysts. This would have maintained secrecy and sped up the process. But he decided on a larger group that would immediately tap into the best judgment of his senior managers, involve them in the improvements that they would play a key role in executing, and educate them in a review process he planned to make an annual event.

Ralph chose to investigate EG's potential value along six lines of analysis. Together these would form a hexagon framework for value creation for the company (see Exhibit 2.2).

The analysis would start with EG's current market value and a comparison of that to EG's intrinsic value based on its historical performance and existing business plans. Next, the team would identify and value operating improvement opportunities such as increasing margins, accelerating core revenue growth, and improving capital efficiency. Third, it would decide whether some businesses should be divested. Fourth, the team would identify potential acquisitions or the formation of new growth initiatives, and estimate their impact on value. Fifth, the team would consider how value might be increased through changing EG's capital structure and enlisting other means of financial engineering.

Current Valuation

Ralph started by reviewing EG's stock performance. He knew that EG had not performed particularly well for its shareholders in recent times and that

Exhibit 2.2 Corporate Strategy Framework

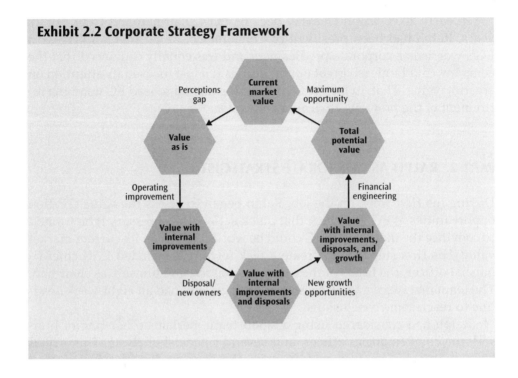

operating returns had been disappointing. But Ralph wanted to be systematic in his review of the market's perspective. His team set about examining EG's performance in the stock market, its underlying financial performance, how it had generated and invested its cash flow, and what the market was assuming about its future performance.

What he found was disturbing—and revealing: EG's return to investors had not only been below the overall market, but also below the returns for comparable companies (see Exhibit 2.3). When he looked at EG's valuation relative to its peers, he was not surprised that his company was valued lower than other companies in terms of the ratio of market value to the book value of invested capital (see Exhibit 2.4 on p. 28).

He also noticed that between 1999 and 2004, when EG had made several acquisitions to build the Woodco furniture businesses, there was a corresponding *decline* in EG's share price (relative to comparable companies and the market around the date of each acquisition). In fact, the decline in EG's total value was about equal to the dollar amount of the premiums over market price EG had paid to acquire the companies. Evidently, Ralph mused, the stock market did not believe EG would add any value to the acquired businesses. In fact, it viewed the acquisition premiums that EG had paid to buy the firms as a damaging transfer of value—from EG investors to the selling shareholders.

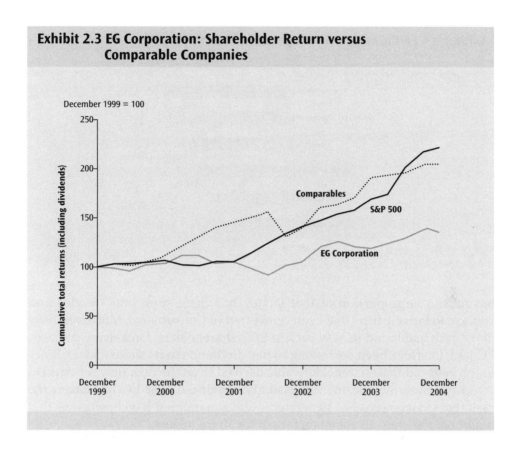

Exhibit 2.3 EG Corporation: Shareholder Return versus Comparable Companies

In fact, EG had not done anything notable with these companies as their owner. There *was* no reason for them to be worth any more than their pre-acquisition value. And it did not matter that the deals had been carefully structured and financed to avoid diluting EG's earnings per share. The market had seen through those cosmetics.

Looking next at the financial results of each of EG's businesses, the team noted that Consumerco had generated high, stable returns on invested capital (30+ percent) for the previous five years (see Exhibit 2.5 on p. 28). However, the earnings of Consumerco were growing at no more than the pace of inflation. Woodco, meanwhile, had suffered steadily declining returns. Foodco's earnings were growing, but returns on investment were low (because of high capital investment requirements in the restaurants). All of these factors had conspired to depress overall EG returns on capital and hamper profit growth.

EG's cash flow map, based on the past five years, was of particular interest to Ralph (see Exhibit 2.6 on p. 29). It showed that while EG had been generating substantial discretionary (or free) cash flow in the Consumerco

Exhibit 2.4 EG Corporation: Comparative Current Valuation

Market-value-to-invested-capital, December 2004

New Moon	4.0
Universal Consumer	3.6
Henry's	3.2
Smith & Smith	3.0
EG Corporation	1.9
Millennium	1.8

business, a large portion of that money had been sunk into Woodco and Foodco. Relatively little had been reinvested in Consumerco. Moreover, little of the cash had found its way back to EG's shareholders. On a five-year basis, EG had, in effect, been borrowing to pay dividends to its shareholders. Since Ralph believed that shareholder value derived from the cash flow returns EG could generate, he became increasingly convinced that EG had taken the cash that Consumerco had generated—and squandered it on businesses that might not generate an adequate return for shareholders.

Ralph next spent a day reading recent analysts' reports. He then visited EG's major investors, and the leading analysts who followed EG's stock. Ralph was surprised at the favorable reception he received. Apparently, the previous CEO rarely met individually with the analysts, and when he did,

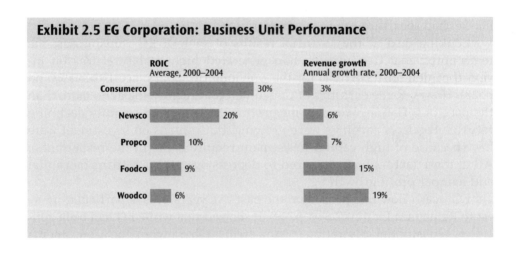

Exhibit 2.5 EG Corporation: Business Unit Performance

Business Unit	ROIC Average, 2000–2004	Revenue growth Annual growth rate, 2000–2004
Consumerco	30%	3%
Newsco	20%	6%
Propco	10%	7%
Foodco	9%	15%
Woodco	6%	19%

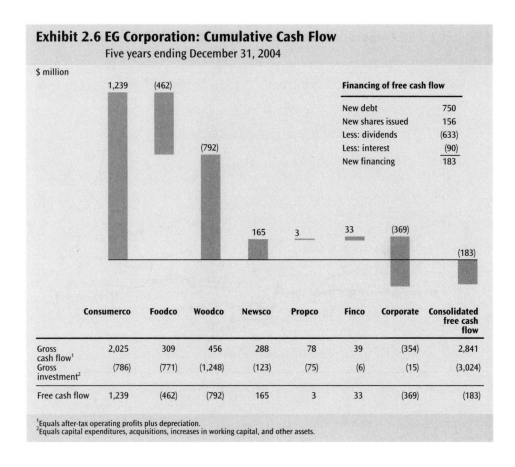

Exhibit 2.6 EG Corporation: Cumulative Cash Flow
Five years ending December 31, 2004

$ million

Financing of free cash flow

New debt	750
New shares issued	156
Less: dividends	(633)
Less: interest	(90)
New financing	183

	Consumerco	Foodco	Woodco	Newsco	Propco	Finco	Corporate	Consolidated free cash flow
Gross cash flow[1]	2,025	309	456	288	78	39	(354)	2,841
Gross investment[2]	(786)	(771)	(1,248)	(123)	(75)	(6)	(15)	(3,024)
Free cash flow	1,239	(462)	(792)	165	3	33	(369)	(183)

[1]Equals after-tax operating profits plus depreciation.
[2]Equals capital expenditures, acquisitions, increases in working capital, and other assets.

never asked them candidly what they thought of the company. When Ralph did ask, one of the analysts showed him why EG lacked credibility: The analysts had to continually revise downward their earnings forecasts for the company (see Exhibit 2.7 on p. 30).

Ralph was not surprised to hear the analysts tell him that EG had been complacent for the past five years. Or that EG had pursued new businesses with little regard for the returns they would generate. Or that EG would remain an unattractive investment candidate unless someone took some action that demonstrated the company's commitment to creating value for shareholders. Ralph was not surprised, because he knew it was true.

EG's "As Is" Value

The team's next step was to assess the value of the EG portfolio, on the basis of projected future cash flow. To do this, the team members developed cash flow models for each business, based on projected sales growth, margins, working capital, and capital spending needs. The finance staff, meanwhile, developed estimates of the cost of capital for each division.

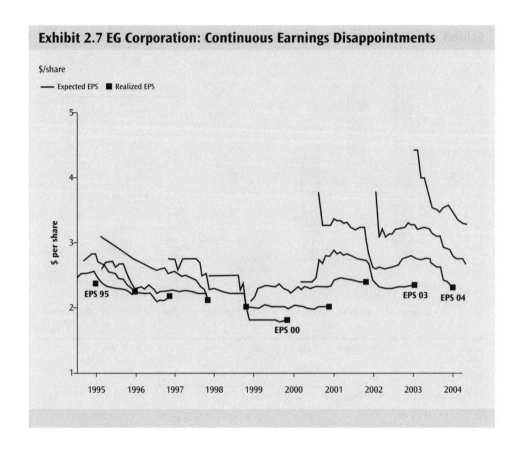

Exhibit 2.7 EG Corporation: Continuous Earnings Disappointments

When these data were assembled, the team ran two sets of discounted cash flow valuations. These served as preliminary benchmarks. The first was based on extrapolations of the previous three years' operating results for each business. These projections were used to estimate the value of each EG business (as well as the cost of corporate headquarters activities and the value of nonoperating investments). Exhibit 2.8 shows the value buildup that the team used to compare the total value to EG's market value.

From this, the team realized that the discounted cash flow value of the company based on historical performance ($5.6 billion) was substantially below EG's value in the marketplace ($7.2 billion). They realized that unless Foodco's performance improved dramatically, Foodco would soon be worth far less than the capital EG had invested in it over the past few years. They also saw that more than 80 percent of EG's value was represented by the cash flow generated by Consumerco. Finally, they realized that corporate headquarters costs, when viewed on a value basis, represented a 25 percent drag on overall EG value.

These were disturbing conclusions, but Ralph asked the team to press on. Next they estimated EG's value—assuming that the performance

Exhibit 2.8 EG Corporation: Value Based on Historical Extrapolation

	DCF value ($ million)	Invested capital ($ million)	Value created/ (destroyed) ($ million)
Consumerco	5,250	2,100	3,150
Foodco	900	900	–
Woodco	600	900	(300)
Newsco	525	360	165
Propco	375	420	(45)
Finco	75	165	(90)
Corporate overhead	(1,275)	0	(1,275)
Total	6,450	4,845	1,605
Debt	(900)	(900)	–
Equity value	**5,550**	**3,945**	**1,605**
Stock market value	7,200		
Value gap	**(1,650)**		
Percent of stock market value	–23%		

estimates in the current business plans were achieved. The results, shown in Exhibit 2.9, indicated that the total discounted cash flow (DCF) value of EG based on its business plan was about 10 percent higher than its current market value.

This seemed good. But Ralph knew that 10 percent was nothing to the stock market. The market took for granted that EG would either improve its performance or fall into the hands of someone who would. Recognizing

Exhibit 2.9 EG Corporation: Value Buildup Comparison

	Historical extrapolation ($ million)	Business plans ($ million)	Difference (percent)
Consumerco	5,250	6,345	21
Foodco	900	825	(8)
Woodco	600	1,800	200
Newsco	525	600	14
Propco	375	450	20
Finco	75	105	40
Corporate overhead	(1,275)	(1,275)	0
Total	6,450	8,850	37
Debt	(900)	(900)	
Equity value	**5,550**	**7,950**	**43**
Stock market value	7,200	7,200	
Value gap	**(1,650)**	**750**	
Percent of stock market value	–23%	10%	

that, Ralph decided that EG would need to come up with something dramatic enough to lift the value of his shareholders' investments much faster than the previous plan.

In thinking this through, Ralph realized that the current plan had problems. Consumerco's plan would increase its value by about 20 percent, which would have a large impact on EG. Foodco's value, however, would actually decline (even though its plan involved substantial growth in the number of outlets and overall sales and earnings).

To Ralph this meant only one thing—the returns on investment at Foodco were too low. Foodco management was focusing more on growth than on returns. In contrast, the Woodco consolidation looked set to improve the value of the furniture businesses dramatically, while the newspaper, finance, and property businesses would improve somewhat too.

At this stage, Ralph decided that Consumerco would have to perform even better, given what it needed to contribute to the company. Foodco, meanwhile, would need to revamp its strategy to make sure that it built value, not simply bulk. And Woodco's consolidation of its companies, already underway, was far more important than he had thought—and would need to succeed to maintain EG's overall value. The bottom line was that EG would need to run hard just to maintain shareholder value, and even harder to exceed it. Any missteps could cause the share price to collapse.

EG's Potential Value with Internal Improvements

After looking at EG's current value, Ralph's team tried to assess how more aggressive plans and strategies might help boost the value of the business.

The managers first conducted a sensitivity analysis, estimating how the value would be affected by an increase in sales growth of 1 percent, then a rise in margins by a percentage point, and finally, the reduction of capital intensity. The results appear in Exhibit 2.10.

Foodco was most sensitive to reductions in capital intensity and increases in margins. If Foodco grew faster at current margins and capital intensity, in fact, its value would actually decrease. Growth would be unprofitable, because Foodco earned a rate of return on invested capital less than its cost of capital. Woodco, meanwhile, would be strengthened most by improvements in its operating margin (which would come with the consolidation of its companies). Consumerco was responsive to sales growth: With its high margins and outstanding capital utilization, each dollar of sales would generate large profits and cash flows.

The team next compared the EG businesses with similar companies, in terms of overall performance as well as relative costs, productivity, and investment. This analysis, coupled with the financial comparisons, convinced Ralph and his team that EG could perform at much higher levels.

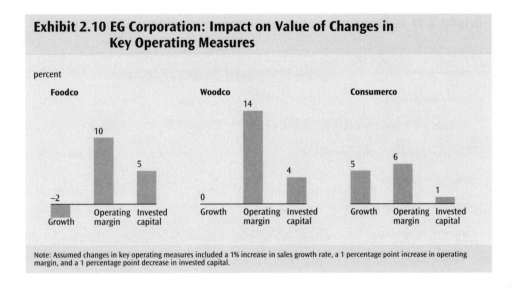

Exhibit 2.10 EG Corporation: Impact on Value of Changes in Key Operating Measures

Note: Assumed changes in key operating measures included a 1% increase in sales growth rate, a 1 percentage point increase in operating margin, and a 1 percentage point decrease in invested capital.

Consumerco seemed to have room to increase revenue significantly and earn even higher margins:

- The team discovered that Consumerco had been restraining R&D and advertising spending to generate cash for EG's diversification efforts and to buffer poor performance in other parts of EG's portfolio. Ralph's team believed the answer lay in boosting short-term spending. This would lead to higher sales volumes in existing EG products and encourage the introduction of additional high-margin products in the future.

- Despite Consumerco's dominant position in its market categories, Consumerco's prices were actually lower than less popular brands. The study revealed that most category leaders were able to charge higher prices. The team estimated that the value created by price increases would more than offset any losses in volume.

- The team discovered that Consumerco's sales force was less than half as productive as sales forces at other companies that sold through the same channels. Ralph had suspected this, and was sure that the productivity of the sales force could be improved.

- The team determined that Consumerco had room to cut costs, particularly in terms of purchases and inventory management. In fact, the cost of sales could easily be reduced by one percentage point.

When the team factored in these possibilities, they found that Consumerco's value could be increased conservatively by 25 percent, as shown in Exhibit 2.11 on page 34.

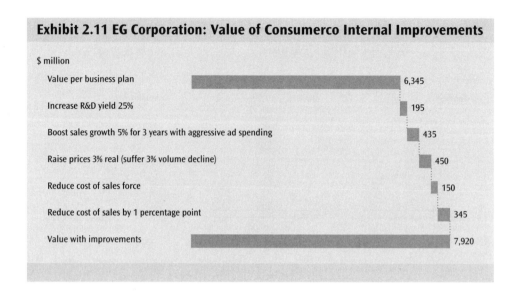

Exhibit 2.11 EG Corporation: Value of Consumerco Internal Improvements

$ million

Value per business plan	6,345
Increase R&D yield 25%	195
Boost sales growth 5% for 3 years with aggressive ad spending	435
Raise prices 3% real (suffer 3% volume decline)	450
Reduce cost of sales force	150
Reduce cost of sales by 1 percentage point	345
Value with improvements	7,920

Woodco could also dramatically improve its performance far beyond the earlier plan. It just needed to be able to perform at the levels of other top furniture companies. This would likely require Woodco to focus less on growth and more on higher margins. To do this, Woodco would need to build better management information and control systems, and stick to its familiar mass-market products, instead of striking out into new upmarket furnishings, as it once planned.

Foodco looked as if it would continue as a poor performer. The industry was extremely competitive. A few large players were earning respectable returns, but even their returns were starting to decline. After further study, the Consumerco brand, which Foodco used, was found to be of little value in building the business. Foodco would be unable to develop significant scale economies, at least in the near future. To make matters worse, Foodco had a voracious appetite for capital to build facilities. But it was not generating a return on new investment sufficient to cover the opportunity cost of the capital. The team decided that Foodco should trim operations back (to its profitable locations) and choose more conservative growth targets.

Similar reviews were carried out for the smaller EG businesses. The team also examined EG's corporate overhead and found opportunities to reduce costs substantially. EG's corporate staff had grown and the divisions had also added staff to the point where they were functioning largely as freestanding operations. Ralph believed that 50 percent of the corporate costs could be eliminated.

Ralph placed the potential internal value of EG's businesses at about $10.9 billion, which would be 50 percent above its current market value (see

Exhibit 2.12 EG Corporation: Potential Value versus Plan Value

	Historical extrapolation ($ million)	Business plans ($ million)	Potential value ($ million)	Improvement (percent)
Consumerco	5,250	6,345	7,920	25
Foodco	900	825	900	9
Woodco	600	1,800	2,400	33
Newsco	525	600	645	8
Propco	375	450	480	7
Finco	75	105	105	0
Corporate overhead	(1,275)	(1,275)	(675)	NA
Total	6,450	8,850	11,775	33
Debt	(900)	(900)	(900)	
Equity value	**5,550**	**7,950**	**10,875**	37
Stock market value	7,200	7,200	7,200	
Value gap	**(1,650)**	**750**	**3,675**	
Percent of stock market value	–23%	10%	51%	

Exhibit 2.12). This was before any incremental value that might accrue through the sale of EG businesses.

Ralph and his team were beginning to feel better about their chances for turning EG into a high-performance company. They were eager to get to the next step: estimating the value of EG's businesses to new owners through a sale or spin-off.

EG's Potential Value to Other Owners

If any of EG's businesses were worth more to someone else than to EG, Ralph realized he should gladly sell them. The buyer might be someone who could create more value from the business through synergies with other businesses or better operational management, or someone who was merely overenthusiastic about the prospects of the business and was ready to buy. In EG's case, Ralph suspected he would find more buyers who could create value (due to synergies or stronger management skills in the relevant industry) than overenthusiastic buyers.

To approximate a selling price, Ralph's team analyzed the external value of EG's businesses under four scenarios: sale to a strategic buyer (another company that could realize operating and strategic synergies); a flotation or spin-off; a leveraged buyout by management or a third party; and a liquidation (see Exhibit 2.13 on p. 36).

The team started by determining how much the EG businesses would trade for in the market if spun off as independent companies. To estimate

Exhibit 2.13 EG Corporation: Comparison of External Value Estimates by Business

	Strategic buyer ($ million)	Spin-off ($ million)	LBO ($ million)	Liquidation ($ million)	Highest value ($ million)
Consumerco	9,750	6,000	7,500	N/A	9,750
Foodco	1,050	840	870	780	1,050
Woodco	465	165	N/A	75	465
Propco	525	N/A	N/A	390	525
Finco	105	75	N/A	150	150
Newsco	570	420	540	N/A	570
Total					12,510
Debt					(900)
Equity value					11,610
Taxes and costs					3,000
Net proceeds					8,610

these values, the team identified a set of publicly traded companies comparable to each EG business. They used current stock market valuation data (e.g., enterprise value-to-EBITA [earnings before interest, taxes, amortization], market-to-book ratios) to estimate the value of the EG businesses as freestanding entities.

To their disappointment, they found that a simple breakup into separate, publicly traded companies would not, at current market prices, provide any gain overall for EG shareholders. Nor did estimates of the value of the businesses as leveraged-buyout candidates suggest that EG as a whole would be worth more than in parts (especially after taking into account the taxes EG would have to pay on the sale of the units). To be sure, the Consumerco business, with its strong, stable cash flow was a natural buyout candidate, but the other businesses were not.

The team then considered the complete or partial liquidation of the businesses. Of the three larger EG businesses, this only made sense for Foodco, and this only because of its real estate holdings: The restaurant property could be sold off piecemeal; the Foodco restaurant division subsequently shut down. But although a few of the restaurants were worth more as real estate, the team soon determined that Foodco was worth more as a going concern than in liquidation.

EG's consumer finance company was a candidate, however. Consumer finance had become so competitive that the spread between borrowing costs and the rates earned on new loans did not cover operating costs. The team discovered that the existing loan portfolio might be sold for more than the entire business was worth. In effect, each year's new business was dissipating some of the value inherent in the existing loan portfolio. The team was also sure that it would be relatively easy to sell the portfolio to other financial companies and exit the business entirely.

Ralph reviewed the team's findings and finally concluded that Consumerco might be worth much more in the hands of another owner than it was now worth to EG. Indeed, to a buyer the opportunities for improvement were plentiful. A merger could offer certain cost savings. The sales forces could be combined and much of Consumerco's direct sales force eliminated. Potential savings could also be realized if Consumerco were merged into an existing management structure at another consumer products company.

In addition to cost savings, an acquirer might inject vigorous marketing expertise into the business, while ramping up the development of new products. Consumerco had grown a bit lazy, thanks to its dominant and essentially unchallenged brand. New energy would undoubtedly bring even richer returns.

All these factors together suggested that Consumerco might be worth more than $9.7 billion to a strategic buyer. This price was much more than its current worth (about $6.3 billion), and even more than Ralph's team believed they could augment its value ($7.9 billion). The implication was clear: Since Consumerco was worth so much more to someone else, and since it was a large part of EG's value, EG itself was at risk of a hostile takeover.

Other EG businesses might attract buyers as well. The team believed that Foodco could attract a restaurant company that could either accelerate Foodco's profitability through better management, or through conversion of the Foodco sites to its own brand. Because Foodco did not fit into EG's larger plans, the team tagged it as a prime sale candidate.

Woodco, meanwhile, might be sold to a company that bought and improved smaller furniture firms. But the team decided that it made little sense to sell Woodco at the present moment—in the midst of the consolidation—when potential buyers might be concerned that the business could fall apart. If the consolidation was successful, EG could sell Woodco for a much higher price in 12 to 18 months. Then again, mused Ralph, if Woodco were performing well, he might be convinced to keep it as the base for making additional furniture company acquisitions.

New Growth Opportunities

Ralph liked the way the analysis was coming together. The big missing piece, however, was growth. For investors to be excited about EG, there had to be a credible plan for long-term growth. Where could it be?

Ralph had often wondered why there was little discussion about incubating new businesses at Consumerco, nor such radical moves as large acquisitions. A quick analysis showed Ralph that if he could find opportunities that generated $1.5 billion to $3 billion in sales, he could increase the market value of Consumerco by $2.4 billion or more. So where was the big idea? Global expansion? New retail services? Direct sales?

Ralph knew that EG's restructuring was his first priority. But he insisted on keeping long-term potential at the top of everyone's mind. As the restructuring analysis continued, Ralph insisted that all the summary charts display the long-term growth imperatives prominently alongside the short-term targets. He was willing to wait nine months while the restructuring was under way, but then he wanted to act on growth.

Potential Value of Financial Engineering

Ralph also urged his CFO to develop an aggressive plan to take advantage of the tax advantages of debt financing. EG had had a policy of maintaining an AA bond rating from Standard & Poor's. EG prided itself as a strong investment-grade company, but Ralph knew that many companies had taken on much higher debt levels and performed equally well. In fact, by taking on debt, these companies were forced to think harder about additional ways to generate cash flow. It also forced them to be smarter about what they needed in terms of investment requirements and fixed expenses.

EG had sizable and stable free cash flows that could support much higher debt. The Consumerco business, which generated the bulk of the cash, was recession-resistant. Ralph also knew that he did not need much reserve financial capacity given the relative maturity of EG's core business and its limited need for capital. He also believed that EG could tap funding for a major expansion or acquisition, if it made economic sense.

Indeed, EG could carry a lot more debt, and that debt level could rise along with an improvement in EG's businesses. At a minimum, EG could raise $1.5 billion in new debt in the next six months, Ralph figured, and use the proceeds to repurchase shares or pay a special dividend. This debt would provide a more tax-efficient capital structure for EG, which would be worth about $600 million in present value to EG's shareholders.

Several bankers had approached Ralph suggesting complex financial transactions, including securitization and leasing. After reviewing some of these with his CFO, however, Ralph was convinced that for an investment-grade company like EG, with little in the way of fungible assets (e.g., airplanes, gas turbine generators, or real estate), these transactions were unlikely to create real shareholder value. He was concerned that they would also distract management from improving the operating performance of the company. So he decided not to put any more time into evaluating those transactions.

EG's New Corporate Strategy

Ralph's team had analyzed EG's value from multiple perspectives. Now they were ready to put them into action, business unit by business unit:

Business	Actions
Consumerco	Increase prices
	Invest in advertising
	Invest in new products
	Rationalize sales force
	Build marketing talent and skills
	Reduce manufacturing costs
Foodco	Sell to strategic buyer
Woodco	Accelerate consolidation
	Focus on basic furniture market rather than expanding in to upscale segments
Propco	Sell
Finco	Sell loan portfolio
	Wind down other activities
Newsco	Sell
Corporate	Decentralize more activities
	Reduce costs by 50 percent
New growth opportunities	To be determined
Financing	Increase debt by $1.5 billion to target BBB rating

If Ralph could successfully execute his plan, it would produce a large gain for EG shareholders. Exhibit 2.14 on page 40 shows the sources of the gain, which would more than double EG's present value. Ralph and his team were confident, and since they could take immediate action, they expected to see quick results.

PART 3: RALPH AS VALUE MANAGER

When EG announced its new corporate strategy, its share price jumped immediately. Then, as it made progress in the first six months of 2005, EG's shares increased 40 percent when the overall stock market was flat. The analysts who followed EG stopped talking about takeovers and applauded the transformation of the company.

Exhibit 2.14 EG Corporation: Value Created through Restructuring

	Historical extrapolation ($ million)	New corporate strategy ($ million)	Difference (percent)
Consumerco	5,250	8,700	66 operating improvements
Foodco	900	1,050	17 sale
Woodco	600	2,400	300 consolidation/sale
Newsco	525	570	9 sale
Propco	375	480	28 sale
Finco	75	135	80 liquidation
Corporate overhead	(1,275)	(675)	47 cuts
Debt tax benefit	NA	600	NA
Total	6,450	13,260	106
Debt	(900)	(900)	
Equity value	**5,550**	**12,360**	**122**
New growth opportunities	0	2,400+	
Equity value with new growth opportunities	**5,550**	**14,760**	**166**

Needless to say, Ralph and his team were pleased with the results. Ralph regretted having to reduce the corporate staff and sell some of EG's businesses. But he took some comfort knowing that he did it in a more orderly and humane way than an outsider would have.

Despite the successes, Ralph knew he had a lot more work ahead to see the restructuring plan through to completion. He also recognized that he needed to orient the company towards managing for value on a permanent basis. Before management became complacent again, he wanted to build on the fragile momentum that had been established.

Ralph planned to take five further steps to build EG's ability to manage value:

1. Focus planning and investment analysis on value creation.
2. Develop value-oriented targets and performance measurement systems.
3. Restructure EG's compensation system to emphasize the creation of shareholder value.
4. Communicate EG's plans, in terms of value creation, more clearly and consistently to investors and analysts.
5. Reshape the role of the company's CFO.

Put Value into Planning and Investment Analysis

Ralph realized that EG was not good at stressing value creation at the corporate and business-unit levels. To change that, Ralph made value creation the responsibility of all senior managers. Value analysis of each of the businesses would be required; in fact, executives would use the hexagon value-creation framework on an annual basis.

At the business level, EG's new focus on value would require some changes, too. Management in the business units would need to think differently about their operations. They would need to focus on what was driving the value of their businesses—whether it was volume growth, margins, or capital utilization.

What would matter in the future was not growth in earnings, but growth in value. Sometimes this would mean dispensing with ambitious growth targets. At other times, it would mean accepting lower earnings when investments in research and development or advertising made economic sense.

EG had been using discounted cash flow analysis to determine capital spending for at least five years. But Ralph saw two problems in this. First, capital spending was not linked tightly enough to the strategic and operating plans for the businesses. Because of this, capital spending proposals were out of context and difficult to evaluate. Ralph intended to tie capital spending closely to strategic and operating plans to ensure that its evaluation was realistic and fact-based. He would also ensure that the finance staff developed appropriate hurdle rates. These would differ by division and reflect the particular opportunity cost of capital.

Second, Ralph knew that one of EG's biggest failures had been in the evaluation of its acquisitions. EG paid too much for the Woodco acquisitions in the 1980s, although the accounting earnings and dilution figures looked good in the first year or two afterward. To Ralph, it was really quite simple: The cash flow value to EG's shareholders had to be higher than the price EG would have to pay, or Ralph would not make the acquisition.

Ralph also believed that EG could assess value much more systematically than in the past. First, EG management would evaluate the target's business on an "as is" basis, just as the team had done for EG. Next, management would use the restructuring hexagon approach to identify improvements that EG management could make to the value of the company, without any EG synergies.

Finally, EG would evaluate the potential for hiking the value of the acquisition through synergies with other EG businesses. Finally, EG management would think about the strategic options the acquisition could create: It might give EG an option on a new technology in one of its businesses or access to a new market, both of which could have substantial value under the right conditions. These would be difficult to evaluate and value, but would be important.

With this information, EG would know how much to pay and what to do with the business after the acquisition. EG would also know the value of the acquisition to other potential buyers, avoiding fruitless bidding contests or the chances of paying too much. (Why give all the potential value of the acquisition to the selling shareholders, when EG will be doing all the work to get there?)

Develop Value-Oriented Targets and Performance Metrics

Ralph knew that his managers needed clear targets and performance metrics to track their progress. Although the stock price was the ultimate metric, something more concrete, particularly to his business unit managers, was required.

During the corporate strategy analysis, Ralph learned what drives a business's value: its long-term revenue growth potential and its return on invested capital (relative to its cost of capital). Return on invested capital (ROIC) is after-tax operating profits divided by sum of working capital and fixed assets. It was obvious to Ralph that these measures—revenue growth and ROIC—were the standards that EG could use to set financial and performance targets at both the business unit and corporate level.

But to make this work, it would be necessary to tailor the growth and ROIC targets to the particular characteristics of the business unit. Consumerco had to emphasize revenue growth. Woodco needed to focus on improving its return on capital. Each business had to be understood before setting its targets.

Ralph recognized that ROIC and other accounting-based measures could be manipulated in the short term so as to obscure performance. ROIC does not reveal whether a business is earning its ROIC, for example, through high prices and declining market share, or stable prices and growing share.

As CEO, Ralph wanted to make sure that business unit leaders focused on long-term value creation. He did not want them pumping up ROIC to look good for one or two years at the expense of the longer term. So he decided that ROIC targets and performance measurement needed to include key operating and strategic drivers, which he thought of as measures of the "health" of the business. On the sales and marketing side, he wanted to set targets for pricing, market share, and new products. On the operating side, he wanted measures such as unit cost, quality, and the ability to meet delivery deadlines.

This was really an integrated system of target setting and performance measurement that combined financial information with health indicators and external market data. Ralph's accounting group, which was accustomed to dealing with accounting results alone, needed to adopt a new mind-set. The accounting group resisted. But Ralph showed them the benefits of integrating financial results with health measures.

Overhaul Business Performance Reviews

Having been at EG for many years, Ralph knew that the monthly and quarterly business unit performance reviews also needed an overhaul. He identified two issues. First, they focused entirely on short-term profits without regard to the drivers of profit. If a business unit hit its budget, there was little discussion of whether the budgeted results were met by true operational improvement or by shortsighted actions that would create hurdles later. Second, corporate management was ill-prepared for the reviews. Corporate executives were not knowledgeable enough about the business units to engage in constructive discussions about the causes of good or bad performance and to work with the business unit managers to identify solutions to problems.

Ralph decided to structure the business unit performance reviews around the new integrated performance measurement system that he had tasked his CFO to develop. He wanted to focus the reviews on the underlying drivers of results, good and bad. He also resolved that he and his CFO would become smarter about the strategic and operating issues and opportunities for each unit so that they could constructively engage the business unit leaders. He figured that if he and the rest of the corporate executive team could not add value to a particular unit, then EG shouldn't own it.

Tie Compensation to Value Creation

Ralph believed that compensation was an important way to motivate employees to focus on value creation. However, EG's system had many flaws. Like many company pay systems, bonuses were calculated based on formulas linked to short-term accounting profits. Executives also received stock options, which helped align their interests with the shareholders, but only loosely.

It was obvious to Ralph that he needed to link EG's compensation system to the new integrated-performance measurement system he was planning. That would lead managers to focus on the "health" of EG by highlighting performance against measures that would drive the long-term value creation of EG, not just short-term financial performance. He was wary, however, about using rigid formulas. He preferred a more subjective approach that allowed senior management to award bonus compensation based on an overall performance assessment, rather than mechanically tying it to a small number of measures. He wanted to be able to reward hard work and creativity, not just luck. Finally, he wanted to defer bonus payouts, even after retirement, so that managers would not have incentives to pump up EG's short-term performance just before they retired or left EG. He knew this would be difficult to implement, but thought it worth the effort.

Ralph decided to keep the stock-option program, but decided to make substantial changes to it. Most important, he changed the exercise price on options from a fixed price to a price indexed to a set of peer companies. That way, the value of the stock options would better reflect EG's own performance, rather than the overall stock market or its industry.

Develop Investor Communications Strategy

Ralph planned to build the company's credibility with Wall Street analysts and investors through some hard work. He wanted to know exactly what investors and analysts thought of EG's performance and prospects.

First, this would help him give the market the information it needed to evaluate the company properly. Second, Ralph knew that the market was smart. It could tell him a lot about the direction of his industry and his competitors. Ralph wasn't trying to fool the market about EG. He would treat the investors and the investing community with the same care that he showed EG's customers and employees. Had previous management taken the time to understand what the market was saying about EG, the company might have avoided the difficult position in which it found itself.

Previously, EG's investor communications had focused on accounting earnings. But Ralph learned that investors and analysts were more interested in the factors that drove earnings than in the earnings themselves. Earning per share driven by stock repurchases would not be viewed as favorably as increased earnings driven by revenue growth through greater market share. Accordingly, Ralph decided to use his investor conference calls and written materials to explain what drove EG's results, so that investors would understand them.

Reshape CFO's Role

Ralph also realized that the role of the CFO needed revising. Managing value takes a lot of work—especially when business strategy and financial strategy are so tightly interlinked. Ralph needed a strong executive to help him.

With the retirement of his current CFO, Ralph was free to create a position that would blend corporate strategy and financial responsibilities. The officer would act as a bridge between the strategic/operating focus of the division heads and the financial requirements of the corporation and its investors. The CFO would take the lead in developing a value-creating corporate strategy for EG, while working with Ralph and the division heads to build a value-management capability throughout the organization.

The CFO would also be responsible for managing the normal financial affairs and financial reporting of the corporation, in particular the new integrated performance-management system. But his or her success would be measured mainly by how well EG made the transition to a corporation that managed value in a superior way.

At the end of the first year, the new CFO's responsibilities would include helping deliver a first-draft corporate strategy and a clearly articulated supporting financial strategy. The CFO would also have trained leading managers to submit plans and proposals in terms of value creation. Investors and securities analysts would also have received a much clearer understanding of EG's strategy and value. Longer term, the CFO's success would be measured by the superior returns to shareholders, the value-creating expansion activities of the company, and the overall establishment of EG in the financial community as a leading-edge, value-managing company.

Ralph expected to spend as long as two years making the crossing—recruiting the new CFO; evaluating all major decisions in terms of impact on value; redesigning the compensation system for senior management; communicating more clearly and consistently with the stock market. All this would help ensure that EG produced outstanding value for shareholders. Moreover, by following this integrated approach, EG would more easily be able to set corporate priorities. Why? Because all major decisions would refer to the common benchmark: their impact on the value of the company.

SUMMARY

The ability to manage value is an essential part of developing sound corporate and business strategies. As the EG Corporation case shows, managing value is not a mysterious process. Valuation techniques can be complex in their details, but they are relatively straightforward in their application. In subsequent chapters we expand on the approaches needed to carry out such corporate value management.

REVIEW QUESTIONS

1. What are two important aspects of becoming value oriented? Apply and discuss the restructuring hexagon to Consumerco. What conclusions might be drawn from the hexagon value analysis to the specific decision alternatives for the Consumerco division?

2. Outline Ralph's five steps to rebuild EG's ability to manage value.

3. Identify how divisional relationships and performance gave rise to the concerns the financial markets had about EG Corp.

4. Identify and define the three steps necessary to develop a value management philosophy.

5. Discuss the value sensitivity analysis of Foodco, Woodco, and Consumerco. What are the strategy implications for each unit?

6. Discuss the different options for divesting business units. What are the advantages and disadvantages of each option?

Fundamental Principles
of Value Creation

This chapter explains the fundamental principles of value and value creation. The first part of the chapter illustrates the basics of value creation with the story of Fred's Hardware. The second part develops the model of value and value creation more formally.

FRED'S HARDWARE

Fred's business undergoes a remarkable transformation. Fred starts out as the owner of a small chain of hardware stores. Then he develops the idea of Fred's Superhardware and converts his stores to the new concept. To expand, Fred takes his company public to raise additional capital. His success leads Fred to develop additional retail concepts, such as Fred's Furniture and Fred's Garden Supplies. In the end, Fred is faced with the complexity of managing a retail conglomerate.

The Early Years

In the early years, Fred owned a small chain of hardware stores. Naive in the ways of finance, he asked us to help him assess his company's financial performance. To keep things simple, we told Fred that he should measure the return on invested capital (after-tax operating profits divided by the capital invested in working capital and property, plant, and equipment) and compare it with what he could earn if he invested his capital elsewhere, for example in the stock market.

Fred calculated his return on invested capital as 18 percent. We suggested that he could earn 10 percent by investing his capital in stocks with

Exhibit 3.1 Fred's Hardware: 2000 Economic Profit

	ROIC (percent)	WACC[1] (percent)	Spread (percent)	Invested capital ($ thousand)	Economic profit ($ thousand)
Entire company	18	10	8	10,000	800
Without low return store	19	10	9	8,000	720

[1]Weighted average cost of capital.

similar risk, so Fred was satisfied, since his investment was earning more than he could earn elsewhere.

Fred had an idea for increasing his company's overall return on invested capital (ROIC). One of his stores was earning only a 14 percent return, and if he closed it, he could increase his average return on invested capital. We told him that what he should care about is not the ROIC itself, but the combination of ROIC (relative to the cost of capital) and the amount of capital invested, expressed as economic profit. We showed him a simple example (see Exhibit 3.1).

Economic profit can be expressed as the spread between ROIC and the cost of capital, multiplied by the amount of invested capital. In Fred's case, economic profit was $800,000. If he closed down his low-returning store, average ROIC would increase, but economic profit would decline. Even though the store earned a lower ROIC than the other stores, it still earned more than its cost of capital.

The objective is to maximize economic profit over the long term, not ROIC. Consider an extreme example: Most investors would prefer to earn a 20 percent return on $1 million of capital, rather than a 50 percent return on $1,000 of capital, even though the rate of return on the smaller capital is higher. Fred was convinced. He set out to maximize economic profit.

A few weeks later, Fred came back perplexed. His sister Sally, who owned Sally's Stores, had just told him about her aggressive expansion plans. As Exhibit 3.2 shows, Sally's operating profit was projected to grow much faster than Fred's. Fred did not like the idea of his sister bettering him.

Wait a minute, we said. How is Sally getting all that growth? What about her economic profit? Fred went back to check and came back with Exhibit 3.3. Indeed, Sally was achieving her growth by investing lots of capital, not through increased efficiency. Her company's ROIC was declining significantly, leading to a decrease in economic profit *despite* the growth in operating profit. Fred was relieved and went off to explain it all to Sally.

Growing Fred's Business

For many years, Fred was happy with the economic profit framework. Then one day he reappeared. He wanted to develop a new business called

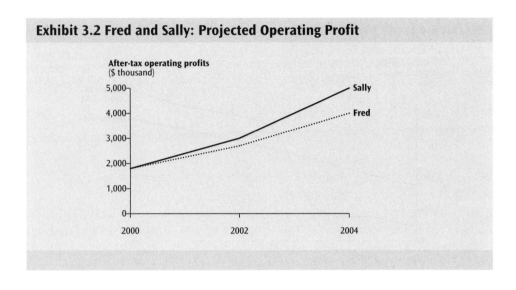

Exhibit 3.2 Fred and Sally: Projected Operating Profit

Fred's Superhardware. But when he looked at the projected results (he now had a financial analysis department), he found that economic profit would decline in the next few years if he converted his stores to the new format because of the new capital investment required (see Exhibit 3.4 on p. 50). After four years, economic profit would be greater, but he did not know how to trade off the short-term decline in economic profit against the long-term improvement.

We said, yes, Fred, you are right. You need some more sophisticated financial tools. At first, we were trying to keep it simple. But now Fred was faced with a decision where the straightforward rule of increasing or

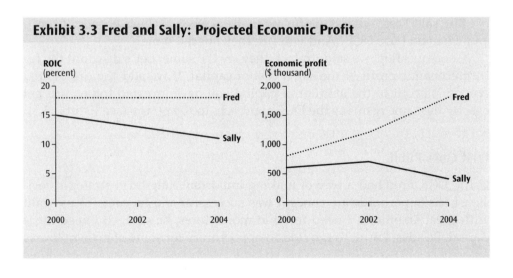

Exhibit 3.3 Fred and Sally: Projected Economic Profit

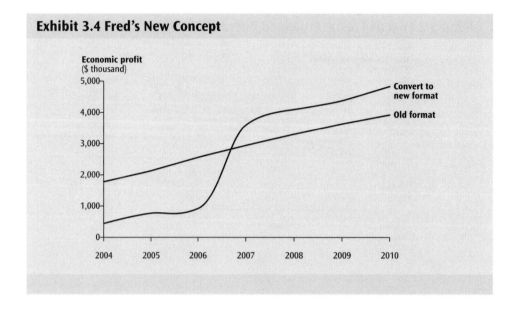

Exhibit 3.4 Fred's New Concept

maximizing economic profit would not offer a clear answer. He needed to aggregate multiple years into a single number to compare the different strategies. One method is to use discounted cash flow (DCF), also known as present value.

Fred said that he knew about DCF. You forecast the future cash flow of a company and discount it to the present at the same opportunity cost of capital discussed earlier. We helped Fred apply DCF to his new store concept. We discounted the projected cash flows at 10 percent. The DCF value of his company without the new concept was $53 million. With the new concept, the DCF value increased to $62 million. He was excited that he could pursue the new concept.

But, said Fred, what is confusing to me is when do I use economic profit and when do I use DCF? And why are they not the same?

Good question, we said. In fact, they *are* the same. Let's discount the future economic profit at the same cost of capital. If we add the discounted economic profit to the amount of capital you have invested today, you get exactly the same result as the DCF approach, to the penny (see Exhibit 3.5).

Fred Goes Public

Using DCF, Fred had a way of making important long-term strategic decisions. His Superhardware concept was successful and he came to us again with great ambitions. I need to build more stores, he said, so I need more capital. Besides, I want to provide an opportunity for some of my employees

Exhibit 3.5 Equivalence of DCF and Economic Profit Valuation[1]

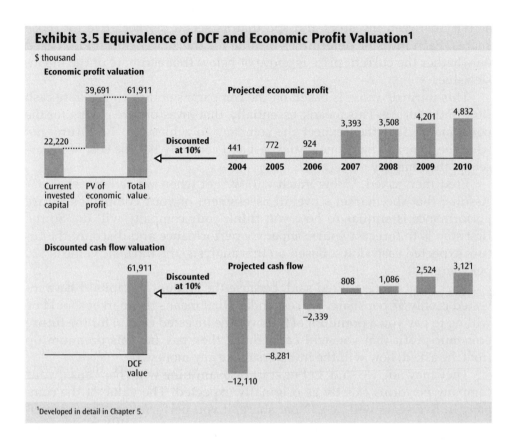

$ thousand

Economic profit valuation

22,220 39,691 61,911

Current invested capital | PV of economic profit | Total value

Discounted at 10% ←

Projected economic profit

441 | 772 | 924 | 3,393 | 3,508 | 4,201 | 4,832
2004 | 2005 | 2006 | 2007 | 2008 | 2009 | 2010

Discounted cash flow valuation

61,911

Discounted at 10% ←

DCF value

Projected cash flow

808 | 1,086 | 2,524 | 3,121
−2,339
−8,281
−12,110

[1]Developed in detail in Chapter 5.

to become owners. So I have decided to take my company public. What is going to happen?

Well, we said, now you need to learn the distinction between financial markets and real markets and how they relate to each other. We need to show you that good performance in one market does not necessarily translate to good performance in another.

Until now, we have been talking about the real market: How much profit and cash flow are you earning relative to the investments you have to make? Are you maximizing your economic profit and cash flow? In the real market, your decision rule is simple: Choose strategies or make operational decisions that maximize the present value of future cash flow or future economic profit.

When a company enters the financial (or capital) market, the real market decision rules are essentially unchanged, but life becomes more complicated because management must simultaneously deal with outside investors and analysts.

When a company goes public, it sells shares to a wide range of investors who can trade those shares in an organized market. The trading activity between investors and speculators sets a market price for those shares. Each investor determines a value for the shares and trades based on whether the current price is above or below that estimate of the intrinsic value.

This intrinsic value is based on the company's ability to generate cash flow in the future. This means, essentially, that investors are paying for the performance that they expect the company to achieve in the future, not what the company has done in the past and certainly not the cost of the assets in the company.

Fred then asked, "How much will we get when we sell our shares?" Assume that the market's overall assessment of your company's future performance is similar to how you think your company will do. So the first step is to forecast your company's performance and discount the future expected cash flows. Based on this analysis, the intrinsic value is $20 per share.

That is interesting, Fred said, because the amount of capital I have invested is only $7 per share. We responded, that means the market should be willing to pay you a premium of $13 over the invested capital for the future economic profit that you will earn. But if they pay me this premium up front, he asked, how will the investors make any money?

They may not, we said. Let us start by examining what happens if your company performs exactly as originally expected. The value of the company in five years will be $32 per share, if you perform exactly as anticipated, expectations beyond five years do not change, and investors continue to expect a 10 percent return from alternative investments. Assume that you have not paid any dividends. So an investor who bought stock for $20 per share today could sell the share for $32 in five years. The annualized return would be 10 percent, exactly the same as the discount rate we used to discount your future performance. The interesting thing is that as long as you perform as expected, the return for your shareholders will be equal to their opportunity cost (assuming the opportunity cost does not change).

If, on the other hand, you did better than expected, your shareholders would earn more than 10 percent. If you did worse than expected, your shareholders would earn less than 10 percent.

Consider the following analogy. Investing in the stock market is like betting on a sports team, but with a point spread (a point spread is the expected difference in points at the end of the game). When a spread exists, you cannot just pick the team you expect to win. You have to beat the spread (if you pick the favorite team, the favorite has to win by more points than the spread for the bet to pay off). Thus, picking a good team is not enough. The team has to beat expectations!

So, Fred said, the return that my investors earn is driven not by the performance of my company but by the performance relative to expectations.

Exactly, we said. Does that mean, asked Fred, that I have to manage my company's performance in the real markets and the financial markets at the same time? Yes, we said. If you create lots of value in the real market (by earning more than your cost of capital and growing fast) but do not do as well as investors expect, they will be disappointed. Your task as manager is to maximize the intrinsic value of the company and to properly manage the expectations of the financial market.

Managing the market's expectations is tricky. You do not want its expectations to be too high or too low. We have seen companies convince investors that they will deliver great performance and then not deliver on those promises. Not only will the share price drop when the market realizes that the company cannot deliver, but it may take years for the company to regain credibility. On the other hand, if the market's expectations are too low and your share price is low relative to the opportunities the company faces, you may be subject to a hostile takeover.

Okay, said Fred, I am ready to go public. Fred initiated an initial public offering (IPO) and raised the capital he needed for the company.

Fred Expands into Related Formats

Fred's Hardware grew quickly and regularly beat expectations, so his share price was a top performer in the market. Fred was confident that his management team could achieve high growth in the Superhardware stores so he decided to try some new concepts: Fred's Furniture and Fred's Garden Supplies. But he was concerned about how to manage the business as it became increasingly complex. He had always had a good feel for the business, but as it grew and he had to delegate decisions he was not sure that things would be managed well.

He told us that his financial people had put in place a planning and control system to closely monitor the economic profit of every store and each division overall. Economic profit targets were set annually for the next three years, progress monitored monthly, and managers' compensation tied to economic profit against these targets. Yet he was not certain that the company was on track for the long-term performance that he and the market were expecting.

You need a planning and control system that tells you about the "health" of the company, the ability of the company to continue growing and creating value, we told Fred. You need a system that incorporates forward-looking metrics, not just backward-looking ones. Tell me more, said Fred.

As Fred had pointed out, the problem with financial metrics is that they cannot tell you how your managers are doing at building the business for the future. For example, in the short term, managers could improve their short-term financial results by cutting back on customer service (the number of employees available in the store at any time to help customers, or employee training), or deferring maintenance or spending on brand-building. You must also incorporate metrics related to customer satisfaction or brand awareness that can give you an idea about the future, not just the current performance.

Finally, Fred was satisfied. He came back from time to time to see us, but only for social visits.

Summarizing Fred's Lessons

Although Fred's story is simple, it highlights the core ideas about creating and measuring value. Here are five important lessons Fred learned:

1. In the real market, you create value by earning a return on your invested capital greater than the opportunity cost of capital.

2. The more you can invest at returns above the cost of capital, the more value you create (growth creates more value as long as the return on capital exceeds the cost of capital).

3. You should select strategies that maximize the present value of expected cash flows or economic profit (you get the same answer regardless of which you choose).

4. The value of a company's shares in the stock market is based on the market's expectations of future performance (which can deviate from intrinsic value if the market is less than fully informed about the company's true prospects).

5. After an initial price is set, the returns that shareholders earn depend more on the changes in expectations about the company's future performance than the actual performance of the company. For example, if a company is expected to earn 25 percent on its investments, but only earns 20 percent, its stock price will drop, even though the company is earning more than its cost of capital.

FORMALIZING THE VALUE CREATION STORY

Fred's story explained the basic principles of value creation. The remainder of this chapter develops the discounted cash flow approach to valuation more formally.

The Intuition behind DCF

To demonstrate the power of discounted cash flow, we start with a simple example. The following table shows the projected earnings for two companies, Value, Inc. and Volume, Inc.:

Earnings	Year				
	1	2	3	4	5
Value, Inc.	$100.0	105.0	110.3	115.8	121.6
Volume, Inc.	$100.0	105.0	110.3	115.8	121.6

Based on this information, would you pay more for Value, Inc. or Volume, Inc.? Since the future earnings of both companies are identical, you might think that they are worth the same. But earnings can be misleading. It is necessary to examine how each company generated its growth. Following is the projected cash flow for the two companies:

Value, Inc.	Year				
	1	2	3	4	5
Earnings	$100.0	$105.0	$110.3	$115.8	$121.6
Net investment	25.0	26.2	27.6	29.0	30.4
Cash flow	$ 75.0	$ 78.8	$ 82.7	$ 86.8	$ 91.2

Volume, Inc.	Year				
	1	2	3	4	5
Earnings	$100.0	$105.0	$110.3	$115.8	$121.6
Net investment	50.0	52.5	55.1	57.9	60.8
Cash flow	$ 50.0	$ 52.5	$ 55.1	$ 57.9	$ 60.8

Now, which company would you pay more for? Most people would pay more for Value, Inc. because it generates higher cash flows. Value, Inc.'s cash flows are higher than Volume, Inc.'s despite identical profits because it invests less than Volume, Inc. to achieve the same profit growth. Value, Inc. invests 25 percent of its profits, whereas Volume, Inc. must invest 50 percent of its profits to generate the same profit growth.

If we assume that both companies have identical risk, we can discount their cash flows at the same discount rate, say 10 percent. If both companies continue to grow cash flow at 5 percent, we can use the growing free cash flow perpetuity formula to value each company.

$$Value = \frac{Cash\ Flow_{t=1}}{Cost\ of\ Capital - g}$$

The formula assumes that a company's cash flow will grow at a constant rate forever.

Using the formula, we compute the value of Value, Inc. to be $1,500 and Volume, Inc. to be $1,000.

We can also calculate an implied earnings multiple for the two companies by dividing their value by their current earnings. Value, Inc. has an earnings multiple of 15 and Volume, Inc. of 10. So despite having identical earnings *and* earnings growth rates, they have *different* earnings multiples. This example illustrates the essential problem with relative value methods such as earnings multiples. Using an earnings multiple approach, you might estimate Volume, Inc.'s value by multiplying Value, Inc.'s multiple and Volume's earnings, particularly if you did not have a forecast of its cash flows. That would clearly overstate Volume's value. Relative value methods do not value directly what matters to investors. Investors cannot buy a house or car with earnings. Only the cash flow generated by the business can be used for consumption or additional investment.

The DCF model accounts for the difference in value by factoring in the capital spending and other cash flows required to generate earnings. DCF has long been used by companies to evaluate capital spending proposals. We can also use DCF to value the entire business, which is effectively just a collection of individual projects.

Drivers of Cash Flow and Value

Technically, once you have estimated and discounted cash flow, you have completed the valuation. However, projected cash flows will not necessarily lead to insights about the performance or the competitive position of the company. Examining only cash flows, you would not be able to answer questions such as these: How does the projection compare with past performance? How does the projection compare with other companies? What are the important factors that could increase or decrease the value of the company?

In addition, short-term cash flows are not good performance measures. A one-year measure of cash flow is meaningless and easy to manipulate. A company can delay capital spending or cut back on advertising or research to improve short-term cash flow. On the other hand, large negative cash flow is not a bad thing if the company is investing to generate even larger cash flows down the road.

As an example, here is the historical and projected cash flow for Heineken, the Dutch brewer:

Historical Free Cash Flow (Euro Millions)		Projected Free Cash Flow (Euro Millions)	
1999	197	2004	(107)
2000	(495)	2005	181
2001	42	2006	320
2002	(685)	2007	477
2003	(1,124)	2008	648

There is not much interesting to say about this series of numbers.

What really matters are the drivers of cash flow. There are two key drivers of cash flow and ultimately value: the rate at which the company can grow its revenues and profits, and its return on invested capital (relative to the cost of capital). A company that earns higher profits per dollar invested will be worth more than a company that cannot generate the same level of returns. Similarly, a faster growing company will be worth more than a slower growing company if they both earn the same return on invested capital (and this return is high enough to satisfy investors).

The following chart shows Heineken's performance from the perspective of growth and return on invested capital:

	1999–2003 Actual (Percent)	2004–2008 Projected (Percent)
Revenue growth	10.7	7.2
EBITA growth	11.9	5.2
ROIC (after goodwill)	13.9	8.9
Cost of capital	8.2	7.5

Comparing this information with what we know about other businesses, we can better assess how Heineken is performing. We can measure the company's growth relative to the industry. We can evaluate whether its ROIC is improving or deteriorating and how it compares with other branded consumer-products companies. In Heineken's case, growth is expected to slow from 10.7 percent per year during the 1999 to 2003 period to 7.2 percent for the next five years. ROIC is projected to drop significantly from around 14 percent historically to less than 9 percent, due to acquisitions and negative currency effects.

To demonstrate the link between ROIC, growth, and free cash flow, we next build a simple valuation model. To do this, we return to the example of

Value, Inc. and model how its cash flows develop year by year. In year 1, Value, Inc.'s earnings equal $100 and net investment equals $25, so cash flow equals $75.

Value, Inc.	Year 1
Earnings	$100.0
Net investment	25.0
Free cash flow	$ 75.0

Value, Inc. invested $25 to grow its profits. Assume that Value, Inc. earns a 20 percent return on its new investment going forward. Year 2's earnings would equal year 1's earnings ($100) plus 20 percent of year 1's investment or $5 ($25 × 20 percent) for a total of $105. (We have also assumed that the earnings on the base level of capital in place at the beginning of year 1 do not change.) Suppose the company reinvests the same percentage of its operating profits each year and earns the same return on new capital. Value, Inc.'s cash flow would look as we presented it previously:

Value, Inc.	Year				
	1	2	3	4	5
Earnings	$100.0	$105.0	$110.3	$115.8	$121.6
Net investment	25.0	26.2	27.6	29.0	30.4
Cash flow	$ 75.0	$ 78.8	$ 82.7	$ 86.8	$ 91.2

Each year Value, Inc.'s earnings and cash flow grow at 5 percent and each year the company reinvests 25 percent of its profits at a return of 20 percent in order to achieve its growth. We can say that in this simple world, a company's growth rate is the product of its return on new capital and its investment rate (net investment divided by operating profits):

Growth Rate = Return on New Invested Capital × Investment Rate

For Value, Inc.,

Growth rate = 20% × 25%
= 5%

Now look at Volume, Inc.'s cash flows. Volume, Inc. also earns $100 in year 1. However, Volume, Inc. earns only a 10 percent return on its capital. For Volume, Inc. to increase its profits in year 2 by $5, it must invest $50 in the first year. Volume, Inc.'s cash flows are as follows:

Volume, Inc.	Year				
	1	2	3	4	5
Earnings	$100.0	$105.0	$110.3	$115.8	$121.6
Net investment	50.0	52.5	55.1	57.9	60.8
Cash flow	$ 50.0	$ 52.5	$ 55.1	$ 57.9	$ 60.8

A greater return on invested capital results in more cash flow, given the same growth rate in operating profits. As noted, Value, Inc. is worth more than Volume, Inc. despite identical earnings and growth rates.

Now look at how growth drives cash flow and value. Suppose Value, Inc. wants to increase its growth rate (and it can invest more capital at the same return). If Value, Inc. wants to grow at 8 percent instead of 5 percent, it must now invest 40 percent of its earnings each year, as shown next (we can use the formula developed earlier to calculate the required investment rate):

Value, Inc.	Year				
	1	2	3	4	5
Earnings	$100.0	$108.0	$116.6	$126.0	$136.0
Net investment	40.0	43.2	46.6	50.4	54.4
Cash flow	$ 60.0	$ 64.8	$ 70.0	$ 75.6	$ 81.6

Note that Value, Inc.'s cash flow is lower each year than it had been in the previous example. At this new higher growth rate, Value, Inc.'s cash flow is lower than the first scenario until year 9, but from then on the cash flow becomes much larger (as shown on Exhibit 3.6 on p. 60). Which scenario results in a higher value? It turns out that as long as the return on new invested capital is greater than the cost of capital used to discount the cash flow, higher growth will generate greater value. In these two scenarios, if we assume that the growth and return patterns continue forever and that Value, Inc.'s cost of capital is 10 percent, then the present value of the 5 percent growth scenario is $1,500 and the present value of the 8 percent growth scenario is $3,000.

So it is worthwhile for investors to accept lower cash flow in the earlier years if they are more than made up for in the later years. This also demonstrates why cash flow in isolation is not a good performance measure. Value, Inc.'s cash flows are lower at 8 percent growth for a number of years, despite the higher value.

Exhibit 3.7 on page 60 shows a matrix of values for a hypothetical company over a range of projected growth rates and returns on invested capital.

Exhibit 3.6 Value, Inc.: Cash Flow at Different Growth Rates

5 percent growth rate

	Year 1	2	3	4	5	6	7	8	9	10	11	12
Earnings	100	105	110	116	122	128	134	141	148	155	163	171
Net investment	25	26	28	29	30	32	34	35	37	39	41	43
Cash flow	**75**	**79**	**83**	**87**	**91**	**96**	**101**	**106**	**111**	**116**	**122**	**128**

8 percent growth rate

	Year 1	2	3	4	5	6	7	8	9	10	11	12
Earnings	100	108	117	126	136	147	159	171	185	200	216	233
Net investment	40	43	47	50	54	59	63	69	74	80	86	93
Cash flow	**60**	**65**	**70**	**76**	**82**	**88**	**95**	**103**	**111**	**120**	**130**	**140**

The exhibit assumes a 10 percent cost of capital. A given value can result from different combinations of growth and return. Since companies cannot always have more of both, a table like this helps managers set targets for long-term performance improvement. A company with an already high ROIC creates more value by increasing growth than by earning ever higher ROIC. Conversely, companies with low ROIC create more value by increasing ROIC. Exhibit 3.7 also demonstrates what happens when the return on new invested capital does not exceed the cost of capital. If the return exactly equals the WACC (weighted average cost of capital), then additional growth neither creates nor destroys value. This makes sense as investors will not pay a premium for additional growth if they can earn the same returns elsewhere. If the return on new invested capital is less than WACC, then additional growth actually destroys value. Investors would earn better returns by investing their capital elsewhere.

Exhibit 3.7 How ROIC and Growth Drive Value[1]

$ million

		ROIC (percent)				
		7.5	10.0	12.5	15.0	20.0
Earnings growth	3	887	1,000	1,058	1,113	1,170
rate (percent)	6	708	1,000	1,117	1,295	1,442
	9	410	1,000	1,354	1,591	1,886

Value destruction ◄─── Value neutral ───► Value creation

[1]Assumes starting NOPLAT = 100, WACC = 10 percent, and a 25-year horizon after which ROIC = WACC.

The Zen of Corporate Finance

Now that we have shown that ROIC and growth drive cash flow and value, we can go a step further and develop a simple formula that captures the essence of valuation. To be consistent, we first introduce some terminology that we will use throughout the book. The terms are defined in detail in Part Two.

- NOPLAT (Net Operating Profits Less Adjusted Taxes) represents the profits generated from the company's core operations after subtracting the income taxes related to the core operations.

- Invested Capital represents the cumulative amount the business has invested in its core operations—primarily property, plant, and equipment and working capital.

- Net Investment is the increase in invested capital from one year to the next.

$$\text{Net Investment} = \text{Invested Capital}_{t+1} - \text{Invested Capital}_{t}$$

- FCF (Free Cash Flow) is the cash flow generated by the core operations of the business after deducting investments in new capital.

$$\text{FCF} = \text{NOPLAT} - \text{Net Investment}$$

- ROIC (Return on Invested Capital) is the return the company earns on each dollar invested in the business. (ROIC can be defined in two ways, as the return on all capital or as the return on new or incremental capital. For now, we assume that both returns are the same.)

$$\text{ROIC} = \frac{\text{NOPLAT}}{\text{Invested Capital}}$$

- IR (Investment Rate) is the portion of NOPLAT invested back into the business.

$$\text{IR} = \frac{\text{Net Investment}}{\text{NOPLAT}}$$

- WACC (Weighted Average Cost of Capital) is the rate of return that investors expect to earn from investing in the company and therefore the appropriate discount rate for the free cash flow. WACC is defined in detail in Chapter 10.

- g (Growth) is the rate at which the company's NOPLAT and cash flow grows each year.

Assume that the company's revenues and NOPLAT grow at a constant rate and the company invests the same proportion of its NOPLAT in its business each year. Investing the same proportion of NOPLAT each year also means that the company's free cash flow will grow at a constant rate.

Since the company grows its cash flows at a constant rate, we can begin by valuing a company using the well-known cash flow perpetuity formula:

$$\text{Value} = \frac{\text{FCF}_{t=1}}{\text{WACC} - g}$$

This formula is well established in the finance and mathematics literature.[1] Next, define free cash flow in terms of NOPLAT and the investment rate.

$$\text{FCF} = \text{NOPLAT} - \text{Net Investment}$$
$$= \text{NOPLAT} - (\text{NOPLAT} \times \text{IR})$$
$$\text{FCF} = \text{NOPLAT} \times (1 - \text{IR})$$

Earlier, we developed the relationship between the investment rate (IR), the company's projected growth in NOPLAT (g), and the return on investment (ROIC).[2]

$$g = \text{ROIC} \times \text{IR}$$

Solving for IR, rather than g, leads to,

$$\text{IR} = \frac{g}{\text{ROIC}}$$

Now build this into the free cash flow definition:

$$\text{FCF} = \text{NOPLAT} \times \left(1 - \frac{g}{\text{ROIC}}\right)$$

Substituting for free cash flow gives the key value driver formula:

$$\text{Value} = \frac{\text{NOPLAT}_{t=1} \left(1 - \dfrac{g}{\text{ROIC}}\right)}{\text{WACC} - g}$$

Substituting the forecast assumptions for Value, Inc. and Volume, Inc. results in the same values we came up with when we discounted their cash flows:

---

[1] For the derivation, see T. E. Copeland and J. Fred Weston, *Financial Theory and Corporate Policy*, 3rd ed. (Reading, MA: Addison Wesley, 1988): Appendix A.

[2] Technically, we should use the return on new, or incremental capital, but for simplicity here, we assume that the ROIC and incremental ROIC are equal.

Company	$NOPLAT_{t=1}$	Growth (Percent)	ROIC (Percent)	WACC (Percent)	Value
Volume, Inc.	100	5	10	10	1,000
Value, Inc. at 5% growth	100	5	20	10	1,500
Value, Inc. at 8% growth	100	8	20	10	3,000

We call the key value driver formula the *Zen of Corporate Finance* because it relates a company's value to the fundamental drivers of economic value: growth, ROIC, and the cost of capital. You might go so far as to say that this formula represents all there is to valuation. Everything else is mere detail.

So why do we not use this formula in practice? In some cases we do, but in most situations, the model is overly restrictive, as it assumes a constant ROIC and growth rate going forward. For companies whose key value drivers are expected to change, we need a model that is more flexible in its forecasts. Therefore, while we do not use this formula in practice, it is extremely useful as a way to keep the mind focused on what drives value.

In Chapter 4, we present the statistical evidence that, in fact, value in the stock market is driven by ROIC and growth, as the Zen formula would predict. In Chapter 6, we provide examples of the actual returns on invested capital and growth rates that companies have historically achieved.

DCF EQUALS THE PRESENT VALUE OF ECONOMIC PROFIT

When we told Fred's story, we introduced the concept of economic profit. You can also value a company using economic profit. The results are identical to the DCF model. (We show the mathematical proof in Appendix A.)

In the economic profit model, the value of a company equals the amount of capital invested, plus a premium equal to the present value of the value created each year. The concept of economic profit is far from new. It dates to at least 1890, when the economist Alfred Marshall wrote: "What remains of the owner's profits after deducting interest on his capital at the current rate may be called his earnings of undertaking or management."[3] Marshall said that the value created by a company during any time period (its economic profit) must take into account not only the expenses recorded in its accounting records but also the opportunity cost of the capital employed in the business.

An advantage of the economic profit model over the DCF model is that economic profit is a useful measure for understanding a company's performance in any single year, whereas free cash flow is not. For example, you would not track a company's progress by comparing actual and projected free cash flow because free cash flow in any year is determined by discretionary, and potentially important, investments in fixed assets and

[3] A. Marshall, *Principles of Economics*, vol. 1. (New York: MacMillan & Co., 1890): 142.

working capital. Management could easily improve free cash flow in a given year at the expense of long-term value creation by simply delaying investments.

Economic profit measures the value created by a company in a single period and is defined as follows:

$$\text{Economic Profit} = \text{Invested Capital} \times (\text{ROIC} - \text{WACC})$$

In other words, economic profit equals the spread between the return on invested capital and the cost of capital times the amount of invested capital. Value, Inc. has invested capital of $500, return on invested capital of 20 percent, and WACC of 10 percent. Its economic profit for the year is $50:

$$
\begin{aligned}
\text{Economic Profit} &= \$500 \times (20\% - 10\%) \\
&= \$500 \times 10\% \\
&= \$50
\end{aligned}
$$

Economic profit translates size, return on capital, and cost of capital into a single measure. When performing an economic profit valuation, we discount and sum all future economic profit.

The above formula for economic profit can be rearranged and defined as after-tax operating profits less a charge for the capital used by the company:

$$
\begin{aligned}
\text{Economic Profit} &= \text{NOPLAT} - \text{Capital Charge} \\
&= \text{NOPLAT} - (\text{Invested Capital} \times \text{WACC})
\end{aligned}
$$

The alternative calculation generates the same value for economic profit.

$$
\begin{aligned}
\text{Economic Profit} &= \$100 - (\$500 \times 10\%) \\
&= \$100 - \$50 \\
&= \$50
\end{aligned}
$$

This approach shows that economic profit is similar in concept to accounting net income, but it explicitly charges a company for *all* its capital, not just the interest on its debt.

Using the economic profit approach, the value of a company equals the amount of capital invested plus a premium or discount equal to the present value of its projected economic profit:

$$\text{Value} = \text{Invested Capital} + \text{Present Value of Projected Economic Profit}$$

Note that if a company earned exactly its WACC every period, then the discounted value of its projected free cash flow should exactly equal its invested capital: Since no value is created by the company, it is worth exactly what was originally invested. A company is worth more or less than its invested capital only to the extent that it earns more or less than its WACC. Therefore, the premium or discount relative to invested capital must equal the present value of the company's future economic profit.

As shown, Value, Inc. earns $50 a year more than investors demand (its economic profit). So the value of Value, Inc. equals $500 (its invested capital at the time of the valuation) plus the present value of its economic profit. In Value, Inc.'s case, its economic profit is $50 in the first year and it grows by 5 percent each year. The present value of its economic profit can be calculated using the growing perpetuity formula:

$$\text{Present Value of Economic Profit} = \frac{\text{EP}}{(\text{WACC} - g)}$$

$$\text{Present Value of Economic Profit} = \frac{\$50}{(10\% - 5\%)} = \$1,000$$

So, Value, Inc.'s value is its invested capital of $500, plus the present value of its economic profit ($1,000) or $1,500, which is exactly equal to the value we came up with when we discounted their cash flows.[4]

ROIC AND GROWTH DRIVE MULTIPLES

Until now, we have focused on how ROIC and growth drive the discounted cash flow and economic profit valuation. We can also use the key value driver formula to show that ROIC and growth drive common multiples, such as price-to-earnings and market-to-book.

To see this, divide both sides of the key value driver formula by NOPLAT:

$$\frac{\text{Value}}{\text{NOPLAT}_{T=1}} = \frac{\left(1 - \dfrac{g}{\text{ROIC}}\right)}{\text{WACC} - g}$$

As the formula shows, a company's earnings multiple is driven by both its expected growth and its return on capital.

You can also turn the formula into a value/invested capital formula. Start with the identity:

---

[4] It appears from the economic profit valuation that the book value of a company drives its economic value. It is true that how we measure a company's current invested capital affects its economic profit. It does not, however, affect its value. If we overstate the company's invested capital, the present value of its future economic profit will be understated by exactly the same amount, so value will not change, and vice versa.

$$\text{NOPLAT} = \text{Invested Capital} \times \text{ROIC}$$

Substituting into the key value driver formula gives:

$$\text{Value} = \frac{\text{Invested Capital} \times \text{ROIC} \times \left(1 - \dfrac{g}{\text{ROIC}}\right)}{\text{WACC} - g}$$

Dividing both sides by Invested capital gives:[5]

$$\frac{\text{Value}}{\text{Invested Capital}} = \text{ROIC} \times \frac{\left(1 - \dfrac{g}{\text{RONIC}}\right)}{\text{WACC} - g}$$

We encounter many executives who think that earnings multiples are primarily driven by growth. As a result, they tend to assume that differences in multiples are primarily due to differences in market expectations about growth. In fact, this idea is perpetuated by the investment community because growth stocks are typically defined as stocks with high earnings multiples. But as the Zen formula demonstrates, multiples are driven by both growth *and* ROIC.

Understanding what drives multiples can be quite helpful. We can use this breakdown of multiples to determine the market's required expectations about a company's long-term future growth. Consider Procter & Gamble and Lowe's, which both trade near 20 times earnings:

Company	Earnings Multiple	ROIC Percent	Implied Long-Term Growth Percent
Procter & Gamble	20	38	5
Lowe's	20	12	9

---

[5] If total ROIC and incremental ROIC are not the same, then this equation becomes:

$$\frac{\text{Value}}{\text{Invested Capital}} = \text{ROIC} \times \frac{\left(1 - \dfrac{g}{\text{RONIC}}\right)}{\text{WACC} - g}$$

Where ROIC equals the return on the company's current capital and RONIC equals the return on incremental capital.

We built DCF models for both companies and asked what assumptions about future ROIC and growth were consistent with each company's earnings multiple. We assumed that ROIC was constant (which appeared reasonable in light of history and analysts' projections) and then solved backwards for growth. Procter & Gamble achieves its earnings multiple of 20 by having a very high ROIC and modest growth. This is consistent with its historical performance and the projected growth of its industry. Lowe's has a much lower ROIC, but is expected to grow much faster (also consistent with its historical and projected performance).

WHY HAVE MULTIPLES ENDURED?

Now that we have explained the logic behind the DCF approach to valuation, you may be asking why earnings multiples are so commonly used in analysts' reports and investment banking pitches. Earnings multiples are a useful shorthand for communications and a useful sanity check for your valuation.

Multiples endure because a discounted cash flow valuation requires projections about ROIC, growth, and free cash flow. Because predicting the future is a difficult task, many financial analysts use multiples to avoid making subjective forecasts. Furthermore, if the expected growth, ROIC, and cost of capital are similar for a set of companies, they should have similar multiples. If you do not have much information about a company's expected performance, you will probably assume that their expected growth and ROIC will match other companies in their industry. So you could value them by assuming that their earnings multiple will equal that of their peers.

Relying on an industry average multiple, however, can be dangerous. Besides the assumption that the ROIC and growth of the typical company in the industry match your company's ROIC and growth, differences in accounting, the effects of inflation, cyclicality, and other factors can distort multiples. At the end of the day, a well-done industry multiple actually takes the same level of effort as a good set of cash-flow forecasts.

Multiples can, however, serve as a useful shorthand, especially for knowledgeable investors. A leading sell side analyst recently told us that he uses discounted cash flow to analyze and value companies, but that he typically communicates his findings in terms of implied multiples. For example, an analyst might say, "Company X deserves a higher multiple than company Y because it is expected to grow faster, earn higher margins, or generate more cash flow."

In practice, we also use multiples as a sanity check. We always compare a company's implied multiple with its peers to see if we can explain why its multiple is higher or lower (due to growth or ROIC). See Chapter 12 for a discussion on how to analyze earnings multiples.

SUMMARY

This chapter showed that value is driven by expected cash flows. Cash flow, in turn, is driven by expected returns on capital and growth. These are the principal lessons of valuation and corporate finance. The remainder of this book discusses how to apply these concepts, both in more technical terms (Part Two) and as a manager (Part Three). Before we move on to the details, however, we first present empirical evidence that long-term ROIC, growth, and cash flow do indeed drive value.

REVIEW QUESTIONS

1. Why should Fred be more interested in economic profit than returns? How does economic profit relate to growth planning?

2. What prompts the need to move from period-to-period metrics, such as ROIC or economic profit, to discounted cash flow?

3. Compare and contrast the economic profit to discounted cash flow approaches. Identify a key advantage of the economic profit model over the discounted cash flow model.

4. Identify the two key drivers to cash flow. How do these drivers impact corporate value?

5. Identify the five key lessons of value creation.

6. The returns that investors earn are driven not by company performance, but by "performance relative to expectations." Discuss.

7. What advantage might exist using a multiples approach to corporate valuation versus either the discounted cash flow model or the economic profit model?

8. Firms A and B are constant growth firms, identical in every aspect except that the ROIC for A is 15 percent and B is 5 percent. Assume that management is in the process of establishing an investment rate of either 40 percent or 60 percent for each firm. Compute the estimated value for each investment rate for each firm given the following information:

Firm A	
Cash flows at $t=1$	$5,000
WACC	10%
Investment rate	1. 40%
	2. 60%
Return on new capital	15%

Firm B	
Cash flows at $t=1$	$5,000
WACC	10%
Investment rate	1. 40%
	2. 60%
Return on new capital	5%

What conclusions should be drawn with respect to the relationship of WACC to ROIC?

4

Do Fundamentals Really Drive the Stock Market?

In the second half of the 1990s, the S&P 500 Index more than tripled in value to an all-time high of almost 1,500. Previous unknowns, such as Amazon and AOL, became stock market superstars, along with a galaxy of other "New Economy" and dot-com entrants. Then the market crashed, and many stars flickered out. In the aftermath, people began to question whether long-held finance theories could really explain such dramatic swings in share prices. Some would even assert that stock markets lead lives of their own, detached from the basics of economic growth and business profitability. Should we abandon the discounted cash flow (DCF) valuations described in Chapter 3 and view the stock market as an arena where emotions rule?

We think not. Although some stocks, in some sectors, can be driven in the short term by irrational behavior, the stock market as a whole follows fundamental laws, grounded in economic growth and returns on investment. In fact, we were surprised at how well this simple, fundamental valuation approach has matched stock market price-to-earnings levels over the past 40 years.

This chapter presents empirical research that supports our view that return on capital, growth, and free cash flows drive value in the capital markets:

- Companies with higher returns and higher growth (at returns above the cost of capital) are valued more highly in the stock market.

- To value stocks, markets primarily focus on the long-term and not short-term economic fundamentals. Although some managers may believe that missing short-term earnings per share (EPS) targets always has devastating share price implications, the evidence shows that share price depends on long-term returns, not short-term EPS performance itself.

- Stock markets are perfectly capable of seeing the economic fundamentals behind accounting information. Therefore, managers should not be overly concerned with the implications of new accounting rules on options or goodwill.

- Stock market valuations correctly reflect underlying economic fundamentals, even when individual investors do not invest on the basis of the fundamentals. While we agree with proponents of "behavioral finance" that emotions can run away with parts of the market, such reactions do not last very long. In fact, we conclude the following for the U.S. and U.K. stock markets:

  —Overall, share price levels have reflected economic fundamentals quite well over the past four decades. The principles that drove share prices in the 1960s still remain valid today, despite significant economic ups and downs, industrial restructurings, and technological and other changes.

  —Market-wide price deviations from fundamentals can occur, but they are the exception, not the rule. In the late 1970s, prices were too low as investors were obsessed with high short-term inflation rates. In the late 1990s, market prices reached excessive levels that could not be justified by the underlying economic fundamentals.

- Market-wide price deviations are short-lived: Over the past four decades, the market corrected itself within a few years to price levels consistent with economic fundamentals.

Our studies indicate that, in most cases, managers can safely assume that share prices reflect the markets' best estimate of intrinsic value. Therefore, managers should continue to make decisions based on discounted cash flow and economic profit. Even when the market undergoes a period of irrational behavior, as we explain in this chapter, smart managers can detect and perhaps exploit these market deviations.

SHAREHOLDER VALUE DRIVEN BY RETURN AND GROWTH

In examining the behavior of the stock market, we first must distinguish between what drives market valuation levels (such as market-value-to-capital ratios) and what drives total return to shareholders (TRS). Market valuation levels are determined by the company's absolute level of long-term performance and growth, that is, expected revenue and earnings growth and return on invested capital (ROIC). TRS is measured by changes in the market valuation of a company over some specific time period and is driven by changes in investor expectations for long-term future returns on capital and growth.

Valuation Levels Driven by Long-Term ROIC and Growth

In Exhibit 4.1, we show that the relative market value of a company, as measured by the market-value-to-capital ratio, is determined by the company's growth and its spread of ROIC over the weighted average cost of capital (WACC). The vertical axis of this graph demonstrates that higher returns (for the same level of growth, as measured on the horizontal axis) lead to higher valuations. Also, when the return on invested capital exceeds the cost of capital, growth leads to higher value. When ROICs fall below the cost of capital, however, higher growth leads to lower valuations. These results, introduced in Chapter 3, are based on a two-stage variant of the key value driver formula (see Chapter 9 for details of the two-stage version underlying Exhibit 4.1).

Although Exhibit 4.1 is a theoretical model, the stock market supports its conclusions. In fact, the empirical results were similar when we compared the market-value-to-capital ratios of more than 500 of the largest U.S. listed companies versus their 10-year growth in sales and 10-year average return on invested capital (ROIC). We grouped the companies by sales

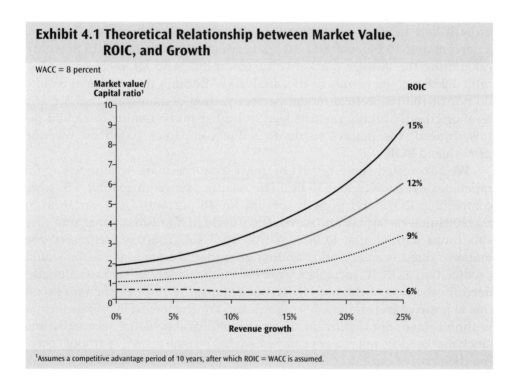

Exhibit 4.1 Theoretical Relationship between Market Value, ROIC, and Growth

WACC = 8 percent

[1]Assumes a competitive advantage period of 10 years, after which ROIC = WACC is assumed.

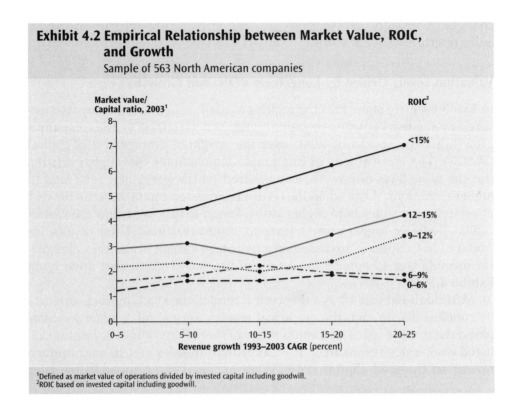

Exhibit 4.2 Empirical Relationship between Market Value, ROIC, and Growth

Sample of 563 North American companies

Market value/Capital ratio, 2003[1]

ROIC[2]

<15%

12–15%

9–12%

6–9%

0–6%

Revenue growth 1993–2003 CAGR (percent)

[1]Defined as market value of operations divided by invested capital including goodwill.
[2]ROIC based on invested capital including goodwill.

growth and ROIC (e.g., companies with average sales growth between 5 percent and 10 percent and ROICs between 12 percent and 15 percent), calculating the average market-value-to-capital ratio for each group. Exhibit 4.2 shows the results of this analysis. Although the empirical results do not fit the theoretical model perfectly, they demonstrate that for any level of growth, higher returns lead to higher market-value-to-capital ratios. Indeed, the market seems to value companies based on revenue growth and ROIC.

We also tested these results by regressing the market-value-to-capital ratios against growth and ROIC. The results, shown in Exhibit 4.3, were compelling: ROIC and growth account for 46 percent of the variation in market-value-to-capital ratios. We then divided the full sample into five subgroups with similar ROICs. Within each subgroup, we regressed the market-value-to-capital ratios against growth and found, as theory would predict, that as ROIC increases, growth is increasingly related to value. Indeed, in the case of the high-ROIC subgroups, the slope of the regression line is positive and statistically significant. For the low-ROIC subgroups, it is almost flat or not significant. Thus, the empirical evidence shows that the stock market does not reward companies that pursue growth without covering their cost of capital.

Exhibit 4.3 Regressions of Market-Value-to-Capital with ROIC and Growth

	Dependent variable	Number of observations	R^2	Variable$_1$	Slope$_1$	t-Stat$_1$	P-value$_1$[2]
Full sample	MV/IC[1]	563	46%	ROIC	19.3	21.5	0%
				Variable$_2$	Slope$_2$	t-Stat$_2$	P-value$_2$
				Growth	2.0	3.4	0%

ROIC cohort	Dependent variable	Number of observations		Variable$_1$	Slope$_1$	t-Stat$_1$	P-value$_1$[2]
0 – 6%	MV/IC[1]	93		Growth	0.25	0.52	60%
6 – 9%	MV/IC[1]	146		Growth	0.76	0.82	41%
9 – 12%	MV/IC[1]	124		Growth	3.22	2.83	1%
12 – 15%	MV/IC[1]	61		Growth	2.14	1.43	16%
>15%	MV/IC[1]	139		Growth	7.99	3.18	0%

[1]Defined as market value of operations divided by invested capital including goodwill.
[2]P-value represents the probability that the tested relationship does not hold, with a P-value of 5% used as the threshold of statistical significance.

On an industry level, we see the same pattern. An analysis of 130 European and U.S. publicly traded chemical companies between 1963 and 2001 showed that companies with higher sales growth achieved a higher market valuation only if they could generate returns above their cost of capital, which is close to the average ROIC in this industry (see Exhibit 4.4 on p. 76). The market penalized companies that attempted growth but earned returns below their cost of capital.

In another test, we applied discounted cash flow to estimate the value of the five leading companies in each of four industry sectors—pharmaceuticals, electric utilities, consumer goods and oil—that had different growth and profitability profiles. We developed forecasts based on long-term historical results and projections from the Institutional Brokers' Estimate System (IBES) analyst consensus estimates.[1] We then discounted the cash flows at the weighted average cost of capital (WACC) for each company. Based on these forecasts, our estimates corresponded very closely to each company's market-value-to-capital ratios for all of the industry sectors, as shown in Exhibit 4.5 on page 77.

Since expected future growth and returns for companies are not directly measurable, we cannot assert scientific proof for our claims. But these tests provide evidence that cash flow, led by the combination of revenue growth and return on capital, drives the value of companies.

[1] Thomson Financial, Institutional Brokers' Estimate System (IBES).

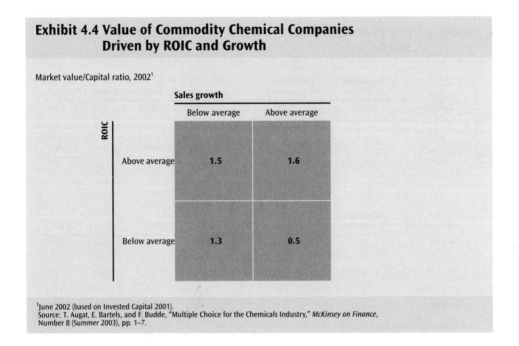

Exhibit 4.4 Value of Commodity Chemical Companies Driven by ROIC and Growth

Market value/Capital ratio, 2002[1]

	Sales growth	
	Below average	Above average
Above average	1.5	1.6
Below average	1.3	0.5

(ROIC shown on vertical axis)

[1]June 2002 (based on Invested Capital 2001).
Source: T. Augat, E. Bartels, and F. Budde, "Multiple Choice for the Chemicals Industry," *McKinsey on Finance*, Number 8 (Summer 2003), pp. 1–7.

Changes in Expectations Drive Total Returns to Shareholders

In Chapter 3, we discussed how total returns to shareholders (TRS) are driven by performance against expectations and not absolute levels of performance. For example, on July 13, 2004, Intel reported a second-quarter net income of $1.76 billion, almost double what it had reported for that period a year earlier. Nevertheless, Intel's share price declined by 11 percent on the day of the announcement, because its sales and margins, considered important indicators for long-term profitability in the sector, were below the market's expectations. Over horizons of 15 years and more, of course, TRS will be linked to earnings, because over the long term, earnings growth will track cash flows. Over shorter periods, however, performance against expectations should generally influence TRS more than the level of earnings and growth itself.

To test what drives TRS, we conducted a statistical analysis, correlating TRS with such traditional performance measures as cash flow and economic profit. We also correlated TRS with changes in cash flow expectations, using consensus earnings forecasts from IBES. As theory would suggest, there is a strong relationship between TRS and changes in performance expectations. However, there is almost no relationship between TRS and the various absolute cash flow or economic profit measures. Exhibit 4.6 on page 78 summarizes the results for the S&P 500 companies over the past 10 years. When we exclude the market bubble years of 1999 to 2001, the analysis shows that 18 percent of the TRS variation across the sample can be explained by the changes in investor expectations (as measured by the R^2 of

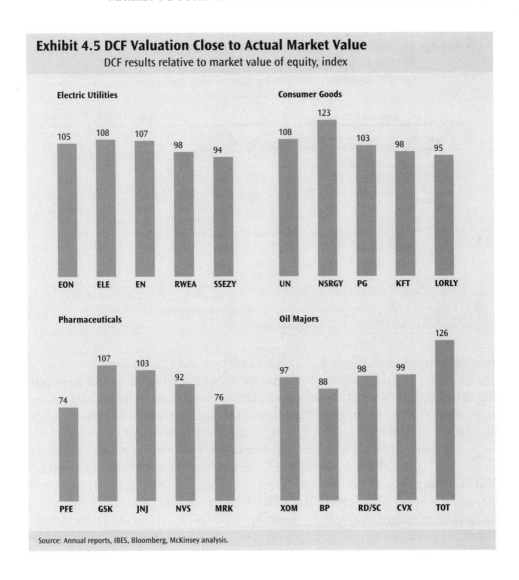

Exhibit 4.5 DCF Valuation Close to Actual Market Value
DCF results relative to market value of equity, index

Source: Annual reports, IBES, Bloomberg, McKinsey analysis.

the regression), far greater than for absolute measures of cash flow and economic profit.

MARKET FOCUSES ON LONG TERM RATHER THAN SHORT TERM

Many managers believe that the stock market focuses too narrowly on near-term earnings, giving companies too little credit for long-term investments. But we disagree: A quick look at the high values for companies without any near-term earnings (such as in biotech or high-tech) indicates that the market indeed takes a long-term view. In September 2004, the stock market capitalization of Sirius Satellite Radio was $4 billion. Yet as of that date, Sirius

Exhibit 4.6 Change in Expectations Is Key Driver of Total Return to Shareholders

S&P 500 companies, 1993–2003

Adjusted R² (percent)		Coefficient	t-Statistic	P-value[3]
Expectations measure[1] — 18.0	FY0	0.15	4.7	0%
	FY1	0.33	10.5	0%
	LTG	1.91	8.6	0%
Change in cash flow — 8.0		0.32	13.5	0%
Actual cash flow[2] — 0.0		0.15	3.0	0%
Change in economic profit — 1.5		0.08	5.1	0%
Actual economic profit[2] — 2.0		0.49	6.9	0%

[1]Expectations measure is based on change in analyst consensus EPS forecast for running fiscal year (FY0), the following fiscal year (FY1) and change in analyst consensus 5-year growth expectation (LTG).
[2]Scaled based on actual revenues.
[3]P-value represents the probability that the tested relationship does not hold, with p-value of 5% used as the threshold of statistical significance.
Source: Datastream, Compustat, IBES, Bloomberg, McKinsey analysis.

had reported sales of only $30 million and was still generating accounting losses. Why the large valuation? Investors believed Sirius would generate significant cash flows at some point in the future. More dramatically, in the late 1990s, the stock market's long-term view was certainly demonstrated in the ascent of Internet stocks, based on companies without concrete products, let alone profits. That time, the market was wrong; long-term earnings never materialized for many of these companies. Nonetheless, the market did not narrowly focus on near-term earnings when valuing these companies. (Chapter 23 describes the valuation of very high growth companies.)

Many managers complain, however, that the markets are increasingly sensitive to short-term earnings surprises. As a result, what some call the "EPS game" has emerged, in which corporations try to meet short-term EPS targets at almost any cost, for fear of missing analysts' expectations. Underscoring this, more than three-quarters of the financial executives in a recent survey said they would forgo economic value creation to avoid missing earnings targets and suffering the associated market reactions.[2]

Missing short-term EPS targets by itself does not lead to lower share prices. In many cases, however, investors have only short-term results by which to gauge long-term corporate performance. In these cases, they interpret the most recent EPS performance as an omen of long-term performance declines and/or loss of management credibility, so the missed target will lower a company's share prices. But if management can convince the market

---

[2]J. Graham, C. Harvey, and S. Rajgopal, "The Economic Implications of Corporate Financial Reporting" (*Journal of Accounting and Economics*, forthcoming).

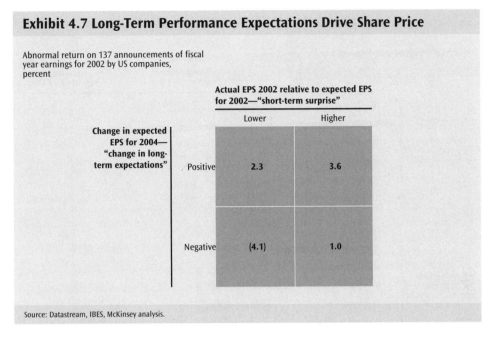

Exhibit 4.7 Long-Term Performance Expectations Drive Share Price

Abnormal return on 137 announcements of fiscal year earnings for 2002 by US companies, percent

Actual EPS 2002 relative to expected EPS for 2002—"short-term surprise"

		Lower	Higher
Change in expected EPS for 2004—"change in long-term expectations"	Positive	2.3	3.6
	Negative	(4.1)	1.0

Source: Datastream, IBES, McKinsey analysis.

that poor short-term earnings will not affect long-term profitability or growth, then the share prices need not fall. Exhibit 4.7 shows the share price reaction to the profit announcements of 137 U.S. companies in 2002.[3] There was no negative share price impact when undershooting earnings did not affect the outlook for longer-term business profitability. But when there was a clear indication of effect on long-term profit expectations, the share price had a strong negative reaction. Reactions had nothing to do with *short-termism* but involved real changes in long-term prospects.

In the pharmaceutical industry, announcements relating to products under development can affect share prices far more than quarterly earnings announcements. This makes sense: Product and pipeline development is a much better indicator of the long-term growth and profitability of pharmaceutical companies than short-term earnings. Markets understand this well, and as Exhibit 4.8 shows on page 80, prices react strongly to pipeline announcements, even when there is no impact on current earnings.

When a high-profile company misses an earnings target, it makes headlines, but the impact of short-term earnings on share prices should not be overstated. In an examination of a large sample of quarterly earnings announcements by U.S. companies between 1992 and 1997, earnings surprises explained less than 2 percent of share price volatility in the four weeks surrounding announcements.[4] In fact, more than 40 percent of companies with

[3] The sample includes selected companies from the S&P 500 Index for which the change in reported EPS and expected EPS was at least 2 percent.
[4] W. Kinney, D. Burgstahler, and R. Martin, "Earnings Surprise 'Materiality' as Measured by Stock Returns," *Journal of Accounting Research*, 40(5) (December 2002): 1297–1329.

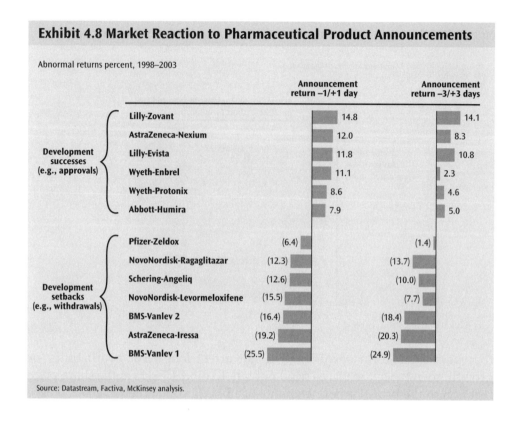

Exhibit 4.8 Market Reaction to Pharmaceutical Product Announcements

Abnormal returns percent, 1998–2003

		Announcement return –1/+1 day	Announcement return –3/+3 days
Development successes (e.g., approvals)	Lilly-Zovant	14.8	14.1
	AstraZeneca-Nexium	12.0	8.3
	Lilly-Evista	11.8	10.8
	Wyeth-Enbrel	11.1	2.3
	Wyeth-Protonix	8.6	4.6
	Abbott-Humira	7.9	5.0
Development setbacks (e.g., withdrawals)	Pfizer-Zeldox	(6.4)	(1.4)
	NovoNordisk-Ragaglitazar	(12.3)	(13.7)
	Schering-Angeliq	(12.6)	(10.0)
	NovoNordisk-Levormeloxifene	(15.5)	(7.7)
	BMS-Vanlev 2	(16.4)	(18.4)
	AstraZeneca-Iressa	(19.2)	(20.3)
	BMS-Vanlev 1	(25.5)	(24.9)

Source: Datastream, Factiva, McKinsey analysis.

a positive (or negative) earnings surprise actually had a negative (or positive) return. This underscores our conclusion that short-term earnings do not drive share prices.

Share prices are determined by long-term cash flows. To test the stock market's time horizon, we examine how much of a company's share price is accounted for by expected cash flows over the next several years. For a subset of S&P 500 companies, dividends expected in the first five years explained less than 9 percent of the market value, on average (see Exhibit 4.9), another illustration of the market's long-term view. Whether considering biotechs or the largest blue chips, investors value long-term cash flows.

The academic literature also finds evidence confirming the long-term view of stock markets:

- In general, stock markets reward R&D and advertising initiatives despite their negative impact on short-term earnings.[5] However, for companies with a weak outlook for future value creation from growth, the

[5] See, for example, K. Chauvin and M. Hirschey, "Advertising, R&D Expenditures and the Market Value of the Firm: Mergers and Acquisitions," *Financial Management*, 22 (1993): 128–140; and R. C. Graham and K. D. Frankenberger, "The Contribution of Changes in Advertising Expenditures to Earnings and Market Values," *Journal of Business Research*, 50 (2001): 149–155.

Exhibit 4.9 Present Value of Expected Dividends[1] for Selected S&P 500 Companies

	Present value of dividends expected over the next five years $	Share price $	Dividends as percentage of stock price (percent)
Abbott Laboratories	4.97	43.59	11.4
Boeing	3.38	42.14	8.0
Campbell Soup	3.23	26.80	12.1
Dow Chemical	6.66	41.57	16.0
Eli Lilly	6.73	70.33	9.6
Ford Motor Co	1.90	16.00	11.9
Gillette	3.36	36.73	9.2
Hewlett-Packard	1.52	22.97	6.6
International Business Machines	3.04	92.68	3.3
Johnson & Johnson	4.80	51.66	9.3
Kellogg	5.26	38.08	13.8
Lockheed Martin	3.07	51.40	6.0
McDonald's	1.98	24.83	8.0
New York Times	2.92	47.79	6.1
Occidental Petroleum	5.45	42.24	12.9
PepsiCo	3.20	46.62	6.9
Rohm & Haas	4.23	42.71	9.9
Sears Roebuck	4.61	45.49	10.1
Texas Instruments	0.40	29.38	1.4
United Parcel Service	4.73	74.55	6.3
Wal-Mart Stores	1.82	53.05	3.4
		Average	8.7

[1]Assuming 7% growth in dividends during next 5 years. Cost of equity based on risk free rate of 4.3%, market risk premium of 5.0% and Bloomberg beta.
Source: Bloomberg, McKinsey analysis.

stock market typically shows a negative price reaction. Further supporting our belief that the stock market has a sophisticated long-term view, investors reward R&D spending only if companies are expected to create value from it.[6]

- Announcements of capital expenditure increases and strategic investments usually boost share prices, even though such moves typically depress current cash flow and earnings.[7] For capital expenditures, growth opportunities are critical in explaining the stock market's

[6]S. Szewczyk, G. Tsetsekos, and Z. Zantout, "The Valuation of Corporate R&D Expenditures: Evidence from Investment Opportunities and Free Cash Flow," *Financial Management,* 25(1) (1996): 105–110.
[7]See, for example, J. R. Woolridge, "Competitive Decline and Corporate Restructuring," *Journal of Applied Corporate Finance,* 1 (1988): 26–36; and J. J. McConnell and C. J. Muscarella, "Corporate Capital Expenditure Decisions and the Market Value of the Firm," *Journal of Financial Economics,* 14(3) (1985): 399–422.

reaction. The market reacts far more favorably, the better the prospects for value-creating growth.[8]

- Stock markets generally react positively to write-offs of bad investments despite their impact on short-term earnings. For example, restructuring write-offs (as opposed to restructuring cash costs) are positively received, and the price reaction is especially strong if the corporation is losing money and has recently changed management.[9]

MARKETS SEE FUNDAMENTALS BEHIND ACCOUNTING INFORMATION

We have shown how market valuations are driven by economic fundamentals such as long-term return on capital and growth, which in turn drive long-term cash flows. Yet many managers remain obsessed with reported earnings, arguing that earnings are the key driver of share prices. Does the market respond primarily to surface accounting numbers, or does it dig down more deeply? As the following examples demonstrate, the market does indeed dig beneath reported earnings—right down to the underlying economic fundamentals.

It is true, however, that share prices will move when companies report higher or lower earnings if the accounting results reflect unexpected changes in underlying cash flows. This may occur with the availability of additional information, perhaps as a consequence of an accounting disclosure, such as a goodwill impairment—if the adjustment reveals lower benefits than expected from past acquisitions. Similarly, the change from last-in-first-out (LIFO) to first-in-first-out (FIFO) inventory accounting can swing share prices, not because of the change in reported earnings, but because of the tax implications of the move.

In addition, fraud or the manipulation of accounting information can cause shares to rise above the real value of the corporation. But markets can be fooled only so long. Sooner or later, cash flows must justify the share price.

Different Accounting Standards Do Not Lead to Different Values

Stock markets do not take reported earnings at face value. Evidence comes from companies that report different accounting results for different stock markets. Non-U.S. companies that have securities listed in the United States, for example, are required to report equity and net profit under U.S.

---

[8] T. J. Brailsford and D. Yeoh, "Agency Problems and Capital Expenditure Announcements," *Journal of Business*, 77(2) (2004): 223–256.

[9] P. K. Chaney, C. E. Hogan, and D. C. Jeter, "The Information Content of Restructuring Charges: A Contextual Analysis" (working paper, Nashville, TN: Vanderbilt University, 2000).

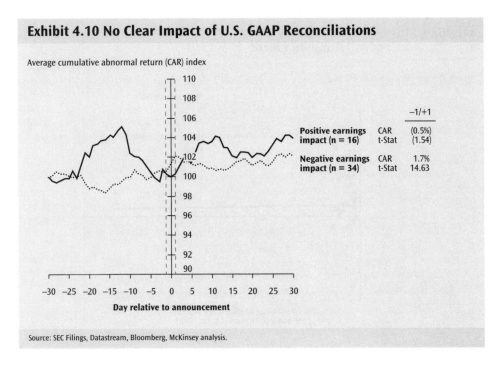

Exhibit 4.10 No Clear Impact of U.S. GAAP Reconciliations

Average cumulative abnormal return (CAR) index

		−1/+1
Positive earnings	CAR	(0.5%)
impact (n = 16)	t-Stat	(1.54)
Negative earnings	CAR	1.7%
impact (n = 34)	t-Stat	14.63

Day relative to announcement

Source: SEC Filings, Datastream, Bloomberg, McKinsey analysis.

Generally Accepted Accounting Principles (GAAP), which can differ significantly from the equity and net profit reported under their domestic accounting standards. If stock prices are truly based on reported earnings, which would investors choose—the earnings reported under U.S. GAAP or domestic accounting standards? To the market, it doesn't matter. The market is not interested in accounting choices; investors care about underlying performance.

To prove the point, we analyzed a sample of 50 European companies that began reporting reconciliations of equity and profit to U.S. GAAP after obtaining U.S. listings between 1997 and 2004. The differences between net income and equity under U.S. and local accounting standards were often quite large: In more than half of the cases, the deviation was more than 30 percent. Many executives probably worried that lower earnings under U.S. GAAP would translate directly to a lower share price. But this was not the case. As shown in Exhibit 4.10, even though two-thirds of the companies in our sample reported lower earnings following U.S. disclosure, the stock market reaction to their disclosure was positive. Evidently, increased disclosure outweighed any artificial accounting effects.

Treatment of Goodwill Does Not Affect Share Price

Since 2001 under U.S. GAAP and 2005 under International Financial Reporting Standards (IFRS) goodwill is no longer amortized on the income statement according to fixed schedules. Instead, companies must write off

Exhibit 4.11 No Consistent Market Reaction to SFAS-142 Goodwill Announcement

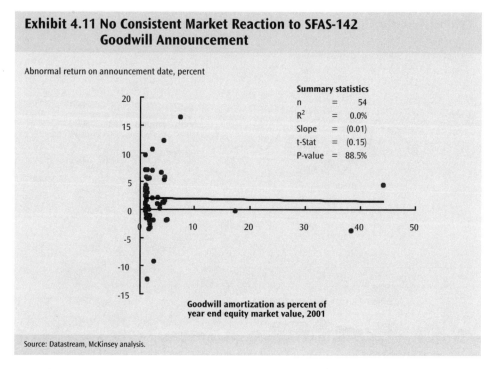

Abnormal return on announcement date, percent

Summary statistics

n	=	54
R^2	=	0.0%
Slope	=	(0.01)
t-Stat	=	(0.15)
P-value	=	88.5%

Goodwill amortization as percent of year end equity market value, 2001

Source: Datastream, McKinsey analysis.

goodwill only when the goodwill is impaired based on business valuations by independent auditors. What effect did changes in accounting for goodwill have on share prices? To answer this question, we looked at this accounting change's impact on share price in two ways.

First, we investigated the share price reactions for companies that stopped amortizing significant amounts of goodwill. These companies would show an increase in reported EPS after this change, since goodwill amortization was no longer charged to the income statement. We analyzed the share price reaction for a sample of 54 U.S. companies with significant goodwill on the day of the announcement in July, 2001 that goodwill amortization in the United States would be abolished.[10] The implied increase in EPS for these companies boosted initial share prices on average, but within two weeks, the prices had returned to normal. Obviously, the market realized that the accounting treatment of goodwill amortization does not affect cash flows. Furthermore, as shown in Exhibit 4.11, the initial share price reaction was not related to the relative amount of goodwill amortization for these companies, and for about a third of the sample the share price actually declined on announcement.

We also looked at 54 companies in the United States and Europe that wrote off significant amounts of impaired goodwill against their profit

---

[10] The sample consists of selected U.S. companies for which annual goodwill amortization was at least 1 percent of the market capitalization.

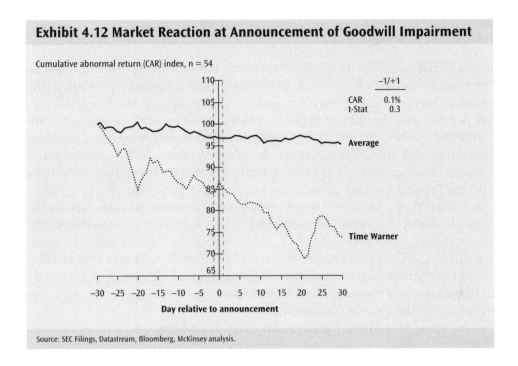

Exhibit 4.12 Market Reaction at Announcement of Goodwill Impairment

Cumulative abnormal return (CAR) index, n = 54

	−1/+1
CAR	0.1%
t-Stat	0.3

Average

Time Warner

Day relative to announcement

Source: SEC Filings, Datastream, Bloomberg, McKinsey analysis.

since January 2002.[11] In this case, as shown in Exhibit 4.12, we did not find a statistically significant drop in share prices on the day of the write-off announcement. Why? The markets already had anticipated the lower benefits from past acquisitions and had reduced the stock price by an average 35 percent in the six months preceding the write-off announcement.

For example, Time Warner announced on January 7, 2002, that it would write off $54 billion in goodwill. Time Warner's stock returns, plotted in Exhibit 4.12, show that the share price actually moved up somewhat on the day of the announcement, relative to major market indexes. However, Time Warner's stock had already lost as much as 37 percent over the six months prior to the announcement. Thus, despite significant changes in reported earnings caused by the changes in accounting from goodwill, there was no immediate impact on share price. The markets looked through current earnings to the underlying long-term cash flow.

Given overwhelming evidence that in the past the stock market looked beyond goodwill amortization when assessing pooling versus purchasing accounting for mergers and acquisitions, these findings should come as no surprise.[12] In fact, goodwill amortization as such never mattered—neither when it showed up in the financial statements nor when it disappeared.

[11] The sample comprises selected U.S. and European companies with a market capitalization of at least $500 million and an impairment charge of at least 2 percent of market capitalization.
[12] See, for example, E. Lindenberg, and M. Ross, "To Purchase or to Pool: Does It Matter?" *Journal of Applied Corporate Finance*, 12(2) (Summer 1999): 32–47.

Accounting for Employee and Management Stock Options Is Irrelevant for Market Value

In the debate over whether employee stock options should be expensed in the income statement, much of the concern has centered on whether the negative earnings impact will drive stock prices lower. From a capital market perspective, the answer is clear: As long as investors have sufficient information on the amount, terms, and conditions of the options granted, new expensing rules will not drive down share prices. In fact, according to a recent study, companies that voluntarily began expensing their employee options *before* it became mandatory experienced positive share price reactions when they announced their intentions to expense options, despite the negative impact on reported earnings.[13] The price reaction was especially strong when companies said they were expensing their options to boost transparency. The same researchers found that when sufficient information about the options is disclosed, the stock market includes the options values in its valuation of the companies—even when these values are not explicitly expensed in the income statement.[14]

We came to a similar conclusion after examining 120 U.S. companies that began voluntarily expensing their stock options in their income statements between July 2002 and May 2004. There was no negative share price impact around the disclosure of earnings; instead, share prices rose on the announcement day. Furthermore, as shown in Exhibit 4.13, there is no relation between the net income impact from option expensing and the abnormal returns during the days surrounding the new policy's announcement. In this case, the market already had the relevant information on the option plans and was not confused by a change in reporting policy.

LIFO/FIFO Inventory Reporting Does Not Influence Share Prices (But the Tax Impact Does)

A classic example of how cash flow matters more than profits can be seen in the impact that different inventory accounting methods have on these two measures. For instance, during periods when prices are rising, changing from FIFO to LIFO can decrease accounting profits yet lead to higher free cash flows. As prices rise, the LIFO inventory method results in lower earnings than the FIFO method, since the cost of goods sold is based on more recent, higher costs. Lower pretax earnings mean lower income taxes. Since the pretax cash flow is the same regardless of the accounting method, LIFO accounting leads to a higher after-tax cash flow than FIFO accounting, despite the lower reported earnings.

---

[13] D. Aboody, M. Barth, and R. Kasznik, "Firms' Voluntary Recognition of Stock-Based Compensation Expense," *Journal of Accounting Research*, 42(2) (December 2004): 251–275.
[14] D. Aboody, M. Barth, and R. Kasznik, "SFAS No. 123 Stock-Based Compensation Expense and Equity Market Values," *Accounting Review*, 79(2) (2004): 251–275.

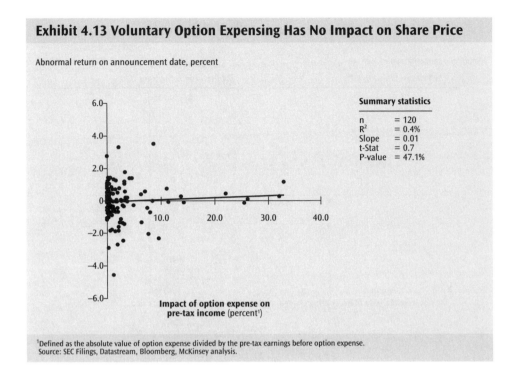

Exhibit 4.13 Voluntary Option Expensing Has No Impact on Share Price

Abnormal return on announcement date, percent

Summary statistics

n   = 120
R^2 = 0.4%
Slope   = 0.01
t-Stat   = 0.7
P-value = 47.1%

**Impact of option expense on
pre-tax income** (percent[1])

[1]Defined as the absolute value of option expense divided by the pre-tax earnings before option expense.
Source: SEC Filings, Datastream, Bloomberg, McKinsey analysis.

Any manager improperly focused solely on earnings would argue that switching from FIFO to LIFO will result in lower share prices as investors react to lower reported earnings. Yet research shows that switching from FIFO to LIFO actually lifts share prices. This is due to increased cash flow, as the DCF model predicts. After adjusting for movements in the broad market and other contemporary effects, companies switching to LIFO experienced significant increases in share prices, whereas firms switching to FIFO saw share prices decline (see Exhibit 4.14 on p. 88). In fact, one study found that the larger the reduction in taxes following the switch to LIFO, the greater the share price increase attributed to the change.[15]

SIGNIFICANT DEVIATIONS FROM INTRINSIC VALUE ARE RELATIVELY RARE AND SHORT-LIVED

When managers make good strategic decisions based on DCF analyses, the financial markets will reward them by setting stock prices according to their company's economic fundamentals. This relationship helps the manager put the company's resources to their best use—and create maximum value for shareholders. Remember, a volatile stock price does not mean

[15] G. Biddle and F. Lindahl, "Stock Price Reactions to LIFO Adoptions: The Association between Excess Returns and LIFO Tax Savings," *Journal of Accounting Research*, 20(2) (1982): 551–588.

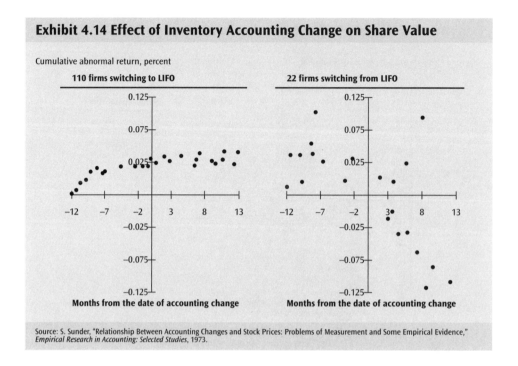

Exhibit 4.14 Effect of Inventory Accounting Change on Share Value

Source: S. Sunder, "Relationship Between Accounting Changes and Stock Prices: Problems of Measurement and Some Empirical Evidence," *Empirical Research in Accounting: Selected Studies*, 1973.

prices do not reflect intrinsic value. For instance, the share price of a biotech company may have reflected its economic fundamentals several years ago, but today the stock may be selling for much less if the company failed to commercialize its products.

Also, while random deviations from intrinsic value can occur in stocks from time to time, managers are still best off assuming that the market will correctly reflect the intrinsic value of their decisions. What managers must be alert to, however, are systematic deviations from intrinsic value, especially those that can affect strategic financial decisions, such as whether and when to issue new shares or pursue acquisitions.

But is there really evidence for such systematic deviations in stock markets? Since the seminal article by Werner DeBondt and Richard Thaler in 1985,[16] some finance academics and practitioners have argued that stock markets are *not* efficient—that they do not necessarily reflect economic fundamentals.[17] According to this "behavioral" point of view, significant and lasting deviations from intrinsic value occur in market valuations.[18] To be

[16] W. DeBondt and R. Thaler, "Does the Stock Market Overreact?" *Journal of Finance*, 40(3) (1985): 793–805.

[17] We loosely define efficient markets here as markets reflecting economic fundamentals.

[18] For an overview of behavioral finance, see N. Barberis and R. Thaler, "A Survey of Behavioral Finance," in *Handbook of the Economics of Finance*, edited by G. M. Constantinides et al. (Boston, MA: Elsevier Science, 2003): 1054–1123; and J. Ritter, "Behavioral Finance," *Pacific-Basin Finance Journal*, 11(4) (September 2003): 429–437.

sure, behavioral finance offers some valuable insights, chief among them that markets are not always right because market imperfections prevent rational investors from correcting mispricing by irrational investors. We cannot disagree with that. But how often do these deviations arise, and are they so significant that they should affect how managers make their financial decisions? Significant deviations from intrinsic value are rare, and markets revert to the economic fundamentals rapidly enough that managers should continue to base their decisions on DCF analyses.

Key Conditions for Market Deviations

In our interpretation of behavioral finance, markets fail to reflect economic fundamentals under three conditions:

1. *Irrational investor behavior.* "Irrational" investors do not process all available information correctly when forming expectations on the stock's future performance. Studies of the investment behavior of professional fund managers and analysts show various forms of such irrationality. For example, individual investors overreact and attach too much importance to recent events and results, so they overprice companies with strong recent performance. Also, individuals are overly conservative in updating expectations, so they underprice stocks that have released positive news on earnings.

2. *Systematic patterns of behavior across different investors.* If individual investors decided to buy or sell without consulting economic fundamentals, the impact on share prices would be limited. Only when they behave irrationally also in a systematic way (i.e., when large groups of investors share particular patterns of behavior) should persistent price deviations occur. Behavioral finance theory argues that patterns of overconfidence, overreaction, and overrepresentation are common to many investors, and such groups can be large enough to prevent a company's share price—at least for some stocks, some of the time—from reflecting underlying economic fundamentals.

3. *Limits to arbitrage in financial markets.* If there are enough rational investors in a market, and there are no barriers to arbitrage, systematic patterns of irrational behavior can be exploited, and they will not have lasting effects on market valuations. In reality, such arbitrage is not always possible. Transaction costs and risks are involved in setting up and running the arbitrage positions.

Assume that a company's share price has dramatically increased over the past few months because the company surprised the market with better-than-expected results. Based solely on this strong recent performance, investors might believe this company will continue to exceed market expectations and thus start bidding for shares. According to behavioral finance theory, many investors will demonstrate this type of myopic behavior, creating upward pressure on the share price.

As long as a sufficient number of investors can identify and take short positions against overpricing on the part of these myopic investors, the share price will return to its fundamental level. In practice, however, this may not be the case; the costs, complexity, and risks involved in setting up a short position may be too high for those who invest on economic fundamentals. One example is so-called "noise trader" risk. It is uncertain how long price deviations will persist, and whether they will increase before finally disappearing. If for some reason investors focused on fundamentals abandon their positions before the share price returns to its fundamental value, they would incur a loss.

When the preceding three conditions all apply, behavioral finance predicts that pricing biases in financial markets can be both significant and persistent.

Some well-known examples of such market deviations can help us understand whether, if, or how these conditions should change our perspectives on how finance theory applies to real-world decision making by corporate managers.

Market Overreaction and Underreaction, Reversal and Momentum

Over the past decade two well-known patterns of price deviations in stock markets have received considerable attention in academic studies: short-term momentum and long-term reversal in share prices. Reversal means that high-performing stocks of the past years typically become low-performing stocks over the next few years.[19] Momentum is a phenomenon in which positive returns for stocks over the past several months are typically followed by several months of continued positive returns.[20] The literature on behavioral finance offers several explanations for these price patterns, but the debate remains far from settled.

Some behaviorists argue reversal is caused by investor overreaction: Investors put too much weight on companies' recent performance. When companies have performed well in recent years, investors are inclined to extrapolate that success into the future. As a result, share prices increase too much, and when cash flows fail to meet projections, investors adjust their expectations, bringing on a reversal. The winning stocks of the past

[19] First documented by DeBondt and Thaler, "Does the Stock Market Overreact?"
[20] See, for example, N. Jegadeesh and S. Titman, "Returns to Buying Winners and Selling Losers: Implications for Stock Market Efficiency," *Journal of Finance*, 48(1) (1993): 65–92; and N. Jegadeesh and S. Titman, "Profitability of Momentum Strategies: An Evaluation of Alternative Explanations," *Journal of Finance*, 56(2) (2001): 699–720.

become low-performing stocks of the future. The same effect may also be responsible for well-known patterns such as the low returns some companies demonstrate following their IPOs and seasoned offerings.[21] Typically, companies issuing new stock previously demonstrated strong business performance, which in turn provides a reason to exploit a favorable track record and issue stock.[22]

Next, momentum can be explained by systematic underreaction: Overly conservative investors are too slow in adjusting their expectations after new information becomes available. Investors may underestimate the true impact of earnings changes, divestitures, share repurchases, and so on.[23] The result is that stock prices do not instantaneously react to good or bad news. This could give rise to short-term momentum in stock returns in which stocks that have outperformed the market as a whole for several months continue to do so over the next couple of months.

But academics are still debating whether irrationality among investors is truly what drives the long-term reversal and short-term momentum patterns found in stock returns. Eugene Fama and Kenneth French,[24] for example, believe that long-term reversals can be explained by risk premiums driven by market-to-book ratio and size. These can be interpreted as indicators of liquidity or distress risk, in addition to the traditional market or beta risk.[25] In Chapter 10, we discuss how such additional risk premiums can affect the cost of capital.

Similarly, short-term momentum in share price returns is not necessarily driven by irrational investors. Profits from these patterns are relatively limited after deducting transaction costs.[26] Thus, these small momentum biases could exist even if all investors were rational.

Furthermore, behavioral finance cannot yet explain why investors overreact under some conditions (such as IPOs) and underreact in others (such

[21] See, for example, J. Ritter, "The Long Run Performance of Initial Public Offerings," *Journal of Finance*, 46(1) (1991): 3–28; T. Loughran and J. Ritter, "The New Issues Puzzle," *Journal of Finance*, 50(1) (1995): 23–51; and B. Dharan and D. Ikenberry, "The Long-Run Negative Drift of Post-Listing Stock Returns," *Journal of Finance*, 50(5) (1995): 1547–1574.

[22] E. Fama, "Market Efficiency, Long-Term Returns, and Behavioral Finance," *Journal of Financial Economics*, 49(3) (1998): 283–306.

[23] Documented by V. Bernard and J. Thomas, "Evidence That Stock Prices Do Not Fully Reflect the Implications of Current Earnings for Future Earnings," *Journal of Accounting and Economics*, 3(4) (1990): 305–340; J. Lakonishok and T. Vermaelen, "Anomalous Price Behavior around Repurchase Tender Offers," *Journal of Finance*, 45(2) (1990): 455–478; and H. Desai and P. Jain, "Long-Run Common Stock Returns Following Stock Splits and Reverse Splits," *Journal of Business*, 70(3) (1997): 409–433.

[24] E. Fama and F. French, "Multifactor Explanation of Asset Pricing Anomalies," *Journal of Finance*, 51(1) (1996): 55–84.

[25] See, for example, J. Cochrane, *Asset Pricing* (Princeton: Princeton University Press, 2001): ch. 20.

[26] Cochrane, ibid., argues that momentum can be explained by a very small autocorrelation in stock returns combined with high volatility and that momentum predictability is too small to be exploited when transaction costs are taken into account.

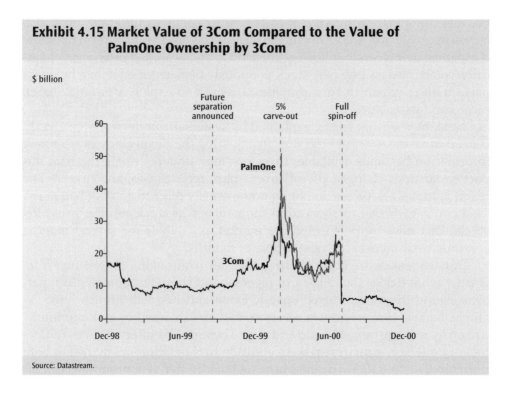

Exhibit 4.15 Market Value of 3Com Compared to the Value of PalmOne Ownership by 3Com

Source: Datastream.

as earnings announcements). Fama considers this puzzle a further indication that markets are efficient: There is no systematic way to predict when markets will over- or underreact.[27] Across all studies, the expected value of an abnormal return is therefore probably still zero. This would imply that managers should still make their decisions based on traditional DCF analyses and efficient-market assumptions.

Persistent Mispricing in Carve-Outs and Dual-Listed Companies

One type of market deviation often suggested to support the validity of behavioral finance is the mispricing of carve-outs and dual-listed companies (see Chapter 16 for more details on carve-outs). A well-documented example is the relative pricing of 3Com versus Palm after the Palm carve-out in March 2000. 3Com had floated 5 percent of its subsidiary Palm in anticipation of a complete spin-off within nine months. Yet immediately after the Palm carve-out, the market capitalization of Palm was higher than the entire market value of 3Com, implying that 3Com's other businesses had negative value (see Exhibit 4.15). Given the size and profitability of their other businesses, this observation clearly implies mispricing. So why did rational investors not exploit

[27] E. Fama, "Market Efficiency, Long-Term Returns, and Behavioral Finance," *Journal of Financial Economics*, 49(3) (1998): 283–306.

the mispricing by going short in Palm shares and long in 3Com shares? They could not, because the free float of Palm shares was too small after the carve-out: 95 percent of all shares were still held by 3Com. Establishing a short position in Palm would have required borrowing the shares from a Palm shareholder. As the share supply via short sales increased steadily over the months following the carve-out, the mispricing gradually decreased.[28]

Additional cases of mispricing for parent companies and their carved-out subsidiaries have been documented.[29] These cases involve similar difficulties in setting up short positions to exploit price differences. This in turn allows mispricing to persist for several weeks or months until the spin-off takes place or is abandoned. These examples expose price differences that appear to be inconsistent with efficient markets (at least in the sense that relevant price information was not quickly and correctly processed). In all cases, however, these price differences resolved within several months.

Another classic example is the price disparity between the shares of Royal Dutch Petroleum and Shell Transport &Trading (T&T), which are separately traded in the Amsterdam and London stock markets, respectively. These twin shares are entitled to a fixed 60:40 portion of the dividends of the combined Royal Dutch/Shell Group. Thus, one would expect that the prices of the Royal Dutch and Shell T&T shares would be priced in a fixed ratio of 60:40.

Over long periods, however, this has not been the case.[30] In fact, for several similar twin-share structures (such as Unilever and Reed-Elsevier), there have been prolonged periods of mispricing, as shown in Exhibit 4.16 on page 94. This phenomenon occurs because, for some reason, investors prefer one of the twin shares over the other and are prepared to pay a premium. The arbitrage opportunity from going short in the overpriced share and going long in the underpriced share is not exploited by rational investors. Not only have such price differentials persisted, they have sometimes been as large as 30 percent. One explanation is that because of noise trader risk, the arbitrage opportunity around dual-listed stocks is actually a risky strategy.[31] Arbitrage investors cannot be sure that prices will converge in the near term; the price gap could even widen.

Does this indict the market's ability to price? We do not think so. In recent years, the price differences for Royal Dutch and stocks with similar

[28] See J. Cochrane, "Stocks as Money: Convenience Yield and the Tech-Stock Bubble" (NBER working paper no. 8987, National Bureau of Economic Research, 2002).

[29] O. Lamont and R. Thaler, "Can the Market Add and Subtract? Mispricing in Tech Stock Carve-Outs," *Journal of Political Economy*, 111(2) (2003): 227–268; and M. Mitchell, T. Pulvino, and E. Stafford, "Limited Arbitrage in Equity Markets," *Journal of Finance*, 57(2) (2002): 551–584.

[30] K. Froot and A. Perold, "Global Equity Markets: The Case of Royal Dutch and Shell," Harvard Business School Case 9-296-077; and K. Froot and E. Dabora, "How Are Stock Prices Affected by the Location of Trade?" *Journal of Financial Economics*, 53(2) (1999): 189–216.

[31] A. de Jong, L. Rosenthal, and M. van Dijk, "The Limits of Arbitrage: Evidence from Dual-Listed Companies" (EFA 2004 Maastricht Meetings paper no. 4695).

Exhibit 4.16 Share Price Disparity of Dual-Listed Companies

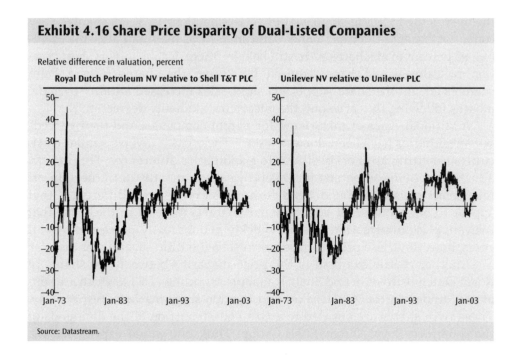

Source: Datastream.

underlying Anglo-Dutch corporate structures all appear to have shrunk. Furthermore, some of these twin-share structures have disappeared as the corporations formally merged, as Royal Dutch and Shell T&T did on October 28, 2004, in announcing the unification of their shares. The disappearance of price differences upon such unification announcements underlines the importance of noise trader risk. As soon as a formal date was set for definitive price convergence, arbitrageurs stepped in to correct any difference.[32] It also underlines the argument that mispricing occurs under special circumstances only—and is by no means a common or long-lasting phenomenon.

Markets and Fundamentals: The Bubble of the 1990s

So do markets reflect economic fundamentals? We believe they do. To verify this conclusion, we estimated the intrinsic valuation level for the U.S. stock market as a whole, based on economic fundamentals, using an equity DCF valuation model. This model is an extended, two-stage version of the value driver formula first presented in Chapter 3 (see Chapter 9 for more details).[33] By using a two-stage model, we could accommodate

[32]See de Jong, Rosenthal, and van Dijk, "The Limits of Arbitrage: Evidence from Dual-Listed Companies." (Note 31)
[33] In the standard value driver formula, we just replace ROIC with return on equity and WACC with cost of equity to obtain the market-to-book ratio of equity instead of invested capital.

both long-term economic fundamentals and short-term fluctuations in key value drivers.

To analyze the valuation levels for the stock market as whole, we forecast each key value driver, such as return on equity (ROE) and growth using economic fundamentals of the entire U.S. economy. For the first stage of the model, we used the actual return on equity, GDP growth, and cost of equity for the year in which we applied the model. In the second stage of the valuation model, we used long-term fundamental values as estimates for the ROE, growth, and cost of equity. Long-term return on equity and growth in the U.S. economy have been remarkably stable for the past 40 years, despite some deep recessions and periods of strong economic growth. The median return on equity for all U.S. companies has been a stable 12 to 15 percent. Long-term gross domestic product (GDP) growth for the U.S. economy has been about 3 percent per year in real terms since 1945.[34] When measured using five- or seven-year rolling averages, it has not deviated significantly from that level in any subperiod. In a separate analysis, we estimated that the inflation-adjusted cost of equity since 1962 has been fairly stable at about 6½ to 7 percent.[35] Using the two-stage DCF valuation model, we estimated the price-to-earnings and market-to-book ratios for the U.S. stock market for each year between 1962 and 2003 (see Exhibit 4.17 on page 96).[36] We did a similar analysis for the U.K. stock market and obtained similar results.

Overall, we were surprised by how well this simple, fundamental valuation model fits the stock market's price-to-earnings levels over the past three decades, despite periods of extremely high economic growth in the 1960s and 1990s, as well as periods of low growth and high inflation in the 1970s and 1980s. Over the long term, the stock market as a whole appears to follow the simple, fundamental economic laws discussed in Chapter 3: Value is driven by returns on capital, growth, and—via the cost of capital—interest rates.

This has led us to three important conclusions: First, by and large, the stock markets in the United States and the United Kingdom have been fairly priced and have oscillated around their intrinsic price-to-earnings ratios. The intrinsic P/E ratio was typically near 15, with the exception of the high-inflation years of the late 1970s and early 1980s, when it was closer to 10.

Second, the late 1970s and late 1990s did indeed produce significant deviations from intrinsic value. In the late 1970s, as investors were obsessed

[34] For the U.S. economy, corporate earnings as a percentage of GDP have been remarkably constant over the past 40 years at around 6 percent.
[35] For estimates of the inflation-adjusted cost of equity for the stock market as a whole, see Chapter 10 and M. Goedhart, T. Koller, and Z. Williams, "The Real Cost of Equity," *McKinsey on Finance*, 5 (Autumn 2002): 11–15.
[36] See M. Goedhart, T. Koller, and Z. Williams, "Living with Lower Market Expectations," *McKinsey on Finance*, 8 (Summer 2003): 7–11.

Exhibit 4.17 Estimating Fundamental Market Valuation Levels

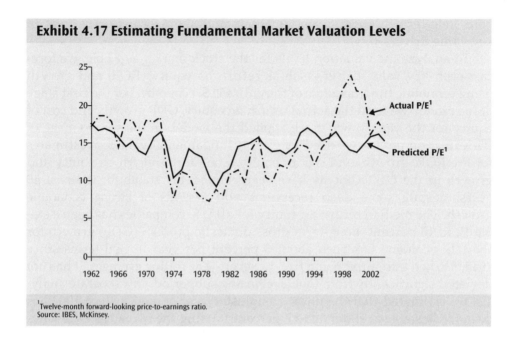

[1]Twelve-month forward-looking price-to-earnings ratio.
Source: IBES, McKinsey.

with high short-term inflation rates, the market was probably valued too conservatively. Based on long-term real GDP growth and returns on equity, the stock market should not have dropped to a P/E level of 7. The other obvious deviation occurred in the late 1990s, when the market valuation rose to a P/E ratio near 25. Such a level for the 12-month forward-looking P/E ratio could not be justified by a long-term real GDP growth of 3 percent and returns on equity of 12 to 15 percent.

Finally, when such deviations occurred, the stock market corrected itself within a few years to its intrinsic valuation level. Thus, although market valuations can apparently be wrong from time to time—even for the stock market as a whole—market valuations return to values justified by economic fundamentals.

When analyzing the relative valuation for the stock market as a whole, keep in mind that during the market bubble of the late 1990s, a limited number of companies with extremely large market capitalizations and extremely high multiples had an enormous impact on the (weighted average) price-to-earnings ratio for the S&P 500 (see Exhibit 4.18). The 12-month trailing P/E ratio for the S&P 500 was about 30 in 1999, whereas the average P/E ratio for almost 95 percent of the constituent companies was only 23. This difference in P/E ratios emerged during the boom of the late 1990s and disappeared by 2001.

Most of these large-capitalization companies with high P/E ratios were clustered in just three sectors: technology, media, and telecommunications

Exhibit 4.18 Impact of Largest Stocks on Overall Market Valuation

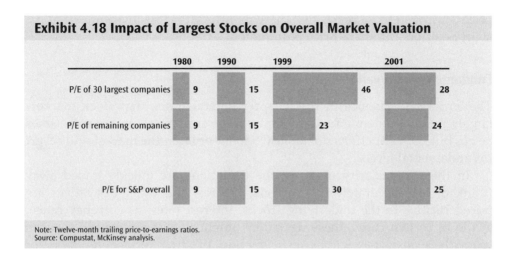

Note: Twelve-month trailing price-to-earnings ratios.
Source: Compustat, McKinsey analysis.

(TMT). In most other U.S. sectors, P/E ratios were significantly lower. Thus, the American stock market bubble of the late 1990s was largely driven by the valuation of the so-called TMT sectors. To illustrate how aggressively investors were valuing the share prices of some of these TMT stocks, we analyzed the value of the 10 highest market capitalization U.S. technology companies. At the end of 1999, these 10 companies had a combined market capitalization of $2.4 trillion, annual revenues of $240 billion, and net income of $37 billion, resulting in an aggregate price-earnings ratio of 64 times. We built a simple DCF model to estimate what performance would be required to justify that market value. For investors to earn an 11 percent return, these companies would have needed to grow their revenues to approximately $2.7 trillion by 2014 and their net income to about $450 billion. To put this in perspective, assuming that GDP grows at a healthy rate from 1999 through 2014 and corporate profits remain a stable share of GDP (as they have for at least the past 80 years), the total corporate profits of all U.S. companies would be about $1.3 to $1.5 trillion by 2014. So these 10 companies would need to earn about one-third of all the profits earned by all U.S. companies.

One would expect rational investors to try to exploit these cases of likely mispricing. But setting up a short position in overpriced stocks is not always easy, and can be costly and risky. The risk arises because although some investors may have recognized, for example, that these companies were overpriced, it was far from clear when this mispricing would disappear. An investor with a short position in these companies would need sufficient liquid assets to maintain the position and patiently sit through possible periods of even deeper mispricing. We know of one experienced investor who set up a short position on an overvalued high-tech stock only to abandon that position at a considerable loss when the share price continued to increase. Just three months after this investor exited his short position, the share price plummeted.

Fundamentals Prevail

The empirical evidence in this chapter demonstrates that stock markets largely reflect economic fundamentals. To be sure, markets can sometimes be off, but such situations do not last. Sooner or later, the market will revert to fundamental levels.

In the vast majority of cases, the deviations are quickly traded away (think of how accurately call options, futures, and other derivatives are priced relative to the underlying stocks, interest rates, or currency rates). While in certain cases, these deviations might persist for months or even years, there ultimately will be sufficient liquidity from rational investors for stock prices to revert to their intrinsic value. In the examples of Royal Dutch/Shell, Unilever, and Reed-Elsevier twin shares, the price differentials decreased significantly or even disappeared. In the 3Com/Palm example, the mispricing disappeared after two months. In the market bubble of the 1990s, the deviation from intrinsic value corrected itself in about three years.

In the end, market value reverts to levels justified by the underlying economic fundamentals—and why not? Irrational investors may cause stock prices to deviate temporarily from intrinsic value, but prices are driven by rational investors with deep pockets, who recognize economic fundamentals because they are focused on the long-term potential of stocks to generate cash dividends.

IMPLICATIONS OF MARKET (IN)EFFICIENCY FOR CORPORATE MANAGERS

Some managers point to evidence of the stock market's inefficiencies to justify a belief that the market behaves irrationally. As evidence, these managers offer the inefficiencies that academics cite, and make the case that arguments supporting the discounted cash flow approach do not square with the real world. Although markets can indeed be inefficient, in the sense that prices sometimes deviate from fundamentals, this does not make discounted cash flow valuation superfluous.

For investors, market deviations may represent an opportunity to make money depending on the practical difficulties and risks of setting up an arbitrage position. Once these inefficiencies become known, however, they usually disappear, and the search is on for new ones.[37] Evidence suggests

---

[37] See, for example, S. Ross, "Neoclassical Finance, Alternative Finance and the Closed End Fund Puzzle," *European Financial Management*, 8(2) (2002): 129–137.

that no investment fund has been able to systematically outperform the market as a whole over the past 35 years.[38] Thus, it appears that the market inefficiencies are not frequent or significant enough to provide investors with systematic excess returns over longer periods.

Paradoxically, given such market deviations, it is even more important for corporate managers and investors to understand the true, intrinsic value of companies. This allows them to exploit any market deviations—if and when they occur. Here are some examples of how corporate managers can benefit from intrinsic value deviations by better timing the implementation of strategic decisions.

- Issuing additional share capital at times when the stock market is attaching too high a value to the company's shares relative to intrinsic value

- Repurchasing company shares when the stock market underprices relative to the intrinsic value

- Paying for acquisitions with shares instead of cash when the stock market overprices the shares relative to intrinsic value

- Divesting particular businesses at times when trading and transaction multiples in that sector are higher than can be justified by underlying fundamentals

Two caveats are important to note in these examples. First, we would not recommend basing a decision to issue or repurchase stock, divest or acquire businesses, or settle in cash or shares for transactions exclusively on a perceived difference between market value and intrinsic value. Instead, these decisions should be grounded in a sound strategic and business rationale that is expected to create value for shareholders. Market deviations are more relevant as tactical considerations regarding the timing and execution details of such decisions—that is, when to issue additional capital or how to pay for a particular transaction.

Second, managers should be critical of analyses claiming to find such market deviations for their company's shares. After careful analysis, most of the alleged deviations that we have come across in our client experience turned out to be insignificant or even nonexistent. Market deviations are typically rare and short-lived. Thus, the evidence for deviations should be compelling before managers act on it. They should be significant in both size and duration, given the cost and time to execute strategic decisions.

As long as your company's share price will eventually return to its long-run, intrinsic DCF value, you should use the DCF approach for strategic

[38] M. Rubinstein, "Rational Markets: Yes or No? The Affirmative Case," *Financial Analyst Journal,* 57(3) (2001): 15–29.

decisions. What matters is the long-term behavior of your company's share price, not whether it is 5 or 10 percent undervalued this week. For strategic business decisions, the evidence strongly suggests that the market uses the DCF approach and reflects intrinsic value. Managers who use the DCF approach to valuation, with their focus on increasing long-term free cash flow, ultimately will be rewarded with higher share prices. The evidence from the market is conclusive. Devoting naive attention to accounting earnings or systematically ignoring price signals by the stock market too often leads to value-destroying decisions.

REVIEW QUESTIONS

1. Define market efficiency.

2. Are financial markets efficient? Provide support for your contention.

3. Chapter 1 included a discussion of the importance of short-term versus long-term financial metrics. Chapter 4 extends this discussion. Discuss the relative importance of the short-term versus the long-term debate with respect to stock value. Does the market focus on the short term or the long term? Provide support for your contention.

4. Many corporate executives focus on NI, EPS, ROI, dividends, and growth rates. In doing so, these executives attempt to manage balance sheet and income statement accounts in order to meet analysts' expectations. Is a manager able to successfully manage these accounts to protect stock price and value?

5. Explain how changing from LIFO to FIFO might lead to a change to DCF value.

6. Under what conditions might the market fail to reflect economic fundamentals?

7. Identify the basic economic laws that direct market behavior. What evidence exists that supports the existence of these laws?

Part Two

Core Valuation Techniques

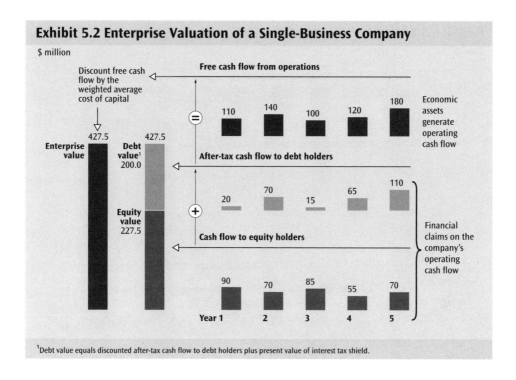

Exhibit 5.2 Enterprise Valuation of a Single-Business Company

$ million

[1]Debt value equals discounted after-tax cash flow to debt holders plus present value of interest tax shield.

Thus, if we want to value the equity (and shares) of a company, we have two choices. We can value the company's operations and subtract the value of all nonequity financial claims (e.g., debt), or we can value the equity cash flows directly. In Exhibit 5.2, we demonstrate the relation between enterprise value and equity value. For this single-business company, equity can be calculated either directly at $227.5 million or by estimating enterprise value ($427.5 million) and subtracting debt ($200.0 million).

Although both methods lead to identical results when applied correctly, the equity method is difficult to implement in practice; matching equity cash flows with the correct cost of equity is challenging (for more on this, see the section on equity valuation later in this chapter). Consequently, to value a company's equity, we recommend valuing the enterprise first and then subtracting the value of any nonequity financial claims.[1]

In addition, the enterprise method is especially valuable when extended to a multibusiness company. As shown in Exhibit 5.3 on page 106, the enterprise value equals the summed value of the individual operating

[1] For financial institutions, such as banks and insurance companies, the choice, size, and structure of financial claims are directly linked to the company's operations (and thus are difficult to separate). In these situations, we prefer the equity cash-flow method. The valuation of financial institutions is addressed in Chapter 25.

Exhibit 5.3 Enterprise Valuation of a Multibusiness Company

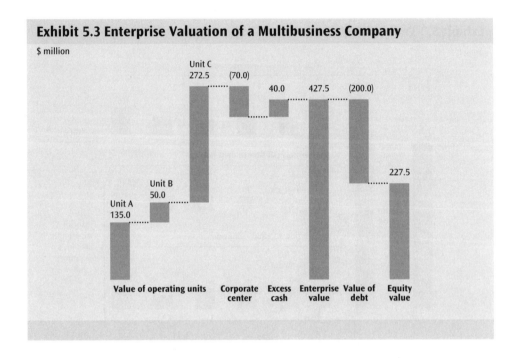

units less the present value of the corporate center costs, plus the value of nonoperating assets. Using enterprise discounted cash flow, instead of the equity cash flow model, enables you to value individual projects, business units, and even the entire company with a consistent methodology.

To value a company's common stock using enterprise DCF:

1. Value the company's operations by discounting free cash flow from operations at the weighted average cost of capital.

2. Value nonoperating assets, such as excess marketable securities, non-consolidated subsidiaries, and other equity investments. Combining the value of operating assets and nonoperating assets leads to enterprise value.

3. Identify and value all nonequity financial claims against the company's assets. Nonequity financial claims include (among others) fixed- and floating-rate debt, pension shortfalls, employee options, and preferred stock.

4. Subtract the value of nonequity financial claims from enterprise value to determine the value of common stock. To determine share price, divide equity value by the number of shares outstanding.

Exhibit 5.4 presents the results of an enterprise DCF valuation for Home Depot, the world's largest retailer of home improvement products.

Exhibit 5.4 Home Depot: Enterprise DCF Valuation

Year	Free cash flow (FCF) ($ million)	Discount factor (@ 9.3%)	Present value of FCF ($ million)
2004	1,930	0.915	1,766
2005	2,219	0.837	1,857
2006	2,539	0.766	1,944
2007	2,893	0.700	2,026
2008	3,283	0.641	2,104
2009	3,711	0.586	2,175
2010	4,180	0.536	2,241
2011	4,691	0.491	2,301
2012	5,246	0.449	2,355
2013	5,849	0.411	2,402
Continuing value	133,360	0.411	54,757
Present value of cash flow			75,928
Mid-year adjustment factor			1.046
Value of operations			**79,384**
Value of excess cash			1,609
Value of other nonoperating assets			84
Enterprise value			**81,077**
Value of debt			(1,365)
Value of capitalized operating leases			(6,554)
Equity value			**73,158**
Number of shares (at fiscal year-end 2003, million)			2,257
Estimated share value (in dollars)			**32.41**

To value Home Depot, future free cash flow is discounted to today's value and then summed across years. For simplicity, the first year's cash flow is discounted by one full year, the second by two full years, and so on. Since cash flows are generated throughout the year, and not as a lump sum, discounting in full-year increments understates the appropriate discount factor. Therefore, we adjust the present value by half a year,[2] leading to the value of operations of $79.4 billion.

To this value, add nonoperating assets (e.g., excess cash and other long-term nonoperating assets) to estimate Home Depot's enterprise value ($81.1 billion). From enterprise value, subtract the present value of nonequity

---

[2] A half-year adjustment is made to the present value for Home Depot because we assume cash flow is generated symmetrically around the midyear point. For companies dependent on year-end holidays, cash flows will be more heavily weighted toward the latter half of the year. In this case the adjustment should be smaller.

claims (traditional debt and capitalized operating leases) to arrive at Home Depot's estimated equity value ($73.2 billion). Dividing the equity value by the number of shares outstanding (2.3 billion) leads to an estimate of share value of $32.41. During the first half of 2004, Home Depot's stock price traded in the mid 30s.

Valuing Operations

The value of operations equals the discounted value of future free cash flow. Free cash flow equals the cash flow generated by the company's operations, less any reinvestment back into the business. Free cash flow is the cash flow available to *all* investors, and is *independent* of leverage. Consistent with this definition, free cash flow must be discounted using the weighted average cost of capital. The WACC is the company's opportunity cost of funds and represents a blended required return by the company's debt and equity holders.

Over the next few pages, we outline the enterprise DCF valuation process. Although we present it sequentially, valuation is an iterative process. To value operations, we analyze the company's historical performance; define and project free cash flow over the short, medium, and long run; and discount the projected free cash flows at the weighted average cost of capital.

Analyzing historical performance   Before projecting future cash flow, examine the company's historical financial performance. A good analysis will focus on the key drivers of value: return on invested capital, growth, and free cash flow. By thoroughly analyzing the past, we can document whether the company has created value, whether it has grown, and how it compares with its competitors.

Although ROIC and FCF are critical to the valuation process, they cannot be computed directly from a company's reported financial statements. Whereas ROIC and FCF are intended to measure the company's operating performance, financial statements mix operating performance, nonoperating performance, and capital structure. Therefore, to calculate ROIC and FCF, first reorganize the accountant's financial statements into new statements that separate operating items, nonoperating items, and financial structure.

This reorganization leads to two new terms: invested capital and net operating profits less adjusted taxes (NOPLAT). Invested capital represents the investor capital required to fund operations, without distinguishing how the capital is financed. NOPLAT represents the total after-tax operating income generated by the company's invested capital, available to *all* financial investors.

Exhibit 5.5 presents the historical NOPLAT and invested capital for Home Depot and one of its direct competitors, Lowe's. To calculate ROIC, divide NOPLAT by average invested capital. In 2003, Home Depot's return on invested capital equaled 18.2 percent (based on a two-year average of invested capital), which exceeds its weighted average cost of capital of 9.3 percent. A detailed discussion of invested capital and NOPLAT, as well as an in-depth historical examination of Home Depot and Lowe's, is presented in Chapter 7.

Next, use the reorganized financial statements to calculate free cash flow, which will be the basis for our valuation. Defined in a manner consistent with ROIC, free cash flow relies on NOPLAT and the change in invested capital. Unlike the accountant's cash flow statement (provided in the company's annual report), free cash flow is independent of nonoperating items and capital structure.

Exhibit 5.6 on page 110 presents historical free cash flow for both Home Depot and Lowe's. As seen in the exhibit, Home Depot is generating nearly

Exhibit 5.5 Home Depot & Lowe's: Historical ROIC Analysis

$ million

	Home Depot			Lowe's		
	2001	2002	2003	2001	2002	2003
Net sales	53,553	58,247	64,816	22,111	26,491	30,838
Cost of merchandise sold	(37,406)	(40,139)	(44,236)	(15,743)	(18,465)	(21,231)
Selling, general and administrative	(10,451)	(11,375)	(12,658)	(4,053)	(4,859)	(5,671)
Depreciation	(756)	(895)	(1,075)	(517)	(626)	(758)
Operating lease interest	288	260	276	106	106	114
Adjusted EBITA	5,228	6,098	7,123	1,904	2,647	3,292
Adjusted taxes	(2,020)	(2,117)	(2,040)	(654)	(825)	(1,069)
NOPLAT	**3,208**	**3,981**	**5,083**	**1,250**	**1,822**	**2,223**
Invested capital						
Operating working capital	2,552	2,746	2,674	1,634	1,451	1,363
Net property and equipment	15,375	17,168	20,063	8,653	10,352	11,945
Capitalized operating leases	5,459	5,890	6,554	2,189	2,373	2,762
Net other assets	(216)	(247)	(524)	134	145	211
Invested capital (excluding goodwill)	23,170	25,557	28,767	12,611	14,321	16,281
Acquired intangibles and goodwill	419	575	833	0	0	0
Cumulative amortization and unreported goodwill	46	54	55	730	730	730
Invested capital (including goodwill)	**23,635**	**26,185**	**29,655**	**13,341**	**15,051**	**17,012**
ROIC excluding goodwill (average)	14.5%	16.3%	18.7%	10.9%	13.5%	14.5%
ROIC including goodwill (average)	14.3%	16.0%	18.2%	10.3%	12.8%	13.9%

Exhibit 5.6 Home Depot and Lowe's: Historical Free Cash Flow

$ million

	Home Depot			Lowe's		
	2001	2002	2003	2001	2002	2003
NOPLAT	3,208	3,981	5,083	1,250	1,822	2,223
Depreciation	756	895	1,075	517	626	758
Gross cash flow	3,964	4,876	6,157	1,767	2,448	2,981
Investment in operating working capital	834	(194)	72	(203)	183	88
Net capital expenditures	(3,063)	(2,688)	(3,970)	(2,135)	(2,325)	(2,351)
Investment in capitalized operating leases	(775)	(430)	(664)	(547)	(184)	(389)
Investments in intangibles and goodwill	(113)	(164)	(259)	0	0	0
Decrease (increase) in other operating assets	105	31	277	(7)	(11)	(66)
Increase (decrease) in accumulated other comprehensive income	(153)	138	172	3	0	0
Gross investment	(3,165)	(3,307)	(4,372)	(2,889)	(2,336)	(2,719)
Free cash flow	799	1,569	1,785	1,122	112	262
After-tax interest income	33	49	36	15	13	9
Decrease (increase) in excess cash	(1,509)	383	(473)	(321)	(189)	(415)
Decrease (increase) in nonoperating assets	9	(24)	23	13	(7)	(140)
Discontinued operations	0	0	0	0	0	15
Cash flow available to investors	(668)	1,977	1,371	(1,415)	(71)	(268)
	2001	2002	2003	2001	2002	2003
After-tax interest expense	17	23	38	123	125	121
After-tax lease interest expense	177	162	170	66	65	71
Decrease (increase) in debt	88	140	(44)	(903)	78	60
Decrease (increase) in capitalized operating leases	(775)	(430)	(664)	(547)	(184)	(389)
Flows to debt holders	(492)	(105)	(500)	(1,261)	85	(138)
Dividends	396	492	595	60	66	87
Net shares repurchased (issued)	(572)	1,590	1,276	(213)	(222)	(217)
Flows to equity holders	(176)	2,082	1,871	(154)	(156)	(130)
Cash flow available to investors	(668)	1,977	1,371	(1,415)	(71)	(268)

$2 billion in free cash flow, whereas Lowe's free cash flow is barely positive. This isn't necessarily a problem for Lowe's. The company's free cash flow is small because it is reinvesting most of its gross cash flow to grow its business.

Projecting revenue growth, ROIC, and free cash flow   To build an enterprise DCF valuation, we project revenue growth, return on invested capital, and free cash flow. Exhibit 5.7 graphs historical and projected ROIC and

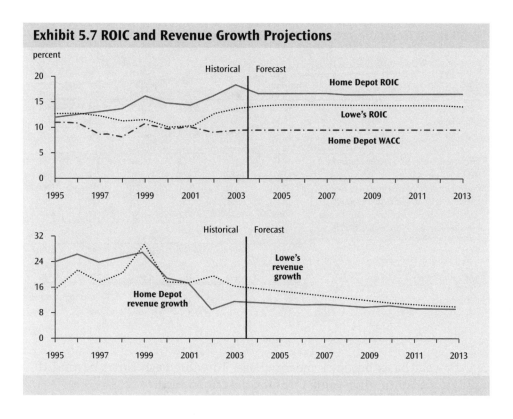

Exhibit 5.7 ROIC and Revenue Growth Projections

revenue growth for Home Depot and Lowe's. As the graphs demonstrate, the two companies are transitioning from a period of high growth (25 percent annually) into mature businesses with strong ROICs (well above Home Depot's 9.3 percent cost of capital) and lower growth rates (currently 10 to 15 percent but falling to 5 percent over the next 10 years).

Free cash flow, which is driven by revenue growth and ROIC, provides the basis for enterprise DCF valuation. Exhibit 5.8 on page 112 shows a summarized free cash flow calculation for Home Depot.[3] To forecast Home Depot's free cash flow, start with forecasts of NOPLAT and invested capital. Over the short run (the first few years), forecast all financial statement line items, such as gross margin, selling expenses, accounts receivable, and inventory. Moving farther out, individual line items become difficult to project. Therefore, over the medium horizon (5 to 10 years), focus on the company's key value drivers, such as operating margin, adjusted tax rate, and capital efficiency. At some point, even projecting key drivers on a

---

[3] Free cash flow does not incorporate any financing-related cash flows such as interest expense or dividends. A good stress test for an enterprise valuation model is to change future interest rates or dividend payout ratios and observe free cash flow. Free cash flow forecasts should *not* change when you adjust the cost of debt or dividend policy.

Exhibit 5.8 Home Depot: Free Cash Flow Summary

$ million

	Historical			Forecast		
	2001	2002	2003	2004	2005	2006
NOPLAT	3,208	3,981	5,083	5,185	5,741	6,342
Depreciation	756	895	1,075	1,193	1,321	1,459
Gross cash flow	3,964	4,876	6,157	6,378	7,062	7,801
Investment in operating working capital	834	(194)	72	(294)	(318)	(344)
Net capital expenditures	(3,063)	(2,688)	(3,970)	(3,399)	(3,708)	(4,036)
Investment in capitalized operating leases	(775)	(430)	(664)	(721)	(780)	(842)
Investments in intangibles and goodwill	(113)	(164)	(259)	(92)	(99)	(107)
Decrease (increase) in other operating assets	105	31	277	58	62	67
Increase (decrease) in accumulated other comprehensive income	(153)	138	172	0	0	0
Gross investment	(3,165)	(3,307)	(4,372)	(4,448)	(4,843)	(5,261)
Free cash flow	799	1,569	1,785	1,930	2,219	2,539

year-by-year basis becomes meaningless. To value cash flows beyond this point, use a continuing-value formula, described next.

Estimating continuing value At the point where predicting the individual key value drivers on a year-by-year basis becomes impractical, do not vary the individual drivers over time. Instead, use a perpetuity-based continuing value, such that:

$$\text{Value of Operations} = \frac{\text{Present Value of Free Cash Flow}}{during \text{ Explicit Forecast Period}} + \frac{\text{Present Value of Free Cash Flow}}{after \text{ Explicit Forecast Period}}$$

Although many continuing-value models exist, we prefer the key value driver model presented in Chapter 3. The key value driver formula is superior to alternative methodologies because it is based on cash flow and links cash flow to growth and ROIC. The key value driver formula is:

$$\text{Continuing Value}_t = \frac{\text{NOPLAT}_{t+1}\left(1 - \dfrac{g}{\text{RONIC}}\right)}{\text{WACC} - g}$$

The formula requires a forecast of net operating profits less adjusted taxes (NOPLAT) in the year following the explicit forecast period, the long-run

Exhibit 5.9 Home Depot: Continuing Value

$ million

NOPLAT $_{2014}$	12,415
Return on incremental invested capital (RONIC)	9.3%
NOPLAT growth rate in perpetuity (g)	4.0%
Weighted average cost of capital (WACC)	9.3%

$$\text{Continuing Value}_t = \frac{\text{NOPLAT}_{t+1}\left(1 - \frac{g}{\text{RONIC}}\right)}{\text{WACC} - g}$$

$$= 133,360$$

forecast for return on new capital (RONIC), the weighted average cost of capital (WACC), and long-run growth in NOPLAT (g).

Exhibit 5.9 presents an estimate for Home Depot's continuing value. Based on a final-year estimate of NOPLAT ($12.4 billion), return on new investment equal to the cost of capital (9.3 percent), and a long-term growth rate of 4 percent, the continuing value is estimated at $133.4 billion. This value is then discounted into today's dollars and added to the value from the explicit forecast period to determine Home Depot's operating value (see Exhibit 5.4).

Alternative methods and additional details for estimating continuing value are provided in Chapter 9.

Discounting free cash flow at the weighted average cost of capital   To determine the value of operations, discount each year's forecast of free cash flow for time and risk. When you discount any set of cash flows, make sure to define the cash flows and discount factor consistently. Since free cash flows are available to *all* investors, the discount factor for free cash flow must represent the risk faced by all investors. The weighted average cost of capital (WACC) blends the required rates of return for debt (k_d) and equity (k_e) based on their market-based target values. For a company financed solely with debt and equity, the WACC is defined as follows:

$$\text{WACC} = \frac{D}{D+E}k_d(1 - T_m) + \frac{E}{D+E}k_e$$

Note how the cost of debt has been reduced by the marginal tax rate (T_m). We do this because the interest tax shield has been *excluded* from free cash flow (remember, interest is tax deductible). Since the interest tax shield has value, it must be incorporated in the valuation. Enterprise DCF values the tax shield by reducing the weighted average cost of capital.

Why move the interest tax shields from free cash flow to the cost of capital? By calculating free cash flow as if the company were financed entirely

Exhibit 5.10 Home Depot: Weighted Average Cost of Capital

percent

Source of capital	Proportion of total capital	Cost of capital	Marginal tax rate	After-tax opportunity cost	Contribution to weighted average
Debt	8.3	4.7	38.2	2.9	0.2
Equity	91.7	9.9		9.9	9.1
WACC	**100.0**				**9.3**

with equity, we can compare operating performance across companies and over time without regard to capital structure. By focusing solely on operations, we can develop a cleaner picture of historical performance, and this leads to better forecasting.

Although applying the weighted average cost of capital is intuitive and relatively straightforward, it comes with some drawbacks. If you discount all future cash flows with a constant cost of capital, as most analysts do, you are implicitly assuming the company manages its capital structure to a target rate. For example, if a company plans to increase its debt-to-value ratio, the current cost of capital will understate the expected tax shields. Although the WACC can be adjusted for a changing capital structure, the process is complicated. In these situations, we recommend an alternative method such as adjusted present value.

The weighted average cost of capital for Home Depot is presented in Exhibit 5.10. For simplicity, the cost of capital in this valuation is based on the company's current capital structure. Since Home Depot has very little debt, the weighted average cost of capital (9.3 percent) is very close to Home Depot's cost of equity (9.9 percent). Chapter 10 provides a more formal discussion of WACC and its components.

This cost of capital is used to discount each year's forecasted cash flow, as well as the continuing value. The result is the value of operations.

Identifying and Valuing Nonoperating Assets

When measured properly, free cash flow from operations should not include any cash flows from nonoperating assets. Instead, nonoperating assets should be valued separately. Nonoperating assets can be segmented into two groups, marketable securities and illiquid investments.

Excess cash and marketable securities   Statement of Financial Accounting Standards (SFAS) No. 115 (1993) and International Accounting Standards

(IAS) No. 39 (1998) require companies to report liquid debt and equity investments (e.g., excess cash and marketable securities) at a fair market value on the company's balance sheet.[4] Therefore, when valuing *liquid* nonoperating assets, use their most recent reported balance sheet value, rather than discount future nonoperating flows.

Illiquid investments, such as nonconsolidated subsidiaries   When valuing a company from the inside, you should value illiquid investments by using enterprise DCF (i.e., project cash flow and discount at the appropriate cost of capital). If you are valuing the company from the outside, valuation of these assets is rough at best. Companies disclose very little information about illiquid investments, such as discontinued operations, excess real estate, nonconsolidated subsidiaries, and other equity investments.

For nonconsolidated subsidiaries, information disclosure depends on the level of ownership. When a company has some influence but not a controlling interest[5] in another company, it records its portion of the subsidiary's profits on its own income statement and the original investment plus its portion of reinvested profits on its own balance sheet. Use this information to create a simple cash flow statement. To discount the cash flow, use a cost of capital commensurate with the risk of the investment, not the parent company's cost of capital (this is why we recommend separation of operating and nonoperating assets).

When ownership is less than 20 percent, investments are reported at historical cost, and the company's portion of profits is recorded *only* when paid out to the parent. In most situations, you will see nothing more than the investment's original cost. In this case, use a multiple of the book value or a tracking portfolio to value the investment. Further details for valuing nonoperating assets are covered in Chapter 11.

Identifying and Valuing Nonequity Claims

Add the value of nonoperating assets to the value of operations to determine enterprise value. To estimate equity value, subtract any nonequity claims, such as debt, unfunded retirement liabilities, capitalized operating leases, and outstanding employee options. Common equity is a residual claimant, receiving cash flows only after the company has fulfilled its other contractual claims. In today's increasingly complex financial markets, *many* claimants have rights to a company's cash flow before equity

---

[4] Liquid investments can appear as either current or long-term assets. Their placement depends on when management intends to sell the assets.

[5] In the United States and Europe, this is generally accepted as between 20 percent and 50 percent ownership.

holders—and they are not always easy to spot. Enron collapsed in 2001 under the weight of hidden debt. The company signed agreements with the creditors of its nonconsolidated subsidiaries, promising to cover loan payments if the subsidiaries could not.[6] Since the subsidiaries were not consolidated, the debt never appeared on Enron's balance sheet, and investors dramatically overestimated the equity's value. When the loans were disclosed in November 2001, the company's stock price fell by more than 50 percent in a single week.

Here are the most common nonequity claims:

- *Debt:* If available, use the market value of all outstanding debt, including fixed and floating rate debt. If that information is unavailable, the book value of debt is a reasonable proxy, unless the probability of default is high or interest rates have changed dramatically since the debt was originally issued. Any valuation of debt, however, should be consistent with your estimates of enterprise value. (See Chapter 11 for more details.)

- *Unfunded retirement liabilities:* The recent weak performance of global stock markets and the rising cost of health care have left many companies with retirement liabilities that are partially unfunded. Although the actual shortfall is not reported on the balance sheet (only a smoothed amount is transferred to the balance sheet), the stock market clearly values unfunded retirement liabilities as an offset against enterprise value. Consider General Motors, which raised nearly $20 billion in debt to fund its pension deficit. The company's stock price actually rose during the month when the new debt was announced and issued. Investors knew a liability existed, even though it wasn't on the balance sheet.

- *Operating leases:* These represent the most common form of off-balance-sheet debt. Under certain conditions, companies can avoid capitalizing leases as debt on their balance sheet, although required payments must be disclosed in the footnotes.

- *Contingent liabilities:* Any other material off-balance-sheet contingencies, such as lawsuits and loan guarantees, will be reported in the footnotes.

- *Preferred stock:* Although the name denotes equity, preferred stock in well-established companies more closely resembles unsecured debt. Therefore, preferred-stock dividends (which are often predetermined and required) should be valued separately, using an appropriate risk-adjusted discount rate.

[6] D. Henry, "Who Else Is Hiding Debt: Moving Financial Obligations into Off-Book Vehicles Is Now a Common Ploy," *BusinessWeek* (January 2002), p. 36.

- *Employee options:* Each year, many companies offer their employees compensation in the form of options. Since options give the employee the right to buy company stock at a potentially discounted price, they can have great value. Employee options can be valued using traditional models, such as Black-Scholes, or advanced techniques such as lattice models.

- *Minority interest:* When a company controls a subsidiary but does not own 100 percent, the investment must be consolidated on the parent company's balance sheet, and the funding other investors provide is recognized on the parent company's balance sheet as minority interest. When valuing minority interest, it is important to realize the minority interest holder does not have a claim on the company's assets, but rather a claim on the subsidiary's assets. Thus, minority interest must be valued separately and not as a percentage of company value.

The identification and valuation of nonequity financial claims are covered in detail in Chapter 11.

A common mistake made when valuing companies is to double-count claims already deducted from cash flow. Consider a company with a pension shortfall. You have been told the company will make extra payments to eliminate the liability. If you deduct the present value of the liability from enterprise value, you should not model the extra payments within free cash flow; that would mean double-counting the shortfall (once in cash flow and once as a claim), leading to an underestimate of equity value.

Valuing Equity

Once you have identified and valued all nonequity claims, we can subtract the claims from enterprise value to determine equity value. Home Depot has traditional debt ($1.4 billion) and capitalized operating leases ($6.6 billion). To value Home Depot's common stock, we subtract each of these claims from Home Depot's enterprise value (see Exhibit 5.4).

To determine Home Depot's share price, divide the estimated common-stock value by the number of undiluted shares outstanding. Do not use diluted shares. We have already valued convertible debt and employee stock options separately. If we were to use diluted shares, we would be double-counting the options' value.

At the end of fiscal year 2003, Home Depot had 2.3 billion shares outstanding. Dividing the equity estimate of $73.2 billion by 2.3 billion shares generates an estimated value of $32 per share. The estimated share value assumes Home Depot can maintain its current ROIC over the forecast period and the growth rate will remain strong, decaying gradually over the next 10 years from its current level of 11 percent to 4 percent in the continuing value. During the first half of 2004, the Home Depot's actual stock price traded between $32 and $38 per share.

ECONOMIC-PROFIT-BASED VALUATION MODELS

The enterprise DCF model is a favorite of academics and practitioners alike because it relies solely on how cash flows in and out of the company. Complex accounting can be replaced with a simple question: Does cash change hands? One shortfall of enterprise DCF, however, is that each year's cash flow provides little insight into the company's performance. Declining free cash flow can signal either poor performance or investment for the future. The economic profit model highlights how and when the company creates value yet leads to a valuation that is identical to that of enterprise DCF.

As stated in Chapter 3, economic profit measures the value created by the company in a single period and is defined as follows:

$$\text{Economic Profit} = \text{Invested Capital} \times (\text{ROIC} - \text{WACC})$$

Since ROIC equals NOPLAT divided by invested capital, we can rewrite the equation as follows:

$$\text{Economic Profit} = \text{NOPLAT} - (\text{Invested Capital} \times \text{WACC})$$

In Exhibit 5.11, we present economic profit calculations for Home Depot using both methods. Since Home Depot has been earning returns greater than its cost of capital, its historical economic profit is positive. Given the company's strong competitive position, we also project positive economic profits going forward. Not every company has positive economic profit. In fact, many companies earn an accounting profit (net income greater than zero) but do not earn their cost of capital.

To demonstrate how economic profit can be used to value a company—and to demonstrate its equivalence to enterprise DCF, consider a stream of growing cash flows valued using the growing-perpetuity formula:

$$\text{Value}_0 = \frac{\text{FCF}_1}{\text{WACC} - g}$$

In Chapter 3, we transformed this cash flow perpetuity into the key value driver model. The key value driver model is superior to the simple cash flow perpetuity model, because it explicitly models the relation between growth and required investment. Using a few additional algebraic

Exhibit 5.11 Home Depot: Economic Profit Summary

$ million

Method 1	Historical 2001	2002	2003	Forecast 2004	2005	2006
Return on invested capital	15.0%	16.8%	19.4%	17.5%	17.4%	17.4%
Weighted average cost of capital	10.1%	9.0%	9.3%	9.3%	9.3%	9.3%
Economic spread	4.9%	7.9%	10.1%	8.2%	8.1%	8.1%
Invested capital	21,379	23,635	26,185	29,655	32,910	36,432
Economic profit	**1,048**	**1,857**	**2,645**	**2,424**	**2,677**	**2,950**
Method 2						
Invested capital	21,379	23,635	26,185	29,655	32,910	36,432
Weighted average cost of capital	10.1%	9.0%	9.3%	9.3%	9.3%	9.3%
Capital charge	2,159	2,124	2,438	2,761	3,064	3,392
NOPLAT	3,208	3,981	5,083	5,185	5,741	6,342
Capital charge	2,159	2,124	2,438	2,761	3,064	3,392
Economic profit	**1,048**	**1,857**	**2,645**	**2,424**	**2,677**	**2,950**

steps (see Appendix A) and the assumption that the company's ROIC on new projects equals historical ROIC, we can transform the cash flow perpetuity into a key value driver model based on economic profits:

$$\text{Value}_0 = \text{Invested Capital}_0 + \frac{\text{Invested Capital}_0 \times (\text{ROIC} - \text{WACC})}{\text{WACC} - g}$$

Finally, we substitute the definition of economic profit:

$$\text{Value}_0 = \text{Invested Capital}_0 + \frac{\text{Economic Profit}_1}{\text{WACC} - g}$$

As can be seen in the economic-profit-based key value driver model, the operating value of a company equals its book value of invested capital plus the present value of all future value created. In this case, the future economic profits are valued using a growing perpetuity, because the company's economic profits are increasing at a constant rate over time. More generally, economic profit can be valued as follows:

$$\text{Value}_0 = \text{Invested Capital}_0 + \sum_{t=1}^{\infty} \frac{\text{Invested Capital}_{t-1} \times (\text{ROIC}_t - \text{WACC})}{(1 + \text{WACC})^t}$$

Since the economic profit valuation was derived directly from the free cash flow model (see Appendix B for a proof of equivalence), any valuation based on discounted economic profits will be identical to enterprise DCF. To assure equivalence, however, you must:

- Use beginning-of-year invested capital (i.e., last year's value).
- Use the same invested-capital number for both economic profit and ROIC. For example, ROIC can be measured either with or without goodwill. If you measure ROIC without goodwill, invested capital must also be measured without goodwill. All told, it doesn't matter how you define invested capital, as long as you are consistent.

Exhibit 5.12 presents the valuation results for Home Depot using economic profit. Economic profits are explicitly forecasted for 10 years; the

Exhibit 5.12 Home Depot: Economic Profit Valuation

Year	Invested capital[1] ($ million)	ROIC (percent)	WACC (percent)	Economic profit ($ million)	Discount factor (@ 9.3%)	Present value of economic profit ($ million)
2004	29,655	17.5	9.3	2,424	0.915	2,217
2005	32,910	17.4	9.3	2,677	0.837	2,241
2006	36,432	17.4	9.3	2,950	0.766	2,259
2007	40,235	17.4	9.3	3,242	0.700	2,271
2008	44,329	17.3	9.3	3,556	0.641	2,278
2009	48,729	17.3	9.3	3,890	0.586	2,281
2010	53,445	17.3	9.3	4,247	0.536	2,278
2011	58,488	17.2	9.3	4,627	0.491	2,270
2012	63,870	17.2	9.3	5,031	0.449	2,258
2013	69,600	17.2	9.3	5,458	0.411	2,241
Continuing value				57,671	0.411	23,679
Present value of economic profit						46,273
Invested capital[1] $_{2004}$						29,655
Invested capital plus present value of economic profit						75,928
Mid-year adjustment factor						1.046
Value of operations						**79,384**
Value of excess cash						1,609
Value of other nonoperating assets						84
Enterprise value						**81,077**
Value of debt						(1,365)
Value of capitalized operating leases						(6,554)
Equity value						**73,158**

[1]Invested capital is measured at the beginning of the year.

remaining years are valued using an economic profit continuing-value for-mula.[7] Comparing the equity value from Exhibit 5.4 with that of Exhibit 5.12, we see that the value of Home Depot's stock is the same, regardless of the method.

The benefit of economic profit becomes apparent when we examine the drivers of economic profit, ROIC and WACC, on a year-by-year basis in Exhibit 5.12. Notice how the valuation depends heavily on Home Depot's ability to maintain current levels of ROIC (17.5 percent) well above the WACC (9.3 percent). If the company's markets become saturated, growth could become elusive, and some companies might compete on price to steal market share. If this occurs, ROICs will drop, and economic profits will re-vert to zero. Explicitly modeling ROIC as a primary driver of economic profit will prominently display this analysis. Conversely, the free cash flow model fails to show this dynamic. Free cash flow could continue to grow, even as ROIC falls.

Another insight generated by the economic profit model occurs when comparing a company's value of operations with its invested capital. For Home Depot, the estimated operating value ($79.4 billion) exceeds the com-pany's invested capital ($29.7 billion) by more than $49.7 billion.

ADJUSTED PRESENT VALUE MODEL

When building an enterprise DCF or economic profit valuation, most finan-cial analysts discount all future flows at a *constant* weighted average cost of capital. Using a constant WACC, however, assumes the company manages its capital structure to a target debt-to-value ratio.

In most situations, debt grows in line with company value. But suppose the company planned to significantly change its capital structure. Indeed, companies with significant debt often pay it down as cash flow improves, thus lowering their future debt-to-value ratios. In these cases, a valuation

---

[7] To calculate continuing value, you can use the economic-profit-based key value driver formula, but only if RONIC equals historical ROIC in the continuing-value year. If RONIC going forward differs from the final year's ROIC, then the equation must be separated into current and future economic profits:

$$\text{Continuing Value}_t = \frac{IC_t\left(ROIC_{t+1} - WACC\right)}{WACC} + \frac{PV(\text{Economic Profit}_{t+2})}{WACC - g}$$

Current Economic Profits   Future Economic Profits

such that

$$PV(\text{Economic Profit}_{t+2}) = \frac{NOPLAT_{t+1}\left(\dfrac{g}{RONIC}\right)(RONIC - WACC)}{WACC}$$

based on a constant WACC would overstate the value of the tax shields. Although the WACC can be adjusted yearly to handle a changing capital structure, the process is complex. Therefore, we turn to an alternative model: adjusted present value.

The adjusted present value (APV) model separates the value of operations into two components: the value of operations as if the company were all-equity financed and the value of tax shields that arise from debt financing:[8]

$$\begin{array}{c} \text{Adjusted} \\ \text{Present Value} \end{array} = \begin{array}{c} \text{Enterprise Value as if the} \\ \text{Company Was All-Equity Financed} \end{array} + \begin{array}{c} \text{Present Value of} \\ \text{Tax Shields} \end{array}$$

The APV valuation model follows directly from the teachings of Modigliani and Miller, who proposed that in a market with no taxes (among other things), a company's choice of financial structure will not affect the value of its economic assets. Only market imperfections, such as taxes and distress costs, affect enterprise value.

When building a valuation model, it is easy to forget these teachings. To see this, imagine a company (in a world with no taxes) that has a 50-50 mix of debt and equity. If the company's debt has an expected return of 5 percent and the company's equity has an expected return of 15 percent, its weighted average cost of capital would be 10 percent. Suppose the company decides to issue more debt, using the proceeds to repurchase shares. Since the cost of debt is lower than the cost of equity, it would appear that issuing debt to retire equity should lower the WACC, raising the company's value.

This line of thinking is flawed, however. In a world without taxes, a change in capital structure would *not* change the cash flow generated by operations, nor the risk of those cash flows. Therefore, neither the company's enterprise value nor its cost of capital would change. So why did we think it would? When adding debt, we adjusted the weights, but we failed to properly increase the cost of equity. Since debt payments have priority over cash flows to equity, adding leverage increases the risk to equity holders. When leverage rises, they demand a higher return. Modigliani and Miller postulated this increase would perfectly offset the change in weights.

In reality, taxes play a part in decision making, and capital structure choice therefore *can* affect cash flows. Since interest is tax deductible, profitable companies can lower taxes by raising debt. But, if the company relies

[8] In this book, we focus on the tax shields generated by interest. On a more general basis, the APV values *any* incremental cash flows associated with capital structure, such as tax shields, issue costs, and distress costs. Distress costs include direct costs, such as court-related fees, and indirect costs, such as the loss of customers and suppliers.

too heavily on debt, the company's customers and suppliers may fear bankruptcy and walk away, restricting future cash flow (academics call this distress costs or deadweight costs). Rather than model the effect of capital structure changes in the weighted average cost of capital, APV explicitly measures and values the cash flow effects of financing separately.

To build an APV-based valuation, value the company as if it were all-equity financed. Do this by discounting free cash flow by the unlevered cost of equity (what the cost of equity would be if the company had no debt). To this value, add any value created by the company's use of debt. Exhibit 5.13 values Home Depot using adjusted present value. Since we assume that Home Depot will manage its capital structure to a target debt-to-value level of 9.3 percent, the APV-based valuation leads to the same value for equity as

Exhibit 5.13 Home Depot: Valuation Using Adjusted Present Value

Year	Free cash flow ($ million)	Interest tax shield (ITS)	Discount factor (@ 9.5%)	Present value of FCF ($ million)	Present value of ITS ($ million)
2004	1,930	113	0.914	1,763	103
2005	2,219	120	0.835	1,852	100
2006	2,539	128	0.763	1,936	98
2007	2,893	136	0.697	2,016	95
2008	3,283	145	0.636	2,090	92
2009	3,711	153	0.581	2,158	89
2010	4,180	162	0.531	2,220	86
2011	4,691	171	0.485	2,276	83
2012	5,246	180	0.443	2,326	80
2013	5,849	189	0.405	2,369	77
Continuing value	129,734	3,626	0.405	52,550	1,469
Present value				73,557	2,372

Present value of FCF using unlevered cost of equity	73,557
Present value of interest tax shields (ITS)	2,372
Present value of FCF and ITS	75,928
Mid-year adjustment factor	1.046
Value of operations	**79,384**
Value of excess cash	1,609
Value of other nonoperating assets	84
Enterprise value	**81,077**
Value of debt	(1,365)
Value of capitalized operating leases	(6,554)
Equity value	**73,158**

did enterprise DCF (see Exhibit 5.4) and economic profit (see Exhibit 5.12). A simplified proof of equivalence between enterprise DCF and adjusted present value can be found in Appendix C. The following subsections explain APV in detail.

Value Free Cash Flow at Unlevered Cost of Equity

When valuing a company using the APV, we explicitly separate the unlevered value of operations (V_u) from any value created by financing, such as tax shields (V_{txa}). For a company with debt (D) and equity (E), this relation is as follows:

$$V_u + V_{txa} = D + E \tag{1}$$

A second result of Modigliani and Miller's work is that the total risk of the company's assets, real and financial, must equal the total risk of the financial claims against those assets. Thus, in equilibrium, the blended cost of capital for operating assets $(k_u,$ which we call the unlevered cost of equity) and financial assets (k_{txa}) must equal the blended cost of capital for debt (k_d) and equity (k_e):

$$\underbrace{\frac{V_u}{V_u + V_{txa}} k_u + \frac{V_{txa}}{V_u + V_{txa}} k_{txa}}_{\text{Operating} \quad \text{Tax Assets}} = \underbrace{\frac{D}{D+E} k_d + \frac{E}{D+E} k_e}_{\text{Debt} \quad \text{Equity}} \tag{2}$$

Operating
Assets

In the corporate finance literature, academics combine Modigliani and Miller's two equations to solve for the cost of equity—to demonstrate the relation between leverage and the cost of equity. In Appendix D, we algebraically rearrange equation 2 to solve for the levered cost of equity:

$$k_e = k_u + \frac{D}{E}\left(k_u - k_d\right) - \frac{V_{txa}}{E}\left(k_u - k_{txa}\right)$$

As this equation indicates, the cost of equity depends on the unlevered cost of equity plus a premium for leverage, less a reduction for the tax deductibility of debt.

Determining the unlevered cost of equity with market data   To use the APV, we need to discount projected free cash flow at the unlevered cost of equity, k_u. However, none of the variables (including k_u) on the left side of equation 2 can be observed. Only the values on the right—that is, those related to debt and equity—can be estimated directly. Because there are so many unknowns and only one equation, we must impose additional restrictions to solve for k_u.

Method 1: Assume k_{txa} equals k_u If you believe the risk associated with tax shields (k_{txa}) equals the risk associated with operating assets (k_u), equation 2 can be simplified dramatically (see Appendix D):

$$k_u = \frac{E}{D+E} k_d + \frac{D}{D+E} k_e \tag{3}$$

We can now determine the unlevered cost of equity because it now relies solely on observable variables, that is, those related to debt and equity. In fact, k_u looks very similar to the weighted average cost of capital, without the interest tax shield.

Equation 3 can be rearranged to solve for the levered cost of equity:

$$k_e = k_u + \frac{D}{E}\left(k_u - k_d\right) \tag{4}$$

Note that when the company has no debt ($D = 0$), k_e equals k_u. This is why k_u is referred to as the unlevered cost of equity.

Method 2: Assume k_{txa} equals k_d If you believe the risk associated with tax shields (k_{txa}) is comparable to the risk of debt (k_d), equation 2 can be rearranged to solve for the unlevered cost of equity:

$$k_u = \frac{D - V_{txa}}{D - V_{txa} + E} k_d + \frac{E}{D - V_{txa} + E} k_e \tag{5}$$

In this equation, k_u relies on observable variables, such as the market value of debt, market value of equity, cost of debt, and cost of equity, as well as one unobservable variable: the present value of tax shields (V_{txa}). To use equation 4, discount expected future tax shields at the cost of debt (to remain consistent) and *then* solve for the unlevered cost of equity.

Many practitioners further refine the last equation by imposing an additional restriction: that the absolute dollar level of debt is constant. If the dollar level of debt is constant, the annual expected tax shield equals ($D \times k_d$) $\times$

T_m, where T_m equals the marginal tax rate. Applying a no-growth perpetuity formula allows us to value the tax shield:

$$V_{txa} = \frac{(D \times k_d) \times T_m}{k_d} = D \times T_m$$

Substituting $D \times T_m$ for the value of the tax shield in the last equation leads to:

$$k_u = \frac{(1-T_m)D}{(1-T_m)D+E} k_d + \frac{E}{(1-T_m)D+E} k_e \qquad (6)$$

Although equation 6 is quite common in practice, its use is limited because the assumptions are extremely restrictive.

Choosing the appropriate formula Which formula should you use to back-solve for the unlevered cost of equity, k_u? It depends on how you see the company managing its capital structure going forward and whether the debt is risk free. If you believe the company will manage its debt-to-value to a target level (the company's debt will grow with the business), then the value of the tax shields will track the value of the operating assets. Thus, the risk of tax shields will equal the risk of operating assets (k_{txa} equals k_u). The majority of companies have relatively stable capital structures (as a percentage of expected value), so we favor the first method.

If you believe the debt to equity ratio will not remain constant, then the value of interest tax shields will be more closely tied to the value of forecasted debt, rather than operating assets. In this case, the risk of tax shields is equivalent to the risk of debt (when a company is unprofitable, it cannot use interest tax shields, the risk of default rises, and the value of debt drops). In this case, equation 5 better approximates the unlevered cost of equity.[9] This situation occurs frequently in periods of high debt such as financial distress and leveraged buyouts.

Value Tax Shields and Other Capital Structure Effects

To complete an APV-based valuation, forecast and discount capital structure side effects such as tax shields, security issue costs, and distress costs. Since Home Depot has little chance of default, we estimated the company's future interest tax shields using the company's promised yield to maturity and marginal tax rate (see Exhibit 5.14). To calculate the expected interest

---

[9] Even if a company's tax shields are predetermined for a given period, eventually they will track value. For instance, successful leveraged buyouts pay down debt for a period of time, but once the debt level becomes reasonable, debt will more likely track value than remain constant.

Exhibit 5.14 Home Depot: Forecast of Interest Tax Shields

Year	Prior year net debt ($ million)	Expected interest rate (percent)	Interest payment ($ million)	Marginal tax rate (percent)	Interest tax shield ($ million)
2004	6,310	4.7	295	38.2	113
2005	6,737	4.7	315	38.2	120
2006	7,179	4.7	336	38.2	128
2007	7,637	4.7	357	38.2	136
2008	8,107	4.7	379	38.2	145
2009	8,589	4.7	402	38.2	153
2010	9,081	4.7	425	38.2	162
2011	9,579	4.7	448	38.2	171
2012	10,081	4.7	472	38.2	180
2013	10,583	4.7	495	38.2	189
Continuing value	11,082	4.7	518	38.2	198

payment in 2004, multiply the prior year's net debt of $6.3 billion by the expected yield of 4.7 percent (net debt equals reported debt plus capitalized operating leases minus excess cash). This led to an expected interest payment of $295 million. Next multiply the expected interest payment by the marginal tax rate of 38.2 percent, for an expected interest tax shield of $113 million in 2004.

Home Depot's conservative use of debt makes tax shield valuation straightforward. For companies with significant leverage, the company may not be able to fully use the tax shields (it may not have enough profits to shield). If there is a significant probability of default, you must model *expected* tax shields, rather than the tax shields based on promised interest payments. To do this, reduce each promised tax shield by the cumulative probability of default.

CAPITAL CASH FLOW MODEL

When a company actively manages its capital structure to a target debt-to-value level, both free cash flow (FCF) and the interest tax shield (ITS) are discounted at the unlevered cost of equity, k_u:

$$V = \sum_{t=1}^{\infty} \frac{\text{FCF}_t}{(1+k_u)^t} + \sum_{t=1}^{\infty} \frac{\text{ITS}_t}{(1+k_u)^t}$$

In 2000, Richard Ruback of the Harvard Business School argued there is no need to separate free cash flow from tax shields when both flows are discounted by the same cost of capital.[10] He combined the two flows and named the resulting cash flow (FCF plus interest tax shields) capital cash flow (CCF):

$$V = PV(\text{Capital Cash Flows}) = \sum_{t=1}^{\infty} \frac{\text{FCF}_t + \text{ITS}_t}{(1 + k_u)^t}$$

Given that Ruback's assumptions match those of the weighted average cost of capital, the capital cash flow and WACC-based valuations will lead to identical results. In fact, we now have detailed three distinct but identical valuation methods created solely around how they treat tax shields: WACC (tax shield valued in the cost of capital), APV (tax shield valued separately), and CCF (tax shield valued in the cash flow).

Although FCF and CCF lead to the same result when debt is proportional to value, we believe free cash flow models are superior to capital cash flow models. Why? By keeping NOPLAT and FCF independent of leverage, we can cleanly evaluate the company's operating performance over time and across competitors. A clean measure of historical operating performance leads to better forecasts.

CASH-FLOW-TO-EQUITY VALUATION MODEL

In each of the preceding valuation models, we determined the value of equity indirectly by subtracting nonequity claims from enterprise value. The equity cash flow model values equity directly by discounting cash flows to equity at the cost of equity, rather than at the weighted average cost of capital.[11]

Exhibit 5.15 details the cash flows to equity for Home Depot. Cash flow to equity can be computed by reorganizing free cash flow found in Exhibit 5.6 or using the traditional method in Exhibit 5.15. In the traditional method, cash flow to equity starts with net income. Next, noncash expenses are added back, and investments in working capital, fixed assets, and non-operating assets are subtracted. Finally, any increases in nonequity financing such as debt are added, and decreases in nonequity financing are subtracted. Alternatively, we can compute cash flow to equity as dividends

[10] Richard S. Ruback, "Capital Cash Flows: A Simple Approach to Valuing Risky Cash Flows," Social Science Research Network (March 2000).
[11] The equity method can be difficult to implement correctly because capital structure is embedded in the cash flow. This makes forecasting difficult. For companies whose operations are related to financing, such as financial institutions, the equity method is appropriate. We discuss valuing financial institutions in Chapter 25.

Exhibit 5.15 Home Depot: Equity Cash Flow Summary

$ million

	Historical 2001	2002	2003	Forecast 2004	2005	2006
Net income	3,044	3,664	4,304	4,796	5,318	5,882
Depreciation	756	895	1,075	1,193	1,321	1,459
Amortization	8	8	1	0	0	0
Increase (decrease) in deferred taxes	(6)	173	605	214	237	262
Gross cash flow	3,802	4,740	5,985	6,203	6,876	7,603
Investment in operating working capital	834	(194)	72	(294)	(318)	(344)
Investment in net long-term assets	(3,224)	(2,683)	(3,780)	(3,433)	(3,745)	(4,076)
Decrease (increase) in excess cash	(1,509)	383	(473)	(177)	(191)	(207)
Investment in other nonoperating assets	9	(24)	23	(9)	(10)	(11)
Increase (decrease) in short-term debt	207	(211)	509	(44)	(54)	(66)
Increase (decrease) in long-term debt	(295)	71	(465)	(73)	(91)	(112)
Cash flow to equity	**(176)**	**2,082**	**1,871**	**2,173**	**2,466**	**2,788**
	2001	2002	2003	2004	2005	2006
Dividends	396	492	595	663	735	813
Share repurchases (issued)	(572)	1,590	1,276	1,510	1,731	1,975
Cash flow to equity	**(176)**	**2,082**	**1,871**	**2,173**	**2,466**	**2,788**

plus share repurchases minus new equity issues. Both methods generate identical results.

To value Home Depot, we discount projected equity cash flows at the cost of equity (see Exhibit 5.16 on p. 130). Unlike enterprise-based models, no adjustments are made for nonoperating assets, debt, or capitalized operating leases. Rather, they are included as part of the equity cash flow.

Once again, note how the valuation, derived using equity cash flows, matches each of the prior valuations.[12] This occurs because we have modeled

---

[12] When performing a stand-alone equity cash flow valuation, you can calculate the continuing value by using a simple growing perpetuity:

$$V_e = \frac{\text{Net Income}\left(1 - \dfrac{g}{\text{ROE}}\right)}{k_e - g}$$

To tie the free cash flow and equity cash flow models, you must convert free cash flow continuing-value inputs into equity cash flow inputs. We did this using:

$$\text{Net Income}\left(1 - \frac{g}{\text{ROE}}\right) = \frac{\text{NOPLAT}\left(1 - \dfrac{g}{\text{ROIC}}\right)}{1 + \dfrac{D}{E}\left(1 - \dfrac{k_e - (1-T)k_d}{k_e - g}\right)}$$

Exhibit 5.16 Home Depot: Cash-Flow-to-Equity Valuation

Year	Cash flow to equity ($ million)	Discount factor (@ 9.9%)	Present value of CFE ($ million)
2004	2,173	0.910	1,978
2005	2,466	0.828	2,042
2006	2,788	0.754	2,101
2007	3,143	0.686	2,155
2008	3,530	0.624	2,203
2009	3,954	0.568	2,245
2010	4,416	0.517	2,282
2011	4,917	0.470	2,312
2012	5,459	0.428	2,336
2013	6,044	0.389	2,353
Continuing value	122,492	0.389	47,695
Present value of cash flow to equity			69,702
Midyear adjustment amount			3,456
Equity value			**73,158**

Home Depot's debt-to-value ratio at a constant level. If debt-to-value instead changes over time, the equity model becomes difficult to implement and can lead to conceptual errors. For example, if leverage is expected to rise, the cost of equity must be adjusted to reflect the additional risk imposed on equity holders. Although formulas exist to adjust the cost of equity, many of the best-known formulas are built under restrictions that may be inconsistent with the way you are implicitly forecasting the company's capital structure via the cash flows. This will cause a mismatch between cash flows and the cost of equity, resulting in an incorrect valuation.

Unwittingly changing the company's capital structure when using the cash-flow-to-equity model occurs too easily—and that is what makes the model so risky. Suppose you plan to value a company whose debt-to-value ratio is 15 percent. You believe the company will pay extra dividends, so you increase debt to raise the dividend payout ratio. Presto! Increased dividends lead to higher equity cash flows and a higher valuation. Even though operating performance has not changed, the equity value has mistakenly increased. What happened? Using new debt to pay dividends causes a rise in net debt to value. Unless you adjust the cost of equity, the valuation will rise incorrectly.

Another shortcoming of the direct equity approach occurs when valuing a company by business unit. The direct equity approach requires allocating debt and interest expense to each unit. This creates extra work yet provides few additional insights.

OTHER APPROACHES TO DISCOUNTED CASH FLOW

You may also come across two variants of enterprise DCF:

1. Using real instead of nominal cash flows and discount rates
2. Discounting pretax cash flows instead of after-tax cash flows

These approaches are well suited only to limited circumstances.

Using Real Cash Flows and Discount Rates

Companies can be valued by projecting cash flow in real terms (e.g., in constant 2004 dollars) and discounting this cash flow at a real discount rate (e.g., the nominal rate less expected inflation). But most managers think in terms of nominal rather than real measures, so nominal measures are often easier to communicate. In addition, interest rates are generally quoted nominally rather than in real terms (excluding expected inflation). Also, since historical financial statements are stated in nominal terms, projecting future statements in real terms is difficult and confusing.

A second difficulty occurs when calculating and interpreting ROIC. The historical statements are nominal, so historical returns on invested capital are nominal. But if the projections for the company use real rather than nominal forecasts, returns on new capital are also real. Projected returns on total capital (new and old) are a combination of nominal and real, so they are impossible to interpret. The only way around this is to restate historical performance on a real basis. This is a complex and time-consuming task. The extra insights gained rarely equal the effort (except in extremely high-inflation environments described in Chapter 22).

Discounting Pretax Cash Flow

For purposes of valuing internal investment opportunities, individual project cash flows are sometimes calculated without taxes. The pretax cash flow is then discounted by a pretax "hurdle rate" (the market-based cost of capital multiplied by 1 plus the marginal tax rate) to determine a pretax value.

This method, however, leads to three fundamental inconsistencies. First, the government calculates taxes on profits after depreciation, not on cash flow after capital expenditures. By discounting pretax cash flow at the pretax cost of capital, you implicitly assume capital investments are tax deductible when made, not as they are depreciated. Furthermore, short-term investments, such as accounts receivable and inventory, are never tax deductible. Selling a product at a profit is what leads to incremental taxes, not holding inventory. By discounting pretax cash flow at the pretax cost of capital, you incorrectly assume investments in operating working capital are tax deductible. Finally, it can be shown that even when net investment equals depreciation, the final result will be downward biased—and the larger the cost of capital, the larger the bias. This bias occurs because the method is only an approximation, not a formal mathematical relation. Because of these inconsistencies, we recommend against discounting pretax cash flows at a pretax hurdle rate.

ALTERNATIVES TO DISCOUNTED CASH FLOW

To this point, we have focused solely on discounted cash flow models. Two additional valuation techniques exist: multiples (comparables) and real options.

Multiples

Assume that you have been asked to value a company that is about to go public. Although you project and discount free cash flow to derive an enterprise value, you worry that your forecasts lack precision. One way to place your DCF model in the proper context is to create a set of comparables. One of the most commonly used comparables is the enterprise-value-to-earnings before interest, taxes, and amortization (EV/EBITA) multiple. To apply the EV/EBITA multiple, look for a set of comparable companies, and multiply a representative EV/EBITA multiple by the company's EBITA. For example, assume the company's EBITA equals $100 million and the typical EV/EBITA multiple in the industry is 15×. Multiplying 15 by $100 million leads to an estimated value of $1.5 billion. Is the enterprise DCF valuation near $1.5 billion? If not, what enables the company to earn better (or worse) returns or grow faster (or slower) than other companies in the industry?

Although the concept of multiples is simple, the methodology is misunderstood and often misapplied. Companies within an industry will have different multiples for valid economic reasons. Computing a representative multiple ignores this fact. In addition, common multiples, such as the price-to-earnings ratio, suffer from the same capital structure problems as equity cash flows. In Chapter 12, we demonstrate how to build and interpret forward-looking comparables, independent of capital structure and other nonoperating items.

Real Options

In 1997 Robert Merton and Myron Scholes won the Nobel Prize in Economics for developing an ingenious method to value derivatives that avoids the need to estimate either cash flows or the cost of capital. (Fischer Black would have been named as a third recipient, but the Nobel Prize is not awarded posthumously.) Their model relies on what today's economists call a "replicating portfolio." They argued that if there exists a portfolio of traded securities whose future cash flows perfectly mimic the security you are attempting to value, the portfolio and security must have the same price. As long as we can find a suitable replicating portfolio, we need not discount future cash flows.

Given the model's power, there have been many recent attempts to translate the concepts of replicating portfolios to corporate valuation. This valuation technique is commonly known as real options. Unlike those for financial options, however, replicating portfolios for companies and their projects may be difficult to create. Therefore, although options-pricing models may teach powerful lessons, today's applications are limited. We cover valuation using options-based models in Chapter 20.

SUMMARY

This chapter described the most common DCF valuation models, with particular focus on the enterprise DCF model and the economic profit model. We explained the rationale for each model and reasons why each model has an important place in corporate valuation. The remaining chapters in Part Two describe a step-by-step approach to valuing a company:

- Chapter 6: Thinking about Return on Invested Capital and Growth
- Chapter 7: Analyzing Historical Performance
- Chapter 8: Forecasting Performance
- Chapter 9: Estimating Continuing Value
- Chapter 10: Estimating the Cost of Capital
- Chapter 11: Calculating and Interpreting Results
- Chapter 12: Using Multiples for Valuation

These chapters explain the technical details of valuation, including how to calculate free cash flow from the accounting statements and how to create and interpret the valuation through careful financial analysis.

REVIEW QUESTIONS

1. What process should a manager employ to compute corporate valuation? In your answer, differentiate between the choice of a process to be followed and the choice of valuation model.

2. Describe the enterprise DCF valuation model.

3. How does growth and return on invested capital drive free cash flow? Illustrate with an example employing constant and nonconstant growth rates.

4. In terms of the enterprise DCF model, how would a manager increase corporate value?

5. Describe the economic profit model. Identify the differences between the economic profit model's value drivers compared to the enterprise DCF model value drivers.

6. Under what conditions would the discounted dividend model of equity value incorrectly define corporate value?

7. Under what circumstances would an executive select the adjusted present value (APV) model of corporate valuation over either the enterprise DCF model or the economic profit model?

8. Why is it important to compute the company's unlevered cost of equity when the APV model is used to determine corporate value?

9. When would a manager use real versus nominal cash flows and rates to value entities?

10. You have been asked to value a stable company (i.e., no growth) whose revenues are $100 million and operating margins are 10 percent. Since the company is not growing, working capital is constant and capital expenditures are spent only to replace depreciation. The company has $50 million in debt outstanding and has a cost of debt equal to 5 percent (the company's bonds trade at par, so interest payments can be computed using the cost of debt). The company has 10 million shares outstanding and its stock is trading at $10.50. The company has a cost of equity equal to 10 percent. The company faces a tax rate of 40 percent.

   a. Compute free cash flow.

   b. Assuming the current capital structure proxies the target capital structure, estimate the weighted average cost of capital.

   c. Using a no-growth perpetuity (FCF divided by WACC), estimate the company's enterprise value, the company's equity value, and its stock price. Is the company undervalued?

   d. If interest taxes shields are discounted at the unlevered cost of equity, what is the unlevered cost of equity?

   e. Compute enterprise value using adjusted present value. How does your result differ from part c?

6

Thinking about Return
on Invested Capital
and Growth

A fully developed discounted cash flow model can be complex. Models that forecast each line item on the income statement and balance sheet can include hundreds of numbers, if not thousands. But in the forest of numbers, it is all too easy to forget the fundamentals: A company's value depends on its return on invested capital (ROIC) and its ability to grow. All other considerations—gross margins, cash tax rates, collection periods, and inventory turns—are, well, just details.

By focusing on ROIC and growth, you can place your forecasts in the proper context. You can measure how well the model's projections fit with the capabilities of the company and the competitive dynamics of the industry. Consider the following example. You are valuing a company in the commodity chemicals business. The company projects operating costs to drop by 3 percent per year over the next 10 years, but because the industry is highly competitive, cost reductions are usually passed on to the consumer. Therefore, you project that the price will fall 2 percent annually. Combined with expected growth in volume, your forecasts lead to a healthy growth in cash flow and a high valuation. After further analysis, however, you realize that because costs are dropping faster than price, ROIC grows from 8 percent to 20 percent over the forecast period. What initially appears to be a reasonable forecast translates to returns on capital not likely to be seen in a commodity business.

Now consider a second model, one that focuses on the economics of the business and not the details. To demonstrate the power of a simple yet insightful model, we present Exhibit 6.1 on page 136, which shows a set of realistic projections for a hypothetical company. We forecast only three line

Exhibit 6.1 The Fundamental Drivers of Value

Forecast	Year 1	2	3	4	5	6	7
Revenue growth (percent)	15.0	14.0	13.0	12.0	11.0	10.0	9.0
After-tax operating margin (percent)	3.0	6.0	8.2	20.0	16.4	11.7	8.3
Capital turns	1.0	1.0	1.1	1.1	1.1	1.2	1.2
ROIC (percent)	3.0	6.0	9.0	22.0	18.0	14.0	10.0

items: revenue growth, after-tax operating margins, and capital turns (the ratio of sales to invested capital). We assume the company's cost of capital equals 10 percent and current revenues equal $1 billion. No other projections are made.

Using the enterprise DCF method outlined in Chapter 5, we value the hypothetical company based solely on the forecasts presented in Exhibit 6.1. The results are presented in Exhibit 6.2. To determine future revenues, we grow current revenues by the forecasted growth rates. After-tax operating profit equals revenue multiplied by after-tax operating margin. To calculate invested capital, we divide each year's revenue by projected capital turnover. Free cash flow equals after-tax operating profit less the increase in invested capital. Adding forecasted discounted free cash flow to continuing value leads to enterprise value.[1] We have been able to build a relatively sophisticated free cash flow model based on only *three* projections.

If simple models provide the necessary flexibility to value a company, why do so many complicated models exist? In some cases, the details *are* unnecessary. In fact, extraneous details can cloud the drivers that really matter. You should make detailed line item forecasts only when they increase the accuracy of key value driver forecasts. For example, perhaps the ROIC you forecast requires dropping the inventory holding period from 50 days to 35 days, an operational improvement beyond the capabilities of the company.

We start the chapter by examining economic theory and how competitive dynamics should affect long-term corporate performance. In the second part of the chapter, we analyze ROIC and growth from an empirical perspective, presenting 40 years of data on the size, timing, and sustainability of ROIC and growth. We find that the typical company's returns on capital gradually regress toward a median ROIC of 9 percent, but many companies show persistence even over 15-year periods. Fast revenue growth,

---

[1] We assume economic profits are zero (i.e., ROIC equals the cost of capital) beyond year 7. When economic profits equal zero, the enterprise value of a company equals its book value. Therefore, the continuing value in year 7 equals the book value of invested capital. To determine today's value, invested capital in year 7 is discounted by seven years.

Exhibit 6.2 A Valuation Based on Fundamentals

$ million

	Year 0	1	2	3	4	5	6	7
Revenues	1,000.0	1,150.0	1,311.0	1,481.4	1,659.2	1,841.7	2,025.9	2,208.2
Operating profits[1]	25.0	34.5	78.7	121.2	331.8	301.4	236.4	184.0
Invested capital	950.0	1,150.0	1,311.0	1,346.8	1,508.4	1,674.3	1,688.2	1,840.2
Free cash flow								
Operating profits[1]		34.5	78.7	121.2	331.8	301.4	236.4	184.0
Net investment		(200.0)	(161.0)	(35.8)	(161.6)	(165.9)	(14.0)	(151.9)
Free cash flow		(165.5)	(82.3)	85.5	170.2	135.5	222.4	32.1
Discount factor		0.91	0.83	0.75	0.68	0.62	0.56	0.51
Discounted cash flow		(150.5)	(68.0)	64.2	116.3	84.1	125.5	16.5
Valuation								
PV(explicit forecasts)	188.1							
Continuing value	944.3							
Enterprise value	1,132.4							

[1]After-tax.

on the other hand, is fleeting. Even the fastest growers struggle to maintain high growth rates, regressing to the long-run median of 6 percent real growth within five years.

A FRAMEWORK FOR VALUE CREATION

In Chapter 3, we introduced a simple, yet powerful, valuation formula that we call the key value driver formula. Derived directly from the growing cash flow perpetuity, the key value driver formula formalized the direct relation between ROIC, growth, and a company's valuation. For some companies, especially companies in mature industries, the key value driver formula works quite well.

For companies growing quickly, however, the key value driver formula is overly restrictive in its assumptions. In many cases, ROIC will change over time as companies and their product markets evolve. Exhibit 6.3 on page 138 presents a *general* pattern for ROIC over time for a single-product company (later in this chapter, we demonstrate how this pattern can take different shapes). The ability to create value for this hypothetical company can be measured in two dimensions: the level of peak ROIC and the sustainability of returns in excess of the cost of capital. In this example, the peak ROIC occurs where the vertical arrow marks the spread between ROIC and cost of capital. The horizontal arrow represents sustainability; the longer a company creates value (ROIC greater than WACC), the greater

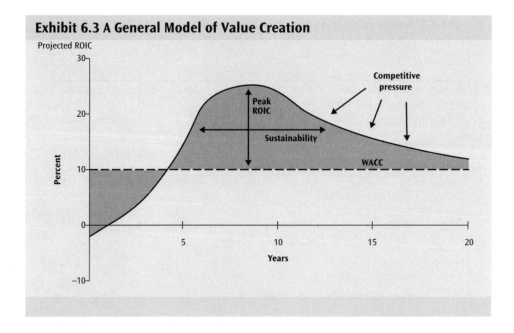

Exhibit 6.3 A General Model of Value Creation

its enterprise value. When it can no longer protect its competitive position, as marked by the downward arrows of competitive pressure, economic theory predicts its ROIC will regress to WACC such that enterprise value equals the book value of invested capital. (Empirical evidence, however, demonstrates this may not be the case; more on this later.)

To better understand the components of value creation, we first examine peak ROIC. Consider the following representation of return on invested capital:

$$\text{ROIC} = (1 - T)\frac{(\text{Unit Price} - \text{Unit Cost}) \times \text{Quantity}}{\text{Invested Capital}}$$

This version of ROIC is identical to the traditional definition of ROIC: NOPLAT divided by invested capital. We segment the ratio, however, into taxes (T), revenue and cost per unit, as well as quantity, to highlight the potential sources of value creation that you should consider when valuing a company.[2] The formula generates a series of questions. Can the company charge a price premium for its products or services? Does the company have lower unit costs than its competition? Can the company sell more products per dollar of invested capital? To justify high future ROICs, you *must* identify at least one source of competitive advantage.

[2] We introduce *units* to motivate a discussion surrounding price, cost, and volume. The formula, however, is not specific to manufacturing. Units can represent the number of hours billed, patients seen, transactions processed, and so on.

Price premium   In commodity markets, companies are price takers. Price takers must sell at the market price to generate business. Alternatively, a price setter has control over the price it charges. To enable price setting, a company cannot sell a commoditized product. It must find a way to differentiate its product so that its competition, if any, is limited.

The beverage company Coca-Cola is a price setter. For the company's primary products, Coke and Diet Coke, Coca-Cola can charge a price well in excess of its marginal costs because most consumers choose soft drinks based on taste, preference, and brand image, not on price. Coca-Cola customers are extremely loyal and rarely switch brands, even when faced with a generic, low-priced alternative. Coke's power to charge a price premium can be seen in the company's ROIC and valuation. At year-end 2003, Coke's ROIC was 48 percent, excluding goodwill, and its enterprise value equaled $125 billion, more than 11 times its book value of invested capital.

Be careful, however. Consumer brand loyalty does not guarantee immunity to competition. Consumer preferences change over time (consider the recent low-carb diet craze in the United States), and as products change, customers may migrate to competing offerings.

Cost competitiveness   A second driver of high ROIC is a company's ability to sell products and services at a lower cost than the competition. The discount retailer Wal-Mart is a low-cost operator. Wal-Mart is well known for using its substantial purchasing volume to lower its costs and force better terms from its suppliers. The company also invests heavily in computing power and other technologies to continually improve its cost position. It stands at the forefront of RFID, a new technology that electronically identifies when inventory enters a stockroom, reaches the main floor, and leaves the store.[3] Data collected is sent to Wal-Mart's Internet-based software, Retail Link, which allows the retailer's 30,000 suppliers to check inventory and sales in near real time. To lower costs further, the company is developing software that will trigger a business process, such as automated restocking or purchasing.

Capital efficiency   Even if profits per unit (or transaction) are small, a company can generate significant value by selling more products per dollar of invested capital than its competition. In the airline industry, an aircraft generates revenue when it is transporting passengers, not when it sits on the ground empty. Thus, the more an airline flies each aircraft in a given day, the more value it can create.

Southwest Airlines is an example of a company with superb capital efficiency. The typical Southwest aircraft can land, deplane, board, and take off

---

[3] L. Sullivan, "Wal-Mart's Way: Heavyweight Retailer Looks Inward to Stay Innovative in Business Technology," *Information Week* (September 27, 2004): 36.

in well under an hour. Conversely, this turnaround process at network carriers, such as American and United, averages over two hours per flight. This difference enables Southwest to spend more time in the air and less time on the ground.

The differences in ground time can be traced directly to differences in corporate strategy. First, Southwest flies point-to-point and does not rely on a hub; network carriers use hubs. A network carrier lands every flight at the same time, transfers passengers, and takes off at the same time. Not only does the congestion cause delays, but any late arrivals cause further delays throughout the system. A point-to-point airline does not face these constraints. Second, Southwest uses a single plane type, whereas network carriers use many. If a pilot calls in sick, an airline that has only one plane type can use any available pilot in the system. A network carrier might have an available pilot, but unless the pilot is certified to fly the given aircraft, the aircraft will sit empty until a qualified pilot becomes available.

Sustainability

To generate a high value, a company must not only excel at pricing power, cost competitiveness, or capital efficiency, but also must be able to sustain this competitive advantage over long periods. If the company cannot prevent competition from duplicating its efforts, high ROIC will be short-lived, and the company's value will be low. Consider a major cost improvement recently implemented by the airlines. The self-service kiosk allows passengers to purchase a ticket or print a boarding pass without waiting in line. From the airlines' perspective, fewer ground personnel can handle more people. So why has this cost improvement not translated into high ROICs for the airlines? Since every company has access to the technology, any cost improvements are passed directly to the consumer in the form of lower prices.

A company can maintain pricing power or a cost advantage only if the company maintains a barrier to imitation (from existing competition) or a barrier to entry (from new competition). The complexity of Microsoft's primary product, Windows, makes switching to an alternative unattractive for individuals and companies. Once users have become well versed in the platform, they are unlikely to switch to a new competitor. Even Linux, a low-cost alternative to Windows, has struggled to gain market share as system administrators and end users remain wary of learning a new way of computing. Or consider Wal-Mart, which located its first stores in rural communities. Rather than build a small store on the town's main street, as did Woolworth, Wal-Mart builds large-scale stores on the outskirts of town. Wal-Mart uses its size to dictate low prices and good terms from its suppliers; but more importantly, by building such a large store in an isolated community, it prevents other large, low-cost competitors from entering the market. A competitor such as Target or Costco could enter the community but, given the scale required to match Wal-Mart's prices, would generate instant overcapacity in the region.

Examples of Peak ROIC and Sustainability

The general pattern of ROIC and sustainability provided in Exhibit 6.3 is flexible and can describe different companies. Some companies have peak ROICs that are very high but offer little sustainability. Other companies have peak ROICs near the cost of capital but can generate excess returns over an extremely long period. Two examples with varying levels of peak ROIC and sustainability are Intel and Johnson & Johnson.

Intel has twice sustained high ROICs over the last 30 years. Exhibit 6.4 plots ROIC for Intel between 1973 and 2003. During that time, Intel has had two distinct periods of significant value creation. In its early life, the company was a pioneer in the computer chips that store data, commonly known as random access memory (RAM) chips. Intel created value for nearly 10 years, but the Japanese government made RAM a high priority, and companies such as NEC and Fujitsu began to flood the market with similar chips at lower prices. The price competition was so intense that it nearly drove Intel out of business. With a financial infusion from IBM, the company reinvented itself, creating the new "brains" of the personal computer. Through

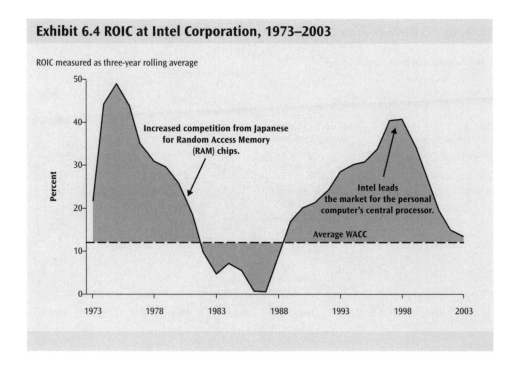

Exhibit 6.4 ROIC at Intel Corporation, 1973–2003

ROIC measured as three-year rolling average

an informal partnership with Microsoft, Intel led the personal-computer microprocessor market. By the late 1990s, however, competitors such as Advanced Micro Devices (AMD) began making inroads, forcing Intel to broaden its product line to include lower-priced chips. Facing increased competition and a general downturn in technology, Intel could no longer post the enormous ROICs of the mid-1990s. Today, Intel is still profitable and remains a strong player in microprocessors for personal computers, but the challenge for Intel is to capture the next major technology shift.

Economic theory dictates that companies earning returns in excess of their cost of capital will invite competition. Yet some companies are able to protect their primary product lines while concurrently expanding into new markets. One such example is Johnson & Johnson. Historically, Johnson & Johnson has earned strong returns on capital through its patented pharmaceuticals and branded consumer products lines, such as Tylenol and Johnson's Baby Shampoo. Through strong brands and capable distribution, the company has been able to maintain a price premium, even in the face of new entrants and alternative products. More recently, the company broadened its product portfolio to health care include medical devices and diagnostics, given the strength of the healthcare industry and expected growth as the baby boomers age.

As shown in Exhibit 6.5, which plots Johnson & Johnson's ROIC over the past 30 years, the company has maintained an ROIC greater than the

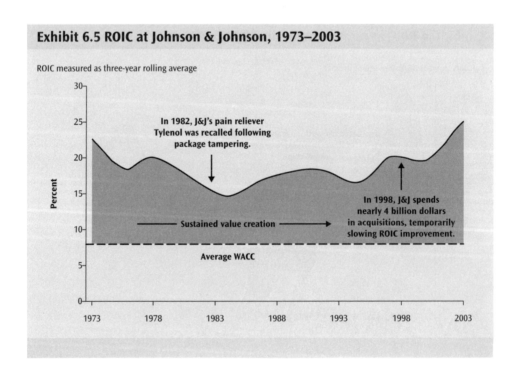

Exhibit 6.5 ROIC at Johnson & Johnson, 1973–2003

cost of capital during the entire period. In fact, given the strength of health care in the 1990s, returns have actually risen from the 1980s. Only the Tylenol tampering scare of the 1980s and the high cost of acquisitions in the late 1990s have dampened the company's continually strong performance.

Recouping Initial Investments or Early Losses

Not every company generates positive spreads. When companies are not earning returns in excess of their cost of capital (or are even losing money), you must assess two questions: (1) How long will it take before the company starts creating value? and (2) How large will the initial investments (or losses) be? We represent these two dimensions as arrows in Exhibit 6.6. The horizontal arrow represents the time to break-even (from a value creation perspective), and the vertical arrow represents the depth of value destruction.

One company that invested for years before creating value (or even earning a profit) is Amgen. Today, Amgen is a global biotechnology company that develops, manufactures, and markets therapeutics based on cellular biology and medicinal chemistry. Founded in 1980 with approximately $20 million in venture capital, the company burned through cash for nearly 10 years. In 1983, company scientists cloned the human protein erythropoietin (EPO), which eventually led to the drug Epogen, a treatment for anemia. Immediately following the drug's FDA approval in 1989, the company's ROIC skyrocketed to nearly 60 percent (see Exhibit 6.7 on p. 144).

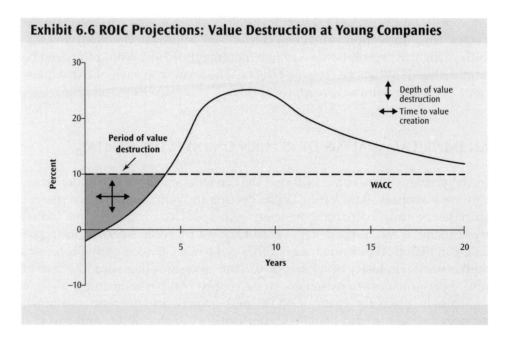

Exhibit 6.6 ROIC Projections: Value Destruction at Young Companies

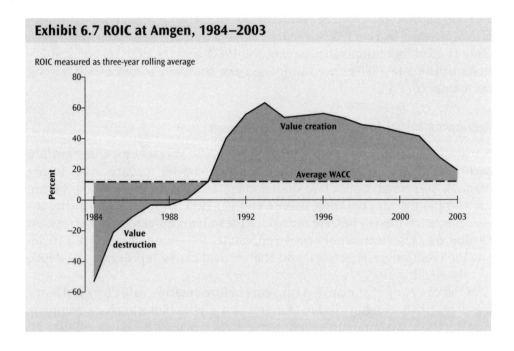

Exhibit 6.7 ROIC at Amgen, 1984–2003

ROIC measured as three-year rolling average

But standing in 1984, how could you predict the depth and length of value destruction? Once EPO was cloned in 1983, it became crucial to thoroughly analyze how much additional research (in dollar terms) would be needed to bring the product to market. In addition, how much would have to be spent for marketing and distribution? Since the drug would not generate cash until it gained FDA approval, it is also necessary to estimate expected time until approval. When considering approval, the FDA will ask: Is the drug truly revolutionary, or just incremental? How would the drug be administered? What are the side effects? The answer to each of these questions has a direct impact on approval time.

AN EMPIRICAL ANALYSIS OF RETURN ON INVESTED CAPITAL

In the previous section, we outlined the economic factors to consider when valuing a company. Any forecasts you develop for ROIC should be consistent with the company's core competencies, its competitive advantage, and industry economics. As a second step, benchmark your forecasts against the *actual* long-run historical performance of other companies. By comparing forecasts with historical industry benchmarks, you can assess whether your forecasts of future performance are reasonable in the context of other companies.

To help place forecasts of ROIC and growth in the proper context, we present the historical financial performance (using ROIC and revenue growth) for more than 5,000 U.S.-based nonfinancial companies over the past 40 years. Our results are generated from McKinsey & Company's corporate performance database, which relies on financial data provided by Standard & Poor's Compustat. Our key findings are as follows:

- The median ROIC between 1963 and 2003 was 9.0 percent and remained relatively constant throughout the period.[4] ROIC does, however, vary dramatically across companies, with only half of observed ROICs between 5 percent and 15 percent.
- Median ROIC differs by industry and growth, but not by company size. Industries that rely on sustainable advantages, such as patents and brands, tend to have high median ROICs (11 percent to 18 percent), whereas companies in basic industries, such as transportation and utilities, tend to earn low ROICs (6 percent to 8 percent).
- Individual-company ROICs gradually regress toward medians over time but are somewhat persistent. Fifty percent of companies that earned ROICs greater than 20 percent in 1994 were still earning at least 20 percent 10 years later.

To analyze historical corporate performance, we first measured median ROIC for each of the past 40 years. In Exhibit 6.8 on page 146, median ROIC is plotted between 1963 and 2003 for U.S.-based nonfinancial companies. ROIC is presented with and without goodwill. The aggregate median ROIC without goodwill equals 9.0 percent, and annual medians oscillate in a relatively tight range between 6.9 percent and 10.6 percent. This oscillation is not random, but instead is tied directly to the overall growth of the economy. When regressing median ROIC versus gross domestic product (GDP), we found that a 100-basis-point increase in GDP growth translates to a 20-basis-point increase in median ROIC.

Although a given year's median ROIC depends on the level of economic growth, it demonstrates no long-term trend. At first, the lack of an upward trend in ROIC may appear counterintuitive; especially given productivity increases over the past 40 years. The U.S. Department of Labor reports manufacturing workers were approximately 3.5 times more productive in 2003 than they were in 1963. So why have productivity increases not translated into improved financial performance? In most industries, healthy competition has transferred the benefits from internal improvements to customers and employees in the form of lower prices and higher salaries, instead of adding to corporate profits.

---

[4] Throughout this section, we report aggregate median ROICs over the entire sample period. To determine an aggregate median ROIC, we average each year's median.

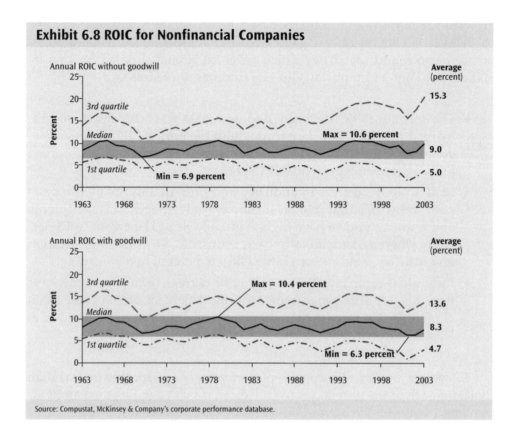

Exhibit 6.8 ROIC for Nonfinancial Companies

Source: Compustat, McKinsey & Company's corporate performance database.

Although median ROICs show little change over the past 40 years, the cross-sectional spread of company ROICs has increased. Over the entire period, half the companies typically had ROICs between 5.0 percent and 15.3 percent. Yet, since 1986, this spread has gradually widened, driven primarily by companies on the top end. In many cases, this improvement has occurred in industries with strong barriers to entry, such as patents or brands, where the drops in raw-material prices and increased productivity have not been transferred to other stakeholders.

The ROIC spreads across companies do not widen, however, when ROIC is measured with goodwill. This implies that top companies are acquiring other top performers yet paying full price for the acquired performance.

To further analyze the spread of ROIC across companies, we present a histogram in Exhibit 6.9. Each bar measures the percentage of observations within a certain range. For instance, approximately 17 percent of the sample has an ROIC between 5.0 percent and 7.5 percent. The aggregate distribution is quite wide, with only half the sample between 5 percent and 15 percent. In fact, in any given year, a particular company can have ROICs well below 0 or above 40 percent. However, 84 percent of the sample had ROIC *below* 20 per-

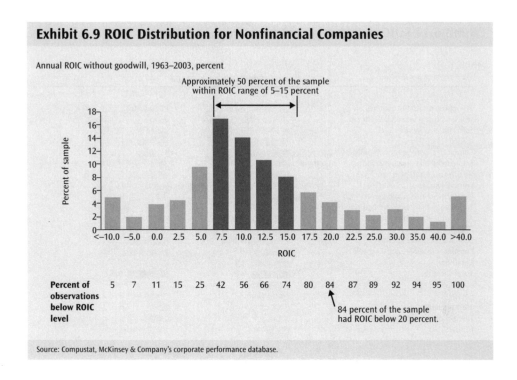

Exhibit 6.9 ROIC Distribution for Nonfinancial Companies

Annual ROIC without goodwill, 1963–2003, percent

Approximately 50 percent of the sample within ROIC range of 5–15 percent

Percent of sample (y-axis)

ROIC (x-axis): <−10.0 −5.0 0.0 2.5 5.0 7.5 10.0 12.5 15.0 17.5 20.0 22.5 25.0 30.0 35.0 40.0 >40.0

| Percent of observations below ROIC level | 5 | 7 | 11 | 15 | 25 | 42 | 56 | 66 | 74 | 80 | 84 | 87 | 89 | 92 | 94 | 95 | 100 |

84 percent of the sample had ROIC below 20 percent.

Source: Compustat, McKinsey & Company's corporate performance database.

cent. Thus, if you project sustained ROICs above 20 percent, you must believe the company is truly exceptional, as only one in six companies achieved this level of performance in a typical year.

Return on Invested Capital by Industry, Size, and Growth

Using aggregate data overlooks the fact that companies with certain characteristics are likely to have different levels of performance. Ideally, we would provide a comprehensive list of segmentation, tying median ROICs directly to the economic principles of pricing power, financial discipline, and competitive barriers to entry. This way, a valuation forecast could be benchmarked against true comparables, rather than overall aggregates. These characteristics, however, are mostly unobservable and difficult to measure quantitatively. Therefore, we instead segmented our sample using proxies, such as industry (different industries have varying competitive barriers to entry), size (for economies of scale), and growth (for the intensity of competition).

In our first segmentation, we examined median ROIC by industry. In Exhibit 6.10 on page 148, we rank 20 nonfinancial industries by median ROIC (based on performance over the past 40 years). To construct an industry, we used S&P's Global Industry Classifications Standard. Each industry classification is broad and encompasses many companies. As the

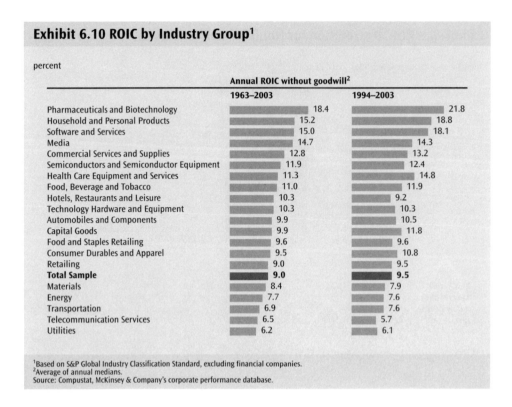

Exhibit 6.10 ROIC by Industry Group[1]

percent

	Annual ROIC without goodwill[2]	
	1963–2003	1994–2003
Pharmaceuticals and Biotechnology	18.4	21.8
Household and Personal Products	15.2	18.8
Software and Services	15.0	18.1
Media	14.7	14.3
Commercial Services and Supplies	12.8	13.2
Semiconductors and Semiconductor Equipment	11.9	12.4
Health Care Equipment and Services	11.3	14.8
Food, Beverage and Tobacco	11.0	11.9
Hotels, Restaurants and Leisure	10.3	9.2
Technology Hardware and Equipment	10.3	10.3
Automobiles and Components	9.9	10.5
Capital Goods	9.9	11.8
Food and Staples Retailing	9.6	9.6
Consumer Durables and Apparel	9.5	10.8
Retailing	9.0	9.5
Total Sample	**9.0**	**9.5**
Materials	8.4	7.9
Energy	7.7	7.6
Transportation	6.9	7.6
Telecommunication Services	6.5	5.7
Utilities	6.2	6.1

[1]Based on S&P Global Industry Classification Standard, excluding financial companies.
[2]Average of annual medians.
Source: Compustat, McKinsey & Company's corporate performance database.

exhibit demonstrates, financial performance varies significantly across industries. Industries that have identifiable sustainable advantages, such as patents and brands, tend to generate higher returns.[5] Pharmaceutical and biotechnology companies had a median ROIC of 18.4 percent; whereas companies in commodity (and often regulated) industries, such as transportation and utilities, had much lower ROICs—6.9 percent and 6.2 percent, respectively. Although performance differs at the extremes, the center is concentrated. Half the industries had median ROICs between 9 percent and 12 percent.

Although not reported, the industry ranking does not vary materially over time. Comparing median ROICs for the 10-year period ending in 2003 versus the entire sample leads to few changes in order (only ROICs of health care equipment companies are noticeably higher). Thus, industry membership can be an important predictor of performance.

We next segment the sample by size and growth. In Exhibit 6.11, we present the median ROICs for 30 separate subgroupings (five categories by

[5]Since R&D and advertising are not capitalized, ROIC will be upward-biased for industries with significant intangible assets. Capitalizing intangible assets, however, requires subjective assessments on amortization periods. Therefore, we present raw results without capitalizing R&D and advertising.

Exhibit 6.11 ROIC Segmented by Size and Growth

Annual ROIC without goodwill, 1963 to 2003

		Revenues				
		<$200M	$200M–$500M	$500M–$1B	$1B–$2.5B	>$2.5B
Three-year real growth rate (percent)	<0	3.3%	5.2%	6.0%	6.5%	7.0%
	0–5	8.0%	7.7%	8.0%	8.1%	9.1%
	5–10	8.9%	9.3%	9.6%	9.5%	10.3%
	10–15	10.8%	10.9%	11.2%	10.9%	11.8%
	15–20	11.9%	11.1%	11.7%	11.5%	11.9%
	>20	12.4%	11.9%	11.8%	11.8%	11.6%

ROIC increases with higher growth rate

No clear relation between size and performance

Source: Compustat, McKinsey & Company's corporate performance database.

total revenue and six categories by revenue growth), each of which has roughly the same number of companies. Moving from the top of this chart to the bottom, we find that median ROICs consistently increase as revenue growth increases, regardless of company size. Do not, however, misinterpret these results. We do *not* believe growth causes strong performance. A company that grows by stealing market share through price reductions is unlikely to maintain high margins—and lower margins often lead to lower ROICs. So why the positive correlation?

First, certain underlying factors enable *both* growth and ROIC. In rapidly expanding sectors with barriers to entry (e.g., high fixed costs), current capacity cannot fulfill continually increasing market demand. Since buyers exceed suppliers, prices and margins remain strong. If growth unexpectedly slows, however, so that industry capacity cannot be filled, companies often lower prices to generate the volume required to cover fixed costs. In this case, as growth drops, so does ROIC.

Second, companies with high ROICs have more incentives and greater opportunities to grow. A company earning a strong ROIC in its core business can create significant value by increasing growth (as demonstrated in

Chapter 3). Conversely, a company with returns at or below the cost of capital is unlikely to create value by accepting new projects (unless economies of scale lower unit costs). In addition, a company with a poor track record for earning high returns on capital in its core business is unlikely to attract funding for new opportunities.

Unlike growth, a company's size (as measured by revenues) shows no clear relation with ROIC. Despite the common perception that economies of should continually lower unit costs, many companies often reach minimum efficient scale at relatively small sizes. At this point, any incremental growth comes at the same unit cost, or even slightly higher costs, as bureaucratic inefficiency and other inflexibilities begin to dominate. To see this, one merely needs to examine Southwest Airlines, a company with only 35 percent of the revenues of American Airlines yet eight times the equity valuation (as of year-end 2004). Or consider Nucor Steel, a company with only 80 percent of the revenues of United States Steel yet 1.5 times the valuation.

Return on Invested Capital Decay Rates

When a company generates ROICs greater than its cost of capital, it invites competition. But how fast does the competition typically replicate a business, steal share, and force lower prices? In Exhibit 6.12, we address this question by forming portfolios based on ROIC. For instance, in each year,

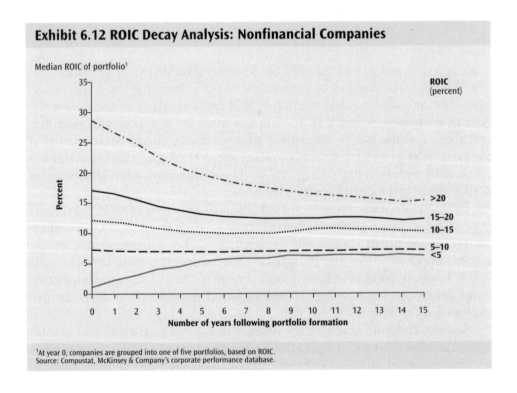

Exhibit 6.12 ROIC Decay Analysis: Nonfinancial Companies

Median ROIC of portfolio[1]

[1]At year 0, companies are grouped into one of five portfolios, based on ROIC.
Source: Compustat, McKinsey & Company's corporate performance database.

we aggregated all companies earning an ROIC greater than 20 percent into a single portfolio. We then tracked the median ROIC for each portfolio over the next 15 years.

Exhibit 6.12 demonstrates a pattern of mean reversion. Companies earning high returns tend to fall gradually over the next 15 years, and companies earning low returns tend to rise over time. Only the portfolio containing companies generating returns between 5 percent and 10 percent (mostly regulated companies) remains constant.

An important result of Exhibit 6.12 is the continued persistence of superior performance beyond 10 years. Although the best companies cannot maintain their current performance, their ROIC does *not* fully regress to the aggregate median of 9 percent. Instead, the top portfolio's median ROIC drops from 29 percent to 15 percent. Since a company's continuing value is highly dependent on long-run forecasts of ROIC and growth, this result has important implications for corporate valuation. Basing a continuing value on the economic concept that ROIC will approach WACC is overly conservative for the *typical* company generating high ROICs (continuing value is the focus of Chapter 9).

When benchmarking historical decay, it is important to segment results by industry (especially if industry is a proxy for competitive barriers to entry). In Exhibit 6.13, we plot the ROIC decay rates for the Consumer Staples

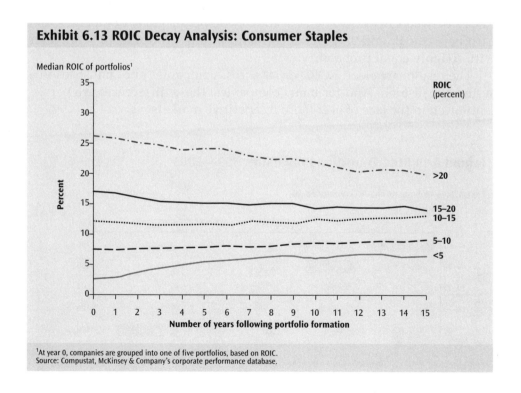

Exhibit 6.13 ROIC Decay Analysis: Consumer Staples

Median ROIC of portfolios[1]

ROIC (percent)

Percent

Number of years following portfolio formation

>20
15–20
10–15
5–10
<5

[1]At year 0, companies are grouped into one of five portfolios, based on ROIC.
Source: Compustat, McKinsey & Company's corporate performance database.

segment of the Food and Staples industry. As the exhibit demonstrates, ROICs once again regress to the mean but at a much slower rate than seen in the full sample. Top performers in Consumer Staples have a median ROIC of 26 percent, which drops to 20 percent after 15 years. (Top performers in the entire sample dropped to 15 percent.) Even after 15 years, the *original* class of best performers still outperforms the worst performers by more than 13 percent.

Although decay rates examine the *rate* of regression toward the mean, decay rates present only aggregate results, not the spread of potential future performance. Does every company generating returns greater than 20 percent eventually migrate to 15 percent, or do some companies actually generate higher returns? Conversely, do some top performers become poor performers? To address this question, we present ROIC transition probabilities in Exhibit 6.14. An ROIC transition probability measures the probability that a company will migrate from one ROIC grouping to another in 10 years. For instance, a company generating an ROIC less than 5 percent in 1994 had a 43 percent chance of earning less than 5 percent in 2003. Transition probabilities read from left to right, and the rows must sum to 100 percent.

As seen in Exhibit 6.14, both high and low performers demonstrate significant persistence in performance. This pattern was consistent throughout the 40-year period. Companies with an ROIC below 5 percent, companies between 5 and 10 percent, and companies greater than 20 percent have a 43 percent, 40 percent, and 50 percent probability, respectively, of remaining in the same grouping 10 years later. Only companies with ROICs between 10 and 20 percent show little persistence. Companies that earn between 10 and 15 percent can land in any grouping 10 years later with roughly equal probability.

The results are clear: ROIC varies across companies and industries in a systematic fashion. And for many companies, these differences are persistent—even in the face of ever more competitive markets.

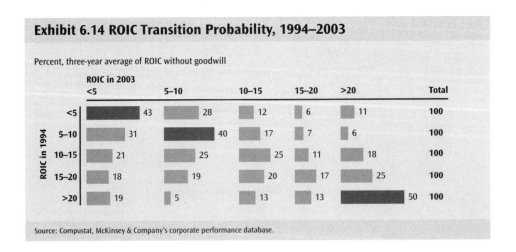

Exhibit 6.14 ROIC Transition Probability, 1994–2003

Percent, three-year average of ROIC without goodwill

ROIC in 1994	ROIC in 2003					Total
	<5	5–10	10–15	15–20	>20	
<5	43	28	12	6	11	100
5–10	31	40	17	7	6	100
10–15	21	25	25	11	18	100
15–20	18	19	20	17	25	100
>20	19	5	13	13	50	100

Source: Compustat, McKinsey & Company's corporate performance database.

AN EMPIRICAL ANALYSIS OF CORPORATE GROWTH

Today's public companies are under tremendous pressure to grow. Sell-side analysts set aggressive growth targets for revenues, earnings per share, and cash flow. Yet growth creates value only when a company's new customers, projects, or acquisitions generate returns greater than the risk-adjusted cost of capital. Finding good projects becomes increasingly difficult as industries become ever more competitive and companies grow ever larger. To generate revenue growth of 26.3 percent in 1990, Wal-Mart added 57,000 new employees. By 2003, the company was so large that it added approximately 100,000 employees, yet grew revenue by only 4.8 percent. To replicate 1990's revenue growth at 2003 productivity levels, Wal-Mart would have needed to add nearly half a million people in a single year—aggressive by any standards.

To help place expectations of long-term growth in a realistic context, we present data on the level and persistence of corporate growth over the past 40 years. Our analysis of revenue growth mirrors that of ROIC, except we now use three-year rolling averages to moderate distortions caused by currency fluctuations and merger and acquisition (M&A) activity.[6] Ideally, we would report statistics on *organic* revenue growth, but current reporting standards do not require companies to disclose the effects of currencies and M&A on revenue growth. Algorithms can be applied to dampen distortions but require overly stringent assumptions.[7] We therefore report raw results.

In addition, all corporate growth results are analyzed using real, rather than nominal, data. We do this because even mature companies saw a dramatic increase in revenue during the 1970s as inflation increased prices. Therefore, to compare growth rates over different time periods, we strip out the effect of inflation by using annual changes in the consumer price index. If you plan to use these data to drive growth forecasts in a valuation model, you *must* add expected inflation to the real results we present. (For more on modeling inflation consistently, see Chapter 22.)

Our general results concerning revenue growth (measured in real terms, except where noted) are as follows:

- The median revenue growth rate between 1963 and 2003 equals 6.3 percent in real terms and 10.2 percent in nominal terms. Real revenue growth fluctuates more than ROIC, ranging from 1.8 percent in 1975 to 10.8 percent in 1998.

---

[6] For more detail on how to define and separate organic, M&A, and currency-driven revenue growth, see Chapter 7.

[7] Acquired growth can be estimated by analyzing the increase in goodwill plus impairments, but doing this has two drawbacks. First, acquired revenue must be estimated using a goodwill-to-revenue ratio. However, profitable companies will have higher ratios, so applying an industry average ratio can cause systematic distortions. Second, goodwill exists only when companies use purchase accounting. Companies that used pooling for M&A would still be incorrectly estimated.

- High growth rates decay very quickly. Companies growing faster than 20 percent (in real terms) typically grow at only 8 percent within 5 years and 5 percent within 10 years.

- Extremely large companies struggle to grow. Excluding the first year, companies entering the *Fortune* 50 grow at an average of only 1 percent (above inflation) over the following 15 years.

We start by examining aggregate levels and trends of corporate growth. Exhibit 6.15 presents median (real) revenue growth rates between 1963 and 2003. The annualized median revenue growth rate between 1963 and 2003 equals 6.3 percent and oscillates between 1.8 percent and 10.8 percent. Median revenue growth demonstrates no trend over time. Even so, real revenue growth of 6.3 percent is quite high, especially when compared with real GDP growth in the United States at 3.3 percent. Why the difference?

Possible explanations abound. They include self-selection, specialization and outsourcing, global expansion, the use of medians, and nonorganic growth. First, companies with good growth opportunities need capital to grow. Since public markets are large and liquid, high-growth companies are more likely to be publicly traded than privately held. We measure only publicly traded companies, so our growth results are likely to be higher. Second, as companies become increasingly specialized and outsource more services, new companies, not picked up by GDP, will grow and develop quickly. Consider Electronic Data Systems (EDS), a company that provides information technology (IT) and data services. As companies move IT from

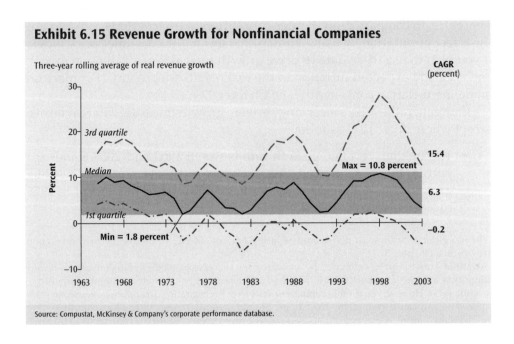

Exhibit 6.15 Revenue Growth for Nonfinancial Companies

Three-year rolling average of real revenue growth

CAGR (percent)

Source: Compustat, McKinsey & Company's corporate performance database.

internal management to EDS, GDP will not change, since it measures aggregate output. Yet EDS's high growth will be part of our sample. A third explanation is that many of the companies in our sample create products and generate revenue outside the United States. This revenue will not be picked up by GDP. Fourth, a significant portion of U.S. GDP is driven by large companies, which tend to grow more slowly. Since we measure the median corporate growth rates, the median company is typically small, and small public companies grow faster. Finally, although we use rolling averages and medians, we can only dampen the effects of M&A and currency fluctuations, not eliminate them entirely.

In addition to mapping median growth, Exhibit 6.15 reveals a second point: beginning in 1973, one-quarter of all companies actually shrank in real terms in a given year. Thus, although most companies publicly project healthy growth over the next five years, reality dictates that many mature firms will shrink in real terms. When you perform a valuation of a mature business, treat projections of strong growth skeptically.

Like the results concerning ROIC, the spread of growth rates across industries varies dramatically. In Exhibit 6.16, we present median revenue growth rates for 20 industries. The median Software and Services company has grown by 20 percent between 1963 and 2003, Semiconductors

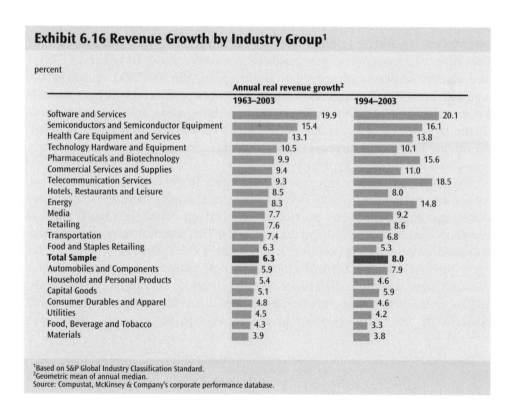

Exhibit 6.16 Revenue Growth by Industry Group[1]

percent

	Annual real revenue growth[2]	
	1963–2003	1994–2003
Software and Services	19.9	20.1
Semiconductors and Semiconductor Equipment	15.4	16.1
Health Care Equipment and Services	13.1	13.8
Technology Hardware and Equipment	10.5	10.1
Pharmaceuticals and Biotechnology	9.9	15.6
Commercial Services and Supplies	9.4	11.0
Telecommunication Services	9.3	18.5
Hotels, Restaurants and Leisure	8.5	8.0
Energy	8.3	14.8
Media	7.7	9.2
Retailing	7.6	8.6
Transportation	7.4	6.8
Food and Staples Retailing	6.3	5.3
Total Sample	**6.3**	**8.0**
Automobiles and Components	5.9	7.9
Household and Personal Products	5.4	4.6
Capital Goods	5.1	5.9
Consumer Durables and Apparel	4.8	4.6
Utilities	4.5	4.2
Food, Beverage and Tobacco	4.3	3.3
Materials	3.9	3.8

[1]Based on S&P Global Industry Classification Standard.
[2]Geometric mean of annual median.
Source: Compustat, McKinsey & Company's corporate performance database.

and Semiconductor Equipment has grown at 15 percent, and Health Care Equipment and Services has grown by 13 percent. Basic staples—such as Consumer Durables and Apparel; Utilities; Food, Beverage, and Tobacco; and Materials—all have grown less than 5 percent in real terms, only slightly higher than real GDP growth.

Yet, unlike the ROIC ranking, the ranking of industries based on growth varies over time. Between 1994 and 2003, Pharmaceuticals and Biotechnology, Telecommunication Services, and Energy each grew at rates well above long-term averages. For Energy, the recent level of higher growth is primarily driven by M&A, as energy companies consolidated during the 1990s (U.S. energy consumption rose by only 1 percent from 1994 to 2003). For Pharmaceuticals and Biotechnology and for Telecommunication Services, the results are a mixture of organic growth and M&A. Although significant consolidation took place during the 1990s, organic pharmaceutical revenues rose substantially with the development of many blockbuster drugs.

Decay Rates for Corporate Growth

Developing an accurate revenue growth forecast is critical to valuation. Yet building tempered projections is challenging, especially given the upward bias shown by research analysts and the media. For instance, empirical research has found that analysts are overly optimistic in their earnings forecasts following initial public offerings (IPOs) relative to a control sample.[8] This upward forecast bias also holds on a broader scale. In Exhibit 6.17, we plot analyst forecasts of aggregate earnings for the S&P 500 versus actual results from 1985 through 2000. Each line plots median earnings forecasts for a particular year and shows how they changed as actual results came closer. In nearly every year, the actual results are lower than forecast. In addition, the longer the forecast (measured up to four years), the more overly optimistic the forecast typically is.

To keep long-term corporate growth rates in their proper perspective, we present historical growth decay rates over the past 40 years. Companies were segmented into five portfolios, depending on their growth rate at portfolio formation. In Exhibit 6.18 on page 158, we plot how each portfolio's median company grows over time. As the exhibit shows, growth decays very quickly; for the typical company, high growth is not sustainable. Within three years, the difference across portfolios dampens considerably, and by year 5, the highest-growth portfolio outperforms the lowest-growth portfolio by less than 5 percentage points. Within 10 years, this difference

---

[8] R. Rajan and H. Servaes, "Analyst Following of Initial Public Offerings," *Journal of Finance*, 52(3) (1997): 507–529.

Exhibit 6.17 Aggregate EPS Forecasts for S&P 500 Constituents

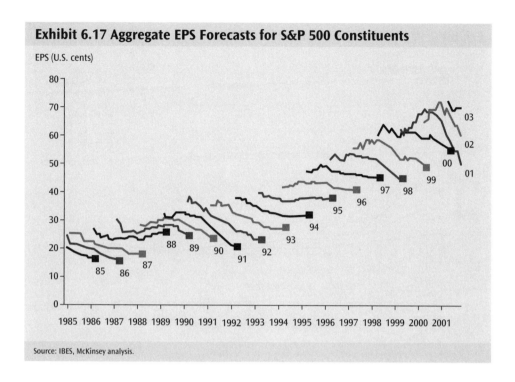

EPS (U.S. cents)

Source: IBES, McKinsey analysis.

drops to less than 2 percentage points. Comparing the decay of growth with that of ROIC, we see that although ROIC is persistent (top companies outperform bottom companies by more than 10 percentage points after 15 years), growth is not.

So why do companies struggle to maintain growth? As with ROIC, strong growth at high returns on capital attracts competition. More importantly, size, saturation, and growth itself are to blame. As the company grows, its revenue base increases, and growing at 20 percent on $200 billion of revenue is much harder than growing at 20 percent on $200 million. Remember, a company that grows at 20 percent will double in size in less than four years. Growth at this rate places many demands on the company and its management, making future growth ever more difficult.

Moreover, since every product market has a limited size, even the best performers must eventually track market growth. Most large companies struggle to grow once they reach a certain size. Exhibit 6.19 on page 159 reports results compiled by the Corporate Executive Board concerning the real revenue growth rate surrounding entrance into the *Fortune* 50.[9] Although

[9] Corporate Executive Board, "Stall Points: Barriers to Growth for the Large Corporate Enterprise" (1998).

Exhibit 6.18 Revenue Growth Decay Analysis

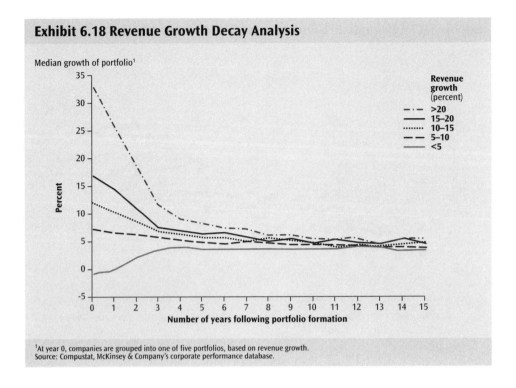

[1]At year 0, companies are grouped into one of five portfolios, based on revenue growth.
Source: Compustat, McKinsey & Company's corporate performance database.

growth is strong before companies enter the *Fortune* 50 (often because of acquisitions), growth drops dramatically after inclusion. In the five years before entrance, real revenue growth varies between 9 percent and 20 percent. And although the year immediately following entrance is high (28.6 percent), in every subsequent year, growth is quite low. In fact, during 5 of the 15 years after inclusion, companies actually shrink (in real terms).

In analyzing Exhibits 6.18 and 6.19 it becomes evident that the *typical* firm cannot maintain supernormal revenue growth. But are there companies that can beat the norm? In short, the answer is no. Exhibit 6.20, which reports the transition probabilities from one grouping to another, shows that maintaining high growth is uncommon. For example, 67 percent of the companies reporting less than 5 percent revenue growth in 1994 continued to report growth below 5 percent 10 years later. The same is also true for high-growth companies: 56 percent of companies growing faster than 20 percent in 1994 grew at real rates below 5 percent 10 years later. Only 13 percent of high-growth companies maintained 20 percent real growth 10 years later, most of which was probably driven by acquisitions.

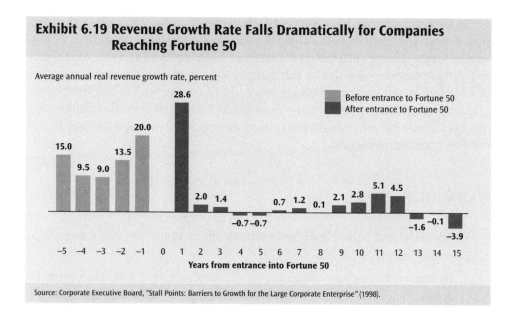

Exhibit 6.19 Revenue Growth Rate Falls Dramatically for Companies Reaching Fortune 50

Average annual real revenue growth rate, percent

- Before entrance to Fortune 50
- After entrance to Fortune 50

Years from entrance into Fortune 50

Source: Corporate Executive Board, "Stall Points: Barriers to Growth for the Large Corporate Enterprise" (1998).

SUMMARY

A valuation based on discounted cash flow is only as good as the model's forecasts. Yet, all too often, we get caught up in the details of a company's financial statements and forget the economic fundamentals: A company's valuation is driven by ROIC and growth. Thus, when you perform a valuation, it is critical to evaluate how your forecasts of ROIC and growth relate to the economics of the industry and how your results compare with the historical performance of companies that came before.

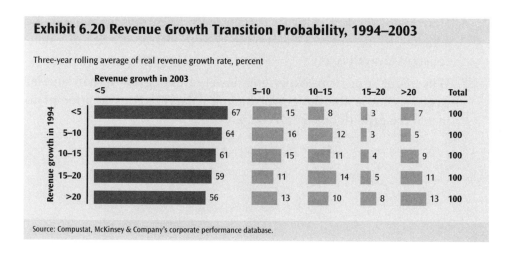

Exhibit 6.20 Revenue Growth Transition Probability, 1994–2003

Three-year rolling average of real revenue growth rate, percent

| Revenue growth in 1994 | Revenue growth in 2003 | | | | | |
	<5	5–10	10–15	15–20	>20	Total
<5	67	15	8	3	7	100
5–10	64	16	12	3	5	100
10–15	61	15	11	4	9	100
15–20	59	11	14	5	11	100
>20	56	13	10	8	13	100

Source: Compustat, McKinsey & Company's corporate performance database.

In this chapter, we have explored elements of value creation: price premium, cost competitiveness, capital efficiency, and sustainability. If you plan to forecast large returns on capital and high levels of growth, make sure you can explicitly point to the company's source of competitive advantage. In addition, make sure any forecasts—even those for which the company's advantages are clear—are within reasonable historical bounds. Otherwise, you may generate an unrealistic valuation and find yourself caught in yet another speculative bubble.

REVIEW QUESTIONS

1. Identify and discuss three sources of competitive advantage that could lead to increases in ROIC.

2. Referring to the key value driver formula, explain why this formula might work well for an established company, whereas for either a startup or rapidly growing company, the key value driver formula is inappropriate.

3. Explain how proper "branding" of corporate products could lead to sustained periods of high ROIC.

4. What factors would lead ROIC to be significantly different across industrial lines? Why might companies operating within the pharmaceutical and biotechnology industries be able to sustain higher ROICs than firms in the technology hardware and equipment and the retailing industries?

5. What does economic theory predict about long-run ROIC? Is historical evidence consistent with these predictions?

6. How might the key value driver approach to corporate valuation be adjusted to incorporate the unique growth characteristics of a non-constant growth firm?

7. Why might large firms experience lower rates of growth than smaller firms? What is the danger of having a large company attempt to match the growth of a small company?

7

Analyzing Historical
Performance

Understanding a company's past is essential for forecasting its future. For that reason, we begin the valuation process by analyzing historical performance. Since the financial statements are not designed for valuation, historical analysis can be challenging. To properly evaluate a company's performance, it is therefore necessary to rearrange the accounting statements, dig for new information in the footnotes, and, where information is missing, make informed assumptions. Only then will the company's previous performance, competitive position, and ability to generate cash in the future come into focus. To analyze a company's historical performance:

- Reorganize the financial statements to reflect economic, instead of accounting, performance, creating such new terms as net operating profit less adjusted taxes (NOPLAT), invested capital, and free cash flow (FCF).

- Measure and analyze the company's return on invested capital (ROIC) and economic profit to evaluate the company's ability to create value.

- Break down revenue growth into its four components: organic revenue growth, currency effects, acquisitions, and accounting changes.

- Assess the company's financial health and capital structure to determine whether it has the financial resources to conduct business and make short- and long-term investments.

The final section of this chapter covers advanced issues in financial analysis, such as capitalizing expenses (e.g., operating leases and R&D), stock-based compensation, retirement plans, provisions and loss reserves, and inflation. Immediately following this chapter, we apply the principles to Heineken, the Dutch brewer. The Heineken case continues through Part Two of the book.

REORGANIZING THE ACCOUNTING STATEMENTS: KEY CONCEPTS

Most companies report in their financial statements return on assets (ROA), return on equity (ROE), and cash flow from operations (CFO). Non-operating items such as nonoperating assets and capital structure, however, bias these measures.[1] To properly ground our historical analysis, we need to separate operating performance from nonoperating items and the financing obtained to support the business. The resulting measures, ROIC and FCF, are independent of leverage and focus solely on the operating performance of a business.

To build ROIC and FCF, we need to reorganize the balance sheet to create invested capital and likewise reorganize the income statement to create net operating profit less adjusted taxes (NOPLAT). Invested capital represents the total investor capital required to fund operations, without distinction to how the capital is financed. NOPLAT represents the total after-tax operating income (generated by the company's invested capital) that is available to *all* financial investors. (Although choice of capital structure will affect valuation, this will be handled through the cost of capital, *not* through ROIC or FCF.) Return on invested capital and free cash flow both rely on NOPLAT and invested capital. ROIC is defined as

$$\text{ROIC} = \frac{\text{NOPLAT}}{\text{Invested Capital}}$$

and free cash flow is defined as

$$\text{FCF} = \text{NOPLAT} + \text{Noncash Operating Expenses} - \text{Investment in Invested Capital}$$

By combining noncash operating expenses, such as depreciation with investment in invested capital, we can also express FCF as[2]

$$\text{FCF} = \text{NOPLAT} - \text{Net Increase in Invested Capital}$$

---

[1] As financial leverage rises, net income will fall due to increased interest expenses. This will cause return on assets to fall, even if the operating performance remains unchanged. Return on equity also commingles operating performance with financial leverage. Specifically, ROE rises with leverage when ROIC is greater than the company's after-tax interest rate on debt, and it falls with leverage when ROIC is less than the company's after-tax interest rate.

[2] This follows directly from the relation that invested capital$_{t+1}$ equals invested capital$_t$ plus investment in invested capital minus any noncash charges that reduce invested capital.

Invested Capital: Key Concepts

To build an economic balance sheet that separates a company's operating assets from its nonoperating assets and financial structure, we start with the traditional balance sheet. The accountant's balance sheet is bound by the most fundamental rule of accounting,

$$\text{Assets} = \text{Liabilities} + \text{Equity}$$

For single-product companies, assets consist primarily of operating assets (OA), such as receivables, inventory, and property, plant, and equipment (PP&E). Liabilities consist of operating liabilities (OL), such as accounts payable and accrued salaries, and interest-bearing debt (D), such as notes payable and long-term debt. Equity (E) will consist of common stock, possibly preferred stock, and retained earnings. Using this more explicit breakdown of assets, liabilities, and equity leads to an expanded version of the balance sheet relation:

$$\text{Operating Assets} = \text{Operating Liabilities} + \text{Debt} + \text{Equity}$$

The traditional balance sheet equation, however, mixes operating liabilities and investor capital on the right side of the equation. Moving operating liabilities to the left side of the equation leads to "invested capital":

$$\text{Operating Assets} - \text{Operating Liabilities} = \textbf{Invested Capital} = \text{Debt} + \text{Equity}$$

With this new equation, we have rearranged the balance sheet to better reflect invested capital used for operations, and net financing provided by investors to fund operations. Note how invested capital can be calculated using the *operating* method, that is, operating assets minus operating liabilities, or the *financing* method, which equals debt plus equity.

For most companies, our last equation is overly simplistic. Assets consist not only of core operating assets, but also of nonoperating assets, such as marketable securities, prepaid pension assets, nonconsolidated subsidiaries, and other equity investments. Liabilities consist not only of operating liabilities and interest-bearing debt, but also of debt equivalents (DE), such as unfunded retirement liabilities and restructuring reserves, and equity equivalents (EE), such as deferred taxes and income-smoothing provisions (we explain equivalents in detail later in the chapter). Expanding our original balance sheet equation:

OA		NOA		OL		D + DE		E + EE
Operating	+	Nonoperating	=	Operating	+	Debt and	+	Equity and
Assets		Assets		Liabilities		Its Equivalents		Its Equivalents

Exhibit 7.1 An Example of Invested Capital

$ million

Accountant's Balance Sheet			Invested Capital			
Assets	Prior year	Current year		Prior year	Current year	
Inventory	200	225	Inventory	200	225	Operating liabilities
Net PP&E	300	350	Accounts payable	(125)	(150)	are netted against
Equity investments	15	25	Operating working capital	75	75	operating assets.
Total assets	515	600				
			Net PP&E	300	350	
Liabilities and equity			Invested capital	375	425	
Accounts payable	125	150				Nonoperating assets
Interest-bearing debt	225	200	Equity investments	15	25	are not included in
Common stock	50	50	Total funds invested	390	450	invested capital.
Retained earnings	115	200				
Total liabilities and equity	515	600	**Total funds invested**			
			Interest-bearing debt	225	200	
			Common stock	50	50	
			Retained earnings	115	200	
			Total funds invested	390	450	

Rearranging leads to the derivation of "total funds invested":

$$
\underset{\substack{\text{Invested} \\ \text{Capital}}}{\text{OA} - \text{OL}} + \underset{\substack{\text{Nonoperating} \\ \text{Assets}}}{\text{NOA}} = \underset{\substack{\text{Funds} \\ \text{Invested}}}{\text{Total}} = \underset{\substack{\text{Debt and} \\ \text{Its Equivalents}}}{\text{D} + \text{DE}} + \underset{\substack{\text{Equity and} \\ \text{Its Equivalents}}}{\text{E} + \text{EE}}
$$

From an investing perspective, total funds invested equals invested capital plus nonoperating assets. From the financing perspective, total funds invested equals debt and its equivalents, plus equity and its equivalents. Exhibit 7.1 rearranges the balance sheet into invested capital for a simple hypothetical company with only a few line items. A more sophisticated example, using real companies, is developed in the next section.

Net Operating Profit Less Adjusted Taxes: Key Concepts

Invested capital makes no distinction between debt and equity. Rather, invested capital combines the two sources of investor funds and treats them equally. In a similar fashion, net operating profit less adjusted taxes (NOPLAT) aggregates the operating income generated by invested capital. Unlike net income, NOPLAT includes profits available to both debt holders and equity holders.

To calculate NOPLAT, we reorganize the accountant's income statement (see Exhibit 7.2) in three fundamental ways. First, interest is not sub-

Exhibit 7.2 An Example of NOPLAT

$ million

Accountant's income statement		NOPLAT		
	Current year		Current year	
Revenues	1,000	Revenues	1,000	
Operating costs	(700)	Operating costs	(700)	
Depreciation	(20)	Depreciation	(20)	
Operating profit	280	Operating profit	280	
				Taxes are calculated on
Interest	(20)	Operating taxes[1]	(70)	operating profits.
Nonoperating income	4	NOPLAT	210	
Earnings before taxes (EBT)	264			Do not include income
		After-tax nonoperating income[1]	3	from any asset excluded from invested capital as
Taxes	(66)	Total income to all investors	213	part of NOPLAT.
Net income	198			
		Reconciliation with net income		Treat interest as a
		Net income	198	financial payout to
		After-tax interest[1]	15	investors, not an
		Total income to all investors	213	expense.

[1]Assumes a flat tax of 25% on all income.

tracted from operating profit. Interest is considered a payment to the company's financial investors, not an operating expense. By reclassifying interest as a financing item, we make NOPLAT independent of the company's capital structure.

Second, when calculating after-tax operating profit, exclude any nonoperating income, gains, or losses generated from assets that were excluded from invested capital. Mistakenly including nonoperating income in NOPLAT, without including the assets in invested capital, will lead to an inconsistent definition of ROIC (the numerator and denominator will consist of different elements).

Finally, since reported taxes are calculated after interest and nonoperating income, they are a function of nonoperating items and capital structure. Keeping NOPLAT focused solely on operations requires that the effects of interest expense and nonoperating income also be removed from taxes. To calculate operating taxes, start with reported taxes, add back the tax shield caused by interest expense, and remove the taxes paid for nonoperating income. The resulting operating taxes should equal the hypothetical taxes that would be reported by an all-equity, pure operating company.

You may wonder how we will take into account the value of the tax shield. Given that interest is tax deductible, the deduction provides an important source of value to the company. But rather than model tax shields in NOPLAT, we will model all financing costs (including interest and its tax shield) in the cost of capital. Similarly, taxes for nonoperating income must be accounted for, and should be netted directly against the nonoperating income, *not* as part of NOPLAT.

Return on Invested Capital: Key Concepts

With our newly reorganized financial statements, we can now measure total investor capital and the after-tax operating income generated from those investments. ROIC measures the ratio of NOPLAT to invested capital:

$$\text{ROIC} = \frac{\text{NOPLAT}}{\text{Invested Capital}}$$

Since NOPLAT and invested capital are independent of financial structure and nonoperating assets, so is ROIC. And by using ROIC, we can now measure how the company's *core* operating performance has changed and how the company compares with its competitors, without the effects of financial structure and other nonoperating items distorting the analysis.

Free Cash Flow: Key Concepts

To value a company's core operations, we discount projected free cash flow at an appropriate risk-adjusted cost of capital. Free cash flow is the after-tax cash flow available to *all* investors: debt holders and equity holders. Unlike "cash flow from operations" reported in a company's financial statement, free cash flow is independent of financing and nonoperating items. It can be thought of as the after-tax cash flow—as if the company held only core operating assets and financed the business entirely with equity. Free cash flow is defined as:

FCF = NOPLAT + Noncash Operating Expenses – Investments in Invested Capital

As shown in Exhibit 7.3, free cash flow excludes nonoperating flows and items related to capital structure. Unlike the accountant's cash flow statement, the free cash flow statement starts with NOPLAT (versus net income). As discussed earlier, NOPLAT excludes nonoperating income and interest expense. Instead, interest (and its tax shield) is treated as a financing cash flow.

Net investments in nonoperating assets and the gains, losses, and income associated with these nonoperating assets are *not* included in free cash flow. Instead, nonoperating cash flows should be valued separately. Combining free cash flow and nonoperating cash flow leads to cash flow available to investors. As is true with total funds invested and profit available to all investors, cash flow available to investors can be calculated using two methodologies: "origin of cash flow" and "to whom the cash flow belongs." Although the two seem redundant, using both methods can help you avoid line item omissions and classification pitfalls.

Exhibit 7.3 An Example of Free Cash Flow

$ million

Accountant's cash flow statement	Current year	Free cash flow	Current year
Net income	198	NOPLAT	210
Depreciation	20	Depreciation	20
Decrease (increase) in inventory	(25)	Gross cash flow	230
Increase (decrease) in accounts payable	25		
Cash flow from operations	218	Decrease (increase) in inventory	(25)
		Increase (decrease) in accounts payable	25
Capital expenditures	(70)	Capital expenditures	(70)
Decrease (increase) in equity investments	(10)	Gross investment	(70)
Cash flow from investing	(80)		
		Free cash flow	**160**
Increase (decrease) in interest-bearing debt	(25)		
Increase (decrease) in common stock	0	After-tax nonoperating income	3
Dividends	(113)	Decrease (increase) in equity investments	(10)
Cash flow from financing	(138)	Cash flow available to investors	153
		After-tax interest expense	15
		Increase (decrease) in interest-bearing debt	25
		Increase (decrease) in common stock	0
		Dividends	113
		Cash flow available to investors	153

• Treat interest as a financial payout to investors, not as an expense.
• Investments in operating items are subtracted from gross cash flow.
• Cash flow from nonoperating assets should be evaluated separately from core operations.

REORGANIZING THE ACCOUNTING STATEMENTS: IN PRACTICE

Reorganizing the statements can be difficult, even for the savviest analyst. Which items are operating assets? Which are nonoperating? Which items should be treated as debt? As equity? In the following pages, we address these questions through an examination of Home Depot, the world's largest home improvement retailer, with stores located throughout North America. The company has grown rapidly over the past 10 years, generating strong returns and cash flow. But its core markets have become increasingly saturated, and the company now faces new challenges.

Invested Capital: In Practice

Invested capital equals operating assets minus operating liabilities. Total funds invested equals invested capital plus nonoperating assets. Alternatively,

Exhibit 7.4 Home Depot and Lowe's: Historical Balance Sheet

$ million

Assets	Home Depot			Lowe's		
	2001	2002	2003	2001	2002	2003
Cash and cash equivalents	2,477	2,188	2,826	799	853	1,446
Short-term investments	69	65	26	54	273	178
Receivables, net	920	1,072	1,097	166	172	131
Merchandise inventories	6,725	8,338	9,076	3,611	3,068	4,584
Other current assets	170	254	303	291	302	348
Total current assets	10,361	11,917	13,328	4,920	5,568	6,687
Net property and equipment	15,375	17,168	20,063	8,653	10,352	11,945
Long-term investments	83	107	84	22	29	169
Acquired intangibles and goodwill	419	575	833	0	0	0
Other assets	156	244	129	141	160	241
Total assets	26,394	30,011	34,437	13,736	16,109	19,042
Liabilities and equity	**2001**	**2002**	**2003**	**2001**	**2002**	**2003**
Short-term debt	211	0	509	159	79	77
Accounts payable	3,436	4,560	5,159	1,715	1,943	2,366
Accrued salaries	717	809	801	347	394	409
Deferred revenue	933	998	1,281	0	0	0
Other accrued expenses	1,204	1,668	1,804	796	1,162	1,516
Total current liabilities	6,501	8,035	9,554	3,017	3,578	4,368
Long-term debt	1,250	1,321	856	3,734	3,736	3,678
Deferred income taxes	189	362	967	305	478	657
Other long-term liabilities	372	491	653	6	15	30
Net common stock and paid-in capital	5,503	3,913	2,637	2,192	2,414	2,631
Retained earnings	12,799	15,971	19,680	4,482	5,887	7,677
Accumulated other comp income	(220)	(82)	90	1	1	1
Total liabilities and equity	26,394	30,011	34,437	13,736	16,109	19,042

total funds invested equals debt and its equivalents plus equity and its equivalents:

$$\underset{\substack{\text{Invested} \\ \text{Capital}}}{\underbrace{OA - OL}} + \underset{\substack{\text{Nonoperating} \\ \text{Assets}}}{\underbrace{NOA}} = \underset{\substack{\text{Total} \\ \text{Funds} \\ \text{Invested}}}{\underbrace{\text{Total}}} = \underset{\substack{\text{Debt and} \\ \text{Its Equivalents}}}{\underbrace{D + DE}} + \underset{\substack{\text{Equity and} \\ \text{Its Equivalents}}}{\underbrace{E + EE}}$$

In Exhibit 7.4, we present balance sheets for Home Depot and Lowe's (a direct competitor of Home Depot). We next set each element of the preceding equation against those figures.

For simplicity, we previously defined invested capital as operating assets minus operating liabilities (OA – OL). Most financial analysts, however, separate invested capital into operating working capital (current operating assets less current operating liabilities), fixed assets (e.g., net property, plant,

Exhibit 7.5 Home Depot and Lowe's: Invested Capital Calculation

$ million

	Home Depot			Lowe's		
	2001	2002	2003	2001	2002	2003
Working cash	1,027	1,117	1,243	424	508	591
Receivables, net	920	1,072	1,097	166	172	131
Merchandise inventories	6,725	8,338	9,076	3,611	3,968	4,584
Other current assets	170	254	303	291	302	348
Operating current assets	8,842	10,781	11,719	4,491	4,950	5,654
Accounts payable	3,436	4,560	5,159	1,715	1,943	2,366
Accrued salaries	717	809	801	347	394	409
Deferred revenue	933	998	1,281	0	0	0
Other accrued expenses	1,204	1,668	1,804	796	1,162	1,516
Operating current liabilities	6,290	8,035	9,045	2,858	3,499	4,291
Operating working capital	2,552	2,746	2,674	1,634	1,451	1,363
Net property and equipment	15,375	17,168	20,063	8,653	10,352	11,945
Capitalized operating leases[1]	5,459	5,890	6,554	2,189	2,373	2,762
Net other assets	(216)	(247)	(524)	134	145	211
Invested capital (excluding goodwill)	23,170	25,557	28,767	12,611	14,321	16,281
Acquired intangibles and goodwill	419	575	833	0	0	0
Cumulative amortization and pooled goodwill[2]	46	54	55	730	730	730
Invested capital (including goodwill)	**23,635**	**26,185**	**29,655**	**13,341**	**15,051**	**17,012**
Excess cash	1,519	1,136	1,609	429	618	1,033
Long-term investments	83	107	84	22	29	169
Total funds invested	**25,237**	**27,428**	**31,348**	**13,792**	**15,698**	**18,213**

	2001	2002	2003	2001	2002	2003
Short-term debt	211	0	509	159	79	77
Long-term debt	1,250	1,321	856	3,734	3,736	3,678
Capitalized operating leases[1]	5,459	5,890	6,554	2,189	2,373	2,762
Debt and debt equivalents	6,920	7,211	7,919	6,082	6,188	6,517
Deferred income taxes	189	362	967	305	478	657
Cumulative amortization and pooled goodwill[2]	46	54	55	730	730	730
Net common stock and paid-in-capital	5,503	3,913	2,637	2,192	2,414	2,631
Retained earnings	12,799	15,971	19,680	4,482	5,887	7,677
Accumulated other comp income	(220)	(82)	90	1	1	1
Equity and equity equivalents	18,317	20,218	23,429	7,709	9,510	11,696
Total funds invested	**25,237**	**27,428**	**31,348**	**13,792**	**15,698**	**18,213**

[1]Capitalized operating lease adjustments are detailed in Exhibit 7.21.
[2]Goodwill and cumulative amortization adjustments are detailed in Exhibit 7.6.

and equipment), intangible assets (e.g., goodwill), and net other long-term operating assets (net of long-term operating liabilities). Exhibit 7.5 demonstrates this line-by-line aggregation for Home Depot and Lowe's. In the following subsections, we examine each element in detail.

Operating working capital   Operating working capital equals operating current assets, net of operating current liabilities. Operating current assets comprise all current assets necessary for the operation of the business, including working cash balances, trade accounts receivable, inventory, and prepaid expenses. Specifically *excluded* are excess cash and marketable securities, that is, cash greater than the operating needs of the business.[3] Excess cash generally represents temporary imbalances in the company's cash position and is discussed later in this section.

Non-interest-bearing operating current liabilities include those liabilities that are related to the ongoing operations of the firm. The most common operating liabilities are those related to suppliers (accounts payable), employees (accrued salaries), customers (deferred revenue),[4] and the government (income taxes payable). If a liability is deemed operating versus financial, it should be netted from operating assets to determine invested capital.

Some argue that operating liabilities, such as accounts payable, are a form of financing and should be treated no differently than debt. This would lead to an *inconsistent* definition of NOPLAT and invested capital. NOPLAT is the income available to both debt and equity holders and therefore, when determining ROIC, should be divided by debt plus equity. Although a supplier may charge customers implicit interest for the right to pay in 30 days, the charge is an indistinguishable part of the price, and hence an indistinguishable part of the cost of goods sold. Since cost of goods sold is subtracted from revenue to determine NOPLAT, operating liabilities must be subtracted from operating assets to determine invested capital.[5]

Net property, plant, and equipment   The book value of net property, plant, and equipment (e.g., production equipment and facilities) is always included in operating assets. Situations that require using the market value or replacement cost are discussed in the section on advanced issues.

Acquired intangibles and goodwill   Whether to include acquired intangibles and goodwill as part of invested capital depends on the type of analysis being performed. To prepare for these later analyses, measure invested capital with and without goodwill. Then, to properly evaluate goodwill, make two adjustments. First, unlike other fixed assets, goodwill does not wear out, nor is it replaceable. Therefore, adjust reported goodwill upward

---

[3] In the company's financial statements, accountants often distinguish between cash and marketable securities, but not between working cash and excess cash. We provide guidance on distinguishing working from excess cash later in the chapter.
[4] Retailers, such as Home Depot and Lowe's, receive customer prepayments from gift cards, prepaid product installations, and anticipated customer returns (for which funds are received but revenue is not recognized).
[5] Alternatively, we could add back the estimated financing cost associated with any operating liabilities to NOPLAT and not subtract the operating liabilities from operating assets. This approach, however, requires information not readily available.

Exhibit 7.6 Home Depot and Lowe's: Adjustments to Goodwill

$ million

Home Depot	1999	2000	2001	2002	2003
Reported goodwill	311	314	419	575	833
Adjustments for merger accounting	0	0	0	0	0
Cumulative amortization and impairments	30	38	46	54	55
Adjusted goodwill	341	352	465	629	888

Lowe's	1999	2000	2001	2002	2003
Reported goodwill	0	0	0	0	0
Adjustments for merger accounting	730	730	730	730	730
Cumulative amortization and impairments	0	0	0	0	0
Adjusted goodwill	730	730	730	730	730

to recapture historical amortization and impairments.[6] (To maintain consistency, amortization and impairments will not be deducted from revenues to determine NOPLAT).

Second, any unrecorded goodwill (due to the old pooling of interest/merger accounting) must be added to recorded goodwill. Consider Lowe's acquisition of Eagle Garden & Hardware. Since the acquisition was recorded using pooling, no goodwill was recognized. Had Lowe's used purchase accounting, the company would have recorded $730 million in goodwill.[7] To include pooling transactions, estimate and record the incremental goodwill while simultaneously adjusting equity to represent the value of shares given away.

In Exhibit 7.6, cumulative amortization and impairments are added back to Home Depot's recorded goodwill. The exhibit also shows Lowe's recapitalized goodwill from the Eagle Garden & Hardware acquisition.

Net other long-term operating assets   If other long-term assets and liabilities are small—and not detailed by the company—we can assume that they are operating. To determine net other long-term operating assets, subtract other long-term liabilities from other long-term assets. This figure should be included as part of invested capital.

[6] The recent implementation of new accounting standards (in 2001 for the United States and 2005 for Europe) radically changed the way that companies account for acquisitions. Today, whether paid in cash or stock, acquisitions must be recorded on the balance sheet using the purchase methodology. Second, goodwill is no longer amortized. Instead, the company periodically tests the level of goodwill to determine whether the acquired business has lost value. If it has, goodwill is impaired (written down).

[7] On the final day of trading, Eagle had 29.1 million shares outstanding at a price of $37.75. Thus, Lowe's paid approximately $1.1 billion. According to its last 10-Q, Eagle had only $370 million in total equity. Goodwill equals $1.1 billion less $370 million, or $730 million.

If, however, the other long-term assets account is relatively large, it might include nonoperating items such as deferred tax assets, prepaid pension assets, intangible assets related to pensions, nonconsolidated subsidiaries, and other equity investments. Nonoperating items should not be included in invested capital.

Long-term liabilities can also include operating and nonoperating items. Long-term *operating* liabilities are liabilities that result directly from an ongoing operating activity. For instance, Home Depot warranties some products beyond one year, collecting customer funds today but recognizing the revenue only as the warranty expires. Most long-term liabilities are not operating liabilities, but rather what we deem debt and equity equivalents. These include unfunded pension liabilities, unfunded postretirement medical costs, restructuring reserves, and deferred taxes.

Where can you find the breakdown of other assets and other liabilities? In some cases, companies provide a table in the footnotes. Most of the time, however, you must work through the footnotes, note by note, searching for items aggregated within other assets and liabilities. For instance, in 2003, Lockheed Martin detailed an intangible asset related to pensions in the pension footnote but nowhere else in its annual report.

Hidden assets and their respective financing   Up to now, we have focused on reorganizing items that appear on the balance sheet. But there are two other items that accountants fail to capitalize: operating leases and investments masquerading as expenses (e.g., research and development). If these hidden assets are significant, we recommend the following adjustments:

- When a company leases an asset under certain conditions, it need not record either an asset or a liability. To properly compare across companies with different leasing policies, you should include the value of the lease as an operating asset, with a corresponding debt recorded as a financing item. Otherwise, companies that lease assets will appear "capital light" relative to identical companies that purchase the assets.

- Given the conservative principles of accounting, accountants expense research and development (R&D), advertising, and certain other expenses in their entirety, even when the economic benefits of the expense continue beyond the current reporting period. If possible, R&D and other quasi investments should be capitalized *and* amortized in a manner similar to capital expenditures. Equity should be adjusted correspondingly to balance the invested capital equation.

The specific treatment of operating leases and R&D expenses is detailed later in this chapter.

Nonoperating assets   Invested capital represents the capital necessary to operate a company's core business. In addition to invested capital, companies can also own nonoperating assets, both liquid and illiquid. Liquid assets include excess cash, marketable securities, and certain financing receivables (e.g., credit card receivables). Illiquid assets include equity investments and excess pension assets. We address excess cash, illiquid investments, and other nonoperating assets like excess pension assets next.

Excess cash and marketable securities   Do not include excess cash in invested capital. By its definition, excess cash is unnecessary for core operations. Rather than mix excess cash with core operations, therefore, you should analyze and value excess cash separately.

Given its liquidity and low risk, excess cash will earn very small returns. Therefore, failing to separate excess cash from core operations will incorrectly depress the company's apparent ROIC. Home Depot's ROIC in 2003 was 18.2 percent. Had excess cash been included as part of invested capital, Home Depot's ROIC would have been incorrectly measured as 17.4 percent.

Companies do not disclose how much cash they deem necessary for operations. Nor does the accountant's definition of cash versus marketable securities distinguish working cash from excess cash. To estimate the size of working cash, we examined the cash holdings of the S&P 500 nonfinancial companies. Between 1993 and 2000, the companies with the smallest cash balances held cash just below 2 percent of sales. If this is a good proxy for working cash, any cash above 2 percent should be considered excess.[8]

This aggregate figure, however, is not a rule. Required cash holdings vary by industry. For instance, one study found that companies in industries with higher cash flow volatility hold higher cash balances.[9] To assess the *minimum* cash needed to support operations, look for a minimum clustering of cash to revenue across the industry.

Illiquid investments, nonconsolidated subsidiaries, and other equity investments   If possible, interest-generating customer loans (e.g., credit card receivables and other long-term customer financing), nonconsolidated subsidiaries, and other equity investments should be measured and valued separately from invested capital. Evaluating customer financing and equity investments

---

[8] Companies in economies with poor shareholder protections tend to hold more cash. Therefore, in economies with poor shareholder protections, median (or bottom quartile) cash holdings might overestimate the amount of working cash truly needed. A. Dittmar, J. Mahrt-Smith, and H. Servaes "International Corporate Governance and Corporate Cash Holdings," *Journal of Financial and Quantitative Analysis* (forthcoming).

[9] T. Opler, L. Pinkowitz, R. Stulz, and R. Williamson, "The Determinants and Implications of Corporate Cash Holdings," *Journal of Financial Economics*, 52(1) (1999): 3–46.

separately requires excluding these accounts from invested capital *and* excluding their respective income from NOPLAT. Companies do not always clearly separate sources of income, so we are sometimes forced to aggregate certain nonoperating assets within invested capital.

Prepaid and intangible pension assets   If a company runs a defined-benefit plan for its employees, it must fund the plan each year. And if a company funds its plan faster than its pension expenses dictate, under U.S. Generally Accepted Accounting Principles (GAAP), the company can recognize a portion of the excess assets on the balance sheet. Pension assets are considered a nonoperating asset and not part of invested capital. Their value is important to the equity holder, so they will be valued later, but separately from core operations. We examine pension assets in detail in the section on advanced issues.

Total funds invested can be calculated as invested capital plus nonoperating assets, or as the sum of net debt, equity, and equity equivalents. We next examine the right-hand side of the "total funds invested" equation.

Other nonoperating assets   Other nonoperating assets, such as excess real estate and discontinued operations, should also be excluded from invested capital.

Debt   Debt includes any short-term or long-term interest-bearing liability. Short-term debt includes commercial paper, notes payable, and the current portion of long-term debt. Long-term debt includes fixed debt, floating debt, and convertible debt with maturities of more than a year.

Debt equivalents such as retirement liabilities and operating leases   If a company's defined-benefit plan is underfunded, it must recognize a portion of the underfunding as a liability. The amount of underfunding is not an operating liability. Rather, we treat unfunded pension expenses and unfunded postretirement medical expenses as a debt equivalent (and treat the net interest expense associated with these liabilities as nonoperating). It is as if the company must borrow money to fund the plan.

Treating unfunded retirement expenses as debt might seem hypothetical, but for some companies the issue has become real. In June 2003, General Motors issued $17 billion in debt, using the proceeds to reduce its pension shortfall, not to fund operations.[10]

---

[10] R. Barley and C. Evans, "GM Plans Record Bond Sale Thursday to Plug Pension Gap," Reuters News (June 26, 2003).

As discussed in the section on hidden assets, a company with substantial operating leases should capitalize those leases, recognizing them both as an asset and as a debt. The resulting liability from capitalizing operating leases should be treated as a debt equivalent. For some companies, such as retailers, operating leases can increase debt dramatically. This helps explain why some retailers, such as the Gap, have sub-A credit ratings even with minimal formal debt.

Other debt equivalents, such as reserves for plant decommissioning and restructuring, are discussed in the section on advanced issues.

Equity (E)   Equity includes original investor funds, such as common stock and additional paid-in capital, as well as investor funds reinvested into the company such as retained earnings and accumulated other comprehensive income (AOCI). In the United States, AOCI consists primarily of currency adjustments and aggregate unrealized gains and losses from liquid assets whose value has changed but have not yet been sold. Any stock repurchased and held in the treasury should be deducted from total equity.

Equity equivalents such as deferred taxes   In certain situations, companies will expense a future cost that has no corresponding cash outlay. Since the expense is noncash, both an expense and an offsetting liability are recognized. The most common noncash expenses are deferred taxes and reserves created for the purpose of income smoothing. Each of these liabilities is an equity equivalent, not an operating liability, so it should *not* be subtracted from operating assets. These liabilities should remain on the right side of the invested-capital equation.

The most common equity equivalent, deferred taxes, arises primarily from tax incentives that governments provide to encourage investment.[11] In many countries, companies use straight-line depreciation to determine taxes reported in their financial statements but can use accelerated depreciation to compute actual taxes owed.[12] Since the delay in taxes is temporary, a liability is recognized. For growing companies, the financial statements will overstate the company's actual tax burden. Thus, rather than using the taxes reported on the income statement to compute NOPLAT, we recommend using taxes actually paid. Using cash taxes, however, means no deferred tax account needs to be recognized. Instead, adjust retained earnings to balance the financial statements. This is why deferred taxes are considered an equity equivalent.

---

[11] In addition to deferred taxes arising from investment, deferred taxes also arise from nonoperating items, such as pensions. When this is the case, deferred taxes should be aggregated with (or netted against) their corresponding nonoperating item. See the company's footnotes for a full breakdown of deferred taxes.

[12] Although not every country allows reported taxes to differ from actual taxes, the practice is becoming more prevalent.

NOPLAT: In Practice

To determine the after-tax income generated by invested capital, we calculate net operating profits less adjusted taxes (NOPLAT). NOPLAT represents total income generated from operations available to all investors. To determine NOPLAT for Home Depot and Lowe's, we turn to their respective income statements (see Exhibit 7.7) and convert the income statement into NOPLAT (see Exhibit 7.8).

Net operating profit (NOP or EBITA)   NOPLAT starts with earnings before interest, taxes, and amortization of goodwill (EBITA), which equals revenue less operating expenses (e.g., cost of goods sold, selling costs, general and administrative costs, depreciation).

Nonoperating income, gains, and losses   To remain consistent with the calculation of invested capital, calculate NOPLAT without interest income, gains, and losses from the corresponding assets that have been excluded. Historical returns on excess cash and other nonoperating assets should be calculated and evaluated separately.

Income adjustments for hidden assets   In the section on invested capital, we outlined certain assets not on the balance sheet: operating leases and capitalized R&D. Corresponding adjustments must also be made to the income statement:

Exhibit 7.7 Home Depot and Lowe's: Historical Income Statement

$ million	Home Depot			Lowe's		
	2001	2002	2003	2001	2002	2003
Net sales	53,553	58,247	64,816	22,111	26,491	30,838
Cost of merchandise sold	(37,406)	(40,139)	(44,236)	(15,743)	(18,465)	(21,231)
Selling, general and administrative	(10,451)	(11,375)	(12,658)	(4,053)	(4,859)	(5,671)
Depreciation	(756)	(895)	(1,075)	(517)	(626)	(758)
Amortization	(8)	(8)	(1)	0	0	0
EBIT	4,932	5,830	6,846	1,798	2,541	3,178
Interest and investment income	53	79	59	25	21	15
Interest expense	(28)	(37)	(62)	(199)	(203)	(195)
Discontinued operations	0	0	0	0	0	15
Earnings before taxes	4,957	5,872	6,843	1,624	2,359	3,013
Income taxes	(1,913)	(2,208)	(2,539)	(601)	(888)	(1,136)
Net earnings	3,044	3,664	4,304	1,023	1,471	1,877

Exhibit 7.8 Home Depot and Lowe's: NOPLAT Calculation

$ million

	Home Depot			Lowe's		
	2001	2002	2003	2001	2002	2003
Net sales	53,553	58,247	64,816	22,111	26,491	30,838
Cost of merchandise sold	(37,406)	(40,139)	(44,236)	(15,743)	(18,465)	(21,231)
Selling, general and administrative	(10,451)	(11,375)	(12,658)	(4,053)	(4,859)	(5,671)
Depreciation	(756)	(895)	(1,075)	(517)	(626)	(758)
Operating lease interest	288	260	276	106	106	114
Adjusted EBITA	5,228	6,098	7,123	1,904	2,647	3,292
Operating cash taxes	(2,020)	(2,117)	(2,040)	(654)	(825)	(1,069)
NOPLAT	3,208	3,981	5,083	1,250	1,822	2,223
Operating taxes						
Reported taxes	1,913	2,208	2,539	601	888	1,136
Taxes on interest income	(20)	(30)	(23)	(9)	(8)	(6)
Tax shield on interest expense	11	14	24	75	78	74
Tax shield on lease interest expense	111	98	105	40	41	44
Operating taxes on EBITA	2,014	2,290	2,645	707	998	1,248
Decrease (increase) in deferred taxes	6	(173)	(605)	(53)	(173)	(179)
Operating cash taxes on EBITA	2,020	2,117	2,040	654	825	1,069
Reconciliation with net income	**2001**	**2002**	**2003**	**2001**	**2002**	**2003**
Net earnings	3,044	3,664	4,304	1,023	1,471	1,877
Increase in deferred taxes	(6)	173	605	53	173	179
Goodwill amortization	8	8	1	0	0	0
Adjusted net income	3,046	3,845	4,910	1,076	1,644	2,056
After-tax interest expense	17	23	38	123	125	121
After-tax lease interest expense	177	162	170	66	65	71
Loss (gain) from discontinued operations	0	0	0	0	0	(15)
Total income available to investors	3,240	4,030	5,119	1,265	1,835	2,232
After-tax interest income	(33)	(49)	(36)	(15)	(13)	(9)
NOPLAT	3,208	3,981	5,083	1,250	1,822	2,223

- Operating lease payments, which consist of interest and depreciation, are expensed within EBITA. Since interest is a financing flow, add back the implied interest expense to determine EBITA and NOPLAT.
- If you decide to capitalize R&D, the R&D expense must not be deducted from revenue to calculate operating profit. Instead, deduct amortization of past R&D, using a reasonable amortization schedule.

Operating leases and capitalized R&D are detailed in the section on advanced issues later in this chapter. Pension expenses and loss provisions may require further adjustments to income. The section on advanced issues also discusses these topics.

Operating cash taxes on EBITA   Since nonoperating items also affect reported taxes, they must be adjusted to an all-equity, operating level. Since interest expense is deductible before taxes, highly leveraged companies will have smaller tax burdens. Although a smaller tax burden can lead to a higher valuation, we recommend valuing all financing effects in the weighted average cost of capital (WACC) or valuing them separately using adjusted present value (APV)—but *not* as part of after-tax operating income.

For Home Depot, compute operating taxes for core operations by starting with reported taxes ($2,539). Next, eliminate the taxes paid on the nonoperating income generated by the company's nonoperating assets ($23). Finally, eliminate the interest expense tax shield (from both traditional debt and capitalized operating leases) by adding the incremental taxes the companies would have paid had Home Depot been entirely financed with equity ($24 and $105 respectively). Home Depot's calculation is as follows:

$ Millions	2001	2002	2003
Reported taxes	1,913	2,208	2,539
Subtract: Taxes on interest income	(20)	(30)	(23)
Add: Tax shield on interest expense	11	14	24
Add: Tax shield on operating lease interest expense	111	98	105
Operating taxes	2,014	2,290	2,645

To eliminate the tax effects of each nonoperating item, multiply each line item's dollar amount by the company's *marginal* tax rate. The marginal tax rate is defined as the tax rate on an extra dollar of income.[13] To calculate marginal taxes, it is necessary to examine the company's financial footnotes. Home Depot reports the following tax schedule in footnote 3 of its annual report:

Tax Rate	2001	2002	2003
Income taxes at federal statutory rate (1)	35.0%	35.0%	35.0%
State income taxes, net of federal (2)	3.5	2.7	3.2
Foreign rate differences	0.1	0.0	−0.4
Other, net	0.0	0.0	−0.6
Accountant's effective (average) tax rate	38.6%	37.6%	37.1%
Marginal tax rate (1 + 2)	38.5%	37.7%	38.2%

[13] Marginal taxes do not equal average taxes, which are computed by dividing reported taxes by earnings before taxes. In fact, whereas marginal taxes are relatively constant, average taxes can vary dramatically. Walt Disney's average tax rate varied between 35 percent and 82 percent from 2001 to 2003, whereas its marginal tax rate varied between 37 percent and 42 percent.

For adjusting reported taxes, marginal taxes are those taxes the company would pay if the financing or nonoperating item were eliminated. If the company eliminated leverage, it would be required to pay additional federal income taxes (line item 1) and state taxes (2). If foreign taxes (3) are based on income and debt is raised abroad, they are marginal. If, however, foreign taxes are based on revenues or debt is raised solely at home, they are not marginal; taxes would not increase as leverage decreased. Whether other taxes (4) are marginal requires further investigation. In this case, we assume they are not. For Home Depot, the marginal tax rate is merely the sum of the federal and state income taxes (1 + 2).

Finally, we recommend using the cash taxes actually paid, versus the taxes reported.[14] The simplest way to calculate cash taxes is to subtract the increase in deferred tax liabilities from operating taxes on EBITA. As shown in Exhibit 7.1, Home Depot's deferred tax liabilities have been growing over time, so reported taxes overstate actual cash taxes. Subtracting the increase in deferred taxes leads to cash taxes:

$ Millions	2001	2002	2003
EBITA	5,228	6,098	7,123
(All-equity) operating taxes on EBITA	2,014	2,290	2,645
Decrease (increase) in deferred taxes	6	(173)	(605)
Operating cash taxes on EBITA	2,020	2,117	2,040
Operating tax rate	38.5%	37.6%	37.1%
× (1 − percent deferred)	−0.3%	7.6%	22.9%
Operating cash tax rate	38.6%	34.7%	28.6%

The cash tax rate at Home Depot has been falling because a greater percentage of operating taxes have been deferred. In 2003, Home Depot was able to defer 22.9 percent of its operating taxes on EBITA.

Reconciliation to net income   To ensure that the reorganization is complete, we recommend reconciling net income to NOPLAT (see the bottom of Exhibit 7.8). To reconcile NOPLAT, start with net income and add back the increase in deferred tax liabilities and goodwill amortization. Next, add back *after-tax* interest expense from both debt and capitalized operating leases. This determines the profits available to all investors. To calculate NOPLAT, subtract after-tax gains and income from nonoperating assets, and you are done. We do this for Home Depot in Exhibit 7.8.

---

[14] If a company reported cash taxes on the income statement, the deferred tax liability would no longer exist, and an offsetting adjustment to retained earnings would be made. Thus, when using cash taxes, you should treat the deferred tax liability as an equity equivalent.

Free Cash Flow: In Practice

Free cash flow is defined as:

$$FCF = NOPLAT + Noncash\,Operating\,Expenses - Investments\,in\,Invested\,Capital$$

Exhibit 7.9 builds the free cash flow calculation and reconciles free cash flow to cash flow available to investors for both Home Depot and Lowe's. The components of free cash flow are as follows:

Gross cash flow   Gross cash flow represents the cash flow generated by the company's operations. It represents the cash available for investment and investor payout, without having to sell nonoperating assets (e.g., excess cash) or raise additional capital. Gross cash flow has two components:

1. *NOPLAT:* As previously defined, net operating profits after taxes are the operating profits available to all investors.
2. *Noncash operating expenses:* Some expenses deducted from revenue to generate NOPLAT are noncash expenses. To convert NOPLAT into cash flow, add back noncash expenses. The two most common noncash expenses are depreciation and employee stock options.[15] Do not add back goodwill amortization and impairments to NOPLAT; they were not subtracted in calculating NOPLAT.

Gross investment   To grow, companies must reinvest a portion of their gross cash flow back into the business. To determine free cash flow, subtract gross investment from gross cash flow. We segment gross investment into four primary areas:

1. *Change in operating working capital:* Growing a business requires investment in operating cash, inventory, and other components of working capital. Operating working capital excludes nonoperating assets, such as excess cash, and financing items, such as short-term debt and dividends payable.
2. *Net capital expenditures:* Net capital expenditures equals investments in property, plant, and equipment, less the book value of any PPE

---

[15] Even though stock options are a noncash expense, they represent value being transferred from shareholders to company employees. Therefore, if you choose to add back noncash compensation to NOPLAT, you must value noncash compensation separately. If you choose not to add back noncash compensation to NOPLAT, there is no need to value them separately. They will be part of enterprise value.

Exhibit 7.9 Home Depot and Lowe's: Historical Free Cash Flow

$ million

	Home Depot			Lowe's		
	2001	2002	2003	2001	2002	2003
NOPLAT	3,208	3,981	5,083	1,250	1,822	2,223
Depreciation	756	895	1,075	517	626	758
Gross cash flow	3,964	4,876	6,157	1,767	2,448	2,981
Investment in operating working capital	834	(194)	72	(203)	183	88
Net capital expenditures	(3,063)	(2,688)	(3,970)	(2,135)	(2,325)	(2,351)
Investment in capitalized operating leases	(775)	(430)	(664)	(547)	(184)	(389)
Investments in intangibles and goodwill	(113)	(164)	(259)	0	0	0
Increase (decrease) in other operating assets	105	31	277	(7)	(11)	(66)
Increase (decrease) in accumulated other comprehensive income	(153)	138	172	3	0	0
Gross investment	(3,165)	(3,307)	(4,372)	(2,889)	(2,336)	(2,719)
Free cash flow	**799**	**1,569**	**1,785**	**1,122**	**112**	**262**
After-tax interest income	33	49	36	15	13	9
Decrease (increase) in excess cash	(1,509)	383	(473)	(321)	(189)	(415)
Decrease (increase) in nonoperating assets	9	(24)	23	13	(7)	(140)
Discontinued operations	0	0	0	0	0	15
Cash flow available to investors	**(668)**	**1,977**	**1,371**	**(1,415)**	**(71)**	**(268)**
	2001	2002	2003	2001	2002	2003
After-tax interest expense	17	23	38	123	125	121
After-tax lease interest expense	177	162	170	66	65	71
Decrease (increase) in debt	88	140	(44)	(903)	78	60
Decrease (increase) in capitalized operating leases	(775)	(430)	(664)	(547)	(184)	(389)
Flows to debt holders	(492)	(105)	(500)	(1,261)	85	(138)
Dividends	396	492	595	60	66	87
Net shares repurchased (issued)	(572)	1,590	1,276	(213)	(222)	(217)
Flows to equity holders	(176)	2,082	1,871	(154)	(156)	(130)
Cash flow available to investors	**(668)**	**1,977**	**1,371**	**(1,415)**	**(71)**	**(268)**

sold. Net capital expenditures are estimated by taking the change in *net* property, plant, and equipment plus depreciation. Do not estimate capital expenditures by taking the change in gross PP&E. Since gross PP&E drops when companies retire assets (which has no cash implications), the change in gross PP&E will often understate the actual amount of capital expenditures.

3. *Change in capitalized operating leases:* To keep the definitions of NOPLAT, invested capital, and free cash flow consistent, include investments in capitalized operating leases in gross investment.[16]

4. *Investment in acquired intangibles and goodwill:* For acquired intangible assets, where cumulative amortization has been added back, we can estimate investment by computing the change in net acquired intangibles. For intangible assets that are being amortized, use the same method as determining net capital expenditures (by taking the change in *net* intangibles plus amortization).

5. *Change in other long-term operating assets, net of long-term liabilities:* Subtract investments in other net *operating* assets. As with invested capital, do not confuse other long-term *operating* assets with other long-term nonoperating assets, such as equity investments and excess pension assets. Changes in equity investments need to be evaluated—but should be measured separately.

Since companies translate foreign balance sheets into their home currency, changes in accounts will capture both true investments (which involve cash) and currency-based restatements (which are merely accounting adjustments). Removing the currency effects line item by line item is impossible. But we can partially undo their effect by subtracting the increase in the equity item titled "foreign currency translation effect," which in the United States is found within the accumulated other comprehensive income account (AOCI).[17] By subtracting the increase, we undo the effect of changing exchange rates.[18]

Reinvestment ratio   Once gross cash flow and gross investment are calculated, we can compare them by dividing gross investment by gross cash flow. The faster the company is growing, the higher the ratio will be. If the ratio is rising without a corresponding increase in growth, examine

---

[16] Since capitalized operating leases are an artificial computation to allow for comparison across companies, we are modeling cash flows that do not really occur. Therefore, some analysts model capitalized operating leases only for ROIC and not for free cash flow. To calculate FCF independent of capitalized operating leases, do not add back after-tax interest when calculating NOPLAT, do not take the change in capitalized operating leases when calculating gross investment, and do not subtract their present value when valuing the company.

[17] Another source of AOCI equals unrealized gains and losses from marketable securities. Each period, marketable securities are *marked to market,* even if the gains and losses are unrealized. Thus, a change in marketable securities might not represent a nonoperating cash flow, but rather an adjustment to their market value. Combining unrealized gains and losses in AOCI with changes in marketable securities will give a more accurate picture of marketable security purchases and sales (which are located in the nonoperating section of cash flow to investors).

[18] For more information on currency adjustments, see FASB Statement 52.

whether the company's investments are taking longer to blossom than expected, or whether the company is adding capital inefficiently.

Cash flow available to investors   Although not included in free cash flow, cash flows related to nonoperating assets are valuable in their own right and must be evaluated separately:

$$
\begin{array}{ccc}
\text{Present Value} & \text{Present Value of After-Tax} & \text{Total Value} \\
\text{of Company's} + & \text{Nonoperating Cash Flow} = & \text{of} \\
\text{Free Cash Flow} & \text{and Marketable Securities} & \text{Enterprise}
\end{array}
$$

To reconcile free cash flow with total cash flow available to investors, include the following nonoperating cash flows:

- *Cash flow related to excess cash and marketable securities:* Excess cash and marketable securities generate cash flow through interest income and asset sales. When you add investment income to cash flow, it must be added-back on an after-tax basis, using the marginal tax rate. This is necessary because NOPLAT includes taxes only on operating profit, not total earnings.

- *Cash flow from other nonoperating assets:* Similar to the treatment of excess cash, add other nonoperating income and gains (or subtract losses) less increases in other nonoperating assets (or add decreases). It is best to combine nonoperating income and changes in nonoperating assets; otherwise a distorted picture could emerge. Consider a company that impaired a $100 million equity investment. If we examine the change in equity investments alone, it appears that the company sold $100 million in nonoperating assets. But this assessment is misleading because no cash actually changed hands; the asset was merely marked down. If we combine the $100 million change (positive cash flow) with the $100 million reported loss (negative cash flow) from the income statement, we see the true impact is zero.

Total financing flow   Cash flow available to investors should be identical to total financing flow. That is, it flows to or from all investors. By modeling cash flow to *and* from investors, you will catch mistakes otherwise missed. Financial flows include flows related to debt, debt equivalents, and equity:

- *After-tax interest expenses:* After-tax interest should be treated as a financing flow. When computing after-tax interest, use the same marginal tax rate used for NOPLAT.

- *Debt issues and repurchases:* The change in debt represents the net borrowing or repayment on *all* the company's interest-bearing debt, including short-term debt, long-term debt, and capitalized operating leases.

- *Dividends:* Dividends include all cash dividends on common and preferred shares. Dividends paid in stock have no cash effects and should be ignored.

- *Share issues and repurchases:* When new equity is issued or shares are repurchased, three accounts will be affected: common stock, additional paid-in capital, and treasury shares. Although different transactions will have varying affects on the individual accounts, we focus on the aggregate change of the three accounts combined. In Exhibit 7.9, we refer to the aggregate change as "Net Shares Repurchased."

- *Change in debt and equity equivalents:* Since accrued pension liabilities and accrued postretirement medical benefits are considered debt equivalents (see advanced topics for more on issues related to retirement benefits), their changes should be treated as a financing flow. Although deferred taxes are treated as an equity equivalent, they should not be included in the financing flow because they are already included as part of NOPLAT.

With our financial statements now reorganized to reflect economic performance versus accounting performance, we are ready to analyze a company's return on invested capital, operating margins, and capital efficiency.

ANALYZING RETURNS ON INVESTED CAPITAL

Having reorganized the financial statements, we have a clean measure of total invested capital and its related after-tax operating income. Return on invested capital (ROIC) measures the ratio of NOPLAT to invested capital:

$$\text{ROIC} = \frac{\text{NOPLAT}}{\text{Invested Capital}}$$

If an asset is included in invested capital, the income related to that asset should be in NOPLAT. Similarly, if a liability is netted against operating assets to determine invested capital, its related expense should be deducted from revenue to determine NOPLAT. Defining the numerator and denominator consistently in this manner is the most important part of correctly calculating the ROIC.

Since profit is measured over an entire year (whereas capital is measured only at a point in time), we also recommend that you average starting

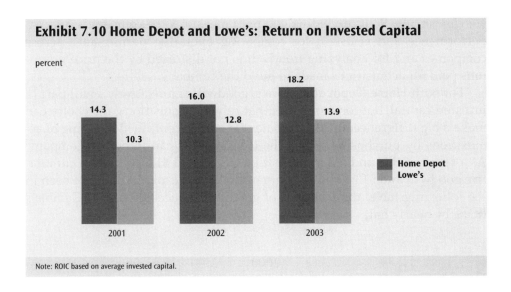

Exhibit 7.10 Home Depot and Lowe's: Return on Invested Capital

percent

Note: ROIC based on average invested capital.

and ending invested capital. Companies that report ROIC in their annual reports often use starting capital. If new assets acquired during the year generate additional income, using only starting capital will overestimate the true ROIC.

Using the NOPLAT and invested capital figures calculated for Home Depot and Lowe's in Exhibits 7.5 and 7.8, we measure the return on invested capital for each company. As can be seen in Exhibit 7.10, Home Depot's ROIC in 2003 exceeds Lowe's ROIC by about 4 percentage points. Both companies have improved their respective ROIC from 2001 to 2003.

Since it focuses solely on a company's operations, ROIC is a better analytical tool for understanding the company's performance than return on equity (ROE) and return on assets (ROA). Return on equity mixes operating performance with capital structure, making peer group analysis and trend analysis less meaningful. Return on assets (even when calculated on a preinterest basis) is inadequate because the ratio double counts any implicit financing charged by suppliers—in the numerator as part of cost of goods sold (COGS) and in the denominator as part of total assets.

Analyzing Return on Invested Capital with and without Goodwill

ROIC should be computed both with and without goodwill because each ratio analyzes different things. For instance, a company that purchases another at a premium to book must spend real resources to acquire valuable economic assets. If the company does not properly compensate investors for the funds spent (or shares given away), it will destroy value. Thus, when you measure historical performance for the company's shareholders, ROIC should be measured with goodwill.

Conversely, ROIC excluding goodwill measures the company's internal performance and is useful for comparing operating performance across companies and for analyzing trends. It is not distorted by the price premiums paid for acquisitions made to build the company.

For both Home Depot and Lowe's, goodwill is a relatively small part of invested capital, but for companies that rely on acquisitions, the choice can make a big difference. In 2003, Procter & Gamble continued its string of acquisitions by purchasing Wella, the German hair-care products company. As a result of this and other acquisitions, P&G had $13.5 billion in cumulative goodwill and $13.8 billion of organic invested capital. As can be seen in the following table, the inclusion of goodwill reduces Procter & Gamble's ROIC by nearly half:

	2000	2001	2002	2003
ROIC excluding goodwill (%)	26.3	24.8	33.2	41.2
ROIC including goodwill (%)	17.8	16.5	19.6	21.3

Economic Profit

In Chapter 5, we demonstrated that the value of a company's operations equals the book value of its invested capital plus the discounted present value of economic profits. Economic profits are calculated as follows:

$$\text{Economic Profit} = \text{Invested Capital} \times (\text{ROIC} - \text{WACC})$$

For an alternative definition of economic profit, substitute NOPLAT/Invested capital for ROIC, and cancel terms:

$$\text{Economic Profit} = \text{NOPLAT} - (\text{Invested Capital} \times \text{WACC})$$

Because it measures whether a company is using its capital more effectively than could be done in the capital markets, economic profit is a powerful tool. In 2003, Home Depot generated $5.1 billion in NOPLAT, yet its capital charge was only $2.4 billion. As can be seen in Exhibit 7.11, both Home Depot and Lowe's were creating value.

Profitable companies do not always create value. In fact, if the capital charge (defined as WACC times invested capital) exceeds NOPLAT, then the company is actually destroying value.

Do not confuse economic profit, which measures how profitably the company used its capital versus the capital markets, with a company's change in market value. In fiscal year 2003, Home Depot generated $2.6 billion in economic profit. During the same year, the company paid $595 mil-

Exhibit 7.11 Home Depot and Lowe's: Economic Profit Calculation

$ million

	Home Depot			Lowe's		
	2001	2002	2003	2001	2002	2003
Invested capital[1]	21,379	23,635	26,185	10,965	13,341	15,051
Weighted average cost of capital	10.1%	9.0%	9.3%	9.8%	8.8%	9.1%
Capital charge	2,159	2,124	2,438	1,071	1,175	1,373
NOPLAT	3,208	3,981	5,083	1,250	1,822	2,223
Capital charge	(2,159)	(2,124)	(2,438)	(1,071)	(1,175)	(1,373)
Economic profit	1,048	1,857	2,645	179	647	850

[1]Invested capital is measured at the beginning of the year.

lion in dividends, and its stock appreciated by $26.4 billion. This generated a total return to shareholders (TRS) of $27.0 billion, substantially more than the economic profit. Economic profit and total returns to shareholders measure different aspects of value: Economic profit measures the one-year performance on *historical book capital*. The change in market value measures changing expectations about *future* economic profits. In Home Depot's case, the market raised its expectations of the company's future performance, based on recent improvements in profitability.

Decomposing Return on Invested Capital to Build an Integrated Perspective

Compared with both its weighted average cost of capital and that of its archrival Lowe's, Home Depot has been earning a superior return on invested capital. But what is driving this performance? Can it be sustained? To better understand ROIC, split apart the ratio as follows:

$$\text{ROIC} = (1 - \text{Cash Tax Rate}) \times \frac{\text{EBITA}}{\text{Revenues}} \times \frac{\text{Revenues}}{\text{Invested Capital}}$$

The preceding equation is one of the most powerful equations in financial analysis. It demonstrates that a company's ROIC is driven by its ability to maximize profitability (operating margin), optimize capital efficiency (turns), or minimize taxes.

Each of these components can be further disaggregated into their respective components, so that each expense and capital item can be compared with revenues. Exhibit 7.12 on page 188 shows how the components can be organized into a tree. On the right side of the tree are operational

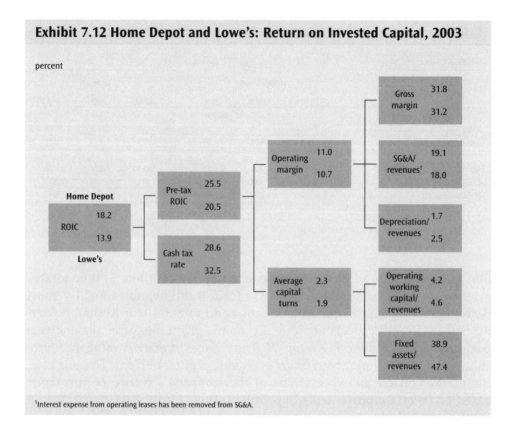

Exhibit 7.12 Home Depot and Lowe's: Return on Invested Capital, 2003

percent

†Interest expense from operating leases has been removed from SG&A.

drivers, over which the manager has control. As we read from right to left, each subsequent box is a function of the boxes to its right. For example, pretax ROIC equals operating margin times capital turnover, and operating margin equals gross margin less SG&A/revenues less depreciation/revenues.

Once you have calculated the historical value drivers, compare them with the drivers of other companies in the same industry. Integrate this perspective with an analysis of the industry structure (opportunities for differentiation, entry/exit barriers, etc.) and a qualitative assessment of the company's strengths and weaknesses.

What is the source of Home Depot's ROIC advantage over Lowe's? Is the advantage sustainable? By examining the ROIC tree in Exhibit 7.12, we can see that Home Depot benefits from a more efficient use of capital and a better cash tax rate. Moving to the right, we see that this capital efficiency comes primarily from fixed assets, which in turn come from more revenues per dollar of store investment. Is this because Home Depot's stores are more efficient or operating at higher-traffic locations? Perhaps, but after further investigation, it appears that a typical Lowe's store is newer and

Exhibit 7.13 Home Depot and Lowe's: Operating Current Assets in Days

Number of days

	Home Depot			Lowe's		
	2001	2002	2003	2001	2002	2003
Operating cash	7.0	7.0	7.0	7.0	7.0	7.0
Receivables, net	6.3	6.7	6.2	2.7	2.4	1.6
Merchandise inventories	45.8	52.2	51.1	59.6	54.7	54.3
Other current assets	1.2	1.6	1.7	4.8	4.2	4.1
Operating current assets	60.3	67.6	66.0	74.1	68.2	66.9

thus more expensive than Home Depot's average store.[19] Newer stores may be a burden today (from a turns perspective) but could be an advantage going forward.

Line item analysis   A comprehensive valuation model will convert every line item in the company's financial statements into some type of ratio. For the income statement, most items are taken as a percentage of sales. (Exceptions exist, however: Taxes should be calculated as a percentage of pretax profits, to determine an average tax rate, not as a percentage of sales.)

For the balance sheet, each line item can also be taken as a percentage of revenues (or for inventories and payables, to avoid the bias caused by changing prices, as a percentage of cost of goods sold). For operating current assets and liabilities, you can also convert each line item into "days," using the following formula:

$$\text{Days} = 365 \times \frac{\text{Balance Sheet Item}}{\text{Revenues}}$$

Although days and a percentage of sales perform a similar cross-company and trend analysis, the use of days lends itself to a more operational interpretation.[20] As can be seen in Exhibit 7.13, the average inventory holding time (using revenue as a base) for Home Depot has risen from 46 to 51 days, whereas the inventory holding time for Lowe's has dropped from 60 to 54. The use of days shows us that what used to be a sizable advantage for Home Depot has turned into a virtual dead heat.

[19] M. E. Lloyd, "Lowe's Execs: Younger Stores, New Programs Distinguish Company," Dow Jones Newswires (May 28, 2004).
[20] If the business is seasonal, operating ratios such as inventories should be calculated using quarterly data.

Exhibit 7.14 Discount Carrier and Network Carrier: Operating Statistics

Operating statistic	Discount carrier 2003	Network carrier 2003
Total revenues ($ millions)	1,000.0	10,000.0
Labor expenses ($ millions)	252.4	4,767.3
Number of employees	5,773.2	53,070.7
Available seat miles (millions)	10,942.9	101,017.1

Source: Company 10-Ks.

Nonfinancial analysis   In an external analysis, ratios are often confined to financial performance. If you are working from inside a company, however, or if the company releases operating data, link operating drivers directly to return on invested capital. By evaluating the operating drivers, you can better assess the sustainability of financial spreads among competitors.

Consider airlines, which are required to release a tremendous amount of operating data. Exhibit 7.14 details operating data from two airlines, a point-to-point discount carrier and a full-service network carrier. The exhibit includes the first two line items from each airline's income statement, total revenue and labor expenses, as well as two operating statistics, total employees and available seat miles (ASMs).[21]

Dividing labor expenses by total revenue (as part of ROIC) shows that the network carrier's labor costs (47.7 percent of revenues) are nearly twice as high as the discount carrier's labor costs (25.2 percent of revenues). But what is driving this differential? Are the discounter's employees more productive? Or are they paid less? Is it that the discount carrier can charge a price premium for its product? To answer these questions, we disaggregated labor expenses to revenue, using the following equation:

$$\frac{\text{Labor Expenses}}{\text{Revenues}} = \frac{\text{Labor Expenses}}{\text{Total Employees}} \times \frac{\text{Total Employees}}{\text{ASMs Flown}} \times \frac{\text{ASMs Flown}}{\text{Revenues}}$$

Note how each term's denominator cancels the next term's numerator, leaving us with the original ratio. Each term has a specific operating interpretation. The first term represents the average salary per full-time employee; the second measures the productivity of each full-time employee (number of employees required to fly one billion ASMs); and the third measures the number of miles flown to generate one dollar of revenue. Companies that can charge a price premium (for such services as frequent-flier miles) need to fly fewer miles per dollar of revenue.

---

[21] Airlines use available seat miles as a proxy for unit capacity. Available seat miles equal the total number of seats available for passengers times the number of miles the airline flies.

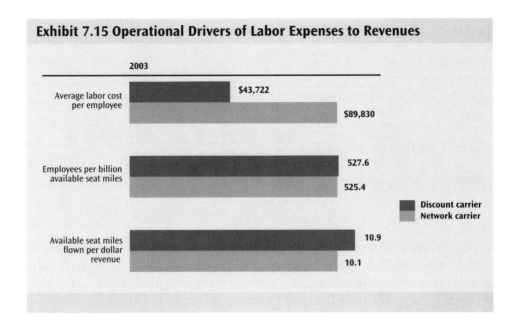

Exhibit 7.15 Operational Drivers of Labor Expenses to Revenues

2003

	Discount carrier	Network carrier
Average labor cost per employee	$43,722	$89,830
Employees per billion available seat miles	527.6	525.4
Available seat miles flown per dollar revenue	10.9	10.1

Exhibit 7.15 illustrates the comparative drivers of total labor expenses for both airlines. Note that the numbers of employees required to fly one billion ASMs are nearly identical (528 employees for the discount carrier versus 525 for the network carrier). The numbers of miles flown to generate one dollar of revenue are also comparable (10.9 miles for the discount carrier and 10.1 for the network carrier). What really drives the difference is average salaries.[22] Based on the calculation, the discounter's employees earn half the salary ($43,722) of their counterparts at the network carrier ($89,830). To assess the network carrier's ability to survive and prosper, we must ask whether the company can close this gap. If it cannot, financial performance will remain poor, and its outlook remains bleak.

ANALYZING REVENUE GROWTH

In Chapter 3 we determined that the value of a company is driven by ROIC, WACC, and growth. Until now, growth has been defined solely as the growth in cash flows. But what drives the long-term growth in cash flows? Assuming profit margins and reinvestment rates stabilize to a long-term level, long-term growth in cash flows will be directly tied to long-term growth in revenues. And by analyzing historical revenue growth, we can assess the potential for growth going forward.

[22] Since the number of employees is reported only once a year, labor costs per employee are only a proxy for average salary. Also, labor costs per employee might differ across airlines because of differences in mix. Both airlines might pay identical salaries for the same position, but the network carrier might employ more higher-paid positions.

Exhibit 7.16 IBM: Revenue Growth Analysis

percent

	2001	2002	2003
Organic revenue growth	0.5	(1.8)	(2.6)
Acquisitions	0.5	2.1	5.4
Divestitures	0.0	(3.3)	0.0
Currency effects	(3.9)	(2.5)	7.0
Reported revenue growth	(2.9)	(5.5)	9.8

Calculating revenue growth directly from the income statement will suffice for most companies. The year-to-year revenue growth results sometimes can be misleading, however. The three prime culprits affecting revenue growth are the effects of changes in currency values for multinational companies, mergers and acquisitions, and changes in accounting policies.

Exhibit 7.16 demonstrates how misleading raw year-to-year revenue growth figures can be. In 2003, when IBM announced its first rise in reported revenues in three years, it became the subject of a *Fortune* magazine cover story.[23] "Things appear to be straightening out dramatically," reported *Fortune*. "Last year Palmisano's company grew for the first time since 2000, posting a 10 percent revenue jump." Although IBM's revenues had technically risen 9.8 percent, *organic revenues* (those attributable to the company's core business, independent of currency fluctuations, acquisitions and divestitures, and accounting changes) actually fell 2.6 percent. Indeed, the rise in IBM's revenue was directly attributable to the general weakening of the U.S. dollar and its acquisitions of Rational Software and of PricewaterhouseCooper's (PwCC) consulting business.

Currency Effects

Multinational companies conduct business in many currencies. At the end of each reporting period, these revenues are converted to the currency of the reporting company. If foreign currencies are rising in value relative to the company's home currency, this translation, at better rates, will lead to higher revenue numbers. Thus, a rise in revenue may not reflect increased pricing power or greater quantities sold, but just a depreciation of the company's home currency.

[23] D. Kirkpatrick and C. Tkaczyk, "Inside Sam's $100 Billion Growth Machine," *Fortune* (June 14, 2004), p. 80.

Companies with extensive foreign business will often comment about revenue growth, using current as well as constant exchange rates. IBM discloses a "year-to-year revenue change" of 9.8 percent but a "year-to-year constant currency" revenue change of only 2.8 percent. Thus, had currencies remained at their prior-year levels, IBM revenue would have been $83.5 billion, rather than the $89.1 billion reported.

Mergers and Acquisitions

Growth through acquisition may have very different ROIC characteristics from internal growth because of the sizable premiums a company must pay to acquire another company. Therefore, it is important to understand how companies have been generating historical revenue growth—through acquisition or internally.

Stripping the effect of acquisitions from reported revenues is difficult. Unless an acquisition is material, company filings do not need to detail or even report an acquisition. For larger acquisitions, a company will sometimes report pro forma statements that recast historical financials as though the acquisition was completed at the beginning of the fiscal year. Revenue growth, then, should be calculated using the pro forma revenue numbers. If the target company publicly reports its own financial data, pro forma statements can be constructed manually by combining revenue of the acquirer and target for the prior year. But beware: The bidder will often include only partial-year revenues from the target for the period *after* the acquisition is completed. To remain consistent, reconstructed prior years also must include only partial-year revenue.

In its 2003 annual report, IBM did not create historical pro forma revenues to account for its February 2003 acquisition of Rational Software. To properly analyze IBM's 2003 organic growth rate, therefore, we create our own estimated historical pro formas (see Exhibit 7.17, p. 194). Since the acquisition closed at the end of February, IBM's 2003 revenue included 10 months of Rational Software's revenues, whereas IBM's 2002 revenues did not. To make the two years comparable, add 10 months of Rational Software's historical revenues to IBM's.

In October 2002, IBM acquired PwCC. IBM's 2003 revenue included an entire year of PwCC revenue, whereas 2002 included only three months of PwCC. To make the two years comparable, add nine months of PwCC's 2002 revenues to IBM's 2002 revenues.[24] Combining IBM's reported revenue with its partial-year revenue from the two acquisitions results in a 2002 pro forma revenue of $85.7 billion. Comparing 2003's constant-currency revenue

---

[24] We assume PwCC was purchased in its entirety by IBM (since PwCC was a private company, a full analysis is difficult). If only a portion of the business were purchased, our estimate of acquired growth would shrink.

Exhibit 7.17 IBM: Calculating Organic Revenue Growth

$ million	Transaction date	Estimated 2002 revenue	Partial year adjustment	Revenue adjustments
IBM reported 2002 revenue				81,186.0
Ten months of Rational Software revenue	2/21/2003	689.8	10/12	574.8
Nine months of PwCC revenue	10/1/2002	5,200.0	9/12	3,900.0
IBM adjusted 2002 revenue				85,660.8
IBM 2003 "constant currency" revenue				83,459.2
IBM adjusted growth rate				(2.6%)

Source: Hoovers On-Line (for Rational Software) and Gartner Group (for PwCC).

of $83.5 billion with the pro forma prior-year revenues of $85.7 billion shows a *decline* in organic revenues of 2.6 percent.

Accounting Changes and Irregularities

Each year, the Financial Accounting Standards Board in the United States and the International Accounting Standards Board make recommendations concerning the financial treatment of certain business transactions. Most changes in revenue recognition policies do not come as formal pronouncements from the boards themselves, but from task forces that issue topic notes. Companies then have a set amount of time to implement the required changes. Changes in a company's revenue recognition policy can significantly affect revenues from year to year.

Consider Emerging Issues Task Force (EITF) 01-14 from the Financial Accounting Standards Board, which concerns reimbursable expenses. Before 2002, U.S. companies accounted for reimbursable expenses by ignoring the pass-through. Today, U.S. companies can recognize the reimbursement as revenue and the outlay as an expense. Although operating profits were unaffected, this dramatically increased year-by-year revenue comparisons for some companies from 2001 to 2002.[25]

If an accounting change is material, a company will document the change in its section on management discussion and analysis (MD&A) and will also recast its historical financial statements. Some companies do not fully document changes in accounting policy, and this can lead to distorted views of performance. For example, a change in consolidation policy can in-

---

[25] One such company, Total System Services (TSYS), a credit-card-processing company, changed its recognition of reimbursable expenses in 2002. From 2001 to 2002, the company increased revenues from $650 million to $955 million, but $250 million of the $305 million in new revenues was attributable solely to the accounting change. Since the change was material, TSYS recast its previous year's financial statements and discussed the change in its management discussion and analysis.

flate revenue growth artificially. In the extreme case, a company that consolidates equity investments one by one can generate artificial revenue growth for years.

Decomposing Revenue Growth to Build an Integrated Perspective

Once the effects of mergers and acquisitions, currency translations, and accounting changes have been removed from the year-to-year revenue growth numbers, analyze revenue growth from an operational perspective. The most standard breakdown is:

$$\text{Revenues} = \frac{\text{Revenue}}{\text{Unit}} \times \text{Units}$$

Using this formula, determine whether prices or quantities are driving growth. Do not, however, confuse revenue per unit with price—they can be different. If revenue per unit is rising, the change could be due to rising prices. Or the company could be shifting its product mix from low-priced to high-priced items.

The operating statistics that companies choose to report (if any) depend on the norms of the industry and the practices of competitors. For instance, most retailers provide information on the number of stores they operate, the number of square feet in those stores, and the number of transactions they conduct annually. By relating different operating statistics to total revenues, we can build a deeper understanding of the business. Consider this retailing standard:

$$\text{Revenues} = \frac{\text{Revenue}}{\text{Stores}} \times \text{Stores}$$

Using the operating statistics reported in Exhibit 7.18, we discover Home Depot not only has more stores than Lowe's, but also generates more revenue

Exhibit 7.18 Home Depot and Lowe's: Operating Data

Operating data	Home Depot			Lowe's		
	2001	2002	2003	2001	2002	2003
Revenue ($ millions)	53,553	58,247	64,816	22,111	26,491	30,838
Number of stores	1,333	1,532	1,707	744	854	952
Number of transactions (millions)	1,091	1,161	1,246	402	466	521
Square feet (thousands)	116,901	157,335	182,649	80,700	94,794	108,528

Source: Company 10-Ks; missing figures estimated using alternative 10-K data.

Exhibit 7.19 Home Depot and Lowe's: Revenue Growth Analysis, 2003

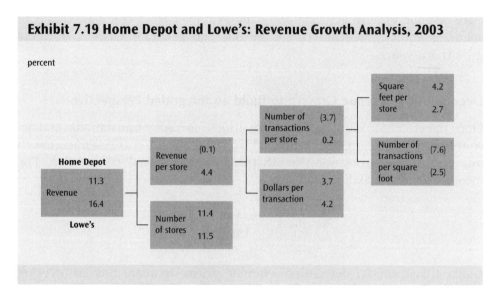

per store ($38 million per store for Home Depot versus $32.4 million for Lowe's). Using the three operating statistics, we can build ratios on revenues per store, transactions per store, square feet per store, dollars per transaction, and number of transactions per square foot.

Although operating ratios are powerful in their own right, what can really change one's thinking about performance is how the ratios are changing over time. Exhibit 7.19 organizes each ratio into a tree similar to the ROIC tree built earlier. Rather than report a calculated ratio, such as revenues per store, however, we report the *change* in the ratio and relate this back to the growth in revenue. At Home Depot and Lowe's, revenues are growing at rates above 10 percent. That growth is respectable by any standard. For Home Depot, however, new store openings, rather than an increase in revenues per store, have been driving growth.

The implications of this analysis are extremely important, to the point that financial analysts have a special name for growth in revenue per store: *comps,* shorthand for "comparables," or year-to-year same-store sales.[26] Why is this revenue growth important? First, new store development is an investment choice, whereas same-store sales growth reflects store-by-store operating performance. Second, new stores require large capital investments, whereas comps growth requires little incremental capital. Higher revenues and less capital lead to higher capital turns, which lead to higher ROIC.

---

[26] Exhibit 7.19 reports only a proxy for comps, as it calculates revenue per store growth directly from each company's reported operating statistics. Given the statistic's importance, both Home Depot and Lowe's report their own calculation of comps growth, defining it as same-store sales for stores open at least one year. How the companies treat closed stores in calculating comps growth is unclear. According to their annual reports, comps growth for Home Depot in 2003 was 3.8 percent, while comps growth for Lowe's was 6.7 percent.

CREDIT HEALTH AND CAPITAL STRUCTURE

To this point, we have focused on the operations of the company and its ability to create value. We have examined the primary drivers of value: a company's return on invested capital, organic revenue growth, and free cash flow. In the final step of historical analysis, we focus on how the company has financed its operations. What proportion of invested capital comes from creditors instead of from equity investors? Is this capital structure sustainable? Can the company survive an industry downturn?

To determine how aggressive a company's capital structure is, we examine two related but distinct concepts, liquidity (via coverage) and leverage. Liquidity measures the company's ability to meet short-term obligations, such as interest expenses, rental payments, and required principal payments. Leverage measures the company's ability to meet obligations over the long term. Since this book's focus is not credit analysis, we detail only a few ratios that credit analysts use to evaluate a company's credit health.

Coverage

To measure the company's ability to meet short-term obligations, compute two ratios: the traditional interest coverage ratio and a more advanced measure, EBITDAR to interest expense plus rental expense.[27] Interest coverage is calculated by dividing either EBITA or EBITDA by interest. The first ratio, EBITA to interest, measures the company's ability to repay interest using profits without having to cut expenditures intended to replace depreciating equipment. The second coverage ratio, EBITDA to interest, measures the company's ability to meet short-term financial commitments, using both current profits and the depreciation dollars earmarked for replacement capital. Although EBITDA provides a good measure of extremely short-term ability to meet interest payments, most companies cannot survive very long without replacing worn assets.

Like the interest coverage ratio, the ratio of EBITDAR to interest expense plus rental expense measures the company's ability to meet its known future obligations, including the effect of operating leases. For many companies, especially retailers, including rental expenses is a critical part of understanding the financial health of the business. Assuming Home Depot can maintain its current level of EBITDAR, it should have no problems meeting either its interest or rental expense commitments (see Exhibit 7.20 on p. 198).[28]

---

[27] EBITDAR is a common acronym for earnings before interest, taxes, depreciation, amortization, and rental expenses.

[28] Profitable, stable companies with small amounts of debt have little bankruptcy risk but forgo the tax benefits of debt. We discuss optimal capital structure in Chapter 17.

Exhibit 7.20 Home Depot: Measuring Coverage

$ million

	1999	2000	2001	2002	2003
EBITA	3,803	4,199	4,940	5,838	6,847
EBITDA	4,258	4,792	5,696	6,733	7,922
EBITDAR	4,647	5,271	6,218	7,266	8,492
Interest	28	21	28	37	62
Rental expense	389	479	522	533	570
Interest plus rental expense	417	500	550	570	632
EBITA / Interest	135.8	199.9	176.4	157.8	110.4
EBITDA / Interest	152.1	228.2	203.4	182.0	127.8
EBITDAR / Interest plus rental	11.1	10.5	11.3	12.7	13.4

Source: Home Depot 10-Ks.

Leverage

To better understand the power (and danger) of leverage, consider the relationship between return on equity (ROE) and return on invested capital (ROIC):

$$ROE = ROIC + \left[ROIC - (1 - T)k_d \right] \frac{D}{E}$$

As the formula demonstrates, a company's ROE is a direct function of its ROIC, its spread of ROIC over its after-tax cost of debt, and its book-based debt-to-equity ratio. Consider a company earning an ROIC of 10 percent, whose after-tax cost of debt is 5 percent. To raise its ROE, the company can either increase its ROIC (through operating improvements) or increase its debt-to-equity ratio (by swapping debt for equity). Although each strategy can lead to an identical change in ROE, increasing the debt-to-equity ratio makes the company's ROE more sensitive to changes in operating performance (ROIC). Thus, while increasing the debt-to-equity ratio can increase ROE, it does so by increasing the risks faced by shareholders.

To assess leverage, measure the company's (market) debt-to-equity ratio over time and against peers. Does the leverage ratio compare favorably with the industry? How much risk is the company taking? We answer these and other questions related to leverage in depth in Chapter 17.

Payout Ratio

The dividend payout ratio equals total common dividends divided by net income available to common shareholders. We can better understand the company's financial situation by analyzing the payout ratio in relation to its cash flow reinvestment ratio (examined earlier). On one hand, if the company has a high dividend payout ratio and a reinvestment ratio greater than 1, then it must be borrowing money to fund negative free cash flow, to pay interest, or to pay dividends. But is this sustainable? On the other hand, a company with positive free cash flow and low dividend payout is probably paying down debt (or aggregating excess cash). In this situation, is the company passing up the valuable tax benefits of debt or hoarding cash unnecessarily?

General Consideration for Historical Analysis

Although it is impossible to provide a comprehensive checklist for analyzing a company's historical financial performance, here are some things to keep in mind:

- Look back as far as possible (at least 10 years). Long-time horizons will allow you to determine whether the company and industry tend to revert to some normal level of performance, and whether short-term trends are likely to be permanent.
- Disaggregate value drivers, both ROIC and revenue growth, as far as possible. If possible, link operational performance measures with each key value driver.
- If there are any radical changes in performance, identify the source. Determine whether the change is temporary or permanent, or merely an accounting effect.

ADVANCED ISSUES

Until now, we have focused on the issues you will typically encounter when analyzing a company. Depending on the company, you may come across difficult (and technical) accounting issues that can affect the estimation of NOPLAT, invested capital, economic profit, and free cash flow. Note, however, that not every issue will lead to material differences in ROIC and growth. Before collecting extra data and estimating required unknowns, decide whether the adjustment will further your understanding of a company and its industry. This section discusses the adjustments most likely to affect results.

Operating Leases

When a company borrows money to purchase an asset, the asset and debt are recorded on the company's balance sheet, and interest is deducted from operating profit. If instead, the company leases that same asset from another company (the *lessor*), it records only the periodic rental expense associated with the lease.[29] Therefore, a company that chooses to lease its assets will have artificially low operating profits (because rental expenses include the implicit interest expense) and artificially high capital productivity (because the assets do not appear on the lessee's balance sheet).

To properly compare operating margins and capital productivity across companies and over time, convert the operating leases into purchased assets and corresponding debt. This is done in two steps. First, value the operating leases. Capitalize the asset value on the balance sheet, and add the implied debt as a liability. (If you do this, remember to increase the company's debt-to-value level in the cost of capital to reflect the higher debt.) Second, break down the rental expense into two components—interest expense and depreciation. Since interest expense is a financing item, the implied interest payment should be added back to EBITA, and taxes should be adjusted to remove the interest tax shield.

To derive the value of operating leases, we examine the determinants of rental expense.[30] To properly compensate the lessor, the rental expense includes compensation for the cost of financing the asset (at the cost of debt, k_d) and the periodic depreciation of the asset (for which we assume straight-line depreciation). Thus, the periodic rental expense equals:

$$\text{Rental Expense}_t = \text{Asset Value}_{t-1} \left(k_d + \frac{1}{\text{Asset Life}} \right)$$

To estimate the asset's value, we rearrange the equation:

$$\text{Asset Value}_{t-1} = \frac{\text{Rental Expense}_t}{k_d + \dfrac{1}{\text{Asset Life}}}$$

In 2003, Home Depot had $570 million in rental expenses. Assuming an average asset life of 20 years and using Home Depot's cost of debt of 4.7 percent, 2002's operating leases are valued at $5.89 billion. Next, we make adjustments to EBITA, operating taxes, and invested capital (see Exhibit 7.21). To determine adjusted EBITA in 2003, we add back the implied interest of operating leases ($276 million) by multiplying the operating lease value

---

[29] SFAS 13 details certain situations when leases must be capitalized (the asset and associated debt must be recorded on the balance sheet). For example, if the asset is transferred to the lessee at the end of the lease, the lease must be capitalized.

[30] We would like to thank McKinsey colleagues Steven Bond, S. R. Rajan, and Werner Rehm for deriving this method of valuing capitalized operating leases.

Exhibit 7.21 Home Depot and Lowe's: Capitalizing Operating Leases

$ million

	Home Depot			Lowe's		
	2001	2002	2003	2001	2002	2003
Reported EBITA	4,940	5,838	6,847	1,798	2,541	3,178
Implied interest	288	260	276	106	106	114
Adjusted EBITA	5,228	6,098	7,123	1,904	2,647	3,292
Operating taxes						
Cash taxes	1,909	2,019	1,935	614	784	1,026
Tax shield on lease interest expense	111	98	105	40	41	44
Adjusted cash taxes	2,020	2,117	2,040	654	825	1,069
NOPLAT (using rental expense)	3,031	3,819	4,912	1,184	1,757	2,152
NOPLAT (capitalizing operating leases)	3,208	3,981	5,083	1,250	1,822	2,223

	Home Depot			Lowe's		
	2001	2002	2003	2001	2002	2003
Invested capital	18,176	20,296	23,101	11,152	12,678	14,250
Capitalized operating leases	5,459	5,890	6,554	2,189	2,373	2,762
Invested capital (with operating leases)	23,635	26,185	29,655	13,341	15,051	17,012
ROIC (using rental expense)	17.4%	19.9%	22.6%	11.6%	14.7%	16.0%
ROIC (capitalizing operating leases)	14.3%	16.0%	18.2%	10.3%	12.8%	13.9%

($5,890 million) times the cost of debt (4.7 percent). The tax shield associated with operating lease interest equals the marginal tax rate (38.2 percent) times the implied interest expense ($276 million). In addition, we increase invested capital by the value of the operating leases.

When we convert from rental expense to capitalized operating leases, Home Depot's ROIC (based on average capital) drops from 22.6 percent to 18.2 percent in 2003. The drop for Lowe's is smaller, but significant nonetheless. However, the smaller percentage does not necessarily imply less value creation. Why? Because the cost of capital will also be lower after adjusting downward for operating leases (we discuss the cost of capital in Chapter 10).

Expensed Investment: Advertising and Research and Development

When a company builds a plant or purchases equipment, the asset is capitalized on the balance sheet and depreciated over time. Conversely, when a company creates an intangible asset, such as a brand name or patent, the entire outlay must be expensed immediately.[31] For firms with significant intangible assets, such as technology companies and pharmaceuticals, failure to recognize intangible assets can lead to a significant underestimation of a company's invested capital and, thus, overstate ROIC.

When you evaluate performance internally, many expenses, such as brand building, customer development, research and development, and training, should be capitalized and amortized (for purposes of internal economic evaluation, not external reporting). But when you examine a company from the outside, you can only evaluate two expensed investments: advertising and research and development (R&D).

The first step in capitalizing an expense like R&D is to choose an amortization period, for example 10 years. Use product and industry characteristics to guide your choice. Next, using the financial statements from 10 years prior (or whatever the amortization period is), treat the year's R&D no differently than you would capital expenditures. This means eliminating the R&D expenditure from the income statement and placing the amount on the balance sheet. Repeat the process for the next year, except that you also deduct R&D amortization from both the income statement (as an expense) and the balance sheet (as a deduction to accumulated R&D).

In Exhibit 7.22, we demonstrate the process by capitalizing R&D expenses for Merck. To adjust 2003 EBITA, start with the original EBITA ($8,651 million), add back the current year's R&D ($3,280 million), and subtract the current amortization ($1,936 million) of the accumulated R&D asset. This leads to an adjusted EBITA of $9,995 million. Although EBITA will change, taxes should *not* be adjusted when capitalizing R&D. The R&D tax shield is real and is related to operations (unlike the interest tax shield). Therefore, the tax shield should remain as part of operations.

To adjust Merck's invested capital, start with 2002's accumulated R&D ($12,163 million), add 2003's R&D ($3,280 million), and subtract 2003's amortization ($1,936 million). Thus, by the end of 2003, Merck's accumulated R&D (based on a 10-year asset life) was $13,506 million. As the exhibit shows, by 2003 nearly one-third of Merck's adjusted invested capital consisted of capitalized R&D. When R&D is expensed, Merck's return on average invested capital is estimated at 21.5 percent. When R&D is capitalized, ROIC drops to 15.2 percent.

Unlike ROIC, free cash flow will not change when expenses are capitalized. When an expense is capitalized, the expense is moved from gross cash flow to gross investment. But since both are components of free cash flow, it remains unaffected. Since amortization is noncash, it also has no

---

[31] Although most development must be expensed, companies can capitalize software development after the product becomes technologically feasible. According FASB's Statement of Position 86, development costs can be capitalized and straight-line amortized over the estimated economic life of the product.

Exhibit 7.22 Merck: Capitalizing R&D

$ million

	1999	2000	2001	2002	2003
EBITA	7,594	9,089	9,728	9,668	8,651
Annual R&D expenditure	2,119	2,344	2,456	2,677	3,280
Annual amortization	(1,347)	(1,484)	(1,633)	(1,780)	(1,936)
Adjusted EBITA	8,367	9,949	10,552	10,565	9,995
Operating taxes (at 38% of EBITA)	(2,886)	(3,454)	(3,697)	(3,674)	(3,288)
NOPLAT	5,481	6,495	6,855	6,891	6,707

	1999	2000	2001	2002	2003
Beginning balance	8,809	9,582	10,442	11,265	12,163
Annual R&D expenditure	2,119	2,344	2,456	2,677	3,280
Annual amortization (10 year life)	(1,347)	(1,484)	(1,633)	(1,780)	(1,936)
Ending accumulated R&D	9,582	10,442	11,265	12,163	13,506
Invested capital	26,533	29,266	33,243	33,885	28,545
Accumulated R&D	9,582	10,442	11,265	12,163	13,506
Adjusted invested capital	36,114	39,707	44,508	46,047	42,051
ROIC (R&D expensed)	22.1%	23.3%	21.9%	20.5%	21.5%
ROIC (R&D capitalized)	16.1%	17.1%	16.3%	15.2%	15.2%

effect (it is deducted to compute NOPLAT but added back to calculate gross cash flow). Thus, capitalizing R&D should have no effect on valuation (beyond how it changes your perceptions of the company's future ability to create value).

Employee Stock Options

By the end of 2003, Home Depot employees held options to buy 2.5 million shares of the company's stock. An alternative to cash compensation, options give the right, but not the obligation, to buy company stock at a specified price. Given the unlimited upside (and limited downside), options can be extremely valuable to the employee. Yet before 2005, companies in the United States and Europe were not required to report the value of options granted as a compensation expense.[32] In fact, before the rule changes requiring expensing, only 117 of the companies in the S&P 500 voluntarily expensed employee stock options. Therefore, to assure

---

[32] Since January 1, 2005, European listed companies are required under IFRS to reflect the cost of all share-based payments, including employee stock options, as an expense. In 2004, the Financial Accounting Standards Board announced its intention to require U.S. listed companies to expense stock-based compensation starting June 15, 2005.

Exhibit 7.23 Home Depot: 10-K Note on Stock-Based Compensation

$ million

	2001	2002	2003
Net earnings, as reported	3,044	3,664	4,304
Stock-based compensation expense included in reported net earnings, net of related tax effects	13	10	42
Total stock-based compensation expense determined under fair value based method for all awards, net of related tax effects	(257)	(260)	(279)
Pro forma net earnings	2,800	3,414	4,067

Source: Home Depot 10-K, 2003.

consistency across years, it is important to analyze and expense historical stock-based compensation.

If the company did not expense options historically, we recommend estimating the impact on ROIC. To determine the value of options not included in Home Depot's income statement, we take the difference between net earnings ($4,304 million) and pro forma net earnings ($4,067 million) found in the company's footnotes (see Exhibit 7.23). For Home Depot, this difference equals $237 million. Since this is an after-tax number, it must be converted to a pretax value, using the company's marginal tax rate (38.2 percent). The pretax compensation expense, estimated at $383 million,[33] is then deducted from EBITA.

Since ROIC is based on cash taxes, and since option expenses are not tax deductible at the time of grant, no adjustment should be made to taxes. For companies that expense options, reported taxes are based on income after option expenses, even though the options are not deductible until exercise. Therefore, accountants create a deferred tax account (since cash taxes are higher than reported taxes). Convert reported taxes to cash taxes (for companies that expense options) by subtracting the increase in deferred tax assets from reported taxes. NOPLAT equals adjusted EBITA less cash taxes.

No adjustment should be made to invested capital. When a company issues options, it is essentially transferring a portion of ownership from one group (current shareholders) to another (employees).

To value a company with significant employee options, you have two choices for treating future stock options compensation: include the future options granted as part of operations (and hence part of free cash flow) or value them separately. Subsequently, the process for adjusting free cash

---

[33] Home Depot's estimated options expense is less than 5 percent of EBIT. For some companies, especially technology companies, the options expense can be quite large. In 2003, Yahoo reported $238 million in net income. Had the company expensed employee stock option grants, net income would have fallen 85 percent to $35 million.

Exhibit 7.24 Treatment of Provisions and Reserves

Classification	Examples	Treatment in NOPLAT	Treatment in invested capital	Treatment in valuation
Ongoing operating provisions	Product returns and warranties	Deduct provision from revenue to determine NOPLAT.	Deduct reserve from operating assets to determine invested capital.	Provision is already part of free cash flow.
Long-term operating provisions	Plant decommissioning costs and retirement plans	Deduct operating portion from revenue to determine NOPLAT and treat interest portion as nonoperating.	Treat reserve as a debt equivalent.	Deduct reserve's present value from the value of operations.
Nonoperating provisions	Restructuring charges, such as expected severance due to layoffs	Convert provision into cash provision and treat as nonoperating.	Treat reserve as a debt equivalent.	Deduct reserve's present value from the value of operations.
Income smoothing provision	Provisions for the sole purpose of income smoothing	Eliminate provision by converting accrual provision into cash provision.	Treat reserve as an equity equivalent.	Since income smoothing provisions are noncash, there is no effect.

flow depends on the choice of valuation method. We defer this discussion to Chapter 11.

Provisions and Reserves

Provisions are *noncash* expenses that reflect future costs or expected losses.[34] Companies take provisions by reducing current income and setting up a corresponding reserve as a liability (or deducting the amount from the relevant asset).

For the purpose of analyzing and valuing a company, we categorize provisions into one of four types: ongoing operating provisions, long-term operating provisions, nonoperating restructuring provisions, or provisions created for the purpose of smoothing income (transferring income from one period to another). Based on the characteristics of each provision, adjust the financial statements to better reflect the company's true operating performance. For example, ongoing operating provisions are treated like any other operating expense, whereas restructuring provisions are converted from an accrual to a cash basis and treated as nonoperating. Exhibit 7.24 summarizes the four provision types.

---

[34] A note on terminology: In the United States, the term *provision* refers to an income statement expense (a charge against income to reflect decline in the value of an asset or expected loss), and the term *reserve* refers to its corresponding liability. In continental Europe, the terms are used interchangeably.

Exhibit 7.25 Provisions and Reserves in the Financial Statements

$ million

Income statement	Year 1	Year 2	Year 3	Year 4
Revenue	1,000	1,200	1,400	1,600
Operating costs	(550)	(660)	(910)	(880)
Provision for product returns	(100)	(120)	(140)	(160)
Provision for plant decommissioning	(24)	(27)	(30)	0
Income smoothing provision	(40)	(40)	80	0
EBITA	286	353	400	560
Provision for restructuring	0	(30)	0	0
Net income	286	323	400	560

Balance sheet	Year 0	Year 1	Year 2	Year 3	Year 4
Operating assets	700	840	980	1,120	0
Reserve for product returns	150	180	210	240	0
Reserve for plant decommissioning	119	144	170	0	0
Reserve for restructuring	0	0	30	0	0
Reserve for income smoothing	0	40	80	0	0
Equity	431	476	490	880	0
Liabilities and shareholder equity	700	840	980	1,120	0

Although reclassification leads to better analysis, the way you adjust the financials for provisions should not affect the company's valuation (no matter how you classify a provision). The company's valuation depends on how and when cash flows through the business, not on accrual-based accounting.

In Exhibit 7.25, we present the financial statements for a hypothetical company that recognizes four types of provisions: a provision for future product returns, an environmental provision for decommissioning the company's plant in four years, an artificial provision for smoothing income, and a restructuring provision for future severance payments. In this example, we reorganized forecasted statements rather than historical statements (whose analysis would be the same) to also demonstrate how each would be treated from a valuation perspective. For simplicity, we assume the company pays no taxes and has no debt.

The process for adjusting the financial statements depends on the type of provision. We use Exhibit 7.26 to discuss each provision in turn. All numbers in parentheses refer to year 1 financials.

Provisions related to ongoing operations   When a company expects that some of its products will be returned, warranties a product, or self-insures

Exhibit 7.26 ROIC with Provisions and Reserves

$ million

NOPLAT		Year 1	Year 2	Year 3	Year 4
Reported EBITA		286	353	400	560
Interest associated with plant decommissioning		12	14	17	0
Increase (decrease) in inc. smoothing reserve		40	40	(80)	0
NOPLAT		337	407	337	560
Reconciliation to net income					
Net income		286	323	400	560
Interest associated with plant decommissioning		12	14	17	0
Increase (decrease) in inc. smoothing reserve		40	40	(80)	0
Provision for restructuring		0	30	0	0
NOPLAT		337	407	337	560

Invested capital	Year 0	Year 1	Year 2	Year 3	Year 4
Operating assets	700	840	980	1,120	0
Reserve for product returns	(150)	(180)	(210)	(240)	0
Invested capital	550	660	770	880	0
Reserve for plant decommissioning	119	144	170	0	0
Reserve for restructuring	0	0	30	0	0
Reserve for income smoothing	0	40	80	0	0
Equity	431	476	490	880	0
Invested capital	550	660	770	880	0
ROIC (on beginning of year capital)		61.4%	61.7%	43.8%	63.6%

a service, it must create a liability when that product or service is sold. If the reserve is related to the ongoing operations and grows in step with sales, the reserve should be treated the same as other noninterest-bearing liabilities (e.g., accounts payable). Specifically, the provision should be deducted from revenues to determine EBITA, and the reserve ($180) should be netted against operating assets ($840). Since the provision and reserve are treated as operating items, they appear as part of free cash flow and should not be valued separately.

Long-term operating provisions Sometimes, when a company decommissions a plant, it must pay for cleanup and other costs. Assume our hypothetical company owns a plant that operates for 10 years and requires $200 million in decommissioning costs. Rather than expense the cash outflow in a lump sum at the time of decommissioning, the company builds a reserve as if the company borrowed the money gradually over time. Thus, if the company borrowed $12.5 million annually at 10 percent, the debt (recorded as a reserve) would grow to $200 million by the plant's final year of operation.[35] If the provision is material, it will be recorded in the company's footnotes as follows:

	Year			
	0	1	2	3
Balance Sheet				
Starting reserve	96.8	119.1	143.5	170.4
Plant decommissioning expense (1)	12.5	12.5	12.5	12.5
Interest cost (2)	9.7	11.9	14.4	17.0
Decommissioning payout	0.0	0.0	0.0	(200.0)
Ending reserve	119.1	143.5	170.4	0.0
Income Statement				
Reported provision (1 + 2)	22.2	24.5	26.9	29.6

In year 1, two years before decommissioning, the reported provision is $24.5 million. The provision consists of the $12.5 million annual decommissioning expense and $11.9 million in hypothetical interest expense (the interest that would have been paid if the company gradually borrowed the decommissioning expense). Therefore, when calculating adjusted EBITA, add back $11.9 million to reported EBITA to remove the interest charges.

To measure NOPLAT and invested capital consistently, treat the reserve ($144 million in year 1) as a source of debt-based capital (and not netted against operating assets to determine invested capital). When you treat the plant closure reserve as a debt equivalent, the final payment will not flow through free cash flow. Therefore, for companies that use the present value methodology with implied interest, the current reported reserve ($119.1 million in year 0) should be subtracted from the value of operations ($1,000.2 million) to determine equity value (see Exhibit 7.27).

One-time restructuring provisions   When management decides to restructure a company, it will often recognize certain future expenses (e.g., severance) immediately. We recommend treating one-time provisions as nonoperating and treating the corresponding reserve as a debt equivalent. In year 2, our hypothetical company declared a $30 million restructuring provision, which will be paid in year 3. Since the restructuring is nonoperating, it is not deducted from revenues to determine NOPLAT. Rather, it is included in the reconciliation to net income. Because we plan to value the provision on a cash basis, the noncash reserve is treated as a debt equivalent and is not netted against operating asset to determine invested capital.

[35] A company that borrows $CF annually at R percent will owe $FV at the end of N years:

$$CF = \frac{R \times FV}{(1+R)^N \left[1 - \frac{1}{(1+R)^N} \right]}$$

Exhibit 7.27 Enterprise DCF with Provisions and Reserves

$ million

	Year 1	Year 2	Year 3	Year 4	
NOPLAT	337	407	337	560	
Net investment in invested capital	(110)	(110)	(110)	880	
Free cash flow	227	297	227	1,440	
From the investor's perspective:					
Provision for restructuring	0	30	0	0	**Present**
(Increase) decrease in restructuring reserve	0	(30)	30	0	**value at 10%**
Cash-based restructuring provision	0	0	30	0	22.5
Interest associated with plant decommissioning	12	14	17	0	
(Increase) decrease in plant closure reserve	(24)	(27)	170	0	
Dividends	240	310	10	1,440	
Free cash flow	227	297	227	1,440	

Free cash flow valuation

	Year 1	Year 2	Year 3	Year 4
Free cash flow	227	297	227	1,440
Discount factor (at 10%)	0.91	0.83	0.75	0.68
Discounted cash flow	206.8	245.8	170.9	983.5

	Year 0	
Value of operations	1,607	
PV (restructuring provision)	(22.5)	Debt equivalent (present value)
Reserve for plant decommissioning	(119.1)	Debt equivalent (reported at time = 0)
Equity value	1,465.4	

Since nonoperating income (and expenses) does not flow through free cash flow, the restructuring expense must be valued separately on a cash basis. To convert accrual-based restructuring expenses to cash, start with the restructuring expense, and subtract the increase in the restructuring reserve. In year 2, this leads to a cash flow of $0 (see Exhibit 7.27). In year 3, this leads to a cash flow of –$30 million. The estimated present value of the nonoperating cash flow stream equals $22.5 million, which must be deducted from the value of operations to determine equity value.

Income-smoothing provisions   In some countries, provisions can be manipulated to smooth earnings. In Exhibit 7.25, our hypothetical company was able to show a smooth growth in reported EBITA and net income by using a smoothing provision. Although we title the account "provision for income smoothing," actual companies use wording more subtle, such as "other provisions." For our hypothetical company, a provision was recorded in years 1 and 2, and was reversed in year 3.[36] By using an income-smoothing provision, the company hid its year 3 decline in operating performance (operating costs rose from 70 percent to 80 percent of sales).

To properly evaluate the company's performance, eliminate any income-smoothing provisions. Do this by adding the income-smoothing provision back to reported EBITA (essentially undoing the income-smoothing provision). In this way, we are converting the provision to a cash (vs. accrual) basis and subsequently need to treat the reserve as an equity equivalent (the process is identical to deferred taxes). Since income-smoothing provisions are entirely noncash, no adjustment must be made to the company's valuation.

Provisions and taxes   In most situations, provisions are tax deductible only when cash is dispersed, not when the provision is reported. Thus, most provisions will give rise to deferred tax assets. We recommend using cash taxes when including provisions in the DCF valuation. This requires netting deferred tax assets against deferred tax liabilities (from depreciation) and subtracting the increase in net deferred tax liabilities from adjusted taxes.

Pensions and Postretirement Medical Benefits

Pension and postretirement medical benefits are a special case of long-term provisions described in the previous section. Retirement benefits differ from other long-term provisions primarily because they (although not always) are prefunded with cash. The cash is held in an off-balance-sheet account titled "plan assets." Since the expected (dollar) return on plan assets is included as part of reported EBITA, retirement provisions can lead to serious distortions in operating performance. Thus, we reorganize the financial statements by allocating pension expenses, prepaid pension assets, and unfunded pension liabilities into operating and nonoperating items.

Pension expenses are composed of four primary items: service cost, interest cost on plan liabilities, expected return on plan assets, and recognized gains and losses.[37] Exhibit 7.28 presents the 10-K pension note for Lockheed Martin. To determine the portion of pension expense that is compensation (and hence operating), we combine service cost and amortization of prior service cost, which represents today's value of promised retirement payments. In 2003, Lockheed Martin had $640 million in service cost and $79 million in prior service cost, for a total operating expense of $719 million.

---

[36] Provisions for income smoothing are often categorized as "general" or "other" provisions.
[37] For more on pension accounting, see D. Kieso, J. Weygandt, and T. Warfield, *Intermediate Accounting* (Hoboken, NJ: Wiley, 2004).

Exhibit 7.28 Lockheed Martin: 10-K Note on Retirement Plans

$ million

	2001	2002	2003	
Service cost	523	565	640	Operating
Amortization of prior service cost	64	72	79	
Interest cost	1,357	1,401	1,453	
Expected return on plan assets	(2,177)	(2,162)	(1,748)	Nonoperating
Recognized net actuarial losses (gains)	(117)	(33)	62	
Amortization of transition asset	(4)	(3)	(2)	
Total net pension expense (income)	(354)	(160)	484	

Source: Lockheed Martin 10-K, 2003.

The remaining items, interest cost and plan returns (both expected and the portion of unexpected returns being recognized), are related to the relative performance of the plan assets, not the operations of the business. If the return on plan assets happened to equal the interest cost on the pension liability, the two would cancel, and only the service cost would remain. Since plan assets fluctuate (with the performance of the market), these two items will not cancel. Consider the bull market of the late 1990s. Strong stock returns drove pension assets up; this raised the expected dollar return on plan assets, driving down reported pension expense. Lockheed Martin's 2001 expected dollar returns were so large, in fact, that the company reported a net pension gain as part of EBITA, rather than as a net expense. As the market fell over the next two years, asset values fell as well. Lockheed Martin wound up adding more than $460 million to its reported operating costs, none of which was actually related to operations.

To remove plan performance from operating expenses (see Exhibit 7.29), we increase reported EBITA ($1,976 million) by the interest cost

Exhibit 7.29 Lockheed Martin: EBITA Pension Adjustment

$ million

	2001	2002	2003
Revenue	23,990	26,578	31,824
EBITA	1,787	1,949	1,976
Add: interest cost[1]	1,357	1,401	1,453
Subtract: return on plan assets[2]	(2,298)	(2,198)	(1,688)
Adjusted EBITA	846	1,152	1,741
EBITA/Revenues (raw)	7.4%	7.3%	6.2%
EBITA/Revenues (adjusted for pension)	3.5%	4.3%	5.5%

[1]Interest cost disclosed in Lockheed Martin 10-K (see Exhibit 7.28).
[2]Return on plan assets equals expected returns plus recognized net actuarial losses plus amortization of transition asset disclosed in Lockheed Martin 10-K (see Exhibit 7.28).

($1,453 million) and decrease it by the combined return on plan assets ($1,688 million). This lowers EBITA in 2003 by more than $200 million. Consider the impact on Lockheed Martin's operating margin over the past three years. In actuality, Lockheed Martin's (adjusted) operating margins have been steadily improving, even though the income statement hides this fact.

Since pension expenses are tax deductible, remove nonoperating pension expenses from reported taxes. At Lockheed Martin's marginal tax rate of 33.1 percent, reported taxes would be increased by $481 million ($1,453 million × 33.1 percent), and decreased by $559 million ($1,688 million × 33.1 percent) to determine operating taxes.

Pension accounting will also affect invested capital. When the reported pension expenses differ from cash payments to the plan, the difference is recorded on the company's balance sheet. The recorded asset (when cash payments exceed expenses) or liability (when expenses exceed cash payments) either is unrelated to operations (e.g., when pension assets rise) or is a debt the company owes (when cash payments are smaller than the present value of the promised benefit). Therefore, any assets should be treated as nonoperating, and any liabilities should be treated as debt equivalents.

Since prepaid pension assets and unfunded liabilities are moved to the balance sheet over long periods of time (under U.S. GAAP and IFRS), they do not reflect current valuation of the plan assets and liabilities. To determine the actual present value of the funding shortfall, you must consult the company's footnotes. (For more on pension valuation, see Chapter 11.)

Minority Interest

A minority interest occurs when a third party owns some percentage of one the company's consolidated subsidiaries. If a minority interest exists, treat the balance sheet amount as an equity equivalent. Treat the earnings attributable to minority interest as a financing cost similar to interest, with an appropriate adjustment for income taxes. Thus, NOPLAT (for use with ROIC and FCF) will exclude the effects of minority interest. After-tax minority interest should be a financing flow.

Inflation

While ROIC provides the single best measure for evaluating the operational performance of a company, it can be distorted by inflation. Consider a company earning $10 in NOPLAT on $100 in invested capital. If inflation doubles both prices and costs, profits will also double. Yet since invested capital is measured at cost, it will remain constant. With profits doubling and capital remaining constant, ROIC will artificially double from 10 percent to 20 percent. If the company's cost of capital equals 10 percent, does this mean the company is now creating value? Probably not. An identical company started today with similar capacity and similar features would require $200 in investment (based on the inflated currency), earn $20, and have an ROIC of 10 percent. Since the two companies are identical from an operating perspective, the older company should not appear superior.[38]

If inflation is significant, such long-term assets as net PP&E should be adjusted upward for inflation. Working backward, you must decompose the fixed assets into layers based on when they were purchased. Each layer is then revalued using a price index. Since depreciation is also based on historical cost, it should be increased as well. Do not adjust taxes, however. Taxes are based on historical depreciation, and increasing depreciation would overestimate the tax shield. To calculate an inflation-adjusted ROIC, divide adjusted NOPLAT by the adjusted invested capital. Since ROIC is now in real terms (excluding inflation), it must be compared with the real cost of capital. (See Chapter 22 for an example of this approach.)

Market versus Book-Invested Capital

The traditional measure of ROIC divides NOPLAT by book-invested capital. Thus, ROIC represents the rate of return on original cost (less depreciation). Although this provides a good ex-post measure of performance, it should not be used to make entry and exit decisions. Consider a company that built a facility for $1 billion. The facility is currently generating $10 million in NOPLAT. Because the facility's 1 percent ROIC is well below its 10 percent cost of capital, the CEO recommends selling the facility. But what if the facility is worth only $50 million on the open market? In this case, the rate of return (based on market-based opportunity costs) is 20 percent. At this price, the CEO would be better off keeping the facility, assuming profits remain constant.

An Alternative Measure: Cash Flow Return on Investment

For companies with large, uneven capital expenditures, ROIC may vary systematically over the asset's life, and this can give a distorted picture about when value is created. In this case, it may be helpful to convert ROIC into a measure similar to internal rate of return (IRR). One common measure based on the principles of IRR is CFROI (cash flow return on investment).[39]

---

[38] In this example, we argue the two companies are comparable because only inflation causes differences in ROIC. If, however, the older company were able to purchase assets at a discount (for a reason other than inflation), it would have a true competitive advantage. Thus, using replacement cost to handle inflation can improperly mask superior performance.

[39] For more information, see B. Madden, *CFROI Valuation: A Total System Approach to Valuing the Firm* (Oxford: Butterworth-Heinemann, 1999).

Consider a livery company that plans to purchase a new taxi for $20,000. The vehicle will operate for four years. Since revenues are independent of the taxi's age, the taxi will earn relatively constant profits over the four years. Assume the company's NOPLAT, invested capital, and ROIC per taxi are as follows:

	Year ($ Thousands)				
	0	1	2	3	4
Revenues		100.0	100.0	100.0	100.0
Operating costs		(93.0)	(93.0)	(93.0)	(93.0)
Depreciation		(5.0)	(5.0)	(5.0)	(5.0)
NOPLAT		2.0	2.0	2.0	2.0
Invested capital	20.0	15.0	10.0	5.0	0.0
ROIC (on beginning of year capital)		10%	13%	20%	40%

Note how the investment's ROIC rises from 10 percent to 40 percent over its life. If the company's cost of capital is 15 percent, it appears that the investment destroys value during its first two years but creates value during the last two years.

Alternatively, you could calculate the internal rate of return for each taxi. Using the classic IRR formula, you would find the taxi earns an IRR of 15 percent over its life. Calculating IRR, however, requires making subjective forecasts, so it does not offer a consistent measure of historical performance.

CFROI removes the subjectivity of year-by-year forecasting yet provides a smoothed measure. To calculate CFROI in a given year, use the traditional IRR methodology of setting the net present value to 0 and then solving for the discount rate. To avoid the subjectivity of forecasting, CFROI assumes a fixed cash flow for a fixed number of periods (the company's estimated asset life). To calculate CFROI, we need three components: the initial investment, the annual cash flow, and residual value. The initial investment equals the gross invested capital measured in the prior period (gross invested capital equals invested capital plus accumulated deprecation). The annual cash flow equals NOPLAT plus depreciation. The residual value equals NOPLAT plus depreciation, plus the return of the original working capital.

Exhibit 7.30 calculates the CFROI in 2003 for Home Depot. To measure initial investment, we add 2002's invested capital ($25,557 million) to 2002's accumulated depreciation ($3,565 million). The annual gross cash flow over 20 years is $6,157 million (as measured by 2003 gross cash flow), and the final year's return of 2002 working capital equals $2,746 million. Using Excel's goal seek function, we arrive at an internal rate of return (CFROI) of 20.7 percent.

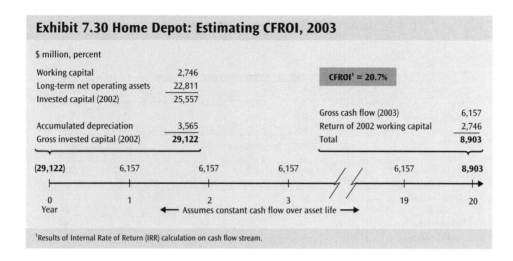

Exhibit 7.30 Home Depot: Estimating CFROI, 2003

$ million, percent

Working capital	2,746		**CFROI[1] = 20.7%**	
Long-term net operating assets	22,811			
Invested capital (2002)	25,557			
			Gross cash flow (2003)	6,157
Accumulated depreciation	3,565		Return of 2002 working capital	2,746
Gross invested capital (2002)	**29,122**		Total	**8,903**

(29,122)	6,157	6,157	6,157			6,157	8,903
0	1	2	3			19	20

Year   ← Assumes constant cash flow over asset life →

[1] Results of Internal Rate of Return (IRR) calculation on cash flow stream.

CFROI captures the lumpiness of the investment better than ROIC. But it is complex to calculate and requires assumptions about the company's estimated asset life. Weighing the simplicity of ROIC versus the smoothness of CFROI, we suggest using CFROI only when companies have the following characteristics:

- Lumpy capital expenditure patterns
- Long-lived fixed assets (over 15 years)
- Large fixed assets to working capital

HEINEKEN CASE

To wrap up this chapter and each of the next four chapters, we present a case study, Heineken N.V.[40] This case will illustrate the concepts from each of the chapters and provide a comprehensive integration of the pieces of an enterprise DCF valuation and economic profit valuation.

Heineken, based in the Netherlands, is the world's third largest beer company, behind Anheuser-Busch and SABMiller. Its main brands are the popular Heineken and Amstel beers. In 2003, the last historical year prior to our valuation, Heineken had net turnover (revenues) of €9.3 billion and employed more than 61,000 people worldwide. The company is also the most international brewer: only 6 percent of its volume comes from the Netherlands. Heineken earns 57 percent of net turnover in Western Europe,

[40] The authors would like to thank Meg Smoot and Yasser Salem for their support of the analysis of Heineken. This case was prepared before the merger of Interbrew and AmBev. The combined company, InBev, is now the world's largest brewer.

Exhibit 7.31 Heineken: Historical Income Statements

€ million

	1998	1999	2000	2001	2002	2003
Net turnover	5,453	6,164	7,014	7,937	9,011	9,255
Raw materials and consumables	(2,593)	(2,890)	(3,246)	(3,645)	(4,011)	(4,461)
Marketing and selling expenses	(790)	(964)	(1,107)	(1,281)	(1,585)	(1,131)
Staff costs	(1,042)	(1,132)	(1,301)	(1,417)	(1,642)	(1,832)
EBITDA	1,028	1,178	1,360	1,594	1,773	1,831
Depreciation	(369)	(379)	(439)	(469)	(491)	(578)
EBITA	659	799	921	1,125	1,282	1,253
Amortization of goodwill	0	0	0	0	0	(31)
Operating profit	659	799	921	1,125	1,282	1,222
Interest paid	(53)	(80)	(109)	(118)	(146)	(180)
Interest received	42	39	43	47	37	40
Profit before tax	648	759	855	1,054	1,173	1,082
Taxation	(235)	(265)	(277)	(327)	(364)	(319)
Results of nonconsolidated participating interest (after tax)	44	51	59	45	48	101
Minority interest	(12)	(28)	(16)	(57)	(62)	(66)
Income before extraordinary items	445	516	621	715	795	798
Extraordinary items (after tax)	0	0	0	52	0	0
Net profit	**445**	**516**	**621**	**767**	**795**	**798**
Shareholders' equity						
Position as of 1 January	2,316	2,299	2,618	2,396	2,758	2,543
Exchange differences	0	0	0	0	(107)	(152)
Reclassification of dividend payable	0	0	0	0	0	94
Revaluations	(69)	35	60	72	32	41
Goodwill written off	(278)	(106)	(778)	(320)	(778)	0
Net profit for the year	445	516	621	767	795	798
Dividends	(115)	(125)	(125)	(157)	(157)	(157)
Position as of 31 December	**2,299**	**2,618**	**2,396**	**2,758**	**2,543**	**3,167**

12 percent in Central/Eastern Europe, 17 percent in North America, 9 percent in Africa and the Middle East, and the remaining 5 percent in the Asia/Pacific region. In addition, only 30 percent of its volume comes from its flagship brands; the rest is from Heineken-owned regional brands.

In this chapter of the case study, we analyze Heineken's historical performance, summarize the beer market, and compare Heineken's performance with the market.

REORGANIZATION OF THE FINANCIAL STATEMENTS

Exhibits 7.31 through 7.38 detail the historical financial analysis of Heineken. Exhibits 7.31 and 7.32 present Heineken's income statement and balance sheet for the years 1998 through 2003, using the British nomenclature that Heineken uses in its English annual report (for example, "turnover" refers to revenues). Exhibits 7.33 through 7.35 present the calculations of Heineken's NOPLAT, invested capital, and

Exhibit 7.32 Heineken: Historical Balance Sheets

€ million

	1998	1999	2000	2001	2002	2003
Operating cash	109	123	140	159	180	185
Excess cash and marketable securities	839	1,084	684	1,016	598	1,231
Accounts receivable	667	746	858	985	1,066	1,205
Stocks (inventory)	452	490	550	692	765	834
Other current assets	108	157	166	207	204	174
Total current assets	2,175	2,600	2,398	3,059	2,813	3,629
Tangible fixed assets	2,605	2,964	3,250	3,605	4,133	5,053
Goodwill	0	0	0	0	0	1,093
Nonconsolidated participating interests	256	189	279	183	412	433
Deferred tax assets	0	0	35	30	22	18
Other financial fixed assets	233	233	301	318	401	671
Total assets	**5,270**	**5,986**	**6,263**	**7,195**	**7,781**	**10,897**
Short-term debt	347	488	428	570	1,039	1,113
Accounts payable	412	457	529	620	629	745
Tax payable	221	289	288	335	322	392
Dividend payable	58	87	78	107	105	16
Other current liabilities	422	538	569	603	554	644
Total current liabilities	**1,460**	**1,860**	**1,892**	**2,235**	**2,649**	**2,910**
Long-term debt	522	490	875	797	1,215	2,721
Deferred tax liabilities	273	295	312	357	381	415
Retirement liabilities	47	48	100	112	352	526
Other provisions	125	158	158	133	133	133
Restructuring provision	289	269	406	422	115	293
Total long-term liabilities	**1,255**	**1,260**	**1,851**	**1,821**	**2,196**	**4,088**
Shareholders' equity	2,299	2,618	2,396	2,758	2,543	3,167
Minority interest	256	248	124	381	393	732
Total equity	**2,555**	**2,866**	**2,520**	**3,139**	**2,936**	**3,899**
Total liabilities and shareholders' equity	**5,270**	**5,986**	**6,263**	**7,195**	**7,781**	**10,897**

free cash flow for each year. Exhibit 7.36 shows the calculations of Heineken's economic profit. The remaining exhibits offer the backup calculations and ratios to be used for forecasting.

Heineken made a significant acquisition in 2003 and changed its accounting policy for discounts provided to distributors and retailers. Therefore, its 2003 results are not directly comparable with those of prior years. For 2003, we calculate ROIC using end-of-year capital rather than average or beginning capital (our standard practice) because Heineken's 2003 income statement contains most of a year's income from the acquired company but its beginning balance sheet contains none of the acquired company's capital.

In our analysis of Heineken's financial statements, several accounting issues merit special attention:

Exhibit 7.33 Heineken: Historical NOPLAT

€ million

	1999	2000	2001	2002	2003
EBITA	799	921	1,125	1,282	1,253
Adjustment for retirement related liability	2	4	4	14	21
Increase/(decrease) in other provisions	34	(0)	(25)	0	0
Adjusted EBITA	835	925	1,104	1,296	1,274
Taxes on EBITA	(280)	(302)	(353)	(406)	(375)
Increase/(decrease) in deferred tax liability	22	(18)	50	32	38
NOPLAT	**577**	**606**	**801**	**922**	**937**
Taxes on EBITA					
Reported taxes	(265)	(277)	(327)	(364)	(319)
Tax shield on interest paid	(28)	(38)	(41)	(50)	(62)
Taxes on interest received	14	15	16	13	14
Tax shield on retirement related liabilities	(1)	(1)	(2)	(5)	(7)
Taxes on EBITA	**(280)**	**(302)**	**(353)**	**(406)**	**(375)**
Reconciliation to net profit					
Net profit	516	621	767	795	798
Increase/(decrease) in other provisions	34	(0)	(25)	0	0
Increase/(decrease) in deferred tax liability	22	(18)	50	32	38
Extraordinary items	0	0	(52)	0	0
Minority interest	28	16	57	62	66
Results of nonconsolidated participating interests	(51)	(59)	(45)	(48)	(101)
Amortization of goodwill	0	0	0	0	31
Adjusted net profit	549	560	752	841	832
Interest paid after tax	52	71	77	96	118
Interest expense on retirement related liabilities	1	3	3	9	14
Total income available to investors	603	633	832	946	964
Interest received after tax	(26)	(28)	(31)	(24)	(26)
NOPLAT	**577**	**606**	**801**	**922**	**937**

- *Net turnover:* Beginning in 2003, Dutch reporting rules changed the method for determining net turnover. Now all discounts and excise duties directly attributable to the turnover must be deducted from gross turnover to determine net turnover. Before 2003, net turnover included excise duties collected from customers. Heineken then showed the transmittal of these duties to the government as an expense. To improve comparability, we have shown net turnover less excise duties for all years. Heineken does not disclose the necessary prior-year information to adjust for discounts.

Exhibit 7.34 Heineken: Historical Invested Capital

€ million

	1998	1999	2000	2001	2002	2003
Operating current assets	1,336	1,516	1,714	2,043	2,215	2,398
Operating current liabilities	(1,055)	(1,284)	(1,386)	(1,558)	(1,505)	(1,781)
Operating working capital	282	232	328	485	710	617
Tangible fixed assets	2,605	2,964	3,250	3,605	4,133	5,053
Operating invested capital (before goodwill)	2,887	3,196	3,578	4,090	4,843	5,670
Goodwill	0	0	0	0	0	1,093
Cumulative goodwill written off and amortized	1,046	1,152	1,930	2,250	3,028	3,059
Operating invested capital (after goodwill)	3,932	4,348	5,508	6,340	7,871	9,822
Excess cash and marketable securities	839	1,084	684	1,016	598	1,231
Nonconsolidated participating interests	256	189	279	183	412	433
Other financial fixed assets	233	233	301	318	401	671
Total investor funds	**5,261**	**5,853**	**6,772**	**7,857**	**9,282**	**12,157**
Shareholders' equity	2,299	2,618	2,396	2,758	2,543	3,167
Cumulative goodwill written off and amortized	1,046	1,152	1,930	2,250	3,028	3,059
Minority interest	256	248	124	381	393	732
Other provisions	125	158	158	133	133	133
Net deferred taxes	273	295	277	327	359	397
Dividend payable	58	87	78	107	105	16
Adjusted equity	4,056	4,558	4,963	5,956	6,561	7,504
Debt	869	978	1,303	1,367	2,254	3,834
Retirement liabilities	47	48	100	112	352	526
Restructuring provision	289	269	406	422	115	293
Total investor funds	**5,261**	**5,853**	**6,772**	**7,857**	**9,282**	**12,157**

- *Acquisitions and treatment of goodwill:* Heineken has consistently used acquisitions for growth, generating more than €3.1 billion in goodwill over the last five years. Before 2003, Heineken followed Dutch accounting policies that permitted the immediate write-off of goodwill. In 2003, these rules were changed, and Heineken began capitalizing and amortizing goodwill. To estimate invested capital with goodwill, we add back the cumulative goodwill written off.

- *Results from nonconsolidated participating interests:* Results from nonconsolidated participating interests represent Heineken's share of income from companies that are not consolidated in its financial statements. Heineken reports these on an after-tax basis. Therefore, when estimating NOPLAT, we do not adjust for taxes on this income.

- *Revaluation reserves:* Each year, Heineken makes an adjustment to its equity called a "revaluation reserve." Although the details of this adjustment are not disclosed, it is most likely due to foreign-currency translation adjustments and

Exhibit 7.35 Heineken: Historical Cash Flow

€ million

	1999	2000	2001	2002	2003
Operating cash flows					
NOPLAT	577	606	801	922	937
Depreciation	379	439	469	491	578
Gross cash flow	956	1,045	1,270	1,413	1,515
(Increase) decrease in working capital	50	(97)	(156)	(225)	93
Capital expenditures	(703)	(665)	(752)	(1,094)	(1,609)
Gross investment	(653)	(762)	(908)	(1,319)	(1,516)
Free cash flow before goodwill	303	283	362	93	0
Investment in goodwill	(106)	(778)	(320)	(778)	(1,124)
Free cash flow after goodwill	197	(495)	42	(685)	(1,124)
After tax interest received	26	28	31	24	26
(Increase) decrease in excess marketable securities	(245)	400	(333)	418	(633)
Results of nonconsolidated participating interests	51	59	45	48	101
(Increase) decrease in non-consolidated participating interests	67	(90)	96	(229)	(21)
Other nonoperating cash flows	1	(68)	35	(83)	(270)
Cash flow to investors	**96**	**(166)**	**(84)**	**(506)**	**(1,921)**
Financing flows					
After tax interest paid	52	71	77	96	118
Interest on retirement liabilities	1	3	3	9	14
Minority interest (income statement)	28	16	57	62	66
(Increase) decrease in minority interest	8	124	(257)	(12)	(339)
(Increase) decrease in debt	(109)	(325)	(64)	(887)	(1,580)
(Increase) decrease in retirement liabilities	(1)	(52)	(12)	(240)	(174)
(Increase) decrease in restructuring provisions	20	(137)	(16)	307	(178)
(Increase) decrease in dividends payable	(28)	9	(29)	2	(5)
Dividends	125	125	157	157	157
Total financing flows	**96**	**(166)**	**(84)**	**(506)**	**(1,921)**

fixed-asset revaluations. We have treated changes in these reserves as nonoperating cash flows.

- *Dividends:* Following changes in Dutch reporting standards in 2003, the year-end equity is reported inclusive of dividends declared but not yet paid. Before 2003, dividends were deducted from equity when declared and shown as a liability until paid to shareholders.

Exhibit 7.36 Heineken: Historical Economic Profit

€ million, percent

Before goodwill	1999	2000	2001	2002	2003
After-tax ROIC (on beginning of year invested capital)	20.0%	18.9%	22.4%	22.5%	16.5%
WACC	8.7%	8.3%	8.4%	7.7%	7.7%
Spread	**11.3%**	**10.6%**	**14.0%**	**14.8%**	**8.8%**
Invested capital (beginning of year)	2,887	3,196	3,578	4,090	5,670
Economic profit	**326**	**340**	**500**	**607**	**501**
NOPLAT	577	606	801	922	937
Capital charge	(251)	(265)	(301)	(315)	(437)
Economic profit	**326**	**340**	**500**	**607**	**501**
After goodwill					
After-tax ROIC (on beginning of year invested capital)	14.7%	13.9%	14.5%	14.5%	9.5%
WACC	8.7%	8.3%	8.4%	7.7%	7.7%
Spread	**6.0%**	**5.6%**	**6.1%**	**6.8%**	**1.8%**
Invested capital (beginning of year)	3,932	4,348	5,508	6,340	9,822
Economic profit	**235**	**245**	**338**	**433**	**181**
NOPLAT	577	606	801	922	937
Capital charge	(342)	(361)	(463)	(488)	(756)
Economic profit	**235**	**245**	**338**	**433**	**181**

- *Taxes:* The statutory tax rate in the Netherlands has been 35 percent in recent years. That rate will be used to calculate the marginal taxes related to interest income and expense.

- *Excess cash:* We have assumed that any cash and marketable securities above 2 percent of turnover are excess to the needs of the business operations. This assumption is approximately the minimum cash level we have historically observed for similar companies. Excess cash is treated as a nonoperating asset, rather than as working capital.

- *Other financial fixed assets:* Other financial fixed assets are primarily loans to customers and related parties.

- *Pension plans:* At the end of 2003, Heineken had an unfunded pension liability of €526 million, primarily related to pensions and annuities that have not been insured with third parties. Unlike U.S. companies, Heineken's financial statements do not disclose the components of pension expense (the portion of expense that is related to interest expense or investment income), so we have assumed a net interest expense at 4 percent of the liability is included in pension expense in operating costs. In estimating NOPLAT, we have reclassified this amount from operating costs to interest expense. (We normally would not adjust for such a small amount, but we do so here to illustrate the technique.)

Exhibit 7.37 Heineken: Historical Operating Ratios

percent

Operating ratios	1999	2000	2001	2002	2003
Adjusted EBITA/net turnover	13.5	13.2	13.9	14.4	13.8
Raw materials, consumables and services/net turnover	46.9	46.3	45.9	44.5	48.2
Marketing and selling expenses/net turnover	15.6	15.8	16.1	17.6	12.2
Staff costs/net turnover	18.4	18.5	17.9	18.2	19.8
Depreciation[1]/net turnover	12.0	12.7	12.6	11.8	11.3
Return on invested capital (beginning)					
Tangible fixed assets/net turnover	48.1	46.3	45.4	45.9	54.6[2]
Working capital/net turnover	4.6	3.3	4.1	5.4	7.7
Net turnover/invested capital (times)	2.1	2.2	2.2	2.2	1.9
Pre-tax ROIC	28.9	28.9	30.9	31.7	26.3
Cash tax rate	30.9	34.5	27.5	28.9	26.4
After-tax ROIC	20.0	18.9	22.4	22.5	19.4[2]
After-tax ROIC (including goodwill)	14.7	13.9	14.5	14.5	11.9[2]
Return on invested capital (average)					
Average tangible fixed assets/net turnover	45.2	44.3	43.2	42.9	54.6[2]
Working capital/net turnover	4.2	4.0	5.1	6.6	7.2
Net turnover/invested capital	2.0	2.1	2.1	2.0	1.6
Pre-tax ROIC	27.5	27.3	28.8	29.0	22.5
After-tax ROIC	19.0	17.9	20.9	20.6	16.5[2]
After-tax ROIC (including goodwill)	13.9	12.3	13.5	13.0	9.5[2]
Growth rates					
Revenue growth rate	13.0	13.8	13.2	13.5	2.7
Adjusted EBITA growth rate	24.7	10.8	19.4	17.3	(1.7)
NOPLAT growth rate	38.6	4.9	32.3	15.0	1.7
Invested capital growth rate	10.7	12.0	14.3	18.4	17.1
Net Income growth rate	16.1	20.3	23.5	3.7	0.4
Investment rates					
Gross investment rate	68.3	72.9	71.5	93.4	100.0
Net investment rate	47.5	53.3	54.9	89.9	100.0
Financing					
Coverage (adjusted EBITA/interest)	10.0	8.4	9.5	8.8	7.0
Cash coverage (gross CF/interest)	11.9	9.6	10.8	9.7	8.4
Debt/total book capitalization	29.9	33.2	36.3	45.0	60.1
Debt/total market capitalization	6.1	6.1	7.6	17.2	24.5
Market value of operating invested capital/book value on invested capital	5.4	6.1	4.7	2.8	3.0
Market value of operating invested capital/adjusted EBITA	21.0	24.0	17.0	11.0	13.0

[1]Depreciation excluding value adjustments.
[2]Ending invested capital used for calculations of ROIC.

Exhibit 7.38 Heineken: Supporting Calculations

€ million

	1999	2000	2001	2002	2003
Change in working capital					
Increase (decrease) in operating cash	14	17	18	21	5
Increase (decrease) in accounts receivable	78	112	127	81	139
Increase (decrease) in stocks	38	60	142	73	69
Increase (decrease) in other current assets	49	9	41	(3)	(30)
(Increase) in accounts payable	(46)	(72)	(91)	(9)	(116)
(Increase) decrease in tax payable	(68)	1	(47)	13	(70)
(Increase) decrease in other current liabilities	(116)	(31)	(34)	49	(90)
Net change in working capital	**(50)**	**97**	**156**	**225**	**(93)**
Capital expenditures					
Increase (decrease) in tangible fixed assets	359	286	355	528	920
Depreciation	379	439	469	491	578
Exchange differences	0	0	0	107	152
Revaluation	(35)	(60)	(72)	(32)	(41)
Capital expenditures (net of disposals)	**703**	**665**	**752**	**1,094**	**1,609**
Investment in goodwill					
Increase (decrease) in goodwill	0	0	0	0	1,093
Increase (decrease) in cumulative goodwill written off and amortized	106	778	320	778	31
Investment in goodwill	**106**	**778**	**320**	**778**	**1,124**
Other nonoperating cash flows					
Extraordinary items	0	0	52	0	0
(Increase) decrease in other financial fixed assets	1	(68)	(17)	(83)	(270)
Nonoperating cash flows	**1**	**(68)**	**35**	**(83)**	**(270)**

- *Deferred taxes:* Heineken has €397 million in net deferred taxes, which we have treated as an equity equivalent, adjusting NOPLAT for the change each year and adding it to equity in the total investor funds reconciliation.

- *Provisions:* We have divided Heineken's provisions—other than pensions and deferred taxes—into restructuring provisions (related to specific plant closings and layoffs) and other provisions (the general income-smoothing provisions that European companies sometimes use), based on information from its footnotes. Similar to deferred taxes, income-smoothing provisions are treated as equity equivalents. Restructuring provisions are treated as a debt equivalent, meaning they are not considered part of NOPLAT, and the change in their value is treated like the change in debt in calculating investor funds and financing flows, as explained earlier in this chapter.

INDUSTRY BACKGROUND

To provide a context for analyzing Heineken's performance, we first outline the competitive landscape of the beer industry. The industry has long been fragmented, regional, and slow growing. Over the five years to 2003, worldwide beer consumption grew 2.0 percent annually in volume terms. Volume is expected to increase by another 2.1 percent per year from 2004 to 2008, primarily from growth in emerging markets (see Exhibit 7.39).

In the past few years, the beer industry has experienced a flurry of mergers and acquisitions, though it remains fragmented. The top 3 brewers have a combined market share of only 23 percent worldwide, and the top 20 brewers have a combined market share of only 61 percent. This fragmentation is due in large part to regional oligopolies. In the top 20 markets by size, the top two players have large market shares, with an average combined market share of 68 percent. However, the leading players vary from country to country (see Exhibit 7.40).

Even as the major brewers have expanded outside their home markets, competition has remained local. The main reasons include consumer preferences for local brands and tastes, high government tariffs, regulations, and limited opportunities for economies of scale or scope across national borders. As a result, when brewers have entered new markets, they typically have focused on transferring skills, such as marketing, rather than building globally integrated businesses. The strength of local com-

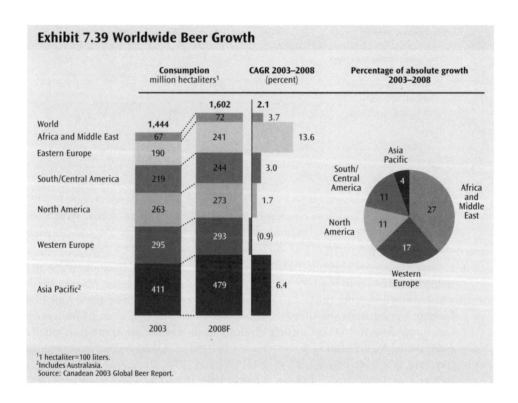

Exhibit 7.39 Worldwide Beer Growth

[1] hectaliter=100 liters.
[2] Includes Australasia.
Source: Canadean 2003 Global Beer Report.

Exhibit 7.40 Beer Industry: National Market Share

percent

Market region	Top players	Market share
Netherlands	Heineken	52
	Interbrew	15
	Grolsch	13
United Kingdom	Scottish & Newcastle	28
	Coors Brewers	20
	Interbrew	17
United States	Anheuser-Busch	47
	Miller	19
	Coors	10
Belgium	Interbrew	55
	Aiken-Maes	14
France	Kronenbourg	40
	Heineken	36
	Interbrew	10
China	Tsingtao	10
	Yanjing	7
	CRE/SAB	5
Brazil	Ambev	68
	Molson	15
	Schincarol	10

Source: Canadean 2003 Global Beer Report.

petition has kept the pace of industry consolidation slow, as local brewers do not feel the need to sell their businesses to the majors to remain competitive.

As tastes converge, technology improves, transportation costs decline, and brewers learn how to better leverage their expertise and brand names, the industry will slowly begin to reach consumers on a global scale. For 6 of the top 10 breweries, at least 20 percent of the volume growth since 1990 has come through acquisitions.

Brewers adopt two distinct strategies: They either specialize by focusing on a specific link in the value chain or become a geographic integrator. The specialization strategy involves focusing on product development, brewing, packaging, distribution, or marketing, and then becoming the global leader in one or two of these tasks. Diageo's Guinness, for example, has focused on a product with a unique flavor supported by aggressive global marketing. Boston Beer Company runs a "virtual" beer company in which it controls product development and marketing but contracts out most production. Geographic integrators such as Heineken and Interbrew, in contrast, purchase underperforming breweries or breweries in developing countries and apply best practices in brewing, distribution, and marketing.

Exhibit 7.41 Heineken: Revenue Growth Analysis

percent

	2000	2001	2002	2003	CAGR 00–03
Organic volume growth	2.0	1.0	2.0	1.5	1.6
Price increase/mix change	3.0	4.0	4.0	3.5	3.6
Underlying organic growth	5.0	5.0	6.0	5.0	5.2
Acquisitions (first time consolidations)	7.0	6.0	7.0	8.0	7.0
Currency changes	1.0	2.0	(1.0)	(4.0)	(0.5)
Accounting change/other	0.8	0.2	1.5	(6.3)	(1.0)
Revenue growth	13.8	13.2	13.5	2.7	10.7

HEINEKEN'S GROWTH AND ROIC

To evaluate Heineken's financial performance, we compared it with other large, publicly traded beer companies: Anheuser-Busch, SABMiller, Coors, and Interbrew (now InBev after the merger with AmBev).

From 1999 through 2003, Heineken increased its revenues by 10.7 percent per year (see Exhibit 7.41). However, organic growth (volume, price increase, and mix) has driven only half of total revenue growth, about 5 percent per year. Acquisitions have added 7 percent per year. The remaining difference is due to currency effects and accounting changes. In 2003, currency changes, primarily the decline in the U.S. dollar, reduced Heineken's revenues by 4 percent. In addition, Heineken changed its method of ac-

Exhibit 7.42 Beer Industry: Revenue Growth Analysis, 1999–2003

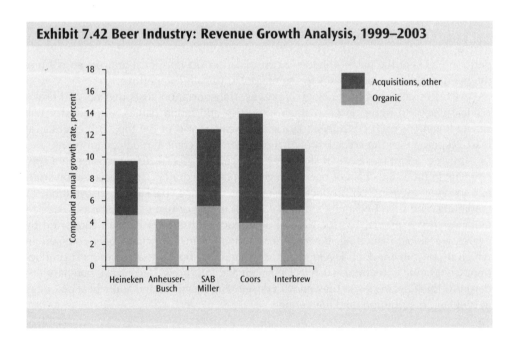

counting for discounts provided to retailers and distributors. Beginning in 2003, turnover (revenue) is shown net of discounts. This accounting change reduced turnover by 6.3 percent in 2003. Heineken does not disclose enough information to restate prior years. This accounting change had no impact on profits, but margins appear to be higher (the same profit divided by smaller turnover).

Exhibit 7.42 compares Heineken's revenue growth with that of its peers. Overall growth from 1999 to 2003 varies from 4.8 percent for Anheuser-Busch to 15.5 percent for Coors. However, these results are not comparable due to acquisitions, accounting changes, and currency effects. The distribution of organic growth was very narrow, ranging from 4.8 percent to 6.1 percent, with Heineken right in the middle.

As all of the companies have similar organic growth rates, the most important driver for explaining the differences in value across peers is ROIC. Heineken increased its ROIC excluding goodwill from 19.4 percent in 1999 to 21.1 percent in 2002 (see Exhibit 7.43). Then ROIC fell in 2003 to 16.5 percent. The decline was largely due to the weaker economics of the Austrian brewer BBAG, which Heineken acquired in 2003. In addition, Heineken's margins were hurt by competition in some markets and by lower margins on beer exported from Europe to the United States, due to the weakening of the

Exhibit 7.43 Beer Industry: Value Drivers

percent

ROIC (including goodwill)	1999	2000	2001	2002	2003
Heineken	13.9	12.3	13.5	13.0	9.5
Anheuser-Busch	16.1	17.2	18.7	21.1	23.8
SABMiller	21.0	27.5	23.6	18.1	12.5
Coors	11.2	12.0	12.2	12.5	6.9
Interbrew	8.2	8.7	10.8	9.7	10.5
ROIC (excluding goodwill)					
Heineken	19.0	17.9	20.9	20.6	16.5
Anheuser-Busch	16.9	18.0	19.6	22.1	24.9
SABMiller	24.7	35.6	36.0	34.3	36.6
Coors	11.6	12.5	13.0	21.3	13.9
Interbrew	13.3	14.6	19.0	18.8	22.1
Operating margin					
Heineken	13.5	13.2	13.9	14.4	13.8
Anheuser-Busch	25.9	26.5	27.1	28.2	29.1
SABMiller	13.8	16.4	19.1	20.3	14.4
Coors	6.3	6.7	7.2	8.3	6.8
Interbrew	10.1	10.4	13.5	13.5	14.1
Capital turnover					
Heineken	2.0	2.1	2.1	2.0	1.6
Anheuser-Busch	1.4	1.5	1.5	1.7	1.8
SABMiller	2.7	2.8	2.6	2.5	3.9
Coors	3.0	2.9	2.9	3.9	3.2
Interbrew	2.0	1.9	1.8	1.8	2.0

U.S. dollar. Heineken's EBITA margin declined from 14.4 percent in 2002 to 13.8 percent in 2003. In addition, BBAG is more capital intensive. Heineken's capital turnover, which had been constant from 1999 to 2002 at 2.1 times, declined to 1.6 times in 2003. (Remember that we used Heineken's ending invested capital to calculate ROIC in 2003.)

We also estimated Heineken's ROIC including goodwill to see the impact of acquisitions. Including goodwill reduces Heineken's ROIC about four to six percentage points in each of the last five years. In 2003, Heineken's ROIC including goodwill was 9.6 percent versus 16.5 percent without goodwill.

Anheuser-Busch and SABMiller had the best underlying performance, with 2003 ROICs before goodwill of 24.9 percent and 36.6 percent, respectively. While Busch's high ROIC comes from strong margins, increasing from 25.9 percent in 1999 to 29.1 percent in 2003, SABMiller was the leader in invested capital turnover, increasing from 2.7 in 1999 to 3.9 in 2003. Exhibit 7.44 shows the breakdown of the capital turnover for each company during 2003. Heineken's low capital turnover has primarily resulted from much higher working capital needs than those of its peers.

Although SABMiller has the highest ROIC excluding goodwill, the company is in line with its peers when taking into account the effects of acquisitions at 12.5 percent in 2003. Since Anheuser-Busch has primarily grown organically, its ROIC including goodwill is roughly the same excluding goodwill at 23.8 percent. Coors has had slight improvements in both margins and capital turnover over the last five years. Interbrew has had constant turnover but has increased margins from 10.1 percent in 1999 to 14.1 percent in 2003. However, ROIC including goodwill has deteriorated for Coors and has increased only slightly for Interbrew, going from 1999 levels of 11.2 percent and 8.2 percent, respectively, to 6.9 percent and 10.5 percent, respectively, in 2003.

PERFORMANCE IN THE STOCK MARKET

As a final assessment of historical performance, we compared the stock market performance of these companies, using two indicators: TRS and the ratio of market value to invested capital. In terms of TRS, Heineken has struggled during the last five years. It is the only company out of its peers to have negative TRS when measured over the one, three, and five years to 2003 (see Exhibit 7.45). Over that period, Heineken's

Exhibit 7.44 Beer Industry: Capital Turnover Analysis, 2003

percent

Company	Working capital/ revenue	Net PPE/ revenue	Other assets/ revenue	Goodwill/ revenue	Capital turnover excluding goodwill	Capital turnover including goodwill
Heineken	7.2	54.6	0.0	11.8	1.6	1.4
Anheuser-Busch	(2.0)	59.5	(1.7)	2.5	1.8	1.7
SABMiller	(2.4)	29.2	(1.0)	49.8	3.9	1.3
Coors	2.2	34.9	(5.7)	31.8	3.2	1.6
Interbrew	0.1	48.7	0.9	55.1	2.0	1.0

shareholder returns have averaged –5 percent per year, much lower than for Anheuser-Busch, at 12 percent, and SABMiller, at 11 percent. (These percentages are based on local currencies, not in a common currency. We tested total returns in U.S. dollars and found the relative performance to be the same.) The market set high standards for Heineken. Unfortunately, Heineken has been unable to keep pace with expectations.

We also compared Heineken's market-value-to-invested-capital ratio with that of its peers. Market-value-to-invested-capital compares the company's market value (both debt and equity) to the amount of capital that has been invested in the company (fixed assets, working capital, and investments in intangibles from acquisitions); it measures the market's perception of the company's ability to create wealth. Heineken's value places it in line with its peers at a market-value-to-invested-capital ratio of 1.6. This means that the market assigns a value of $1.60 for every dollar invested in the company. Anheuser-Busch was the only company that truly stood out from its peers, with a market-value-to-invested-capital ratio of 6.1. Busch's high value to invested capital including goodwill is primarily driven by a greater ROIC including goodwill: 23.8 percent in 2003 versus its peer average of 12.9 percent.

Exhibit 7.45 Beer Industry: Stock Market Performance

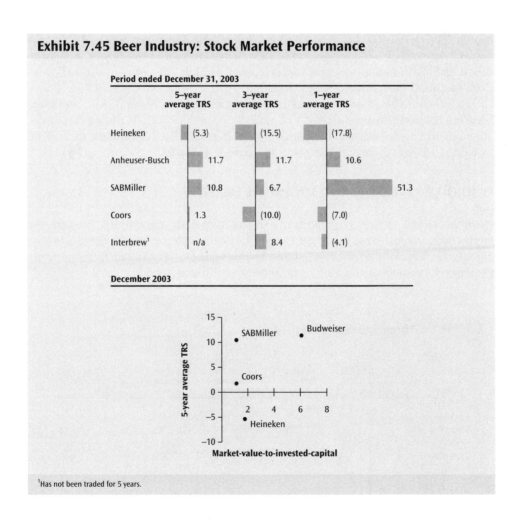

Period ended December 31, 2003

	5–year average TRS	3–year average TRS	1–year average TRS
Heineken	(5.3)	(15.5)	(17.8)
Anheuser-Busch	11.7	11.7	10.6
SABMiller	10.8	6.7	51.3
Coors	1.3	(10.0)	(7.0)
Interbrew[1]	n/a	8.4	(4.1)

December 2003

[1]Has not been traded for 5 years.

Exhibit 7.46 Beer Industry: Value Multiples

Excluding goodwill	Value/invested capital	Operating value/EBITA	2003 ROIC (percent)	1999–2003 ROIC (percent)
Heineken	2.8	12.1	16.5	19.0
Anheuser-Busch	6.4	15.7	24.8	20.3
SABMiller	4.5	11.0	36.6	33.5
Coors	2.8	12.3	13.9	14.5
Interbrew	4.0	13.7	22.1	17.6
Including goodwill				
Heineken	1.6	12.1	9.5	12.5
Anheuser-Busch	6.1	15.7	23.8	19.4
SABMiller	1.5	11.0	12.5	20.5
Coors	1.4	12.3	6.9	11.0
Interbrew	1.2	13.7	10.5	9.6

The matrix on the bottom of Exhibit 7.45 shows TRS and market-value-to-invested-capital simultaneously. Heineken is valued in line with Coors and SABMiller, but the market historically had high expectations for Heineken, so its TRS is lower. Anheuser-Busch had high value to invested capital as well as high TRS. Anheuser-Busch positively surprised the market during this period.

Heineken is valued at 12.1 times EBITA, in line with SABMiller, Coors, and Interbrew but below Anheuser-Busch at 15.7 times (see Exhibit 7.46). As the exhibit shows, all the peers have similar organic growth, so it is no surprise that differences in ROIC (without goodwill) drive the differences in earnings multiples.

LIQUIDITY, LEVERAGE, AND FINANCIAL HEALTH

Heineken's debt increased significantly in 2003, due to acquisitions. Despite the higher debt, interest coverage in 2003 was 7.2 times, a strong investment-grade level and also in line with peers (see Exhibit 7.47). Heineken retains significant financial flexibility for additional acquisitions or to weather difficult periods.

Exhibit 7.47 Beer Industry: Credit Ratios

Company	Adjusted EBITA $ million	Interest expense $ million	Adjusted EBITA/ interest expense	Gross cash flow/ interest expense	Debt to MV of investor funds (percent)
Heineken	1,605	227	7.1	8.4	24.5
Anheuser-Busch	3,201	376	8.5	2.8	14.5
SABMiller	1,198	163	7.3	6.9	33.8
Coors	272	70	4.0	6.0	33.9
Interbrew	996	131	8.0	10.0	21.2

REVIEW QUESTIONS

1. Why is it important to convert the balance sheet and income statement to reflect economic performance versus accounting performance?

2. Identify and explain the key steps to restate the company's balance sheet and income statement.

3. How do operating assets differ from nonoperating assets? How do operating assets differ from invested capital? Why is this differentiation important?

4. How does a manager adjust the income statement to compute NOPLAT? Why are the adjustments important?

5. Explain how net income differs from free cash flow. Why is the difference important when valuing a corporation?

6. Define ROIC. How does ROIC differ from ROA or ROI? Explain the process and importance of decomposing the ROIC ratio.

7. How does a corporation's choice of pension plan (defined contribution versus defined benefit) impact the computation of ROIC? What additional factors must be evaluated when computing invested capital, NOPLAT, and ROIC?

8. When should goodwill be included in the computation of ROIC?

Historical Balance Sheet for MKM, Inc.

$ millions	2003	2004
Cash	5	10
Marketable securities	155	107
Inventory	250	300
Current assets	410	417
Property, plant, and equipment	400	500
Equity investments at cost	100	75
Total assets	910	992
Accounts payable	200	210
Current portion of long-term debt	20	20
Current liabilities	220	230
Long-term debt	200	200
Equity	100	100
Retained earnings	390	462
Total liabilities and shareholder equity	910	992

Historical Income Statement for MKM, Inc.

$ millions	2003	2004
Revenue	810	880
Operating expenses	-600	-640
Depreciation	-80	-90
Operating profit	130	150
Interest income	5	5
Interest expense	-10	-10
Loss on equity investment	0	-25
Earnings before taxes	125	120
Taxes	-50	-48
Net income	75	72

9. Assuming the marginal tax rate equals 40 percent, compute MKM's EBITDA, NOPLAT, Invested Capital, and ROIC (for simplicity, use year-end invested capital). Is ROIC increasing or decreasing?

10. Decompose MKM's ROIC and explain how each component of the decomposition leads to an integrated perspective of performance. Address whether operating margins or capital turnover is driving the drop in ROIC.

11. Develop an economic profit statement for MKM. Assume an 11.1 percent weighted average cost of capital. Interpret the results from year to year.

12. Compute MKM's free cash flow in 2004. How can the company have negative free cash flow, even though it is creating value?

13. Compute MKM's interest coverage ratio. Is the interest coverage ratio improving?

8

Forecasting Performance

In Chapter 6 we focused on how to forecast long-run value drivers that are consistent with economic theory and historical evidence. In this chapter we focus on the mechanics of forecasting—specifically, how to develop an integrated set of financial forecasts that reflect the company's expected performance.

Although the future is unknowable, careful analysis can yield insights into how a company may develop. This chapter shows how to build a well-structured spreadsheet model: one that separates raw inputs from computations, flows from one worksheet to the next, and is flexible enough to handle multiple scenarios. Next we discuss the process of forecasting. To arrive at future cash flow, we forecast the income statement, balance sheet, and statement of retained earnings. The forecasted financial statements provide the information we need for computing ROIC and free cash flow.

While you are building a forecast, it is easy to become engrossed in the details of individual line items. But we stress, once again, that you must place your *aggregate* results in the proper context. You can do much more to improve your valuation by matching future ROIC against a company's competitive advantage than by precisely (but perhaps inaccurately) forecasting accounts receivable 10 years out. For this reason, we start by discussing the proper length and detail of a forecast.

DETERMINE LENGTH AND DETAIL OF THE FORECAST

Before you begin forecasting individual line items, you must determine how many years to forecast and how detailed your forecast should be. The typical solution, described in Chapter 5, is to develop an explicit forecast for

233

a number of years and then to value the remaining years by using a formula, such as the key value driver formula introduced in Chapter 3. But whatever formula you choose, all the continuing-value approaches assume steady-state performance. Thus, the explicit forecast period must be long enough for the company to reach a steady state, defined by the following characteristics:

- The company grows at a constant rate and reinvests a constant proportion of its operating profits into the business each year.
- The company earns a constant rate of return on new capital invested.
- The company earns a constant return on its base level of invested capital.

As a result, free cash flow will grow at a constant rate and can be valued using a growth perpetuity. The explicit forecast period should be long enough that the company's growth rate is less than or equal to that of the economy. Higher growth rates would eventually make companies unrealistically large, relative to the aggregate economy.

In general, we recommend using a forecast period of 10 to 15 years—perhaps longer for cyclical companies or those experiencing very rapid growth. Using a short explicit forecast period, such as five years, typically results in a significant undervaluation of a company or requires heroic long-term growth assumptions in the continuing value. Even so, a long forecast period raises its own issues, namely the difficulty of forecasting individual line items 10 to 15 years into the future. To simplify the model and avoid the error of false precision, we often split the explicit forecast into two periods:

1. A detailed five- to seven-year forecast, which develops complete balance sheets and income statements with as many links to real variables (e.g., unit volumes, cost per unit) as possible
2. A simplified forecast for the remaining years, focusing on a few important variables, such as revenue growth, margins, and capital turnover

This approach not only simplifies the forecast, it also forces you to focus on the business's long-term economics, rather than the individual line items of the forecast. The Heineken case at the end of the chapter demonstrates how this works.

COMPONENTS OF A GOOD MODEL

If you combine 15 years of financial forecasts with 10 years of historical analysis, any valuation spreadsheet becomes complex. Therefore, you need

Exhibit 8.1 Sample Excel Workbook

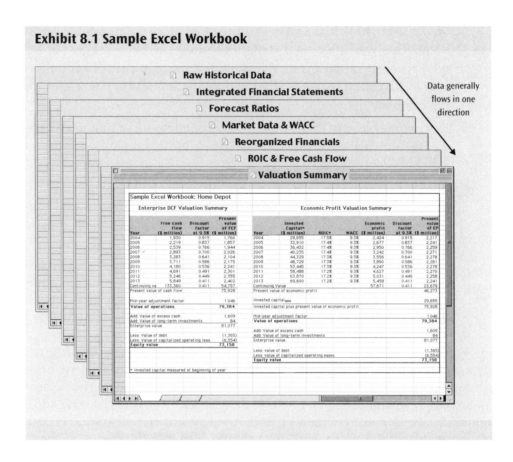

to design and structure your model before starting to forecast. Many designs are possible. In our example (see Exhibit 8.1), the Excel workbook contains seven worksheets:

1. *Raw historical data:* Collect raw data from the company's financial statements, footnotes, and external reports in one place. Report the raw data in its original form.

2. *Integrated financial statements:* Using figures from the raw-data worksheet, create a set of historical financials that find the right level of detail. The income statement should be linked with the balance sheet through retained earnings. This worksheet will contain historical and forecasted financial statements.

3. *Historical analysis and forecast ratios:* For each line item in the financial statements, build historical ratios, as well as forecasts of future ratios. These ratios will generate the forecasted financial statements contained on the previous sheet.

4. *Market data and WACC:* Collect all financial market data on one worksheet. This worksheet will contain estimates of beta, the cost of equity, the cost of debt, and the weighted average cost of capital, as well as historical market values and valuation/trading multiples for the company.

5. *Reorganized financial statements:* Once a complete set of financial statements (both historical and forecasted) are built, reorganize the financial statements to calculate NOPLAT, its reconciliation to net income, invested capital, and its reconciliation to total funds invested.

6. *ROIC and free cash flow:* Use the reorganized financials to build return on invested capital, economic profit, and free cash flow. Future free cash flow will be the basis of your valuation.

7. *Valuation summary:* This worksheet presents discounted cash flows, discounted economic profits, and final results. The valuation summary includes the value of operations, nonoperating asset valuations, valuation of nonequity claims, and the resulting equity value.

Well-built valuation models have certain characteristics. First, original data and user input are collected in only a few places. For instance, we limit original data and user input to just three worksheets: raw data (worksheet 1), forecasts (worksheet 3), and market data (worksheet 4). To provide additional clarity, denote raw data or user input in a different color. Second, whenever possible, a given worksheet should feed into the next worksheet. Formulas should not bounce from sheet to sheet without clear direction. Raw data should feed into integrated financials, which, in turn, should feed into ROIC and free cash flow. Finally, unless specified as data input, numbers should *never* be hard-coded into a formula. Hard-coded numbers are easily lost as the spreadsheet grows in complexity.

MECHANICS OF FORECASTING

The enterprise DCF relies on forecasted free cash flow. But as noted at the beginning of this chapter, free cash flow forecasts should be created indirectly by first forecasting the income statement, balance sheet, and statement of retained earnings. Compute forecasted free cash flow in the same way as when analyzing historical performance. (A well-built spreadsheet will use the same formulas for historical and forecasted periods without any modification.)

We can break the forecasting process into six steps:

1. *Prepare and analyze historical financials.* Before forecasting future financials, you must build and analyze historical financials.

2. *Build the revenue forecast.* Almost every line item will rely directly or indirectly on revenue. You can estimate future revenue by using either a top-down (market-based) or bottom-up (customer-based) approach. Forecasts should be consistent with historical economy-wide evidence on growth.

3. *Forecast the income statement.* Use the appropriate economic drivers to forecast operating expenses, depreciation, interest income, interest expense, and reported taxes.

4. *Forecast the balance sheet: invested capital and nonoperating assets.* On the balance sheet, forecast operating working capital; net property, plant, and equipment; goodwill; and nonoperating assets.

5. *Forecast the balance sheet: investor funds.* Complete the balance sheet by computing retained earnings and forecasting other equity accounts. Use excess cash and/or new debt to balance the balance sheet.

6. *Calculate ROIC and FCF.* Calculate ROIC to assure forecasts are consistent with economic principles, industry dynamics, and the company's ability to compete. To complete the forecast, calculate free cash flow as the basis for valuation. Future FCF should be calculated the same way as historical FCF.

Give extra emphasis to forecasting revenue. Almost every line item in the spreadsheet will be either directly or indirectly driven by revenues, so you should devote enough time to arrive at a good revenue forecast, especially for rapidly growing businesses.

Step 1: Prepare and Analyze Historical Financials

Before you start building a forecast, you must input the company's historical financials into a spreadsheet program. To do this, you can rely on data from a professional service, such as Standard & Poor's Compustat, or you can use financials directly from the company's filings. Professional services offer the benefit of standardized data (i.e., financial data formatted into a set number of categories). Since data items do not change across companies, a single model can analyze any company. However, using a standardized data set carries a *significant* cost. Many of the specified categories aggregate important items, hiding critical information. For instance, Compustat groups "advances to sales staff" (an operating asset) and "pension and other special funds" (a nonoperating asset) into a single category titled "other assets." Because of this, models based solely on preformatted data can lead to significant errors in the estimation of value drivers, and hence to poor valuations.

Alternatively, you can build a model using financials from the company's annual report. To use raw data, however, you must dig. Often, companies

Exhibit 8.2 Boeing: Current Liabilities in Balance Sheet

$ million

Balance sheet	2002	2003
Accounts payable and other liabilities	13,739	13,563
Advances in excess of related costs	3,123	3,464
Income taxes payable	1,134	277
Short-term debt and current portion of long-term debt	1,814	1,144
Current liabilities	**19,810**	**18,448**
From note 12–Accounts payable and other liabilities:		
Accounts payable	4,431	3,822
Accrued compensation and employee benefit costs	2,876	2,930
Pension liabilities	1,177	1,138
Product warranty liabilities	898	825
Lease and other deposits	280	316
Dividends payable	143	143
Other	3,934	4,389
Accounts payable and other liabilities	**13,739**	**13,563**

Source: Boeing 10-K, 2003.

aggregate critical information to simplify their financial statements. Consider, for instance, the financials for Boeing presented in Exhibit 8.2. On Boeing's reported balance sheet, the company consolidates many items into the account titled "accounts payable and other liabilities." In the notes to the balance sheet, note 12 details this line item. Some of the components (such as accounts payable), are operating liabilities, and others (such as dividends payable) are nonoperating.

We prefer to collect raw data on a separate worksheet. On the raw-data sheet, record financial data as originally reported, and never combine multiple data into a single cell. Once you have collected raw data from the reported financials *and* notes, use the data to build a set of financial statements: the income statement, balance sheet, and statement of retained earnings. Although the statement of retained earnings appears redundant, it will be critical for error checking during the forecasting process, because it connects the income statement to the balance sheet.

As you build the integrated financials, you must decide whether to aggregate immaterial line items. Analyzing and forecasting numerous immaterial items can lead to confusion, introduce mistakes, and cause the model to become unwieldy. Returning to the Boeing example presented in Exhibit 8.2, "lease and other deposits" are well under 1 percent of Boeing's revenue. Therefore, the valuation model can be simplified by combining this account with other (operating) liabilities. When aggregating, make sure never to combine operating and nonoperating items into a single category. If the two accounts are combined, you cannot calculate ROIC and FCF properly.

Step 2: Build the Revenue Forecast

To build a revenue forecast, you can use a top-down forecast, in which you estimate revenues by sizing the total market, determining market share, and forecasting prices. Or with the bottom-up approach, use the company's own forecasts of demand from existing customers, customer turnover, and the potential for new customers. When possible, use both methods to establish bounds for the forecast.

The top-down approach can be applied to any company. For companies in mature industries, the aggregate market grows slowly and is closely tied to economic growth and other long-term trends, such as changing consumer preferences. In these situations, you can rely on professional forecasts of the aggregate market and instead focus on market share by competitor.[1] To do this, you must determine which companies have the capabilities and resources to compete effectively and capture share. A good place to start, of course, is with historical financial analysis. But more importantly, make sure to address how the company is positioned for the future. Does it have the required products and services to capture share? Do other competitors have products and services that will displace your company's market position? A good forecast will address each of these issues.

Over the short-term, top-down forecasts should build on the company's announced intentions and capabilities for growth. For instance, retailers like Wal-Mart have well-mapped plans for new store openings, which is their primary driver of revenue growth. Oil companies like BP have proven reserves and relatively fixed amounts of refining capacity. And pharmaceutical companies like Merck have a fixed set of drugs under patent and in clinical trials.

In emerging-product markets, the top-down approach is especially helpful but often requires more work than for established markets. For instance, consider the recent launch of the digital video recorder (DVR). Given its lack of history, how do you estimate the potential size and speed of penetration for companies in the DVR market? You could start by sizing the current (or peak) VCR market. Analyze whether DVRs, given their greater ease of use, will incur even greater adoption. Next, forecast how quickly DVRs will penetrate households. To do this, look at the speed of penetration for other household electronics, such as the CD player or the

---

[1] For the automobile industry, for instance, Datamonitor publishes the *Automobile Manufacturers Global Industry Guide*. The report includes a five-year forecast of aggregate unit volume by geographic region.

DVD player. It is necessary to determine the characteristics that drive penetration speeds in each of these markets and how the DVR compares with these characteristics. Finally, what price (and margin) do you expect from the DVR? How many companies are developing the product, and how competitive will the market be? As you can see, there are more questions than answers. The key is structuring the analysis and applying historical evidence from comparable markets whenever possible.

Whereas a top-down approach starts with the aggregate market and predicts penetration rates, price changes, and market shares, a bottom-up approach relies on projections of customer demand. In some industries, customers have projected their own revenue forecasts and will give suppliers a rough estimate of their own purchase projections. By aggregating across customers, you can determine short-term forecasts of revenue from the current customer base. Next, estimate the rate of customer turnover. If customer turnover is significant, you have to eliminate a portion of estimated revenues. As a final step, project how many new customers the company will attract and how much revenue those customers will contribute. The resulting bottom-up forecast combines new customers with revenues from existing customers.

Regardless of the method, forecasting revenues over long time periods is imprecise. Customer preferences, technologies, and corporate strategies change. These often unpredictable changes can profoundly influence the winners and losers in the marketplace. Therefore, you must constantly reevaluate whether the current forecast is consistent with industry dynamics, competitive positioning, and the historical evidence on corporate growth. If you lack confidence in your revenue forecast, use multiple scenarios to model uncertainty. Doing this will not only bound the forecast, but will also help company management make better decisions.

Step 3: Forecast the Income Statement

With a revenue forecast in place, next forecast individual line items related to the income statement. To forecast a line item, use a three-step process:

1. *Decide what economically drives the line item.* For most line items, forecasts will be tied directly to revenue. Some line items will be economically tied to a specific asset (or liability). For instance, interest income is usually generated by liquid securities; if this is the case, forecasts of interest income should be tied to liquid securities.

2. *Estimate the forecast ratio.* For each line item on the income statement, compute historical values for each ratio, followed by estimates for each of the forecast periods. To get the model working properly, initially set the forecast ratio equal to the previous year's value. Once the entire model is complete, return to the forecast page, and input your best estimates.

3. *Multiply the forecast ratio by an estimate of its driver.* Since most line items are driven by revenue, most forecast ratios, such as COGS to revenue, should be applied to estimates of future revenue. This is why a good revenue forecast is critical. Any error in the revenue forecast will be carried through the entire model. Other ratios should be multiplied by their respective drivers.

Exhibit 8.3 presents the historical income statement and partially completed forecast for a hypothetical company. To demonstrate the three-step process, we forecast cost of goods sold. In the first step, we calculate historical COGS as a function of revenue. Then we compute the historical ratio of COGS to revenue, which equals 37.5 percent. For simplicity, we initially set next year's ratio equal to 37.5 percent as well. Finally, we multiply the forecasted ratio by an estimate of next year's revenue: 37.5 percent × $288 million = $108 million.

Note that we did not forecast COGS by increasing the account by 20 percent (the same growth rate as revenue). Although this process leads to the same initial answer, it dramatically reduces flexibility. Because we used a forecast ratio, we can either vary estimates of revenue (and COGS will change in step) or vary the forecast ratio (for instance, to value a potential improvement). If we had increased the COGS directly, however, we could only vary the growth rate.

Exhibit 8.3 Partial Forecast of the Income Statement

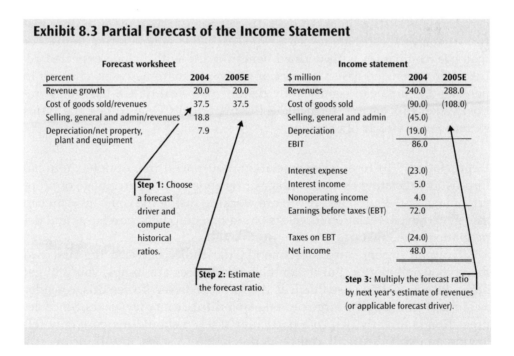

Forecast worksheet				Income statement		
percent		2004	2005E	$ million	2004	2005E
Revenue growth		20.0	20.0	Revenues	240.0	288.0
Cost of goods sold/revenues		37.5	37.5	Cost of goods sold	(90.0)	(108.0)
Selling, general and admin/revenues		18.8		Selling, general and admin	(45.0)	
Depreciation/net property, plant and equipment		7.9		Depreciation	(19.0)	
				EBIT	86.0	
				Interest expense	(23.0)	
Step 1: Choose a forecast driver and compute historical ratios.				Interest income	5.0	
				Nonoperating income	4.0	
				Earnings before taxes (EBT)	72.0	
				Taxes on EBT	(24.0)	
				Net income	48.0	

Step 2: Estimate the forecast ratio.

Step 3: Multiply the forecast ratio by next year's estimate of revenues (or applicable forecast driver).

Exhibit 8.4 Typical Forecast Drivers for the Income Statement

	Line item	Recommended forecast driver	Recommended forecast ratio
Operating	Cost of goods sold (COGS)	Revenue	COGS/revenue
	Selling, general, and administrative (SG&A)	Revenue	SG&A/revenue
	Depreciation	Prior year net property, plant, and equipment (PP&E)	Depreciation/net PP&E
Nonoperating	Nonoperating income	Appropriate nonoperating asset, if any	Nonoperating income/ nonoperating asset or growth in nonoperating income
	Interest expense	Prior year total debt	Interest expense (t)/total debt (t-1)
	Interest income	Prior year excess cash	Interest income (t)/excess cash (t-1)

Exhibit 8.4 presents typical forecast drivers and forecast ratios for the most common financial statement line items. The appropriate choice for a forecast driver, however, depends on the company and the industry in which it competes.

Operating expenses   For each operating expense on the income statement—such as cost of goods sold; selling, general, and administrative; and research and development—we recommend generating forecasts based on revenue. In most cases, the process for operating expenses is straightforward. However, as we outlined in Chapter 7, accountants sometimes include certain nonoperating items in operating expenses. As done in proper historical analysis, estimate forecast ratios *excluding* nonoperating items. For instance, companies with defined-benefit plans will include expected returns from pension assets as part of COGS. In extreme cases, changes in pension accounts can significantly distort historical COGS-to-revenue ratios. When this occurs, recalculate the historical COGS-to-revenue ratios excluding the effects of pensions.

Depreciation   To forecast depreciation, you have three options. You can forecast depreciation as a percentage of revenue or as a percentage of property, plant, and equipment. If you are working inside the company, you can also generate depreciation forecasts based on equipment purchases and depreciation schedules.

If capital expenditures are smooth, the choice between the first two methods won't matter. But if capital expenditures are lumpy, you will get better forecasts if you use PP&E as the forecast driver. To see this, consider a company that makes a large capital expenditure every few years. Since depreciation is directly tied to a particular asset, it should increase only following an expenditure. If you tie depreciation to sales, it will incorrectly grow as revenues grow, even when expenditures haven't been made.

Exhibit 8.5 Completed Forecast of the Income Statement

Forecast worksheet			Income statement		
percent	2004	2005E	$ million	2004	2005E
Revenue growth	20.0	20.0	Revenues	240.0	288.0
Cost of goods sold/revenue	37.5	37.5	Cost of goods sold	(90.0)	(108.0)
Selling, general and admin/revenue	18.8	18.8	Selling, general and admin	(45.0)	(54.0)
Depreciation/revenue	7.9	7.9	Depreciation	(19.0)	(22.8)
EBIT/revenue	35.8	35.8	EBIT	86.0	103.2
Nonoperating items			Interest expense	(23.0)	(22.2)
Nonoperating income growth	33.3	33.3	Interest income	5.0	3.0
			Nonoperating income	4.0	5.3
Interest rates			Earnings before taxes (EBT)	72.0	89.4
Interest expense	7.6	7.6			
Interest income	5.0	5.0	Taxes on EBT	(24.0)	(30.0)
			Net income	48.0	59.4
Taxes					
Operating tax rate	34.4	34.4			
Marginal tax rate	40.0	40.0			
Average tax rate	33.3	33.6			

When using PP&E as the forecast driver, tie depreciation to *net* PP&E, rather than gross PP&E. Ideally, depreciation would be tied to gross PP&E. Otherwise, a company that purchases only one asset would see an annual drop in depreciation as the asset depreciates (the ratio of depreciation to net PP&E is fixed, not the dollar amount). But tying depreciation to gross PP&E requires forecasting asset retirements. Specifically, when assets are fully depreciated, they must be removed from gross PP&E, or else you will over-estimate depreciation (and its tax shield) in the outer years.

If you have access to detailed, internal information about the company's assets, you can build formal depreciation tables. For each asset, project depreciation using an appropriate depreciation schedule, asset life, and salvage value. To determine companywide depreciation, combine the annual depreciation of each asset.

In Exhibit 8.5, we present a forecast of depreciation, as well as the remaining line items on the income statement. In this example, we assume capital expenditures are smooth. Therefore, we forecast depreciation as a percentage of sales.

Nonoperating income   Nonoperating income is generated by nonoperating assets, such as customer financing, nonconsolidated subsidiaries, and other equity investments.[2] For nonconsolidated subsidiaries and other

[2] See Chapter 11 for additional information on the accounting treatment and valuation of non-operating assets.

equity investments, the forecast methodology depends on how much information is reported. For investments in which the parent company owns less than 20 percent, the company records only dividends received and asset sales. The nonoperating asset is recorded at cost, which remains unchanged until sold. For these investments, you cannot use traditional drivers to forecast cash flows; instead, estimate future nonoperating income by examining historical growth in nonoperating income or by examining the revenue and profit forecasts of publicly traded comparables (comparable to the equity investment).

For nonconsolidated subsidiaries with greater than 20 percent ownership, the parent company records income even when it is not paid out. Also, the recorded asset grows as the investment's retained earnings grow. Thus, you can estimate future income from the nonconsolidated investment either by forecasting a nonoperating income growth rate or by forecasting return on equity (nonoperating income as a percentage of the appropriate nonoperating asset) based on industry dynamics and the competitive position of the subsidiary.

Interest expense and interest income   Interest expense (income) should be tied directly to the liability (asset) that generates the expense (income). The appropriate driver for interest expense is total debt. Total debt, however, is a function of interest expense, and this circularity leads to implementation problems. To see this, consider a rise in operating costs. If the company uses debt to fund short-term needs, total debt will rise to cover the financing gap caused by lower profits. This increased debt load will cause interest expense to rise, dropping profits even further. Lower profits, once again, requires more debt. To avoid the complexity of this feedback effect, compute interest expense as a function of the previous year's debt load. This shortcut will simplify the model and lead to minimal estimation error.[3]

To forecast interest expense using the prior year's debt, we need the historical income statement (see Exhibit 8.5) and balance sheet (see Exhibit 8.6) of our hypothetical company. To estimate future interest expense, start with 2004 interest expense ($23 million), and divide by 2003's total debt ($304 million, found by aggregating short-term debt of $224 million plus long-term debt of $80 million). This ratio equals 7.6 percent. To estimate 2005 interest expense, multiply the estimated forecast ratio (7.6 percent) by 2004 total debt ($293 million), which leads to a forecast of $22.2 million. Note how interest expense is falling, even while revenue rises, because total debt is shrinking. Thus, net income can change as a percentage of revenue, even when forecast ratios are constant.

---

[3] If you are using last year's debt multiplied by current interest rates to forecast interest expense, the forecast error will be greatest when year-to-year changes in debt are significant.

Exhibit 8.6 Historical Balance Sheet

$ million

Assets	2003	2004	Liabilities and equity	2003	2004
Cash	5.0	5.0	Accounts payable	15.0	20.0
Excess cash	100.0	60.0	Short-term debt	224.0	213.0
Inventory	35.0	45.0	Current liabilities	239.0	233.0
Current assets	140.0	110.0			
			Long-term debt	80.0	80.0
Net property, plant, and equipment	200.0	250.0	Common stock	65.0	65.0
Equity investments	100.0	100.0	Retained earnings	56.0	82.0
Total assets	440.0	460.0	Total liabilities and equity	440.0	460.0

Using historical interest rates to forecast interest expense is a simple, straightforward estimation method. And since interest expense is not part of free cash flow, the choice of how to forecast interest expense will *not* affect the company's valuation (the cost of debt is modeled as part of the weighted average cost of capital). When a company's financial structure is a critical part of the forecast, however, split debt (and interest expense) into two categories, existing debt and new debt. Until repaid, existing debt should generate interest expense consistent with historical rates. Interest expense based on new debt, in contrast, should be paid at current market rates. Unless management specifically projects particular maturities, assume the company will raise 10-year bonds. Thus, projected interest expense should be calculated using the 10-year yield to maturity for comparably rated debt.

Estimate interest income the same way, with forecasts based on the asset generating the income. Be careful: interest income can be generated by a number of different investments, including excess cash, short-term investments, customer financing, and other long-term investments. If a footnote details the historical relation between interest income and the assets that generate the income (and the relation is material), develop a separate calculation for each asset.

Taxes   In a simple model, you can estimate reported taxes as a percentage of earnings before taxes. When the company's average tax rate does not equal its marginal tax rate, as is the case for most companies, you need a more complicated forecasting approach.[4] Otherwise, ROIC and free cash flow in forecast years will inadvertently change as leverage and nonoperating income change. Therefore, base free cash flow forecasts on the operating tax rate, not on the

---

[4] To compute the average tax rate, divide taxes by earnings before taxes. The marginal tax rate equals the tax rate on the next dollar of income.

average tax rate. As described in Chapter 7, calculate the historical operating tax rate as follows:

$$\text{Operating Tax Rate} = \frac{\text{Reported Taxes} + \Sigma T_m(\text{NOE}) - \Sigma T_m(\text{NOI})}{\text{EBITA}}$$

where T_m = Marginal tax rate by nonoperating item
NOE = Nonoperating expense, such as interest expense
NOI = Nonoperating income, such as income from liquid securities

Exhibit 8.7 calculates operating taxes (for 2003 and 2004) for our sample company. In 2004, reported taxes equal $24.0 million and operating taxes equal $29.6 million. Dividing operating taxes by EBITA gives us the operating tax rate, which in 2004 is 34.4 percent.

Next, to forecast *reported* taxes, proceed in two steps. First, estimate operating taxes going forward: multiply the forecasted operating tax rate by the forecast of EBITA (in our example, we assume the operating tax rate will remain constant). Next, to determine reported taxes, subtract the projected interest tax shield (interest times the marginal tax rate), and add any marginal taxes on nonoperating income. You now have a forecast of both operating and reported taxes, calculated such that future values of FCF and ROIC will not change with leverage.

For our sample company, the operating tax rate differs from the marginal tax rate. Often this occurs because of special tax credits that are granted for certain investments. If you use historical tax rates to forecast future tax rates, you implicitly assume that these special incentives will grow in line with EBITA. If this is not the case, EBITA should be taxed at the marginal rate, and tax credits should be forecast one by one.

Exhibit 8.7 Forecast of Reported Taxes

$ million

	2003	2004	2005E	
Reported taxes	17.0	24.0	30.0	
Taxes on interest expense	6.8	9.2	8.9	Forecast operating taxes
Taxes on interest income	(1.2)	(2.0)	(1.2)	first and work backwards
Taxes on nonoperating income	(1.2)	(1.6)	(2.1)	to estimate reported taxes
Operating taxes	21.4	29.6	**35.5**	
Forecast driver				
EBITA	64.0	86.0	103.2	
Operating tax rate (percent)	33.4	34.4	34.4	
Operating taxes	21.4	29.6	35.5	

Step 4: Forecast the Balance Sheet: Invested Capital and Nonoperating Assets

To forecast the balance sheet, we first forecast invested capital and nonoperating assets. We do not, however, forecast excess cash or sources of financing (such as debt and equity). Excess cash and sources of financing require special treatment and will be handled in Step 5.

When you forecast the balance sheet, one of the first issues you face is whether to forecast the line items in the balance sheet directly (in stocks) or indirectly by forecasting changes (in flows). For example, the stocks approach forecasts end-of-year receivables as a function of revenue, and the flow approach forecasts the change in receivables as a function of the growth in revenue. We favor the stocks approach. The relationship between the balance sheet accounts and revenue (or other volume measures) is more stable than that between balance sheet changes and changes in revenue. Consider the example presented in Exhibit 8.8. The ratio of accounts receivable to revenue remains within a tight band between 9.5 percent and 10.4 percent, while the ratio of changes in accounts receivable to changes in revenues ranges from 5 percent to 18 percent.

To forecast the balance sheet, start with items related to invested capital and nonoperating assets. Exhibit 8.9 on page 248 summarizes forecast drivers and forecast ratios for the most common line items.

Operating working capital   To start the balance sheet, forecast items within operating working capital, such as accounts receivable, inventories, accounts payable, and accrued expenses. Remember, operating working capital excludes any nonoperating items, such as excess cash (cash not needed to operate the business), short-term debt, and dividends payable.

When forecasting operating working capital, estimate most line items as a percentage of revenue. Possible exceptions are inventories and accounts payable. Since these two accounts are tied to input prices, estimate them instead as a percentage of cost of goods sold (which is also tied to input prices).

Exhibit 8.8 Stock versus Flow Example

	Year 1	Year 2	Year 3	Year 4
Revenue ($)	1,000	1,100	1,200	1,300
Accounts receivable ($)	100	105	117	135
Stock method				
Accounts receivable as a percentage of revenue	10.0	9.5	9.8	10.4
Flow method				
Change in accounts receivable as a percentage of the change in revenue		5.0	12.0	18.0

Exhibit 8.9 Typical Forecast Drivers and Ratios for the Balance Sheet

	Line item	Typical forecast driver	Typical forecast ratio
Operating line items	Accounts receivable	Revenue	Accounts receivable/revenue
	Inventories	Cost of goods sold	Inventories/COGS
	Accounts payable	Cost of goods sold	Accounts payable/COGS
	Accrued expenses	Revenue	Accrued expenses/revenue
	Net PP&E	Revenue	Net PP&E/revenue
	Goodwill	Acquired revenues	Goodwill/acquired revenue
Nonoperating line items	Nonoperating assets	None	Growth in nonoperating assets
	Pension assets or liabilities	None	Trend towards zero
	Deferred taxes	Adjusted taxes	Change in deferred taxes/adjusted taxes

However, as a practical matter, we usually simplify the forecast model by projecting each working capital item using revenues. The distinction is material only when price is expected to deviate significantly away from cost per unit.

In Exhibit 8.10, we present a forecast of operating working capital, long-term operating assets, and nonoperating assets (investor funds will be detailed later). All working capital items are forecasted in days, computed

Exhibit 8.10 Partial Forecast of the Balance Sheet

Forecast worksheet			Balance sheet		
Forecast ratio	2004	2005E	$ million	2004	2005E
Cash (in days)	7.6	7.6	Cash	5.0	6.0
Inventory (in days)	68.4	68.4	Excess cash	60.0	
Accounts payable (in days)	(30.4)	(30.4)	Inventory	45.0	54.0
Net working capital (in days)	45.6	45.6	Current assets	110.0	
Fixed assets (percent)			Net PP&E	250.0	300.0
Net PP&E/revenues	104.2	104.2	Equity investments	100.0	100.0
			Total assets	**460.0**	**460.0**
Nonoperating assets (percent)					
Growth in equity investments	0.0	0.0	**Liabilities and equity**		
			Accounts payable	20.0	24.0
			Short-term debt	213.0	
			Current liabilities	233.0	
			Long-term debt	80.0	
			Newly issued debt	0.0	
			Common stock	65.0	
			Retained earnings	82.0	
			Total liabilities and equity	**460.0**	

using revenues. Working cash is estimated at 7.6 days of revenue, inventory at 68.4 days of revenue, and accounts payable at 30.4 days of revenue. We forecast in days for the added benefit of tying forecasts more closely to operations. For instance, if management announces its intention to reduce its inventory holding period from 45 days to 30 days, we can compute changes in value by adjusting the forecast directly.

Property, plant, and equipment   Consistent with our earlier argument concerning stocks and flows, net PP&E should be forecast as a percentage of revenues. A common alternative is to forecast capital expenditures as a percentage of revenues. However, this method too easily leads to unintended increases or decreases in capital turnover (the ratio of PP&E to revenues). Over long periods, companies' ratios of net PP&E to revenues tend to be quite stable, so we favor the following approach for PP&E:

- Forecast net PP&E as a percentage of revenues.
- Forecast depreciation, typically as a percentage of gross or net PP&E.
- Calculate capital expenditures by computing the increase in net PP&E plus depreciation.

To continue our example, we use the forecasts presented in Exhibit 8.10 to estimate expected capital expenditures. In 2004, net PP&E equaled 104.2 percent of revenues. If this ratio is held constant for 2005, the forecast of net PP&E equals $300 million. To estimate capital expenditures, compute the increase in net PP&E ($50 million), and add depreciation ($22.8 million). Capital expenditures, therefore, are projected to equal $72.8 million.

If you forecast PP&E as a percentage of sales, always calculate and analyze implied capital expenditures. For companies with low growth rates and projected improvements in capital efficiency, the resulting capital expenditure projections may be negative (implying asset sales), which in turn, leads to positive cash flow. Although asset sales at book value are possible, they are unlikely.

Goodwill   A company records goodwill when the price it paid for an acquisition exceeds the target's book value. For most companies, we choose not to explicitly model potential acquisitions, so we set revenue growth from acquisitions equal to zero and hold goodwill constant at its current level. We prefer this approach because of the empirical literature documenting how the *typical* acquisition fails to create value (any synergies are transferred to the target through high premiums). Since adding a zero-NPV investment will not increase the company's value, forecasting acquisitions is unnecessary. In fact, by forecasting acquired growth in combination with the company's current financial results, you make implicit (and often hidden) assumptions about the present value of acquisitions. For instance, if the forecast ratio of goodwill to acquired revenue implies positive NPV for acquired growth, increasing the growth rate from acquired revenue can dramatically increase the resulting valuation, even when good deals are hard to find.

If you decide to forecast acquisitions, first assess what proportion of future revenue growth they are likely to provide. For example, consider a company with $100 million in revenue that has announced an intention to grow by 10 percent annually—5 percent organically and 5 percent through acquisitions. In this case, measure historical ratios of goodwill to acquired revenue and apply those ratios to acquired revenue. For instance, assume the company historically adds $3 in goodwill for every $1 of acquired revenue. Multiplying the expected $5 million of acquired growth by 3, we obtain an expected increase of $15 million in goodwill. Make sure, however, to perform a reality check on your results by varying acquired growth and observing the resulting changes in company value. Confirm that your results are consistent with the company's historical performance concerning recent acquisitions and marketwide empirical evidence.

Nonoperating assets, debt, and equity equivalents Next, forecast nonoperating assets (such as nonconsolidated subsidiaries and equity investments), existing debt, and equity equivalents (such as pension liabilities and deferred taxes). Because many nonoperating items are valued using methods other than discounted cash flow (see Chapter 11), we usually create forecasts solely for the purpose of financial planning. For instance, consider unfunded pension liabilities. Assume management announces its intention to reduce unfunded pensions by 50 percent over the next five years. To value unfunded pensions, do *not* discount the projected outflows over the next five years. Instead, use the *current* actuarial assessments of the shortfall, which appears in the footnote on pensions. The rate of reduction will have no valuation implications but will affect the ability to pay dividends or require additional debt at particular times. To this end, model a reasonable time frame for eliminating pension shortfalls.

We are extremely cautious about forecasting (and valuing) nonconsolidated subsidiaries and other equity investments. Valuations should be based on assessing the investments currently owned, not on discounting the forecasted changes in their book values and resulting income. If a forecast is necessary for planning, consider that nonoperating assets often grow in a lumpy fashion, unrelated to a company's revenues. To forecast equity investments, rely on historical precedent to determine the appropriate level of growth.

Regarding deferred taxes, those used to occur primarily through differences in depreciation schedules (investor and tax authorities use different depreciation schedules to determine taxable income). Today, deferred taxes arise for many reasons, including tax adjustments for pensions, stock-based compensation, goodwill amortization, and deferred revenues. For sophisticated valuations that require extremely detailed forecasts, forecast deferred taxes line by line, tying each tax to its appropriate driver. In most situations, forecasting deferred taxes by computing the proportion of taxes likely to be deferred will lead to reasonable results. For instance, if operating taxes are estimated at 34.4 percent of EBITA and the company historically has been able to incrementally defer one-fifth of taxes paid, we assume it can defer $\frac{1}{5} \times 34.4$ percent going forward. Liabilities will then increase by the amount deferred.

Step 5: Forecast the Balance Sheet: Investor Funds

To complete the balance sheet, forecast the company's sources of financing. To do this, rely on the rules of accounting. First, use the principle of clean surplus accounting:

$$\text{Retained Earnings}_{(t+1)} = \text{Retained Earnings}_t + \text{Net Income} - \text{Dividends}$$

Returning to our earlier example, Exhibit 8.11 presents the statement of retained earnings. To estimate retained earnings in 2005, start with 2004 retained earnings of $82.0 million. To this value, add the 2005 forecast of net income (from the income statement) of $59.4 million. Next, estimate the dividend payout. In 2004, the company paid out 45.8 percent of net income in the form of dividends. Applying a 45.8 percent payout ratio to estimated net income leads to $27.2 million in expected dividends. Using the clean surplus relation, we estimate 2005 retained earnings at $114.2 million.

At this point, five line items remain: excess cash, short-term debt, long-term debt, a new account titled newly issued debt, and common stock. Some combination of these line items must make the balance sheet balance. For this reason, these items are often referred to as "the plug." In simple models, assume common stock remains constant and existing debt either remains constant or is retired on schedule. To complete the balance sheet, set one of the remaining two items (excess cash or newly issued debt) equal to

Exhibit 8.11 Statement of Retained Earnings

$ million

	2003	2004	2005E
Starting retained earnings	36.0	56.0	82.0
Net income	36.0	48.0	59.4
Dividends declared	(16.0)	(22.0)	(27.2)
Ending retained earnings	56.0	82.0	114.2
Dividends/net income (percent)	44.4	45.8	45.8

Exhibit 8.12: Forecast Balance Sheet: Sources of Financing

$ million

	2003	2004	2005E	Completed 2005E	
Cash	5.0	5.0	6.0	6.0	**Step 1:** Determine retained
Excess cash	100.0	60.0		36.2	earnings using the clean
Inventory	35.0	45.0	54.0	54.0	surplus relation, forecast
Current assets	140.0	110.0		96.2	existing debt using
					contractual terms, and keep
Net PP&E	200.0	250.0	300.0	300.0	equity constant.
Equity investments	100.0	100.0	100.0	100.0	
Total assets	**440.0**	**460.0**		**496.2**	**Step 2:** Test which is higher, assets
					excluding excess cash or
Liabilities and equity					liabilities and equity,
Accounts payable	15.0	20.0	24.0	24.0	excluding newly issued
Short-term debt	224.0	213.0	213.0	213.0	debt.
Current liabilities	239.0	233.0	237.0	237.0	
					Step 3: If assets excluding excess
Long-term debt	80.0	80.0	80.0	80.0	cash are higher, set excess
Newly issued debt	0.0	0.0		0.0	cash equal to zero and plug
Common stock	65.0	65.0	65.0	65.0	the difference with newly
Retained earnings	56.0	82.0	114.2	114.2	issued debt. Otherwise, plug
Total liabilities and equity	**440.0**	**460.0**		**496.2**	with excess cash.

zero. Then use the primary accounting identity—assets equal liabilities plus shareholder's equity—to value the remaining item.

Exhibit 8.12 presents the elements of this process for our example. First, hold short-term debt, long-term debt, and common stock constant. Next, sum total assets, excluding excess cash: cash ($6 million), inventory ($54 million), net PP&E ($300 million), and equity investments ($100 million) total $460 million. Then sum total liabilities and equity, excluding newly issued debt: accounts payable ($24 million), short-term debt ($213 million), long-term debt ($80 million), common stock ($65 million), and retained earnings ($114.2 million) total $496.2 million. Because residual liabilities and equity (excluding newly issued debt) are greater than residual assets (excluding excess marketable securities), newly issued debt is set to zero. Now total liabilities and equity equal $496.2 million. To assure the balance sheet balances, we set the only remaining item, excess cash, equal to $36.2 million. This increases total assets to $496.2 million, and the balance sheet is complete.

To implement this procedure in a spreadsheet, use Microsoft Excel's prebuilt "IF" function. Use the function to set excess cash to zero when assets (excluding excess cash) exceed liabilities and equity (excluding newly issued debt). Conversely, if assets are less than liabilities and equity, use the function to set short-term debt equal to zero and excess cash equal to the difference.

How capital structure affects valuation   When using excess cash and newly issued debt to complete the balance sheet, you will likely encounter one common side effect: as growth drops, newly issued debt will drop to zero, and excess cash will become very large. But what if a drop in leverage is inconsistent with your long-term assessments concerning capital structure? From a valuation perspective, this side effect does not matter. Excess cash and debt are not included as part of free cash flow, so they do not affect the enterprise valuation. Capital structure only affects enterprise DCF through the weighted average cost of capital. Thus, only an adjustment to WACC will lead to a change in valuation.

To bring capital structure in the balance sheet in line with capital structure implied by WACC, adjust the dividend payout ratio or amount of net share repurchases. For instance, as the dividend payout is increased, retained earnings will drop, and this should cause excess cash to drop as well. By varying the payout ratio, you can also test the robustness of your FCF model. Specifically, ROIC and FCF, and hence value, should not change when the dividend rate is adjusted.

How you choose to model the payout ratio depends on the requirements of the model. In most situations, you can adjust the dividend payout ratio by hand when needed (remember, the ratio does not affect value but rather brings excess cash and newly issued debt closer to reality). For more complex models, determine net debt (total debt less excess cash) by applying the target net-debt-to-value ratio modeled in the WACC at each point in time. Next, using the target debt-to-value ratio, solve for the required dividend payout. To do this, however, a valuation must be performed in each forecast year and iterated backwards—a time-consuming process for a feature that will not affect the final valuation.

Step 6: Calculate ROIC and FCF

Once you have completed your income statement and balance sheet forecasts, calculate ROIC and FCF for each forecast year. This process should be straightforward if you have already computed ROIC and FCF historically. Since a full set of forecasted financials are available, merely copy the two calculations across from historical financials to projected financials.

The resulting ROIC projections should be consistent with the empirical evidence provided in Chapter 6. For companies that are creating value, future ROICs should fit one of three general patterns. ROIC should either remain near current levels (when the company has a distinguishable sustainable advantage), trend toward an industry or economic median, or trend to the cost of capital. Think through the economics of the business to decide what is appropriate.

ADDITIONAL ISSUES

The preceding sections detailed the process for creating a comprehensive set of financial forecasts. When forecasting, you are likely to come across three additional issues: forecasting using nonfinancial operating drivers, forecasting using fixed and variable costs, and handling the impact of inflation.

Nonfinancial Operating Drivers

Until now, we have created forecasts that rely solely on financial drivers. In industries where prices are changing or technology is advancing, forecasts should incorporate nonfinancial ratios, such as volume and productivity.

Consider the recent turmoil in the airline industry. Fares requiring Saturday-night stays and advance purchases disappeared as competition intensified. Network carriers could no longer distinguish business travelers, their primary source of profit, from leisure travelers. As the average price dropped, costs rose as a percentage of sales. But were airlines truly becoming higher-cost? And how would this trend continue? To forecast changes more accurately, we need to separate price from volume (as measured by seat miles). Then, instead of forecasting costs as a percentage of revenues, forecast costs as a function of expected quantity, in this case seat miles. For instance, rather than forecast fuel cost as a percentage of revenues, project it using gallons of fuel per seat mile, combined with a market forecast for the price of oil.

The same concept applies to advances in technology. For instance, rather than estimate labor as a percentage of revenues, one could forecast units per employee and average salary per employee. By separating these two drivers of labor costs, you can model a direct relation between productivity improvements from new technology and estimated changes in units per employee.

Fixed versus Variable Costs

When you are valuing a small project, it is important to distinguish fixed costs (incurred once to create a basic infrastructure) from variable costs (correlated with volume). When you are valuing an individual project, only variable costs should be increased as revenues grow.

At the scale of most publicly traded companies, however, the distinction between fixed and variable costs is often immaterial, because nearly every cost is variable. For instance, consider a mobile-phone company that transmits calls using radio-frequency towers. In spite of the common perception that the tower is a fixed cost, this is only true for a given number of subscribers. As subscribers increase beyond a certain limit, new towers must be added, even in an area with preexisting coverage. The same holds true for technology purchases (such as servers) and support functions (such as human resources). What is a fixed cost in the short run for small increases in activity becomes variable over the long run even at reasonable growth rates (remember, 10 percent annual growth doubles the size of a company in about seven years). Since corporate valuation is about long-run profitability and growth, nearly every cost should be treated as variable.

When an asset, such as computer software, is truly scalable, it should be treated as a fixed cost. Be careful, however. Many technologies, such as computer software, quickly become obsolete, requiring new incremental expenditures for the company to remain competitive. In this case, a cost deemed fixed actually requires repeated cash outflows.

Inflation

In Chapter 5, we recommended that forecasts and the cost of capital be estimated in nominal (with price inflation) rather than real (without price inflation) currency units. To remain consistent, the nominally based financial forecast and the nominally based cost of capital must reflect the same expected general inflation rate. This means that the inflation rate built into the forecast must be derived from an inflation rate implicit in the cost of capital.[5]

When possible, derive the expected inflation rate from the term structure of government bond rates. The nominal interest rate on government bonds reflects investor demands for a real return plus a premium for expected inflation. Estimate expected inflation as the nominal rate of interest less an estimate of the real rate of interest, using the following formula:

$$\text{Expected Inflation} = \frac{(1 + \text{Nominal Rate})}{(1 + \text{Real Rate})} - 1$$

To estimate expected inflation, start by calculating the nominal yield to maturity on a 10-year government bond. But how do you find the real rate? Starting in 1981, the British government began issuing "linkers." A linker is a bond that protects against inflation by growing the bond's coupons and principal at the consumer price index. Consequently, the yield to maturity

---

[5] Individual line items may have specific inflation rates that are higher or lower than the general rate, but they should still derive from the general rate. For example, the revenue forecast should reflect the growth in units sold and the expected increase in unit prices. The increase in unit prices, in turn, should reflect the generally expected level of inflation in the economy plus or minus an inflation rate differential for that specific product. Suppose general inflation is expected to be 4.0 percent and unit prices for the company's products are expected to increase at 1 percent lower than general inflation. Overall, the company's prices would be expected to increase at 3.0 percent per year. If we assume a 3.0 percent annual increase in units sold, we would forecast 6.1 percent annual revenue growth ($1.03 \times 1.03 - 1$).

Exhibit 8.13 Expected Inflation versus Growth in the Consumer Price Index

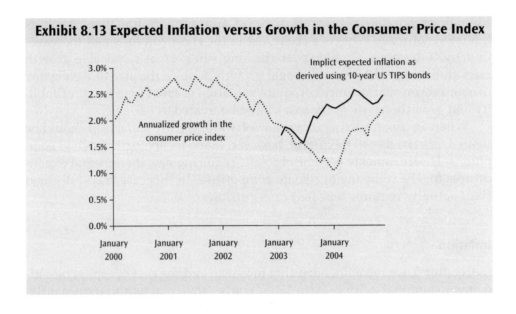

on a linker is the market's expectation of the real interest rate for the life of the bond. Since the British first introduced inflation-indexed bonds, more than 20 countries have followed suit, including Brazil, the European Central Bank, Israel, South Africa, and the United States. In December 2004, the yield on a 10-year U.S. treasury bond equaled 4.2 percent, and the yield on a U.S. TIPS (inflation-indexed) bond equaled 1.7 percent. To determine expected inflation, apply the previous formula:

$$\text{Expected Inflation} = \frac{1.042}{1.017} - 1 = 0.025$$

Expected inflation, as measured by the difference in nominal and real bonds, thus equals 2.5 percent annually over the next 10 years.

Data from the past few years in the United States supports this approach. Exhibit 8.13 presents annualized growth in the U.S. consumer price index versus expected inflation implied by traditional U.S. Treasury bonds and U.S. TIPS.[6] In the exhibit, expected inflation (as measured by the formula) precedes changes in the actual consumer price index, which is a measure of historical inflation. The two sets of numbers track quite closely, and near the end of 2004, both rates were roughly 2 percent annually.

---

[6] Although the U.S. TIPS bond began trading in 1997, the U.S. government only began disseminating comparable 10-year yields in 2003.

Inflation will also distort historical analysis, especially when it exceeds 5 percent annually. In these situations, historical financials should be adjusted to better reflect operating performance, independent of inflation. We discuss the impact of high inflation rates in Chapter 22, in the context of emerging markets.

HEINEKEN CASE

In this section of the Heineken case, we develop a forecast for Heineken's financial performance, following the approach laid out in the chapter. First, we offer a strategic perspective on Heineken and describe several scenarios. We then translate the base case scenario into a financial forecast.

For this case, we use a five-year detailed forecast, followed by a summary forecast for 10 years. The continuing value follows after the 15-year forecast (discussed in the next chapter).

CREATING SCENARIOS

The beer industry grows slowly and is fragmented on a global basis but concentrated on a regional (or country) basis. Growth opportunities in the emerging markets are expected to outpace those of Europe and North America. Most markets have consolidated; as a result, apart from a mega merger, the integrators can anticipate only the relatively slow growth they can squeeze out organically or through acquisitions in emerging markets.

Heineken's strategy is to leverage its brand and its manufacturing and marketing skills worldwide. That strategy has several key features:

- *Product development:* Heineken has a global standard for the recipe of its main brands. This standard minimizes product development costs and ensures consistent quality worldwide.
- *Brewing:* Heineken controls quality by using a roving staff of brewmasters, who employ best practices in production sites worldwide. This helps the company lower brewing costs in developed markets and add value to sites it purchases or develops in new markets. To maximize penetration into new markets, Heineken combines exports, licensed brewing, and acquisition of production capacity and local brands.
- *Packaging:* Although Heineken standardizes images on beer labels to support brand awareness, it also tailors packaging to satisfy local customers' tastes. This may add variable costs, but the impact is more than offset by the company's success in penetrating markets.

- *Marketing:* Leveraging its brand is an important part of Heineken's success. Heineken is the most global player in the market; its beer can be found in more than 170 countries. Heineken bills its major brands (Heineken and Amstel) as premium products in non-European markets and as mainstream products in European markets. It segments marketing and advertising campaigns to capture the highest possible premium.

Heineken supports this business strategy with acquisitions. The company has purchased a large number of producers and distributors since its major expansion in Europe during the 1980s. In 2003 alone, Heineken consolidated Karlsberg International Brand (Germany), Dinal LLP (Kazakhstan), CCU (Chile), Karlovacka Pivovara (Croatia), and BBAG (Austria with operations in Romania, Hungary, and the Czech Republic). The company has grown faster through acquisitions than any other major brewer except Interbrew and SABMiller.

For valuing Heineken, we developed three scenarios that could describe the company's potential strategy and business climate:

1. *Business as usual:* Under the business-as-usual scenario, the industry experiences no major shocks, Heineken continues to grow organically at a modest rate, and its margins and capital efficiency remain constant at 2004 levels (after a projected decline from 2003). Heineken also makes a series of small acquisitions.

2. *Aggressive acquisition:* Heineken and its competitors accelerate their growth through acquisitions. This strategy drives up acquisition prices, reducing returns on capital.

3. *Operating improvement:* In this scenario, Heineken focuses on improving its operations, ultimately increasing its margins and return on capital to the levels it achieved in 2001.

For the remainder of this chapter and in Chapter 9, we will analyze only the business-as-usual scenario in detail. The resulting valuations of the other two scenarios will be summarized in Chapter 11.

THE FIVE-YEAR FORECAST

We typically create an explicit forecast of 10 to 15 years, so the company can reach a steady-state financial performance before we apply a continuing value. We divide the explicit forecast period into two subperiods. For the first subperiod (five years in Heineken's case), we forecast complete income statements and balance sheets. For the remaining subperiod (10 years in Heineken's case), we use a condensed forecast.

As with most forecasts, Heineken's forecast is driven by revenues (or "turnover," as it is called in Heineken's financial statements). In other words, we derive most income statement and balance sheet line items from the revenue forecast. The detailed projections for the first five years are laid out in Exhibit 8.14 on page 259 and Exhibit 8.15 on page 260.

Exibit 8.14 Heineken: Short-Term Financial Forecast

	Historical					Forecast				
	1999	2000	2001	2002	2003	2004	2005	2006	2007	2008
Turnover growth (percent)										
Organic volume growth	0.0	2.0	1.0	2.0	1.5	1.5	1.5	1.5	1.5	1.5
Price increase/mix change	2.0	3.0	4.0	4.0	3.5	1.5	1.5	1.5	1.5	1.5
Underlying organic growth	2.0	5.0	5.0	6.0	5.0	3.0	3.0	3.0	3.0	3.0
Acquisitions	8.0	7.0	6.0	7.0	8.0	8.0	5.0	4.0	3.0	2.0
Currency changes	2.0	1.0	2.0	-1.0	-4.0	-1.0	0.0	0.0	0.0	0.0
Accounting change/other	1.0	0.8	0.2	1.5	-6.3	0.0	0.0	0.0	0.0	0.0
Turnover growth	13.0	13.8	13.2	13.5	2.7	10.0	8.0	7.0	6.0	5.0
Operating expense ratios (percent)										
Raw materials, consumables and services (of net turnover)	46.9	46.3	45.9	44.5	48.2	48.9	48.9	48.9	48.9	48.9
Marketing and selling expenses (of net turnover)	15.6	15.8	16.1	17.6	12.2	12.8	12.8	12.8	12.8	12.8
Staff costs (of net turnover)	18.4	18.5	17.9	18.2	19.8	19.8	19.8	19.8	19.8	19.8
Depreciation (of fixed assets)	12.0	12.7	12.6	11.8	11.3	11.3	11.3	11.3	11.3	11.3
Interest rates (percent)										
Interest rate on existing debt (on beginning of year balance)	8.2	8.4	8.6	6.5	4.7	4.5	4.5	4.5	4.5	4.5
Interest rate on new debt	0.0	0.0	0.0	0.0	0.0	4.5	4.5	4.5	4.5	4.5
Interest rate on retirement related liabilities	4.0	4.0	4.0	4.0	4.0	4.0	4.0	4.0	4.0	4.0
Interest rate on excess cash (on beginning of year balance)	4.7	4.0	6.9	3.6	6.7	1.9	1.9	1.9	1.9	1.9
Taxes (percent)										
Statutory tax rate in Netherlands	34.9	35.0	35.0	34.5	34.5	34.5	34.5	34.5	34.5	34.5
Operating tax rate	33.2	31.8	31.2	30.4	28.5	28.5	28.5	28.5	28.5	28.5
Minority interest (percent)										
Minority interest (of profit before tax and goodwill amortization)	3.7	1.9	5.4	5.3	6.3	6.3	6.3	6.3	6.3	6.3
Dividends (€ millions)										
Dividends	125	125	157	157	157	157	157	157	157	157
Other										
Amortization of goodwill	0	0	0	0	31	55	79	95	109	121
Results of nonconsolidated participating interests (€ millions)	51	59	45	48	101	31	33	36	38	40

Turnover

Each year's turnover equals the prior year's turnover grown at a projected rate. The projected growth rate is the sum of volume growth, price/mix changes, currency effects, and growth from acquisitions.

The 2004 forecast was based on analyst projections. The 2004 forecast includes volume growth of 1.5 percent, a price/mix increase of 1.5 percent, 8 percent growth

Exhibit 8.15 Heineken: Balance Sheet Forecast Assumptions

| | Historical | | | | | Forecast | | | | |
	1999	2000	2001	2002	2003	2004	2005	2006	2007	2008
Working capital										
Operating cash (percent of net turnover)	2.0	2.0	2.0	2.0	2.0	2.0	2.0	2.0	2.0	2.0
Accounts receivable (days)	44.1	44.6	45.3	43.2	47.5	47.5	47.5	47.5	47.5	47.5
Stocks (days)	29	28.6	31.8	31	32.9	32.9	32.9	32.9	32.9	32.9
Other current assets (days)	9.3	8.6	9.5	8.3	6.9	6.9	6.9	6.9	6.9	6.9
Accounts payable (days)	27.1	27.5	28.5	25.5	29.4	29.4	29.4	29.4	29.4	29.4
Tax payable (days)	17.1	15	15.4	13	15.5	15.5	15.5	15.5	15.5	15.5
Other current liabilities (days)	31.8	29.6	27.7	22.4	25.4	25.4	25.4	25.4	25.4	25.4
Capital expenditure										
Tangible fixed assets (percent of net turnover)	48.1	46.3	45.4	45.9	54.6	54.6	54.6	54.6	54.6	54.6
Other assets										
Nonconsolidated participating interests (shares and loans, percent of net turnover)	3.1	4.0	2.3	4.6	4.7	4.7	4.7	4.7	4.7	4.7
Deferred tax assets (percent of turnover)	0	35	30	22	18	18	18	18	18	18
Other financial fixed assets (€ million)	233	301	318	401	671	671	671	671	671	671
Other liabilities (€ million)										
Retirement related liability	48	100	112	352	526	526	526	526	526	526
Short-tem debt	488	428	570	1,039	1,113	283	283	283	283	283
Long-term debt	490	875	797	1,215	2,721	2,438	2,154	1,871	1,587	1,304
Deferred tax liabilities	295	312	357	381	415	427	440	453	467	481
Other provisions	158	158	133	133	133	146	158	169	179	188
Minority interest	**248**	**124**	**381**	**393**	**732**	**763**	**798**	**835**	**876**	**918**

from acquisitions, and a 1 percent decline due to currency effects. Normally, we would not forecast currency changes, but Heineken had partially hedged its results against a decline in the dollar in 2002 and 2003. Unless the dollar strengthened in 2004, the decline in the dollar in 2002 and 2003 would reduce 2004 turnover because the hedges have expired.

For the next four years, we projected Heineken's underlying volume growth to average 1.5 percent per year, somewhat lower than the industry because of Heineken's stronger presence in the slower-growing developed markets. The geographic mix of sales affects average prices realized, since prices are lower in emerging markets. We forecast effective price increases to drop to 1.5 percent per year and continue at that level throughout the explicit forecast period, as more sales shift to developing markets. This is somewhat lower than historical price increases. Finally, we assumed that the pace of acquisitions growth will decline over the course of the five-year forecast. We forecast turnover growth from acquisitions to be 8 percent in 2004, declining to zero in 2009.

Operating Expenses

We forecast operating expenses as a percentage of turnover. The accounting change for discounts makes historical comparisons difficult. Before 2003, turnover was reported before subtracting discounts, and discounts were treated as an expense. Beginning in 2003, discounts were netted against turnover, so operating expenses as a percent of turnover appears to decline in 2003. From 1999 to 2002, the sum of operating expenses was roughly constant as a percent of sales. The changes in 2003 were due to the accounting change for discounts and the acquisitions made during the year.

We projected 2004 operating expenses using analysts' forecasts, which expect an increase in costs relative to turnover versus 2003. A significant portion of the cost increase is due to the weakening of the dollar. (Heineken receives U.S. dollars from sales in the United States but produces the beer in Holland at euro costs.) Given the historical consistency in operating-expense ratios, we projected operating costs at a constant percent to turnover from 2005 through 2008.

Depreciation

Most of the depreciable assets purchased by Heineken are related to the company's breweries; they include buildings and large machinery. In the years 1999 to 2003, depreciation was between 11 and 13 percent of net tangible fixed assets. We assumed that depreciation remains constant as a percentage of net tangible fixed assets, given the slow growth and industrial nature of the business.

Interest Expense and Income

We estimated each year's interest expense based on the level of debt at the beginning of that year, rather than the average for the year, to avoid circular calculations. We forecast the interest rate on Heineken's debt to be 4.5 percent, its current borrowing rate and close to its effective rate in 2003. To estimate the interest rate on excess marketable securities, we used the interest rate on one-year bonds in the Netherlands (1.9 percent).

Taxes

We estimated Heineken's marginal tax rate as 34.5 percent, the statutory tax rate in the Netherlands. Heineken's effective tax rate on operating profits is expected to remain at its 2003 level of 28.5 percent, with cash taxes somewhat lower due to deferred taxes.

Minority Interest

We assumed that minority interest will remain at about 6.3 percent of profits before taxes and goodwill amortization.

Dividends

Heineken maintains a conservative dividend policy, so we assumed that its dividend will remain constant over the next five years.

Goodwill Amortization

We projected goodwill amortization using the prior year's amortization plus one-twentieth of the increase in goodwill.[7]

Results of Nonconsolidated Participating Interests

The results from nonconsolidated participating interests represent Heineken's share of the income of nonconsolidated affiliates. In 2003, Heineken reported nonconsolidated participating interests income of €101 million. Most of this, however, came from the sale of investments, not ongoing income. The ongoing income represented about 6.5 percent of the balance sheet account for nonconsolidated participating interests. We assumed that future income would remain at 6.5 percent of the balance sheet amount.

Working Capital

Operating working capital comprises operating cash, accounts receivable, stocks (inventories), and other current assets (such as prepaid expenses) less accounts payable and other current liabilities (such as taxes payable). Working capital does not include financing items such as short-term debt or dividends payable. Between 1999 and 2003, net working capital increased from 2.3 percent to 6.7 percent, driven mainly by an increase in accounts receivable. We forecast that net working capital will remain at 6.7 percent of net turnover. To simplify later analysis, we express working capital forecasts in day's sales.

Tangible Fixed Assets

To forecast tangible fixed assets (called property, plant, and equipment in the United States), we used a simple approach. We made an assumption about the amount of net fixed assets it takes to generate each dollar of sales. Because of Heineken's acquisitions of companies with higher fixed assets and the effect of the revenue accounting change in 2003, the company's net fixed assets to net turnover increased from 48.1 percent in 1999 to 54.6 percent in 2003. We forecast that net fixed assets will remain the same as in 2003. Note that this simplified forecast approach might not hold for a high-growth company or one operating in an inflationary environment.

Goodwill

Since our forecast of turnover growth includes acquisitions, we also had to forecast goodwill associated with the acquisitions. We forecast that goodwill would equal 155

---

[7] This forecast was developed using accounting rules for goodwill amortization that are no longer in effect. As explained in Chapter 7, the change in accounting for goodwill has no impact on value or performance.

percent of the turnover from acquisitions in the year of the acquisition. This is consistent with historical relationships.

Nonconsolidated Participating Interests

Nonconsolidated participating interests were 4.7 percent of turnover in 2003. We kept this amount constant going forward.

Deferred Tax Assets

Since the deferred tax assets are very small, we held them constant.

Other Financial Fixed Assets

Other financial fixed assets are primarily loans to customers. We assumed these remain constant.

Retirement-Related Liability

The retirement-related liability is the difference between the company's retirement assets and the actuarial liability for current and former employees. We assumed this remains constant.

Short- and Long-Term Debt

We forecast long-term debt based on the retirement schedules in Heineken's annual report footnotes. Short-term debt includes both debt due within one year and the current portion of long-term debt. We assumed that true short-term debt is paid down and only the current portion of long-term debt remains on the balance sheet. We used a line called "New long-term debt" to reflect future financing needs.

Deferred Tax Liabilities

Deferred tax liabilities were projected to grow at the same rate as EBITA.

Provisions

We projected that Heineken would pay off its restructuring provision in 2004. Its other provisions would grow at the same rate as turnover.

Minority Interest

Minority interest on the balance sheet increases each year by the minority interest on the income statement less an assumed 50 percent dividend. This forecast is based on the assumption that the subsidiaries with minority interests are mature and therefore can be expected to pay out a high percentage of profits as dividends.

Exhibit 8.16 Heineken: Forecast Income Statement

€ million

	Historical 2003	Forecast 2004	2005	2006	2007	2008
Net turnover	9,255	10,181	10,995	11,765	12,470	13,094
Raw materials and consumables	(4,461)	(4,978)	(5,377)	(5,753)	(6,098)	(6,403)
Marketing and selling expenses	(1,131)	(1,303)	(1,407)	(1,506)	(1,596)	(1,676)
Staff costs	(1,832)	(2,015)	(2,176)	(2,329)	(2,468)	(2,592)
EBITDA	1,831	1,884	2,035	2,177	2,308	2,423
Depreciation	(578)	(628)	(678)	(726)	(769)	(808)
EBITA	1,253	1,256	1,356	1,451	1,538	1,615
Amortization of goodwill	(31)	(55)	(79)	(95)	(109)	(121)
Operating profit	1,222	1,201	1,278	1,356	1,429	1,495
Interest paid	(180)	(173)	(96)	(66)	(44)	(29)
Interest received	40	24	0	0	0	0
Profit before tax	1,082	1,052	1,182	1,290	1,385	1,465
Taxation	(319)	(307)	(354)	(391)	(424)	(451)
Results of nonconsolidated participating interests (after tax)	101	31	33	36	38	40
Minority interest	(66)	(63)	(69)	(75)	(80)	(84)
Income before extraordinary items	798	714	792	860	919	970
Extraordinary items (after tax)	0	0	0	0	0	0
Net profit	**798**	**714**	**792**	**860**	**919**	**970**
Shareholders' equity						
Position as of 1 January	2,543	3,167	3,724	4,359	5,061	5,824
Exchange differences	(152)	0	0	0	0	0
Reclassification of dividend payable	94	0	0	0	0	0
Revaluations	41	0	0	0	0	0
Goodwill written off	0	0	0	0	0	0
Net profit for the year	798	714	792	860	919	970
Dividends	(157)	(157)	(157)	(157)	(157)	(157)
Position as of 31 December	**3,167**	**3,724**	**4,359**	**5,061**	**5,824**	**6,637**

Exhibits 8.16 to 8.22 show the resulting projected income statements, balance sheets, and calculations of NOPLAT, invested capital, free cash flow, and economic profit for the years 2003 to 2008. (The weighted average cost of capital is calculated in Chapter 10.)

MEDIUM-TERM FORECAST

For the years 2009 to 2018, we used a streamlined model, projecting only core value drivers such as net turnover growth, EBITA margin, the ratio of working capital to revenues, and the ratio of fixed assets to revenues. Our forecast assumes that Heineken reaches a steady state, with constant growth, margins, and ROIC beginning in 2009. We could have applied the terminal value at this point but have instead presented the 10-year forecast to illustrate what the streamlined forecast looks like. The assumptions

Exhibit 8.17 Heineken: Forecast Balance Sheets

€ million

	Historical 2003	Forecast 2004	2005	2006	2007	2008
Operating cash	185	204	220	235	249	262
Excess cash and marketable securities	1,231	0	0	0	0	0
Accounts receivable	1,205	1,326	1,432	1,532	1,624	1,705
Stocks (inventory)	834	917	991	1,060	1,124	1,180
Other current assets	174	191	207	221	234	246
Total current assets	3,629	2,638	2,849	3,048	3,231	3,393
Tangible fixed assets	5,053	5,558	6,003	6,423	6,809	7,149
Goodwill	1,093	1,516	1,766	1,954	2,073	2,113
Nonconsolidated participating interests	433	476	514	550	583	613
Deferred tax assets	18	18	18	18	18	18
Other financial fixed assets	671	671	671	671	671	671
Total assets	**10,897**	**10,877**	**11,821**	**12,665**	**13,385**	**13,957**
Short-term debt	1,113	283	283	283	283	283
Accounts payable	745	820	885	947	1,004	1,054
Tax payable	392	431	466	498	528	555
Dividend payable	16	18	19	20	22	23
Other current liabilities	644	708	765	819	868	911
Total current debt	**2,910**	**2,260**	**2,418**	**2,568**	**2,705**	**2,826**
Long-term debt	2,721	2,438	2,154	1,871	1,587	1,304
New debt	0	593	967	1,181	1,221	1,077
Deferred tax liabilities	415	427	440	453	467	481
Retirement liabilities	526	526	526	526	526	526
Other provisions	133	146	158	169	179	188
Restructuring provision	293	0	0	0	0	0
Total long-term liabilities	**4,088**	**4,130**	**4,246**	**4,201**	**3,981**	**3,576**
Shareholders' equity	3,167	3,724	4,359	5,061	5,824	6,637
Minority interest	732	763	798	835	876	918
Total equity	**3,899**	**4,487**	**5,157**	**5,897**	**6,699**	**7,555**
Total liabilities and shareholders' equity	**10,897**	**10,877**	**11,821**	**12,665**	**13,385**	**13,957**

are laid out in Exhibit 8.23, and the resulting summary financial statements appear in Exhibit 8.24.

CHECK FOR REASONABLENESS

Exhibit 8.25 summarizes Heineken's performance in the business-as-usual scenario. Heineken's growth falls significantly from its historically high level, as Heineken slows down its acquisitions strategy. ROIC declines somewhat, primarily reflecting the weak performance expected in 2004. Future acquisitions also reduce Heineken's ROIC (including goodwill). Overall, the results are consistent with the scenario and current strategy we have described.

Exhibit 8.18 Heineken: Forecast NOPLAT

€ million

	Historical 2003	Forecast 2004	2005	2006	2007	2008
EBITA	1,253	1,256	1,356	1,451	1,538	1,615
Adjustment for retirement liability	21	21	21	21	21	21
Increase (decrease) in other provisions	0	13	12	11	10	9
Adjusted EBITA	1,274	1,290	1,389	1,483	1,569	1,645
Taxes on EBITA	(375)	(365)	(394)	(421)	(446)	(468)
Increase (decrease) in deferred tax liability	38	12	13	13	14	14
NOPLAT	**937**	**937**	**1,008**	**1,075**	**1,137**	**1,191**
Taxes on EBITA						
Reported taxes	(319)	(307)	(354)	(391)	(424)	(451)
Tax shield on interest paid	(62)	(60)	(33)	(23)	(15)	(10)
Taxes on interest received	14	8	0	0	0	0
Tax shield on retirement liabilities	(7)	(7)	(7)	(7)	(7)	(7)
Taxes on EBITA	**(375)**	**(365)**	**(394)**	**(421)**	**(446)**	**(468)**
Reconciliation to net profit						
Net profit	798	714	792	860	919	970
Increase (decrease) in other provisions	0	13	12	11	10	9
Increase (decrease) in deferred tax liability	38	12	13	13	14	14
Extraordinary items	0	0	0	0	0	0
Minority interest	66	63	69	75	80	84
Results of nonconsolidated participating interests	(101)	(31)	(33)	(36)	(38)	(40)
Amortization of goodwill	31	55	79	95	109	121
Adjusted net profit	832	826	931	1,018	1,095	1,158
Interest paid after tax	118	113	63	43	29	19
Interest expense on retirement liabilities	14	14	14	14	14	14
Total income available to investors	964	953	1,008	1,075	1,137	1,191
Interest received after tax	(26)	(15)	0	0	0	0
NOPLAT	**937**	**937**	**1,008**	**1,075**	**1,137**	**1,191**

Exhibit 8.19 Heineken: Forecast Invested Capital

€ million

	Historical 2003	Forecast 2004	2005	2006	2007	2008
Operating current assets	2,398	2,638	2,849	3,048	3,231	3,393
Operating current liabilities	(1,781)	(1,959)	(2,116)	(2,264)	(2,400)	(2,520)
Operating working capital	617	679	733	784	831	873
Tangible fixed assets	5,053	5,558	6,003	6,423	6,809	7,149
Operating invested capital (before goodwill)	5,670	6,237	6,736	7,208	7,640	8,022
Goodwill	1,093	1,516	1,766	1,954	2,073	2,113
Cumulative goodwill written off and amortized	3,059	3,114	3,192	3,287	3,396	3,517
Operating invested capital (after goodwill)	9,822	10,867	11,694	12,449	13,109	13,652
Excess cash and marketable securities	1,231	0	0	0	0	0
Nonconsolidated participating interests	433	476	514	550	583	613
Other financial fixed assets	671	671	671	671	671	671
Total investor funds	**12,157**	**12,014**	**12,879**	**13,670**	**14,364**	**14,936**
Shareholders' equity	3,167	3,724	4,359	5,061	5,824	6,637
Cumulative goodwill written off and amortized	3,059	3,114	3,192	3,287	3,396	3,517
Minority interests	732	763	798	835	876	918
Other provisions	133	146	158	169	179	188
Net deferred taxes	397	409	422	435	449	463
Dividend payable	16	18	19	20	22	23
Adjusted equity	7,504	8,174	8,948	9,809	10,746	11,745
Debt	3,834	3,314	3,405	3,336	3,092	2,664
Retirement liabilities	526	526	526	526	526	526
Restructuring provision	293	0	0	0	0	0
Total investor funds	**12,157**	**12,014**	**12,879**	**13,670**	**14,364**	**14,936**

Exhibit 8.20 Heineken: Forecast Cash Flow

€ million

	Historical 2003	Forecast 2004	2005	2006	2007	2008
Operating cash flows						
NOPLAT	937	937	1,008	1,075	1,137	1,191
Depreciation	578	628	678	726	769	808
Gross cash flow	1,515	1,565	1,686	1,801	1,907	1,999
(Increase) decrease in working capital	93	(62)	(54)	(51)	(47)	(42)
Capital expenditures	(1,609)	(1,133)	(1,123)	(1,146)	(1,155)	(1,148)
Gross investment	(1,516)	(1,195)	(1,177)	(1,197)	(1,202)	(1,190)
Free cash flow before goodwill	0	370	509	604	705	809
Investment in goodwill	(1,124)	(478)	(328)	(284)	(228)	(161)
Free cash flow after goodwill	(1,124)	(107)	181	320	477	648
After-tax interest received	26	15	0	0	0	0
(Increase) decrease in excess marketable securities	(633)	1,231	0	0	0	0
Results of nonconsolidated participating interests	101	31	33	36	38	40
(Increase) decrease in nonconsolidated participating interests	(21)	(43)	(38)	(36)	(33)	(29)
Cash flow to investors	**(1,921)**	**1,126**	**176**	**320**	**482**	**659**
Financing flows						
After tax interest paid	118	113	63	43	29	19
Interest on retirement related liabilities	14	14	14	14	14	14
Minority interest (income statement)	66	63	69	75	80	84
(Increase) decrease in minority interest	(339)	(31)	(35)	(38)	(40)	(42)
(Increase) decrease in debt	(1,580)	520	(91)	70	243	428
(Increase) decrease in retirement related liabilities	(174)	0	0	0	0	0
(Increase) decrease in restructuring provisions	(178)	293	0	0	0	0
Dividends	157	157	157	157	157	157
Total financing flows	**(1,921)**	**1,126**	**176**	**320**	**482**	**659**

Exhibit 8.21 Heineken: Forecast Economic Profit

€ million, percent

Before goodwill	Historical 2003	Forecast 2004	2005	2006	2007	2008
After-tax ROIC (on beginning of year invested capital)	16.5%	16.5%	16.2%	16.0%	15.8%	15.6%
WACC	7.7%	7.5%	7.5%	7.5%	7.5%	7.5%
Spread	**8.8%**	**9.0%**	**8.7%**	**8.5%**	**8.3%**	**8.1%**
Invested capital (beginning of year)	5,670	5,670	6,237	6,736	7,208	7,640
Economic profit	**501**	**512**	**540**	**570**	**597**	**618**
NOPLAT	937	937	1,008	1,075	1,137	1,191
Capital charge	(437)	(425)	(468)	(505)	(541)	(573)
Economic profit	**501**	**512**	**540**	**570**	**597**	**618**
After goodwill						
After-tax ROIC (on beginning of year invested capital)	11.9%	9.5%	9.3%	9.2%	9.1%	9.1%
WACC	7.7%	7.5%	7.5%	7.5%	7.5%	7.5%
Spread	**4.2%**	**2.0%**	**1.8%**	**1.7%**	**1.6%**	**1.6%**
Invested capital (beginning of year)	9,822	9,822	10,867	11,694	12,449	13,109
Economic profit	**181**	**201**	**193**	**198**	**203**	**208**
NOPLAT	937	937	1,008	1,075	1,137	1,191
Capital charge	(756)	(737)	(815)	(877)	(934)	(1,024)
Economic profit	**181**	**201**	**193**	**198**	**203**	**208**

Exhibit 8.22 Heineken: Supporting Calculations

€ million

	Historical 2003	Forecast 2004	2005	2006	2007	2008
Change in working capital						
Increase (decrease) in operating cash	5	19	16	15	14	12
Increase (decrease) in accounts receivable	139	121	106	100	92	81
Increase (decrease) in stocks	69	83	73	69	64	56
Increase (decrease) in other current assets	(30)	17	15	14	13	12
(Increase) in accounts payable	(116)	(75)	(66)	(62)	(57)	(50)
(Increase) decrease in tax payable	(70)	(39)	(34)	(33)	(30)	(26)
(Increase) decrease in other current liabilities	(90)	(64)	(57)	(54)	(49)	(43)
Net change in working capital	**(93)**	**62**	**54**	**51**	**47**	**42**
Capital expenditures						
Increase (decrease) in tangible fixed assets	920	505	445	420	385	340
Depreciation	578	628	678	726	769	808
Exchange differences	152	0	0	0	0	0
Revaluation	(41)	0	0	0	0	0
Capital expenditures (net of disposals)	**1,609**	**1,133**	**1,123**	**1,146**	**1,155**	**1,148**
Investment in goodwill						
Increase (decrease) in software and other	1,093	423	250	189	119	40
Increase (decrease) in cumulative goodwill written off and amortized	31	55	79	95	109	121
Investment in goodwill	**1,124**	**478**	**328**	**284**	**228**	**161**
Other nonoperating cash flows						
(Increase) decrease in other financial fixed assets	(270)	0	0	0	0	0
Nonoperating cash flows	**(270)**	**0**	**0**	**0**	**0**	**0**

Exhibit 8.23 Heineken: Forecast Medium-Term Operating Ratios

percent

	Historical 2003	Forecast 2004	2005	2006	2007	2008	2009	2010	2011	2012	2013	2014	2015	2016	2017	2018
Turnover growth																
Organic volume growth	1.5	1.5	1.5	1.5	1.5	1.5	1.5	1.5	1.5	1.5	1.5	1.5	1.5	1.5	1.5	1.5
Price increase/mix change	3.5	1.5	1.5	1.5	1.5	1.5	1.5	1.5	1.5	1.5	1.5	1.5	1.5	1.5	1.5	1.5
Underlying organic growth	5.0	3.0	3.0	3.0	3.0	3.0	3.0	3.0	3.0	3.0	3.0	3.0	3.0	3.0	3.0	3.0
Acquisitions	8.0	8.0	5.0	4.0	3.0	2.0	0.0	0.0	0.0	0.0	0.0	0.0	0.0	0.0	0.0	0.0
Currency changes	(4.0)	(1.0)	0.0	0.0	0.0	0.0	0.0	0.0	0.0	0.0	0.0	0.0	0.0	0.0	0.0	0.0
Accounting change/other	(6.3)	0.0	0.0	0.0	0.0	0.0	0.0	0.0	0.0	0.0	0.0	0.0	0.0	0.0	0.0	0.0
Turnover growth	**2.7**	**10.0**	**8.0**	**7.0**	**6.0**	**5.0**	**3.0**	**3.0**	**3.0**	**3.0**	**3.0**	**3.0**	**3.0**	**3.0**	**3.0**	**3.0**
Adjusted EBITA margin	13.8	12.7	12.6	12.6	12.6	12.6	12.5	12.5	12.5	12.5	12.5	12.5	12.5	12.5	12.5	12.5
Cash tax rate	26.4	27.4	27.4	27.5	27.5	27.6	27.6	27.6	27.6	27.6	27.6	27.6	27.6	27.6	27.6	27.6
Operating working capital/net turnover	6.7	6.7	6.7	6.7	6.7	6.7	6.7	6.7	6.7	6.7	6.7	6.7	6.7	6.7	6.7	6.7
Tangible fixed assets/net turnover	54.6	54.6	54.6	54.6	54.6	54.6	54.6	54.6	54.6	54.6	54.6	54.6	54.6	54.6	54.6	54.6
Net turnover/invested capital (times)	1.6	1.7	1.7	1.7	1.7	1.7	1.7	1.7	1.7	1.7	1.7	1.7	1.7	1.7	1.7	1.7
Pre-tax ROIC	22.5	21.7	21.4	21.3	21.1	21.0	20.7	20.7	20.7	20.7	20.7	20.7	20.7	20.7	20.7	20.7
ROIC	16.5	15.7	15.5	15.4	15.3	15.2	15.0	15.0	15.0	15.0	15.0	15.0	15.0	15.0	15.0	15.0
ROIC including goodwill	9.5	9.1	8.9	8.9	8.9	8.9	8.9	9.0	9.1	9.2	9.3	9.4	9.5	9.6	9.7	9.8
Invested capital growth	17.1	10.0	8.0	7.0	6.0	5.0	3.1	3.0	3.0	3.0	3.0	3.0	3.0	3.0	3.0	3.0
Adjusted EBITA growth	(1.7)	1.3	7.7	6.8	5.8	4.8	2.5	3.0	3.0	3.0	3.0	3.0	3.0	3.0	3.0	3.0
NOPLAT growth	1.7	0.0	7.5	6.7	5.7	4.8	2.5	3.0	3.0	3.0	3.0	3.0	3.0	3.0	3.0	3.0
Continuing value																
ROIC			15.0													
NOPLAT growth			3.0													

Exhibit 8.24 Heineken: Forecast Medium-Term Financial Results

	Historical 2003[1]	Forecast 2004	2005	2006	2007	2008	2009	2010	2011	2012	2013	2014	2015	2016	2017	2018
Invested capital																
Operating working capital	617	679	733	784	831	873	904	931	959	987	1,017	1,048	1,079	1,111	1,145	1,179
Tangible fixed assets	5,053	5,558	6,003	6,423	6,809	7,149	7,364	7,585	7,812	8,047	8,288	8,537	8,793	9,057	9,328	9,608
Invested capital	**5,670**	**6,237**	**6,736**	**7,208**	**7,640**	**8,022**	**8,267**	**8,515**	**8,771**	**9,034**	**9,305**	**9,584**	**9,872**	**10,168**	**10,473**	**10,787**
Goodwill	1,093	1,516	1,766	1,954	2,073	2,113	1,985	1,857	1,729	1,601	1,473	1,345	1,217	1,089	961	833
Cumulative goodwill written off and amortized	3,059	3,114	3,192	3,287	3,396	3,517	3,645	3,773	3,901	4,029	4,157	4,285	4,413	4,541	4,669	4,797
Invested capital (after goodwill)	**9,822**	**10,867**	**11,694**	**12,449**	**13,109**	**13,652**	**13,897**	**14,145**	**14,401**	**14,664**	**14,935**	**15,214**	**15,502**	**15,798**	**16,103**	**16,417**
Revenues	9,255	10,181	10,995	11,765	12,470	13,094	13,487	13,891	14,308	14,737	15,180	15,635	16,104	16,587	17,085	17,597
Adjusted EBITA	1,274	1,290	1,389	1,483	1,569	1,645	1,686	1,736	1,789	1,842	1,897	1,954	2,013	2,073	2,136	2,200
Cash taxes on EBITA	(337)	(353)	(381)	(408)	(432)	(454)	(465)	(479)	(494)	(508)	(524)	(539)	(556)	(572)	(589)	(607)
NOPLAT	**937**	**937**	**1,008**	**1,075**	**1,137**	**1,191**	**1,221**	**1,257**	**1,295**	**1,334**	**1,374**	**1,415**	**1,457**	**1,501**	**1,546**	**1,593**
Free cash flow																
NOPLAT	937	937	1,008	1,075	1,137	1,191	1,221	1,257	1,295	1,334	1,374	1,415	1,457	1,501	1,546	1,593
Increase in operating invested capital	(938)	(567)	(499)	(472)	(432)	(382)	(245)	(248)	(255)	(263)	(271)	(279)	(288)	(296)	(305)	(314)
Investment in goodwill	(1,124)	(478)	(328)	(284)	(228)	(161)	0	0	0	0	0	0	0	0	0	0
Free cash flow	**(1,124)**	**(107)**	**181**	**320**	**477**	**648**	**975**	**1,009**	**1,039**	**1,071**	**1,103**	**1,136**	**1,170**	**1,205**	**1,241**	**1,278**
Economic profit (before goodwill)																
Invested capital (beginning of year)	5,670	5,670	6,237	6,736	7,208	7,640	8,022	8,267	8,515	8,771	9,034	9,305	9,584	9,872	10,168	10,473
WACC (percent)	7.7%	7.5%	7.5%	7.5%	7.5%	7.5%	7.5%	7.5%	7.5%	7.5%	7.5%	7.5%	7.5%	7.5%	7.5%	7.5%
Annual capital charge	**437**	**425**	**468**	**505**	**541**	**573**	**602**	**620**	**639**	**658**	**678**	**698**	**719**	**740**	**763**	**785**
NOPLAT	937	937	1,008	1,075	1,137	1,191	1,221	1,257	1,295	1,334	1,374	1,415	1,457	1,501	1,546	1,593
Annual capital charge	(437)	(425)	(468)	(505)	(541)	(573)	(602)	(620)	(639)	(658)	(678)	(698)	(719)	(740)	(763)	(785)
Economic profit (before goodwill)	**501**	**512**	**540**	**570**	**597**	**618**	**619**	**637**	**656**	**676**	**696**	**717**	**739**	**761**	**784**	**807**
Economic profit (after goodwill)																
Invested capital (beginning of year)	9,822	9,822	10,867	11,694	12,449	13,109	13,652	13,897	14,145	14,401	14,664	14,935	15,214	15,502	15,798	16,103
WACC (percent)	7.7%	7.5%	7.5%	7.5%	7.5%	7.5%	7.5%	7.5%	7.5%	7.5%	7.5%	7.5%	7.5%	7.5%	7.5%	7.5%
Annual capital charge	**756**	**737**	**815**	**877**	**934**	**983**	**1,024**	**1,042**	**1,061**	**1,080**	**1,100**	**1,120**	**1,141**	**1,163**	**1,185**	**1,208**
NOPLAT	937	937	1,008	1,075	1,137	1,191	1,221	1,257	1,295	1,334	1,374	1,415	1,457	1,501	1,546	1,593
Annual capital charge	(756)	(737)	(815)	(877)	(934)	(983)	(1,024)	(1,042)	(1,061)	(1,080)	(1,100)	(1,120)	(1,141)	(1,163)	(1,185)	(1,208)
Economic profit (after goodwill)	**181**	**201**	**193**	**198**	**203**	**208**	**197**	**215**	**234**	**254**	**274**	**295**	**316**	**339**	**361**	**385**

[1]For 2003, used end of year invested capital due to acquisitions.

Exhibit 8.25 Heineken: Business as Usual Scenario Summary

percent

	Historical 1999–2002	2003	Forecast 2004	2005–2008	2009–2018
Turnover growth					
Organic	5.3	5.0	3.0	3.0	3.0
Acquisitions	6.7	8.0	8.0	3.7	0.0
Other	1.5	(10.3)	(1.0)	0.0	0.0
Turnover growth	**13.5**	**2.7**	**10.0**	**6.7**	**3.0**
Adjusted EBITA growth	15.8	(1.7)	1.3	6.3	3.0
Invested capital growth	14.9	17.1	10.0	6.0	3.0
Adjusted EBITA/revenues	13.8	13.8	12.7	12.6	12.5
Turnovers/invested capital (times)	1.9	1.6	1.7	1.7	1.7
Tax rate on EBITA	30.5	26.4	27.4	27.5	27.6
ROIC (after tax, before goodwill)	19.6	16.5	15.7	15.4	15.0
ROIC (after tax, after goodwill)	13.2	9.5	9.1	8.9	9.4
WACC	8.3	7.7	7.5	7.5	7.5

REVIEW QUESTIONS

1. Identify the six-step process for creating a valuation forecast. What is the most important step in this process? Explain.

2. What is the benefit of a short-term performance forecast? What is the benefit of a long-term performance forecast? How might a manager combine the benefits of both short-term and long-term performance forecasts to develop a more accurate value forecast?

3. Identify and explain the benefits of a bottom-up forecast process. Identify and explain the benefits of a top-down forecast process. Which process would likely provide a company better results?

4. Identify the differences between a marginal tax rate, an average tax rate, and an operating tax rate. Which tax rate is most appropriate for performance forecasting?

5. Discuss how capital structure affects corporate valuation. Use the enterprise DCF model to illustrate your position.

6. It has been said repeatedly that adding value translates to ROIC being greater than WACC. How does this result from the competitive advantages of strategic positioning?

7. Given the historical data, construct the following two scenarios for IMT's valuation:

Aggressive (AG): IMT introduces significant changes and increases to its product line and ability to meet technological change in the industry. *Goal: Improve all expense structures at high levels of sales growth over the near term;* Operating Expense/Sales of 74 percent, 73 percent, 73 percent for three years, SG&A/Sales of 16 percent, three years of sales growth of 40 percent per year.

Conservative (CO): IMT is barely able to hold its own in the global arena of faster paced technological change and customer demands. *Goal: maintain historical sales, operating and general expense structures;* Operating Expense/Sales of 74 percent in perpetuity, SG&A/Sales of 19 percent, three years of sales growth at 20 percent per year.

International Machine Tools Inc. (IMT):

	2000	2001	2002	2003	2004
Current assets	499	489	443	429	484
Current liabilities	240	236	255	237	369
Debt in current liabilities	25	12	7	21	78
Long-term debt	218	200	244	207	236
Total assets	686	693	598	579	730
Capital expenditures	34	34	16	18	23
Change in deferred taxes	4	(5)	3	2	2
Sales	851	838	754	789	1,029
Operating expenses	626	624	579	592	765
General expenses	151	157	132	134	191
Depreciation	23	24	24	21	26
Investment income	4	2	2	3	2
Interest expense	22	20	19	19	16
Miscellaneous income, net	3	(33)	(75)	–	(70)
Income taxes	18	4	10	11	8

9

Estimating
Continuing Value

As described in Chapter 5, the concept of continuing value (CV) provides a useful method for simplifying company valuations. To estimate a company's value, we separate a company's expected cash flow into two periods and define the company's value as follows:

$$\text{Value} = \frac{\text{Present Value of Cash Flow}}{\textit{during } \text{Explicit Forecast Period}} + \frac{\text{Present Value of Cash Flow}}{\textit{after } \text{Explicit Forecast Period}}$$

The second term is the continuing value: the value of the company's expected cash flow beyond the explicit forecast period. Making simplifying assumptions about the company's performance during this period (e.g., assuming a constant rate of growth and return on capital), we can estimate continuing value by using formulas instead of explicitly forecasting and discounting cash flows over an extended period.

A thoughtful estimate of continuing value is essential to any valuation because continuing value often accounts for a large percentage of a company's total value. Exhibit 9.1 on page 276 shows continuing value as a percentage of total value for companies in four industries, given an eight-year explicit forecast. In these examples, continuing value accounts for 56 percent to 125 percent of total value. These large percentages do not necessarily mean that most of a company's value will be created in the continuing-value period. Often continuing value is large because profits and other inflows in the early years are offset by outflows for capital spending and working capital investment—investments that should generate higher cash

Exhibit 9.1 Continuing Value as a Percentage of Total Value

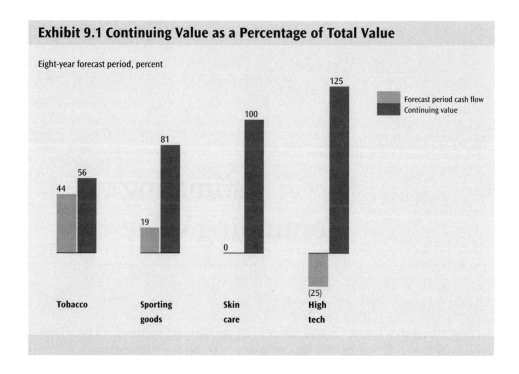

Eight-year forecast period, percent

Legend:
- Forecast period cash flow
- Continuing value

Data points:
- Tobacco: 44, 56
- Sporting goods: 19, 81
- Skin care: 0, 100
- High tech: (25), 125

flow in later years. We discuss the interpretation of continuing value in more detail later in this chapter.

This chapter begins with the recommended continuing-value formulas for discounted cash flow (DCF) and economic profit valuation. We then discuss issues commonly raised about how to interpret continuing value and suggest some best practices in estimating continuing-value parameters such as growth and return on invested capital. Finally, we compare the recommended formulas with other continuing-value techniques and discuss more advanced formulas.

The continuing-value formulas developed over the next few pages are consistent with the frameworks for discounted cash flow and economic profit. This is important because continuing value is sometimes treated as though it differs from the discounted cash flow of the explicit forecast period. For example, some acquirers estimate continuing value for a target company by applying the same price-to-earnings multiple five years in the future as the multiple they are currently paying for the target. By doing this, they are assuming that someone would be willing to pay the same multiple for the target company five years from now, regardless of changes in growth and return prospects over that period. This type of circular reasoning leads to inaccurate valuations. Instead, acquirers should try to estimate what the multiple should be at the end of the forecast period, given the industry conditions at *that* time.

RECOMMENDED FORMULA FOR DISCOUNTED CASH FLOW VALUATION

If you are using the enterprise DCF model, you should estimate continuing value by using the value driver formula derived in Chapter 3:

$$\text{Continuing Value}_t = \frac{\text{NOPLAT}_{t+1}\left(1 - \dfrac{g}{\text{RONIC}}\right)}{\text{WACC} - g}$$

where NOPLAT_{t+1} = Normalized level of NOPLAT in the first year after the explicit forecast period

g = Expected growth rate in NOPLAT in perpetuity

RONIC = Expected rate of return on new invested capital

WACC = Weighted average cost of capital

A simple example demonstrates that the value driver formula does, in fact, replicate the process of projecting the cash flows and discounting them to the present. Begin with the following cash flow projections:

	Year				
	1	2	3	4	5
NOPLAT	$100	$106	$112	$119	$126
Net investment	50	53	56	60	63
Free cash flow	$ 50	$ 53	$ 56	$ 60	$ 63

The same pattern continues after the first five years presented. In this example, the growth rate in NOPLAT and free cash flow each period is 6 percent. The rate of return on net new investment is 12 percent, calculated as the increase in NOPLAT from one year to the next, divided by the net investment in the prior year. The WACC is assumed to be 11 percent. First, discount a long forecast—say, 150 years:

$$CV = \frac{50}{1.11} + \frac{53}{(1.11)^2} + \frac{56}{(1.11)^3} + \cdots + \frac{50(1.06)^{149}}{(1.11)^{150}}$$

$$CV = 999$$

Next, use the growing free cash flow perpetuity formula:

$$CV = \frac{50}{11\% - 6\%}$$

$$CV = 1,000$$

Finally, use the value driver formula:

$$CV = \frac{100\left(1 - \dfrac{6\%}{12\%}\right)}{11\% - 6\%}$$

$$CV = 1,000$$

All three approaches yield the same result. (If we had carried out the discounted cash flow beyond 150 years, the result would have been the same.)

Although the value driver formula and the growing free cash flow (FCF) perpetuity formula are technically equivalent, applying the FCF perpetuity is tricky, and it is easy to make a common conceptual error. The typical error is to incorrectly estimate the level of free cash flow that is consistent with the growth rate you are forecasting. If growth in the continuing-value period is forecast to be less than the growth in the explicit forecast period (as is normally the case), then the proportion of NOPLAT that must be invested to generate growth also is likely to be less. In the continuing-value period, more of each dollar of NOPLAT becomes free cash flow available for the investors. If this transition is not explicitly taken into consideration, the continuing value could be significantly underestimated. Later in this chapter, we provide an example that illustrates what can go wrong when using the value driver formula.

Because perpetuity-based formulas rely on parameters that never change, use a continuing-value formula only when the company has reached a steady state, with constant growth, margins, capital turnover, and WACC. Chapter 6 provided guidance for thinking about long-term growth and return on capital. In addition, when estimating the continuing-value parameters, keep in mind the following technical considerations:

- *NOPLAT:* The level of NOPLAT should be based on a normalized level of revenues and sustainable margin and ROIC. The normalized level of revenues should reflect the midpoint of its business cycle and cycle average profit margins.

- *RONIC:* The expected rate of return on new invested capital (RONIC) should be consistent with expected competitive conditions. Economic theory suggests that competition will eventually eliminate abnormal returns, so for many companies, set RONIC equal to WACC. However, for companies with sustainable competitive advantages (e.g., brands and patents), you might set RONIC equal to the return the company is forecast to earn during later years of the explicit forecast period. Chapter 6 contains data on the long-term returns on capital for companies in different industries.

- *Growth rate:* Few companies can be expected to grow faster than the economy for long periods. The best estimate is probably the expected long-term rate of consumption growth for the industry's products, plus inflation. Sensitivity analyses also are useful for understanding how the growth rate affects continuing-value estimates. Again, Chapter 6 provides empirical evidence on historical corporate growth rates.

- *WACC:* The weighted average cost of capital should incorporate a sustainable capital structure and an underlying estimate of business risk consistent with expected industry conditions.

The key value driver formula is highly sensitive to the formula's parameters. Exhibit 9.2 shows how continuing value (calculated using the value driver formula) is affected by various combinations of growth rate and rate of return on new investment. The example assumes a $100 million base level of NOPLAT and a 10 percent WACC. At a 14 percent expected rate of return on new capital, changing the growth rate from 6 percent to 8 percent increases the continuing value by 50 percent, from about $1.4 billion to about $2.1 billion.

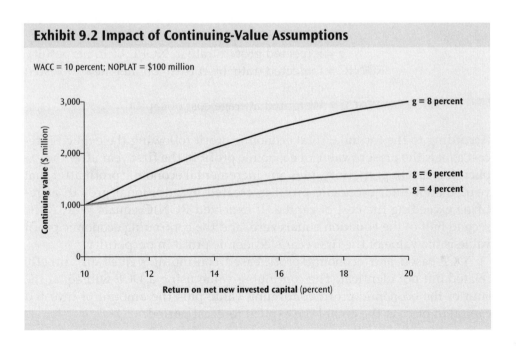

Exhibit 9.2 Impact of Continuing-Value Assumptions

WACC = 10 percent; NOPLAT = $100 million

RECOMMENDED FORMULA FOR ECONOMIC PROFIT VALUATION

With the economic profit approach, the continuing value does not equal the value of the company following the explicit forecast period. Instead, it is the incremental value over the company's invested capital at the end of the explicit forecast period. The total value of the company is as follows:

$$\text{Value} = \begin{array}{c}\text{Invested Capital}\\\text{at Beginning}\\\text{of Forecast}\end{array} + \begin{array}{c}\text{Present Value of Forecasted}\\\text{Economic Profit } during\\\text{Explicit Forecast Period}\end{array} + \begin{array}{c}\text{Present Value of Forecasted}\\\text{Economic Profit } after \text{ the}\\\text{Explicit Forecast Period}\end{array}$$

The economic profit continuing value is the last term in the preceding equation. Although this continuing value differs from the DCF continuing value, the value of the company will be the same, given the same projected financial performance.

The economic profit formula* is:

$$CV_t = \frac{\text{Economic Profit}_{t+1}}{\text{WACC}} + \frac{(\text{NOPLAT}_{t+1})\left(\dfrac{g}{\text{RONIC}}\right)(\text{RONIC} - \text{WACC})}{\text{WACC}(\text{WACC} - g)}$$

where Economic profit$_{t+1}$ = Normalized economic profit in the first year after the explicit forecast period

NOPLAT$_{t+1}$ = Normalized NOPLAT in the first year after the explicit forecast period

g = Expected growth rate in NOPLAT in perpetuity

RONIC = Expected rate of return on net new invested capital

WACC = Weighted average cost of capital

According to the formula, total economic profit following the explicit forecast equals the present value of economic profit in the first year after the explicit forecast in perpetuity, plus any incremental economic profit after that year. Incremental economic profit is created by additional growth at returns exceeding the cost of capital. If expected RONIC equals WACC, the second half of the equation equals zero, and the continuing economic profit value is the value of the first year's economic profit in perpetuity.

DCF-based and economic-profit-based continuing values are directly related but not identical. The continuing value using a DCF will equal the sum of the economic profit continuing value plus the amount of invested capital in place at the end of the explicit forecast period.

* See footnote 7 on page 121 for the derivation.

SUBTLETIES OF CONTINUING VALUE

Three misunderstandings about continuing value are common. First is the misperception that the length of the explicit forecast affects the company's value. Second, there is confusion about the relationship of continuing value to the length of time a company is forecast to earn returns on invested capital greater than its cost of capital—its competitive advantage period. Finally, some analysts incorrectly infer that a large continuing value relative to the company's total value implies that value creation occurs primarily after the explicit forecast period.

Does the Length of Forecast Affect the Company's Value?

While the length of the explicit forecast period you choose is important, it does not affect the value of the company; it only affects the distribution of the company's value between the explicit forecast period and the years that follow. In Exhibit 9.3, the company value is $893, regardless of how long the forecast period is. Exhibit 9.4 on page 282 details the calculations for the first two scenarios. With a forecast horizon of five years, the present value of the continuing value accounts for 79 percent of total value. With a 10-year horizon, the present value of continuing value accounts for only 60 percent of total value.

The choice of forecast horizon will indirectly affect value if it is associated with changes in the economic assumptions underlying the continuing-value estimate. You can unknowingly change your performance forecasts when you change your forecast horizon. Many forecasters assume that the rate of return on new invested capital will equal the cost of capital in the

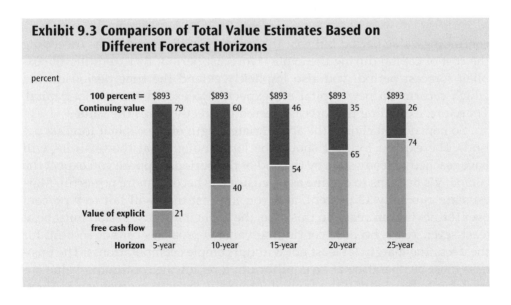

Exhibit 9.3 Comparison of Total Value Estimates Based on Different Forecast Horizons

Exhibit 9.4 Comparison of Total Value Calculations for 5-Year and 10-Year Horizons

$ million

5-year horizon	1	2	3	4	5	Base for CV
NOPLAT	100.0	109.0	118.8	129.5	141.2	149.6
Depreciation	20.0	21.8	23.8	25.9	28.2	
Gross cash flow	120.0	130.8	142.6	155.4	169.4	
Gross investment	76.3	83.1	90.6	98.7	107.6	
FCF	43.8	47.7	52.0	56.7	61.8	
Discount factor	0.893	0.797	0.712	0.636	0.567	
Present value of cash flow	39.1	38.0	37.0	36.0	35.0	

Overall assumptions (percent)	Years 1–5	Years 6+
Return on investment (RONIC)	16	12
Growth rate (g)	9	6
WACC	12	12

$$\text{Present value of continuing value} = \frac{\text{NOPLAT } (1 - g/\text{RONIC})}{\text{WACC} - g} [1 / (1 + \text{WACC})]^5 = \frac{\$149.6 \, (1 - 6\%/12\%)}{12\% - 6\%} \, (0.5674) = \$707.5$$

Present value of FCF 1 – 5 185.1
Continuing value   707.5
Total value   892.6

10-year horizon	1	2	3	4	5	6	7	8	9	10	Base for CV
NOPLAT	100.0	109.0	118.8	129.5	141.2	149.6	158.6	168.1	178.2	188.9	200.2
Depreciation	20.0	21.8	23.8	25.9	28.2	29.9	31.7	33.6	35.6	37.8	
Gross cash flow	120.0	130.8	142.6	155.4	169.4	179.6	190.3	201.7	213.9	226.7	
Gross investment	76.3	83.1	90.6	98.7	107.6	104.7	111.0	117.7	124.7	132.2	
FCF	43.8	47.7	52.0	56.7	61.8	74.8	79.3	84.1	89.1	94.5	
Discount factor	0.893	0.797	0.712	0.636	0.567	0.507	0.452	0.404	0.361	0.322	
Present value of cash flow	39.1	38.0	37.0	36.0	35.0	37.9	35.9	34.0	32.1	30.4	

$$\text{Present value of continuing value} = \frac{\text{NOPLAT } (1 - g/\text{RONIC})}{\text{WACC} - g} [1 / (1 + \text{WACC})]^{10} = \frac{\$200.2 \, (1 - 6\%/12\%)}{12\% - 6\%} \, (0.322) = \$537.2$$

Present value of FCF 1–10 355.4
Continuing value   537.2
Total value   892.6

continuing-value period but that the company will earn returns exceeding the cost of capital during the explicit forecast period. By extending the explicit forecast period, you also implicitly extend the time period during which returns on new capital are expected to exceed the cost of capital. Therefore, extending the forecast period indirectly raises the value.

So how do you choose the appropriate length of the explicit forecast period? The explicit forecast should be long enough that the business will have reached a steady state by the end of the period. Suppose you expect the company's margins to decline as its customers become more powerful. Margins are currently 12 percent, and you forecast they will fall to 9 percent over the next seven years. In this case, the explicit forecast period must be at least seven years, because continuing-value approaches cannot account for the declining margin (at least not without complex computations). The business must be operating at an equilibrium level for the continuing-value approaches to be useful. If the explicit forecast is more than seven years, there will be no effect on the total value of the company.

Confusion about Competitive Advantage Period

A related issue is the concept of a company's competitive advantage period, or period of supernormal returns. This is the notion that companies will earn returns above the cost of capital for a period of time, followed by a decline to the cost of capital. While this concept is useful, linking it to the length of the forecast is dangerous. One reason is simply that, as we just showed, there is no direct connection between the length of the forecast and the value of a company.

More important is that the length of competitive advantage is sometimes inappropriately linked to the explicit forecast period. Remember, the key value driver formula is based on *incremental* returns on capital, not companywide average returns. If you assume that incremental returns in the continuing-value period will just equal the cost of capital, you are not assuming that the return on total capital (old and new) will equal the cost of capital. The original capital (prior to the continuing value period) will continue to earn the returns projected in the last forecast period. In other words, the company's competitive advantage period has *not* come to an end once the continuing-value period is reached. Exhibit 9.5 shows the implied average ROIC, assuming that projected continuing-value growth is 4.5 percent, the return on base capital is 18 percent, the return on new capital (RONIC) is 10 percent, and the WACC is 10 percent. The average return on all capital declines gradually. From its starting point at 18 percent, it declines to 14 percent (the halfway point to the RONIC) after 11 years. It reaches 12 percent after 23 years and 11 percent after 37 years.

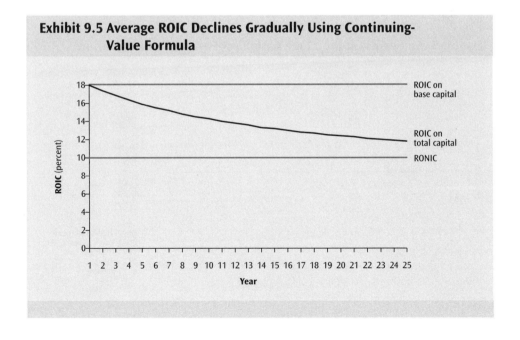

Exhibit 9.5 Average ROIC Declines Gradually Using Continuing-Value Formula

When Is Value Created?

Executives often state uncomfortably that "all the value is in the continuing value." Exhibit 9.6 illustrates the problem for Innovation Inc. It appears that 85 percent of Innovation's value comes from the continuing value. But there are other ways to interpret the source of value.

Exhibit 9.7 suggests an alternative: a business components approach. Innovation Inc. has a base business that earns a steady 12 percent return on capital and is growing at 4 percent per year. It also has developed a new product line that will require several years of negative cash flow for construction of a new plant. As shown in Exhibit 9.7, the base business has a value of $877, or 71 percent of Innovation's total value. So 71 percent of the company's value comes from operations that are currently generating strong cash flow. But the company has decided to reinvest this cash flow in a profitable new product line. This does not mean that 85 percent of the value is more than eight years out. It just means that the cash flow pattern mechanically results in the appearance that most of the value is a long way off.

We can use the economic profit model to generate another interpretation of continuing value. Exhibit 9.8 compares the components of value for Innovation Inc., using the two interpretations discussed earlier as well as the economic profit model. Under the economic profit model, 62 percent of Innovation's value is simply its invested capital. The rest of the value is the present value of projected economic profit (8 percent for economic profit before year 9 and 30 percent for economic profit after year 9).

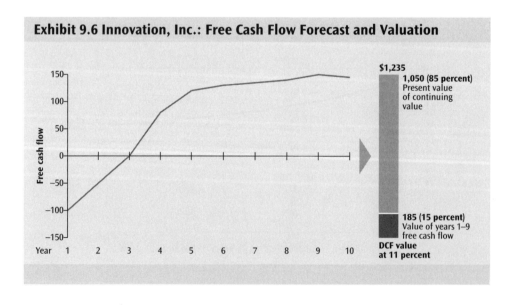

Exhibit 9.6 Innovation, Inc.: Free Cash Flow Forecast and Valuation

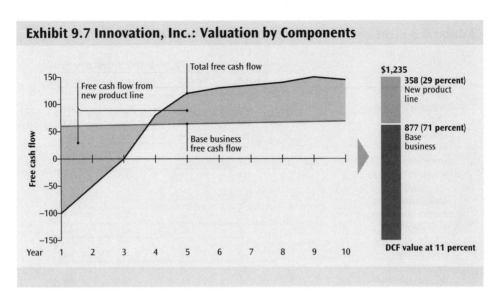

Exhibit 9.7 Innovation, Inc.: Valuation by Components

COMMON PITFALLS

Estimating a company's performance 10 to 15 years out is not a precise process. Common mistakes in estimating continuing value include naive base-year extrapolation and both naive and purposeful conservatism.

Naive Base-Year Extrapolation

Exhibit 9.9 on page 286 illustrates a common error in forecasting the base level of free cash flow: assuming that the investment rate is constant, so NOPLAT, investment, and FCF all grow at the same rate. From year 9 to

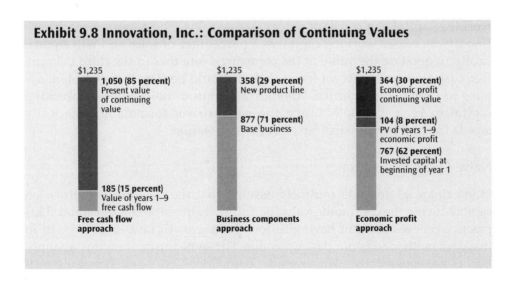

Exhibit 9.8 Innovation, Inc.: Comparison of Continuing Values

Exhibit 9.9 Right and Wrong Ways to Forecast the Base Free Cash Flow

	Year 9	Year 10	Year 11 (5 percent growth)	
			Incorrect	Correct
Sales	1,000	1,100	1,155	1,155
Operating expenses	(850)	(935)	(982)	(982)
EBIT	150	165	173	173
Cash taxes	(60)	(66)	(69)	(69)
NOPLAT	90	99	104	104
Depreciation	27	30	32	32
Gross cash flow	117	129	136	136
Capital expenditures	30	33	35	35
Increase in working capital	27	30	32	17
Gross investment	57	63	67	52
Free cash flow	60	66	69	84
Memo: year-end working capital	300	330	362	347
Working capital/sales (percent)	30	30	31	30
Increase in working capital/sales (percent)	2.7	2.7	2.7	1.5

year 10 (the last forecast year), the company's earnings and cash flow grow by 10 percent. The forecast suggests that growth in the continuing-value period will be 5 percent per year. A naive, and incorrect, forecast for year 11 (the continuing-value base year) simply increases every cash flow from year 10 by 5 percent, as shown in the third column. This forecast is wrong because the increase in working capital is far too large, given the projected increase in sales. Since sales are growing more slowly, the proportion of gross cash flow devoted to increasing working capital should decline significantly, as shown in the last column. In the final column, the increase in working capital should be the amount necessary to maintain the year-end working capital at a constant percentage of sales. The naive approach continually increases working capital as a percentage of sales and will significantly understate the value of the company. Note that in the third column, free cash flow is 18 percent lower than it should be. The same problem applies to capital expenditures, though we limited the example to working capital to keep it simple. Using the value driver formula automatically avoids the problem of naive base-year extrapolation.

Naive Overconservatism

Many financial analysts routinely assume that the incremental return on capital during the continuing-value period will equal the cost of capital. This practice relieves them of having to forecast a growth rate, since growth in this case neither adds nor destroys value. For some businesses, this assumption is too conservative. For example, both Coca-Cola's and PepsiCo's soft-drink businesses earn high returns on invested capital, and their returns are unlikely to fall substantially as they continue to grow due to the strength of their brands. An assumption that RONIC equals WACC for these businesses would substantially understate their values. This problem applies equally to almost any business selling a product or service that is unlikely to be duplicated, including many pharmaceutical companies, consumer products companies, and some software companies.

Purposeful Overconservatism

Analysts sometimes are overly conservative because of the uncertainty and size of the continuing value. But, if continuing value is to be estimated properly, the uncertainty should cut both ways: The results are just as likely to be higher than an unbiased estimate as they are to be lower. So conservatism overcompensates for uncertainty. Uncertainty matters, but it should be modeled using scenarios, and not through conservatism.

EVALUATING OTHER APPROACHES TO CONTINUING VALUE

Several alternative approaches to continuing value are used in practice, often with misleading results. A few approaches are acceptable if used carefully, but we prefer the methods recommended earlier because they explicitly rely on the underlying economic assumptions embodied in the company analysis. Other approaches tend to hide the underlying economic assumptions. Exhibit 9.10 illustrates, for a sporting goods company, the wide dispersion of continuing-value estimates arrived at by different techniques. This section explains why we prefer the recommended approaches. We classify the most common techniques into two categories: (1) other DCF approaches, and (2) non-cash-flow approaches.

Exhibit 9.10 Continuing-Value Estimates for a Sporting Goods Company

Technique	Assumptions	Continuing value ($ million)
Book value	Per accounting records	268
Liquidation value	80 percent of working capital 70 percent of net fixed assets	186
Price-to-earnings ratio	Industry average of 15X	624
Market-to-book ratio	Industry average of 1.4X	375
Replacement cost	Book value adjusted for inflation	275
Perpetuity based on final year's cash flow	Normalized FCF growing at inflation rate	428

Other Discounted Cash Flow Approaches

The recommended DCF formulas can be modified to derive additional continuing-value formulas with more restrictive (and sometimes unreasonable) assumptions.

One variation is the convergence formula. For many companies in competitive industries, we expect the return on net new investment to eventually converge to the cost of capital as all the excess profits are competed away. This assumption allows a simpler version of the value driver formula, as follows:

$$CV = \frac{NOPLAT_{t+1}}{WACC}$$

The derivation begins with the value driver formula:

$$CV = \frac{NOPLAT_{t+1}\left(1 - \dfrac{g}{RONIC}\right)}{WACC - g}$$

Assume that RONIC = WACC (that is, the return on incremental invested capital equals the cost of capital):

$$CV = \frac{NOPLAT_{t+1}\left(1 - \dfrac{g}{WACC}\right)}{WACC - g}$$

$$CV = \frac{NOPLAT_{t+1}\left(\dfrac{WACC - g}{WACC}\right)}{WACC - g}$$

Canceling the term $WACC - g$ leaves a simple formula:

$$CV = \frac{NOPLAT_{t+1}}{WACC}$$

The fact that the growth term has disappeared from the equation does not mean that the nominal growth in NOPLAT will be zero. The growth term drops out because new growth adds nothing to value, as the return associated with growth equals the cost of capital. This formula is sometimes interpreted as implying zero growth (not even with inflation), but this is not the case.

Misinterpretation of the convergence formula has led to another variant: the *aggressive-growth* formula. This formula assumes that earnings in the continuing-value period will grow at some rate, most often the inflation rate. The conclusion is then drawn that earnings should be discounted at the real WACC rather than the nominal WACC. The resulting formula is as follows:

$$CV = \frac{NOPLAT_{t+1}}{WACC - g}$$

Here, g is the inflation rate. This formula can substantially overstate continuing value because it assumes that NOPLAT can grow without any incremental capital investment. This is unlikely (or impossible), because any growth will probably require additional working capital and fixed assets.

To see how this formula relates to the key value driver formula, assume that the return on incremental capital investment (RONIC) approaches infinity:

$$CV = \frac{NOPLAT_{t+1}\left(1 - \dfrac{g}{RONIC}\right)}{WACC - g}$$

$$RONIC \to \infty \text{ therefore } \frac{g}{RONIC} \to 0$$

$$CV = \frac{NOPLAT_{t+1}(1 - 0)}{WACC - g}$$

$$CV = \frac{NOPLAT_{t+1}}{WACC - g}$$

Exhibit 9.11 on page 290 compares the two variations of the key value driver formula. This exhibit shows how the average return on invested capital (both existing and new investment) behaves under the two assumptions. In the aggressive-growth case, NOPLAT grows without any new investment, so the return on invested capital eventually approaches infinity. In the convergence case, the average return on invested capital moves toward the weighted average cost of capital as new capital becomes a larger portion of the total capital base.

Exhibit 9.11 Rates of Return Implied by Alternative Continuing-Value Formulas

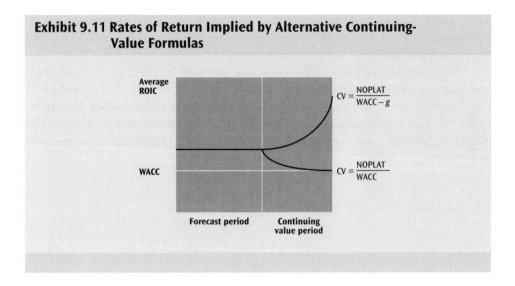

Non-Cash-Flow Approaches

In addition to DCF techniques, non-cash-flow approaches to continuing value are sometimes used. Three common approaches are multiples, liquidation value, and replacement cost.

Multiples

Multiples approaches assume that a company will be worth some multiple of future earnings or book value in the continuing period. But how do you estimate an appropriate future multiple?

A common approach is to assume that the company will be worth a multiple of earnings or book value based on the multiple for the company today. Suppose we choose today's current industry average price-to-earnings (P/E) ratio. This ratio reflects the economic prospects of the industry during the explicit forecast period as well as the continuing-value period. In maturing industries, however, prospects at the end of the explicit forecast period are likely to be very different from today's. Therefore, we need a different P/E ratio that reflects the company's prospects at the end of the forecast period. What factors will determine that ratio? As discussed in Chapter 3, the primary determinants are the company's expected growth, the rate of return on new capital, and the cost of capital. The same factors are in the key value driver formula. Unless you are comfortable using an arbitrary P/E ratio, you are much better off with the value driver formula.

When valuing an acquisition, companies sometimes fall into the circular reasoning that the P/E ratio for the continuing value should equal the P/E ratio paid for the acquisition. In other words, if I pay 18 times earnings today, I should be able to sell the business for 18 times earnings at the end of the explicit forecast period. In most cases, the reason a company is willing to pay a particular P/E for an acquisition is that it plans to improve the target's earnings. So the effective P/E it is paying on the improved level of earnings will be much less than 18. Once the improvements are in place and earnings are higher, buyers will not be willing to pay the same P/E unless they can make additional improvements. Chapter 12 describes other common mistakes made when using multiples.

Liquidation Value

The liquidation value approach sets the continuing value equal to the estimated proceeds from the sale of the assets, after paying off liabilities at the end of the explicit forecast period. Liquidation value is often far different from the value of the company as a going concern. In a growing, profitable industry, a company's liquidation value is probably well below the going-concern value. In a dying industry, liquidation value may exceed going-concern value. Do not use this approach unless liquidation is likely at the end of the forecast period.

Replacement Cost

The replacement cost approach sets the continuing value equal to the expected cost to replace the company's assets. This approach has several drawbacks. First, not all tangible assets are replaceable. The company's *organizational capital* can be valued only on the basis of the cash flow the company generates. The replacement cost of just the company's tangible assets may greatly understate the value of the company.

Second, not all the company's assets will ever be replaced. Consider a machine used only by this particular industry. As long as it generates a positive cash flow, the asset is valuable to the ongoing business of the company. But the replacement cost of the asset may be so high that replacing it is not economical. Here, the replacement cost may exceed the value of the business as an ongoing entity.

ADVANCED FORMULAS FOR CONTINUING VALUE

In certain situations, you may want to break up the continuing-value (CV) period into two periods with different growth and ROIC assumptions. You might assume that during the first eight years *after* the explicit forecast period, the company will grow at 8 percent per year and earn an incremental ROIC of 15 percent. After those eight years, the company's growth rate will slow to 5 percent, and incremental ROIC will drop to 11 percent. In a situation such as this, you can use a two-stage variation of the value driver formula for DCF valuations:

$$
CV = \left[\frac{NOPLAT_{t+1}\left(1 - \dfrac{g_A}{RONIC_A}\right)}{WACC - g_A} \right]\left[1 - \left(\frac{1+g_A}{1+WACC}\right)^N \right]
$$

$$
+ \left[\frac{NOPLAT_{t+1}\,(1+g_A)^N\left(1 - \dfrac{g_B}{RONIC_B}\right)}{(WACC - g_B)(1+WACC)^N} \right]
$$

where N = Number of years in the first stage of the CV period

g_A = Expected growth rate in the first stage of the CV period

g_B = Expected growth rate in the second stage of the CV period

$RONIC_A$ = Expected incremental ROIC during the first stage of the CV period

$RONIC_B$ = Expected incremental ROIC during the second stage of the CV period

Note that g_B must be less than WACC for this formula to be valid. (Otherwise the company would eventually take over the entire world economy.)

A two-stage variation can also be used for the economic profit continuing-value formula:[1]

$$
CV = \frac{Economic\ Profit_{t+1}}{WACC}
$$

$$
+ \left[\frac{NOPLAT_{t+1}\left(\dfrac{g_A}{RONIC_A}\right)(RONIC_A - WACC)}{WACC\left(WACC - g_A\right)} \right]\left[1 - \left(\frac{1+g_A}{1+WACC}\right)^N \right]
$$

$$
+ \frac{NOPLAT\,(1+g_A)^N\left(\dfrac{g_B}{RONIC_B}\right)(RONIC_B - WACC)}{WACC(WACC - g_B)(1+WACC)^N}
$$

---

[1] Thanks to Pieter de Wit and David Krieger for deriving this formula.

These formulas always assume that the return on the base level of capital remains constant at the level of the last year of the explicit forecast.

If you want to model a decline in ROIC for all capital, including the base level of capital, it is best to model this into the explicit forecast. It is difficult to model changes in average ROIC with formulas because the growth rate in revenues and NOPLAT will not equal the growth rate in FCF, and there are multiple ways for the ROIC to decline. You could model declining ROIC by setting the growth rate for capital and reducing NOPLAT over time (in which case NOPLAT will grow much slower than capital). Or you could set the growth rate for NOPLAT and adjust FCF each period (so FCF growth again will be slower than NOPLAT growth). The dynamics of these relationships are complex, and we do not recommend embedding the dynamics in continuing-value formulas, especially when the key value drivers become less transparent.

HEINEKEN CASE

We used the value driver model to estimate Heineken's DCF continuing value. For the business-as-usual scenario, the values of the parameters are estimated as follows:

- The first year of the continuing-value period is 2019 (one year after the last forecasted year). We project Heineken's 2019 NOPLAT to be €1.641 billion.

- Heineken's WACC is projected to remain at 7.5 percent. We do not foresee any significant change in Heineken's target capital structure or business risk.

- Heineken's return on new invested capital before goodwill beyond 2018 is forecast to be 15.0 percent. This is consistent with the forecast performance in the years leading up to 2018 in this scenario. This forecast for RONIC implies that Heineken, like other branded consumer product companies, owns brands that will allow it to achieve returns above its cost of capital for a long time.

- We expect that Heineken's NOPLAT will grow at 3 percent, based on 1.5 percent volume growth, 1.5 percent price increases, and constant margins. This forecast for growth is less than nominal GDP growth but consistent with the earlier years in the forecast.

By using these parameters in the recommended continuing-value formula, we obtain an estimated continuing value of €29.173 billion in 2018:

$$CV = \frac{NOPLAT_{2019}\left(1 - \frac{g}{RONIC}\right)}{WACC - g}$$

$$= \frac{1{,}641\left(1 - \frac{3.0\%}{15\%}\right)}{7.5\% - 3.0\%}$$

$$= €29.173 \text{ billion}$$

Using the economic profit approach and the same parameters, we obtain a continuing value of economic profit after 2018 equal to €18.387 billion, calculated as follows:

$$\text{CV of Economic Profit} = \frac{\text{Economic Profit}_{2019}}{\text{WACC}} + \frac{\text{NOPLAT}_{2019}\left(\dfrac{g}{\text{RONIC}}\right)(\text{RONIC}-\text{WACC})}{\text{WACC}(\text{WACC}-g)}$$

$$= \frac{832}{7.5\%} + \frac{1,641\left(\dfrac{3.0\%}{15\%}\right)(15\%-7.5\%)}{7.5\%(7.5\%-3.0\%)}$$

$$= €18.387 \text{ billion}$$

The continuing value is a large portion of Heineken's value because Heineken is expected to earn more than its cost of capital during and after the explicit forecast. However, the economic profit continuing value is smaller than the DCF continuing value. Adding the amount of invested capital at the end of 2018 to the continuing value of economic profit gives a total continuing value of €29.173 billion, the same value calculated using the DCF approach:

$$\text{CV} = \text{Invested capital}_{2018} + \text{CV of economic profit}$$
$$= €10.787 \text{ billion} + €18.387 \text{ billion}$$
$$= €29.173 \text{ billion}$$

REVIEW QUESTIONS

1. Identify three common errors executives make when estimating continuing value using the value driver formulas.

2. Identify and define four technical considerations to be analyzed when estimating continuing value using the value driver formula.

3. A client explains that her firm's value must be affected by the choice of explicit forecast horizon. Build a model to test her claim. NOPLAT, depreciation, and gross investment for year 1 have been forecasted to be $10.0, $2.5, and $13.61, respectively.

   a. To evaluate your client's claim, first assume a short horizon of three years.

   b. Compare the results of this three-year horizon to a six-year forecasted horizon. The company's management team forecasted RONIC for years 1 to 3 to be 18 percent and 11 percent thereafter. The company executives also forecasted NOPLAT to grow at 20 percent for years 1 to 3 and a decline to continuing growth rate of 5 percent thereafter. Finally, the management team has estimated an initial WACC of 14 percent for years 1 to 3, and declining to 12 percent after the initial forecasted period.

c. Compare your computed value for both time horizons. Provide an explanation of your results.

4. Your client remains skeptical. Why use two different representations of value: free cash flow and economic profit? Show her that the present value of economic profit plus beginning invested capital equals the present value of free cash flows.

5. Demonstrate for your client the equivalence between the free cash flow model and the economic profit model using the three-year horizon model described in question 4. Identify and discuss the similarities, differences and usefulness of each model.

6. Identify the strengths and weaknesses of the Enterprise DCF, Economic Profit, and Multiples approaches to estimating continuing value.

10

Estimating the Cost
of Capital

To value a company using enterprise DCF, we discount free cash flow by the weighted average cost of capital (WACC). The weighted average cost of capital represents the opportunity cost that investors face for investing their funds in one particular business instead of others with similar risk.

The most important principle underlying successful implementation of the cost of capital is consistency between the components of WACC and free cash flow. Since free cash flow is the cash flow available to all financial investors (debt, equity, and hybrid securities), the company's WACC must include the required return for each investor. In addition, the duration and risk of the financial securities used to estimate the WACC must match that of the free cash flow being discounted. To assure consistency, the cost of capital must meet several criteria:

- It must include the opportunity costs from *all* sources of capital—debt, equity, and so on—since free cash flow is available to all investors, who expect compensation for the risks they take.

- It must weight each security's required return by its target market-based weight, not by its historical book value.

- It must be computed after corporate taxes (since free cash flow is calculated in after-tax terms). Any financing-related tax shields not included in free cash flow must be incorporated into the cost of capital or valued separately (as done in the adjusted present value).

- It must be denominated in the same currency as free cash flow.

- It must be denominated in nominal terms when cash flows are stated in nominal terms.

For most companies, discounting free cash flow at the WACC is a simple, accurate, and robust method of corporate valuation. If, however, the company's target capital structure is expected to change significantly, for instance in a leveraged buyout (LBO), a constant WACC can overstate (or understate) the impact of interest tax shields. In this situation, discount free cash flow at the unlevered cost of equity, described later in this chapter, and value tax shields and other financing effects separately (as described in Chapter 5).

To determine the weighted average cost of capital, calculate its three components: the cost of equity, the after-tax cost of debt, and the company's target capital structure. Since *none* of the variables are directly observable, we employ various models, assumptions, and approximations to estimate each component.

In this chapter, we begin by defining the components of WACC and introducing the assumptions underlying these metrics. The next three sections detail how to estimate the cost of equity, cost of debt, and target capital structure, respectively. The chapter concludes with a discussion of WACC estimation when the company employs a complex capital structure, using hybrid securities such as convertible debt.

WEIGHTED AVERAGE COST OF CAPITAL

In its simplest form, the weighted average cost of capital is the market-based weighted average of the after-tax cost of debt and cost of equity:

$$\text{WACC} = \frac{D}{V} k_d (1 - T_m) + \frac{E}{V} k_e$$

where D/V = Target level of debt to enterprise value using market-based (not book) values

E/V = Target level of equity to enterprise value using market-based values

k_d = Cost of debt

k_e = Cost of equity

T_m = Company's marginal income tax rate

For companies with other securities, such as preferred stock, additional terms must be added to the cost of capital, representing each security's expected rate of return and percentage of total enterprise value.

The cost of capital does not include expected returns of operating liabilities, such as accounts payable. Required compensation for funds from customers, suppliers, and employees is included in operating expenses, such as cost of goods sold, so it is already incorporated in free cash flow. Including operating liabilities in the WACC would incorrectly double-count their cost of financing.

Exhibit 10.1 Home Depot: Weighted Average Cost of Capital

percent

Source of capital	Proportion of total capital	Cost of capital	Marginal tax rate	After-tax opportunity cost	Contribution to weighted average
Debt	8.3	4.7	38.2	2.9	0.2
Equity	91.7	9.9		9.9	9.1
WACC	**100.0**				**9.3**

To determine the cost of equity, we rely on the capital asset pricing model (CAPM), one of many theoretical models that convert a stock's risk into expected return.[1] The CAPM uses three variables to determine a stock's expected return: the risk-free rate, the market risk premium (i.e., the expected return of the market over risk-free bonds), and the stock's beta. In the CAPM, beta measures a stock's co-movement with the market and represents the stock's ability to further diversity the market portfolio. Stocks with high betas must have excess returns that exceed the market risk premium; the converse is true for low-beta stocks.

To approximate the cost of debt for an investment-grade firm, use the company's yield to maturity on its long-term debt. For companies with publicly traded debt, calculate yield to maturity directly from the bond's price and promised cash flows. For companies with illiquid debt, use the company's debt rating to estimate the yield to maturity. Since free cash flow is measured without interest tax shields, measure the cost of debt on an after-tax basis.

Finally, the after-tax cost of debt and cost of equity should be weighted using target levels of debt to value and equity to value. For mature companies, the target capital structure is often approximated by the company's current debt-to-value ratio, using market values of debt and equity. As will be explained later, you should not use book values.

In Exhibit 10.1, we present the WACC calculation for Home Depot. The company's cost of equity was determined using the CAPM, which led to a required equity return of 9.9 percent. To apply the CAPM, we used the December 2003 10-year U.S. government bond rate of 4.3 percent, a market risk premium of 4.5 percent, and a relevered industry beta of 1.23. As a

---

[1] Depending on the context, we use the terms *expected return, required return,* and *opportunity cost* interchangeably. Expected return refers to an investor's expected return on a security, given its level of risk. Financial managers refer to a "required return" because the return on an internal project must exceed the expected return on comparable investments. Otherwise, the investor would generate better returns outside the company. This is why the term *opportunity cost* also is quite common.

proxy for Home Depot's pretax cost of debt, we used the yield to maturity on AA-rated debt (4.7 percent). In Chapter 7, we estimated Home Depot's marginal tax rate at 38.2 percent, so its after-tax cost of debt equals 2.9 percent. Finally, we assume Home Depot will maintain a current debt-to-value ratio of 8.3 percent going forward.[2] Adding the weighted contributions from debt and equity, we arrive at a WACC equal to 9.3 percent.

We discuss each component of the weighted average cost of capital next.

ESTIMATING THE COST OF EQUITY

To estimate the cost of equity, we must determine the expected rate of return of the company's stock. Since expected rates of return are unobservable, we rely on asset-pricing models that translate risk into expected return.

The most common asset-pricing model is the capital asset pricing model (CAPM). Other models include the Fama-French three-factor model and the arbitrage pricing theory (APT). The three models differ primarily in how they define risk. The CAPM defines a stock's risk as its sensitivity to the stock market,[3] whereas the Fama-French three-factor model defines risk as a stock's sensitivity to three portfolios: the stock market, a portfolio based on firm size, and a portfolio based on book-to-market ratios. The CAPM is the most common method for estimating expected returns, so we begin our analysis with that model.

Capital Asset Pricing Model

Because the CAPM is discussed at length in modern finance textbooks,[4] we will not delve into the theory here. Instead, we focus on best practices for implementation.

The CAPM postulates that the expected rate of return on any security equals the risk-free rate plus the security's beta times the market risk premium:

$$E(R_i) = r_f + \beta_i \, [E(R_m) - r_f]$$

---

[2] Net debt equals reported debt plus the present value of operating leases, less excess cash. Although net debt to value at 8.3 percent is probably overly conservative, there is no evidence that Home Depot plans to increase its debt-to-value ratio.

[3] In theory, the market portfolio represents the value-weighted portfolio of all assets, both traded (such as stocks) and untraded (such as a person's skill set). Throughout this chapter, we use a well-diversified stock portfolio, such as the S&P 500 or the Morgan Stanley Capital International World Index, as a proxy for the market portfolio.

[4] For example, Richard Brealey and Stewart Myers, *Principles of Corporate Finance* (New York: McGraw-Hill, 2002); and Thomas Copeland, Fred Weston, and Kuldeep Shastri, *Financial Theory and Corporate Policy* (Boston: Addison-Wesley, 2005).

where $E(R_i)$ = Security i's expected return
r_f = Risk-free rate
β_i = Stock's sensitivity to the market
$E(R_m)$ = Expected return of the market

In the CAPM, the risk-free rate and market risk premium (defined as the difference between $E(R_m)$ and r_f) are common to all companies; only beta varies across companies. Beta represents a stock's incremental risk to a diversified investor, where risk is defined by how much the stock covaries with the aggregate stock market. Consider General Mills, a cereal manufacturer, and Cisco, a maker of network routers. Consumer cereal purchases are relatively independent of the stock market's value, so the beta for General Mills is low; we estimated it at 0.4. Based on a risk-free rate of 4.3 percent and a market risk premium of 5 percent, the cost of equity for General Mills is estimated at 6.3 percent (see Exhibit 10.2). In contrast, technology companies tend to have high betas. When the economy struggles, the stock market drops, and companies stop purchasing new technology. Thus, Cisco's value is highly correlated with the market's value, and its beta is high. Based on a beta of 1.4, Cisco's expected rate of return is 11.3 percent. Since General Mills offers greater protection against market downturns than Cisco, investors are willing to pay a premium for the stock, driving down expected returns. Conversely, since Cisco offers little diversification to the market portfolio, the company must earn higher returns to entice investors.

Although the CAPM is based on solid theory (the 1990 Nobel Prize in Economics was awarded to the model's primary author, William Sharpe),

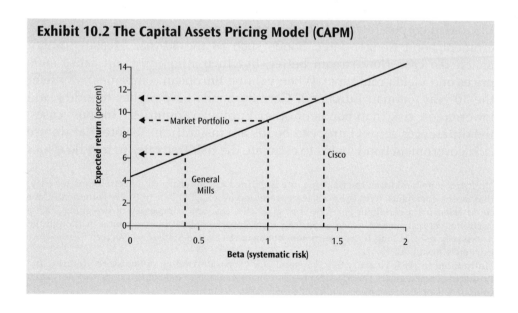

Exhibit 10.2 The Capital Assets Pricing Model (CAPM)

the model provides little guidance for implementation. For instance, when valuing a company, which risk-free rate should you use? How do you estimate the market risk premium and beta? In the following section, we address these issues. Our general conclusions are as follows:

- To estimate the risk-free rate in developed economies, use highly liquid, long-term government securities, such as the 10-year zero-coupon strip.
- Based on historical averages and forward-looking estimates, the appropriate market risk premium is currently between 4.5 and 5.5 percent.
- To estimate a company's beta, use an industry-derived unlevered beta levered to the company's target capital structure.

Estimating the risk-free rate   To estimate the risk-free rate, we look to government default-free bonds.[5] Government bonds come in many maturities. For instance, the U.S. Treasury issues bonds with maturities ranging from one month to 20 years. Since different maturities can generate different yields to maturity, which maturity should you use?

Ideally, each cash flow should be discounted using a government bond with a similar maturity. For instance, a cash flow generated 10 years from today should be discounted by a cost of capital derived from a 10-year zero-coupon government bond. We prefer zero-coupon government strips because long-term government bonds make interim interest payments,[6] causing their effective maturity to be shorter than their stated maturity.

In practice, few people discount each cash flow using a matched maturity. For simplicity, most choose a single yield to maturity from one government bond that best matches the entire cash flow stream being valued. For U.S.-based corporate valuation, the most common proxy is the 10-year government bond (longer-dated bonds such as the 30-year Treasury might match the cash flow stream better, but their illiquidity can cause stale prices and yield premiums). When valuing European companies, we prefer the 10-year German Eurobond. German bonds have higher liquidity and lower credit risk than bonds of other European countries. (In most cases, the differences across European bonds are insignificant.) Note that we use *local* government bond yields to estimate the risk-free rate. To handle issues

---

[5] In its most general form, the risk-free rate is defined as the return on a portfolio (or security) that has no covariance with the market (represented by a CAPM beta of 0). Hypothetically, one could construct a zero-beta portfolio, but given the cost and complexity of designing such a portfolio, we recommend focusing on long-term government *default-free* bonds. Although not necessarily *risk free*, long-term government bonds in the United States and Western Europe have extremely low betas.

[6] Introduced in 1985, Treasury STRIPS stands for "Separate Trading of Registered Interest and Principal of Securities." The STRIPS program enables investors to hold and trade the individual components of Treasury notes and bonds as separate securities.

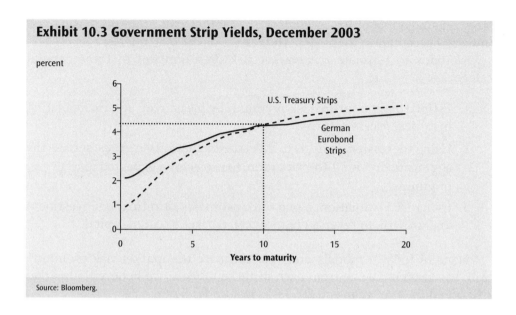

Exhibit 10.3 Government Strip Yields, December 2003

percent

- U.S. Treasury Strips
- German Eurobond Strips

Years to maturity

Source: Bloomberg.

like inflation consistently, we must ensure that cash flows and the cost of capital are denominated in the same currency.

In Exhibit 10.3, we plot the yield to maturity for various U.S. and German zero-coupon strips versus their years to maturity (a relation commonly known as the yield curve or term structure of interest rates). As of December 2003, the 10-year U.S. and German treasury strips were both trading at 4.3 percent.

If you are valuing a company or long-term project, do *not* use a short-term Treasury bill to determine the risk-free rate. When finance textbooks calculate the CAPM, they typically use a short-term Treasury rate because they are estimating expected returns for the next *month*. As can be seen in Exhibit 10.3, short-term Treasury bills (near the *y*-axis) traded well below 10-year bonds (0.9 percent versus 4.3 percent) in December 2003. Investors typically demand higher interest rates from long-term bonds when they believe short-term interest rates will rise over time. Using the yield from a short-term bond as the risk-free rate in a valuation fails to recognize that a bondholder must reinvest at higher rates when the short-term bond matures. Thus, the short-term bond rate misestimates the opportunity cost of investment for longer-term projects.

Estimating the market risk premium   Sizing the market risk premium—the difference between the market's expected return and the risk-free rate—is arguably the most debated issue in finance. The ability of stocks to outperform bonds over the long run has implications for corporate valuation, portfolio composition, and retirement savings. But similar to a stock's expected return, the expected return on the market is unobservable. And since no single model for estimating the market risk premium has gained universal acceptance, we present the results of various models.

Methods to estimate the market risk premium fall in three general categories:

1. Estimating the future risk premium by measuring and extrapolating historical excess returns.
2. Using regression analysis to link current market variables, such as the aggregate dividend-to-price ratio, to project the expected market risk premium.
3. Using DCF valuation, along with estimates of return on investment and growth, to reverse engineer the market's cost of capital.

None of today's models precisely estimate the market risk premium. Still, based on evidence from each of these models, we believe the market risk premium as of year-end 2003 was just under 5 percent.

Historical market risk premium   Investors, being risk-averse, demand a premium for holding stocks rather than bonds. If the level of risk aversion hasn't changed over the last 75 years, then historical excess returns are a reasonable proxy for future premiums (assuming measurement issues, such as survivorship bias, aren't overly problematic). To best measure the risk premium using historical data, follow these guidelines:

- Calculate the premium relative to long-term government bonds.
- Use the longest period possible.
- Use an arithmetic average of longer-dated intervals (such as five years).
- Adjust the result for econometric issues, such as survivorship bias.

Use long-term government bonds   When calculating the market risk premium, compare historical market returns with the return on 10-year government bonds. As discussed in the previous section, long-term government bonds better match the duration of a company's cash flows than do short-term bonds.

Use the longest period possible   When using historical observations to predict future results, the issue is what length of history to examine. If the market risk premium is stable, a longer history will reduce estimation error. Alternatively, if the premium changes and estimation error is small, a shorter period is better. To determine the appropriate historical period, we consider any trends in the market risk premium compared with the noise associated with short-term estimates.

To test for the presence of a long-term trend, we regress the U.S. market risk premium versus time. Over the last 100 years, no statistically significant trend is observable.[7] Based on regression results, the average excess return has fallen by 3.3 basis points a year, but this result is well below its standard error (leading to a low t-statistic). In addition, premiums calculated over sub-periods, even as long as 10 years, are extremely noisy. For instance, U.S. stocks outperformed bonds by 18 percent in the 1950s but offered no premium in the 1970s. Given the lack of any discernible trend and the significant volatility of shorter periods, you should use the longest time series possible.

Use arithmetic average of longer-dated intervals   When reporting market risk premiums, most data providers report an annual number, such as 6.2 percent per year. But how do they convert a century of data into an annual number? And is an annualized number even important?

Annual returns can be calculated using either an arithmetic average or a geometric average. An arithmetic (simple) average sums each year's observed premium and divides by the number of observations:

$$\text{Arithmetic Average} = \frac{1}{T}\sum_{t=1}^{T}\frac{1+R_m(t)}{1+r_f(t)}-1$$

A geometric average compounds each year's excess return and takes the root of the resulting product:

$$\text{Geometric Average} = \left(\prod_{t=1}^{T}\frac{1+R_m(t)}{1+r_f(t)}\right)^{1/T}-1$$

The choice of averaging methodology will affect the results. For instance, between 1903 and 2002, U.S. stocks outperformed long-term government bonds by 6.2 percent per year when averaged arithmetically. Using a geometric average, the number drops to 4.4 percent. This difference is not random; arithmetic averages always exceed geometric averages when returns are volatile.

So which averaging method on historical data best estimates the *expected* future rate of return? To estimate the mean (expectation) for any random variable, well-accepted statistical principles dictate that the arithmetic average is the best unbiased estimator. Therefore, to determine a security's

---

[7] Some authors, such as Lewellen, argue that the market risk premium does change over time—and can be measured using financial ratios, such as the dividend yield. We address these models separately. J. Lewellen, "Predicting Returns with Financial Ratios," *Journal of Financial Economics*, 74(2) (2004): 209–235.

expected return for one period, the best unbiased predictor is the arithmetic average of many one-period returns. A one-period risk premium, however, can't value a company with many years of cash flow. Instead, long-dated cash flows must be discounted using a compounded rate of return. But when compounded, the arithmetic average will be *biased* upward (too high).

This bias is caused by estimation error and autocorrelation in returns. Let's examine the effect of estimation error first. To estimate the mean of a distribution, statistical theory instructs you to average the observations. In a finite sample, the sample average (R_A) will equal the true mean (μ) plus an error term (ε):

$$R_A = \mu + \varepsilon$$

Sometimes the error term is positive, so the sample average overestimates the true mean, and at other times, the error term is negative. But the average error term equals 0, so the sample average is an unbiased estimator of the true mean.

To value a cash flow *beyond* one period, we must determine the discount factor by raising R_A to a given power. For instance, to estimate a two-period discount rate, we calculate R_A squared. Squaring R_A leads to the following equation:

$$R_A = (\mu + \varepsilon)^2 = \mu^2 + \varepsilon^2 + 2\mu\varepsilon$$

Since the true mean, μ, is a constant and the expectation of ε is 0, the expectation of $2\mu\varepsilon$ equals 0. The expectation of ε^2, however, is not 0, but a positive number (the square of any nonzero number is greater than zero). Therefore, R_A^2 will be greater than μ^2 (the true mean squared), and a compounded sample average will be too high.

The compounded arithmetic average will also be biased upward when returns are negatively autocorrelated (meaning low returns follow high returns and high returns follow low returns). Although there is disagreement in the academic community, the general consensus is that the aggregate stock market exhibits negative autocorrelation.[8] In this case, the arithmetic mean is biased upward.

---

[8] Empirical evidence presented by James Poterba, Lawrence Summers, and others indicates that a significant long-term negative autocorrelation exists in stock returns. See J. Poterba and L. Summers, "Mean Reversion in Stock Prices," *Journal of Financial Economics* (October 1988): 27–60. However, subsequent studies by Matthew Richardson and others challenge the statistical significance of earlier studies. See M. Richardson, "Temporary Components of Stock Prices: A Skeptic's View," *Journal of Business and Economic Statistics*, 11 (1993): 199–207.

Exhibit 10.4 Expected Value When Returns Exhibit Negative Autocorrelation

	Potential return		Unconditional probability			
	20%		50%			
	(10%)		50%			

Scenario	Current value	Return in period one	Return in period two	Future value	Expected value when returns are independent		Expected value when returns are negatively autocorrelated	
1	100	1.2	1.2	144	25%	36.0	15%	21.6
2	100	1.2	0.9	108	25%	27.0	35%	37.8
3	100	0.9	1.2	108	25%	27.0	35%	37.8
4	100	0.9	0.9	81	25%	20.3	15%	12.2
					100%	110.3	100%	109.4

To better understand the effect of negative autocorrelation, consider a portfolio that can either grow by 20 percent or fall by 10 percent in a given period (see Exhibit 10.4). Since both returns are equally likely, the one period average return equals 5 percent. In addition, if returns are independently and identically distributed, after two periods there is:

1. A 25 percent probability that an initial investment of $100 will grow to $144

2. A 50 percent probability (two equally probable scenarios) that $100 will grow to $108

3. A 25 percent probability that $100 will shrink to $81

The expected value in two periods equals $110.3, the same as if $100 had grown consistently at the *arithmetic* average of 5 percent for two periods. But if the four scenarios are not equally likely, the expected value in two periods will not equal $110.3. For instance, if there is a 70 percent probability that low returns will be followed by high returns (or vice versa), the expected value in two periods is only $109.4. In this case, compounding the arithmetic mean will lead to an upward bias in expected return.

To correct for the bias caused by estimation error and negative autocorrelation in returns, we have two choices. First, we can calculate multiperiod holding returns directly from the data, rather than compound single-period averages. Using this method, a cash flow received in five years will be discounted by the average five-year market risk premium, not by the annual

Exhibit 10.5 Cumulative Returns for Various Intervals, 1903–2002

percent

| | | Cumulative returns | | | Annualized returns | |
Arithmetic mean of	Number of observations	U.S. stocks	U.S. government bonds	U.S. excess return	U.S. excess returns	Blume estimator
1-year holding periods	100	11.3	5.3	6.2	6.2	6.2
2-year holding periods	50	24.1	10.9	12.6	6.1	6.1
4-year holding periods	25	49.9	23.1	23.0	5.3	6.0
5-year holding periods	20	68.2	29.5	32.3	5.8	5.9
10-year holding periods	10	165.6	72.1	70.1	5.5	5.6

Source: Ibbotson Associates, McKinsey analysis.

market risk premium compounded five times.[9] In Exhibit 10.5, we present arithmetic averages for holding periods of 1, 2, 4, 5, and 10 years. To avoid placing too little weight on either early or recent observations, we use nonoverlapping returns. The downside of this method is that 5- and 10-year holding periods have very few observations. As shown in the exhibit, the annualized excess return trends downward from 6.2 percent to 5.5 percent as the length of the holding period increases.

Alternatively, researchers have used simulation to show that an estimator proposed by Marshall Blume best adjusts for problems caused by estimation error and autocorrelation of returns:[10]

$$R = \frac{T-N}{T-1}R_A + \frac{N-1}{T-1}R_G$$

where T = Number of historical observations

N = Forecast period

R_A = Arithmetic average

R_G = Geometric average

In the last column of Exhibit 10.5, we report Blume's estimate for the market risk premium. Blume's method generates the same downward-trending estimate of the market risk premium (albeit more smoothly than the raw holding period averages). Based on both estimation techniques, it appears 5.5 percent is a reasonable approximation for *historical* excess returns.

[9] Jay Ritter writes, "There is no theoretical reason why one year is the appropriate holding period. People are used to thinking of interest rates as a rate per year, so reporting annualized numbers makes it easy for people to focus on the numbers. But I can think of no reason other than convenience for the use of annual returns." J. Ritter, "The Biggest Mistakes We Teach," *Journal of Financial Research*, 25 (2002): 159–168.

[10] D. C. Indro and W. Y. Lee, "Biases in Arithmetic and Geometric Averages Premia," *Financial Management*, 26(4) (Winter 1997); M. E. Blume, "Unbiased Estimators of Long Run Expected Rates of Return," *Journal of the American Statistical Association*, 69(347) (September 1974).

Survivorship bias   Other statistical difficulties exist with historical risk premiums. According to one argument,[11] even properly measured historical premiums can't predict future returns, because the observable sample will include only countries with strong historical returns. Statisticians refer to this phenomenon as survivorship bias. The U.S. market outperformed all others during the twentieth century, averaging 4.3 percent in real terms (deflating by the wholesale price index) versus a median of 0.8 percent for other countries.[12] A concurring study[13] notes that the −100 percent returns from China, Russia, and Poland are too often ignored in discussions of stock market performance.

Since it is unlikely that the U.S. stock market will replicate its performance over the next century, we adjust downward the historical arithmetic average market risk premium. Using data from Philippe Jorion and William Goetzmann, we find that between 1926 and 1996, the U.S. arithmetic annual return exceeded the median return on a set of 11 countries with continuous histories dating to the 1920s by 1.9 percent in real terms, or 1.4 percent in nominal terms. If we subtract a 1 percent to 2 percent survivorship bias from the long-term arithmetic average of 5.5 percent, the difference implies the future range of the U.S. market risk premium should be 3.5 to 4.5 percent.

Market risk premium regressions   Although we find no long-term trend in the historical risk premium, many argue that the market risk premium is predictable using observable variables, such as the aggregate dividend-to-price ratio, the aggregate book-to-market ratio, or the aggregate ratio of earnings to price.

The use of current financial ratios to estimate the expected return on stocks is well documented and dates back to Charles Dow in the 1920s. The concept has been tested by many authors.[14] To predict the market risk premium using financial ratios, excess market returns are regressed against a financial ratio, such as the market's aggregate dividend-to-price ratio:

$$R_m - r_f = \alpha + \beta \ \ln\left(\frac{\text{Dividend}}{\text{Price}}\right) + \varepsilon$$

---

[11] S. Brown, W. Goetzmann, and S. Ross, "Survivorship Bias," *Journal of Finance* (July 1995): 853–873.

[12] P. Jorion and W. Goetzmann, "Global Stock Markets in the Twentieth Century," *Journal of Finance,* 54(3) (June 1999): 953–974.

[13] Elroy Dimson, Paul Marsh, and Michael Staunton, *Triumph of the Optimists* (Princeton: Princeton University Press, 2002).

[14] E. Fama and K. French, "Dividend Yields and Expected Stock Returns," *Journal of Financial Economics,* 22(1) (1988): 3–25; R. F. Stambaugh, "Predictive Regressions," *Journal of Financial Economics,* 54(3) (1999): 375–421; and J. Lewellen, "Predicting Returns with Financial Ratios," *Journal of Financial Economics,* 74(2) (2004): 209–235.

Exhibit 10.6 Expected Market Risk Premium Based on Dividend Yield

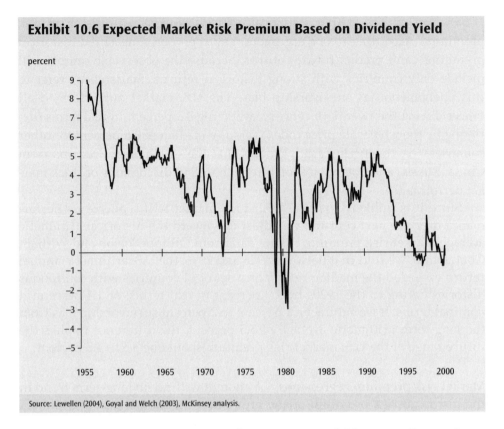

Source: Lewellen (2004), Goyal and Welch (2003), McKinsey analysis.

Using advanced regression techniques unavailable to earlier authors, Jonathan Lewellen found that dividend yields *do* predict future market returns. But as shown in Exhibit 10.6, the model has a major drawback: the risk premium prediction can be negative (as it was in the late 1990s). Other authors question the explanatory power of financial ratios, arguing that a financial analyst relying solely on data available at the time would have done better using unconditional historical averages (as we did in the last section) in place of more sophisticated regression techniques.[15]

Forward-looking models   A stock's price equals the present value of its dividends. Assuming dividends are expected to grow at a constant rate, we can rearrange the growing perpetuity to solve for the market's expected return:

$$P = \frac{\text{DIV}}{k_e - g} \quad \text{converts to} \quad k_e = \frac{\text{DIV}}{P} + g$$

In the previous section, we reviewed regression models that compare market returns (k_e) to the dividend-price ratio (DIV/P). Using a simple re-

[15] A. Goyal and I. Welch, "Predicting the Equity Premium with Dividend Ratios," *Management Science*, 4, 9(5) (2003): 639–654.

gression, however, ignores valuable information and oversimplifies a few market realities. First, the dividend-price yield itself depends on the expected growth in dividends (g), which simple regressions ignore (the regression's intercept is determined by the data). Second, dividends are only one form of corporate payout. Companies can use free cash flow to repurchase shares or hold excess cash for significant periods of time; consider Microsoft, which accumulated more than $50 billion in liquid securities before paying its first dividend.

Using the principles of discounted cash flow, along with estimates of growth, various authors have attempted to reverse engineer the market risk premium. Two studies used analyst forecasts to estimate growth,[16] but many argue that analyst forecasts focus on the short term and are severely upward biased. Fama and French use long-term dividend growth rates as a proxy for future growth, but they focus on dividend yields, not on available cash flow.[17] Alternatively, our own research has focused on *all* cash flow available to equity holders, as measured by a modified version of the key value driver formula (detailed in Chapter 3):[18]

$$k_e = \frac{\text{Earnings}\left(1 - \dfrac{g}{\text{ROE}}\right)}{P} + g \text{ such that } CF_e = \text{Earnings}\left(1 - \frac{g}{\text{ROE}}\right)$$

Based on this formula, we used the long-run return on equity (13 percent) and the long-run growth in real GDP (3.5 percent) to convert a given year's S&P 500 median earnings-to-price ratio into the cost of equity.[19]

Exhibit 10.7 on page 312 plots the nominal and real expected market returns between 1962 and 2002. The results are striking. After stripping out inflation, the expected market return (*not* excess return) is remarkably constant, averaging 7.0 percent. For the United Kingdom, the real market return is slightly more volatile, averaging 6.0 percent. Based on these results, we estimate the current market risk premium by subtracting the current real long-term risk-free rate from the real equity return of 7.0 percent (for U.S. markets). At year-end 2003, the yield on a U.S. Treasury inflation-protected security (TIPS) equaled 2.1 percent. Subtracting 2.1

[16] J. Claus and J. Thomas, "Equity Premia as Low as Three Percent? Evidence from Analysts' Earnings Forecasts for Domestic and International Stocks," *Journal of Finance,* 56(5) (October 2001): 1629–1666; and W. R. Gebhardt, C. M. C. Lee, and B. Swaminathan, "Toward an Implied Cost of Capital," *Journal of Accounting Research,* 39(1) (2001): 135–176.

[17] Eugene F. Fama and Kenneth R. French, "The Equity Premium," Center for Research in Security Prices Working Paper No. 522 (April 2001).

[18] Marc H. Goedhart, Timothy M. Koller, and Zane D. Williams, "The Real Cost of Equity," *McKinsey on Finance* (Autumn 2002): 11–15.

[19] Using a two-stage model (i.e., short-term ROE and growth rate projections, followed by long-term estimates) did not change the results in a meaningful way.

Exhibit 10.7 Real and Nominal Expected Market Returns

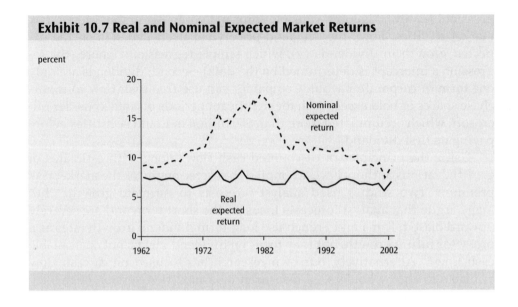

percent from 7.0 percent gives an estimate of the risk premium at just under 5 percent.

Although many in the finance profession disagree about how to measure the market risk premium, we believe 4.5 to 5.5 percent is an appropriate range. Historical estimates found in most textbooks (and locked in the mind of many), which often report numbers near 8 percent, are too high for valuation purposes because they compare the market risk premium versus short-term bonds, use only 75 years of data, and are biased by the historical strength of the U.S. market.

Estimating beta   According to the CAPM, a stock's expected return is driven by beta, which measures how much the stock and market move together. Since beta cannot be observed directly, we must *estimate* its value. To do this, we first measure a raw beta using regression and then improve the estimate by using industry comparables and smoothing techniques. The most common regression used to estimate a company's raw beta is the market model:

$$R_i = \alpha + \beta R_m + \varepsilon$$

In the market model, the stock's return (not price) is regressed against the market's return.

In Exhibit 10.8, we plot 60 months of Home Depot stock returns versus S&P 500 returns between 1999 and 2003. The solid line represents the "best

Exhibit 10.8 Home Depot: Stock Returns versus S&P 500 Returns, 1999–2003

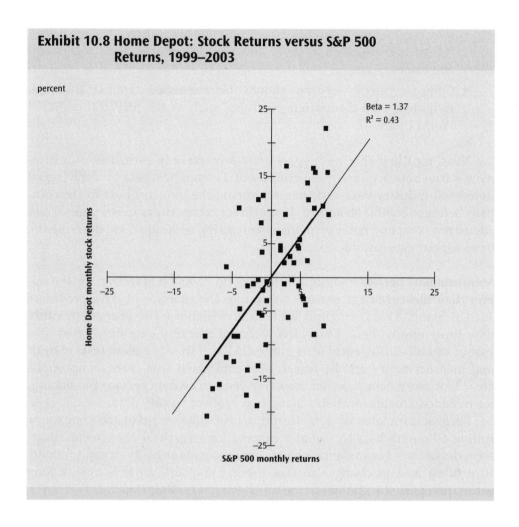

fit" relation between Home Depot's stock returns and the stock market. The slope of this line is commonly denoted as beta. For Home Depot, the company's raw beta (slope) is 1.37. Since typical betas range between 0 and 2, with the value-weighted average beta equaling 1, this raw result implies Home Depot is riskier than the typical stock.

But why did we choose to measure Home Depot's returns in months? Why did we use five years of data? And how precise is this measurement? The CAPM is a one-period model and provides little guidance on implementation. Yet, based on certain market characteristics and a variety of empirical tests, we reach several conclusions:

- Raw regressions should use at least 60 data points (e.g., five years of monthly returns). Rolling betas should be graphed to examine any systematic changes in a stock's risk.

- Raw regressions should be based on monthly returns. Using shorter return periods, such as daily and weekly returns, leads to systematic biases.
- Company stock returns should be regressed against a value-weighted, well-diversified portfolio, such as the S&P 500 or MSCI World Index.

Next, recalling that raw regressions provide only estimates of a company's true beta, we improve estimates of a company's beta by deriving an unlevered industry beta and then relevering the industry beta to the company's target capital structure. If no direct competitors exist, you should adjust raw company betas by using a smoothing technique. We describe the basis for our conclusions next.

Measurement period   Although there is no common standard for the appropriate measurement period, we follow the practice of data providers such as Standard & Poor's and Value Line, which use five years of monthly data to determine beta. Using five years of monthly data originated as a rule of thumb during early tests of the CAPM.[20] In subsequent tests of optimal measurement periods, researchers confirmed five years as appropriate.[21] Not every data provider uses five years. The data service Bloomberg, for instance, creates raw betas using two years of weekly data.

Because estimates of beta are imprecise, however, plot the company's rolling 60-month beta to visually inspect for structural changes or short-term deviations. For instance, changes in corporate strategy or capital structure often lead to changes in risk for stockholders. In this case, a long estimation period would place too much weight on stale data.

In Exhibit 10.9, we graph IBM's raw beta between 1985 and 2004. As the exhibit shows, IBM's beta hovered near 0.7 in the 1980s but rose dramatically in the mid-1990s and now measures near 1.3. This rise in beta occurred during a period of great change for IBM, as the company moved from hardware (such as mainframes) to services (such as consulting). Subsequently, using a long estimation period (for instance, 10 years) would underestimate the risk of the company's new business model.

Frequency of measurement   In 1980, Nobel laureate Robert Merton argued that estimates of covariance, and subsequently beta, improve as returns are

---

[20] F. Black, M. Jensen, and M. Scholes, "The Capital Asset Pricing Model: Some Empirical Tests," in *Studies in Theory of Capital Markets*, ed. M. Jensen (New York: Praeger, 1972).

[21] Alexander and Chervany tested the accuracy of estimation periods from one to nine years. They found four-year and six-year estimation periods performed best but were statistically indistinguishable. G. Alexander and N. Chervany, "On the Estimation and Stability of Beta," *Journal of Financial and Quantitative Analysis*, 15 (1980): 123–137.

Exhibit 10.9 IBM: Market Beta, 1985–2004

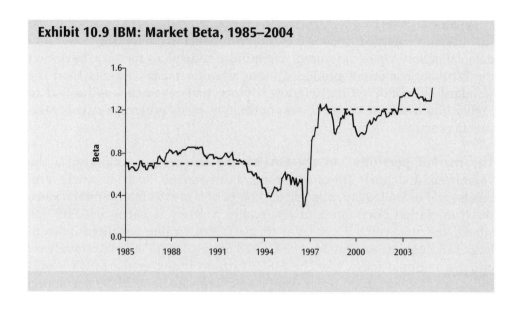

measured more frequently.[22] Implementing Merton's theory, however, has proven elusive. Empirical problems make high-frequency beta estimation unreliable. Therefore, we recommend using monthly data.

Using daily or even weekly returns is especially problematic when the stock is rarely traded. An illiquid stock will have many reported returns equal to zero, not because the stock's value is constant but because it hasn't traded (only the last trade is recorded). Consequently, estimates of beta on illiquid stocks are biased downward. Using longer-dated returns, such as monthly returns, lessens this effect. One proposal for stocks that trade infrequently even on a monthly basis is to sum lagged betas.[23] In lagged-beta models, a stock's return is simultaneously regressed on concurrent market returns and market returns from the prior period. The two betas from the regression are then summed.

A second problem with using high-frequency data is the bid/ask bounce. Periodic stock prices are recorded at the last trade, and the recorded price depends on whether the last trade was a purchase (using the ask price) or a sale (using the bid price). A stock whose intrinsic value remains unchanged will therefore "bounce" between the bid and ask price, causing distortions in beta estimation. Using longer-period returns dampens this distortion.

[22] R. Merton, "On Estimating the Expected Return on the Market," *Journal of Financial Economics,* 8 (1980): 323–361.

[23] M. Scholes and J. T. Williams, "Estimating Betas from Nonsynchronous Data," *Journal of Financial Economics,* 5 (1977): 309–327. See also E. Dimson, "Risk Measurement When Shares Are Subject to Infrequent Trading," *Journal of Financial Economics,* 7 (1979): 197–226.

Over the past few years, promising research on high-frequency beta estimation has emerged, spawned by improvements in computing power and data collection. One study used five-minute returns to measure beta, and the estimation method produced more accurate measurements than the standard 60-month rolling window.[24] Since that research was limited to highly liquid stocks, however, we continue to focus on longer-dated intervals in practice.

The market portfolio   In the CAPM, the market portfolio equals the value-weighted portfolio of all assets, both traded (such as stocks and bonds) and untraded (such as private companies and human capital). Since the true market portfolio is unobservable, a proxy is necessary. For U.S. stocks, the most common proxy is the S&P 500, a value-weighted index of large U.S. companies. Outside the United States, financial analysts rely on either a regional index like the MSCI Europe Index or the MSCI World Index, a value-weighted index comprising large stocks from 23 developed countries (including the United States).

Most well-diversified indexes, such as the S&P 500 and MSCI World Index, are highly correlated (the two indexes had an 85.4 percent correlation between 1999 and 2003). Thus, the choice of index will have little effect on beta. For instance, Home Depot's beta with respect to the S&P 500 is 1.37, whereas the company's beta with respect to the MSCI World Index is nearly identical at 1.35. Do *not*, however, use a local market index. Most countries are heavily weighted in only a few industries and, in some cases, a few companies. Consequently, when measuring beta versus a local index, you are not measuring market-wide systematic risk, but rather a company's sensitivity to a particular industry.

The internet bubble distorted the market portfolio   In the late 1990s, equity markets rose dramatically, but this increase was confined primarily to extremely large capitalization stocks and stocks in the telecommunications, media, and technology sectors (commonly known as TMT). Historically, TMT stocks contribute approximately 20 percent of the market value of the S&P 500. Between 1999 and 2001, this percentage rose to nearly 50 percent. And as the market portfolio changed, so too did industry betas. As shown by the historical betas for 10 industries in Exhibit 10.10, betas related to TMT rose dramatically during the tech boom, while betas outside the TMT sector fell. For instance, between 1990 and 1997, the food industry had an average beta of 0.85. Immediately following the tech boom, the food industry's beta dropped to zero.

---

[24] T. Bollerslev and B. Y. B. Zhang, "Measuring and Modeling Systematic Risk in Factor Pricing Models Using High-Frequency Data," *Journal of Empirical Finance*, 10 (2003): 533–558.

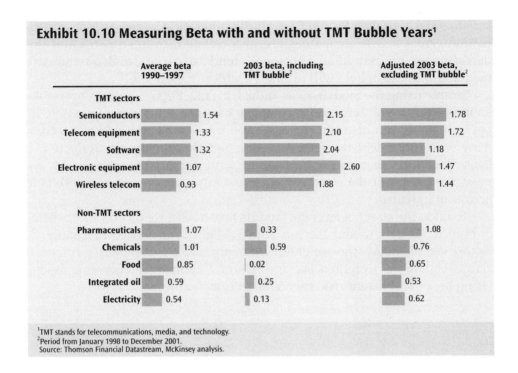

Exhibit 10.10 Measuring Beta with and without TMT Bubble Years[1]

	Average beta 1990–1997	2003 beta, including TMT bubble[2]	Adjusted 2003 beta, excluding TMT bubble[2]
TMT sectors			
Semiconductors	1.54	2.15	1.78
Telecom equipment	1.33	2.10	1.72
Software	1.32	2.04	1.18
Electronic equipment	1.07	2.60	1.47
Wireless telecom	0.93	1.88	1.44
Non-TMT sectors			
Pharmaceuticals	1.07	0.33	1.08
Chemicals	1.01	0.59	0.76
Food	0.85	0.02	0.65
Integrated oil	0.59	0.25	0.53
Electricity	0.54	0.13	0.62

[1]TMT stands for telecommunications, media, and technology.
[2]Period from January 1998 to December 2001.
Source: Thomson Financial Datastream, McKinsey analysis.

But will these new, widely dispersed, betas continue? Probably not. Since 2001, the market portfolio has returned to its traditional composition. Therefore, betas are likely to normalize as well. To this end, we argue that estimates of future beta should exclude observations from 1998 to 2001.[25] Remember, the end goal is not to measure beta historically, but rather to use the historical estimate as a predictor of future value. In this case, recent history isn't very useful and should not be overweighted.

Improving estimates of beta: Industry betas   Estimating beta is an imprecise process. Earlier, we used historical regression to estimate Home Depot's raw beta at 1.37. But the regression's R-squared was only 43 percent, and the standard error of the beta estimate was 0.20. Using two standard errors as a guide, we feel confident Home Depot's true beta lies between 0.97 and 1.77—hardly a tight range.

To improve the precision of beta estimation, use industry, rather than company-specific, betas.[26] Companies in the same industry face similar

---

[25] André Annema and Marc Goedhart, "Better Betas," *McKinsey on Finance* (Winter 2003): 10–13.
[26] If unlevered industry betas are drawn from the same distribution, the standard error of the industry average equals the volatility of the beta distribution divided by the square root of the number of observations. Thus, the standard error of an industry beta falls as the number of beta observations rises.

operating risks, so they should have similar operating betas. As long as estimation errors across companies are uncorrelated, overestimates and underestimates of individual betas will tend to cancel, and an industry median (or average) beta will produce a superior estimate.[27]

Simply using the median of an industry's raw betas, however, overlooks an important factor: leverage. A company's beta is a function of not only its operating risk, but also the financial risk it takes. Shareholders of a company with more debt face greater risks, and this increase is reflected in beta. Therefore, to compare companies with similar operating risks, we must first strip out the effect of leverage. Only then can we compare beta across an industry.

To undo the effect of leverage (and its tax shield), we rely on the theories of Franco Modigliani and Merton Miller (M&M), introduced in Chapter 5. According to M&M, the weighted average risk of a company's financial claims equals the weighted average risk of a company's economic assets. Using beta to represent risk, this relation is as follows:

$$\underbrace{\frac{V_u}{V_u + V_{txa}}\beta_u}_{\text{Operating Assets}} + \underbrace{\frac{V_{txa}}{V_u + V_{txa}}\beta_{txa}}_{\text{Tax Asset}} = \underbrace{\frac{D}{D+E}\beta_d}_{\text{Debt}} + \underbrace{\frac{E}{D+E}\beta_e}_{\text{Equity}}$$

where V_u = Value of the company's operating assets
V_{txa} = Value of the company's interest tax shields
D = Market value of the company's debt
E = Market value of the company's equity

In Appendix D, we rearrange the equation to solve for the beta of equity (β_e). This leads to:

$$\beta_e = \beta_u + \frac{D}{E}(\beta_u - \beta_d) - \frac{V_{txa}}{E}(\beta_u - \beta_{txa})$$

To simplify the formula further, most practitioners impose two additional restrictions.[28] First, because debt claims have first priority, the beta of

---

[27] Statistically speaking, the sample average will have the lowest mean squared error. However, because sample averages are heavily influenced by outliers, we recommend examining both the mean and median beta.

[28] In Chapter 5, we detailed alternative restrictions that can be imposed to simplify the general equation regarding risk. Rather than repeat the analysis, we focus on the least restrictive assumption for mature companies: that debt remains proportional to value. For a full discussion of which restrictions to impose and how they affect the cost of capital, please see the section on adjusted present value in Chapter 5.

debt tends to be low. Thus, many assume (for simplicity) the beta of debt is 0. Second, if the company maintains a constant capital structure, the value of tax shields will fluctuate with the value of operating assets and beta of the tax shields (β_{txa}) will equal the beta of the unlevered company (β_u). Setting β_{txa} equal to β_u eliminates the final term:

$$\beta_e = \beta_u \left(1 + \frac{D}{E} \right) \tag{1}$$

Thus, a company's equity beta equals the company's operating beta (commonly known as the unlevered beta) times a leverage factor. As leverage rises, so will the company's equity beta. Using this relation, we can convert equity betas into unlevered betas. Since unlevered betas focus solely on operating risk, they can be averaged across an industry (assuming industry competitors have similar operating characteristics).

To estimate an industry-adjusted company beta, use the following four-step process. First, regress each company's stock returns against the S&P 500 to determine raw beta. In Exhibit 10.11 on page 320, we report regression betas for Home Depot (1.37) and Lowe's (1.15). Next, to unlever each beta, calculate each company's market-debt-to-equity ratio. To calculate net debt ($6.310 billion for Home Depot), add the book value of reported debt ($1.365 billion) to the estimated value of operating leases ($6.554 billion) and then subtract excess cash ($1.609 billion).[29] To determine equity value ($80.101 billion), we multiply the company's stock price ($35.49) by the number of shares outstanding (2.257 billion). With debt and equity in hand, compute debt to equity (.079). Applying equation 1 leads to an unlevered beta of 1.27 for Home Depot and 1.02 for Lowe's. In step three, determine the industry unlevered beta by calculating the median (in this case, the median and average betas are the same).[30] In the final step, relever the industry unlevered beta is to each company's *target* debt-to-equity ratio (using current market values as proxies).

Unlevered cost of equity   As demonstrated, we can unlever an equity beta in order to improve beta estimation for use in the CAPM and WACC. We also can use unlevered industry betas to estimate a company's unlevered cost of equity. To estimate the unlevered cost of equity for use in an adjusted present value (APV) valuation, simply apply the CAPM to the industry unlevered beta.

---

[29] The process for valuing operating leases and excess cash is detailed in Chapter 7.
[30] In most valuations, more than two company betas are available. For Home Depot, Lowe's is the only publicly traded competitor. As a general rule, use as many direct comparables as possible.

Exhibit 10.11 Determining the Industry Beta

$ million

Capital structure	Home Depot	Lowe's
Debt	1,365	3,755
Operating leases	6,554	2,762
Excess cash	(1,609)	(948)
Total net debt	6,310	5,569
Shares outstanding (millions)	2,257	787
Share price ($)	35.49	55.39
Market value of equity	80,101	43,592
Debt/equity	0.079	0.128

Beta calculations	Home Depot	Lowe's
Raw beta (step 1)	1.37	1.15
Unlevered beta (step 2)	1.27	1.02
Industry average unlevered beta (step 3)	1.14	1.14
Relevered beta (step 4)	1.23	1.30

Improving estimates of beta: Smoothing   For well-defined industries, an industry beta will suffice. But if few direct comparables exist, an alternative is beta smoothing. Consider the simple smoothing process used by Bloomberg:

$$\text{Adjusted Beta} = (.33) + (.67)\ \text{Raw Beta}$$

Using this formula "smooths" raw estimates toward 1. For instance, a raw beta of 0.5 leads to an adjusted beta of 0.67, while a raw beta of 1.5 leads to an adjusted beta of 1.34. Bloomberg's smoothing mechanism dates back to Blume's observation that betas revert to the mean.[31] Today, more advanced smoothing techniques exist.[32] Although the proof is beyond the scope of this book, the following adjustment will reduce beta estimation error:

$$\beta_{adj} = \frac{\sigma_\varepsilon^2}{\sigma_\varepsilon^2 + \sigma_b^2}(1) + \left(1 - \frac{\sigma_\varepsilon^2}{\sigma_\varepsilon^2 + \sigma_b^2}\right)\beta_{raw}$$

[31] M. Blume, "Betas and Their Regression Tendencies," *Journal of Finance,* 30 (1975): 1–10.
[32] For instance, see P. Jorion, "Bayes-Stein Estimation for Portfolio Analysis," *Journal of Financial and Quantitative Analysis,* 21 (1986): 279–292.

where σ_ε = The standard error of the regression beta

$\quad\quad$ σ_b = The cross-sectional standard deviation of all betas

The raw regression beta receives the most weight when the standard error of beta from the regression (σ_ε) is smallest. In fact, when beta is measured perfectly ($\sigma_\varepsilon = 0$), the raw beta receives all the weight. Conversely, if the regression provides no meaningful results (σ_ε is very large), you should set beta equal to 1.

For Home Depot, the standard error of the beta estimate equals 0.20, and in 2004 the cross-sectional standard deviation of beta (across all S&P 500 stocks) equaled 0.590. Therefore, the adjusted beta equals 0.103 + (1 – 0.103) × 1.37, or 1.33.

Alternatives to the CAPM: Fama-French Three-Factor Model

In 1992, Eugene Fama and Kenneth French published a paper in the *Journal of Finance* that received a great deal of attention because they concluded, "In short, our tests do not support the most basic prediction of the SLB [Sharpe-Lintner-Black] Capital Asset Pricing Model that average stock returns are positively related to market betas."[33] At the time, theirs was the most recent in a series of empirical studies that questioned the usefulness of estimated betas in explaining the risk premium on equities. Among the factors negatively or positively associated with equity returns were the size of the company, a seasonal (January) effect, the degree of financial leverage, and the firm's book-to-market ratio.[34] Based on prior research and their own comprehensive regressions, Fama and French concluded that equity returns are inversely related to the size of a company (as measured by market capitalization) and positively related to the ratio of a company's book value to its market value of equity.

Given the strength of Fama and French's empirical results, the academic community has begun measuring risk with a model commonly known as the Fama-French three-factor model. With this model, a stock's excess returns are regressed on excess market returns (similar to the CAPM), the excess

[33] E. Fama and K. French, "The Cross-Section of Expected Stock Returns," *Journal of Finance* (June 1992): 427–465.

[34] R. Blanz, "The Relationship between Return and the Market Value of Common Stocks," *Journal of Financial Economics* (March 1981): 3–18; M. Reinganum, "Misspecification of Capital Asset Pricing: Empirical Anomalies Based on Earnings Yields and Market Values," *Journal of Financial Economics* (March 1981): 19–46; S. Basu, "The Relationship between Earnings Yield, Market Value and Return for NYSE Common Stocks: Further Evidence," *Journal of Financial Economics* (June 1983): 129–156; L. Bhandari, "Debt/Equity Ratio and Expected Common Stock Returns: Empirical Evidence," *Journal of Finance* (April 1988): 507–528; D. Stattman, "Book Values and Stock Returns," *The Chicago MBA: A Journal of Selected Papers* (1980): 25–45; and B. Rosenberg, K. Reid, and R. Lanstein, "Persuasive Evidence of Market Inefficiency," *Journal of Portfolio Management* (1985): 9–17.

Exhibit 10.12 Home Depot's Fama-French Cost of Equity

Factor	Average monthly premium (percent)	Average annual premium (percent)	Regression beta	Contribution to expected return (percent)
Market risk premium		4.5	1.35	6.1
SMB premium	0.25	3.0	(0.04)	(0.1)
HML premium	0.36	4.4	(0.10)	(0.5)
Premium over risk free rate				5.5
			Risk free rate	4.3
			Cost of equity	9.8

returns of small stocks over big stocks (SMB), and the excess returns of high book-to-market stocks over low book-to-market stocks (HML).[35] Because the risk premium is determined by a regression on the SMB and HML stock portfolios, a company does not receive a premium for being small. Instead, the company receives a risk premium if its stock returns are correlated with those of small stocks or high book-to-market companies. The SMB and HML portfolios are meant to replicate unobservable risk factors, factors that caused small companies with high book-to-market values to outperform their CAPM expected returns.

To run a Fama-French regression, we need monthly returns for three portfolios: the market portfolio, the SMB portfolio, and the HML portfolio. Given the model's popularity, Fama-French portfolio returns are now available from professional data providers.

We use the Fama-French three-factor model to estimate Home Depot's cost of equity in Exhibit 10.12. To determine the company's three betas, regress Home Depot stock returns against the excess market portfolio, SMB, and HML. The regression in Exhibit 10.12 used monthly returns and was specified as follows:

$$R_i - r_f = \alpha + \beta_1(R_m - r_f) + \beta_2 \left(R_S - R_B \right) + \beta_3 \left(R_H - R_L \right) + \varepsilon$$

As the exhibit indicates, Home Depot's traditional beta remains unchanged, but its cost of equity is lower in the Fama-French model because Home Depot is correlated with other large companies (small companies outperform large companies) and other companies with a low book-to-market ratio (high book-to-market companies outperform low book-to-

---

[35] For a complete description of the factor returns, see E. Fama and K. French, "Common Risk Factors in the Returns on Stocks and Bonds," *Journal of Financial Economics,* 33 (1993): 3–56.

market companies). Based on the historical annualized premiums for SMB (3.0 percent) and HML (4.4 percent), Home Depot's cost of capital equals 9.8 percent, versus 10.4 percent according to the standard CAPM. (These values are not comparable to the cost of equity presented in Exhibit 10.1, which used industry betas.)

The Fama-French model suffers from the same implementation issues as the CAPM. For instance, how much data should you use to determine the each factor's risk premium? Since 1926, small companies have outperformed large companies, but since 1982, they have not. Should returns be regressed using monthly data? Should regressions use five years of data? Given the model's recent development, many of these questions are still under investigation.

Alternatives to the CAPM: The Arbitrage Pricing Theory

Another alternative to the CAPM, the arbitrage pricing theory (APT), resembles a generalized version of the Fama-French three-factor model. In the APT, a security's actual returns are *fully* specified by k factors and random noise:

$$\tilde{R}_i = \alpha + \beta_1 \tilde{F}_1 + \beta_2 \tilde{F}_2 + \cdots + \beta_k \tilde{F}_k + \varepsilon$$

By creating well-diversified factor portfolios, it can be shown that a security's expected return must equal the risk-free rate plus the cumulative sum of its exposure to each factor times the factor's risk premium (λ):

$$E[R_i] = r_f + \beta_1 \lambda_1 + \beta_2 \lambda + \cdots + \beta_k \lambda_k$$

Otherwise, arbitrage is possible (positive return with zero risk).

On paper, the theory is extremely powerful. Any deviations from the model result in unlimited returns with no risk. In practice, implementation of the model has been elusive, as there is little agreement about how many factors there are, what the factors represent, or how to measure the factors. For this reason, use of the APT resides primarily in the classroom.

In Defense of Beta

Fama and French significantly damaged the credibility of the CAPM and beta. Today, most academics rely on three-factor models to measure historical risk and return. Even so, the three-factor model has its critics. To start, the CAPM is based on solid theory about risk and return (albeit with strong assumptions), whereas the Fama-French model is based purely on empirical evidence. Although the latter model has been loosely tied to risk factors such as illiquidity (size premium) and default risk (book-to-market premium), no theory has gained universal acceptance.

In addition, S. P. Kothari, Jay Shanken, and Richard Sloan argue that beta may work better than portrayed in Fama and French. They point out that Fama and French's statistical tests were of low enough power that the tests could not reject a nontrivial (beta-related) risk premium of 6 percent over the post-1940 period.[36] Second, when they used annual returns, rather than monthly returns, to estimate beta (to avoid seasonality in returns), they found a significant linear relationship between beta and returns. Finally, they argue that the economic magnitude of size is quite small, and book-to-market premiums could be a result of survivorship bias.

Other research argues that the Fama-French three-factor model historically outperforms the CAPM because either beta or the market portfolio has been improperly measured. In a recent study, a one-factor model based on time-varying conditional betas eliminated the book-to-market effect.[37] Another article argues that regressions based on equity-only portfolios, such as the S&P 500, leads to the incorrect measurement of beta.[38] This mismeasurement is correlated with leverage, which in turn is correlated with size and book-to-market. When the researchers controlled for leverage, excess returns associated with HMB and SML disappeared.

The bottom line? It takes a better theory to kill an existing theory, and we have yet to see the better theory. Therefore, we continue to use the CAPM while keeping a watchful eye on new research in the area.

ESTIMATING THE AFTER-TAX COST OF DEBT

To estimate the cost of debt, use the yield to maturity of the company's long-term, option-free bonds. Technically speaking, yield to maturity is only a proxy for expected return, because the yield is actually a *promised* rate of return on a company's debt (it assumes all coupon payments are made on time and the debt is paid in full). An enterprise valuation based indirectly on the yield to maturity is therefore theoretically inconsistent: expected free cash flows should not be discounted by a promised yield. For companies with highly rated debt, however, this inconsistency is

---

[36] S. Kothari, J. Shanken, and R. Sloan, "Another Look at the Cross-Section of Expected Returns," *Journal of Finance* (December 1995).

[37] A. Ang and J. Chen, "CAPM over the Long Run: 1926–2001," (working paper, Los Angeles: University of Southern California, 2004).

[38] M. Ferguson and R. Shockley, "Equilibrium 'Anomalies,'" *Journal of Finance, 58*(6) (2003): 2549–2580.

immaterial, especially when compared with the estimation error surrounding beta and the market risk premium. Thus, for estimating the cost of debt for a company with investment-grade debt (debt rated at BBB or better), yield to maturity is a suitable proxy.

When calculating yield to maturity, use *long-term* bonds. As discussed earlier, short-term bonds do not match the duration of the company's free cash flow. To solve for yield to maturity (ytm), reverse engineer the discount rate required to set the present value of the bond's promised cash flows equal to its price:

$$\text{Price} = \frac{\text{Coupon}}{(1+\text{ytm})} + \frac{\text{Coupon}}{(1+\text{ytm})^2} + \cdots + \frac{\text{Face} + \text{Coupon}}{(1+\text{ytm})^N}$$

Ideally, yield to maturity should be calculated on liquid, option-free, long-term debt. If the bond is rarely traded, the bond price will be stale. Using stale prices will lead to an outdated yield to maturity. Yield to maturity will also be distorted when corporate bonds have attached options, such as callability or convertibility, as their value will affect the bond's price but not its promised cash flows.

Bond Ratings and Yield to Maturity

For companies with only short-term bonds or bonds that rarely trade, determine yield to maturity by using an indirect method. First, determine the company's credit rating on unsecured long-term debt. Next, examine the average yield to maturity on a portfolio of long-term bonds with the same credit rating. Use this yield as a proxy for the company's implied yield on long-term debt.

Investing in corporate debt is not risk free. Each year, a number of companies default on their obligations. In 2002, corporate bond defaults reached $163.6 billion worldwide. Since the probability of default is critical to bond pricing, professional rating agencies, such as Standard & Poor's (S&P) and Moody's, will rate a company's debt. To determine a company's bond rating, a ratings agency will examine the company's most recent financial ratios, analyze the company's competitive environment, and interview senior management. Corporate bond ratings are freely available to the public and can be downloaded from rating agency Web sites. For example, consider Home Depot. On June 10, 2004, Moody's reaffirmed its credit rating for Home Depot at Aa3 for its long-term debt. During that same time period, S&P rated Home Depot slightly higher at AA. In this case, the two agencies' ratings were different. Split ratings occur, but relatively infrequently.

Exhibit 10.13 Yield Spread over U.S. Treasuries by Bond Rating, December 2003

Basis points

Rating	Maturity in Years						
	1	2	3	5	7	10	30
Aaa/AAA	34	28	35	21	22	28	50
Aa1/AA+	37	31	33	34	40	29	62
Aa2/AA	39	33	34	35	42	34	64
Aa3/AA–	40	34	36	37	43	37	65
A2/A	57	49	49	57	65	48	82
Baa2/BBB	79	91	96	108	111	102	134
Ba2/BB	228	245	260	257	250	236	263
B2/B	387	384	384	349	332	303	319

Source: Bloomberg.

Once you have a rating, convert the rating into a yield to maturity. Exhibit 10.13 presents U.S. corporate yield spreads over U.S. government bonds. All quotes are presented in basis points, where 100 basis points equals 1 percent. Since Home Depot is rated AA by S&P and Aa3 by Moody's, we estimate that the 10-year yield to maturity is between 34 and 37 basis points over the 10-year Treasury. Adding 34 basis points to the risk-free rate of 4.34 percent equals 4.68 percent.

Using the company's bond ratings to determine the yield to maturity is a good alternative to calculating the yield to maturity directly. Never, however, approximate the yield to maturity using a bond's coupon rate. Coupon rates are set by the company at time of issuance and only approximate the yield if the bond trades near its par value. When valuing a company, you must estimate expected returns relative to *today's* alternative investments. Thus, when you measure the cost of debt, estimate what a comparable investment would earn if bought or sold today.

Below-Investment-Grade Debt

In practice, few financial analysts distinguish between expected and promised returns. But for debt below investment grade, using the yield to maturity as a proxy for the cost of debt can cause significant error.

To better understand the difference between expected returns and yield to maturity, consider the following example. You have been asked to value a one-year zero-coupon bond whose face value is $100. The bond is risky; there is a 25 percent chance the bond will default and you will recover only half the final payment. Finally, the cost of debt (not yield to maturity), estimated using the CAPM, equals 6 percent. Based on this information,

Exhibit 10.14 Beta by Bond Class, 1990–2000

Asset class	Beta
Treasury bonds	0.19
Investment-grade corporate debt	0.27
High-yield corporate debt	0.37

Source: Lehman Brothers, "Global Family of Indices, Fixed Income Research"; Morgan Stanley Capital International; U.S. Treasury, Paul Sweeting.

you estimate the bond's price by discounting expected cash flows by the cost of debt:

$$\text{Price} = \frac{E[CF]}{1 + k_d} = \frac{(.75)(\$100) + (.25)(\$50)}{1.06} = \$82.55$$

Next, to determine the bond's yield to maturity, place promised cash flows, rather than expected cash flows, into the numerator. Then solve for the yield to maturity:

$$\text{Price} = \frac{\text{Promised}[CF]}{1 + \text{ytm}} = \frac{\$100}{1 + \text{ytm}} = \$82.55$$

The $82.55 price leads to a 21.1 percent yield to maturity, *much* higher than the cost of debt. So what drives the yield to maturity? Three factors: the cost of debt, the probability of default, and the recovery rate. When the probability of default is high and the recovery rate is low, the yield to maturity will deviate significantly from the cost of debt. Thus, for companies with high default risk and low ratings, the yield to maturity is a poor proxy for the cost of debt.

To estimate the cost of high-yield debt, we rely on the CAPM (a general pricing model, applicable to any security). Bond indexes are used to generate betas, since individual bonds rarely trade. Exhibit 10.14 presents the market beta for investment-grade and high-yield bonds. As reported in the exhibit, high-yield bonds have a beta 0.1 higher than investment-grade bonds. Assuming a 5 percent market risk premium, this translates to a premium of 0.5 percent over investment-grade bonds. Thus, to calculate the cost of debt for a company with debt rated BB or below, use the BBB yield to maturity and add 0.5 percent.

Incorporating the Interest Tax Shield

To calculate free cash flow (using techniques detailed in Chapter 7), we compute taxes as if the company were entirely financed by equity. By using all-equity taxes, we can make comparisons across companies and over time, without regard to capital structure. Yet, since the tax shield has value, it must be accounted for. In an enterprise DCF using the WACC, the tax shield is valued as part of the cost of capital. To value the tax shield, reduce the cost of debt by the marginal tax rate:

$$\text{After-Tax Cost of Debt} = \text{Cost of Debt} \times (1 - T_m)$$

Chapter 7 detailed how to calculate the marginal tax rate for historical analysis. For use in the cost of capital, you should calculate the marginal tax rate in a consistent manner, with one potential modification to account for the timing of future tax payments. According to research by John Graham, the statutory marginal tax rate overstates the *future* marginal tax rate because of rules related to tax-loss carryforwards, tax-loss carrybacks, investment tax credits, and alternative minimum taxes.[39] For instance, when a company loses money, it will receive a cash credit only if it has been profitable in the past three years; otherwise, it must carry the loss forward until it is once again profitable.

Graham uses simulation to estimate the realizable marginal tax rate on a company-by-company basis. For investment-grade companies, use the statutory rate. For instance, because Home Depot is highly profitable, Graham's model estimates the company's future marginal statutory tax rate at the full 35 percent. The typical company, however, does not always fully use its tax shields. Graham estimates the marginal tax rate is on average 5 percentage points below the statutory rate.

USE TARGET WEIGHTS TO DETERMINE COST OF CAPITAL

With our estimates of the cost of equity and cost of debt, we can now blend the two expected returns into a single number. To do this, we use the target weights of debt and equity to enterprise value, on a market (not book) basis:

$$\text{WACC} = \frac{D}{V} k_d (1 - T_m) + \frac{E}{V} k_e$$

Using market values to weight expected returns in the cost of capital follows directly from the formula's derivation (see Appendix C for a derivation of free cash flow and WACC). But consider a more intuitive explanation: the WACC represents the expected return on an *alternative* investment with identical risk. Rather than reinvest in the company, management could return capital to investors, who could reinvest elsewhere. To return capital without changing the capital structure, management can repay debt and re-

[39] J. Graham, "Debt and the Marginal Tax Rate," *Journal of Financial Economics*, 41 (1996): 41–73; and J. Graham, "Proxies for the Corporate Marginal Tax Rate," *Journal of Financial Economics*, 42 (1996): 187–221.

purchase shares, but must do so at their *market* value. Conversely, book value represents a sunk cost, so it is no longer relevant.

The cost of capital should rely on target weights, rather than current weights, because at any point, a company's current capital structure may not reflect the level expected to prevail over the life of the business. The current capital structure may merely reflect a short-term swing in the company's stock price, a swing that has yet to be rebalanced by management. Thus, using today's capital structure may cause you to overestimate (or underestimate) the value of tax shields for companies whose leverage is expected to drop (or rise).

Many companies are already near their target capital structure. If yours is not, decide how quickly the company will achieve the target. In the simplest scenario, the company will rebalance immediately and maintain the new capital structure. In this case, using the target weights and a constant WACC (for all future years) will lead to a reasonable valuation. If you expect the rebalancing to happen over a significant period of time, then use a different cost of capital each year, reflecting the capital structure at the time. In practice, this procedure is complex; you must correctly model not only the weights, but also the changes in the cost of debt and equity (because of increased default risk and higher betas). For extreme changes in capital structure, modeling enterprise DCF using a constant WACC can lead to significant error. In this case, value the company with adjusted present value (APV).

To develop a target capital structure for a company, use a combination of three approaches:

1. Estimate the company's current market-value-based capital structure.
2. Review the capital structure of comparable companies.
3. Review management's implicit or explicit approach to financing the business and its implications for the target capital structure.

Estimating Current Capital Structure

To determine the company's current capital structure, measure the market value of all claims against enterprise value. For most companies, the claims will consist primarily of debt and equity (we address more complex securities in the last section). If a company's debt and equity are publicly traded, simply multiply the quantity of each security by its most recent price. Most difficulties arise when securities are not traded such that prices can be readily observed.

Debt If an observable market value is not readily available, you can value debt securities at book or use discounted cash flow. In most cases, book value reasonably approximates the current market value. This will not be the case, however, if interest rates have changed dramatically since the time of issuance or the company is in financial distress. In these two situations, the current price will differ from book value because either expected cash flows have changed (increased probability of default lowers expected cash flow) or the discount rate has changed (interest rates drive discount rates) from their original levels.[40]

In these situations, value each bond separately by discounting promised cash flows at the appropriate yield to maturity. Promised cash flows will be disclosed in the notes of a company's annual report. Determine the appropriate yield to maturity by examining the yields from comparably rated debt with similar maturities.

Debt equivalent claims   Next, value off-balance-sheet debt, such as operating leases and pension liabilities. As detailed in Chapter 7, operating leases can be valued using the following formula:

$$\text{Lease Value}_{t-1} = \frac{\text{Rental Expense}_t}{k_d + \dfrac{1}{\text{Asset Life}}}$$

Only include operating leases in debt if you plan to adjust free cash flow for operating leases as well. Consistency between free cash flow and the cost of capital is paramount. Any pension adjustments made to free cash flow must be properly represented in the debt portion of the cost of capital. Specifically, if you add back any tax shields during adjustments to NOPLAT, you must account for the tax shields in the present value of pension liabilities and the cost of debt.

Equity   If common stock is publicly traded, multiply the market price by the number of shares *outstanding*. The market value of equity should be based on shares outstanding in the capital market. Therefore, do not use shares issued, as they may include shares repurchased by the company.

At this point, you may be wondering why you are valuing the company if you are going to rely on the market's value of equity in the cost of capital. Shouldn't we be using the estimated equity value? The answer is no. Remember, we are only estimating today's market value to frame management's philosophy concerning capital structure. To value the company, use *target* weights.

For privately held companies, no market-based values are available. In this case, you must determine equity value (for the cost of capital) either using a

---

[40] For floating-rate bonds, changes in Treasury rates won't affect value, since coupons float with Treasury yields. Changes in market-based default premiums, however, will affect the market value of floating-rate bonds, since bonds are priced at a fixed spread above Treasury yields.

multiples approach or through DCF iteratively. To perform an iterative valuation, assume a reasonable capital structure, and value the enterprise using DCF. Using the estimate of debt to enterprise value, repeat the valuation. Continue this process until the valuation no longer materially changes.

Minority interest   If minority interest—claims by outside shareholders on a portion of a company's business (often a subsidiary acquired by the company)—is publicly traded, then you can determine their approximate value directly from the market price for the shares. When the minority interest is not publicly traded, you must estimate its current value. To do this, apply a company-specific or industry price-to-earnings ratio directly to the income generated for minority interest.

Review Capital Structure of Comparable Companies

To place the company's current capital structure in the proper context, compare its capital structure with those of similar companies. Exhibit 10.15 presents the median debt-to-value levels for 11 industries. As the exhibit shows, industries with heavy fixed investment in tangible assets tend to have higher debt levels. High-growth industries, especially those

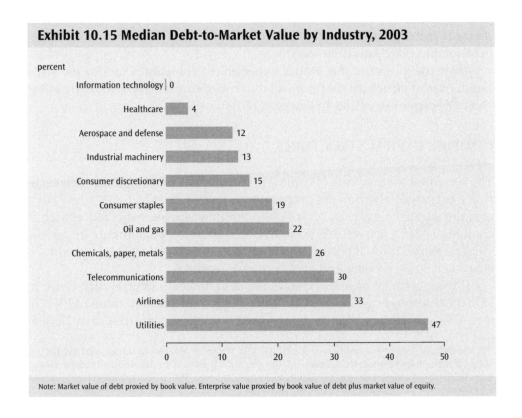

Exhibit 10.15 Median Debt-to-Market Value by Industry, 2003

percent

Information technology	0
Healthcare	4
Aerospace and defense	12
Industrial machinery	13
Consumer discretionary	15
Consumer staples	19
Oil and gas	22
Chemicals, paper, metals	26
Telecommunications	30
Airlines	33
Utilities	47

Note: Market value of debt proxied by book value. Enterprise value proxied by book value of debt plus market value of equity.

with intangible investments, tend to use very little debt. Economy-wide, the median debt-to-value ratio for the S&P 500 is 13.1 percent, and the median debt-to-equity ratio is 19.7 percent.

Having a company with a different capital structure is perfectly acceptable, but you should understand why. For instance, is the company by philosophy more aggressive or innovative in the use of debt financing, or is the capital structure only a temporary deviation from a more conservative target? Often, companies finance acquisitions with debt they plan to quickly retire or refinance with a stock offering. Alternatively, is there anything different about the company's cash flow or asset intensity that can explain the difference? Always use comparables to help you assess the reasonableness of estimated debt-to-equity levels.

Review Management's Philosophy

As a final step, review management's historical financing philosophy (or question management outright). Has the current team been actively managing the company's capital structure? Is the management team aggressive in its use of debt? Or is it overly conservative? Consider UPS, a company with a well-known conservative culture. Although cash flow is strong and stable, the company rarely issues debt. From a financing perspective, it doesn't need to issue additional securities; investments can be funded with current profits. Since the company is primarily employee owned, there is little threat of outside takeover. Therefore, UPS is unlikely to increase its target debt-to-value ratio anytime soon.

Over the long run, one would expect most companies to aim toward a target capital structure that minimizes cost of capital. We will address the choice of capital structure in Chapter 17.

COMPLEX CAPITAL STRUCTURES

The weighted average cost of capital is determined by weighting each security's expected return by its proportional contribution to total value. For a complex security, such as convertible debt, measuring expected return is challenging. Is a convertible bond like straight debt, enabling us to use the yield to maturity? Is it equity, enabling us to use the CAPM? In actuality, it is neither, so we recommend an alternative method.

If the treatment of hybrid securities will make a material difference in valuation results,[41] we recommend using adjusted present value (APV). In the APV, enterprise value is determined by discounting free cash flow at

---

[41] If the hybrid security is unlikely to be converted, it can be treated as traditional debt. Conversely, if the hybrid security is well "in the money," it should be treated as traditional equity. In these situations, errors are likely to be small, and a WACC-based valuation remains appropriate.

the unlevered cost of equity. The value of incremental cash flows related to financing, such as interest tax shields, is then computed separately. To determine the company's unlevered cost of equity, use the unlevered industry beta. This avoids the need to compute company specific components, such as the debt-to-equity ratio, a required input in the unlevering equation.

In some situations, you may still desire an accurate representation of the cost of capital. In these cases, split hybrid securities into their individual components. For instance, you can replicate a convertible bond by combining a traditional bond with a call option on the company's stock. You can further disaggregate a call option into a portfolio consisting of a risk-free bond and the company's stock. By converting a complex security into a portfolio of debt and equity, you once again have the components required for the traditional cost of capital. The process of creating replicating portfolios to value options is discussed in Chapter 20.

HEINEKEN CASE

In the case for this chapter, we explain how we estimated Heineken's WACC. Our estimate of Heineken's WACC is 7.5 percent as of the end of February 2004, as shown in Exhibit 10.16, based on a target market value capital structure of 10 percent debt to 90 percent equity, with the cost of equity at 8.0 percent and pretax cost of debt at 4.5 percent.

Our estimate of Heineken's target capital structure (10 percent debt to 90 percent equity) is based on historical analysis. Heineken's current capital structure using market values is 24 percent debt to 76 percent equity, as shown in Exhibit 10.17 on page 334, but the current capital structure is higher than Heineken's historical norm (see Exhibit 10.18 on p. 334). Heineken historically has had less than 10 percent debt. Its debt in 2002 and 2003 is higher because of recent acquisitions. In light of Heineken's excess cash balances, significant cash flow, and conservative dividend, we expect the company to reduce its debt levels significantly within a few years. So we selected a conservative long-term capital structure of 10 percent debt.

Exhibit 10.16 Heineken: Weighted Average Cost of Capital

percent

	Target capital structure	Cost	Tax benefit	Weighted cost
Debt	10.0	4.5	35	0.3
Common equity	90.0	8.0		7.2
Total	100.0			7.5

Exhibit 10.17 Heineken: Current Capital Structure

	Book value € million	Percent of total capitalization	Market value € million	Percent of total capitalization
Short term debt	1,113	14	1,113	6
Long term debt	2,721	33	2,809	15
Retirement related liabilities	526	6	526	3
Total debt	4,360	53	4,448	24
Common equity	3,167	38	13,171	71
Minority interest	732	9	1,030	5
Total equity	3,899	47	14,201	76
Total capitalization	8,259	100	18,649	100

Even though we did not use Heineken's year-end 2003 capital structure, we present its calculation in Exhibit 10.17, as follows:

- *Short-term debt:* Short-term debt matures within one year, so in most cases, book value approximates market value.
- *Long-term debt:* None of Heineken's debt is publicly traded, so market quotes were unavailable. Heineken supplied limited information on its long-term debt issues. For the debt instruments for which we had information, we used the current face value, years to maturity, coupon rate, and opportunity cost of debt to estimate the market value by discounting the expected cash flows to the present (see Exhibit 10.19). For long-term debt where no information was available, we assumed the current book value was a reasonable proxy for market value.

Exhibit 10.18 Heineken: Historical Capital Structure

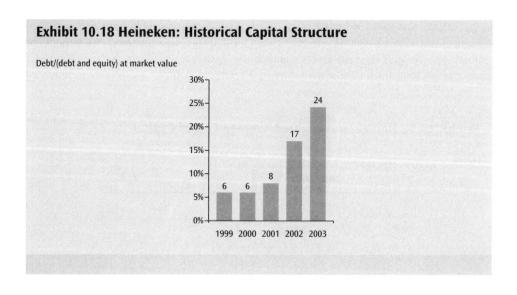

Debt/(debt and equity) at market value

Exhibit 10.19 Heineken: Market Value of Long-Term Debt

Debt issue	Coupon rate percent	Book value € million	Year of maturity	Market value € million
Bond loan from credit institution	4.4	497	2010	496
Bond loan from credit institution	5.0	596	2013	624
Loan from credit institution	5.3	387	2008	414
Loan from credit institution	4.1	506	2008	540
Other issues		735		735
Total long-term debt		**2,721**		**2,809**

- *Retirement-related liabilities:* We estimated the market value of net retirement-related liabilities to be equal to the actuarial value in the footnotes, which for Heineken also equals its book value.

- *Common equity:* In late February 2004, the market value of Heineken's equity was €13.2 billion, based on a share price of €33.65 and a total of 392 million shares outstanding.

- *Minority interest:* To estimate a market value for minority interest, we applied a peer-average P/E multiple of 15.6 to Heineken's minority-interest income in 2003. Given minority-interest income in 2003 of 66 million, we estimated the market value of minority interest to be €1.0 billion.

We estimated the cost of Heineken's debt and equity as follows:

- *Cost of debt:* We assumed that Heineken's opportunity cost of debt equals that of the similarly rated companies (as expressed as a premium over the risk-free rate). Although Heineken has not been rated by S&P or Moody's, we have assumed that its rating would be similar to highly rated beer companies. In the Netherlands, the default premium for investment-grade companies comparable to Heineken was about 40 basis points in February 2004. Since the euro risk-free rate in February was 4.1 percent, the opportunity cost of debt is 4.5 percent before taxes, or 2.9 percent after taxes.

- *Cost of equity:* Using the capital asset pricing model, we estimated Heineken's cost of equity to be 8.0 percent based on a euro risk-free rate of 4.1 percent,[42] a market risk premium of 5.2 percent,[43] and a levered beta of approximately 0.75 rounded. The levered beta is based on the median of the unlevered betas for a sample of brewers (0.66), shown in Exhibit 10.20 on page 336, relevered to Heineken's target capital structure (debt-to-value ratio of 10 percent). To un-lever and relever the betas, we used the formula $\beta_l = \beta_u \times (1 + D/E)$, as explained

---

[42] We used the yield on German treasury bonds for the risk-free rate, as they are the most liquid and have the lowest yield to maturity.
[43] The market risk premium is based on a 7.0 percent real return on equities less the real return on the risk-free rate of 1.8 percent at the time of the Heineken valuation.

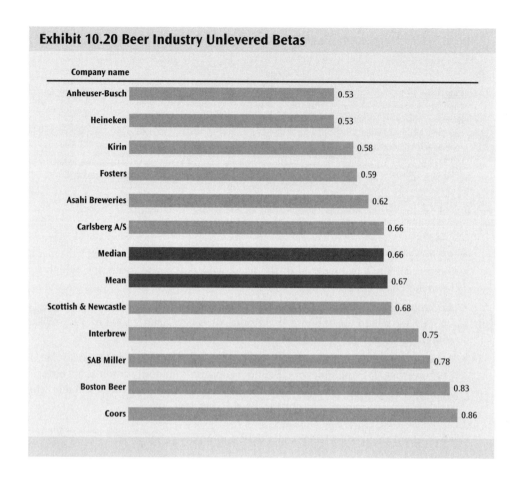

Exhibit 10.20 Beer Industry Unlevered Betas

Company name	
Anheuser-Busch	0.53
Heineken	0.53
Kirin	0.58
Fosters	0.59
Asahi Breweries	0.62
Carlsberg A/S	0.66
Median	0.66
Mean	0.67
Scottish & Newcastle	0.68
Interbrew	0.75
SAB Miller	0.78
Boston Beer	0.83
Coors	0.86

earlier in this chapter. In the brewing industry, the range of unlevered betas was 0.53 to 0.86, and the median and mean were almost identical (0.66 and 0.67, respectively). As we mentioned earlier, individual companies' betas are difficult to measure, so we typically use the industry median rather than a company's measured beta unless we have specific reasons to believe that the company's beta should differ from the industry.

REVIEW QUESTIONS

1. Identify and describe five key principles of computing WACC.
2. Present, in its simplest form, the WACC formula. Why should a manager compute an after-tax cost of debt and not an after-tax cost of equity when determining WACC?
3. Present, in its simplest form, the $E(R_i)$ formula, based upon the CAPM. What should a manager consider when selecting an appropriate risk free rate of return?

4. How does an arithmetic average differ from a geometric average? When might one approach be preferred over the other?

5. What is survivorship bias? How does survivorship bias impact a manager's computation and use of historical market returns?

6. Using an average of historical returns to determine the market risk premium is often described as backward looking while reverse engineering the key value driver formula is described as forward looking. Identify the differences between the two approaches in terms of the data used in the computation of $E[R_i]$ or k_e for each model.

7. Identify three key characteristics of the raw data needed for computing the CAPM.

8. What is the purpose of unlevering beta? What useful information can be gained from comparing the unlevered beta of a company compared to the unlevered beta of its industry? What is the purpose of relevering the industry's beta by the market value of your corporation's debt position?

9. Identify the strengths and weaknesses of the three $E[R_i]$ or k_e models presented in Chapter 10 (CAPM, APT, and Fama-French). Which model would you recommend a manager select to compute a company's estimate of $E[R_i]$ or k_e? Explain.

10. What is the basis for using the company's target capital structure versus the current capital structure when estimating WACC?

11

Calculating and Interpreting Results

After finishing your financial projections and continuing-value estimate, you are ready to conclude your valuation. In this chapter, we show how to take the final steps to create a complete valuation:

- Discount forecasted cash flows or economic profits and continuing value to determine the present value of operations.
- Calculate equity value from the present value of operations by adding the value of nonoperating assets and subtracting the value of nonequity claims.
- Use scenarios to deal better with the uncertainty underlying the final valuation.
- Examine valuation results to ensure that your findings are technically correct, your assumptions realistic, and your interpretations plausible.

This chapter focuses on calculating and interpreting results for the two most widely used approaches: enterprise DCF and discounted economic profit. In Chapter 5, we also discussed several valuation alternatives such as the APV, capital cash flow, and cash-flow-to-equity approach. To a large extent, the key messages about calculation and interpretation of results also apply to the alternative approaches. When they do not, we will state this explicitly.

CALCULATE VALUE OF OPERATIONS

From the free cash flow and economic profit projections, calculate the present value of operations in three steps: discount free cash flows, discount continuing value, and sum the resulting values to determine the value of operations.

Discount Free Cash Flows

The first step is to discount each year's free cash flow (or economic profit) to the present, using the WACC. For most valuations, future cash flow is discounted by a constant WACC. If you have chosen to vary the WACC over time, however, ensure that you are consistent in the way you discount future cash flows.[1] A time-varying WACC is appropriate if the yield curve is sharply increasing or decreasing or if significant changes are expected in, for example, the capital market weights for debt and equity, the cost of debt, or the tax rate. Such changes could occur for a company that is at a very low or high leverage and will converge to a sustainable, long-term capital structure. In that case, however, the APV approach is preferable, because it more easily allows for explicit modeling of the capital structure and debt-related tax shields over time.

Discount the Continuing Value

Next, discount the continuing value to the present. If you calculate continuing value using the perpetuity-based approach we presented in Chapter 9, bear in mind that the continuing value is already expressed as a value in the last year of the explicit forecast period. Therefore, you should discount it by the number of years in the explicit forecast. For example, if the forecast has 10 years, discount the continuing value by 10 years, not 11 years. In addition, if WACC varies over the explicit forecast period, remember to follow the approach described in the previous section when discounting continuing value.

Calculate the Value of Operations

The third and final step is to add the present value of free cash flow in the explicit period to the present value of the continuing value. The resulting value is called the value of operations. In the economic profit approach, invested capital at the beginning of the forecast period must be added to discounted economic profits and continuing value.[2]

---

[1] If the WACC varies over time, ensure that the discount factor DF_T for the free cash flow in year T is properly defined as:

$$DF_T = \prod_{t=1}^{T}(1 + WACC_t)$$

where $WACC_t$ = Cost of capital for year t

[2] This should be the invested capital at the end of the last historical year.

The value of operations should be adjusted for midyear discounting. We often assume that cash flows occur continuously throughout the year rather than in a lump sum at the end of the year. To adjust for this discrepancy, we grow the discounted value of operations at the WACC for six months.

CALCULATE EQUITY VALUE

Discounting cash flows or economic profits to obtain the value of operations was fairly straightforward. Calculating the equity value from the value of operations is a bit more complex. For all the valuation approaches discussed in Chapter 5, except the cash-flow-to-equity approach, there are two general rules:

1. All assets and liabilities whose cash flows are not included in the DCF value of operations must be separately valued and added to or subtracted from the DCF valuation. This holds for both on-balance-sheet and off-balance-sheet assets and liabilities (see Exhibit 11.1 on p. 342).

2. The best valuation approach for these assets and liabilities depends on the degree to which their value changes with the DCF value of operations. For example, the value of employee stock options and convertible bonds will increase as the value of operations increases, and your valuation approach should reflect this.
   - If there is a strong dependency between nonoperating assets and nonequity claims on one hand and the value of operations on the other, make sure the assumptions underlying your estimates are fully consistent with those underlying the DCF value of operations. This applies to employee stock options, convertible bonds, debt in distressed companies, and sometimes to nonconsolidated subsidiaries.[3]
   - If there is little or no dependency, as in the case of marketable securities, you can use the current market value when available or perform a DCF valuation if not. Use book values only when they are a good approximation of market value or as a method of last resort.

---

[3] Assume that your DCF valuation of operations implies a value per share significantly above the current market price per share. In this case, you should not deduct convertibles or options as nonequity claims at their current market value but at the higher value implied by your DCF results. Similarly, the current market value of nonconsolidated subsidiaries may need upward adjustment if their operations are closely related to those of the parent company. Finally, if the company is in financial distress with debt trading at a significant discount, deducting debt at the current market value will lead to an overestimation of equity value because the value of debt should increase with the value of operations.

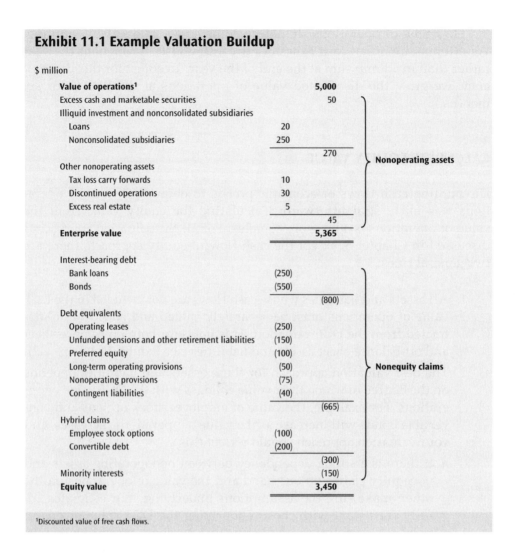

Exhibit 11.1 Example Valuation Buildup

$ million

Value of operations[1]		**5,000**
Excess cash and marketable securities		50
Illiquid investment and nonconsolidated subsidiaries		
Loans	20	
Nonconsolidated subsidiaries	250	
		270
Other nonoperating assets		
Tax loss carry forwards	10	
Discontinued operations	30	
Excess real estate	5	
		45
Enterprise value		**5,365**
Interest-bearing debt		
Bank loans	(250)	
Bonds	(550)	
		(800)
Debt equivalents		
Operating leases	(250)	
Unfunded pensions and other retirement liabilities	(150)	
Preferred equity	(100)	
Long-term operating provisions	(50)	
Nonoperating provisions	(75)	
Contingent liabilities	(40)	
		(665)
Hybrid claims		
Employee stock options	(100)	
Convertible debt	(200)	
		(300)
Minority interests		(150)
Equity value		**3,450**

Nonoperating assets

Nonequity claims

[1]Discounted value of free cash flows.

If you have applied the cash-flow-to-equity approach, there are fewer adjustments to the DCF result because the valuation already represents an estimate of the (undiluted) equity value. However, in some cases, you must still adjust for outstanding stock options or other convertible securities.

Nonoperating Assets

When reorganizing the company's accounting statements in Chapter 7, we classified particular assets as nonoperating assets. Cash flows related to these assets are not included in the free cash flow (or economic profit), and therefore are not accounted for in the value of operations. Although not included in operations, they still represent value to the shareholder. Thus, you must assess the present value of each nonoperating asset separately and add the resulting value to the value of operations. In this section, we identify the most common nonoperating assets and describe how to handle these in the valuation.

If necessary, you should take into account any special circumstances that could affect shareholders' ability to capture the full market value of these assets. For example, if the company has announced it will sell off a nonoperating asset in the near term, you should deduct the estimated capital gains taxes (if any) on the asset from its market value.

Excess cash and marketable securities Nonoperating assets that can be converted into cash on short notice and at low cost are classified as excess cash and marketable securities. Under U.S. GAAP and IFRS, companies must report such assets at their fair market value on the balance sheet. Therefore, you can use the most recent book values as a proxy for the market value—unless you have reason to believe they have significantly changed in value since the reporting date (as in the case of high-risk equity holdings).

In general, we do not recommend valuing highly liquid nonoperating assets if the market values are available. If you decide to perform a DCF valuation of nonoperating securities, estimate meaningful cash flow projections, and discount these at the appropriate cost of capital, which in general is *not* equal to the company's WACC. For example, discounting future cash flows from government bonds and Treasury bills at the company's WACC will lead to an undervaluation because the appropriate cost of capital is the risk-free rate.

Illiquid investments and nonconsolidated subsidiaries This category of nonoperating assets typically includes loans and equity stakes in subsidiaries that are not consolidated in the company's financial statements. These assets are not easily converted into cash, so they are recorded on the balance sheet at historical cost, not at fair market value.

For *loans* to other companies, use the reported book value. This is a reasonable approximation of market value if the loans were given at fair market terms and if the borrower's credit risk and general interest rates have not changed significantly since issuance. If this is not the case, you should perform a separate DCF valuation of the promised interest and principal payments at the yield to maturity for corporate bonds with similar risk and maturity.

Nonconsolidated subsidiaries are companies in which the parent company holds a noncontrolling equity stake. Under U.S. GAAP and IFRS, this generally applies to equity stakes below 50 percent.[4] Because the parent company does not have formal control over these subsidiaries, their financials are not

---

[4] See Chapter 21 for more details on consolidation under U.S. GAAP and IFRS.

consolidated. Under U.S. GAAP and IFRS, there are two ways in which non-consolidated subsidiaries can appear in the parent company's accounts:

1. For equity stakes between 20 percent and 50 percent, the parent company is assumed to have *influence but not control* over the subsidiary. The equity holding in the subsidiary is reported in the parent balance sheet at the investment's historical cost plus profits and additional investment, less dividends received. The parent company's portion of the subsidiary's profits is shown below EBIT on the income statement.

2. For equity stakes below 20 percent, the parent company is assumed to have *no influence*. The equity holdings are shown at historical cost on the parent's balance sheet. The parent's portion of the subsidiary's dividends is included below EBIT on the income statement.

The best approach to handling these subsidiaries depends on the information available:

- If the subsidiary is publicly listed, use the market value for the company's equity stake. Verify that the market value is indeed a good indicator of intrinsic value. In some cases, these listed subsidiaries have very limited free float and/or very low liquidity, so the share price may not properly reflect current information.

- If the subsidiary is not listed but you have access to its financial statements, perform a separate DCF valuation of the equity stake. Discount the cash flows at the appropriate cost of capital, which is not necessarily the parent company's WACC. Also, when completing the parent valuation, include only the value of the parent's *equity stake* and not the subsidiary's entire enterprise value or equity value.

If the parent company's accounts are the only source of financial information for the subsidiary, we suggest the following alternatives:

- *Simplified cash-flow-to-equity valuation:* This is a feasible approach when the parent has a 20 to 50 percent equity stake, because the subsidiary's net income and approximate book equity[5] are disclosed in the parent's accounts. Build forecasts for how the key value drivers (net income growth and return on equity) will develop, so you can project future cash flows to equity. Discount these cash flows at the cost of equity for the subsidiary in question and not at the parent company's WACC.

- *Multiples valuation:* If the parent has a 20 to 50 percent equity stake, you can also build a valuation based on the price-to-earnings and/or

---

[5] The book value of the subsidiary equals the historical acquisition cost plus retained profits, which is a reasonable approximation of book equity. In case any goodwill is included in the book value of the subsidiary, this should be deducted.

market-to-book multiple. Net income and approximate book equity for the subsidiary are available, and you can estimate an appropriate multiple from a group of listed peers.

- *Tracking portfolio:* For parent equity stakes below 20 percent, you may have no information beyond the investment's original cost, that is, the book value shown in the parent's balance sheet. Even applying a multiple is difficult because neither net income nor the *current* book value of equity is reported. If you know when the stake was acquired, you can approximate its current market value by adding the relative price increase for a portfolio of comparable stocks over the same holding period.

You should triangulate your results as much as possible, given the lack of precision for these valuation approaches.

Other nonoperating assets The preceding categories are typically the most significant nonoperating assets from a valuation perspective. But companies can also have several other types of nonoperating assets such as tax loss carryforwards, excess real estate, and pension assets, to name a few. These assets are not necessarily reported separately on a company's balance sheet, so they can be hard to identify.

Tax loss carryforwards—or net operating losses (NOLs), as they are called in the United States—represent accumulated historical losses that a company can use to compensate future tax charges. Tax loss carryforwards are included in the tax assets on the balance sheet and discussed in the company's footnotes. From an outsider's perspective, it is difficult to accurately estimate the true value of tax loss carryforwards, because they do not necessarily offset the cash taxes as derived from the consolidated income statement. For example, for companies with foreign subsidiaries, you would need to know tax losses and future taxable profits on a country-by-country basis, because domestic tax losses cannot offset foreign taxable profits, and vice versa.

Do not confuse tax loss carryforwards with ongoing deferred tax assets as defined in Chapter 7. Ongoing deferred tax assets should not be included in nonoperating assets because they are already explicitly accounted for in the calculation of the cash tax rate.

Estimate the value of the tax loss carryforwards separately and not as part of free cash flow. Create a separate account for the accumulated tax loss carryforwards, and forecast the development of this account by adding any future losses and subtracting any future taxable profits on a year-by-year basis. For each year in which the account is used to offset taxable profits, discount the tax savings at the cost of debt.[6] Some practitioners

---

[6] If the tax loss carryforwards are relatively small compared with near-term taxable profits, the amount of future tax savings will not fluctuate much with the company's profitability, and the cost of debt is most appropriate. The higher the tax losses relative to near-term profits, the more

simply set the carryforward's value at the tax rate times the accumulated tax losses.

A second, more complex alternative, is to adjust both the tax rate used in the free cash flow projections and in the WACC during years for which the company can offset (part of) its tax charges. In this case, the value of tax loss carryforwards is included in the DCF value of operations and should not be double counted as a nonoperating asset.

Discontinued operations are businesses being sold or closed down. The earnings from discontinued operations are explicitly shown in the income statement, and the associated net asset position is disclosed on the balance sheet. Because discontinued operations are no longer part of a company's operations, their value should not be modeled as part of free cash flow or included in the DCF value of operations. Under U.S. GAAP and IFRS, the assets and liabilities associated with the discontinued operations are written down to their fair value and disclosed as a net asset on the balance sheet, so the most recent book value is usually a reasonable approximation.[7]

Excess real estate and other unutilized assets are assets no longer required for the company's operations. As a result, any cash flows that the assets could generate are excluded from the free cash flow projection, and the assets are not included in the DCF value of operations. Identifying these assets in an outside-in valuation is nearly impossible unless they are specifically disclosed in the company's footnotes. Therefore, including their value separately as a nonoperating asset is often limited to internal valuations. For excess real estate, use the most recent appraisal value when available. Alternatively, estimate the real estate value either by using an appraisal multiple such as value per square meter or by discounting expected future cash flows from rentals at the appropriate cost of capital. Of course, be careful to exclude any *operating* real estate from these figures, because that value is implicitly included in the free cash flow projections and value of operations.

We do not recommend a separate valuation for unutilized operating assets unless they are expected to be sold in the near-term. If the financial projections for the company reflect growth, the value of any underutilized assets should instead be captured in lower future capital expenditures.

Surpluses in a company's pension funds show up as net *pension assets* in the balance sheet. We will describe in detail how to value pension assets during our discussion of pension liabilities.

---

the value of tax savings will fluctuate with profits, and the more appropriate the unlevered cost of capital becomes. This is consistent with our recommendation in Chapter 5 to use the unlevered cost of capital to discount the expected future tax savings from the interest on debt.

[7] Any upward adjustment to the original book value of assets and liabilities is limited to the cumulative historical impairments on the assets. Thus, the fair market value of discontinued operations *could* be higher than the net asset value disclosed in the balance sheet.

Nonequity Claims

The value of operations plus nonoperating assets equals the enterprise value. To calculate the value of common equity, you need to deduct the value of all the nonequity claims from the enterprise value. Although non-equity claims include a long array of items, they can be grouped into four categories (shown in Exhibit 11.1):

1. Debt such as bonds, short-term and long-term bank loans
2. Debt equivalents such as operating leases, pensions, specific types of provisions, preferred stock, and contingent liabilities (e.g., outstanding claims from litigation)
3. Hybrid claims such as employee stock options and convertible bonds
4. Minority interests

For the purpose of exposition, we use the term *nonequity claims* to represent all financial claims other than those from current common stockholders. For example, even though convertible debt and employee options can be converted into common equity, we group them under nonequity claims. Note that even in a discounted-cash-flow-to-equity valuation, you must deduct the value of employee stock options and convertible debt or convertible preferred equity[8] to estimate the value of common equity.

In this section, we provide an overview of the most frequently encountered nonequity claims and recommend how to include them in a company valuation.

Debt   Corporate debt comes in many forms: commercial paper, notes payable, fixed and floating bank loans, corporate bonds, and capitalized leases. If the debt is relatively secure and actively traded, use its market value. If the debt instrument is not traded, discount the promised interest payments and the principal repayment at the yield to maturity to estimate current value. The book value of debt is a reasonable approximation for fixed-rate debt if interest rates and default risk have not significantly changed since the debt issuance. For floating-rate debt, market value is not sensitive to interest rates, and book value is a reasonable approximation if the company's default risk has been fairly stable.

For companies in *financial distress,* you must be careful when valuing debt. For distressed companies, the value of the debt will be at a significant discount to its book value and will fluctuate with the value of the enterprise. Essentially, the debt has become similar to equity: its value will depend

---

[8] For convertible debt (preferred equity), only the interest (preferred dividend) payments are included in the equity cash flow projections. The value of the conversion option still needs to be deducted from the equity DCF result.

directly on your estimate for the enterprise value, and you should not simply deduct the current market value of debt. If sound economic forecasts put your DCF estimate of enterprise value significantly above its current market value and you deduct the current market value of debt to determine equity, you are underestimating the true value of debt and overestimating the equity value. The reason is that as the enterprise value increases, the value of debt increases as well.

For distressed companies, apply an integrated-scenario approach to value operations as well as equity. For each scenario, estimate the enterprise value conditional on your financial forecasts, deduct the full value[9] of the debt and other nonequity claims,[10] and calculate the equity value as the residual (which should be zero for any scenario where the conditional enterprise value is less than the value of debt plus other nonequity claims). Next, weight each scenario's conditional value of equity by its probability of occurrence to obtain an estimate for the value of equity. In the same way, you can calculate the point estimates for enterprise value and debt value (for an example, see the section on scenario valuation later in this chapter).

Operating leases These are the most common form of off-balance-sheet debt. Under certain restrictions, companies can avoid capitalizing leases on their balance sheet. For these so-called operating leases, rental charges are included in operating costs, and required future payments are disclosed in the notes to the balance sheet.

Following the guidelines outlined in Chapter 7, capitalize the value of the operating leases as part of invested capital and as a debt-equivalent liability. Add the estimated after-tax interest component from the lease back to operating profit on the income statement. By doing this, you effectively treat the leased assets as if they were owned and financed with straight debt. Therefore, you need to deduct the capitalized value of operating leases as a nonequity claim. Estimate this value with the following formula:

$$\text{Capitalized Operating Leases} = \text{Asset Value} = \frac{\text{Rental Expense}}{\left(k_d + \dfrac{1}{\text{Asset Life}}\right)}$$

where k_d = Cost of debt

Unfunded pension and other postretirement liabilities Unfunded retirement liabilities should be treated as debt-equivalents. They can make a signif-

---

[9] That is, the value of the debt for a nondistressed company—typically close to book value.

[10] All nonequity claims need to be included in the scenario approach for distressed companies. The order in which they are entitled to claim the enterprise value will make a difference for the value of debt and other claims, but not for the equity value.

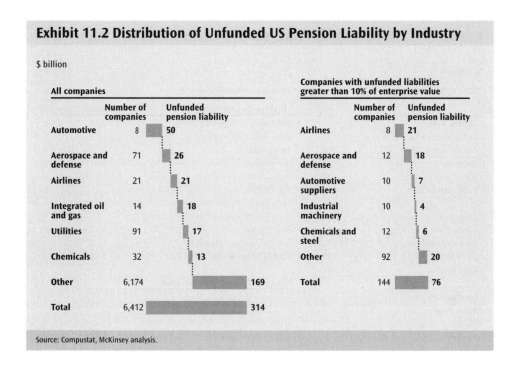

Exhibit 11.2 Distribution of Unfunded US Pension Liability by Industry

$ billion

All companies	Number of companies	Unfunded pension liability		Companies with unfunded liabilities greater than 10% of enterprise value	Number of companies	Unfunded pension liability
Automotive	8	50		Airlines	8	21
Aerospace and defense	71	26		Aerospace and defense	12	18
Airlines	21	21		Automotive suppliers	10	7
Integrated oil and gas	14	18		Industrial machinery	10	4
Utilities	91	17		Chemicals and steel	12	6
Chemicals	32	13		Other	92	20
Other	6,174	169		Total	144	76
Total	6,412	314				

Source: Compustat, McKinsey analysis.

icant difference when calculating equity value, especially for older companies. As Exhibit 11.2 shows, unfunded pension liabilities are significant, amounting to $314 billion for listed U.S. companies in 2002. These liabilities are concentrated in the automotive, aerospace, airline, oil and gas, and utility sectors.

Postretirement liabilities typically originate from pension plans and postretirement medical benefit plans. Plans are designated as either defined contribution or defined benefit. If a plan is structured on a *defined-contribution* basis, it is not relevant from a valuation perspective. In this case, the company makes fixed contributions into a fund, whose investment performance determines an employee's eventual benefits. The company is only liable to contribute a predetermined amount, and the employees bear the risk of inadequate performance of fund assets.

However, for *defined-benefit* plans, the company is obliged to provide specific retirement benefits to employees irrespective of the actual performance of the plan's funds. Under U.S. GAAP and IFRS, the fair market value of the plan's assets and liabilities are disclosed in the financial statements, but only in the footnotes. The resulting surplus (deficit) should be added to (subtracted from) enterprise value on an after-tax basis.

Do not use the book value of net retirement assets or liabilities as reported on the balance sheet. That amount does not include all of the capital gains and losses on the fund assets, nor recent changes to the fund's liabilities.

We illustrate our recommended approach through an analysis of the retirement liabilities for a large U.S. company. Exhibit 11.3 on page 350 shows a

Exhibit 11.3 Company Pension and Postretirement Liabilities, 2004

$ million

2004 Balance Sheet		2004 Notes to the balance sheet		
		Change in benefit obligation	**Pension**	**Non-pension**
Current assets		**Obligation at beginning of year**	**1,798**	**373**
Cash and cash equivalents	32	Acquisition adjustment	–	–
Accounts receivable	490	Service cost	50	4
Inventories	795	Interest cost	111	23
Other current assets	164	Plan amendments	(3)	(21)
Total current assets	**1,481**	Actuarial loss	23	(19)
		Participant contributions	3	–
Plant assets, net of depreciation	1,901	Curtailment/special termination benefits	3	–
Goodwill	1,900	Benefits paid	(119)	(27)
Other intangible assets	1,095	Foreign currency adjustment	27	–
Other assets	298	**Benefit obligation at end of year**	**1,893**	**333**
Total assets	**6,675**			
		Change in fair value of plan assets		
Current liabilities		Fair value at beginning of year	1,472	
Notes payable	810	Acquisition adjustment	–	
Payable to suppliers and others	607	Actual return on plan assets	184	
Accrued liabilities[1]	607	Employer contributions	65	
Dividend payable	65	Participants contributions	3	
Accrued income taxes	250	Benefits paid	(115)	
Total current liabilities	**2,339**	Foreign currency adjustment	18	
		Fair value at end of year	**1,627**	
Long-term debt	2,543			
Nonpension postretirement benefits	298	**Funded status recognized**		
Other liabilities	621	**Funded status at end of year**	**(266)**	**(333)**
Total liabilities	**5,801**	Unrecognized prior service cost	42	(33)
		Unrecognized loss	661	49
Shareowners' equity		**Net amount recognized**	**437**	**(317)**
Preferred stock	0			
Capital stock	20	**Amounts recognized**		
Additional paid-in capital	264	Prepaid benefit cost (included in Other Assets)	103	
Earnings retained in the business	5,642	Intangible asset (incl. in Other Intangible Assets)	27	
Capital stock in treasury	(4,848)	Accumulated other comprehensive loss	307	
Accum. other comprehensive loss	(204)	**Net amount recognized**	**437**	
Total shareowners' equity	**874**			
Total liabilities and equity	**6,675**			

[1]The current portion of nonpension postretirement liabilities included in accrued liabilities was $19 million at August 1, 2004 and August 3, 2003.

summary of the company's balance sheet and the overview of retirement liabilities in the footnotes. As of August 2004, the balance sheet has just one specific entry for retirement-related liabilities of $298 million. However, this is an incomplete picture. First, this liability represents only the nonpension postretirement benefits that the company provides. The assets and liabilities for pension benefits are hidden within other entries in the balance sheet.

Second, under U.S. GAAP, the amounts recognized in the balance sheet for pension and other retirement liabilities do not necessarily represent the fair value of the liabilities. In fact, for many companies, the book values in the balance sheet differ significantly from the fair value.

The notes to the balance sheet provide critical information for analyzing and valuing the company's retirement liabilities. Focus first on the pension benefits. The fair value of the total pension liabilities is $1,893 million, whereas the fair value of the fund assets is $1,627 million. Because of this underfunding, the pension plan represents a net liability to the company with a fair value of $266 million. However, since a portion of the losses and prior costs for the plan are classified as unrecognized losses and costs under U.S. GAAP, the book value in the balance sheet is higher. This occurs because annual gains and losses from plan assets are not charged to the income statement immediately, but only gradually over the course of several years. In our example, the company recognizes the pension plan as a net asset of $437 million (instead of a net liability of $266 million). The notes discuss how this net amount is spread out across multiple balance sheet categories: Other Assets, Other Intangible Assets, and Shareholders' Equity.

For the nonpension postretirement benefits, the fair value of the liability is $333 million, another net liability because there are no fund assets. Again, this value differs from the $317 million recognized as book value on the balance sheet—although not by a large amount. The book amount corresponds to the $298 million explicitly shown as a line item on the balance sheet plus an additional $19 million included in Accrued Liabilities.

In this case, the company's total net liability at fair value equals $599 million ($266 million for pension benefits plus $333 million for nonpension retirement benefits). On an after-tax basis, this converts to $389 million, which should be subtracted from enterprise value as a nonequity claim.[11]

To avoid double counting, make sure all other nonequity claims or nonoperating assets do not include retirement assets and liabilities. For example, in our case, $103 million of pension assets are included on the balance sheet under Other Assets. In the event you classify Other Assets as nonoperating assets, you should at least take out the $103 million before adding Other Assets to the equity value buildup.

Preferred equity The name *preferred equity* is somewhat misleading; preferred stock more closely resembles unsecured debt than equity and should be treated as a debt equivalent. Preferred stock dividends are similar to interest payments because they are often predetermined and can be withheld only under special conditions. If preferred equity is traded, use the market

[11] This example uses a nominal tax rate of 35 percent.

value to deduct from enterprise value. In other cases, make a separate DCF valuation, discounting the expected preferred dividends in perpetuity at the cost of unsecured debt.

Other debt equivalents   This category includes all remaining liabilities for which no cash flows are included in the company's free cash flow projections. Here we discuss two examples: provisions and contingent liabilities.

Certain *provisions* other than retirement-related liabilities need to be deducted as nonequity financial claims. Following the guidelines in Chapter 7, we distinguish four types of provisions:

1. Ongoing operating provisions (e.g., for warranties and product returns) are already accounted for in the free cash flows and should therefore not be deducted from enterprise value.

2. Long-term operating provisions (e.g., for plant-decommissioning costs) should be deducted from enterprise value as debt equivalents. Because these provisions cover cash expenses that become payable in the long term, they are typically recorded at the discounted value in the balance sheet. In this case, there is no need to perform a separate DCF analysis, and you can use the book value of the liability in your valuation. Note that the book value does not equal the present value of all future expenses because the provision is gradually accumulated over the years until the expense becomes payable (see Chapter 7 for more details).

3. Nonoperating provisions (e.g., for restructuring charges resulting from layoffs) must be deducted from enterprise value as a debt equivalent. Although a discounted value would be ideal, the book value from the balance sheet is often a reasonable approximation. These provisions are recorded at a nondiscounted value because outlays are usually in the near term.

4. Income-smoothing provisions do not represent actual future cash outlays, so they should not be deducted from enterprise value. These provisions were common in several European countries but will disappear after 2005, when most European countries adopt IFRS.

Contingent liabilities are usually not disclosed in the balance sheet but are separately discussed in the notes to the balance sheet. Examples are possible liabilities from pending litigation and loan guarantees. When possible, estimate the associated expected after-tax cash flows (if the costs are tax deductible), and discount these at the cost of debt. Unfortunately, assessing the probability of such cash flows materializing is difficult, so the valuation should be interpreted with caution. Therefore, estimate the value of contingent liabilities for a range of probabilities to provide some boundaries on your final valuation.

Employee stock options Many companies offer their employees stock options as part of their compensation. Options give the holder the right, but not the obligation, to buy company stock at a specified price, known as the exercise price. Since employee stock options have long maturities and the company's stock price could eventually rise above the exercise price, options can have great value.

Employee stock options affect a company valuation in two ways. First, the value of options that will be granted in the future needs to be captured in the free cash flow projections or in a separate DCF valuation, following the guidelines in Chapter 7. When captured in the free cash flow projections, the value of future options grants is included in the value of operations and should not be treated as a nonequity claim. Second, the value of options currently outstanding must be subtracted from enterprise value as a nonequity claim. Note, however, that the value of the options will depend on your estimate of enterprise value, and your option valuation should reflect this.

Under U.S. GAAP and IFRS, the notes disclose considerable information about employee options, including the number of options currently outstanding grouped by exercise prices and maturities, as well as the number of options that are vested. In general, employee options are unvested at the time of granting. Options can be exercised or sold only after they are vested, which usually happens over several years of continuous employment. For valuation purposes, deduct the value of all vested options. For unvested options, make an adjustment to account for the likelihood that some employees will leave the company and never exercise their options.

The following approaches can be used for valuing employee options:

- We recommend using the estimated market value from *option-valuation models*, such as Black-Scholes or more advanced binomial (lattice) models. Under U.S. GAAP and IFRS, the notes to the balance sheet report the total value of all employee stock options outstanding, as estimated by such option-pricing models. Note that this value is a good approximation only if your estimate of share price is close to the one underlying the option values in the annual report. Otherwise, you need to create a new valuation using an option-pricing model. The notes disclose the information required for valuation.[12]

- A second method, the *exercise value approach*, provides only a lower bound for the value of employee options. It assumes that all options are exercised immediately and thereby ignores the time value of the options. The resulting valuation error increases as options have longer time to maturity, the company's stock has higher volatility,

---

[12] For more on the valuation of employee stock options, see, for example, J. Hull and A. White, "How to Value Employee Stock Options," *Financial Analysts Journal*, 60(1) (January/February 2004): 114–119.

Exhibit 11.4 Employee Stock Options Example

Company data		Option value method	Exercise value method
Enterprise value ($ million)	11,000		
Debt value ($ million)	(1,000)		
Nondiluted equity value ($ million)	10,000		
Number of shares nondiluted	90.0		
Value per share nondiluted	111.1		
Stock options			
Number of options outstanding	10.0		
Option exercise price	90.0		
Option maturity (years)	5.0		
Stock volatility (annualized percent)	35.0		
Risk free rate (percent)	5.5		

	Option value method	Exercise value method
Enterprise value ($ million)	11,000	11,000
Debt value ($ million)	(1,000)	(1,000)
Option exercise proceeds ($ million)		900
Option value ($ million)	(481)	
Equity value ($ million)	9,519	10,900
Number of shares nondiluted	90.0	90.0
Number of new shares	–	10.0
Number of shares diluted	90.0	100.0
Value per share	105.8	109.0

and the company's share price is closer to the exercise price. Given that a more accurate valuation is already disclosed in the annual report, we do not recommend this method. However, it is still quite common among practitioners.

Exhibit 11.4 provides a brief example of these two methods. Assume that you have estimated the enterprise value of a company at $11 billion. The company has straight debt with a market value of $1 billion and 10 million unexercised, fully vested stock options. The number of common shares currently outstanding is 90 million. The exercise price for all options is $90, which will acquire one share of common stock. If you did not value the options separately but simply divided the nondiluted equity value by the number of undiluted shares, you would overestimate the value per share at $111.1 instead of the true value of $105.8, derived next.

The column titled "Option value method" in Exhibit 11.4 shows the equity value per share when employee options are incorporated using an option valuation model. We assume a remaining time to maturity of five years for the options, a risk-free rate of 5.5 percent, and a volatility of the company's stock of 35 percent. Applying a Black-Scholes option-pricing model adjusted for the dilution effect, the estimated market value of the options amounts to $481 million.[13] The value per share of common equity is then $105.8.

---

[13] For illustration purposes, we adjusted the Black-Scholes option price only for the dilution effect of new-share issuance by multiplying the option price by the following expression:

$$\frac{\text{Number of Existing Shares Outstanding}}{\left(\text{Number of Existing Shares Outstanding} + \text{Number of New Shares Issued}\right)}$$

The exercise value method overestimates the value per share of common equity because it assumes immediate conversion of all options. The only advantage of the method is that it is simple to apply. Assuming full conversion, the company in this example receives $900 million in exercise proceeds and would have to provide 10 million common shares to the option holders. In the exercise value method, the company either retains the exercise proceeds or uses these to repay debt so that the resulting equity value will amount to $10.9 billion. Taking into account the 10 million shares handed out to the options holders, the resulting value per share is $109.

In this simplified example, the valuation error from applying the exercise value method is only 3 percent. However, for companies with a relatively large number of options outstanding or exercise prices well above the current stock price, the difference can be quite significant.

Convertible debt Convertible bonds are corporate bonds that can be exchanged for common equity at a predetermined conversion ratio. A convertible bond is essentially a package of a straight corporate bond plus a call option on equity (the conversion option).[14] Because the conversion option can have significant value, this form of debt requires treatment different from that of regular corporate debt.

The value of convertibles depends on the enterprise value. In contrast to straight debt, neither the book value nor the simple DCF value of bond cash flows is a good proxy for the value of convertibles. If the convertible bonds are actively traded, you could use their market values, but these are suitable only if your estimated stock price is near the traded stock price. If not, there are two alternatives:

1. We recommend using an *option-based valuation* for convertible debt. In contrast to the treatment of stock options, however, annual reports do not provide any information on the value of convertible debt. Accurate valuation of convertible bonds with option-based models is not straightforward, but following methods outlined by John Ingersoll,[15] you can apply an adjusted Black-Scholes option-pricing model for a reasonable approximation.

2. The *conversion value approach* assumes that all convertible bonds are immediately exchanged for equity and ignores the time value of the

---

[14] See R. Brealey and S. Myers, *Principles of Corporate Finance,* 7th ed. (New York: McGraw-Hill, 2002), ch. 23. If you are doing a discounted-cash-flow-to-equity valuation, you subtract only the value of the conversion option from your DCF valuation. The straight-debt component of the convertible debt has already been included in the equity cash flows.

[15] The convertible bond can be modeled as a call option on the fraction of equity that the bondholders receive after conversion, with the face value of the bond as exercise price. See J. Ingersoll, "A Contingent Claims Valuation of Convertible Securities," *Journal of Financial Economics,* 4 (1977): 289–322.

conversion option. It leads to reasonable results when the conversion option is deep in the money, meaning the bond is more valuable when converted into equity than held for future coupon and principal payments.

We illustrate both methods in Exhibit 11.5. This exhibit presents an example similar to the one used for the valuation of stock options. In this case, the company has no options outstanding but instead 10 million convertible bonds with a face value of $100. The coupon is 2 percent per year, and the bonds have five years to maturity. The cost of debt is 6.5 percent. The conversion ratio for the bonds is 0.8, meaning 10 bonds can be converted into 8 common shares of equity.

Using a simple convertible-bond valuation model, we estimate a value of $108.2 per bond. This value consists of the present value of coupons and principal repayment of $81.3 plus a conversion option value of $26.9. Deducting the value of all convertible bonds and straight debt from the enterprise value, we arrive at an equity value of $8,918 million and a value per share of $99.1.

Under the conversion value approach, we convert all bonds into equity and simply divide the undiluted equity value by a total of $90 + 0.8 \times 10 = 98$ shares. In contrast to the exercise of stock options, there is no cash inflow

Exhibit 11.5 Convertible Debt Example

Company data			Convertible valuation method	Conversion value method
Enterprise value ($ million)	11,000	Enterprise value ($ million)	11,000	11,000
Debt value ($ million)	(1,000)	Debt value ($ million)	(1,000)	(1,000)
Convertibles face value ($ million)	(1,000)	Convertibles value ($ million)	(1,082)	–
Nondiluted equity value ($ million)	9,000	**Equity value ($ million)**	**8,918**	**10,000**
Number of shares nondiluted	90.0			
Value per share nondiluted	100.0	Number of shares nondiluted	90.0	90.0
		Number of new shares	–	8.0
Convertible bond		**Number of shares diluted**	90.0	98.0
Number of bonds	10			
Face value	100.0	**Value per share**	**99.1**	**102.0**
Coupon rate (percent)	2.0			
Years to maturity	5			
Conversion ratio	0.8			
Value per bond				
Bond component	81.3			
Conversion option	26.9			
Total	108.2			
Stock volatility (annualized percent)	35.0			
Risk free rate (percent)	5.5			
Cost of debt (percent)	6.5			

for the company. Instead, we exclude the value of the convertible bonds from the nonequity claims. This leads to an estimated value per share of $102, which overestimates the true value.

Minority interests   When a company controls a subsidiary without full ownership, the subsidiary's financial statements still must be fully consolidated in the group accounts. Without any further adjustment, the full value of the subsidiary would be improperly included in the parent company valuation. Therefore, you need to deduct the value of the third-party minority stake in the subsidiary as a nonequity financial claim.

Because minority stakes are to a certain extent the mirror image of nonconsolidated subsidiaries, the recommended valuation for minority interest is similar to that of nonconsolidated subsidiaries; see the corresponding section for more details. If the minority stake is publicly listed, as in the case of minority carve-outs (see Chapter 16), use the proportional market value owned by outsiders to deduct from enterprise value. Alternatively, you can perform a separate valuation using a DCF approach, multiples, or a tracking portfolio, depending on the amount of information available. Remember, however, that minority interest is a claim on a subsidiary, not the entire company. Thus, any valuation should be directly related to the subsidiary and not the company as a whole.

Calculating Value per Share

The final step in a valuation is to calculate the value per share. Assuming that you have used an option-based-valuation approach for all options and convertible securities, you should divide the total equity value by the number of *undiluted* shares outstanding. Use the undiluted number of shares because the values of convertible debt and stock options have already been deducted from the enterprise value as nonequity claims.

The number of shares outstanding is the gross number of shares issued, less the number of shares held in treasury. Most U.S. and European companies report the number of shares issued and those held in treasury under shareholders' equity. However, some companies show treasury shares as an investment asset, which they are not from an economic perspective. Treat them, instead, as a reduction in the number of shares outstanding.

If you use the conversion and exercise value method to account for convertible debt and stock options, you generate a different value for equity and should divide by the *diluted* number of shares.

VALUATION UNDER MULTIPLE SCENARIOS

The purpose of valuing a company is often to guide a management decision related to acquisition, divestiture, or adoption of internal strategic initiatives. Since most of these decisions involve uncertainty and risk, consider making financial projections under multiple scenarios. The scenarios should reflect different assumptions regarding future macro-economic, industry, or business developments, as well as the corresponding strategic response by the company. Collectively, the scenarios should capture the future states of the world that would have the most impact on future value creation and a reasonable chance of occurrence.

Assess how likely it is that the key assumptions underlying each scenario will change, and assign each scenario a probability of occurrence. When analyzing the scenarios, critically review your assumptions on the following variables:

- *Broad economic conditions:* How critical are these forecasts to the results? Some industries are more dependent on basic economic conditions than others. Home building, for example, is highly correlated with the overall health of the economy. Branded food processing, in contrast, is less affected by broad economic trends.

- *Competitive structure of the industry:* A scenario that assumes substantial increases in market share is less likely in a highly competitive and concentrated market than in an industry with fragmented and inefficient competition.

- *Internal capabilities of the company* that are necessary to achieve the business results predicted in the scenario: Can the company develop its products on time and manufacture them within the expected range of costs?

- *Financing capabilities of the company* (which are often implicit in the valuation): If debt or excess marketable securities are excessive relative to the company's targets, how will the company resolve the imbalance? Should the company raise equity if too much debt is projected? Should the company be willing to raise equity at its current market price?

Complete the alternative scenarios suggested by the preceding analyses. The process of examining initial results may well uncover unanticipated questions that are best resolved by creating additional scenarios. In this way, the valuation process is inherently circular. Performing a valuation often provides insights that lead to additional scenarios and analyses. Scenarios not only help you deal with the uncertainty in your financial projections, they also enable you to value nonoperating assets and nonequity claims more consistently, as we discussed in the beginning of this chapter.

In Exhibit 11.6, we provide a simplified example of a scenario approach to DCF valuation. The company being valued faces great uncertainty because of a new product launch for which it has spent considerable R&D.

Exhibit 11.6 Example of a Scenario Approach to DCF Valuation

$, percent

Probability weighted equity value:
1,766

67% Probability

Scenario #1

Value of operations	5,522
Nonoperating assets	614
Interest-bearing debt	(3,500)
Equity value	2,635

Financial projections

	2004	2005	2006	2007	2008	2009	2010	CV
Growth (percent)	5.0	6.0	8.0	9.0	6.0	5.0	3.5	3.5
Operating margin[1] (percent)	7.5	10.0	12.0	10.0	10.0	10.0	10.0	
Capital turns	1.00	1.00	1.05	1.10	1.05	1.00	1.00	
ROIC (percent)	7.5	10.0	12.6	11.0	10.5	10.0	10.0	10.0
Revenues	3,000	3,180	3,434	3,743	3,968	4,167	4,312	
NOPLAT	225	318	412	374	397	417	431	
Invested capital	3,000	3,180	3,271	3,403	3,779	4,167	4,312	
NOPLAT		318	412	374	397	417	431	
Net investment		(180)	(91)	(132)	(376)	(387)	(146)	
Free cash flow (FCF)		138	321	242	21	29	285	7,253
Discount factor		0.93	0.87	0.80	0.75	0.70	0.65	0.65
PV(FCF)		128	278	195	16	20	185	4,700

33% Probability

Scenario #2

Value of operations	2,165
Nonoperating assets	241
Interest-bearing debt	(2,406)
Equity value	—

	2004	2005	2006	2007	2008	2009	2010	CV
Growth (percent)	5.0	3.0	(1.0)	(1.0)	1.5	1.5	1.5	1.5
Operating margin[1] (percent)	7.5	5.0	3.0	2.0	3.0	4.0	6.5	
Capital turns	1.00	1.03	1.00	0.97	0.97	0.97	0.97	
ROIC (percent)	7.5	5.2	3.0	1.9	2.9	3.9	6.3	7.5
Revenues	3,000	3,090	3,059	3,029	3,074	3,120	3,167	
NOPLAT	225	155	92	61	92	125	206	
Invested capital	3,000	3,000	3,059	3,122	3,169	3,217	3,265	
NOPLAT		155	92	61	92	125	206	
Net investment		—	(59)	(63)	(47)	(48)	(48)	
Free cash flow (FCF)		155	33	(3)	45	77	158	2,786
Discount factor		0.93	0.87	0.80	0.75	0.70	0.65	0.65
PV(FCF)		144	28	(2)	34	54	102	1,805

Note: WACC: 7.5%, Tax rate: 35%, Debt at face value: $3,500.
[1]After-tax operating margin.

If the product succeeds, revenue growth will nearly double over the next few years. Returns on capital will peak at above 12 percent and remain at 10 percent in perpetuity. If the product launch fails, however, growth will continue to erode as the company's current products become obsolete. Operating margins and returns on capital will decline to levels below the cost of capital. The company only earns its cost of capital in the long term beyond 2010.

The two scenarios in Exhibit 11.6 reflect this double-or-quit future. Under the favorable scenario, the DCF value of operations equals $5,522. The nonoperating assets consist primarily of nonconsolidated subsidiaries, and given their own reliance on the product launch, they are valued at the implied NOPLAT multiple for the parent company, $614. We next deduct the face value of the debt outstanding at $3,500, as the bond was issued at par and interest rates have not changed significantly since the debt was issued. The resulting equity value is $2,635 million.

Under the unfavorable scenario, the product launch fails and the DCF value of operations is only $2,165. In this scenario, the value of the subsidiaries is much lower ($241), as their business outlook has deteriorated due to the failure of the new product. The value of the debt is no longer $3,500 in this scenario. Instead, the debt holders would end up with $2,406 by seizing the enterprise. Obviously, the common equity would have no value.

Given the approximately two-thirds probability of success for the product, the probability-weighted equity value across both scenarios amounts to $1,766. Note that the probability-weighted value of the debt would be $3,139—below its face value.

When using the scenario approach, make sure to generate a complete valuation buildup from value of operations to equity value. For example, using a scenario approach solely for the value of operations and subsidiaries and then deducting debt at its face value would seriously underestimate the equity value. In this case, the equity value would be $361 too low ($3,500 face value minus $3,139 probability-weighted value of debt).[16] A similar argument holds for nonoperating assets.

By creating scenarios, you can also better understand the company's key priorities. In our example, it appears that searching for ways to improve the financial performance in the downside scenario by, for example, reducing costs or cutting capital expenditures is unlikely to affect shareholder value, unless the changes can generate at least $1,100 in present value. Given the current operating profit of $225, this seems unlikely. In contrast,

---

[16] This also explains why using the market price of bonds or debt in your valuation can lead to errors if the bonds trade at a significant discount to their face value due to default risk (see this chapter's discussion on the treatment of debt as a nonequity claim). Deducting the market price of such bonds from the probability-weighted value of operations would be correct only if your assumptions on default scenarios and probabilities precisely reflect those of bond investors in the capital market.

increasing the odds of a successful launch has a much greater impact on shareholder value. Increasing the success probability from two-thirds to three-fourths would boost shareholder value by 12 percent.

VERIFYING VALUATION RESULTS

After estimating the equity value, you should perform several checks to test the logic of your results, minimize the possibility of errors, and ensure that you have a good understanding of the forces driving the valuation.

Consistency Check

The first series of checks concerns the logic of your model and valuation: Are the outcomes consistent with your assumptions?

Ensure that all *checks and balances* in your model are in place. Your model should reflect the following fundamental equilibrium relations:

- For the unadjusted financial statements, does the balance sheet balance in every year? Does the net income flow correctly into dividends paid and retained earnings? Are the sources of cash equal to the uses of cash?

- For the rearranged financial statements, does the sum of invested capital plus nonoperating assets balance with the financing sources? Is NOPLAT identical when calculated top down from sales and bottom up from net income? Does net income correctly link to dividends and retained earnings in adjusted equity? Does the change in excess cash and debt line up with the cash flow statement?

If these relations do not hold, there is a logical error in the model.

The next step is to check that your valuation results correctly reflect *value driver economics.* If the projected returns on invested capital are above the WACC, the value of operations should be above the book value of invested capital. If, in addition, growth is high, value of operations should be considerably above book value. If not, a computational error has probably been made. Compare your valuation results with a back-of-the-envelope value estimate based on the key value driver formula, taking long-term average growth and return on capital as key inputs.

Finally, make sure that patterns of *key financial and operating ratios* are consistent with economic logic:

- Are the patterns intended? For example, does invested capital turnover increase over time for sound economic reasons or simply because you modeled future capital expenditures as a fixed percentage of revenues? Are future cash tax rates changing dramatically because you forecasted deferred tax assets as a percentage of revenues or operating profit?

- Are the patterns reasonable? Avoid large step-changes in key assumptions from one year to the next because these will distort key ratios and could lead to false interpretations. For example, a strong single-year improvement in capital efficiency could make capital expenditures in that year negative, leading to an unrealistically high cash flow.

- Is a steady state reached for the company's economics by the end of the explicit forecasting period, that is, when you apply a continuing-value formula? A company achieves a steady state only when its free cash flows are growing at a constant rate. If this is not the case, extend the explicit forecast period while keeping the key performance ratios constant.

Sensitivity Analysis

The second step is to check whether your model's results are robust under alternative assumptions. Start with the *key value drivers* such as growth and return on invested capital, which you can further break down into operating margins and capital turnover. If you change the projected growth and returns, does the valuation change in the way it should? For example, if the return on invested capital is near the WACC, is value fairly insensitive to changes in growth, as it should be? If you increase capital turnover assumptions, do ROIC and value rise?

Next, dive deeper into the model's logic and check how changes in sector-specific *operating value drivers* affect the final valuation. For example, if you increase customer churn rates for a telecommunications company, does company value decrease? Can you explain with back-of-the-envelope estimates why the change is so large (or so small)?

Plausibility Analysis

Once you believe the model's logic is correct, you should test whether the final results are plausible.

If the company is listed, compare your results with the *market value*. If your estimate is far from the market value, do not jump to the conclusion that the market is wrong. Your default assumption should be that the market is right, unless you have specific indications that not all relevant information has been incorporated in the share price, for example due to low free float or low liquidity of the stock.

Perform a sound *multiples analysis.* Calculate the implied forward-looking valuation multiples of the operating value over, for example, EBITA, and compare these with equivalently defined multiples of traded peer-group companies. We explain in Chapter 12 how to do a proper multiples analysis. Make sure you can explain any significant differences with peer-group companies in terms of the companies' value drivers and underlying business characteristics or strategy.

The Art of Valuation

Valuation can be highly sensitive to small changes in assumptions about the future. Take a look at the sensitivity of a typical company with a forward-looking P/E ratio of 15 to 16. Increasing the cost of capital for this company by 0.5 percentage points will decrease the value by approximately 10 percent. Changing the growth rate for the next 15 years by 1 percentage point annually will change the value by about 6 percent. For high-growth companies, the sensitivity is even greater. The sensitivity is highest when interest rates are low, as they have been since the late 1990s.

In light of this sensitivity, it should be no surprise that the market value of a company fluctuates over time. Historical volatilities for a typical stock over the past several years have been around 25 percent per annum. Taking this as an estimate for future volatility, the market value of a typical company could well fluctuate around its expected value by 15 percent over the next month.[17]

We typically aim for a valuation range of plus or minus 15 percent, which is similar to the range used by many investment bankers. Even valuation professionals cannot always generate exact estimates. In other words, keep your aspirations for precision in check.

HEINEKEN CASE

In this chapter's case, we complete and analyze the Heineken valuation. First, we calculate the equity value of Heineken for the business-as-usual scenario. We then value

---

[17] Based on a 95 percent confidence interval for the end-of-month price of a stock with an expected return of 9 percent per year.

the other two scenarios we developed for the case in Chapter 8. Finally, we estimate a probability-weighted value.

VALUE IN THE BUSINESS-AS-USUAL SCENARIO

Exhibits 11.7 and 11.8 show the calculation of the value of Heineken's operations, using the DCF and economic profit approaches, respectively. Under both methods, the value of Heineken's operations is €16.855 billion.

The value of operations includes a midyear adjustment equal to one-half of a year's value discounted at Heineken's WACC. This is to adjust for the fact that we conservatively discounted the free cash flows and economic profits as if they were entirely realized at the end of each year, when, in fact, cash flows occur (cycles notwithstanding) evenly throughout the year. The six-month factor assumes that cash flows will come in on average in the middle of the year.

Under the business-as-usual scenario, Heineken's equity value is €13.466 billion, or €34.35 per share, as shown in Exhibit 11.9 on page 366. To calculate the market equity value, we added the market value of nonoperating assets such as excess cash, financial fixed assets, and nonconsolidated participating interests to the value of operations; this sum is the enterprise value. We then subtract debt, retirement liabilities, minority interest, and the restructuring provision to obtain the equity value.

Exhibit 11.7 Heineken: DCF Valuation

€ million

	Free cash flow	Discount factor	Present value of FCF
2004	(107)	0.9302	(100)
2005	181	0.8653	156
2006	320	0.8050	258
2007	477	0.7488	357
2008	648	0.6966	452
2009	975	0.6480	632
2010	1,009	0.6028	608
2011	1,039	0.5607	583
2012	1,071	0.5216	558
2013	1,103	0.4852	535
2014	1,136	0.4513	513
2015	1,170	0.4199	491
2016	1,205	0.3906	471
2017	1,241	0.3633	451
2018	1,278	0.3380	432
Continuing value	29,173	0.3380	9,860
Operating value			16,257
Mid-year adjustment factor			1.04
Operating value (discounted to current month)			**16,855**

Exhibit 11.8 Heineken: Economic Profit Valuation

€ million

	Economic profit before goodwill	Discount factor	Present value of economic profit
2004	512	0.9302	476
2005	540	0.8653	467
2006	570	0.8050	459
2007	597	0.7488	447
2008	618	0.6966	431
2009	619	0.6480	401
2010	637	0.6028	384
2011	656	0.5607	368
2012	676	0.5216	353
2013	696	0.4852	338
2014	717	0.4513	324
2015	739	0.4199	310
2016	761	0.3906	297
2017	784	0.3633	285
2018	807	0.3380	273
Continuing value	18,387	0.3380	6,214
Present value of economic profit			11,826
Invested capital excluding goodwill (beginning of forecast)			5,670
Less: present value of investments in goodwill			(1,239)
Value of operations			16,257
Mid-year adjustment factor			1.04
Operating value (discounted to current month)			**16,855**

Heineken's enterprise value includes three nonoperating assets:

1. Financial fixed assets of €671 million are primarily receivables from customers. We valued these loans at book value.

2. Nonconsolidated participating interests are less than 50 percent investments in other companies. We valued these at a multiple of income from these investments, similar to the multiples for all brewers. Heineken's share of income from these companies was €30 million in 2003 (excluding a one-time gain from the sale of investments of €71 million), which we multiplied by a typical brewer's multiple of 16 to estimate the value of Heineken's interest at €480 million.

3. Heineken's excess cash of €1.231 billion is valued at book value.

By adding the nonoperating assets to the value of operations, we determine an enterprise value of €19.237 billion. The value of Heineken's debt, minority interest, and retirement liabilities were estimated in Chapter 10 when we estimated Heineken's

Exhibit 11.9 Heineken: Value of Equity

€ million

Value of operations	16,855
Value of financial fixed assets	671
Value of nonconsolidated participating interests	480
Excess cash	1,231
Enterprise value	**19,237**
Value of debt	(3,922)
Value of retirement liabilities	(526)
Minority interest	(1,030)
Restructuring provision	(293)
Equity value	**13,466**
Number of shares outstanding (million)	392
Value per share	**€34.35**

cost of capital. We also subtract the restructuring provision, which we expect to be paid out in the next year. (Since the payout of the restructuring provision will not flow through free cash flow, it must be subtracted here.) There is no adjustment for executive stock options because Heineken does not use options to compensate its managers.

The value of operations for the business-as-usual case is about three times the invested capital (excluding goodwill). This is consistent with Heineken's projected ROIC being about twice its cost of capital with modest growth. (With zero growth, the ratio of DCF value to invested capital will equal the ratio of ROIC to WACC.)

ADDITIONAL SCENARIOS AND PROBABILITY WEIGHTING

We also valued the other two scenarios for Heineken, the operating-improvement scenario and the aggressive-acquisitions scenario. The results are summarized in Exhibit 11.10.

In the operating-improvement scenario, we projected that Heineken could improve margins and capital turnover near to the peak levels it achieved over the last five years. This brings Heineken's ROIC up to 21 percent by the end of the forecast, versus 15 percent in the business-as-usual scenario. Under the operating-improvement scenario, Heineken's value is €47.00 per share, a 37 percent premium to the business-as-usual scenario.

For the aggressive-acquisitions scenario, we forecast growth from acquisitions at the five-year average historical level of 7.2 percent from 2005 to 2010, then slowing

Exhibit 11.10 Heineken: Summary of Scenario Values

	Scenario		
	Operating capital utilization improvements	Business as usual	High premium acquisitions
Average revenue growth, 2004–2008 (percent)	6.5	6.5	10.2
Average EBITA/turnover 2004–2008 (percent)	13.8	12.6	12.6
Average ROIC (excluding goodwill) 2004–2008 (percent)	20.0	16.0	16.0
Enterprise value (€ million)	23.9	19.2	15.1
Equity value (€ million)	18.4	13.5	9.6
Equity value per share (€ million)	46.97	34.35	24.55
Probability	25%	60%	15%
Expected value per share		€36.03	

by 1 percent per year. Under this scenario, competition for acquisitions heats up, and Heineken is forced to pay high premiums to continue its acquisition growth. We forecast goodwill to increase to 150 percent of revenues from acquisitions during the acquisition year. Operating performance remains constant. Under the aggressive-acquisitions scenario, Heineken's value is €24.55 per share, a 29 percent discount relative to the business-as-usual case.

Finally, we weighted the scenario values with probabilities and arrived at an estimated value of €36.03 per share, as shown in Exhibit 11.10. The estimated value is about 7 percent higher than Heineken's market value of €33.65 per share as of February 2004. We assigned a higher probability to the upside scenario because we believe that the recent pressures on margins will force Heineken management to focus on operating improvement rather than acquisition growth. That said, the temptation of growth through acquisitions is always lurking and may overcome the focus on operations.

While the scenario approach estimates a value close to the market value, the real insight from the scenario approach is the spread of values. Even in the case of a profitable but modestly growing company like Heineken, the spread of values across the scenarios is plus or minus 30 percent, a substantial opportunity (or risk) for both investors and managers.

Finally, we conducted a sensitivity analysis to complement the scenario analysis. Exhibit 11.11 on page 368 summarizes the impact on Heineken's value when we change the forecasts for revenue growth, margins, capital turnover, and cost of capital. It is impossible to compare the sensitivities directly, because we don't know whether the changes in variables are equally likely or difficult. For example, we don't know whether it is more or less difficult to increase capital turnover by 0.1 times or to increase margins by 1 percent.

Exhibit 11.11 Heineken: Sensitivity Analysis

	Base value 2004–2008 (percent)	Change	Change in equity value (€ billions)	(percent)
Organic revenue growth	3.0	1.0 %	1.6	11.5
Adjusted EBITA margin	12.7	1.0 %	1.8	13.0
Capital turnover	1.6	0.1 times	0.2	1.1
WACC	7.5	(0.5) %	2.4	17.5

In any case, it is evident that Heineken's value is highly sensitive to changes in its cost of capital (a 17 percent change in value for a 0.5 percentage point change in WACC). Given the uncertainty in estimating WACC, this suggests a range of accuracy for the valuation. On the operating front, the value is moderately sensitive to both revenue growth and margin, although we suspect that margin increases might be more achievable and sustainable than accelerating growth in a mature market like beer.

REVIEW QUESTIONS

1. From a manager's perspective, what is the purpose of computing the firm's enterprise value?

2. Once a manager computes enterprise value, what additional process steps need to be undertaken to determine the value of its equity position? Compare and contrast these additional steps to those of the cash-flow-to-equity model.

3. Identify the accounting standards specifying the manner and methods to be followed when consolidating a subsidiary's financial statements into those of the parent's financial statements.

4. If a parent company is not able to consolidate a subsidiary's financial position, explain how the degree of equity ownership impacts the parent company's cash flow position.

5. Discuss the relationship of the following nonoperating assets to the estimation of enterprise value: tax loss carry forwards, discontinued operations, investment in excess real estate, and investments in underutilized assets.

6. Identify and define the basic categories of nonequity claims. Discuss how each of the following nonequity claims could lead to significant adjustments to a corporate valuation model: preferred equity and convertible bonds, employee stock options, and unfunded pension liabilities.

7. What should a company consider when estimating the value of employee stock options? Identify the main factors that impact the value of employee stock options.

8. Define scenario analysis. What benefits are likely to accrue to a manager when scenario analysis is undertaken in conjunction with computing enterprise value?

9. Identify the steps that should be taken to verify the results obtained from estimating enterprise value.

10. How are convertible debt instruments defined in an annual report? Discuss the impact of the financial statement treatment of convertible debt to the estimation of equity value.

12

Using Multiples
for Valuation

Discounted cash flow analysis is the most accurate and flexible method for valuing projects, divisions, and companies. Any analysis, however, is only as accurate as the forecasts it relies on. Errors in estimating the key ingredients of corporate value—ingredients such as a company's ROIC, growth rate, and WACC—can lead to mistakes in valuation and, ultimately, to strategic errors.

A careful multiples analysis—comparing a company's multiples versus those of comparable companies—can be useful in making such forecasts and the DCF valuations they inform more accurate. Properly executed, such an analysis can help test the plausibility of cash flow forecasts, explain mismatches between a company's performance and that of its competitors, and support useful discussions about whether the company is strategically positioned to create more value than other industry players. As you seek to understand why a company's multiples are higher or lower than those of the competition, multiples analysis can also generate insights into the key factors creating value in an industry.

Yet multiples are frequently misunderstood and even more often misapplied. Many financial analysts, for example, calculate an industry-average price-to-earnings (P/E) ratio and multiply it by a company's earnings to establish a "fair" valuation. The use of the industry average, however, overlooks the fact that companies, even in the same industry, can have drastically different expected growth rates, returns on invested capital, and capital structures. The P/E ratio can exhibit flaws even when comparing companies with identical prospects, since it commingles operating and nonoperating items. By contrast, a carefully designed multiples analysis *can* provide valuable insights about a company and its competitors.

In this chapter, we step through the process of how to create, interpret, and apply multiples in a valuation setting. We examine how to choose which multiples are the most effective and how to create multiples that reflect a company's core operations. Although many claim multiples are an easy-to-apply valuation method, the converse is true. As you will see, a well-done multiples analysis requires many of the same adjustments (and effort) as traditional DCF.

COMPARABLES ANALYSIS: AN EXAMPLE

Each week, investment banking research analysts report the stock market performance of Home Depot and other American retailers by creating a valuation *comps* table (*comps* means "comparable companies"). Exhibit 12.1 is an abridged version of a typical valuation summary. We use the exhibit to demonstrate how multiples are created and reported.

Reported in the summary are each company's week-end closing price and market capitalization. The table also reports analyst projections for each company's earnings per share (EPS). To compare the valuations across companies, each company's share price is divided by the projected EPS to obtain a forward-looking P/E ratio. To derive Home Depot's forward-looking P/E ratio of 13.3, divide its week-end closing price of $33 by its projected 2005 EPS of $2.48. Although the calculation is not detailed in the summary tables, a forward-looking enterprise-value-to-EBITDA ratio is also reported.

A challenge of using these ratios involves selecting the appropriate companies for comparison. For the period covered in Exhibit 12.1, Home

Exhibit 12.1 Hardline Retailing Valuation Summary, July 2004

Hardline retailing	Ticker	Stock price ($) July 23, 2004	Market capitalization $ million	Earnings per share (EPS), ($)[1] 2004	2005	Foward-looking multiples, 2005 EBITDA[2]	P/E
Home improvement							
Home Depot	HD	33.00	74,250	2.18	2.48	7.1	13.3
Lowe's	LOW	48.39	39,075	2.86	3.36	7.3	14.4
Home furnishing							
Bed Bath & Beyond	BBBY	34.89	10,697	1.58	1.83	9.9	19.1
Linens 'n Things	LIN	25.86	1,152	1.86	2.13	5.1	12.1
Consumer electronics							
Best Buy	BBY	47.11	15,537	2.88	3.41	6.3	13.8
Circuit City	CC	13.58	2,708	0.55	0.61	4.4	22.3
Benchmark index							
S&P 500	SPX	1,086.20		64.74	69.76		15.6

[1]Credit Suisse First Boston (CSFB) analysts' projections for EPS by calendar year.
[2]EBITDA = earnings before interest, taxes, depreciation, and amortization; EBITDA and P/E are reported by calendar year.
 Source: *Hardlines Retailing: Weekly Review*, CSFB, New York, July 26, 2004.

Depot and its primary competitor, Lowe's, traded at nearly identical multiples. The price-to-earnings ratios for the two companies differed by only 8 percent, and their enterprise-to-EBITDA ratios differed by only 3 percent. This similarity does not hold, however, when we expand the set of comparables. For the entire hardline retailing group, enterprise multiples vary from 4.4 to 9.9. Why such a large range? Investors have different expectations for each company's ability to create value going forward. Therefore, from a valuation perspective, not every company in the sample is truly comparable.

Understanding what drives these systematic differences in multiples is critical to using multiples appropriately. We discuss the drivers of multiples next.

WHAT BESIDES GROWTH DRIVES MULTIPLES?

Many investors and corporate managers swayed by the teachings of Wall Street pundits believe that multiples are driven by earnings growth. David and Tom Gardner of The Motley Fool investor web site write, "The P/E generally reflects the market's expectations for the growth of a given company."[1] Academics further this perception in their own writings. In their core finance text, Professors Richard Brealey and Stewart Myers write, "The high P/E shows that investors think that the firm has good growth opportunities, that its earnings are relatively safe and deserve a low [cost of capital], or both."[2]

Growth does indeed drive multiples, but *only* when combined with a healthy return on invested capital. To see how both ROIC and growth drive multiples, we reexamine the key value driver formula, introduced in Chapter 3:

$$V = \frac{\text{NOPLAT}\left(1 - \dfrac{g}{\text{ROIC}}\right)}{\text{WACC} - g}$$

The key value driver is a cash-flow-based formula that has been rearranged to focus on NOPLAT, ROIC, growth (g), and the WACC. To build a pretax enterprise-value multiple, disaggregate NOPLAT into EBITA and the company's cash tax rate (T):

[1] David Gardner and Tom Gardner, "The Fool Ratio: The Growth Rate Examined," www.fool.com/School/TheGrowthRate.htm.
[2] Many readers interpret "good growth opportunities" as implying "plentiful growth opportunities." This is incorrect. Instead, Brealey and Myers write "good growth opportunities" to imply "value-creating growth opportunities." This difference is critical. Richard Brealey and Stewart Myers, *Principles of Corporate Finance* (New York: McGraw-Hill, 2002).

$$V = \frac{\text{EBITA}\,(1-T)\left(1-\dfrac{g}{\text{ROIC}}\right)}{\text{WACC}-g}$$

and divide both sides by EBITA:

$$\frac{V}{\text{EBITA}} = \frac{(1-T)\left(1-\dfrac{g}{\text{ROIC}}\right)}{\text{WACC}-g}$$

The resulting equation is an algebraic representation of a commonly used multiple, enterprise value to EBITA. The multiple is similar to the P/E ratio but focuses on enterprise value, rather than equity. (We return to this fundamental difference in the next section.) From the equation, four factors drive the enterprise-value-to-EBITA multiple: the company's growth rate, return on invested capital, the cash tax rate, and the cost of capital. In most situations, the average cash tax rate and cost of capital will be similar across companies within the industry (because they face the same tax policies and have similar operating risks). This similarity does *not* hold for ROIC and growth, which can vary dramatically across companies, even within an industry. Thus, the same industry can include companies with drastically different multiples for perfectly valid reasons.

To demonstrate how different values of ROIC and growth will generate different multiples, Exhibit 12.2 uses the key value driver formula to create a set of hypothetical multiples for a company whose cash tax rate equals 30

Exhibit 12.2 How ROIC and Growth Drive Multiples

Enterprise value to EBITA[1]

Long-term growth rate (percent)	Return on invested capital (percent)				
	6	9	15	20	25
4.0	4.7	7.8	10.3	11.2	11.8
4.5	3.9	7.8	10.9	12.1	12.8
5.0	2.9	7.8	11.7	13.1	14.0
5.5	1.7	7.8	12.7	14.5	15.6
6.0	n/a	7.8	14.0	16.3	17.7

[1]Based on the key value driver formula, assuming a 30 percent cash tax rate and a 9 percent cost of capital.

percent and whose cost of capital equals 9 percent, rates similar to those for Home Depot.[3] In the exhibit, high multiples result from high returns on invested capital *and* from high growth rates.

As Exhibit 12.2 demonstrates, the enterprise-value-to-EBITA multiple increases with growth only if the company's ROIC is greater than the cost of capital. When ROIC equals the WACC, the enterprise-value-to-EBITA multiple is constant and equals $(1 - T)/\text{WACC}$. In this example, the WACC is 9 percent, and expected cash taxes are 30 percent, so the enterprise-value multiple is estimated at 7.8 times, regardless of expected growth. (Home Depot's actual enterprise value multiple of 2005 EBITA equals 8.7.) The exhibit also demonstrates that different combinations can lead to the same results. If the company grows at 6 percent and generates a 15 percent return on invested capital, it will have the same multiple (according to the formula) as if the company grew at only 5 percent but generated returns of 25 percent.

BEST PRACTICES FOR USING MULTIPLES

A thoughtful multiples analysis can provide valuable insights about a company and its competitors. Conversely, a poor analysis can result in confusion. In Exhibit 12.3 on page 376, we create a set of multiples analyses for Home Depot using various methodologies. For each comparison, we compute whether Home Depot is trading at a premium (i.e., has a higher multiple) to other companies or trading at a discount. In the first comparison, a trailing P/E ratio (based on earnings from the last fiscal year) is computed to benchmark Home Depot against all hardline retailers. Based on this comparison, the company trades at a 19 percent discount to its "peers." This discount is misleading, however, because the backward-looking price-to-earnings ratio measures past performance, not future performance, which is the basis for value. The ratio also commingles operating, nonoperating, and financial characteristics. Therefore, we make a series of adjustments to focus on future operating performance.

Because the listed retailers are extremely diverse, with varying prospects for ROIC and growth, we first reduce the peer group to Home Depot's closest competitor, Lowe's. (We would prefer to include other home improvement competitors, such as Menards, but it and other large-scale home improvement retailers are not publicly traded.) After this adjustment, the trailing P/E ratio discount drops to 17 percent. We next replace historical earnings with estimates for next year's earnings, which further lowers the discount to 8 percent.

---

[3] The key value driver formula is a perpetuity-based formula that assumes ROIC and growth never change. Since this assumption is overly restrictive for most companies, we use the formula to demonstrate levers, rather than predict accurate enterprise-value multiples.

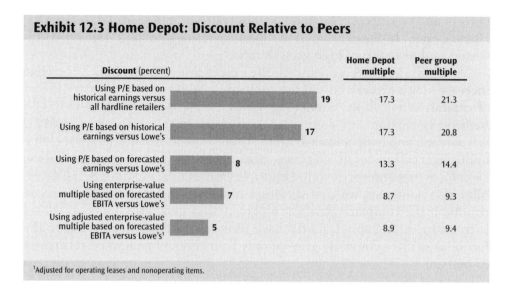

Exhibit 12.3 Home Depot: Discount Relative to Peers

Discount (percent)		Home Depot multiple	Peer group multiple
Using P/E based on historical earnings versus all hardline retailers	19	17.3	21.3
Using P/E based on historical earnings versus Lowe's	17	17.3	20.8
Using P/E based on forecasted earnings versus Lowe's	8	13.3	14.4
Using enterprise-value multiple based on forecasted EBITA versus Lowe's	7	8.7	9.3
Using adjusted enterprise-value multiple based on forecasted EBITA versus Lowe's[1]	5	8.9	9.4

[1] Adjusted for operating leases and nonoperating items.

To improve the comparison further, we switch to an enterprise-value multiple. This avoids any bias caused by capital structure and nonoperating gains and losses. Using an enterprise-value-to-EBITA multiple causes the difference to drop to 7 percent. Finally, we strip out excess cash and adjust for capitalized operating leases (the same two adjustments we made when calculating Home Depot's enterprise DCF value) from the enterprise-value multiple. Based on the adjusted enterprise-value multiple, Home Depot and Lowe's trade within 5 percent of one another.

As the Home Depot example demonstrates, using the wrong multiple can lead to errors in assessment and potentially valuation. When we used trailing P/E to compare Home Depot with the hardline retailers, the company seemed to be undervalued by 20 percent. But with an adjusted enterprise-value multiple, the valuation differences are small.

To apply multiples properly, use the following four best practices:

1. Choose comparables with similar prospects for ROIC and growth.
2. Use multiples based on forward-looking estimates.
3. Use enterprise-value multiples based on EBITA to mitigate problems with capital structure and one-time gains and losses.
4. Adjust the enterprise-value multiple for nonoperating items, such as excess cash, operating leases, employee stock options, and pension expenses (the same items for which we adjusted ROIC and free cash flow).

Choose Comparables with Similar Prospects

To analyze a company using comparables, you must first create a peer group. Most analysts start by examining the company's industry. But how do you define an industry? Sometimes, a company lists its competitors in its annual report. If the company doesn't disclose its competition, you can use an industry classification system such as Standard Industrial Classification (SIC) codes.[4] Home Depot's SIC code, however, contains more than 20 companies, many of which are not directly comparable because they sell very different products or rely on different business models. A slightly better but proprietary system is the Global Industry Classifications Standard (GICS) system, recently developed by Standard & Poor's and Morgan Stanley. A recent study found GICS classifications do a significantly better job of explaining cross-sectional variations in valuation multiples, forecasted and realized growth rates, R&D expenditures, and key financial ratios.[5]

Once you have collected a list and properly measured the multiples, the digging begins. You must answer a series of questions: Why are the multiples different across the peer group? Do certain companies in the group have superior products, better access to customers, recurring revenues, or economies of scale? If these strategic advantages translate to superior ROIC and growth rates, better-positioned companies should trade at higher multiples. You must understand what products they sell, how they generate revenue and profits, and how they grow. Only then will a company's multiple appear in the appropriate context with other companies.

In general, we recommend analyzing a set of multiples to better understand how a company is valued relative to its peers. In limited situations, you may need a representative multiple for use in valuation. For example, valuing minority interest from an outside perspective is difficult using traditional DCF because the required information to reconstruct cash flows is unavailable. (See Chapter 11 for more on minority interest.) Although missing information can be estimated, an alternative is to apply a representative earnings-based multiple to minority interest.

To develop a representative multiple, first limit the set to companies with similar characteristics, as we described above. Next, compute the median or harmonic mean of the sample.[6] To calculate the harmonic mean, compute the peer group's average EBITA-to-enterprise-value ratio (the reciprocal of the traditional ratio), and then take the reciprocal of the average. Do not use the average multiple outright, which can lead to major

---

[4] Beginning in 1997, SIC codes were replaced by a major revision called the North American Industry Classification System (NAICS). The NAICS six-digit code not only provides for newer industries, but also reorganizes the categories on a production/process-oriented basis. The Securities and Exchange Commission (SEC), however, still lists companies by SIC code.

[5] S. Bhojraj, C. M. C. Lee, and D. Oler, "What's My Line? A Comparison of Industry Classification Schemes for Capital Market Research" (working paper, Ithaca, NY: Cornell University, May 2003), http://ssrn.com/abstract=356840.

[6] Malcolm Baker and Richard Ruback use simulation to demonstrate that the harmonic mean leads to superior results. M. Baker and R. S. Ruback, "Estimating Industry Multiples" (working paper, Cambridge, MA: Harvard Business School, 1999).

distortions. Companies whose earnings are small on a temporary basis will have extremely large multiples that will inappropriately dominate the average. The sample median is less sensitive to outliers.

In some industries, the peer group will contain companies with negative earnings. For these companies, the multiples are not meaningful. In most situations, these companies can be excluded from the peer set because they are not comparable (a company with poor prospects should not be used to value a company with good prospects). If you are truly unclear about your company's future prospects, then including only companies with positive earnings will bias the industry multiple. In this case, switch to a multiple whose denominator is positive. Companies with negative earnings often have positive EBITDA and always have positive sales. Use this option sparingly, however. Moving up the income statement imposes further restrictions on the comparability of margins, returns on capital, and so on.

The retailers examined in Exhibit 12.1 are "pure play" businesses, meaning the vast majority of their revenues and profits come from one business type. When valuing or analyzing a company with multiple business units, each with different prospects for ROIC and growth, you should use a separate peer group for each business unit. (For more on valuing multibusiness companies, see Chapter 19.)

Use Forward-Looking Multiples

When building a multiple, the denominator should use a forecast of profits, rather than historical profits. Unlike backward-looking multiples, forward-looking multiples are consistent with the principles of valuation—in particular, that a company's value equals the present value of future cash flow, not sunk costs.

Empirical evidence shows that forward-looking multiples are indeed more accurate predictors of value. One empirical study examined the characteristics and performance of historical multiples versus forward industry multiples for a large sample of companies trading on the New York Stock Exchange (NYSE), the American Stock Exchange (AMEX), and NASDAQ.[7] When companies were measured versus their industry, their historical earnings-to-price (E/P) ratios had 1.6 times the standard deviation of one-year forward E/P ratios (6.0 percent versus 3.7 percent). In addition, the study found forward-looking multiples led to greater pricing accuracy.[8] The median pricing error equaled 23 percent for historical multiples and 18

---

[7] J. Liu, D. Nissim, and J. Thomas, "Equity Valuation Using Multiples," *Journal of Accounting Research*, 40 (2002): 135–172.

[8] To forecast a company's price, the authors multiplied the company's earnings by the industry median multiple. Pricing error equals the difference between forecasted price and actual price, divided by actual price.

percent for one-year forecasted earnings. Two-year forecasts worked even better, lowering the median pricing error to 16 percent.

Other research, which used multiples to predict the price of 142 initial public offerings, also found multiples based on forecasted earnings outperformed those based on historical earnings.[9] As the analysis moved from multiples based on historical earnings to multiples based on one- and two-year forecasts, the average pricing error fell from 55.0 percent to 43.7 percent to 28.5 percent, respectively, and the percentage of firms valued within 15 percent of their actual trading multiple increased from 15.4 percent to 18.9 percent to 36.4 percent.

Based on the principles of valuation and on empirical evidence, we recommend building multiples based on forecasted profits, not on historical profits.[10] If you must use historical data, make sure to use the most recent data possible and eliminate any one-time events.

Use Enterprise-Value Multiples

Although widely used, the price-earnings multiple has two major flaws. First, the price-earnings ratio is systematically affected by capital structure. Second, unlike EBITA, net income is calculated after nonoperating gains and losses. Thus, a nonoperating loss, such as a noncash write-off, can significantly lower earnings (without a comparable effect on value), causing the P/E ratio to be artificially high. Given the shortcomings of P/E ratios, we recommend using forward-looking enterprise-value multiples—debt plus equity to forecasted EBITA.[11] The following paragraphs examine the effects of capital structure and one-time items in detail.

Throughout this book, we have focused on the drivers of operating performance—ROIC, growth, and free cash flow—because the traditional ratios, such as return on assets and return on equity, commingle the effects of operations and capital structure. The same principles hold true with multiples. Price-earnings multiples commingle expectations about operating performance, capital structure, and nonoperating items.

To effectively analyze valuation multiples across an industry, we need a multiple that is independent of capital structure. The price-to-earnings ratio does not meet this criterion. In Appendix E, we derive the explicit

[9] M. Kim and J. R. Ritter, "Valuing IPOs," *Journal of Financial Economics,* 53(3) (1999): 409–437.

[10] A cautionary note about using forward multiples: Some analysts forecast future earnings by assuming an industry multiple and backing out the required earnings based on the current price. In this case, any multiples you calculate will merely reflect the analyst's assumptions about the appropriate forward multiple, and dispersion (even when warranted) will be nonexistent.

[11] If the company has nonoperating assets, such as excess cash or nonconsolidated subsidiaries, the enterprise-value ratio must be adjusted. Otherwise, the numerator (which includes the value from nonoperating assets) and the denominator (which excludes their income) will be inconsistent. We discuss adjustments in the next section.

Exhibit 12.4 The Relation between Leverage and P/E

Price to earnings multiple[1]

Debt to value	Price to earnings for an all-equity company				
	10	15	20	25	40
10%	9.5	14.6	20.0	25.7	45.0
20%	8.9	14.1	20.0	26.7	53.3
30%	8.2	13.5	20.0	28.0	70.0
40%	7.5	12.9	20.0	30.0	120.0
50%	6.7	12.0	20.0	33.3	n/m

[1]Assumes a cost of debt equal to 5% and no taxes.

relation between a company's actual P/E ratio and its unlevered P/E ratio (PE_u)—the P/E ratio as if the company were entirely financed with equity. Assuming no taxes, a company's P/E ratio can be expressed as follows:

$$\frac{P}{E} = \bar{K} + \frac{\bar{K} - PE_u}{\left(\frac{D}{V}\right)(k_d)(PE_u) - 1} \quad \text{such that } \bar{K} = \frac{1}{k_d}$$

where k_d = cost of debt
             D/V = the ratio of debt to value

As the formula demonstrates, when the unlevered P/E equals the reciprocal of the cost of debt, the numerator of the fraction equals zero, and leverage has no effect on the P/E ratio. For companies with large unlevered P/Es (i.e., companies with significant opportunities for future value creation), P/E systematically increases with leverage. Conversely, companies with small unlevered P/Es would exhibit a drop in P/E as leverage rises.

Based on this formula for the P/E ratio, Exhibit 12.4 compares the relation between leverage and P/E. To build the table, we assume a cost of debt equal to 5 percent and no taxes. For unlevered P/E ratios greater than 20, the P/E ratio increases with leverage. This occurs because, for high-P/E companies, the drop in equity (which occurs when debt is used to repurchase shares) is less than the drop in earnings (because of new interest). For companies with significantly high unlevered P/Es, such as 40, increased leverage will cause the levered P/E to explode. In this example, a company with an unlevered P/E of 40 and debt to value of 50 percent is not meaningful, because interest causes earnings to be negative.

An alternative to the P/E ratio is enterprise value to EBITA. In a world with no taxes and no distress costs, the enterprise-value-to-EBITA ratio is unaffected by leverage. In actuality, even the enterprise-value-to-EBITA ratio depends somewhat on a company's capital structure. The reason is that although EBITA is independent of capital structure, enterprise value is higher for companies with more efficient capital structures. Remember, enterprise value depends on ROIC, growth, *and* the weighted average cost of capital. Thus, improvements in WACC translate to increases in enterprise value.

In theory, we would like to remove the present value of tax shields and distress costs from enterprise value. This would allow us to create a purely operating multiple, completely independent of a company's capital structure. In practice, the complexity of removing these effects outweighs the potential errors they cause if left in place.

A second problem with the P/E ratio is that earnings include many non-operating items, such as restructuring charges and write-offs. Since many nonoperating items are one-time events, multiples based on P/Es can be misleading. In 2002, AOL-Time Warner wrote off nearly $100 billion in goodwill and other intangibles. Even though EBITA equaled $6.4 billion, the company recorded a $98 billion loss. Since earnings were negative, the company's 2002 P/E ratio was meaningless.

Adjust Enterprise-Value Multiple for Nonoperating Items

Although EBITA is superior to earnings for calculating multiples, even enterprise-value multiples must be adjusted for nonoperating items included within enterprise value or reported EBITA. This is similar to the discussion in Chapter 7, where we demonstrated how financial statements based on today's accounting principles commingle operating and nonoperating items. This caused us to reorganize the company's financial statements, allowing us to compute ROIC and free cash flow, both of which are independent of capital structure and nonoperating items.

To build a clean set of multiples, we apply the same principles. The market-based enterprise value must be adjusted for nonoperating items, such as excess cash and operating leases. Although reported EBITA appears independent of nonoperating items, it *must* be adjusted as well. For instance, reported EBITA includes the implicit interest expense from operating leases. Failing to adjust EBITA can generate misleading results. See Chapter 7 for a detailed description of the reorganization process; here are the most common adjustments:

- *Excess cash and other nonoperating assets:* Since EBITA excludes interest income from excess cash, enterprise value should not include excess cash either. To calculate an enterprise-value multiple, sum the market values of debt and equity, subtract excess cash, and divide the remainder by EBITA. The same holds true for other nonoperating assets, whose income is not part of EBITA. Nonoperating assets must be evaluated separately.

- *Operating leases:* Companies with significant operating leases will have an artificially low enterprise value (because we are ignoring the value of lease-based debt) and an artificially low EBITA (because rental expense includes interest costs). To calculate an enterprise-value multiple, add the value of leased assets to the market value of debt and equity. Add back the implied interest expense to EBITA.

- *Employee stock options:* For companies that fail to expense stock options, EBITA will be artificially high. To properly calculate an enterprise-value multiple, subtract the after-tax value of *newly issued* employee option grants from EBITA (as reported in the footnotes). To adjust enterprise value, add the present value of employee grants *outstanding* to the sum of debt and equity. Enterprise value should be adjusted for any company with outstanding options, regardless of its expensing policy.

- *Pensions:* To adjust enterprise value, add the after-tax present value of pension liabilities to debt plus equity. To remove the nonoperating gains and losses related to plan assets, start with EBITA, add the pension interest expense, and deduct the recognized returns on plan assets (as reported in the footnotes).

To see the distortions caused by nonoperating assets, consider once again the multiples analysis presented in Exhibit 12.1. Best Buy trades at a premium to Circuit City Stores, according to their respective enterprise-value multiples (6.3 versus 4.4), but it trades at a discount based on P/E ratios (13.8 versus 22.3). So which is it, premium or discount? In reality, Circuit City's P/E multiple is meaningless. In July 2004, Circuit City's total equity value was approximately $2.7 billion, but the company held nearly $1 billion in cash. Since cash generates very little income, the P/E ratio of cash is very high (a 2 percent after-tax return on investment translates to a P/E of 50). Thus, the extremely high P/E of cash will artificially increase the P/E of Circuit City's operating business. When we remove cash from equity value ($2,708 million − $990 million) and divide by earnings less after-tax interest income ($122 million − $8 million), Circuit City's P/E drops from 22.3 to 15.1.

In Exhibit 12.5, we adjust the enterprise multiples of Home Depot and Lowe's for excess cash and operating leases. To adjust enterprise value, we start with Home Depot's market value of debt plus equity ($75.6 billion), add back the value of leased assets ($6.6 billion), and subtract excess cash ($1.6 billion). This leads to an adjusted enterprise value of $80.6 billion. Next, we adjust 2005 estimated EBITA ($8.7 billion) for implied interest on operating leases ($340 million). Before adjustments, Home Depot's enterprise-value multiple is within 6.6 percent of that for Lowe's. After adjustments, the difference drops to 5.1 percent.

Exhibit 12.5 Home Depot and Lowe's: Adjusted to Enterprise Value Multiples

$ million	Home Depot	Lowe's	
Outstanding debt	1,365	3,755	
Market value of equity	74,250	39,075	
Enterprise value	75,615	42,830	
Capitalized operating leases	6,554	2,762	
Excess cash	(1,609)	(1,033)	
Adjusted enterprise value	80,560	44,559	
2005 EBITA	8,691	4,589	
Implied interest from leases	340	154	
Adjusted 2005 EBITA	9,031	4,743	
	Home Depot	Lowe's	Difference
Raw enterprise value multiple	8.7	9.3	(6.6%)
Adjusted enterprise value multiple	8.9	9.4	(5.1%)

Throughout this chapter, we emphasize enterprise-value multiples based on EBITA. This approach enables us to tie the enterprise-value multiple directly to the key value driver formula. A common alternative to the EBITA multiple is the EBITDA multiple.[12] Many financial analysts use EBITDA multiples because depreciation is a noncash expense, reflecting sunk costs, not future investment.

To see this, consider two companies, each of which owns a machine that produces identical products. Both machines have the same cash-based operating costs, and each company's products sell for the same price. If one company paid more for its equipment (for whatever reason—perhaps poor negotiation), it will have higher depreciation going forward and, thus, lower EBITA. Valuation, however, is based on discounted cash flow, not discounted profits. And since both companies have identical cash flow, they should have identical values.[13] We would therefore expect the two companies to have identical multiples. Yet, because EBITA differs across the two companies, their multiples will differ as well.

Since valuation is based on future cash flows, EBITDA might seem superior to EBITA. But this is not always the case. Exhibit 12.6 on page 384 presents two companies that differ in only one aspect. Company A manufactures its

---

[12] EBITDA stands for earnings before interest, taxes, depreciation, and amortization.

[13] Since depreciation is tax deductible, a company with higher depreciation will have a smaller tax burden. Lower taxes lead to higher cash flows and a higher valuation. Therefore, even companies with identical EBITDAs will have different EBITDA multiples. The distortion, however, is less pronounced.

Exhibit 12.6 Comparing EBITA and EBITDA Multiples

$ million	Company A	Company B	
Revenues	100	100	
Raw materials	(10)	(35)	Company B outsources manufacturing to another company
Operating costs	(40)	(40)	
EBITDA	50	25	
Depreciation	(30)	(5)	
EBITA	20	20	

Multiples	Company A	Company B
Enterprise value ($ million)	150.0	150.0
Enterprise value / EBITDA	3.0	6.0
Enterprise value / EBITA	7.5	7.5

products using its own equipment, whereas Company B outsources manufacturing to a supplier. Since Company A owns its equipment, it recognizes significant depreciation—in this case, $30 million. Company B has less equipment, so its depreciation is only $5 million. However, Company B's supplier will include its own depreciation costs in its price, and Company B will subsequently pay more for its raw materials. Because of this difference, Company B generates EBITDA of only $25 million, versus $50 million for Company A. This difference in EBITDA will lead to differing multiples. Yet, when Company A's depreciation is accounted for, both companies trade at 7.5 times EBITA.

When computing the enterprise-value-to-EBITDA multiple in the previous example, we failed to recognize that Company A (the company that owns its equipment) will have to expend cash to replace aging equipment. Since capital expenditures are recorded as an investing cash flow they do not appear on the income statement, causing the discrepancy. Some analysts overcome this reinvestment problem by adjusting EBITDA for expected investments in working capital and property, plant, and equipment. This adjustment is highly subjective (capital expenditures are lumpy, so smoothing is required) and can result in a negative denominator, making the multiple meaningless.

ALTERNATIVE MULTIPLES

Although we have so far focused on enterprise-value multiples based on EBITA and EBITDA, other multiples can prove helpful in certain situations.

In the following subsections, we discuss three alternatives: the price-to-sales ratio, the price-to-earnings-growth ratio (known as the PEG ratio), and regression-based analysis using nonfinancial data.

Price-to-Sales Multiples

Generally speaking, price-to-sales multiples are not particularly useful for explaining company valuations. As shown earlier, an enterprise-value-to-EBITA multiple assumes similar growth rates and returns on incremental capital. An enterprise-value-to-sales multiple imposes an additional important restriction: similar operating margins on the company's existing business. For most industries, this restriction is overly burdensome.

The multiples chart in Exhibit 12.7 is often analyzed by investment bankers. In the chart, Home Depot's stock value is estimated using peer multiples. Each horizontal set of dots represents a different multiple. The top row estimates Home Depot's stock price based on each peer company's enterprise-value-to-sales ratio, the middle row uses an enterprise-value-to-EBITA ratio, and the bottom row shows a price-to-earnings ratio. The vertical line represents Home Depot's actual stock price at the time of the analysis and intersects Home Depot's actual multiples.

In this example, Circuit City trades at 0.1 times forecasted sales; applying that ratio to Home Depot's forecasted revenues would place Home Depot's stock price at $4 per share. At the other extreme, Bed, Bath, & Beyond trades at 1.7 times sales, generating an estimate of $60 for Home Depot's stock. Thus, we have narrowed the company's stock price to somewhere between $4 and $60 per share—a range too wide to provide any useful insight.

Given how imprecise price-to-sales ratios are, limit their use to situations where the company in question or its peers have extremely small or

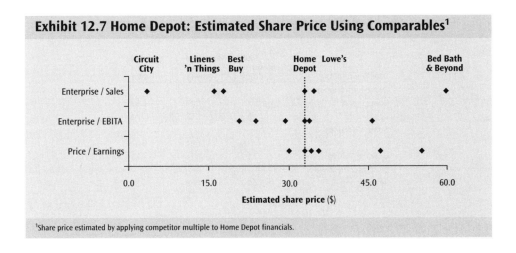

Exhibit 12.7 Home Depot: Estimated Share Price Using Comparables[1]

[1]Share price estimated by applying competitor multiple to Home Depot financials.

even negative operating profits. Revenue multiples are most common to venture capital because many start-ups will not turn a profit for years. If your situation demands a price-to-sales multiple, make sure to follow the fundamental principles presented in this chapter: Use enterprise value, not equity value; use forward-looking sales projections; and focus on companies with similar growth, ROICs, and expected operating margins.

PEG Ratios

Whereas a price-to-sales ratio further restricts the enterprise-value-to-EBITA multiple by assuming operating margins are common across companies, the price-earnings-growth (PEG) ratio is more flexible than the enterprise-value-to-EBITA ratio, because it allows expected growth to vary across companies. If you use a PEG ratio, you can expand a company's peer group to include competitors that are in different stages of their life cycle (from a growth perspective).

Traditionally, PEG ratios are calculated by dividing the P/E ratio by expected growth in earnings per share, but our modified version is based on the enterprise-value multiple:

$$\text{Adjusted PEG Ratio} = 100 \times \frac{\text{Enterprise-Value Multiple}}{\text{Expected EBITA Growth Rate}}$$

Exhibit 12.8 calculates the adjusted PEG ratios for our sample of retailers. To calculate Home Depot's adjusted PEG ratio (0.6 times), divide the company's forward-looking enterprise-value multiple (7.1 times) by its expected operating profit growth rate (11.8 percent). Based on the adjusted PEG ratio, Home Depot trades at a significant premium to Lowe's. Using the

Exhibit 12.8 Adjusted PEG Ratio

Hardline retailing	2005 enterprise multiple	Expected profit growth	Adjusted PEG ratio
Home improvement			
Home Depot	7.1	11.8	0.60
Lowe's	7.3	17.2	0.42
Home furnishing			
Bed Bath & Beyond	9.9	16.1	0.61
Linens 'n Things	5.1	15.4	0.33
Consumer electronics			
Best Buy	6.3	18.8	0.34
Circuit City	4.4	7.6	0.58

Source: CSFB estimates on hardline retailing, July 26, 2004.

key value driver formula as our guide, this is not surprising. Since the PEG ratio controls only for growth, companies with higher ROICs *should* trade at higher levels. According to analyst estimates, Home Depot's ROIC is expected to equal 17 percent, whereas the estimate of ROIC for Lowe's is only 14 percent.

The PEG ratio's ability to analyze companies with varying growth rates appears to give it a leg up on the standard enterprise-value multiple. Yet the PEG ratio has its own drawbacks that can lead to valuation errors. First, there is no standard time frame for measuring expected growth. You may find yourself wondering whether to use one-year, two-year, or long-term growth. Exhibit 12.8 used analyst projections for two-year expected EBITA growth.

Second, PEG ratios assume a linear relation between multiples and growth, such that no growth implies zero value. Exhibit 12.9 uses the average PEG ratio to value a hypothetical industry with five companies. Each company has a long-term expected ROIC of 15 percent, has a WACC equal to 9 percent, and pays cash taxes at 30 percent. The five hypothetical companies differ only in their growth rates (which vary from 2 percent to 6 percent). Using the key value driver formula, we estimate each company's enterprise-value multiple. Note how the dotted line, which plots enterprise value versus

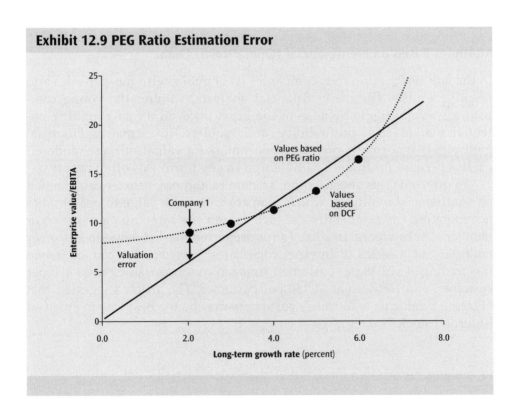

Exhibit 12.9 PEG Ratio Estimation Error

growth, is curved and has a positive intercept (even zero-growth firms have positive values). Conversely, the PEG ratio is linear and has a zero intercept. Since PEG is multiplied by growth to approximate firm value, a company with constant profits would have an implied value of zero. As a result, the typical application of industry PEG ratios will systematically undervalue companies with low growth rates.

To avoid undervaluing low-growth companies, some financial analysts (and most academics) use a regression analysis to determine a representative multiple. The regression is based on the following equation:

$$EV/EBITA_i = a + b \text{ (Expected Growth}_i)$$

For the six hardline retailers presented in Exhibit 12.8, this regression leads to an intercept of 3.5 and a slope coefficient of 0.2. Thus, a zero-growth company should be valued at 3.5 times EBITA, not zero, and a company expected to grow at 5 percent would be valued at 4.5 times EBITA. This regression analysis, however, does not adjust for the nonlinear relation between growth and value. More advanced regression techniques can be employed, but unless the sample is large, the regression often fails to provide useful insight.

Multiples Based on Nonfinancial (Operational) Data

In the late 1990s, numerous companies went public with meager sales and negative profits. For many financial analysts, valuing the young companies was a struggle because of the great uncertainty surrounding potential market size, profitability, and required investments. Financial multiples that normally provide a benchmark for valuation were rendered useless because profitability (measured in any form) was often negative.

To overcome this shortcoming, academics and practitioners alike relied on nonfinancial multiples, which compare enterprise value to one or more nonoperating financial statistics, such as web site hits, unique visitors, or number of subscribers. In 2000, *Fortune* reported market-value-to-customer multiples for a series of Internet companies.[14] *Fortune* determined Yahoo was trading at $2,038 per customer, Amazon.com was trading at $1,400 per customer, and NetZero at $1,140 per customer. The article suggested that "Placing a value on a Website's customers may be the best way to judge an [Internet] stock."

[14] E. Schonfeld, "How Much Are Your Eyeballs Worth?" *Fortune* (February 21, 2000), pp. 197–200.

To use a nonfinancial multiple effectively, you must follow the same guidelines outlined earlier in this chapter. The nonfinancial metric must be a reasonable predictor of future value creation, and thus somehow tied to ROIC and growth. In the example cited previously, Yahoo trades at a higher multiple than Amazon.com because Yahoo's incremental costs per user are much smaller, an advantage that translates into higher profits.

Nonfinancial measures did play an important role in the early valuation of Internet stocks. The first academic study about Internet valuations examined a sample of 63 publicly traded Internet firms in the late 1990s.[15] The study found that the number of unique visitors to a web site or the number of pages on a site viewed per visit were directly correlated to a company's stock price even after controlling for the company's current financial performance. The power of a given nonfinancial metric, however, depended on the company. For portal and content companies such as Yahoo, page views and unique visitors were both correlated to a company's market value. For e-tailers such as Amazon.com, only the page views per visit were correlated with value. Evidently, the market believed "stopping by" would not translate to future value for e-tailers.

For Internet companies in the late 1990s, investors focused on nonfinancial metrics because early financial results were unrelated to long-term valuation creation. As the industry matured, however, financial metrics became increasingly important. Later research found gross profit and R&D spending became increasingly predictive, whereas nonfinancial data lost power.[16] This research indicates a return to traditional valuation metrics even for the "new economy" stocks, as the relevance of nonfinancial metrics diminished over the 24-month testing period.

Two cautionary notes about using nonfinancial multiples to analyze and value companies: First, nonfinancial multiples should be used only when they provide incremental explanatory power above financial multiples. If a company cannot translate visitors, page views, or subscribers into profits and cash flow, the nonfinancial metric is meaningless, and a multiple based on financial forecasts is better. Second, nonfinancial multiples, like all multiples, are *relative* valuation tools. They measure one company's valuation relative to another, normalized by some measure of size. They do not measure absolute valuation levels. To value a company correctly, one must always remember to ask: Is a value of $2,038 per customer too much?

---

[15] B. Trueman, M. H. F. Wong, and X. J. Zhang, "The Eyeballs Have It: Searching for the Value in Internet Stocks," *Journal of Accounting Research,* 38 (2000): 137–162.

[16] P. Jorion and E. Talmor, "Value Relevance of Financial and Non Financial Information in Emerging Industries: The Changing Role of Web Traffic Data" (working paper no. 021, London Business School Accounting Subject Area, 2001).

SUMMARY

Of the available valuation tools, discounted cash flow continues to deliver the best results. However, a thoughtful multiples analysis merits a place in your tool kit as well. When that analysis is careful and well reasoned, it not only provides a useful check of your DCF forecasts but also provides critical insights into what drives value in a given industry. Just be sure that you analyze the underlying reasons that multiples differ from company to company. When possible, base your analysis on forward-looking numbers. Focus on enterprise value and remove nonoperating items from your analysis. Never view multiples as a shortcut. Instead, approach your multiples analysis with as much care as you bring to DCF analysis.

REVIEW QUESTIONS

1. Compare and contrast the following relative valuation models: P/E Model, PEG Model, P/B Model, P/S Model.

2. Why is it important that management perform a supplemental valuation analysis employing a relative valuation model?

3. Discuss the importance of selecting comparable companies when estimating the appropriate relative valuation model.

4. Identify and discuss the four best practices applied to the construction of a relative valuation multiplier.

5. Compare and contrast the relative P/E valuation model to the DCF valuation model.

6. How does the relative valuation model differ from the enterprise valuation model?

Part Three

Making Value Happen

13

Performance Measurement

Part One of this book explained the basic principles of value creation, and Part Two detailed how to estimate a company's value. Part Three, beginning with this chapter, looks at value creation from a managerial perspective, examining several topics: managing performance to increase ROIC and growth; creating value through mergers, acquisitions, and divestitures; using capital structure to support value creation; and communicating effectively with investors to ensure that the company's stock price reflects its intrinsic value.

To address these topics, we need a way to decide if a company is doing a good job of creating value. That requires measurement of corporate performance, a task that is more difficult than most think. Many investors, boards of directors, and executives are happy and, to some extent, complacent when earnings per share and stock price are increasing. That certainly was the case in the late 1990s, when most share prices were rising, the economy was strong, and corporate profits were robust. But some of the profits reported were not sustainable (some were even based on accounting fraud), and in some cases, stock prices became disconnected from the companies' underlying performance. Conversely, a declining share price may not signal poor performance. Home Depot's share price declined between 1999 and 2003, yet as you will see later in this chapter, the company surpassed every North American retailer except Wal-Mart in creating value.

The Internet bubble and recent corporate scandals have prodded boards of directors, senior managers, and investors to rethink how they assess corporate performance. Good accounting results and a rising stock price can be misleading and may not indicate whether a company is fundamentally "healthy" in the sense of being able to improve current performance and profitably build future business. True assessment of a company's health requires dissecting and understanding the underlying drivers of earnings

Special thanks to Richard Dobbs, who co-wrote this chapter.

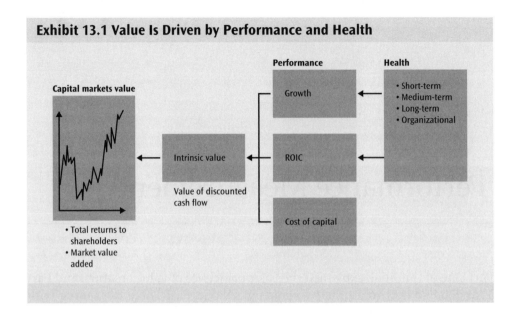

Exhibit 13.1 Value Is Driven by Performance and Health

growth and stock price increases. Board members, as representatives of the company's stockholders with access to internal information, have a special obligation to dig deeper into their companies' operating and financial performance to assess long-term health.

The framework presented in Exhibit 13.1 demonstrates the links between shareholder value, as measured by the stock market, and the drivers of value. The left side of the exhibit reports recent performance in the stock market and the company's stock price. As we demonstrated in Chapters 3 and 4, a company's market value is driven by the discounted value of its expected cash flows, its "intrinsic" value. While a valuable tool for strategic analysis, intrinsic DCF cannot be used to evaluate historical performance because it is based on subjective projections. But DCF value can be linked to key financial indicators. The financial drivers of cash flow and DCF value are growth (in revenues and profits) and return on invested capital (relative to a company's cost of capital).

Since only a company's historical growth and returns on capital—not its future performance—can be measured directly, the potential for future growth and returns must be inferred. To do so, it is necessary to devise metrics for the longer-term health of companies to complement the metrics for their short-term performance. Think of a patient visiting his doctor. The patient may be feeling fine, in the sense of meeting requirements for weight, strength, and energy. But if his cholesterol is too high, he may need to take corrective action now to prevent future heart disease. Similarly, if a company shows strong growth and return on capital, it still needs to determine if the performance is sustainable. Understanding these health indicators can tell us how a company achieved its financial results. For example, did it sacrifice long-term value creation for short-term financial results? Evaluating value drivers will also help us identify value creation opportunities so the organization can focus on high-priority opportunities.

With this framework in mind, we can organize performance measurement around three questions:

1. Historically, how much economic value has the company created (as measured by the company's financial statements)? We will refer to this measure as *performance*.

2. How well positioned is the company to create additional economic value in the future, and what risks may prevent this value creation? We will refer to this set of metrics as the company's *health*.

3. Is the company's current market value in line with its historical performance and potential economic value creation? What accounts for recent changes in its stock price?

The first question addresses historical financial performance. This appears straightforward, but some ways of measuring historical financial performance are better than others. Financial metrics that can be linked directly to value creation (e.g., economic profit, ROIC, and growth) are more meaningful than traditional accounting metrics, such as earnings per share. However, every historical measure has two potential flaws. First, historical financial metrics are subjective; accountants and managers must make judgments about when to record revenues and costs. Often, this judgment is colored by personal incentives (e.g., their boss wants the current quarter to look good). The second, and perhaps more important, flaw is that historical financial metrics cannot capture the trade-offs managers constantly make between achieving short-term financial results and investing for the future.

The second question addresses the company's health by examining the underlying drivers of a company's financial performance. Specifically, how did the company achieve its recent financial results, and did the company sacrifice future performance to achieve those results? Health metrics compensate for the shortcomings of historical performance metrics and give us a glimpse into the future. For instance, does the company have the products, people, and processes to create additional value? Another important dimension of corporate health is an assessment of the risks the company faces and the procedures in place to mitigate those risks.

As a final assessment of corporate performance, we examine the performance of the company's stock price. Given that stock price improvement is the ultimate objective of the company's shareholders and that stock prices often provide more objective assessments of value than management, we might expect to examine stock price performance first, not last.

Yet examining stock price without the proper context too easily leads to mistaken impressions. For instance, consider an oil company whose improving stock price reflects rising oil prices, rather than improved techniques in exploration, or a bank's rising stock price that reflects falling interest rates, not increased efficiencies. A board of directors that is complacent with strong stock price performance caused by factors outside management control will all too quickly despair when outside factors eventually turn against the company.

When evaluating changes in stock price, management must also ask whether the company's stock price properly reflects the company's historical performance and future prospects. If not, does the difference result from the market's failure to understand the company's potential or from management's excessive optimism about what has been and can be achieved?

A holistic assessment of corporate performance that answers all three questions is far superior to any single performance measure. The process helps managers make trade-offs between short- and long-term value creation and determine how to best communicate the company's value to investors. It helps board members assess the actions managers are taking. It helps investors decide whether the current price is fair.

PERFORMANCE: VALUE DELIVERED

As we demonstrated in Chapter 3, value and value creation are driven by growth and return on capital, so it is natural that growth and return on invested capital will be the starting point for measuring corporate performance. Specifically, how does the company's ROIC compare with its cost of capital and the ROICs of its peers? Has ROIC been increasing or decreasing? How fast has the company grown, both absolutely and relative to peers? Is its growth accelerating or decelerating?

Why not use the most common measure of corporate performance, earnings per share? Although companies that grow with an ROIC greater than the cost of capital will also generate attractive EPS growth, the inverse is not true. Companies with strong EPS growth may not be creating value if EPS growth comes from heavy investment or changes in the company's financial structure.

One disadvantage of ROIC and growth, however, is that both are measured as percentages. Neither incorporates the magnitude of value creation, so a small company or business unit with a 30 percent ROIC will appear more successful than an enormous company with a 20 percent ROIC. To overcome this, economic profit converts ROIC into a dollar measure, so the size of value creation can be incorporated into comparisons with other companies. Furthermore, economic profit can also be used to measure the trade-off between growth and ROIC.

We can see this in a comparison of two companies. Recall from Chapter 3 the definition of economic profit:

$$\text{Economic Profit} = \text{Invested Capital} \times (\text{ROIC} - \text{WACC})$$

Assume two companies have identical WACCs equal to 10 percent. Company A earns a 20 percent ROIC on $10 billion of invested capital, so its economic profit equals $1 billion. Company B earns a 30 percent ROIC on only $2 billion of invested capital, so its economic profit equals $400 million. Which company is performing better? Company A creates more economic profit, but Company B has a higher ROIC. It is impossible to say one company is better than the other. Instead, an assessment of the companies should consider their performance relative to peers, the size of their product markets, and similar factors.

To illustrate key points of corporate performance measurement, we compare Home Depot with a broad sample of retailers. Our sample includes all American retailers with 2003 revenues of more than $6 billion (given industry differences, we exclude grocery retailers). For presentation purposes, we show only about three companies from each retail subsector. Even though most large retailers do not compete directly with Home Depot, it is insightful to see Home Depot's performance relative to all other large retailers.

Home Depot's average ROIC over the five years ended in 2003 was 15.6 percent, higher than its 9.2 percent cost of capital during this period. While Home Depot's ROIC is the highest among the large American retailers (see Exhibit 13.2 on p. 398), many companies have ROICs greater than 25 percent in other industries, including pharmaceuticals, consumer packaged goods, and high-performing industrials. But is the performance of other industries even relevant? In the case of Home Depot, we believe the proper comparison is other retailers. Retailers, by nature, require significant physical assets (buildings and fixtures) and inventories. Further, they sell the same or very similar products as other retailers, so competition constrains their margins.

As Exhibit 13.2 also demonstrates, there are winners and losers in retail. Relatively young retailers (those less than 35 years old) are earning ROICs in the midteens (more than the cost of capital). Older companies are struggling to earn their cost of capital.

Home Depot's revenues grew an average of 16.5 percent annually between 1999 and 2003, once again at the high end of large retailers. This performance is exceptional for a company that was already one of the largest retailers in the United States. Even so, the company's primary competitor, Lowe's, grew faster. Its faster growth, however, started from a smaller base. Thus, by 2003, Home Depot's revenues of $65 billion were still more than twice the $31 billion earned by Lowe's. From a growth perspective, we again see winners and losers among the large retailers. In general, the older

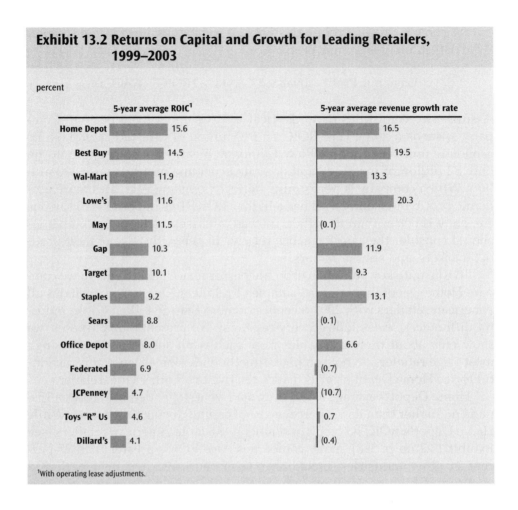

Exhibit 13.2 Returns on Capital and Growth for Leading Retailers, 1999–2003

percent

	5-year average ROIC[1]	5-year average revenue growth rate
Home Depot	15.6	16.5
Best Buy	14.5	19.5
Wal-Mart	11.9	13.3
Lowe's	11.6	20.3
May	11.5	(0.1)
Gap	10.3	11.9
Target	10.1	9.3
Staples	9.2	13.1
Sears	8.8	(0.1)
Office Depot	8.0	6.6
Federated	6.9	(0.7)
JCPenney	4.7	(10.7)
Toys "R" Us	4.6	0.7
Dillard's	4.1	(0.4)

[1] With operating lease adjustments.

retailers were shrinking while the successful companies grew much faster than the American economy.

We next consider economic profit, to counter the disadvantage of ROIC and growth being percentage metrics that fail to factor company size into comparisons. Exhibit 13.3 shows the economic profit for the large retailers. Second only to Wal-Mart, Home Depot generated $7.1 billion in economic profit over the five years through 2003.

Examining the retailers as a group, rankings based on economic profit differ from those compiled using ROIC and growth, with Wal-Mart and Home Depot moving into a class of their own. Highfliers, such as Best Buy, may have high ROIC and superior growth, but they generate those results on much less capital than Wal-Mart and Home Depot.

EPS may be the most often cited metric of historical financial performance, but it is not very useful for assessing corporate performance. It combines financing, one-time items, and other factors that hide a company's true performance, rather than illuminating it. The perception that net in-

Exhibit 13.3 Cumulative Economic Profit for Leading Retailers, 1999–2003

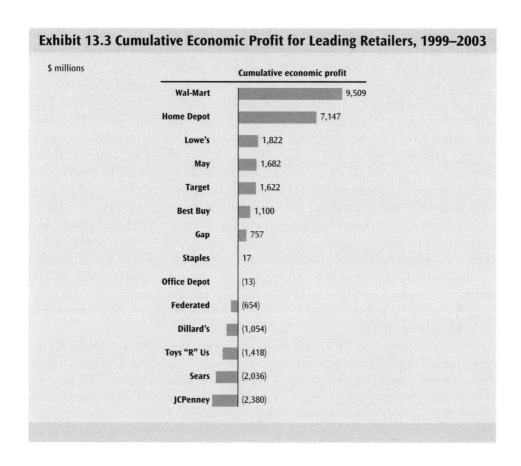

$ millions

Cumulative economic profit

Wal-Mart	9,509
Home Depot	7,147
Lowe's	1,822
May	1,682
Target	1,622
Best Buy	1,100
Gap	757
Staples	17
Office Depot	(13)
Federated	(654)
Dillard's	(1,054)
Toys "R" Us	(1,418)
Sears	(2,036)
JCPenney	(2,380)

come and EPS collapse performance into a single number is simply mistaken. Measuring performance using EPS alone is flawed, in that it ignores the opportunity cost of equity capital. In addition, it is surprisingly easy to manipulate net income and EPS, in particular, through financing decisions unrelated to the company's operating performance.

For example, let's say a company you are analyzing is considering a $1 billion acquisition, which it plans to finance with new debt. The company's cost of debt equals 6 percent, and its weighted average cost of capital is 9 percent. As a result of the acquisition, the company would earn an extra $100 million in operating profits and pay $60 million in interest expense (it borrows at 6 percent) and $16 million in income taxes (assuming a 40 percent tax rate). Thus, following the acquisition, the acquirer's net income would increase by $24 million.

What would be the impact on economic profit? Based on the figures given, the company's economic profit would decline by $30 million, calculated as follows. The company's after-tax return on new capital (6 percent) equals the extra after-tax operating profits ($100 million less taxes of $40 million, or $60 million) divided by the required investment ($1 billion).

Subtracting the 9 percent cost of capital from the 6 percent return on capital yields a spread of –3 percent. Multiply the spread by the new capital; the result is a $30 million decline in economic profit.

Net income would increase by $24 million, but economic profit would decline by $30 million. Which figure better captures value creation? Economic profit does. The key assumption in generating additional EPS is that the acquisition can be financed entirely with debt. This assumption is wrong. The only reason the company can finance the acquisition with all debt is that its remaining businesses would act as collateral. In reality, the company would borrow against its other businesses' cash flow, not just the cash flow from the acquisition. The acquisition is supported by, say, only 25 percent debt and 75 percent equity, where the opportunity cost of equity (especially on an after-tax basis) will be much higher than the after-tax cost of debt, even though the cost of equity doesn't show up in the EPS calculation.

To break even in terms of value creation, the acquisition must earn $90 million after taxes or $150 million in pretax operating profits. So the company would have a shortfall of $50 million in operating profits, despite increasing its net income.

In fact, to generate EPS growth, there is no reason even to make an acquisition. EPS growth can be generated through financing decisions alone. For example, many companies repurchase shares solely to meet EPS targets. While there are many legitimate reasons to repurchase shares, increasing EPS is not one of them. For most companies, repurchasing shares will mechanically increase EPS regardless of value creation. As long as the price paid for the shares (in terms of a price-earnings multiple) is less than the multiple on the debt assumed or cash used, EPS will increase.

To see how this works, assume a company borrows at 6 percent and gets a tax benefit of 40 percent for its borrowing. The implied P/E ratio on new debt is $1/[0.06 \times (1 - 0.40)]$, or 27.8 times. As long as the company repurchases its shares at less than 27.8 times earnings (as about 90 percent of companies can), earnings per share will increase as income decreases more slowly than shares outstanding. However, if a company takes on more debt, all else equal, its shares become riskier, and its cost of equity will increase, which should reduce its P/E ratio. Financial statements explicitly recognize only the gains from share repurchases, and not the costs.

Net income and EPS also are subject to one-time gains and losses. While these gains and losses are real, too often companies use one-time gains and losses to smooth out their operating performance or hit earnings targets. Among the large retailers analyzed earlier, the largest increase in EPS was generated by Sears, which increased its EPS by 34 percent from 1999 to 2003. Yet most of this increase was due to one-time gains from asset sales and the impact of share repurchases, rather than increases in operating performance. We know of one company whose annual report cover proudly advertised the company's nearly 20 percent EPS growth over four years. But when we stripped out one-time items and the impact of share repurchases, operating profits were up only 4 percent a year. Not surprisingly, the company's stock price failed to increase in line with EPS.

Despite our critique of net income and EPS, we don't advocate ignoring them entirely. Companies that generate strong growth and earn high returns on capital will *also* post strong increases in net income and EPS. But keep in mind that, particularly over a one- to three-year period, it is easy to boost net income and EPS *without* strong operating performance as measured by revenue growth, ROIC, and economic profit.

HEALTH: SCOPE TO CREATE ADDITIONAL VALUE

Even though financial metrics like ROIC and growth outperform EPS in measuring historical performance, they cannot capture the trade-offs between short-term financial results and investment for future earnings. To do this, we need to measure the company's health. This second dimension of corporate performance measurement examines the underlying drivers of a company's financial performance to determine whether the company is prepared to create value in the future.

To see the critical difference between performance and health, consider the dynamics in the pharmaceutical industry. In the year after the patent on a drug expires, sales of that drug often decline by 50 percent to 75 percent or more, as generic producers lower prices and steal market share. When a major product will be going off patent in a couple of years with no replacement on the horizon, investors know future profits will suffer. In such a case, the company could have strong current performance but a low market value. In retailing, chains can sometimes maintain margins by scrimping on store refurbishment and brand building. Consider the aging Kmart and Toys "R" Us chains, both seriously wounded by Wal-Mart's and Target's new, clean stores.

To identify a company's key health metrics, start with a value creation tree, as shown in Exhibit 13.4 on page 402. The value creation tree illustrates the connections between intrinsic value and generic categories of health metrics. Value is ultimately driven by a company's long-term growth and its return on invested capital (relative to its cost of capital). The health metrics are the short-, medium-, and long-term metrics that ultimately determine a company's long-term growth and ROIC.

The framework in Exhibit 13.4 shares some elements with a popular framework known as the "balanced scorecard." Based on a 1992 *Harvard Business Review* article by Robert Kaplan and David Norton,[1] the idea of a

---

[1] Robert S. Kaplan and David P. Norton, "The Balanced Scorecard: Measures That Drive Performance," *Harvard Business Review*, 80(1) (January 1992): 71–79.

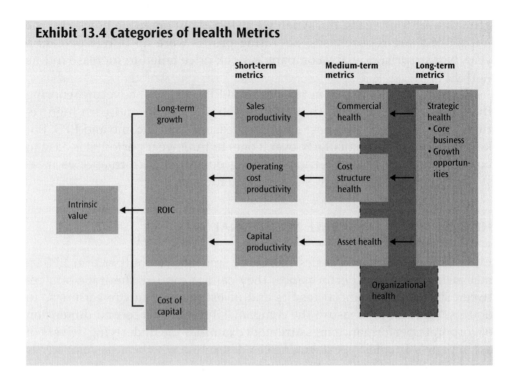

Exhibit 13.4 Categories of Health Metrics

balanced scorecard has spawned numerous nonprofit and for-profit organizations to advocate and implement the idea. The premise of the balanced scorecard is that financial performance is only one aspect of performance. Kaplan and Norton point to three equally important perspectives on performance: customer satisfaction, internal business processes, and learning and growth. Although our concept of health metrics resembles Kaplan and Norton's nonfinancial metrics, we differ in advocating that companies develop their own metrics tailored to their industry and strategy, based on rigorous analytics, and linked as explicitly as possible to metrics for value creation. Tailoring is critical; without it, setting strategic priorities is difficult. For example, product innovation is important in some industries, while in others, tight cost control and customer service matter more.

Every company will have its own health metrics, but the eight generic categories presented in Exhibit 13.4 ensure that a company has systematically explored all the important ones. Short-term metrics, on the left side of the exhibit, are typically the easiest to quantify and measure. They also can be measured and monitored more frequently (monthly or quarterly). Moving to the right, medium-term and long-term metrics may be difficult to quantify and may be measured annually or over even longer periods. In addition, as you move farther to the right, the performance metrics are increasingly difficult for outside parties, such as investors, to use.

Short-term metrics   Short-term metrics are the immediate drivers of historical ROIC and growth. They are indicators of whether growth and ROIC over the short term can be sustained, or whether they will improve or decline. They might include metrics such as cost per unit for a manufacturing company or same-store sales growth for a retailer.

Following the growth and ROIC framework, short-term metrics fall into three categories:

1. *Sales productivity* metrics are the drivers of recent sales growth, such as price and quantity, market share, the company's ability to charge higher prices relative to peers (or charge a premium for its product or services), sales force productivity, and same-store sales growth versus new-store growth for a retailer.

2. *Operating cost productivity* metrics are typically drivers of unit costs, such as the component costs for building an automobile or delivering a package. UPS, for example, is well known for charting out the optimal delivery path of its drivers to enhance their productivity and for developing well-defined standards on how to deliver packages.

3. *Capital productivity* measures how well a company uses its working capital (inventories, receivables, and payables) and its property, plant, and equipment. Dell revolutionized the personal-computer business by building to order so it could minimize inventories. Because the company keeps inventory levels so low and has few receivables to boot, it can operate with negative working capital.

Home Depot's short-term health was strong across a number of fronts. From a growth perspective, Home Depot increased its store count by about 13.4 percent a year between 1999 and 2003, while simultaneously increasing same-store sales (known as comps) by 3.5 percent. From a profitability perspective, Home Depot's ROIC increased from 14.9 percent to 18.2 percent, due to improvements in margins, partly offset by a drop in capital efficiency. Gross margin (revenues less cost of goods sold), increased from 30.9 percent to 33.4 percent, due largely to improving purchasing and the development of exclusive product lines from manufacturers. The increase in gross margin was partly offset by higher selling, general, and administrative expenses due to increased investment in advertising and store modernization. In addition, management of working capital improved slightly, though this was offset by additional investment in the stores.

When assessing short-term corporate performance, separate the effects of forces that are outside management's control (both good and bad) from things management can influence. For instance, upstream oil company executives shouldn't get much credit for higher profits that result from higher oil prices, nor should real estate executives get much credit for higher real estate prices (and the resulting higher commissions). Oil company performance should be evaluated with an emphasis on reserves and production growth, exploration costs, and drilling costs. Real estate brokerages should be evaluated primarily on the number of sales and ability to cross-sell.

Medium-term metrics   Medium-term metrics go beyond short-term performance by looking forward to indicate whether a company can maintain and improve its growth and ROIC over the next one to five years (or longer for companies, such as pharmaceutical manufacturers, that have long product cycles). The medium-term metrics fall into three categories:

1. *Commercial health* metrics indicate whether the company can sustain or improve its current revenue growth. These metrics include the company's product pipeline (talent and technology to bring new products to market over the medium term), brand strength (investment in brand building), and customer satisfaction. Commercial health metrics vary widely by industry. For a pharmaceutical company, the obvious priority is its product pipeline. For an online retailer, customer satisfaction and brand strength may be the most important components of medium-term commercial health.

2. *Cost structure health* measures a company's ability to manage its costs relative to competitors over three to five years. These metrics might include assessments of programs such as Six Sigma, which companies including General Electric use to reduce their costs continually and to maintain a cost advantage relative to their competitors across most of their businesses.

3. *Asset structure health* measures how well a company maintains and develops its assets. For a hotel or restaurant chain, the average time between remodeling projects may be an important driver of health.

In the quest for growth during the 1990s, Home Depot temporarily lost sight of its medium-term health as measured by its customer service and the quality of its stores. Recognizing the problem, in 2001 the company began to reinvest in its existing locations, with the intention of making them more appealing to customers, and to refocus on customer service—for example, by raising its incentives for employees. It also offered installation services and do-it-yourself clinics and set up sales desks specifically for professional customers. Continued success will depend on its ability to go on satisfying its customers by carefully measuring and monitoring its customer service, its customer traffic, and the age and condition of its stores.

Long-term strategic health   Metrics for long-term strategic health show the ability of an enterprise to sustain its current operating activities and to identify and exploit new growth areas. A company must periodically assess and measure the threats—including new technologies, changes in customer preferences, and new ways of serving customers—that could make its current business less profitable. In assessing a company's long-term strategic health, it can be hard to identify specific metrics; those situations require more qualitative milestones, such as progress in selecting partners for mergers or for entering a market.

While Home Depot's leading position in the home improvement business appears to be solid in the medium term, a longer term threat comes from Wal-Mart, which sells many of the same fast-moving items, such as light bulbs. The cost base of Wal-Mart is lower because it provides less in-store help than does Home Depot, which must therefore ensure that store associates focus on higher-margin areas where support is critical (such as plumbing) rather than on products whose price doesn't incorporate assistance to customers.

Besides guarding against threats, companies must continually watch for new growth opportunities, whether in related industries or new geographies. For example, many Western companies have begun preparing for China's enormous, fast-growing markets. Microsoft has sought other profitable businesses beyond Windows by investing heavily in games, Internet services, and software for handheld devices.

Adding new services helped Home Depot to squeeze more profits from its existing stores, but it has been less successful at expanding abroad and at developing new store formats. By 2003, only 7 percent of its revenues came from outside North America, and though it has experimented with new store formats, such as its Expo Design Center, only 4 percent of its stores used them as of 2003.

Organizational health   The final element of corporate health, organizational health, measures whether the company has the people, skills, and culture to sustain and improve its performance. Diagnostics of organizational health typically measure the skills and capabilities of a company, its ability to retain its employees and keep them satisfied, its culture and values, and the depth of its management talent. Again, what is important varies by industry. Pharmaceutical companies need deep scientific-innovation capabilities but relatively few managers. Retailers need lots of trained stored managers, a few great merchandisers, and in most cases, store staff with a customer service orientation.

Given Home Depot's rapid growth and substantial size, one of its core challenges continues to be attracting and retaining skilled employees at a competitive cost. When it took on lower-cost part-time workers, who often knew much less than its traditional store associates did, customers began to wonder what made the company special. Even holding on to its store managers became a problem, since the drive for efficiency through centralization stifled the company's original entrepreneurial spirit. To address the long-term challenges, the company began offering incentive programs for management and added more full-time staff in stores—moves that have been credited with helping to improve same-store sales.[2]

Identify and Analyze Potential Risks

A final dimension of corporate health that investors and boards should evaluate is risk. What risks is the company exposed to, and how has the management team decided to manage each risk? Most risks come from outside the company—for example, commodity price risk, technology risk, and competitive risk. But some risks come from inside the company, including the risk of employee malfeasance or system failures. Risks can be mitigated through a conservative capital structure, hedging, or backup systems. In any case, risk and risk mitigation are a necessary element of corporate performance measurement.

STOCK MARKET PERFORMANCE

The final step in assessing a company's performance is examining its stock price performance, viewing performance in the stock market as an external assessment of a company's performance and health. In an ideal world, we would only have to look in the newspapers to understand how well a company was doing in the stock market. But performance in the stock market is anything but easy to interpret.

The most common approach to measuring stock market performance is to measure total returns to shareholders (TRS) over a period of time, where TRS is defined as share price appreciation plus dividends. TRS has severe limitations; however, it doesn't measure actual performance, but rather performance against expectations, which can severely penalize the best-performing companies. To mitigate this problem, we introduce another set of metrics for stock market performance: market value added (MVA) and market-value-to-capital. Both statistics measure the stock market's assessment of how much value a company can create in the future.

A second problem with metrics for stock market performance is that the stock market has limited information about a company's performance and potential, so a company's value in the stock market can sometimes deviate from its intrinsic value. The only way to solve this problem is to limit how

---

[2]Justin Lahart, "Housing Just Keeps Going Up," *Fortune* (June 8, 2003), http://www.fortune .com/fortune/subs/article/0,15114,455936-2,00.html; and Betty Schiffman, "Home Depot Remodels Its Growth Plans," *Forbes* (November 30, 2001), http://www.forbes.com/2001/11/30 /1130homedepot.html.

we use stock market metrics. Management teams and boards of directors should use these metrics as a secondary source of performance insight, asking only, "Does the stock market value of a company accurately reflect its value creation potential?"

Measuring Stock Market Performance: The Expectations Treadmill

The problem with TRS as a performance measure is that, over shorter periods, TRS represents more about changes in expectations of performance than about performance itself. As a result, companies that have consistently met high performance standards can have difficulty delivering high TRS. The market may believe that management is doing an outstanding job, but its approval has already been factored into the share price.

One way to understand the problem is by analogy to a treadmill. The speed of the treadmill represents the expectations for future performance implicit in the share price. If managers beat these expectations, the market raises the company's stock price but also accelerates the treadmill. Thus, as performance improves, the expectations treadmill turns faster. The better managers perform, the more the market expects from them; they have to run the treadmill ever faster just to keep up.

For outstanding companies, the treadmill moves faster than for anyone else. It is difficult for management to deliver at the expected level without faltering. Accelerating the treadmill will be hard; continuing to do so will eventually become impossible. Consider the case of Tina Turnaround. Tina has just been hired as CEO of Widgets "R" Us. The company's margins and growth are below those of competitors. The market doesn't expect much, so its share price is low. Tina hires a top-notch team and gets to work. After two years, Widgets is catching up to its peers in margins and return on capital, and market share is rising. Widgets' stock price rises twice as fast as its peers' stock prices, because the market wasn't expecting the company's turnaround.

Tina and her team continue their hard work. After two more years, Widgets has become the industry leader, with the highest ROIC. Its share price has risen at four times the rate of the industry. Given the company's consistent performance, the market expects the company to continue earning above-average returns and revenue growth. As time goes by, Widgets maintains its high ROIC and leading market share. But two years later, Tina is surprised to see that the shares of Widgets have done no better than its peers' stock prices, even though the company has outperformed its rivals in both ROIC and growth. Tina has been caught by the expectations treadmill. She and her team have done such a good job that the expectation of continued high performance is already incorporated into the company's share price. As long as she delivers results in line with the market's expectations, her company's share price performance will be no better than average.

This explains why extraordinary managers may deliver only ordinary TRS in the short run. Conversely, managers of companies with low performance expectations might find it easy to earn high TRS. This predicament illustrates the old saying about the difference between a good company and a good investment: in the short term, good companies may not be good investments, and vice versa.

One way to overcome the limitations of TRS is to employ complementary metrics for stock market performance. One such measure is market value added (MVA), popularized by the consulting firm Stern Stewart & Co. MVA is the difference between the market value of a company's debt and equity and the amount of capital invested. A related measure, expressed as a ratio, is the market-value-to-capital ratio—the ratio of a company's debt and equity to the amount of capital invested.

MVA and the market-value-to-capital ratio complement TRS by measuring different aspects of a company's performance. TRS can be likened to a treadmill's *change* in speed; it measures performance against the expectations of the financial markets and changes in these expectations. MVA and market-value-to-capital, in contrast, can be likened to the current speed of the treadmill. They measure the financial market's view of the future performance relative to the capital invested in the business, so they assess expectations for the absolute level of performance.

Let's examine Home Depot and the other large retailers in terms of their performance in the stock market. The market value of Home Depot's debt and equity (including capitalized operating leases) was $88 billion at the end of 2003, with $8 billion in debt and operating leases and $80 billion in equity. At the end of 2003, the company had invested $29 billion in operating capital (working capital, the capitalized value of operating leases, and property, plant, and equipment). Therefore, Home Depot's MVA was $59 billion, and its market-value-to-capital ratio was 3.1.

The MVA of Home Depot was the industry's second highest, behind only Wal-Mart and far ahead of the others (see Exhibit 13.5). In terms of market-value-to-capital, Home Depot is also at the high end of the scale. It is not expected to generate as much value per dollar of capital as some high-fliers (such as Best Buy), but it makes up for that with its size.

What about TRS? Over the five years ended 2003, Home Depot's—at –2.3 percent per year—was near the bottom of the group. The company delivered a strong economic profit, the second-highest MVA, and a strong market-value-to-capital ratio but also had very low TRS. Evidently, Home Depot's performance over this period was below the level the market expected at the beginning of the measurement period (1999). We'll explore the reasons for Home Depot's low TRS a bit later, but first we will introduce the "expectations treadmill matrix," a snapshot of the market performance for a group of companies—in this case, large American retailers.

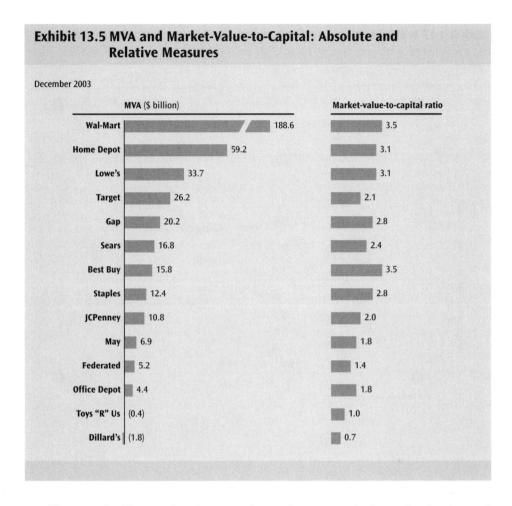

Exhibit 13.5 MVA and Market-Value-to-Capital: Absolute and Relative Measures

December 2003

	MVA ($ billion)	Market-value-to-capital ratio
Wal-Mart	188.6	3.5
Home Depot	59.2	3.1
Lowe's	33.7	3.1
Target	26.2	2.1
Gap	20.2	2.8
Sears	16.8	2.4
Best Buy	15.8	3.5
Staples	12.4	2.8
JCPenney	10.8	2.0
May	6.9	1.8
Federated	5.2	1.4
Office Depot	4.4	1.8
Toys "R" Us	(0.4)	1.0
Dillard's	(1.8)	0.7

The treadmill matrix plots market value to capital on the horizontal axis and TRS on the vertical axis. (We use the market-value-to-capital ratio in this example because a size-based measure, such as MVA, is difficult to graph effectively.) Exhibit 13.6 on page 410 presents the treadmill matrix for the large American retailers. The dashed lines represent the median TRS and market-value-to-capital. Companies fall into each of the quadrants created by these medians.

Quadrant 1 companies have both a high TRS and high market value to capital. These highfliers include Best Buy and Lowe's. Quadrant 3 companies are the opposite, with low TRS and low market-value-to-capital ratios. Examples include Dillard's and Toys "R" Us. Companies in Quadrants 1 and 3 are straightforward to evaluate because both performance metrics are high or low.

The results of Quadrants 2 and 4 are more interesting. Quadrant 2 companies are recovering underperformers. This group includes the Limited

Exhibit 13.6 Market-Value-to-Capital and TRS for Leading Retailers

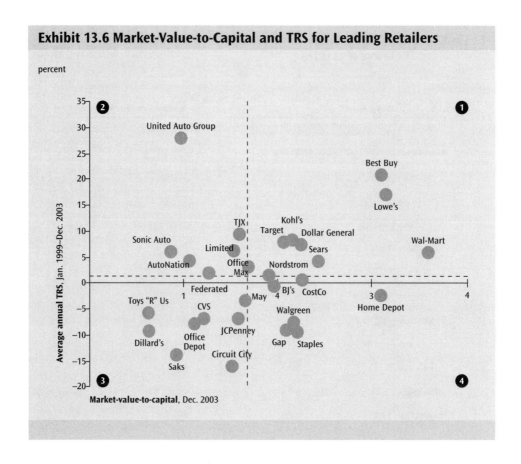

and United Auto Group. These companies have higher than median TRS but low-market-value-to-capital. Five years ago, when expectations of their performance were low, their market-value-to-capital ratios were even poorer. The companies have since demonstrated better than expected performance, accelerating their treadmill, but their market-value-to-capital ratios are nowhere near those of their top competitors.

Home Depot is in Quadrant 4, with low TRS but a higher than median market-value-to-capital ratio. Home Depot is joined in this quadrant by Walgreens, Staples, and the Gap. Historically, these retailers have been some of the best in the United States. What's going on? It is impossible to say whether their position results from unrealistic market expectations at the beginning of the period or from managers' inability to realize their companies' potential. But consider that the beginning of our TRS measurement period is 1999, near the top of the stock market cycle. As we noted in Chapter 4, around 1999 the large-capitalization stocks had much higher P/E ratios, probably at unreasonably high levels. This gap has since closed. But this example demonstrates one of the pitfalls of using

TRS as a performance measure: The results are highly dependent on the starting date.

Is the Market Value in Line with Value Creation Potential?

The final step in assessing a company's performance is linking the company's market value to its intrinsic value creation potential. We can do this by reverse engineering the company's share price, essentially using a DCF model and estimating the required performance (growth and ROIC) to generate the current share price. We can then evaluate how difficult it will be for the company to achieve the required level of performance.

In Chapter 5, we summarized a DCF valuation of Home Depot in which the value approximated Home Depot's market value at the end of 2003. The underlying projections assumed that Home Depot would continue to earn an ROIC of about 18 to 19 percent per year, the same as its 2003 ROIC, yet higher than its ROIC range over the three prior years of 14.9 percent to 16.3 percent. The DCF valuation also assumed that Home Depot's growth would slow from its historically high rates. Revenue growth averaged 16.5 percent during the five years ended 2003. Our projection assumed declining growth from approximately 12 percent in 2004 to 5 percent annually by 2013. This forecast of declining growth and constant ROIC resulted in a DCF equity value of $73 billion, which is within the trading range of Home Depot's shares. Other projections—for example, high growth and lower ROIC—could lead to the same value, but we'll explore this scenario.

Is the market value consistent with Home Depot's intrinsic value creation potential? First, let's examine the required growth. Using the growth rates in our simple estimation leads to $83 billion of new revenues by 2013. One equity analyst projects same-store sales growth of 3 percent to 4 percent, which is consistent with Home Depot's historical rate of same-store sales growth. With 4 percent same-store sales growth, Home Depot would need to add 900 stores over the next 10 years (about 50 percent of its current base). Yet one equity analyst estimated that the U.S. market for home improvement superstores was approximately 78 percent saturated at the end of 2003. Therefore, the growth rates in this scenario are plausible but difficult to achieve, bringing Home Depot close to estimates of market saturation. The growth implied by the share price appears reasonable and is consistent with Home Depot's recent announcement that it would open new stores at a slower rate than previously. Instead, the company plans to invest in infrastructure improvements on its current base.

Second, we need to consider whether Home Depot can maintain its ROIC at 18 percent to 19 percent. As Home Depot's growth slows and it focuses on core operations, some of its earlier issues with managing growth should be easier to deal with. But even as growth slows, competition with Lowe's could intensify. Furthermore, Wal-Mart has been selling more and more of the fast-moving items that Home Depot sells, potentially siphoning off customers.

Home Depot's current market value reflects business as usual with healthy growth in a maturing market. As the market nears saturation, Home Depot will face challenges in maintaining its ROIC while continuing to grow, especially since it has not demonstrated much success outside North America or with new store formats.

Having examined Home Depot's current market value relative to its performance potential, we return to the company's negative five-year TRS. Exhibit 13.7 shows an analysis of the change in Home Depot's value over the five years through 2003. We start with the market value in 1999 of $132 billion. If Home Depot had performed exactly as expected, its equity value would have increased by the cost of equity (less dividends and share repurchases) to $197 billion at the end of 2003. The difference between that number and its $80 billion market value at the end of 2003 is due to changes in performance expectations.

Assume that in 1999 the market estimated that margins and capital turnover would remain at 1998 levels. Since operating margins actually increased, we estimate the market *should have* increased the company's value by $50 billion. The cost of equity, capital efficiency, and cash tax rate did not change significantly during this period, so we attribute most of the remainder to changes in expectations for revenue growth. In Home Depot's case,

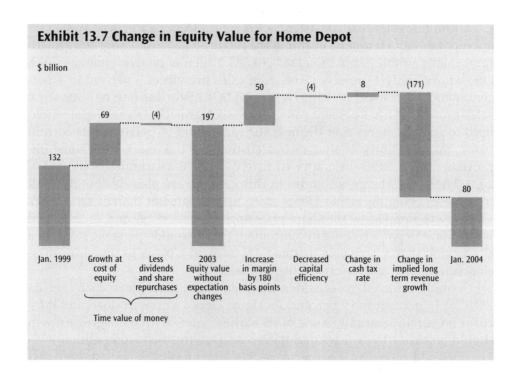

Exhibit 13.7 Change in Equity Value for Home Depot

growth expectations declined significantly, accounting for a $171 billion drop in value. At the end of 2003, we estimated the revenue growth consistent with Home Depot's share price to be about 8 percent annually for the next 10 years. At the end of 1998 investors would have had to expect Home Depot to grow 26 percent a year to justify the market value at the time. Such high growth expectations would have required Home Depot to triple its store count over 10 years, from 760 in 1998 to more than 2,300 in 2008, with continued healthy growth until at least 2013, far beyond the saturation level estimated by the equity analyst mentioned earlier. From this analysis, we are tempted to conclude that Home Depot's poor TRS since 1999 results more from an overly optimistic market value at the beginning of the period than from ineffective management.

SUMMARY

Insightful measurement of corporate performance is difficult. Simple approaches, such as EPS growth and TRS metrics, are inadequate. TRS is problematic because it does not consider how the market valued the company at the start of the measurement period, a problem that can be remedied with market valued added (MVA) and similar metrics. EPS does not take into consideration the opportunity cost of capital and can be manipulated by short-term actions. Revenue growth and ROIC are better measures of historical financial performance. However, all financial metrics—EPS, ROIC, and TRS—are backward looking. Measurement of corporate performance must also address a company's health: how well it is positioned to sustain and improve performance. Corporate health metrics explain how financial results were achieved and provide insights into future performance that are essential for truly understanding a company's performance.

REVIEW QUESTIONS

1. Identify the three dimensions of performance that should be considered when managers and investors evaluate the performance of a company.

2. What is the relationship between ROIC and economic profit? Develop a rationale that will lead a manager to conclude that economic profit is superior to ROIC.

3. Demonstrate how a manager either might smooth earnings or meet EPS targets by repurchasing shares of their company's common stock.

4. What is meant by the implied P/E on debt model? Explain how changing a company's leverage could be used to meet P/E or earnings targets.

5. Describe a value creation tree. What benefit does a manager gain by employing a value creation tree analysis as an integral component of performance measurement and analysis?

6. Define *market value added*. Does market value added provide the same performance insights to the corporate executive as economic profit?

7. Go to the internet and gather information for Hutchinson Technologies (HTCH). From the information gathered:

   a. Compute Hutchinson's ROIC.

   b. How much economic value has HTCH created?

   c. How well positioned is the company to create additional economic value in the future?

   d. Is the company's current market value in line with its historical performance and potential value creation?

14

Performance Management

Value managers have a holy grail as unattainable as the object of the knightly quests in the legend of King Arthur: a value creation purpose instilled in each of the thousands of business decisions made at the company every day. A single CEO or a small group of executives cannot make all these decisions, which range from the profound to the mundane. Companies have therefore established systems to ensure that decisions are consistent with short- and long-term objectives and that the management team can clearly see how those myriad decisions affect value creation.

These systems, called performance management systems, typically include long-term strategic plans, short-term budgets, capital budgeting systems, performance reporting and reviews, and compensation systems. Successful value creation requires that all components of these management systems are aligned to the company's strategy so as to encourage decisions that maximize value. For example, if product development is important to the strategic plan, the short-term budget and capital budget must include the necessary spending in the current year to develop the new product, and performance reviews must evaluate progress on new products, not just short-term profits.

Performance management is where managers spend most of their time, yet they are often dissatisfied with the results. They ask for the mystery formula that will make the system work, or even the secret metric everyone can work toward. Performance management is difficult, however, and offers no quick solutions. That said, a few lessons will make the process more effective.

Special thanks to Richard Dobbs, who co-wrote this chapter.

EVOLUTION OF PERFORMANCE MANAGEMENT SYSTEMS

Until the mid-1980s, most companies' performance management systems focused on maintaining the company as an ongoing enterprise and occasionally on achieving targets for net income or EPS. Often, shareholders' interests were lined up only loosely with the interests of managers; compensation primarily took the form of salary, and any bonuses were linked to short-term earnings. Hostile takeovers were rare, so managers were comfortable in their jobs.

In the late 1970s, theorists and practitioners including Joel Stern and Alfred Rappaport advocated a stronger link between the creation of shareholder value and the way companies were managed. This approach to performance management became known as Value-Based Management (VBM). The original, powerful idea behind VBM was to align the company's measurement system with economic value creation in a way that traditional accounting-based measurement systems did not. The focus of these early programs was ensuring that the measurement system fully took into account the cost of the capital tied up in the business. They did this by emphasizing metrics such as economic profit and economic value added (EVA),[1] which we discussed in Chapter 3. All these measures take into account the economic cost of the capital deployed in the business. For economic profit or EVA, calculation of the metric includes a specific charge for the economic cost of the capital tied up in the business.

Aligning managerial compensation more closely with shareholder value creation took root and gained wider acceptance. Companies linked management compensation explicitly to performance on economic profit or EVA. Companies also made greater use of stock-based compensation, particularly executive stock options.

The ideas behind VBM were important advances in management. Today, many businesses accept the ideas of linking management compensation to shareholder value creation and of explicitly recognizing the opportunity cost of equity capital. However, the results of many VBM programs were mixed. For example, we examined the shareholder returns of a sample of companies that publicly announced the adoption of VBM programs and found that the number of companies outperforming their industry peers three and five years later was not greater than the number that underperformed their peers. More than 20 years after VBM came onto the scene, many managers are still struggling with their performance management system and feel they somehow could be doing it more effectively.

The failure of many early VBM programs stemmed from two management mistakes. First, many managers ended up with VBM programs that

---

[1] EVA is a registered trademark of Stern Stewart & Co. and is synonymous with the generic term *economic profit.*

continued to emphasize short-term performance. Second, managers tended to overemphasize measurement and neglect the wider management processes, such as integration of these new metrics into planning, performance reviews, and compensation. In this chapter, we explore each of these problems.

Many VBM programs replaced net income or EPS with metrics such as EVA or economic profit. Although the new metric was better than those it replaced because it factored in the economic cost of the capital deployed in the business, it was still essentially a one-year measure, focusing on short-term performance. The new metric did not measure the company's long-term health, so it encouraged managers to boost short-term performance at the expense of investing in the long term. Managers had no incentive to invest in product development, brand building, customer satisfaction, or employee development. These VBM programs delivered short-term results that were not sustainable or that traded away opportunities for future growth.

Another reason early VBM programs failed was that companies focused too much on measurement and neglected to change the way the new metrics were used. In effect, these companies developed first-rate *value-based measurement* systems but had forgotten the management part. Some companies never linked their performance measurement system to the way they evaluated their people, so employees did not change what they focused on. Others treated their VBM program as just something else to do or something run by the finance department independently of the line managers. One company, for instance, spent years setting up a so-called VBM system featuring metrics that cascaded down throughout the business, elegant monthly management information reports, and a first-rate scorecard covering financial performance, operating drivers, organizational health, and customer service. But management did nothing to extend it from a discrete program in the finance department and engage the entire company. Nearly a year later, the program had made no discernible impact. Beyond top-level conversations, few managers used or understood the scorecard; some did not even know what it was. They had no involvement in the program's development, little understanding of the need for the new scorecard, and no incentive to use it.

EFFECTIVE VALUE-BASED MANAGEMENT

Successful as well as unsuccessful companies have seen that there are no magic bullets for creating a successful performance management system. Managers cannot delegate what is effectively their job to a "system." Managers must still invest most of their time in performance management. The success or failure of performance management depends not on a set of metrics, corporate calendars or templates, but mostly on the rigor and honesty of the process. Does the CEO add value by understanding the economics of the business units and being able to negotiate performance targets that are both challenging and achievable? Are trade-offs between the short and long term transparent?

When performance management is working well, it helps the layers of the organization communicate frankly and effectively. It gives managers space to manage, while assuring their bosses that the agreed-on level of performance will be achieved. In many companies, the only communication between layers of management involves whether a particular unit is reaching its profit target. With a good performance management system, just as much attention goes to the reason behind the profit achieved relative to target, and there is dialogue about concrete steps to improve performance.

Although we can offer no simple formulas, successful performance management includes some important ingredients:

- *Complete buy-in at all levels on the priority and mind-set of value creation.* Midlevel managers are unlikely to buy into managing for longer-term value creation if top management regularly cuts R&D, advertising, or employee development to make short-term profit targets. Without leadership from the top, a company cannot build a successful performance management system.

- *Clarity on which value drivers are fundamental to the performance and health of the business.* Many companies lack systematic processes for identifying a business's underlying value drivers and developing metrics against these value drivers, such as product launch speed in pharmaceuticals or the timing of new plant investments in commodity businesses like chemicals and paper.

- *A target- and aspiration-setting process that provides real challenge and builds commitment.* The process should result in targets for which business unit managers feel responsible. Targets must be difficult to achieve but not so unreasonable that the managers treat them as fanciful.

- *A fact-based performance review process that balances short-term performance and long-term growth.* In too many performance reviews, senior management does not understand enough about the business to assess whether a business unit's performance resulted from the management team's smarts and hard work or simply from good or bad luck.

- *A strong link to accountability and the process for evaluating and remunerating people.* The evaluation and remuneration of managers cannot be reduced to simple formulas tied to accounting results; it must be based on a deeper assessment of accomplishments.

In the remainder of this chapter we explore these essentials in detail.

PERVASIVE VALUE CREATION MIND-SET

Companies that succeed at performance management instill a value creation mind-set throughout the business. Their employees at all levels understand the principle of value thinking, know why it matters, and make decisions in the context of the impact on value. They achieve this because their top managers consistently reinforce the importance of the value mind-set in all their communications, build the capabilities to understand value creation, and (as discussed later) link value creation to the reward process.

Often, managing value is mistakenly viewed as the responsibility of a small group of managers. Typically this group includes the CEO, the board, and those in the finance function charged with ensuring that performance reports are appropriately designed and completed in a timely manner, and that any deviations showing up in the performance metrics against targets are identified and explained. This finance group is usually distinct from the business managers in charge of the day-to-day operations. Consequently, there is often a gap in accountability and limited understanding of how day-to-day decisions affect value.

When designing the performance management system, successful organizations bridge this gap by investing time in two-way discussions that include the business managers in the system's development. Also, they physically break down the barrier between the finance team and the line managers. Many organizations have no dedicated finance career track beyond the roles requiring technical skills such as tax law and accounting. Instead, they move personnel between operating the business and running the planning and performance management, so they can learn how business decisions affect value.

Companies instill the value mind-set when the top management team models that mind-set in each interaction. It is important that employees see executives walk the talk. Companies where top management pulls back on advertising expenditures to hit a quarterly earnings forecast typically have difficulty building a value mind-set. At companies with strong value mind-sets, CEOs take a stock market perspective in many of their interactions. CEOs use internal and external addresses to instill the importance of shareholder value creation by reminding their colleagues who the investors in their company really are. In a recent speech Lord Browne, the CEO of British Petroleum, said:

> Successful business creates wealth for many different people. We take our shareholders' money, put it to work applying skills and technology, and we create additional wealth for them. The money invested doesn't come from . . . the sort of capitalists who always used to be drawn in cartoons wearing tall black hats. It comes from ordinary savers—directly and through investment funds. Most of our

investors . . . are individuals and families saving for their retirement. They depend on the investments they make with us, and that is a considerable responsibility. . . . The role of business in society is to take people's savings, to use them productively and to add to the wealth with which we have been entrusted.[2]

VALUE DRIVERS AND VALUE METRICS

A value mind-set centers on understanding the company's value drivers. A *value driver* is an action that affects business performance in the short or long term and thereby creates value. Value drivers include increasing the number of stores for a supermarket chain, reducing the levels of working capital for a consumer goods company, and building employee loyalty in a software company. They also include more strategic actions, such as merging divisions with those of a competitor to remove excess capacity or offshoring activities to a lower-cost country such as India.

To measure how well the business is performing in relation to these value drivers, companies use a mix of *value metrics* and *value milestones*. Value metrics measure quantitatively how well the business is doing in terms of a value driver; for example, percentage addition of new space is a metric for growth of new stores. For some value drivers (particularly those that are more strategic), it is hard to identify specific metrics, so the company uses value milestones instead. These measure how well the business is doing on the activities related to the value driver. In a mature commodity materials manufacturing industry, a significant value driver is consolidating businesses with competitors to remove excess capacity (without the consolidation, none of the players have an incentive to remove capacity). To measure progress on this value driver, a company might use milestones in an acquisition program, such as approaching potential partners, getting approval from antitrust authorities, and closing the transaction. Finally, the top 10 to 15 value metrics and value milestones that matter for the business, given its strategy and industry, are called the company's *key performance indicators* (KPIs).

As we saw in Chapter 13, the primary elements of historical performance are growth and return on capital, but measuring historical growth and return on capital does not tell us about the potential for future growth and return on capital—the business's health. These historical measures also do not tell managers what to do to improve growth and return on capital. Therefore, in this chapter, we take the concept of measures to a deeper level, discussing how effective performance management requires an understanding of the underlying drivers of value and how these can be used by a management team to provide focus on how and where they can create value.

---

[2] The Botwinick Lecture, Columbia Business School, November 2004.

What Are the Value Drivers?

Value depends on performance in both the short term and the long term, so the value drivers must include those related to short-term performance and those related to the long-term health of the business. Thus, applying appropriate cost controls to manage short-term earnings and cash flow are normally part of a company's value drivers. The company must also identify what will drive longer-term value, so managers do not cut short-term costs at the expense of, say, product development or maintenance of a manufacturing plant's physical assets.

The relative importance of different value drivers in a particular business depends on its fundamental microeconomics. Improving customer loyalty matters much more in branded consumer goods than it does in commodity chemicals, where costs and production uptime have a disproportionate impact on value.

The importance of different value drivers also depends on strategy; even in the same industry, two companies might have different value drivers. In retail, some companies such as Wal-Mart compete on price, and some such as 7-Eleven compete on convenience. For companies that compete on price, managing the supply chain's cost effectiveness is much more important than it is for companies that compete on convenience, because an efficient supply chain allows the retailer to attract customers through low prices. In contrast, managing the supply chain to improve product availability (number of products in stock) in stores is a much bigger value driver for retailers that compete on convenience. Customers looking for convenience need to have the product available when they visit the store.

Clarity about what the business's value drivers are and how each driver affects value has several advantages. First, if managers know the value drivers, they can make explicit choices requiring a trade-off between pursuing one value driver and allowing performance against another to deteriorate. This is particularly true for trade-offs between the delivery of short-term performance and the activities that build the long-term health of the business to sustain future performance. These trade-offs are real. Increasing investment for the long term will cause short-term returns to decline, as management expenses some of the costs such as R&D or advertising in the year they occur, not in the year the investments achieve their benefits. Other costs are capitalized but will not earn a return before the project is commissioned, so they will suppress overall returns in the short term.

Another benefit of clarity about value drivers is that it enables the management team to assign priorities to actions so that activities expected to create substantially more value take precedence over others. Setting priorities encourages focus that often adds more to value than efforts to improve on multiple dimensions simultaneously. Without an explicit discussion of priorities and trade-offs, different members of the management team could interpret and execute the business strategy in numerous ways. Distinctive planning and performance management systems promote a common language—the value-driver approach—that shapes the way top management and employees think about creating value at each level of the organization. For example, in a pharmaceutical company setting such an approach would encourage discussion and coordinated action across the organization regarding specific steps to increase the speed of product launches in order to accelerate value creation.

Developing Value Drivers and Value Metrics

Some companies develop their value drivers and metrics in a two-step process. First, they develop an understanding of the economic links within the business and identify potential value drivers. Second, they identify which value drivers have the highest priority because they have the most potential to create value.

Step 1: Understand economic links in the business, and identify potential value drivers   The core activity of this first phase is to develop value trees for a business unit. The value tree is a systematic method of analytically and visually linking the business's operational metrics to financial metrics and shareholder value. Each element of financial performance is broken down into operational metrics. Value drivers are associated with each of these metrics. Exhibit 14.1 shows a simple value tree for a manufacturing company.

Managers should develop different initial versions of trees based on different hypotheses and business knowledge in order to stimulate identification of unconventional sources of value. The information from these versions should then be integrated into one tree (or in some cases, a few trees) that best reflects the understanding of the business. Managers should develop separate trees for different parts of a business unit if the parts are clearly different (for example a unit that includes a retail business and wholesale trading).

We illustrate this process by applying it to a temporary-help company. Exhibit 14.2 on page 424 shows four different approaches used to develop a value tree for this company. A tree based on profit-and-loss structure often seems to managers to be the most natural and easiest to complete. Such a tree, however, is unlikely to provide the insight gained by looking at the business from a customer's perspective, or from that of a branch or other relevant vantage point. Exhibit 14.3 on page 425 is a summary value tree. To create it, management has adopted the most useful insights provided by other trees, a process that forms the basis for further development.

When you develop value trees, pay particular attention to growth value drivers. Initiatives in the different growth horizons pay off over different time periods. Yet the timing of the payoffs has little to do with those points in time when management must nurture the opportunity with attention and invest-

Exhibit 14.1 Simple Value Driver Tree: Manufacturing Company

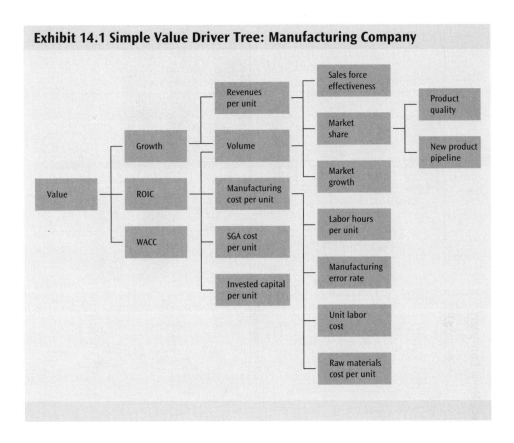

ment in order to bring it to fruition. Continuing the example of the temporary-help company, Exhibit 14.4 on page 426 illustrates a value tree created for developing business in a new geographic market. Important value drivers included developing the market and staff capabilities in the new country.

Step 2: Identify highest-priority value drivers   Every tip of a value tree is a potential value driver, so a full disaggregation would result in a large number of value drivers, certainly more than management could feasibly focus on. As a result, the second step after creating the value trees is to ask questions to filter out the business's key value drivers:

1. *Is the value driver material?* The simplest way to test this is to estimate the sensitivities of the value driver by changing the appropriate metric in the value tree; for example, a 1 percent increase in the shipping costs increases the overall logistics cost of a business by x percent. However, it is not easy to represent some inputs to a value tree by arithmetic formulas, such as the relationship between advertising spending in a beer business and value in a certain niche consumer brand channel. In this case, testing whether advertising expense is a

Exhibit 14.2 Value Trees from Four Perspectives: Temporary-Help Company

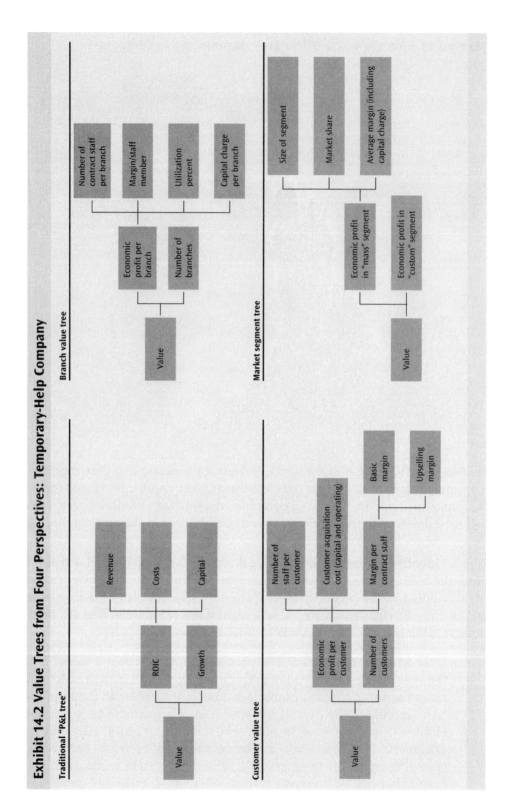

Traditional "P&L tree"

Branch value tree

Customer value tree

Market segment tree

424

Exhibit 14.3 Summary Short-Term Value Tree: Temporary-Help Company

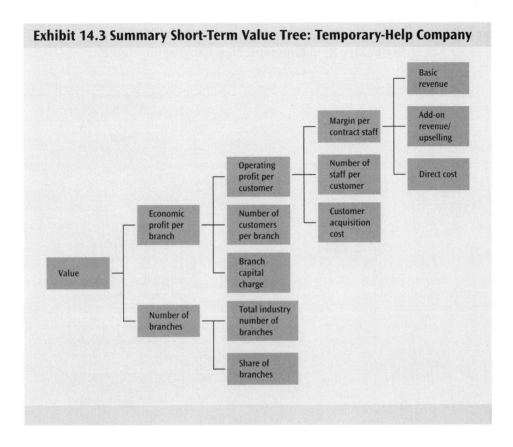

material driver of value depends on thoroughly understanding the effectiveness of marketing expenses in the beer industry. The input-output relationship would be constructed using research on past marketing, experience of the business managers, and historical "bang for the buck" analysis.

2. *How much impact can the business have on the value driver?* This second filter assesses the extent to which the business can stimulate and affect change. To prioritize the value drivers, managers have to estimate how much they can affect each one and then use the value tree to understand the relative impact on value. Several considerations are helpful for assessing the business's possible impact on each value driver:

- Does the external environment allow change? For example, growing the number of stores is not meaningful as a key value driver for a retail business if planning authorities are unlikely to grant permission for further store expansion.

- Do the current business assets offer room for improvement? If the current reliability of the company's manufacturing plants is already near the technical limits for a process or a best-in-class industry

Exhibit 14.4 Summary Medium-Term Value Tree: Temporary-Help Company, New Geographic Market

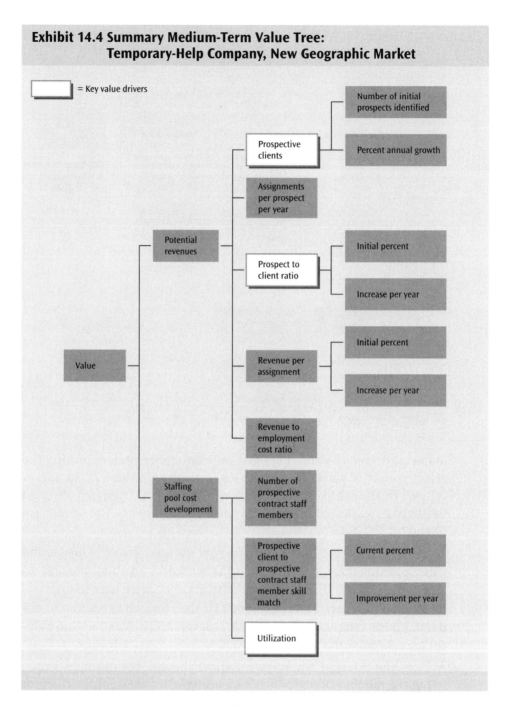

benchmark, the potential for further improvement is likely to be small. In that case, improving reliability is less likely to be a key value driver.

- Do the existing skill set and capabilities offer the appropriate foundation for change? It is very well coming up with a set of value drivers, but if the business lacks the necessary human resources to apply them, then management should focus first on developing capabilities as a precursor to value creation.

3. *Have unintended consequences been considered?* Focusing too much on one value driver will often have unintended consequences; for example, performance against other value drivers could slip. One manufacturing company focused on improving factory availability (the proportion of the time the plant was able to produce) as the main value driver. During a high-margin period, its marginal production generated significant economic returns. However, unintended consequences included excessive maintenance, overinvestment to build redundancy, and an overstocking of replacement parts. When margins returned to a more normal level, these consequences drained profitability. A better alternative is to develop a balanced set of value drivers that manage for unintended consequences. For the manufacturing company, improving availability had to be supplemented with managing maintenance effectiveness.

4. *Is the value driver sustainable?* Value drivers that deliver value once (e.g., delivering one-time cost synergies from integrating a newly acquired business unit) should be distinguished from those that consistently create value for the business. Technology leadership over competitors cannot be a key value driver for a manufacturing business if there is no patent protection and much competition.

By answering these questions, management should rank the 10 to 15 value drivers that really matter at different levels of the business and identify the appropriate value metrics. Ideally, these value drivers cascade through the organization. The CEO might focus on overall productivity, and the shift managers would focus on productivity of particular units during their shift.

Applying this process to an example, Exhibit 14.5 on page 428 illustrates the key value drivers and metrics for a pharmaceutical company. The exhibit shows the key value metrics, the company's current performance relative to best and worst in class, its aspirations for each driver, and the potential value impact from meeting its targets. The greatest value creation would come from three areas: accelerating the rate of release of new products from 0.5 to 0.8 per year, reducing from six years to four the time it takes for a new drug to reach 80 percent of peak sales, and cutting cost of goods sold from 26 percent to 23 percent of sales. Some of the value drivers (such as new-drug development) are long term, whereas others (such as reducing COGS) have a shorter term focus.

A well-defined and appropriately selected set of key value drivers ought to allow management to articulate how the organization's strategy

Exhibit 14.5 Key Value Drivers: Pharmaceutical Company

Value driver	Performance and targets			Increase in value (€ billion)
	Worst in peer group		Best in peer group	

Top-line growth

- Rate of release of major products, per year
- Optimizing product lifecycle
  - Time to market in years
  - Time to 80 percent of peak sales in years
- Market share in high value segments, such as share of sales of major products in U.S.

Efficiency/effectiveness

- Research and development effectiveness, such as product tail
  - Sales of non-major products as a percent of total sales
- Optimizing industrial operations
  - Cost of goods sold in percent of sales
- Optimizing marketing and sales and general and administrative costs, such as general and administrative expenses as percent of sales

Performance and targets values:

Rate of release: Worst 0.1 — Current 0.5 — Target 0.8 — Best 1.0 | Increase in value: 15.3

Time to market: Worst 14 — Target 10 — Current 6 — Best 9 | Increase in value: 4.5

Time to 80 percent of peak sales: Worst 7 — Current 6 — Target 4 — Best 3 | Increase in value: 9.8

Market share: Worst 25% — Current 40% — Target 50% — Best 70% | Increase in value: 2.3

Sales of non-major products: Worst 50% — Current 35% — Target 25% — Best 10% | Increase in value: 6.3

Cost of goods sold: Worst 35% — Current 26% — Target 23% — Best 14% | Increase in value: 11.3

General and administrative expenses: Worst 6% — Current 5% — Target (3%) — Best 3% | Increase in value: 4.8

● Current position

➤ All arrows represent an equivalent implementation effort

creates value. If it is impossible to represent some component of the strategy using the key value drivers, or if some key value driver does not serve as a building block in the strategy, then managers should reexamine the value trees, the filters, or both.

Disseminating the Value Drivers and Metrics

Although the value driver approach underpins the entire performance management system from longer-term strategic planning to yearly and monthly performance management, the key value metrics could vary depending on their purpose. For example, the executive board would focus on financial and operational metrics associated with overall business performance and health, and line managers would focus on operational metrics relating to day-to-day performance, especially monthly performance assessment.

For the company to realize the benefits of clarity on the value drivers and metrics, managers at all levels must understand them. The process of developing the value drivers and metrics is therefore as important as the drivers and metrics themselves. The management team at all levels of the business must be involved in coming up with the value drivers. A chemicals business engaged its top 30 people in drawing up value trees and testing to determine the most important value drivers. At workshops, the participants debated the relative importance of the emerging key value drivers and how they linked to the strategic context for each business unit. At the start, some managers were skeptical, believing that their collective business experience would make arriving at the key value drivers an obvious and non-value-adding exercise. However, the discussions yielded some surprises in the form of material differences in people's assumed priorities. Exchanges provided a healthy test of how well management was aligned and whether it could clearly articulate how to create value in the business. By the end of the process managers understood their business much better.

EFFECTIVE TARGET SETTING

The third key element of effective performance management is setting targets that are challenging but realistic enough to be "owned" by the managers responsible for meeting them. We focus on target setting for a business unit, but the ideas apply at all levels of a company. The process should ensure that targets do not appear theoretical and unrealistic to those who are supposed to deliver the performance required to meet them. It also helps to make sure the organization views the targets as a set of aspirations embraced by the entire management team (albeit with challenges from above and from peers), rather than as something simply imposed by others.

Aligning top-down and bottom-up targets requires negotiation between the corporate center and business units. The process is iterative, and its most important prerequisite is a well-informed corporate center. Top management, particularly the CEO, must understand the economics and operating environment of each business, independent of information that the business provides.

Targets should be based on actual opportunities for improvement associated with the key value drivers and the underlying economics of the business unit. Companies can identify opportunities by benchmarking performance on a particular value metric or milestone based on the following considerations:

- *Fundamental economic analysis:* This involves estimating the potential for revenue growth and ROIC based on the product market and competitive environment. The company might estimate the potential size of a business's market and convert that estimate into market share and revenue targets based on a competitive assessment. ROIC targets can be based on the competitiveness of the market and the experience of companies in similar markets.

- *External benchmarks:* These benchmarks compare the company's performance on a value driver with similar companies in the same industry. The analysis can clarify how the company is performing against competitors, including a sense of where it enjoys superior performance and where it lags. External benchmarks are credible because they are based on companies actually delivering levels of performance. Companies often benefit from benchmarking themselves against companies in other, similar industries. A petroleum company might benchmark product availability in its service station shops against a traditional grocery retailer. External benchmarks may also extend beyond direct competitors. Even if companies' products and services are in different sectors, their processes may be similar; if so, they may have similar value drivers and may benefit from benchmarking. Lean manufacturing approaches developed by automakers have been successfully transplanted into many other industries, including retailing and services. For example, measuring the proportion of activities that require rework can suggest how well one business operates a process relative to other companies.

- *Internal benchmarks:* These benchmarks compare the performance of similar units within the company. They may be less challenging than external benchmarks, as they do not necessarily involve looking at world-class players. However, internal benchmarks deliver a number of benefits. The data are likely to be more readily available, since sharing the information poses no competitive or antitrust problems. Also, unearthing the causes of differences in performance is much easier, as the unit heads can visit the benchmark unit. Finally, these comparisons facilitate peer review, a point that we explore later.

- *Benchmarks against itself:* These measures involve analyzing the historical performance of the same business over time on a particular value metric. If the business can show that it has delivered high performance with the same management team on the same equipment, it overcomes the major objection to external benchmarks: that they do not apply to the particular unit in the company. One company found that its daily production varied widely. Management ranked the days by production level, as shown in Exhibit 14.6, demonstrating that the business could deliver outstanding performance on some days—proof that it was not impossible. The effort also helped managers understand what actions they could use to improve daily production (in this case, reducing variation in daily production, rather than eliminating bottlenecks or adding capacity).

- *Theoretical limits:* Some processes or activities have physical limits on their efficiency. For example, with no wastage, a pump might require 18 kilowatt-hours of energy. If it actually uses 25 kilowatt-hours, it is

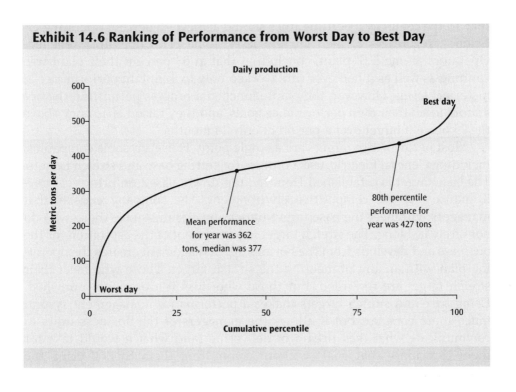

Exhibit 14.6 Ranking of Performance from Worst Day to Best Day

operating at 72 percent of the theoretical limit. Particularly in manufacturing, identifying theoretical limits indicates how far performance can be improved, that is, the extent to which a value driver can improve efficiency.

To clearly understand and carefully apply these measures, analysis is necessary. Some companies establish a separate analytic group whose role is to compile this analysis.

Some of the most effective companies supplement the top-down challenge with a challenge from peers running similar businesses. Colleagues running similar businesses will be familiar with opportunities for improvement, so they will be much more effective than staff managers at providing challenge. Companies that have excelled at performance management arrange peer challenge not only on overall profitability during the year but also on the plans for capital expenditure, growth, pricing, and costs. An additional benefit of this peer challenge is that it can encourage colleagues to support one another in improving the performance of the business. One of Canada's largest privately held companies assigns the strongest performers to help colleagues who are not performing as well.

When those assigned to meet targets also actively help in setting them, a company has a chance to generate the understanding and commitment needed for outstanding performance. Consider the experience of one global consumer goods company. When the corporate technical manager ordered that all the company's bottling lines should achieve 75 percent operating efficiency, regardless of their current level, some plant operators rebelled. Operators at one U.S. plant, concluding that at 53 percent their plant was running as well as it had ever run, worked only to maintain performance at historical levels. However, the plant launched a process permitting the operators to set their own performance goals, and they raised efficiency above the 75 percent target over a period of only 14 months.

Most performance targets are a single point. However, some companies, including General Electric, use a process for setting base and stretch targets. The base target is established from the top down, based on prior-year performance and the competitive environment. The company expects that managers will meet the base target under any circumstance; those who do not rarely last long. The stretch target is a statement of the aspiration for the business and develops from the bottom up. Management creates the operating plan with an aim of meeting the stretch target. Those who meet their stretch target are rewarded, but those who miss it are seldom punished. Using base and stretch targets makes a performance management system much more complex, but it allows the managers of the business units to communicate what they dream of delivering (and what it would take for them to achieve that goal) without committing them to delivering the stretch target.

FACT-BASED PERFORMANCE REVIEWS

Performance reviews should not be anecdotal, but should be based on measurable facts. Companies should consider using performance and health scorecards to fuel the conversation between manager and subordinate by clearly showing individual performance. Performance reviews based on facts keep leaders and managers honest and help make corrective action effective.

What to Measure

The best information for fact-based reviews is a scorecard incorporating the key value metrics from the value driver analysis. Managers may be tempted to think that financial reports alone can serve as the basis for performance discussions. Financial results are only part of the review process, however. Key value metrics show the operating performance behind the financial results.

The consumer goods company in Exhibit 14.7 illustrates the importance of having a set of key value metrics. For several years, a business unit showed consistent double-digit growth in economic profit. Since the financial results were consistently strong—in fact, the strongest across all the business units—corporate managers were pleased and did not ask many questions of the business unit. One year, the unit's economic profit unexpectedly began to decline. Corporate management began digging deeper into the unit's results. They discovered that for the preceding three years the unit had been increasing its economic profit by raising

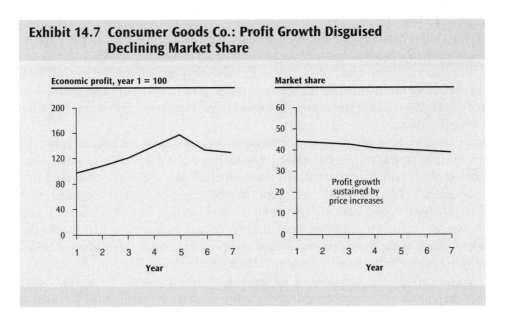

Exhibit 14.7 Consumer Goods Co.: Profit Growth Disguised Declining Market Share

prices and cutting back on product promotion. That created the conditions for competitors to take away market share. The unit's strong short-term performance was coming at the expense of its long-term health. The company changed the unit's management team, but lower profits continued for several years as the unit recovered its position with consumers.

Corporate centers also find it convenient to impose one scorecard on all business units. This is shortsighted. Although a single scorecard makes it easier to compare units, management forgoes the chance to understand each unit's unique value drivers. Ideally, companies should have custom-tailored scorecards that cascade through each business, so that each manager can monitor the key value drivers most important to him or her.

Problem Solving

Managers should use reviews as problem-solving sessions to determine the root causes of bad performance. Instead of identifying who is to blame, managers can use review sessions to fix problems so they do not recur. Reviewers should be required to prepare thoroughly for reviews and turn traditionally one-sided discussions ("boss tells, subordinate does") into collaborative sessions. Doing so in front of peers brings together a group of individuals with well-informed insights and respected perspectives. This makes problem solving more effective, increases the sense of accountability, and virtually eliminates any sandbagging. Orchestrated with care, the review helps motivate frontline managers and employees, rather than deflating them. One public transport authority winnows down to a few the issues to debate and invites a select number of people to the table to resolve them, with minor data questions delegated to separate channels. Whatever the chosen format, however, this is an area where the manager or leader has a crucial role in setting the tone of the organization and the level of honesty. Reviewing performance together in a constructive environment encourages managers to be open and take more responsibility. But if the manager has a blame mind-set, subversive behavior will follow.

Consider how one chemical company designed a more effective way to review performance. A year after introducing a VBM approach to make reported data more transparent, the company had yet to see the expected improvements. Worse, nearly everyone in the organization recognized that official discussions about performance were something of a sham. Some managers misrepresented reports of their actual performance to create the appearance of meeting targets; others built enough slack into future performance targets to make sure they would easily be met.

The company's response: Change the review process. What had been one-on-one review involving the division head and unit leader became a broader discussion between the division head and all unit leaders together. Rather than simply reviewing the data, the meeting focused on the most important lessons from the previous reporting period, as well as the greatest risks and opportunities expected in the coming period. Emphasis in the meeting shifted away from individual successes and failures to a combination of shared lessons and problem solving on future risks and opportunities. Next, the company introduced a series of peer meetings among unit leaders without the division heads present. These meetings aimed to review plans and identify risks and opportunities in order to set priorities for allocating capital and resources. In the first year of the new processes, capital outlays dropped 25 percent, and underlying profits, adjusted for the usual modulations of the business cycle, rose by 10 percent.

ACCOUNTABILITY IN EVALUATION AND REMUNERATION

The final element of successful performance management is creating accountability and rewards for individual managers and employees. The rewards are typically financial and, according to some critics, have become excessive. During the past decade, financial compensation, particularly stock options, reached new heights. As the long bull market extended into the late 1990s, executives received extraordinary rewards that had little to do with their own performance and everything to do with factors beyond their reach, such as declining interest rates. When the stock market fell, companies maintained the higher level of rewards.

Many have argued that current compensation systems are broken because they rarely link compensation to the company's long-term value creation. But development of better approaches will take years, and the nature of these changes is unclear. In the meantime, here are several emerging ideas on how to better align incentives and value creation:

- Link stock-based compensation to the specific performance of the company, stripping out broad macro and industry effects.
- Tie some portion of compensation for senior executives to corporate results several years after the executive's departure.
- Link bonuses as much to health metrics as to short-term financial results.
- Move away from formulaic compensation to more judgment-based systems.

In addition to financial rewards, companies motivate their people through nonfinancial means. One of these is career progression. Another links to the company's values and beliefs; employees gain inherent satisfaction from living up to a distinctive "XYZ" way of doing business.

SUMMARY

For many companies, performance management is the most important driver of value creation. Yet performance management is difficult to describe, let alone execute well. The rewards, however, are great for companies that can build a value creation mind-set, clarify the business's short- and long-term value drivers, set stretch targets that people believe are achievable, conduct fact-based performance reviews, and effectively motivate their people.

REVIEW QUESTIONS

1. Identify and define the components of an effective performance management system. How does an effective performance management system differ from early value-based management systems?

2. What is the difference among a value driver, value metric, and milestone? Describe the relationship among milestones, metrics, and value drivers.

3. What are the advantages/disadvantages of tailored value drivers versus the balance scorecard?

4. Why is it important for a manager to understand a business's value drivers and how each driver affects value?

5. Describe the process employed to determine a company's value drivers.

6. What is the purpose of creating a value tree analysis? Identify the critical components and the processes for creating a company's value tree diagram.

7. What is the purpose of identifying an appropriate benchmark? Describe two classifications of benchmarks. Present the differences in how the two classifications of benchmarks are defined and used.

15

Creating Value through Mergers and Acquisitions

Mergers, divestitures, joint ventures, and other change-of-ownership transactions are important ways for corporations to reallocate resources and execute strategies. At some point in their careers, senior executives can expect to receive an overture from another company, bid on a business offered for sale, or debate with colleagues the merits of a deal.

Mergers and acquisitions (M&A) have long been features of the corporate landscape. They first became notorious in the late 1800s in the United States with the activity of the "robber barons," followed by the consolidations of J. P. Morgan and others in the early 1900s. Since then, there have been several waves of M&A activity in the United States—during the booming economy of the late 1960s, in the controversial restructuring wave of the mid-1980s, and most recently with the megadeals signed during the late 1990s (see Exhibit 15.1 on p. 438).

Mergers and acquisitions have become a global phenomenon. Europe has seen increased M&A activity, driven by overcapacity and the introduction of a common currency. The M&A market in Japan is also expanding, fueled by strong competition and local concerns about foreign investors targeting domestic companies. In fact, many deals are now cross-border, with companies either entering new markets or consolidating industries globally. And for some companies, pursuing acquisitions and divestitures can become corporate strategy in itself. Private equity shops and other industry consolidators show that superior M&A capabilities can be translated into shareholder value.

Today, change-of-ownership transactions are supported and even encouraged by a large infrastructure developed to facilitate such deals, including investment bankers, corporate lawyers, management consultants, accountants,

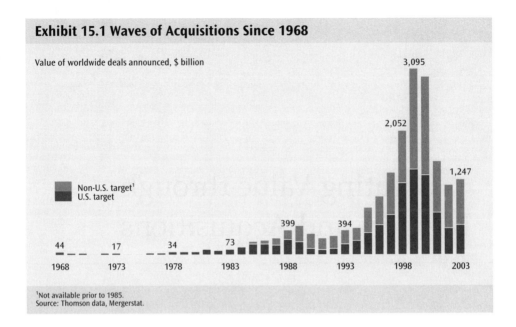

Exhibit 15.1 Waves of Acquisitions Since 1968

Value of worldwide deals announced, $ billion

[1]Not available prior to 1985.
Source: Thomson data, Mergerstat.

public relations firms, deal magazines, and private investigators. Considering that most investment banks did not even have M&A departments in the late 1970s, the transformation has been remarkable.

In this chapter, we focus on the most common change-of-ownership transactions, mergers and acquisitions, and specifically how to create value by acquiring another business. We address the following topics:

- The debate over who benefits from M&A.
- How and when to use M&A as a strategic tool.
- How to measure value creation using a structured framework.
- Methods for estimating and capturing synergies.
- How to pay for an acquisition.
- The need to emphasize value creation over accounting treatment.
- Techniques for being a successful acquirer.

DO SHAREHOLDERS BENEFIT FROM M&A?

Economists, politicians, journalists, and the public constantly debate who benefits from mergers and acquisitions. A merger can be beneficial for shareholders but harmful to consumers if it creates a monopolistic position and higher prices. Alternatively, real improvements in efficiency can lead to higher quality and less costly products. The economy overall will be more vibrant, offer greater opportunities, and create more jobs if resources are continuously moved to their best uses. These developments, of course, are of little consolation to the workers who lose their jobs when merged companies reduce excess capacity and eliminate redundant positions.

Although a successful M&A strategy will consider an acquisition's impact on customers, employees, and the community, this book's focus is on how to create and manage value for a company's shareholders. And creating value through acquisition is tricky. Today's market for corporate control is fairly efficient: Easy, good deals are hard to come by, if they exist at all. Most successful deals result from highly disciplined deal making—and sometimes just good luck.

Numerous empirical studies have examined whether M&A transactions create value for shareholders. Based on strong empirical evidence, few question that the typical acquisition creates value for sellers. It is difficult to argue the contrary when target shareholders receive, on average, 30 percent premiums over their stock's pre-announcement market price. For acquirers, the evidence of value creation is far less conclusive. Empirical studies examining the reaction of capital markets to M&A announcements find that the value-weighted average deal lowers the acquirer's stock price between 1 and 3 percent.[1] Using a sample of U.S. and European transactions larger than $500 million between January 1996 and September 1998, our own analysis found that for half the deals with a statistically significant reaction in the capital markets, the acquirer's share price decreases in the 10-day window around the announcement of the transaction.[2] Stock returns following the acquisition are no better. Mark Mitchell and Erik Stafford find that acquirers underperform comparable companies by 5 percent during the three years following the acquisitions.[3]

Although the market frowns on the *average* deal, many deals do create value for the bidding company. Therefore, it is important to distinguish what separates value-creating from value-destroying transactions. Academic research points to three characteristics:

1. *Strong operators are more successful.* According to empirical research, acquirers whose earnings and share price grow at a rate above industry average for three years before the acquisition earn statistically significant positive returns on announcement.[4] Another study found

---

[1] Although 1 to 3 percent appears small, this decline in stock price translates to $218 billion in lost value for companies performing acquisitions between 1980 and 2001. For additional details, see S. B. Moeller, F. P. Schlingemann, and R. M. Stulz, "Do Shareholders of Acquiring Firms Gain from Acquisitions?" (NBER working paper no. W9523, Ohio State University, 2003).

[2] The analysis included 506 deals in Europe and the United States with available data. Of these, 276 saw statistically significant positive or negative reactions of the buyer's share price.

[3] M. L. Mitchell and E. Stafford, "Managerial Decisions and Long-Term Stock Price Performance," *Journal of Business,* 73 (2000): 287–329.

[4] R. Morck, A. Shleifer, and R. Vishny, "Do Managerial Objectives Drive Bad Acquisitions?" *Journal of Finance,* 45 (1990): 31–48.

similar results using the market-to-book ratio as a measure of corporate performance.[5]

2. *Low transaction premiums are better.* Researchers have found that acquirers paying a high premium earn negative returns on announcement.[6]

3. *Being the sole bidder helps.* Several studies have found that acquirer stock returns are negatively correlated with the number of bidders; the more companies attempting to buy the target, the higher the price.[7]

Overall, the statistical evidence demonstrates that the typical acquisition will not create value for the acquirer. However, the specifics of each transaction matter more than summary statistics. Is your company a superior operator? Will your company's superior performance translate to better performance in the target? Even if you are the appropriate owner, will you overpay during the heat of an auction? There are always outliers in the statistics, and your deal might be one. We therefore return to the fundamentals: Only a relentless focus on value creation helps to turn the odds in favor of acquirers.

MERGERS AND ACQUISITIONS VERSUS ORGANIC GROWTH AS STRATEGY

M&A can be a strategy. Rolling up an industry by purchasing several smaller players and improving the economics by exploiting economies of scale can generate large economic profits. When NationsBank acquired 31 retail banks in the United States between 1988 and 1997, it rolled out well-documented best practices across each function that reduced costs at the regional level. During this time period, net income rose an average of 32 percent annually, with shareholder returns near 22 percent per year.

Many other strategic themes rely on M&A to create value. You may want to enter a market with an innovative product but lack the capabilities to develop the product fast enough to capture the value. In this situation, the best way to achieve your goal might be to purchase a small company with a product already under development. Or if you want to enter a new geographic market, you might need a local sales force that would take years to build—but only a few months to acquire.

---

[5] H. Servaes, "Tobin's Q and the Gains from Takeovers," *Journal of Finance,* 46 (1991): 409–419.
[6] M. L. Sirower, *The Synergy Trap* (New York: Free Press, 1997); and N. G. Travlos, "Corporate Takeover Bids, Methods of Payment, and Bidding Firms' Stock Return," *Journal of Finance,* 42 (1987): 943–963. The result was statistically significant in Sirower but not significant in Travlos.
[7] R. Morck, A. Shleifer, and R. Vishny, "Do Managerial Objectives Drive Bad Acquisitions?" *Journal of Finance,* 45 (1990): 31–48; and D. K. Datta, V. K. Narayanan, and G. E. Pinches, "Factors Influencing Wealth Creation from Mergers and Acquisitions: A Meta-Analysis," *Strategic Management Journal,* 13 (1992): 67–84.

However, it is important to first ask whether M&A is the right step for your company. Fundamentally, when purchasing another company, you purchase the company's assets—tangible assets such as property and equipment, and intangible assets such as patents, customer lists, and the know-how of the employees. Alternatively, you could have invested a similar amount of money to create (or purchase) the same assets internally. Assuming your company has opportunities for this type of organic growth, internal investments tend to return more money for each invested dollar than acquisitions of other companies through the capital markets.

To examine the implications of organic versus acquired growth, consider the hypothetical company detailed in Exhibit 15.2. In its current state, our company has revenues of $20 billion, after-tax operating profits (NOPLAT) of $1.2 billion, and an ROIC of 20 percent. The company is currently growing at 4 percent annually. Based on discounted cash flows, the company's value is $16 billion (we assume 10 percent cost of capital).

Suppose the company decides to grow (beyond current expectations) through an internally generated product line extension. The company invests $300 million in the new product line. Since the new investment has similar profit and growth potential as the existing base, the value of the company will increase by $500 million, or 3.1 percent above the base case.

Next, consider what will happen if management decides to acquire another company, rather than create the new product line itself. The third column in Exhibit 15.2 presents the characteristics of a target company

Exhibit 15.2 Creating Value through Acquisitions Is Hard to Do

$ million, percent

			Acquired growth		
	Acquirer	Organic growth	No synergies	Increase profits by 50%	Increase growth by 50%
Revenues	20,000	1,000	1,000	1,000	1,000
Expected growth	4%	4%	4%	4%	6%
NOPLAT	1,200	60	60	90	60
Invested capital	6,000	300	300	300	300
ROIC	20%	20%	20%	30%	20%
DCF value	16,000	800	800	1,300	1,050
Market value		(300)[1]	(800)	(800)	(800)
Premium (30%)			(240)	(240)	(240)
Value creation	16,000	500	(240)	260	10
Value creation/ acquirer value		3.1%	(1.5%)	1.6%	0.1%

[1] Initial investment.

performing identically to the acquirer's internal growth opportunity: The target's revenues are $1 billion, its ROIC equals 20 percent, and the target is expected to grow at 4 percent. The target has a DCF value of $800 million. But since the typical acquisition requires a 30 percent premium, the price to the acquirer would be $1,040 million. If no value is created beyond the market's current expectations, the acquirer overpays, and its value would drop by 1.5 percent.

If the acquirer's management can increase the target's profitability by 50 percent (e.g., by eliminating redundant positions in the two companies) or increase the target's growth rate by 50 percent (e.g., through the cross-selling of products), the new company would generate higher cash flows than the two companies on a stand-alone basis. Therefore, the value of the target would be higher, as detailed in the fourth and fifth columns of Exhibit 15.2. However, because of the 30 percent premium, the majority of new value is *transferred* to the target's shareholders. Thus, whereas organic growth could have increased value 5 percent, an acquisition enhances value by only 1.6 percent (with a profit increase) or 0.1 percent (with a growth rate increase). Even though the acquirer has invested more than $1 billion, its share price would rise less than 2 percent. So even with optimistic assumptions for synergies, the net value generated by acquiring $1 billion in revenue is far smaller than the value generated by investing internally.

Note, however, that this hypothetical example assumes that organic growth is a potential substitute for M&A. As mentioned previously, requirements for speed, limits in acquirer capabilities, or barriers to imitation of competitor products may make organic growth sometimes impossible or extremely expensive. Nevertheless, the required premiums make it difficult to create value from an acquisition, so you need a good rationale for investing shareholder capital in an acquisition—and you need to execute relentlessly to realize the promised synergies incorporated in the transaction's price.

A FRAMEWORK FOR CREATING VALUE THROUGH MERGERS AND ACQUISITIONS

If the market value of the target incorporates the value of its discounted free cash flows, the required investment (in the form of the acquisition price including premium) will be equal to or higher than the current value of the stand-alone business. Value creation, therefore, requires increasing the expected free cash flows of the combined entities *beyond* current expectations.

When evaluating M&A opportunities, we rely on a simple framework to measure how much value will be created for an acquirer's shareholders. In its simplest form, an acquirer's net value creation equals the target's value to the acquirer less the price paid:

Exhibit 15.3 How to Think about Value Creation in M&A

$ million

Value		Price	
Intrinsic value		Market value	
of target	900	of target	800
NPV of synergies	400	Premium paid	240
Gross value of			
acquired assets	1,300	Total price paid	1,040

Value to shareholders of the acquirer: 260

- *Value (what you get):* The gross value acquired is the intrinsic value of the target (based on discounted cash flows) plus the net present value of the synergies that the business combination will generate.
- *Price (what you pay):* The acquirer pays the market value of the target before the deal was announced plus any premium that must be paid.

Exhibit 15.3 applies this framework to a hypothetical transaction. The value of the target including synergies equals $1.3 billion, while the price paid equals $1.04 billion. Therefore, the value created by the transaction equals $260 million.

This framework explicitly models something experienced managers already know: What really drives value creation from M&A is the value of the synergies versus the required premium (the amount above the current market value the acquirer has to pay). The following subsections examine the framework's components in detail.

Market Value versus Intrinsic Value

When using the framework in Exhibit 15.3, you must first analyze whether the target's current market value equals its stand-alone intrinsic value. We too often hear executives rationalize an acquisition by insisting the target company is "undervalued by the market." But how often does the intrinsic value of a company *really* exceed the market value?

Although market values revert to intrinsic values over longer periods, we believe that pockets of short-term opportunities can exist. Markets sometimes overreact to negative news, such as the criminal investigation of an executive or the failure of a single product in a portfolio of many strong products. In cyclical industries, assets are often undervalued at the bottom of the cycle. Managers with good information, analysis, and foresight can acquire assets when they are cheap compared with their actual economic potential. Comparing actual market valuations with intrinsic values based on a "perfect foresight" model, we found companies could more than double shareholder returns (relative to actual returns) if they acquired assets at the bottom of a cycle and sold at the top.[8] Just as informed investors may profit by timing the market, a strategic buyer may be able to acquire assets below their intrinsic value.

But since market values can deviate from intrinsic values, management must also be wary of overvaluation. Consider the stock market bubble during the late 1990s. Companies that merged with or acquired technology, media, and telecommunications companies saw their share price plummet when the market reverted to earlier levels. Overpaying when the market is inflated deserves serious consideration because M&A activity seems to rise following periods of strong market performance. If (and when) prices are artificially high, large synergies are necessary to justify an acquisition even when the target can be purchased without a premium to market value.

In our experience, opportunities to create value by buying low and selling high are rare and relatively small. To truly create value, the acquiring company must be able to increase the future cash flows of the combined entity.

Value Creation through Synergies

When acquiring another company, you will have to take actions to improve future cash flows of the combined businesses. These opportunities for improvement are called synergies. For a thorough analysis of synergies, it helps again to remember the fundamentals of value creation: An increase in value has to come from better revenue growth, higher margins, more efficient capital utilization, or a lower cost of capital.

The source of synergies depends on the strategies and capabilities of your company. If your company is the most efficient operator in its industry, synergies will likely come from improving the target's return on invested capital. Similarly, if your strategy is to consolidate a lot of smaller businesses in a niche, you will reduce cost—most likely in purchasing, sales, and administration—and perhaps reduce the industry capacity overall, increasing the capital efficiency. In these cases, revenue synergies will play a minor role.

Conversely, if your company's distribution network is unparalleled, you can create value by purchasing a smaller company with a superior product yet limited distribution capabilities. Many large pharmaceutical companies purchase small, single-product drug companies that have a potential block-

---

[8] T. Koller and M. de Heer, "Valuing Cyclical Companies," *The McKinsey Quarterly*, 2 (2000): 62–69.

buster product but lack access to the available product markets. Based on its superior distribution network, the larger company will not only increase total absolute sales (by accessing untapped markets), but also speed up penetration in current markets.

Paying Dearly to Capture Synergies

To gain control of the target, the acquirer must pay the target's shareholders a premium over the current market value (known as the control premium). Although premiums can vary widely, the average control premiums have been fairly stable, near 30 percent of the preannouncement price of the target's equity. For targets pursued by multiple acquirers, the premium rises dramatically.

In many cases, the required premium meets (or exceeds) the level of captured synergies. Academic theory points to several reasons why buyers pay such high prices:

- *The winner's curse:* If several companies evaluate a given target, and all have roughly the same synergies available to them, the one who most overestimates potential synergies will offer the highest price. Since the offer price is based on overestimation, and not value creation, the "winner" overpays.[9]

- *The free-rider problem:* When an acquirer cannot easily "squeeze out" minority shareholders after a takeover, shareholders who choose not to tender will receive ownership in the newly combined business. If the gross acquired value exceeds the purchase price plus a premium, these shareholders will receive a higher value than those who tendered at the offer price. Since target shareholders prefer to "free ride" on the acquirer's synergies rather than tender at the offer price, nobody has an incentive to tender. To convince target shareholders to sell, all value creation must be paid to the target's shareholders.[10]

- *Hubris:* The acquirer's management overestimates its ability to generate and capture synergies.[11]

Premiums for private deals tend to be smaller, although comprehensive evidence is difficult to collect due to the lack of publicly available data. In many private deals, the seller is a corporation that wants to divest a business unit. Since the majority shareholder controls the tender decision, these deals are not subject to the free-rider problem. Also, private acquisitions

[9] K. Rock, "Why New Issues Are Underpriced," *Journal of Financial Economics,* 15 (1986): 187–212.
[10] S. J. Grossman and O. Hart, "Takeover Bids, the Free-Rider Problem, and the Theory of the Corporation," *Bell Journal of Economics,* 11 (1980): 42–64.
[11] R. Roll, "The Hubris Hypothesis of Corporate Takeovers," *Journal of Business,* 59 (1986): 197–216.

often stem from the seller's desire to get out, rather than the buyer's desire for a purchase.

In general, an acquirer will almost always pay a premium over the price at which the company is traded in the market. That means management must properly identify, estimate, and capture potential synergies.

ESTIMATING AND CAPTURING SYNERGIES

History teaches us that the word *synergy* represents either the pipe dreams of management or the hard-nosed rationale for a deal. Sometimes it is a little of both. Consider the following example: A large health services company paid several billion dollars for a profitable company in a related industry segment. For the company to create value on the acquisition, the target's after-tax earnings would have to more than double, from the current level of $225 million to approximately $500 million. But how would this happen? Was there enough extra revenue growth or incremental cost savings to make this happen?

In practice, the acquirer was unable to make improvements of this magnitude, so the acquisition resulted in the destruction of significant shareholder value. During the years following the acquisition, the acquirer's stock price consistently fell, even while the market rose. For this company, the estimation of deal benefits became disconnected from reality. Too often, a visionary CEO's idea of an industry-transforming deal collides with the reality of day-to-day business.

In this section, we explain the following elements of synergy estimation:

- Process for estimating cost and revenue synergies
- Level of accuracy to expect from synergy estimates
- Cost and timing of implementation
- Top-down approach to checking your synergies
- Alternative deal structures to consider

Estimating Cost Synergies

Too often, managers estimate cost synergies by simply calculating the difference in financial performance between the bidder and target. Having an EBITA margin 200 basis points higher than the target, however, will not necessarily translate into better performance. So how should you go about estimating cost synergies?

There are two parts to estimating and capturing synergies. First, estimate synergies using an *outside-in* approach based on publicly available data

Exhibit 15.4 Sample Framework for Estimating Cost Synergies

	Example synergies
Research and development	• Stopping redundant projects • Eliminating overlap in research personnel • Developing new products through transferred technology
Procurement	• Pooled purchasing (higher volume) • Standardizing products
Manufacturing	• Eliminating overcapacity • Transferring best operating practices
Sales and marketing	• Cross-selling of products • Using common channels • Transferring of best practices • Lowering combined marketing budget
Distribution	• Consolidating warehouses and truck routes
Administration	• Exploiting economies of scale in finance/accounting and other back office functions • Consolidating strategy and leadership functions

and data provided by the target's management team (through a due diligence request). Second, after the deal is signed, start a *bottom-up* process together with representatives from both companies to define the actions needed to capture the synergies. It is helpful to use the company's business system as a guide for structuring the work. Exhibit 15.4 shows a generic business system as an example, identifying synergies related to research and development, procurement, manufacturing, sales and marketing, distribution, and administration. The analysis should be structured using the following four steps:

1. Develop an industry-specific business system.

2. Develop a baseline for costs as if the two companies remained independent. Make sure the baseline costs are consistent with the intrinsic valuations.

3. Estimate the synergies for each cost category based on the expertise of experienced line managers.

4. Compare aggregate improvements with margin and capital efficiency benchmarks to judge whether the estimates are realistic given industry economics.

An insightful business system will fulfill three criteria. First, it assigns every cost item of the target and each cost-saving idea to one (and only one) segment of the business system. This will assure that you examine the entire cost structure of the target without double-counting cost savings. Second, if you believe there will be cost savings in the bidder's organization, you must be able to assign these savings to the appropriate segments in the business system. Last, the business system should be designed such that each segment has sufficient detail. The analysis will not provide much insight if 90 percent of the cost synergies are labeled "Administration." In this case, you should disaggregate the system further into organizational units such as finance, accounting, treasury, and investor relations.

Once the business system is completed, forecast baseline costs for both the acquirer and target. The base level of costs equals the costs as if both companies had continued as stand-alone entities. Only by developing a solid forecast of expected costs will you be able to distinguish real synergies from stand-alone improvements.

For an accurate estimate of potential cost savings (beyond the expected baseline cost development), explicitly tie the financial savings to operational activities in the business. What is the equivalent headcount reduction of the SG&A cost synergy? What is the resulting revenue per headcount? How much will distribution costs fall when trucks are fully loaded, rather than partially loaded? Are revenues sufficient to guarantee fully loaded trucks? And so on.

When tying cost savings to operational drivers, involve experienced line managers in the process. An integrated team that includes both financial analysts and experienced line managers is more likely than a pure finance team to be accurate. In addition, experienced line managers will often already know details about the target. If so, you will generate insights on capacity, quality issues, and unit sales not easily found in the public domain.

Consider one acquisition, where the head of operations took the lead in estimating the savings from rationalizing manufacturing capacity, distribution networks, and suppliers.[12] His in-depth knowledge about the unusual manufacturing requirements for a key product line and looming investment needs at the target's main plant substantially improved synergy estimates. In addition, this manager conducted a due diligence interview with the target's head of operations, learning the target did not have an enterprise resource planning (ERP) system. Each of these facts improved negotiations and deal structuring (e.g., permitting management to promise that the target's primary European location would be retained while maintaining flexibility at the target's primary U.S. facility). Moreover, involving the operations manager ensured that the company was prepared to act quickly and decisively to capture synergies following the deal's closure.

---

[12] This and other examples can also be found in S. A. Christofferson, R. S. McNish, and D. L. Sias, "Where Mergers Go Wrong," *McKinsey Quarterly*, 2 (2004): 93–99.

After you complete the synergy assessment, always compare the aggregate results for the combined companies with industry benchmarks for operating margins and capital efficiency. Ask whether the resulting ROIC and growth projections make sense given the overall expected economics of the industry. Only a fully developed integrated income statement and balance sheet will ensure that synergy estimates are in line with economic reality.

To illustrate the detail required in estimating synergies, Exhibit 15.5 presents the result of an outside-in synergy estimate for a merger in the automotive industry. Overall, the acquirer estimated that the combined entity could reduce total costs by about 10 percent. However, the relative savings varied widely by business system category. For example, although procurement costs are the single largest cost for automotive manufacturers, most companies already have the necessary size to negotiate favorable contracts. Therefore, savings from procurement were estimated at only 5 percent. In contrast, research and development reductions were estimated at 33 percent, as the two companies consolidated new-product development, paring down the number of expected offerings. This reduction also had a follow-on effect in manufacturing, as product designs would move toward a common platform, lowering overall manufacturing costs. Finally, while sales and distribution expenses could be lowered, management decided to preserve the combined company's marketing budget.

Exhibit 15.5 Automotive Merger: Estimating Cost Synergies

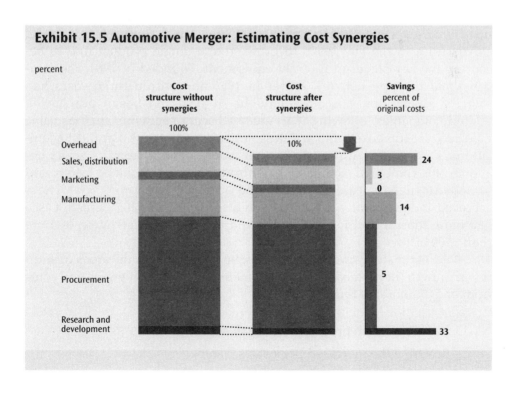

Estimating Revenue Synergies

Although it is tempting to assume revenues for the newly combined company will equal stand-alone sales plus new cross-selling, the reality is often quite different. First, the merger often disrupts existing customer relationships, leading to a loss of business. Also, smart competitors use mergers as a prime opportunity to recruit star salespeople and product specialists. Some customers may have used the acquirer and target as dual sources, so they will move part of their business to another company (to assure a minimum of two suppliers). Finally, customers who decide to stay during the merger will not be shy in asking for price and other concessions that salespeople will be eager to offer for fear of losing the business.

Make sure to develop estimates of pricing power and market share that are consistent with market growth and competitive reality. As in the process for cost synergies, calibrate the pro forma assumptions with the realities of the marketplace. One global financial company estimated that an acquisition would net €1 billion in top-line synergies within the next five years, including double-digit profit growth in the first year. However, overall market growth was limited, so the only way to achieve these goals was by increasing market share through lower prices. Actual profit growth was a mere 2 percent.

Revenue synergies often involve acquiring a specific technology or product. A large company that uses its established distribution network to bring a superior product from a small start-up to market within months instead of years can create tremendous value. Cisco relied on this model successfully in the late 1990s to grow from a single product line to becoming the key player in Internet equipment. Founded in 1984, the company sold the first network router in 1986 and within three years had sales of $28 million. Cisco went public in 1990 and began purchasing related companies, allowing it to enter adjacent segments such as cable modems, set-top boxes, and wireless network equipment. For most acquisitions, Cisco targeted companies that would benefit from its scale, enabling the combined company to introduce new products faster and to achieve higher peak sales than the acquired companies could have achieved independently. In 2004, even after the technology crash, Cisco had more than $22 billion in revenue and a market capitalization of more than $100 billion.

When estimating revenue synergies, be explicit about the areas of additional growth (beyond base case assessments). Revenue synergies will come from one (or more) of four sources:

1. Increasing each product's peak sales level
2. Reaching the increased peak sales faster

3. Extending each product's life

4. Adding new products (or features) that could not have been developed if the two companies had remained independent

Alternatively, revenue increases could come from higher prices through reduced competition. In reality, antitrust regulations are in place precisely to prevent companies from using this lever (which de facto would transfer value from customers to shareholders). Instead, any increase in price must be directly attributable to an increase in value to the customer and not to reduced choice.

Evaluating the Quality and Accuracy of Synergy Estimates

The four sources of synergies—higher margins, increased capital efficiency, higher growth, and lower cost of capital—typically have a rank order of confidence. We find that cost reduction synergies are estimated fairly well, especially when companies acquire a business with similar characteristics.

In Exhibit 15.6, we present the results of 90 acquisitions analyzed by McKinsey's Post-Merger Management practice. According to their research, 88 percent of the acquirers were able to capture at least 70 percent of the

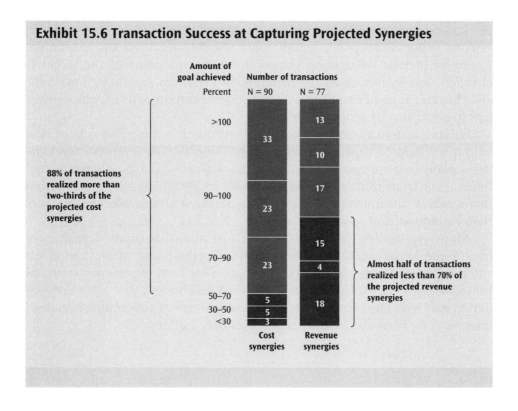

Exhibit 15.6 Transaction Success at Capturing Projected Synergies

estimated cost savings.[13] Contrast this with the revenue synergies. Just half of the acquirers realized more than 70 percent of the targeted revenue synergies. In almost one-quarter of the observed acquisitions, the acquirer realized less than 30 percent of the targeted revenue synergies.

In our experience, too many managers in low-growth businesses believe they can create value merely by purchasing a high-growth business. This is not so; to create a true synergy, the transaction has to enable one or both of the companies to grow faster than *originally expected.* In fact, many companies have difficulty even maintaining the baseline revenue growth because a portion of the combined company's customers leave due to uncertainty, demand larger discounts, or simply need a new source now that two of their suppliers have merged.

Finally, we are skeptical of synergies that stem from a perceived lower cost of capital. Combining companies may smooth earnings, but since investors can already diversify their own stock portfolios, combining companies will not lower the aggregate risk they face. Optimizing the target's capital structure to either reduce taxes or lower financial distress costs may provide some value but should not be the deciding factor.[14]

Implementation Costs, Requirements, and Timing

Make no mistake; there are *always* implementation costs to capture synergies. Some costs are obvious, such as the costs to decommission a plant and the severance that must be paid to employees. Yet subtle costs, forgotten even by experienced practitioners, must also be identified and estimated. Examples include rebranding campaigns when the name of the target is changed, integration costs for different information technology systems, and the retraining of employees. Total implementation costs may be equivalent to a full year of synergies or more.

Second, acquirers often make overly optimistic assumptions about how long it will take to capture synergies. Ensuring a stable supply while closing a plant is more complicated than the acquirer expects, disparate customer lists from multiple sources can be tricky to integrate, examining thousands of line items in the purchasing database always takes more hours than estimated, and so on.

Moreover, timing problems are not just about discounted cash flow (cash today being worth more than cash tomorrow): Bad timing can affect whether the synergies are captured at all. Our own experience suggests that synergies not captured within the first full budget year after consolidation may never be captured, as the circumstances are overtaken by subsequent events. Persistent management attention matters.

---

[13] See note 12.
[14] In Chapter 17, we discuss the valuation impact of changes in capital structure.

Neglecting the fixed lifetime of certain synergies can be equally problematic. Many savings, while real, are not perpetual. For example, one source of cost savings is to eliminate excess capacity. But if the industry is growing, the excess capacity would eventually be eliminated through natural growth. Thus, *incremental* savings from capacity reductions are accumulated only during the expected duration of excess capacity.

Checking Your Estimates with a Simple Top-Down Approach

Checking how reasonable a synergy estimate is turns out to be easier than you think. Just return to the basics: Any real synergy has to show up as an increase in expected growth, operating margin, or capital efficiency. Assume you are analyzing a potential target with a market value of $800 million. The company has revenue of $1 billion, after-tax operating profits equal to $60 million (operating margins are 10 percent and the tax rate is 40 percent), and invested capital equal to $300 million. The company's ROIC equals 20 percent, and its cost of capital is 10 percent. Assuming the company can maintain a stable return on capital and growth rate, we can use discounted cash flow and the company's market value to reverse engineer its long-term growth rate, which in this case equals 4 percent. Now assume that a 30 percent premium is required to complete the acquisition (for a total price of $1.04 billion). How large do the synergies have to be to justify this premium?

If synergies come primarily from operating improvements to the target, the simplest way to answer this question is to discount cash flows to find the necessary combinations of growth and margin that justify the price, and compare these with the base assumptions.[15] The left side of Exhibit 15.7 on page 454 shows the growth and margin combinations implied by the current valuation and the acquisition price under consideration. You can already see that a 30 percent premium requires significant improvements in margins and/or growth over the base case.

The right side of Exhibit 15.7 quantifies the required improvements in growth and operating margins (both analyses keep the capital intensity constant for simplicity). Each point on the line represents one combination of growth and margin improvement of the target that justifies paying a 30 percent premium. If synergies come entirely from margin improvements, operating margins must increase by 2.4 percentage points to justify the premium. Assuming a 10 percent operating margin in the base case, getting the value of the premium back therefore requires nearly a 25 percent improvement in operating profit of the target in perpetuity. Alternatively, if all synergies are revenue synergies, growth has to increase by about 1.9 percent perpetually.

---

[15] This approach can be adapted if synergies show up in the acquirer's organization as well.

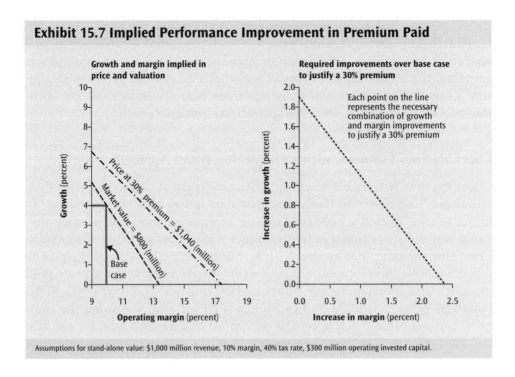

Exhibit 15.7 Implied Performance Improvement in Premium Paid

Assumptions for stand-alone value: $1,000 million revenue, 10% margin, 40% tax rate, $300 million operating invested capital.

Alternatives to Acquisition

Always question whether a full acquisition is required to capture the bulk of the synergies. Perhaps assets can be combined in a joint venture, or the two companies might enter into a marketing and distribution alliance.

Joint ventures differ from acquisitions in several ways. First, their creation does not usually require a takeover premium. Second, joint ventures can focus on individual parts of the business system—the parts where synergies will be greatest. Third, joint ventures can be renegotiated or even dissolved after a period of time. While the potential reward of a joint venture might be lower, the risks can be lower as well.

Alliances and joint ventures have their downside. The legal arrangements for joint ventures and alliances tend to be more complicated than for an acquisition, since they need to consider items such as governance, dispute resolution, and exit strategies.

The bottom line: think before you buy. Even if synergies in an alliance or joint venture are lower than in an outright purchase, the lack of a sizable premium and ability to unwind the position could make these alternatives attractive. And do not forget to look inside your organization. Could your company build the target's business internally? Maybe there is a way to create the same value without the risk of a large transaction.

HOW TO PAY: CASH VERSUS STOCK

Should you pay in cash or shares? Empirical evidence shows that, on average, an acquirer's stock returns surrounding the acquisition announcement are higher when the acquirer offers cash than when it offers shares. We are hesitant, however, to draw a conclusion solely based on aggregate statistics—after all, even companies that offer cash can pay too much.

Assuming that your company is not capital constrained, the real issue is whether the risks and rewards of the deal should be shared with the target's shareholders. When paying in cash, the acquirer's shareholders carry the entire risk of capturing synergies and paying too much. If you exchange shares, the target's shareholders assume a portion of the risk.

Exhibit 15.8 outlines the impact on value of paying in cash versus shares for a hypothetical transaction. Assume that the acquirer and the target have a market capitalization of $1 billion and $500 million, respectively. The acquirer pays a 30 percent premium for a total price of $650 million. Estimated DCF values after the transaction are calculated under two scenarios: (1) synergies are $50 million less than the premium paid and (2) synergies are $50 million higher. (To simplify, we assume that market value equals intrinsic value for both the target and the acquirer.) If the payment is entirely

Exhibit 15.8 Paying with Stock Means Sharing the Risk and Rewards

Value to shareholders after a transaction, $ million

Fair market value before the deal
- Acquirer: 1,000
- Target: 500
- **Price paid** 650
- (30% premium)

		Downside scenario Synergies = 100	Upside scenario Synergies = 200
Consideration in cash	Acquirer shareholders	950	1,050
	Target shareholders	650	650
	Acquirer value creation (destruction)	(50)	50
Consideration in stock	Acquirer shareholders	970	1,030
	Target shareholders	630	670
	Acquirer value creation (destruction)	(30)	30

cash, the target's shareholders get $650 million, regardless of whether the synergies are high enough to justify the premium. These shareholders do not share in the implementation risk. The acquirer's shareholders see the value of their stake increase by $50 million in the upside case and decrease by the same amount in the downside case. They carry the full risk.

Next, consider a transaction in which shares are exchanged. The target's shareholders participate in the implementation risk by virtue of being shareholders in the new combined entity.[16] In the upside case, their payout from the acquisition increases as synergies increase: They receive $670 million in value as opposed to $650 million. Effectively, even more value has been transferred from the acquirer's shareholders to the target's shareholders. The acquirer's shareholders are willing to allow this transfer because they are protected if implementation goes poorly. If the deal destroys value, the target's shareholders now get less than before—albeit still at a nice premium, since their portion of the combined company is worth $630 million, compared with the $500 million market value before the deal.

From this perspective, two key issues should influence your choice of payment:

1. Whether you think the target and/or your company is overvalued or undervalued. In a bubble scenario, you will be more inclined to pay in shares, as everybody will share the burden of the market correction. In such a scenario, develop a perspective on relative overvaluation of the two businesses. If you believe your shares are more overvalued than the target's, they are valuable in their own right as transaction currency.[17]

2. How confident you are in the overall value creation of the deal. The more confident you are in the value creation, the more you should be inclined to pay in cash.

Along with risk sharing, consider the optimal capital structure. Can your company raise enough cash through a debt offering to pay for the target entirely in cash? Overextending credit lines to acquire a company can devastate the borrower. One company, an automotive supplier, paid cash for a string of acquisitions. Synergies did not materialize as originally expected (partially for lack of rigorous execution), and the company ended up with a debt burden that it could not bear. In the end, the company was forced to restructure its obligations in bankruptcy.

---

[16] Target shareholders with small stakes can sell their shares in the public market to avoid implementation risk. Influential shareholders with large stakes, such as company founders and senior executives, will often agree not to sell shares for a specified period. In this case, they share the risk of implementation.

[17] The signaling effect of a share consideration is similar to that of share issuance. The capital markets will use this new information (that the shares might be overvalued) when pricing the shares.

If the capital structure of the combined entity cannot take the debt from the original acquisition, you need to consider paying partially or fully in shares, regardless of desired risk sharing.

FOCUS ON VALUE CREATION, NOT ACCOUNTING

Many managers focus on the accretion and dilution of earnings, instead of value creation. They do so despite numerous studies showing that market valuation does not depend on an acquisition's accounting treatment, but on the estimated value creation from the deal. Therefore, a focus on accounting measures is dangerous and can easily lead to poor decisions, as described in Chapter 4.

By 2005, both International Financial Reporting Standards (IFRS) and U.S. Generally Accepted Accounting Principles (U.S. GAAP) eliminated amortization of goodwill. This change means earnings dilution in acquisitions with goodwill is now smaller than under the old accounting rules. Consequently, most acquisitions paid with cash will now be accretive, since a major source of dilution has vanished. In the case of share deals, the deal is accretive if the acquirer's price-to-earnings ratio is higher than the target's.

The new rule creates a new danger zone: acquisitions that are accretive but value destroying. Consider the hypothetical deal in Exhibit 15.9. You are evaluating the purchase of a company currently priced in the market at $400 million for $500 million in cash. Your company, the acquirer, is worth $1.6 billion and has a net income of $80 million. For simplicity, assume there are no synergies from the deal. You decide to finance this deal by raising debt at

Exhibit 15.9 EPS Accretion with Value Destruction

Assumptions	Acquirer	Target
Net income ($ million)	80.0	30.0
Shares outstanding (million)	40.0	10.0
EPS ($)	2.0	3.0
Preannouncement share price ($)	40.0	40.0
P/E ($ per share)	20.0	13.3
Market value ($ million)	1,600.0	400.0
Price paid ($ million)		500.0

Impact on EPS	Cash deal	Stock deal
Net income from acquirer ($ million)	80.0	80.0
Net income from target ($ million)	30.0	30.0
Additional interest[1] ($ million)	(19.5)	0.0
Net income after acquisition ($ million)	90.5	110.0
Original shares (million)	40.0	40.0
New shares (million)	0.0	12.5
Number of shares (million)	40.0	52.5
EPS before acquisition ($)	2.0	2.0
EPS accretion ($)	0.3	0.1
EPS after acquisition ($)	2.3	2.1

[1]Pre-tax cost of debt at 6 percent, tax rate of 35 percent.

a pretax interest rate of 6 percent. This deal destroys value: You pay $100 million over fair value (remember, no synergies). Even so, next year's earnings and EPS actually increase because the after-tax earnings from the acquired company ($30 million) exceed the after-tax interest required for the new debt ($19.5 million). But how can a deal increase earnings yet destroy value? The answer is simple. The acquirer is borrowing 100 percent of the deal value using its existing asset base as collateral. In actuality, the acquired business could not sustain this level of debt on a stand-alone basis. And since the acquirer puts an increased debt burden on the existing shareholders without properly compensating them for the additional risk, value is destroyed. Only when the ROIC is greater than the target's stand-alone cost of capital are shareholders appropriately compensated. In our hypothetical deal, the investment is $500 million, and the after-tax profit is $30 million—a mere 6 percent return on invested capital. While this is above the after-tax cost of financing the debt of 3.9 percent, it is below the appropriate cost of capital.

Now suppose the same target is acquired through an exchange of shares. The acquirer would need to issue 12.5 million new shares to provide a 25 percent acquisition premium to the target company's shareholders.[18] After the deal, the combined company would have 52.5 million shares outstanding and earnings of $110 million. The earnings per share for the new company rises to $2.10, so the deal is again accretive without any underlying value creation. The new EPS is merely the weighted average of the individual companies' EPS, so the increase is a result of mathematics and not indicative of value creation.

Financial markets understand the priority of value creation over accounting results. In a study of 117 transactions larger than $3 billion that took place in the United States during 1999 and 2000, we found that earnings accretion or dilution resulting from the deal was not a factor in the market's reaction (Exhibit 15.10). Regardless of whether the expected EPS was greater, smaller, or the same two years after the deal, about 41 percent of the acquirers saw a positive market reaction. Results were fairly robust for both year 1 and year 2 impact on earnings per share, across different time periods, and for both risk-adjusted return and raw return. Also, companies that used purchase accounting (which creates goodwill) were just as likely to see significant positive market returns as companies that used pooling accounting (which avoids goodwill but is now disallowed under U.S. GAAP and IFRS).

---

[18] The exchange ratio in this hypothetical deal is 1.25 shares of the acquiring company for one share of the target company. We assume that the capital market does not penalize the acquirer and the exchange ratio can be set in relation to the preannouncement share price plus the 25 percent acquisition premium.

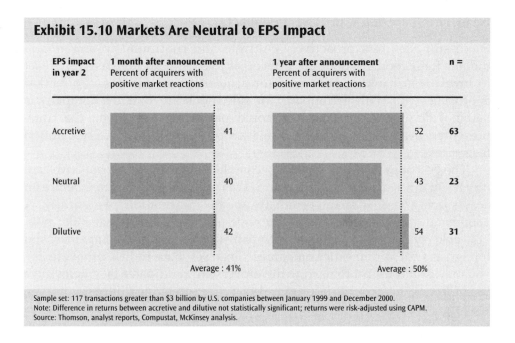

Exhibit 15.10 Markets Are Neutral to EPS Impact

EPS impact in year 2	1 month after announcement Percent of acquirers with positive market reactions	1 year after announcement Percent of acquirers with positive market reactions	n =
Accretive	41	52	63
Neutral	40	43	23
Dilutive	42	54	31
	Average : 41%	Average : 50%	

Sample set: 117 transactions greater than $3 billion by U.S. companies between January 1999 and December 2000.
Note: Difference in returns between accretive and dilutive not statistically significant; returns were risk-adjusted using CAPM.
Source: Thomson, analyst reports, Compustat, McKinsey analysis.

HOW TO BE A SUCCESSFUL ACQUIRER

Disciplined acquirers can extract value from mergers and acquisitions. To become a successful acquirer and create value for the shareholders, you must:

- Earn the right to acquire by having a strong core business.
- Consider only targets for which you can improve future free cash flow.
- Excel in estimating overall value creation.
- Maintain discipline during negotiation.
- Rigorously plan and execute the integration.

Earn the Right to Grow through M&A

Are you strong enough to acquire another company? Before considering a deal, reflect on whether your company's operating and financial performance (as measured by competitive benchmarking) makes it a superior competitor.

Time and again, we see transactions in which a weak player tries to swallow another weak player in the hope of creating a stronger force in the market. Although some deals might realize these hopes, studies have shown that, by and large, you have to be a strong player to create value from M&A. Remember the proverb: Two dogs do not make a lion.

Focus on Where You Can Have an Impact

Successful acquirers proactively cultivate and continuously screen candidates for a good strategic fit. Conversely, you should not passively react to investment banking proposals for acquisition candidates. If a banker approaches you with a company for sale, odds are that the company is being widely shopped, and you could pay top dollar given the time-pressured evaluation and due diligence process—hardly a prescription for success.

The best approach is to develop a complete database on prospective candidates in areas of strategic interest. Since it may be several years before an acquisition arises, it is important to update information periodically. A good candidate database will cast a wide net. Make sure to consider publicly held companies, divisions of companies, privately held companies, and foreign as well as domestic companies. Once you have built a complete list, you may find it useful to narrow the universe of candidates by employing a list of knock-out criteria (a process known as screening). Targets that are too large, too small, or contain too many unrelated divisions can be eliminated. A key set of criteria should reflect the value-creating mechanism you envision. If your company is best in class in operations, consider buying underperforming companies that you could turn around. If you have a unique sales channel, search for companies with great products but a sales force that requires better management.

Consider General Electric, which acquired a continuous stream of companies in seemingly low-tech areas over the past two decades. Throughout this growth period, the company's return on invested capital (excluding goodwill) in the industrial businesses increased from less than 20 percent to well over 50 percent. Excluding the growth from acquisition, GE's internal growth mirrored that of the U.S. GDP. The company's strategy for value creation is clear: Find businesses where GE can improve operations to world class.

A clear understanding of how you plan to increase value enough to make the acquisition worthwhile will also help you succeed in the next step: estimating the deal's value.

Properly Estimate Synergies

Many companies destroy value during the acquisition process because they are overly optimistic about the potential synergies. To develop a good estimate of the value from a deal, be vigilant in applying the guidelines we outlined earlier: Compare your estimates with outside benchmarks, back out required synergies to justify premiums, and do not underestimate implementation cost and timing issues.

Be a Disciplined Negotiator

Even when synergies are properly estimated, acquirers too often bid up the price beyond the limits of realistic synergies and industry economics. It is all too easy to find a benchmark that justifies a higher price or to bargain away important nonprice terms that restrict the acquirer's ability to achieve potential synergies. Remember the winner's curse: Your competitors either dropped out or failed to bid because they could not justify the price. Make sure to understand why your company is still in the race.

At a minimum, you need to quantify all deal terms that have any influence on potential value creation. A seller might insist on guaranteed employment levels at the hometown manufacturing plant or require lucrative contracts for key employees. A buyer, in the heat of negotiation, might agree to guarantee service levels for products that the synergy team assumed would be discontinued. Or simply, the premium discussed around the table creeps up over the course of the negotiation. On-the-fly changes can significantly affect value creation for shareholders, and executives should keep track of the value creation framework diligently as negotiations progress.

It is vitally important that the negotiation team and the financial team act as one. The value creation framework should be updated daily, and changes should be well documented. Quantify important items that will enable the lead negotiator to trade one item versus another. The financial team should be able to scrutinize draft agreements to flag issues that are at odds with the initial assumptions about sources of synergies.

Plan and Control the Integration

Although post-merger management is beyond the scope of this book, the following three themes should guide you through the post-merger integration: Start early, put a strong team in place, and track implementation using both financial and nonfinancial (operating) benchmarks.

Start the integration process early—before announcement   In a recent study, McKinsey's Post-Merger Management practice found a direct correlation between the speed of execution and the ability to capture estimated synergies. Experience shows that synergies not captured quickly may never be captured. We recommend starting implementation planning in parallel with the valuation and negotiation process. At the time of announcement, you should have a clear picture of who will run the integration team, the merged company's new organizational structure, and ideally who should fill the new company's key positions.

Put a strong integration team in charge   The manager of the integration team should *not* be a poor performer looking to leave the company. Quite the contrary, he or she should be a strong performer, and the assignment should hold the promise of a continued fast-track career in the combined entity. The team supporting the integration manager should be equally strong and have good prospects for long-term advancement.

Use nonfinancial benchmarks in tracking implementation Throughout the implementation phase, from the bottom-up development of an action plan to dissolution of the integration team, the nonfinancial benchmarks that you developed to set synergy targets will be critical to track success. Remember to drill down to significant detail, such as headcount targets by functional group. A fairly complex database is often necessary to track implementation success and monitor the implementation status of individual action items. Ensure you have adequate resources for this task.

SUMMARY

Corporate valuation plays a central role during the merger and acquisition process. A well-done valuation keeps the potential for success in perspective and attaches hard numbers to sometimes vague or smoky ideas. Accounting measures, strategic visions, and gut feelings are of little guidance in today's ultracompetitive markets.

The simple framework of market value, intrinsic value, synergies, and required premiums puts value creation in the proper perspective. You will need to model the individual entities, the synergies, and the combined entity down to the level of free cash flow. The reward for this hard work is a clear view of whether the acquisition creates value for your shareholders.

Finally, do not forget that you must control the process. Find your own targets, starting with a self-analysis that identifies your abilities to create value. You might even discover that you must first improve your own organization before you earn the right to buy and operate another company. Decide on your maximum price, and stick to it as part of a carefully planned negotiation strategy. After you complete the transaction, continue to manage the integration process carefully, moving as quickly as possible to capture the synergies that may quickly disappear.

REVIEW QUESTIONS

1. What are the principal lessons to be learned from the analysis of M&A activity at the announcement of a change?

2. Identify three characteristics that differentiate between value creating and value destroying transactions. Should academic evidence

sway an executive from engaging in a merger or acquisition transaction? Explain.

3. Define *organic growth*. How does organic growth differ from growth via merger and acquisition?

4. Define *synergy*. Describe how synergies might enhance a corporation's value.

5. Exhibit 15.4 provides a generic business system structure useful for estimating the value of synergies related to an acquisition or merger. The construction of a business system structure unique to and useful for a specific corporation must fulfill three fundamental criteria. Identify the criteria and explain their importance.

6. Identify five characteristics that should lead to successful corporate value creation through acquisition and merger activity.

7. Outline the immediate actions management must take when in a merger integration. Relate these actions to specific sources of value change.

8. You are trying to decide between paying for an acquisition in cash or with shares of common stock. What factors should you consider in selecting your choice of payment?

9. You have just completed a merger with the one firm that can possibly salvage your R&D efforts for remaining competitive. Your consultants remind you that most firms do not realize their expectations for value-creating growth. Outline several steps to ensure post-merger integration.

10. Why you should consider a joint venture as opposed to a merger or acquisition?

16

Creating Value
through Divestitures

As the story of EG Corp. in Chapter 2 illustrated, any value creation program should include periodically and systematically cleaning out your portfolio of businesses. But the the role divestitures should play in value creation and the role they typically play in the modern corporation are often distinctly different.

Divestitures, like mergers and acquisitions, tend to occur in waves. In the decade following the conglomerate excesses of the 1960s and 1970s, many companies refocused their portfolios. These divestitures were generally sales to other companies or private buyout firms. During the 1990s, another wave included many more transactions involving public ownership, such as spin-offs, carve-outs, and tracking stocks (see Exhibit 16.1 on p. 466).

Evidence shows that divestitures create value for corporations, both in the short term, around their announcement, and in the long term. Furthermore, companies employing a balanced portfolio approach of both acquisitions and divestitures have outperformed companies that rarely divested. Despite their potential, divestitures usually occur as a reaction to pressure from outside the corporation, rather than as a proactive and systematic divestiture program. Executives seem to shy away from divestitures and usually delay them too long. In their view, portfolio expansion is a clearer sign of success—and easier to manage—than the sale of part of the business

Special thanks to André Annema for coauthoring this chapter, and to Lee Dranikoff and Antoon Schneider, whose work on divestitures forms a core part of this chapter.

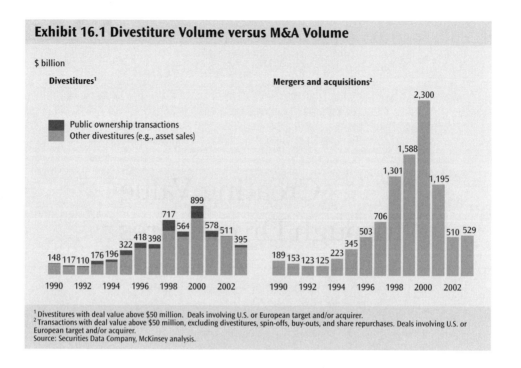

Exhibit 16.1 Divestiture Volume versus M&A Volume

$ billion

Divestitures[1]

■ Public ownership transactions
■ Other divestitures (e.g., asset sales)

Mergers and acquisitions[2]

[1] Divestitures with deal value above $50 million. Deals involving U.S. or European target and/or acquirer.
[2] Transactions with deal value above $50 million, excluding divestitures, spin-offs, buy-outs, and share repurchases. Deals involving U.S. or European target and/or acquirer.
Source: Securities Data Company, McKinsey analysis.

portfolio, especially of profitable businesses. Developing an active portfolio approach requires many companies to adopt a novel set of values in which all businesses will most likely be considered for divestiture at some point in their life cycle.

In this chapter, we apply an active portfolio approach to decisions about divestitures. We begin by reviewing the evidence that divestitures can create value for a corporation. Then we answer three basic questions:

1. Why does an active approach to divestitures create value?
2. What is an effective approach to making decisions about divestitures?
3. How should management choose the specific transaction type for a divestiture?

VALUE CREATION FROM DIVESTITURES

Divestitures create value for corporations, both in the short term and over the long term. Executives should focus on the potential for value creation and not refrain from divesting assets out of concern for issues related to size or earnings dilution.

Exhibit 16.2 Market-Adjusted Announcement Returns of Divestitures[1]

	All	Spin-offs	Carve-outs	Asset sales
Mean	3.0%	4.5%	2.3%	2.6%
Median	1.8%	3.6%	0.9%	1.6%
Number of transactions	370	106	125	139

[1]Cumulative abnormal returns measured from one day before to one day after announcement.
Source: J. H. Mulherin and A. L. Boone, "Comparing Acquisitions and Divestitures," *Journal of Corporate Finance*, Number 6 (2000): 117–139.

Academic research provides abundant evidence for divestitures' potential to create value.[1] A study of 370 private and public companies[2] found significant positive excess returns around the announcement of different types of divestitures (see Exhibit 16.2). Most of the companies the researchers studied were reactive in their use of divestitures, waiting until they had to respond to economic, technological, or regulatory shocks. In August 2004, Agfa-Gevaert announced that it was selling its consumer film and photo labs division to focus on its more profitable activities in medical imaging and graphic arts. The increased popularity of digital cameras had caused a decline in sales of traditional rolls of film. The photo activities had been the company's original business, and according to the CEO, "divesting them was not an easy decision, but with changing market conditions you have to make a choice."

Most research looking at divestitures' impact on value has focused on the short term. But what about the impact over a longer term? A study of 200 large U.S. companies from 1990 to 2000 showed that companies with a passive portfolio approach—those that did not sell businesses or only sold poor businesses under pressure—underperformed companies with an active portfolio approach.[3] The best performers systematically divested as well as acquired companies (see Exhibit 16.3 on p. 468).

---

[1] See, for example, J. Miles and J. Rosenfeld, "The Effect of Voluntary Spin-Off Announcements on Shareholder Wealth," *Journal of Finance*, 38 (1983): 1597–1606; K. Schipper and A. Smith, "A Comparison of Equity Carve-Outs and Seasoned Equity Offerings: Share Price Effects and Corporate Restructuring," *Journal of Financial Economics*, 15 (1986): 153–186; K. Schipper and A. Smith, "Effects of Recontracting on Shareholder Wealth: The Case of Voluntary Spin-Offs," *Journal of Financial Economics* 12 (1983): 437–468; J. Allen and J. McConnell, "Equity Carve-Outs and Managerial Discretion," *Journal of Finance*, 53 (1998): 163–186; and R. Michaely and W. Shaw, "The Choice of Going Public: Spin-Offs vs. Carve-Outs," *Financial Management*, 24 (1995): 5–21.

[2] J. Mulherin and A. Boone, "Comparing Acquisitions and Divestitures," *Journal of Corporate Finance*, 6 (2000): 117–139.

[3] J. Brandimarte, W. Fallon, and R. McNish, "Trading the Corporate Portfolio," *McKinsey on Finance* (Fall 2001): 1–5.

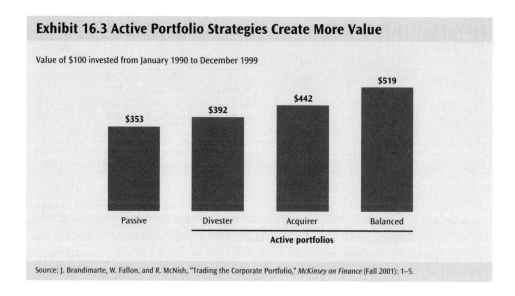

Exhibit 16.3 Active Portfolio Strategies Create More Value

Value of $100 invested from January 1990 to December 1999

			$519
		$442	
	$392		
$353			
Passive	Divester	Acquirer	Balanced
	Active portfolios		

Source: J. Brandimarte, W. Fallon, and R. McNish, "Trading the Corporate Portfolio," *McKinsey on Finance* (Fall 2001): 1–5.

General Dynamics, a U.S. defense company, provides an interesting example of an active portfolio approach that created considerable value. In the beginning of the 1990s, General Dynamics faced an unattractive industry environment. According to forecasts at that time, U.S. defense spending would be cut significantly, and General Dynamics—a broad and varied producer of weapons systems—was expected to be affected severely. When CEO William A. Anders took control in 1991, he initiated a series of divestitures. Revenues were halved in a period of two years, but shareholder returns were extraordinary: an annualized rate of 58 percent between 1991 and 1995, more than double the shareholder returns of General Dynamics' major peers. Then, beginning in 1995, Anders began acquiring companies in attractive subsectors. Over the next seven years, General Dynamics' annualized return exceeded 20 percent, again more than double the typical returns in the sector.

In contrast, most managers seem to shy away from divestitures. The research mentioned earlier on 200 U.S. companies found a clear bias against divestitures. Almost 60 percent of the companies executed two or fewer divestitures over the 10-year period. Furthermore, according to an analysis of a random subsample of divestitures, at least 75 percent of the transactions were a reactive move under some form of pressure, due to underperformance of the corporate parent, the business unit, or both. In addition, the majority of reactive deals occurred only after the business had been underperforming for many years. Because underperformance is transparent to the market, investors exert continuous pressure on the cor-

Exhibit 16.4 Earnings Dilution through Portfolio Management

	Company	Divested business unit	Use of proceeds		
			Hold cash	Debt repayment	Share buyback
Operating value	2,500	400	2,100	2,100	2,100
Cash	–		500	–	–
Enterprise value	2,500		2,600	2,100	2,100
Debt	(600)		(600)	(100)	(600)
Market value of equity	1,900		2,000	2,000	1,500
Shares outstanding	100		100	100	75
Share price	19.0		20.0	20.0	20.0
EBIT	266.8	55.0	211.8	211.8	211.8
Interest income (2%)	–	–	10.0	–	–
Interest expenses (6%)	(36.0)	–	(36 0)	(6.0)	(36.0)
Pre-tax income	230.8	55.0	185.8	205.8	175.8
Taxes (35%)	(80.8)	(19.3)	(65.0)	(72.0)	(61.5)
Net income	150.0	35.8	120.8	133.8	114.3
Earnings per share	1.50		1.21	1.34	1.52
Price-earnings ratio	12.7		16.6	15.0	13.1

poration to divest. In an analysis of voluntary asset sales,[4] companies that decided to sell assets tended to be poor performers and were highly leveraged, suggesting that most voluntary asset sales are reactive and not part of proactive divestiture programs. Other researchers[5] have confirmed this view of parent companies holding on to underperforming businesses too long.

In our experience, many managers dislike divestitures because these transactions dilute corporate earnings. However, if another party is willing to pay more for the subsidiary than the value the parent company expects to extract, the divestiture will create value and should be pursued. Although earnings per share may fall, the company's price-to-earnings (P/E) ratio will rise. The example in Exhibit 16.4 illustrates this. The company described in the left two columns receives an offer to sell a mature business for $500 million in cash. In the hands of the parent company, the value of the

[4] L. Lang, A. Poulsen, and R. Stulz, "Asset Sales, Firm Performance, and the Agency Costs of Managerial Discretion," *Journal of Financial Economics*, 37 (1994): 3–37.

[5] D. Ravenscraft and F. Scherer, "Mergers, Sell-Offs, and Economic Efficiency," (The Brookings Institution, 1987), p. 167; and M. Cho and M. Cohen, "The Economic Causes and Consequences of Corporate Divestiture," *Managerial and Decision Economics*, 18 (1997): 367–374.

business is estimated to be $400 million. Such a divestiture creates value, no matter how the parent company uses the proceeds:

- If the parent company simply holds on to the proceeds, it will dilute its earnings per share. The reason is straightforward: The interest rate earned on the cash is lower than the earnings yield (earnings relative to value) of the divested business unit. In other words, the interest income earned is lower than the forgone earnings of the business unit. This is just simple mathematics. However, the equity value increases, and the company's P/E ratio is higher than before.

- If the company uses the proceeds to repay some debt instead, earnings per share will still be lower than before the divestiture if the interest rate on the debt is lower than the earnings yield of the divested business. Dilution is less than in the scenario of holding on to the proceeds because the interest rate on the debt is usually higher than the investment yield on the cash holdings.

- The company can also use the proceeds to buy back shares. If the ratio of sales proceeds to earnings of the divested business unit is lower than the P/E ratio of the remaining business, the divestiture will dilute earnings per share after the share buyback has occurred: The relative change in earnings is less than the relative change in the number of shares outstanding. Because divested units are typically the most mature businesses in a company's portfolio, divestitures often lead to earnings dilution. But as the example shows, a divestiture followed by a share buyback can also increase earnings per share if the proceeds are high enough.

Against this background, it is perhaps not surprising that a change in corporate leadership seems to be one of the key triggers for divestitures. Among the previously mentioned 200 companies we researched, about half of their major divestitures (those reported on the front page of the *Wall Street Journal*) took place in companies where the chief executive officer had a fairly early tenure.

WHY DIVESTITURES CREATE VALUE

In short, divestitures create value when the business unit is worth more to some other owner or in some other ownership structure. Business units can be worth more in another ownership structure because the current structure may impose unique costs on the parent and/or the business unit. Some of these costs can be hidden, such as when the parent company culture is dominated by a mature business and limits innovation. In other cases the costs can be more explicit, for example when a company lacks core skills to be an effective operator in an industry. An active portfolio management approach creates value by avoiding, eliminating, or at least minimizing these costs.

Although divesting underperforming businesses avoids the direct costs of bearing the deteriorating results, divesting profitable and/or growing businesses can also benefit both the parent and the business unit. In these situations, a divestiture may create value because the subsidiary will become more competitive, due to increased freedom for tailored financing and investment decisions, improved management incentives, or better focus. Divestitures also may create value by taking advantage of information asymmetry when fully informed executives take advantage of imperfectly informed investors or financial/strategic buyers. This is a more tactical rationale and may work only in limited situations.

Because of these potential benefits, companies should regularly divest businesses—even good, healthy ones—so the corporation can grow stronger and the remaining businesses can reach their full potential. This means that divestitures could include companies at different stages of their life cycle. The divested business unit may very well be a profitable, cash-generating business or a business with relatively high growth potential. The costs of holding on to supposedly healthy businesses can in many cases far outweigh the benefits. Consider what some of these costs might be.

Costs to the Parent

Well-established, mature businesses provide a company with stability and cash flows. But this stability can be a mixed blessing, since holding on to a mature business can strap the parent with substantial costs. Quite often, these costs are hidden and may not seem to be pressing.

The hidden costs take several forms. As a business unit matures, its culture may become incompatible with the culture that the parent company wants to create, hindering the rest of the group's efforts for change. Stable units can also remove the impetus to innovate, resulting in incremental changes rather than substantial improvements. Because the mature units typically are relatively large, scarce management time is often diverted into operating a business unit that is not really part of the company's future. The relative impact of management time spent may also differ. If management time spent on new, high-growth initiatives creates relatively more value than spending that same amount of time on a lower-performing mature business, the company would benefit from divesting the mature business.

In 1999, Pactiv—a producer of specialty packaging products—sold its aluminum business, despite the business's strong cash flow. According to management, the aluminum business was using resources and management time that could have been better used elsewhere. In addition, the cyclical nature of the aluminum business made the company more difficult for investors to understand. Alternately, mismatched business units can lead to suboptimal decision-making because of conflicts of interest and cross-subsidization. During the early 1990s, Lucent—at that time a business unit of AT&T and a successful maker of telecom equipment—was selling its products to many of AT&T's competitors. To avoid conflict and ease possible customer concerns, AT&T arranged to spin off Lucent in 1996.

Costs to the Unit

A second class of costs includes those that affect the business unit. These costs relate to a poor fit between the parent company and the business unit during the unit's life cycle. The life cycle of a business consists of three different phases:

1. *Start-up:* Establishing a viable business
2. *Expansion:* Enabling growth of the business
3. *Maturity:* Driving efficiency and rationalizing industry structure

At each phase in a business unit's life cycle, the business requires a different type of parent company.

In particular, as a business moves through the phases of its life cycle, the critical skills to manage it successfully will change—from innovation-focused skills in the start-up phase to cost management skills in the maturity phase. Many corporations lack the full breadth and depth of skill and have only two or three world-class capabilities. These core capabilities tend to be relatively static over time, so the parent company's skills can become obsolete for a unit as it develops through its life cycle.

As a result, divestitures may be appropriate for a business in any of the three stages of its life cycle. Divestitures in the start-up phase could result from frequently reviewing the "bets" the corporation has in its portfolio. Divestitures in the expansion phase may be necessary for a parent lacking the right skills to push a business to its next level. Finally, divestitures in the maturing phase may be proper when the parent does not have the best skills to drive efficiency.

For example, pharmaceutical company executives face the challenge of managing two different types of business. The major pharmaceutical companies emphasize innovation. They typically have core skills in the discovery, development, and marketing of innovative drugs. As these drugs come to the market, they require a specialized sales force that interacts with medical practitioners. The products are patent protected and can be highly profitable in the case of blockbuster products with annual sales of more than $1 billion. As a patent's expiration date nears, however, generic competition usually enters the market. After expiration, prices plummet, and the pharmaceutical company loses significant market share to competitors with generic products. The changed market dynamics require a very different set

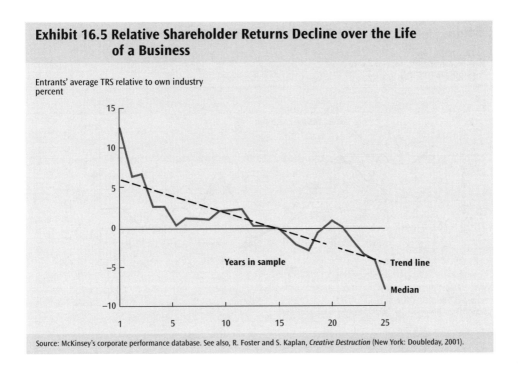

Exhibit 16.5 Relative Shareholder Returns Decline over the Life of a Business

Entrants' average TRS relative to own industry
percent

Source: McKinsey's corporate performance database. See also, R. Foster and S. Kaplan, *Creative Destruction* (New York: Doubleday, 2001).

of skills in cost-effective manufacturing and sales to maximize the value of these products. The question is whether these skills are sufficiently present in the pharmaceutical companies that hold onto their prescription drugs after the patent expires.

Depressed Exit Prices

Holding on to a business unit too long can reduce the company's shareholder returns and value. Companies that hold on to seriously underperforming business too long risk bringing down the value of the entire corporation. By the time the company is forced to conduct a fire sale of the assets, it has already destroyed substantial value and generally will receive limited proceeds from the divestiture.

As businesses become more mature and competitive challenges increase, the level of expected future value creation generally declines. Exhibit 16.5 shows this by plotting a company's total return to shareholders (TRS) relative to the TRS of the company's industry sector.[6] As the business matures, the company's returns fall lower and lower relative to its industry. Even in a growing industry, TRS can grow slowly or decline, as shown in Exhibit 16.6 on page 474, which indicates decreasing valuation levels.

[6] R. Foster and S. Kaplan, *Creative Destruction* (New York: Doubleday, 2001).

Exhibit 16.6 Shareholder Returns Can Decline Despite Ongoing Growth

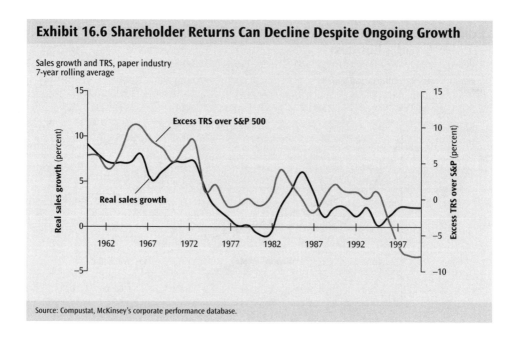

Sales growth and TRS, paper industry
7-year rolling average

Source: Compustat, McKinsey's corporate performance database.

TRS reflects the market's expectations for future performance. Relative to outsiders, managers should be in a better position to determine a business's true performance prospects. When managers detect that market valuations in an industry segment do not (yet) reflect the lower future performance potential, they have arrived at an opportune moment to divest the business.

HOW TO APPROACH DIVESTITURES

Given that a value-creating approach to divestitures may result in divesting both good and bad businesses throughout all stages of their life cycle, executives need a way to decide which businesses to divest. Obviously, divesting a good business is often not an intuitive choice. Furthermore, the selection of divestiture candidates goes beyond an assessment of the competitive position within the industry. Although this is important, portfolio decisions should also be based on whether the parent company is the right owner of a business. That is, does the parent company add value to the business?

More than Business Positioning

The classic approach to managing a business portfolio evaluates a business's competitive position within its industry, as well as the industry's overall attractiveness. Many considerations go into the evaluation, including a company's ability to compete in the industry. The ability to compete may come from access to specific resources, such as talent, or specific capabilities. Judging industry attractiveness entails a broad assessment of economic factors, including growth potential and levels of competition. The classic approach calls for divesting all businesses whose relative ability to compete and whose industry attractiveness is low, and to invest in those capable of competing vigorously in attractive industries.

Parent and Business Unit Fit

Still, the classic approach has a weakness. It assumes that synergies between different businesses are negligible and that the corporation is the best owner of all types of businesses. But keeping in mind that the corporate skills required to manage a business will differ at specific phases in its life cycle, we conclude that the portfolio management approach should also consider the fit between parent and business unit.

A more sophisticated approach to portfolio management assesses the business portfolio based on business attractiveness and whether the corporation is the natural owner of the business, as illustrated in Exhibit 16.7. This approach defines attractiveness (the horizontal axis in Exhibit 16.7) as

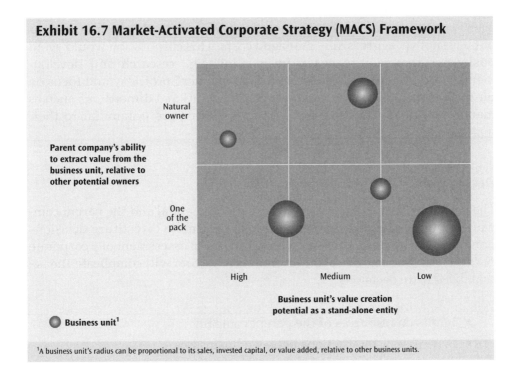

Exhibit 16.7 Market-Activated Corporate Strategy (MACS) Framework

Natural owner

Parent company's ability to extract value from the business unit, relative to other potential owners

One of the pack

High   Medium   Low

Business unit's value creation potential as a stand-alone entity

● Business unit[1]

[1]A business unit's radius can be proportional to its sales, invested capital, or value added, relative to other business units.

the business's value creation potential as a stand-alone enterprise. This measure captures both the typical dimensions of the classic approach—the industry attractiveness and the business's competitive position. Note that the ownership of the business does not affect its stand-alone value creation potential. Instead, this dimension represents the maximum value that could be obtained if the business were to operate independently. Businesses with relatively large stand-alone value creation potential should perhaps be divested anyway because other companies may better extract that value. By selling the business, the parent can capture some of that value, for example through a premium.

Being the natural owner of the business unit means a corporation has greater capabilities to extract value from the business unit than other possible owners have. Most corporations have a few distinctive competencies (e.g., operational planning, cost management, brand management). We define a core competency as a world-class skill or process that distinguishes the company from its competition, drives value creation, is sustainable and not easily imitated, and can be applied across existing and new businesses. Core competencies typically are the focus of senior management time and effort and usually are one of the defining factors of a company's culture. Such skills can focus on driving either the performance of existing businesses or the growth of existing and new businesses.

An individual company's profile of core competencies has implications for its business portfolio. A corporation with a "cost and capital manager" profile would own businesses that generate steady revenue streams but have not yet aggressively managed costs. This corporation would avoid businesses that require heavy investment (e.g., research and development). Corporations with an "operational planner" profile would focus on businesses that could compete on specific operational dimensions such as manufacturing, and would avoid operations that are unfamiliar to their managers.

Deciding on a Divestiture

The principle that a business's value-creation potential and the parent company's ability to extract that value should determine divestiture decisions provides a strong framework for making an initial assessment of a corporate portfolio. In practice, however, several other factors will complicate the actual divestiture decisions:

- Limits on resources of the parent company
- Synergies or transactions between businesses

- Pricing of the asset/business
- Legal, contractual, or regulatory barriers and transaction costs
- Liquidity of the market for the asset/business

Management time is one of the critical resources that limit a company. Even a portfolio of attractive businesses with a good fit may have to be pruned to ensure that all businesses receive the appropriate management attention. This factor was important in the earlier example of Pactiv.

Divesting a business unit from the portfolio may also affect the remaining businesses. A divestiture can eliminate synergies between businesses or change the competitive position of businesses remaining within the portfolio. Companies with a highly integrated business model—where business units share significant assets—tend to have difficulty capturing value with divestitures. Consider a bank that would like to sell a particular product line. Without the bank's customer base, the value of the product line might be limited. In that case, a divestiture of the product line may not generate any significant value.

The potential sales price of assets can also affect the decision to divest a business. If the market currently attaches more value to a business than the intrinsic value estimated by management, these conditions are favorable to a near-term divestiture. Most likely, many of the high-tech ownership restructuring transactions at the end of the 1990s were at least partly motivated by the favorable valuation levels at that time. As discussed in Chapter 4, market valuation levels are generally in line with intrinsic value potential in the long term but can deviate for periods. Executives should use their superior insight into their businesses to assess such possible value gaps with regard to divestiture.

Even though a transaction might make strategic sense, legal, contractual, or regulatory barriers may limit its feasibility. In certain regulated markets, it may be impossible to divest specific assets. Certain contractual obligations can also limit divestiture possibilities. In addition, transaction costs, including taxes, often affect transaction decisions. Asset sales may be fully taxable, whereas public ownership transactions may provide more tax-efficient structures. Furthermore, some businesses are not stand-alone entities before divestiture. Preparing a business for divestiture can require extensive legal restructuring. A new legal entity may have to be created, perhaps requiring multiple internal transactions to transfer different assets into the new legal entity. Some countries tax capital gains on such internal transactions.

The decision to divest a business will also depend on the liquidity of the market for those particular assets. A recent study concludes that liquidity is a key driver in explaining the difference in divestment behavior between companies that seem to have similar fundamental reasons to divest.[7]

DECIDING ON TRANSACTION TYPE

Once a corporation has identified businesses for divestiture, it must decide what transaction structure to use. There are different types of private and public transaction structures. Deciding on a specific transaction type depends on the availability of strategic or financial buyers, the need to raise cash, and the benefits of retaining some level of control during the first phase of the separation. Although the reason for pursuing a divestiture should be to increase the value of the corporation, a parent's urgent need for cash may lead it to choose transaction types that deliver the maximum amount of cash, rather than one that maximizes value.

In the remainder of this chapter, we provide a brief overview of different transaction types and discuss the trade-offs among alternative forms of public ownership transactions, their impact on long-term performance, and the dynamics of ownership structures over time.

Alternative Forms of Divestitures

Executives can choose from many different types of transaction structures, both private and public transactions:

Private Transactions

- *Trade sale:* sale of part or all of a business to a strategic or a financial investor
- *Joint venture:* combining part or all of a business with other industry players, other companies in the value chain, or venture capitalists

Public Transactions

- *Initial public offering:* sale of all shares of a subsidiary to new shareholders in the stock market
- *Carve-out:* sale of part of the shares in a subsidiary to new shareholders in the stock market
- *Spin-off:* distribution of all shares in a subsidiary to existing shareholders of the parent company

---

[7] F. Schlingemann, R. Stulz, and R. Walkling, "Divestitures and the Liquidity of the Market for Corporate Assets," *Journal of Financial Economics*, 64 (2002): 117–144.

- *Split-off:* an offer to existing shareholders of the parent company to exchange their shares in the parent company for shares in the subsidiary
- *Tracking stock:* separate class of parent shares that is distributed to existing shareholders of the parent company through a spin-off or sold to new shareholders through a carve-out

In most cases, companies should choose a private transaction if they can identify other parties that are better owners of the business. Private transactions allow the company to sell the business unit at a premium and capture value immediately. In most situations, the counterparties will be strategic buyers, that is, other industry players. However, the company should also consider financial buyers. Fiscal implications may affect this decision in practice, because asset sales for cash typically generate a taxable profit and therefore may turn out to be less favorable.

If the company cannot identify better owners, it will have to choose a public restructuring alternative. All the public transactions in the preceding list involve the creation of a new public security, but not all of them actually result in cash proceeds. Full IPOs and carve-outs result in cash proceeds as securities are sold to new shareholders. In the other public transactions, new securities are offered to existing shareholders, sometimes in exchange for other existing shares (split-offs). When industry consolidation is expected, a public transaction may be more beneficial for the shareholders in the long term if the newly floated business unit would drive the consolidation or would be a takeover candidate. In that case, shareholders do not earn a premium from the divestiture itself, but significant value may be created for shareholders in the future.

Spin-offs The most common form of public ownership transactions is a spin-off. In this case, the parent company gives up control over the business unit by distributing the subsidiary shares to the parent shareholders. This full separation maximizes the strategic flexibility of the subsidiary, provides the greatest freedom to improve operations by sourcing from more competitive companies (instead of the former parent), and avoids conflicts of interest between the parent company and the business unit. Spin-offs are usually carried out to improve operating performance of the business units.

Many spin-offs are executed in two steps: a minority IPO (carve-out) followed by a full spin-off relatively shortly thereafter. A one-step spin-off is typically less complex and does not depend on market circumstances, as no shares need to be issued. However, a two-step spin-off has benefits as well. The minority IPO already establishes dedicated equity coverage, creates market making in the shares, and may reduce the risk of flow-back by developing an interested investor base.

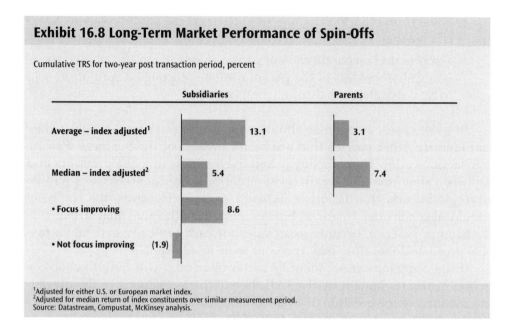

Exhibit 16.8 Long-Term Market Performance of Spin-Offs

Cumulative TRS for two-year post transaction period, percent

According to McKinsey's research on operating and capital market performance after completion of the transaction, spin-offs typically meet or exceed expectations for value creation. Analysis of parent and subsidiary performance of a sample of spin-off transactions shows that the operating margin of spin-off subsidiaries improves by one-third during the three years after completion of the transaction. Operating margins of the parent companies on average show a very modest increase. Other researchers[8] confirm the improvements in operating performance, with larger improvements for the subsidiary than for the parent company. In a later study,[9] operating improvements were significant only for focus-improving spin-offs—where the business spun off was different from the parent's core line of business.

Post-transaction shareholder returns for spin-off parents and subsidiaries are consistent with the results on operating improvements. As Exhibit 16.8 shows, market-adjusted shareholder returns during a two-year period after completion are positive for both parents and spun-off subsidiaries. However, the positive performance of the subsidiaries is driven by focus-improving spin-offs. Transactions that did not improve focus had mostly negative post-transaction returns.[10]

---

[8] P. Cusatis, J. Miles, and J. Woolridge, "Some New Evidence That Spinoffs Create Value," *Journal of Applied Corporate Finance* 7 (1994): 100–107.

[9] L. Daley, V. Mehrotra, and R. Sivakumar, "Corporate Focus and Value Creation: Evidence from Spinoffs," *Journal of Financial Economics*, 45 (1997): 257–281.

[10] Cusatis, Miles, and Woolridge (see note 8) find similar shareholder returns for parents and subsidiaries.

Carve-outs   Sometimes parent companies do not want to give up control over a business unit. The reason could be a desire to maintain some synergies between parent and subsidiary, or to shelter the subsidiary from market forces such as mergers and acquisitions. If the company does not want to give up control, it should consider a minority carve-out or possibly a tracking stock.

Carve-out subsidiaries typically have higher growth rates than their parents but do not differ much in terms of operating performance. For high-growth subsidiaries, a carve-out results in proceeds that can be used to fund this growth.

The downside of ownership restructuring where the parent retains a controlling stake in the subsidiary is the possibility of unclear governance. If the parent enforces a minimum stake to retain control, this may restrict growth and value creation by the separated business, which would destroy the benefits that the carve-out was intended to deliver. In addition, these companies risk further conflicts as the business unit's executives pursue the best interests of their own company and shareholders.

France Telecom's carve out of mobile-phone operator Orange provides an example of these conflicts. In 2001 France Telecom carved out a 14 percent stake of Orange after acquiring the business from Vodafone, which had to divest it after acquiring Mannesman. The carve-out's main objective was to raise cash to reduce France Telecom's high leverage at the time. In a consolidating industry Orange could not use its equity for acquisitions without further diluting France Telecom's stake. Using debt financing for acquisitions would have worsened France Telecom's balance sheet. Early in 2004, France Telecom reacquired the Orange shares from the market. The delisting supported the implementation of France Telecom's new integrated fixed-mobile operator strategy at a time when the rationale for a separate listing was becoming unclear. Valuations had come down, and incorporating Orange's cash flows into group structure would deliver financing and fiscal benefits.

On average, the market-adjusted long-term performance for carve-out parents and subsidiaries is negative. For a variety of reasons, however, there is significant divergence of performance among carve-out transactions. Research indicates that carve-outs from financially distressed parent companies on average show negative market-adjusted returns, whereas other carve-out companies earn positive market-adjusted returns.[11] The subsidiaries from distressed parents continue to have relatively low operating performance, indicating that they were partly contributing to the distress. Additional evidence suggests that market performance is better for focus-improving carve-out transactions.[12]

[11] J. Madura and T. Nixon, "The Long-Term Performance of Parent and Units Following Equity Carve-Outs," *Applied Financial Economics*, 12 (2002): 171–181.
[12] A. Vijh, "Long-Term Returns from Equity Carveouts," *Journal of Financial Economics*, 51 (1999): 273–308.

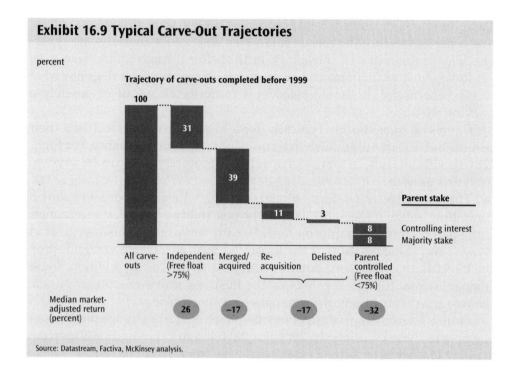

Exhibit 16.9 Typical Carve-Out Trajectories

Source: Datastream, Factiva, McKinsey analysis.

In addition, there is a clear relation between the success in the capital markets of carve-out subsidiaries and the evolution of their ownership structure. Research on a relatively small sample found that virtually all minority carve-outs were either fully sold or reacquired at a later stage.[13] Carve-out subsidiaries that were reacquired earned negative shareholder returns in the period between the first issue and parent reacquisition. In our research on more than 200 carve-outs announced before 1998, the majority of the carve-out entities did not last.[14] As shown in Exhibit 16.9, only 8 percent of the carve-out subsidiaries we analyzed remained majority-controlled by the parent. The majority of the subsidiaries were spun off further, acquired, or merged with other players. Most of these acquisitions or parent buybacks happened within a four-year period after the carve-out. During the two years after completion, shareholder returns of the carve-out entities showed a clear performance difference. Carve-outs with positive shareholder returns, when adjusted for market returns, were typically

[13] A. Klein, J. Rosenfeld, and W. Beranek, "The Two Stages of an Equity Carve-Out and the Price Response of Parent and Subsidiary Stock," *Managerial and Decision Economics,* 12 (1991): 449–460.

[14] A. Annema, W. Fallon, and M. Goedhart, "Do Carve-Outs Make Sense?" *McKinsey on Finance* (Fall 2001): 6–10.

spun off. Carve-outs with negative returns were usually acquired or bought back by the parent, suggesting that they were less successful than had been anticipated.

Recent examples of parent buybacks are France Telecom's Wanadoo and Deutsche Telekom's T-Online. Both telecom companies had previously carved out minority stakes in their Internet service providers. France Telecom floated a minority stake in Wanadoo around mid-year 2000 at €9 per share—the shares peaked around €22 in September 2000—and reacquired the minority stake in early 2004 at €8.9 per share. Deutsche Telekom floated a minority stake in T-Online in early 2000 at €27 per share—the shares peaked around €47 in May 2000—and announced an offer to buy back the shares in October 2004 at €9.0 per share. As separate companies, these Internet businesses no longer fitted with the strategy of their telecom parents to integrate Internet operations with fixed-line business to spur growth.

Carve-outs that lasted as parent-controlled companies with a free float of less than 75 percent showed significant negative returns. In our research, these carve-out subsidiaries typically had lower growth rates than other carve-outs. This underperformance may indicate that the rationale of the carve-out was flawed; the carve-outs may have happened for opportunistic reasons unrelated to value creation. The parent companies most likely did not intend to fully separate these businesses when they were carved out. The low market returns could have resulted from the subsidiary lacking the opportunity to maximize its potential under continued parent control, or the parent taking advantage of high market valuation levels at the time, without considering real ongoing benefits of full separation.

When thinking about partial ownership separation of a business unit through a carve-out, executives need to plan for full separation. Although a minority carve-out might initially shelter the unit from market forces such as acquisitions, it is very unlikely that the parent can hold on to its majority stake for long. In most situations, the separation is irreversible. The separated businesses may attract new equity financing to fund their growth or perhaps pursue acquisitions, both of which will most likely dilute the parent's stake in the carved-out business, ultimately leading to loss of control.

Tracking stock   An alternative form of public ownership restructuring is the issuance of tracking stock. Tracking stock offers a parent the advantage of maintaining control over a separated subsidiary, but often complicates corporate governance. Because there is no formal, legal separation between the subsidiary and the parent, a single board of directors needs to decide on potentially competing needs of common and tracking stock shareholders. Furthermore, both entities are liable for each other's debt, which precludes flexible capital raising. Although there may be specific tax or legal barriers for separation that would favor the use of a tracking stock alternative, the evidence for tracking stock is far from convincing. In an analysis of tracking stocks,[15] this kind of transaction appeared to destroy value in the long term. On the elimination of tracking stock, the announcement effect for the parent was positive, reflecting the market's relief that the structure had been discontinued. Furthermore, tracking stock is used far less often than carve-out and spin-off transactions, implying that this form of ownership restructuring fails to bring the benefits that executives are looking for.

SUMMARY

As businesses go through their life cycles, corporations face renewed challenges for portfolio restructuring through divestiture. This process is natural and never-ending. A divested unit may very well pursue further separations later in its lifetime, especially in dynamic industries undergoing rapid growth and technological change. A good example of these ownership dynamics is AT&T, as shown in Exhibit 16.10. After the company's original breakup in the 1980s, AT&T continued the process of ownership separation in 1996, leading to five new public companies within five years. AT&T first split off Lucent Technologies (telecom equipment and networking), which subsequently spun off Avaya (communication networks) in 2000 and executed a carve-out of Agere Systems (semiconductors) in the same year. AT&T also spun off NCR (information technology hardware and software) in 1996 and carved out AT&T Wireless in 2000.

In contrast to AT&T, most corporations divest businesses only after resisting shareholder pressure. In delaying, they risk forgoing the significant value creation potential from an active approach to divestitures. Ideally, executives should pursue an ongoing, proactive divestiture program to evaluate the corporate portfolio as its businesses evolve through their life cycles and the industry itself changes.

Senior executives should prepare the organization for this cultural shift to a more active approach. They should deliver the message that divestitures of good businesses will happen and should not be considered failures. Because divesting good businesses may be hard for managers, corporations should build forcing mechanisms into their divestiture program. For example, management could have regular dedicated exit review meetings to ensure that the topic remains on the executive agenda.

Furthermore, each business could have a "date stamp" of estimated exit. Although this may not result in a definite exit, it would require regular

---

[15] M. Billett and A. Vijh, "The Market Performance of Tracking Stocks" (working paper, Henry B. Tippie College of Business, University of Iowa, February 2001).

Exhibit 16.10 Dynamics of Ownership Restructuring

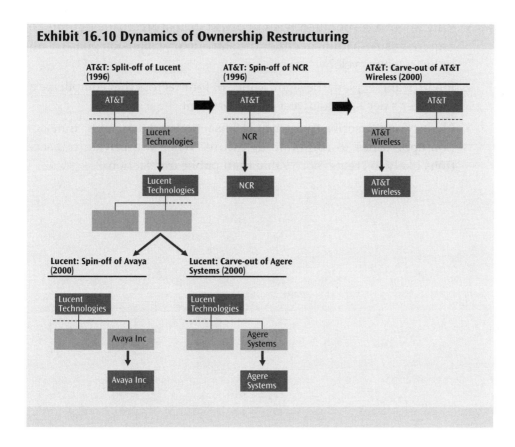

evaluations of all businesses. Other approaches could be to limit the number of businesses in the corporate portfolio or to strive for a target balance in acquisitions and divestitures. Such practices help transform divestitures from evidence of failure into shrewd strategies for building value.

REVIEW QUESTIONS

1. Many corporate managers view a change in earnings (EPS) as a signal to the capital markets. Explain under what conditions a divestiture will lead to EPS dilution or accretion if the proceeds from the divestiture are used (1) to repay debt or (2) to repurchase common shares. What does this mean for the value created by a divestiture?

2. Describe the key reasons why divesting a business can create value for shareholders, even when the business is still in the early stages of its lifecycle.

3. Why might a corporation wish to divest its mature business units to acquire business units in either the start-up or expansion phase of an industry's life cycle?

4. Identify and explain the significance of four factors that complicate a manager's decision to divest a business unit.

5. Identify and describe two private transaction and two public transaction approaches to corporate divesture. When are private transactions likely to create more value than public transactions?

17

Capital Structure

As the number of companies facing financial distress has risen over the past several years, executives have assigned ever greater importance to decisions that affect capital structure. Careful design and management of a company's capital structure do more to prevent value destruction than to boost value creation. When managers make decisions about capital structure, they usually have much more to lose than to gain in terms of value.

In this chapter, we discuss tools and frameworks that can help managers make two levels of decisions about capital structure. The first level is the strategic decision about the company's long-term target capital structure. This includes issues such as the desired level of debt financing and dividend payout ratios. The second level is more tactical and concerns the best short-term steps to handle deviations from these long-term targets. A typical tactical issue is what the company should do with any excess cash—increase dividends, repurchase shares, or hold on to the cash. Specifically, this chapter addresses the following topics:

- The impact of capital structure on value creation for shareholders
- The role of credit ratings in capital structure decisions
- The establishment of long-term capital structure targets
- The choice of specific steps to change a capital structure
- The impact on value creation for shareholders of financial engineering, such as hedging strategies or structured finance

CAPITAL STRUCTURE AND VALUE CREATION

Over the past several decades, the diversity of financing instruments has increased dramatically. Today debt comes in many different forms, including straight debt, convertible bonds, commodity-linked bonds, and other structured debt. Equity instruments include "traditional" common and preferred equity shares, employee stock options, convertible preferred stock, and more exotic forms such as tracking stocks. Still, the fundamental question in designing a company's capital structure is simply the choice between debt (which represents a fixed claim on the enterprise value) and equity (the residual claim). We can further simplify this choice to asking what the company's leverage should be, as measured in terms of debt to total enterprise value.

Value Trade-Offs in Designing Capital Structure

Although academic researchers have investigated the issue for decades, there is still no clear model for a company's optimal leverage ratio, the leverage that would create most value for shareholders.[1] But there is evidence that leverage delivers key benefits as well as giving rise to certain costs (Exhibit 17.1).

Tax savings The most obvious benefit of debt versus equity is the reduction of taxes. Interest charges for debt are tax deductible, whereas payments to shareholders as dividends and share repurchases are not. Replacing equity with debt reduces taxable income and therefore increases the value of the firm.[2] However, this tax reduction does not make full debt funding optimal. For example, more debt funding may reduce corporate taxes but could actually lead to higher taxes for investors. In many countries, investor taxes are higher on interest income than on capital gains on shares. That situation could actually make equity funding more attractive, depending on the relevant tax rates for corporations and investors.[3]

Reduction of corporate overinvestment The so-called *free-cash-flow hypothesis*[4] argues that debt can help impose investment discipline on managers, as private equity firms have known well for decades. Especially in companies with strong cash flows and low growth opportunities, managers may be tempted to loosen controls and increase corporate spending on perks or investment projects and acquisitions that boost growth at the expense of value. If share ownership is widely dispersed, it is difficult and costly for shareholders to assess when managers are engaging in such overinvestment.

---

[1] For an overview of the literature, see M. Barclay and C. Smith, "The Capital Structure Puzzle: Another Look at the Evidence," *Journal of Applied Corporate Finance*, 12(1) (1999): 8–20.

[2] For an overview, see M. Grinblatt and S. Titman, *Financial Markets and Corporate Strategy*, 2nd ed. (New York: McGraw-Hill, 2002), Chapter 14; R. Brealey and S. Myers, *Principles of Corporate Finance*, 7th ed. (New York, McGraw-Hill, 2003), Chapter 18.

[3] M. Miller, "Debt and Taxes," *Journal of Finance*, 32(2) (1977): 261–275.

[4] M. Jensen, "Agency Costs of Free Cash Flow, Corporate Finance and Takeovers," *American Economic Review*, 76(2) (1986): 323–339.

Exhibit 17.1 Capital Structure Value Trade-Offs

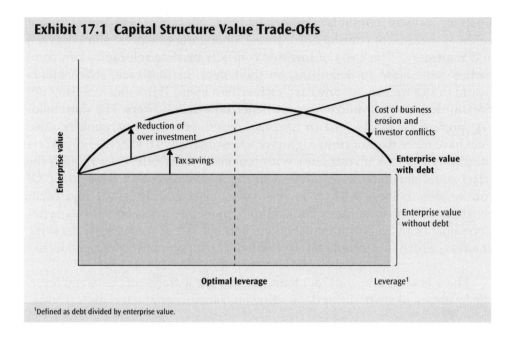

Debt curbs such managerial behavior by forcing the company to pay out free cash flow according to scheduled interest and principal obligations.

Costs of business erosion and bankruptcy   But higher levels of debt also give rise to costs. Most notably, bankruptcy costs are the legal and administrative costs of liquidating or restructuring the company for the debt holders after it has defaulted on its debt. Academic research indicates that these costs are relatively small, around 3 percent of a company's market value.[5] However, the costs of business erosion[6] are probably much higher. Highly leveraged companies are more likely to forgo investment opportunities or reduce budgets for research and development and other costs for which the payoffs are further in the future. As a result, these companies may lose significant value creation opportunities. Furthermore, as the risk of financial distress increases, companies become more likely to lose customers, employees, and suppliers. The risk of losing business is high, particularly when the products require long-term service and maintenance. A well-documented example is that of Chrysler, which faced a 40 percent reduction of its car sales amid consumer concerns over a possible bankruptcy in 1979.[7]

[5] See, for example, L. Weiss, "Bankruptcy Resolution: Direct Costs and Violation of Priority of Claims," *Journal of Financial Economics*, 27(2) (1990): 285–314.
[6] We prefer the term *business erosion* to the more often used *financial distress* because the associated costs arise very gradually and long before there may be an actual distress event, such as nonperformance on debt.
[7] See, for example, T. Opler, M. Saron, and S. Titman, "Corporate Liability Management: Designing Capital Structure to Create Shareholder Value," *Journal of Applied Corporate Finance*, 10(1) (1997): 21–32.

Costs of investor conflicts Higher leverage may cause additional loss of value as a result of conflicts of interest among debt holders, shareholders, and managers.[8] The costs of investor conflicts become relevant when companies come close to defaulting on their debt. In that case, shareholders would prefer to take out any cash rather than invest it in value-creating opportunities, which would primarily benefit the debt holders. The shareholders' preference would lead to *corporate underinvestment*. Shareholders also may have more to gain from high-risk investments with short-term payoffs than from low-risk investments with longer-term payoffs, even though the latter could generate more value—leading to so-called *asset substitution*. Of course, debt holders will try to protect themselves from these and other conflicts with shareholders. For example, they may insist on various types of covenants and monitor management actions. All of these measures come at a cost, which will ultimately be carried by the company's shareholders.

There is some empirical evidence on how these trade-offs between leverage levels are likely to differ depending on company characteristics:

- The higher a company's returns, the lower its growth and business risk, and the more fungible its assets and capabilities, the more highly it should be leveraged. Such companies are more likely to benefit from tax savings because they have stable profits. Imposing discipline on management is more important because the cost of overinvesting is likely to be high for these low-growth companies. Because the company's assets and capabilities have alternative uses, the expected costs of business erosion are lower: even after a bankruptcy, the assets and capabilities would have significant value to new owners. This explains why airlines can sustain high leverage[9] in spite of their low returns and high risk: airplanes are easily deployed for use by other airline companies in case of bankruptcy.

- For companies with lower returns, higher growth potential and risk, and highly specific assets and capabilities, leverage should be lower. In this case, the potential tax savings are small because taxable profits are low in the near term. Management should not be too financially restricted because investments are essential to capture future growth. In addition, because of the high growth and the uniqueness of the assets and capabilities, the expected costs of business erosion are high, too. If such companies go into bankruptcy, they lose valuable growth opportunities, and any remaining assets have very little value to third parties.

[8] See, for example, S. Ross, R. Westerfield, and J. Jaffe, *Corporate Finance*, 6th ed. (New York: McGraw-Hill, 2001), pp. 427–430.
[9] Specifically, leverage is high when the operating leases of aircraft are taken into account.

These patterns are supported by ample evidence from academic research. The most highly leveraged industries are indeed typically mature and asset-intensive; examples are steel, paper, and cement. Industries with the lowest leverage, such as software, biotech, and high-tech start-ups, have larger opportunities for growth and investment. Companies with greater tangible assets usually sustain greater debt, because they have more assets that can serve as collateral, reducing the costs of business erosion and bankruptcy.[10] Companies with higher earnings volatility and higher advertising and R&D costs tend to be financed with less debt.[11] Leverage also proves to be higher for companies with more fungible assets and lower for companies producing durable goods, such as machinery and equipment, requiring long-term maintenance and support.[12]

Pecking-order theory   An alternative to the view that there is a trade-off between equity and debt is a school of thought in finance theory that sees a "pecking order" in financing.[13] According to this theory, companies meet their investment needs first by using internal funds (from retained earnings), then by issuing debt, and finally by issuing equity. One of the causes for this pecking order is that investors interpret financing decisions by managers as signals of a company's financial prospects. For example, investors will interpret an equity issue as a signal that management believes shares are overvalued. Because of this interpretation, rational managers will turn to equity funding only as a last resort because it could cause the share price to fall. An analogous argument holds for debt issues, although the overvaluation signal is much smaller because the value of debt is much less sensitive to a company's financial success.[14]

According to the theory, companies will have lower leverage when they are more mature and profitable, simply because they can fund internally and do not need any debt or equity funding. However, the empirical evidence for the theory is not conclusive. For example, mature companies generating strong cash flows are among the most highly leveraged companies, whereas the pecking-order theory would predict they would have

[10] R. Rajan and L. Zingales, "What Do We Know about Capital Structure? Some Evidence from International Data," *Journal of Finance,* 50(5) (1995): 1421–1460.

[11] M. Bradley, G. Jarell, and E. Kim, "On the Existence of an Optimal Capital Structure: Theory and Evidence," *Journal of Finance,* 39(3) (1984): 857–878; and M. Long and I. Malitz, "The Investment-Financing Nexus: Some Empirical Evidence," *Midland Corporate Finance Journal,* 3(3) (1985): 53–59.

[12] See note 1 and S. Titman and R. Wessels, "The Determinants of Capital Structure Choice," *Journal of Finance,* 43(1) (1988): 1–19.

[13] See G. Donaldson, "Corporate Debt Capacity: A Study of Corporate Debt Policy and the Determination of Corporate Debt Capacity," Harvard Graduate School of Business (Boston, 1961); and S. Myers, "The Capital Structure Puzzle," *Journal of Finance,* 39(3) (1974): 575–592.

[14] An exception is, of course, the value of debt in a financially distressed company.

the lowest leverage. High-tech start-up companies are among the least leveraged, rather than debt-loaded, as the theory would predict.[15]

In light of the evidence, it seems that the signaling hypotheses underlying the pecking-order theory are quite relevant for financial managers, but more so for selecting and timing specific funding alternatives than for setting capital structure targets.[16] Recent research among financial executives confirms that this interpretation corresponds closely to current management practice.[17]

Is There an Optimal Capital Structure?

Although the costs and benefits of leverage are clear, there is less clarity on how to determine the optimal capital structure for a given company. How should managers decide on the best target leverage for their companies? The bad news is that there seems to be no exact answer. The good news is twofold. First, for most companies, the answer is not as critical for shareholder value as some practitioners think. Second, managers can find meaningful indications of an *effective* capital structure, that is, a structure that is hard to improve on in terms of creating shareholder value (see the following section).

How critical is leverage for shareholder value anyway? Exhibit 17.2 shows the distribution of credit ratings for all U.S. and European companies with a market capitalization over $1 billion according to Standard & Poor's. The ratings are a measure of a company's credit quality between AAA (highest quality) and D (defaulted), with ratings of BBB– and higher indicating so-called investment-grade quality. The vast majority of the companies are in the rating category of A+ to BBB–. Credit ratings are fairly persistent over time, so most companies probably do not move in and out of this range. Below the BBB-rating level interest rates are much higher because many investors cannot invest in debt that is not investment grade, and the flexibility to raise capital is limited, especially in periods when credit is tight.

---

[15] See note 1 and M. Baker and J. Wurgler, "Market Timing and Capital Structure," *Journal of Finance,* 52(1) (2002): 1–32.

[16] See also A. Hovakimian, T. Opler, and S. Titman, "The Debt-Equity Choice," *Journal of Financial and Quantitative Analysis,* 36(1) (2001): 1–24, for evidence that the pecking-order theory predicts short-term movements in corporate debt levels but that long-term changes are more in line with the trade-offs discussed earlier in this section.

[17] J. Graham and H. Campbell, "How Do CFOs Make Capital Budgeting and Capital Structure Decisions?" *Journal of Applied Corporate Finance,* 15(1) (2002): 8–23.

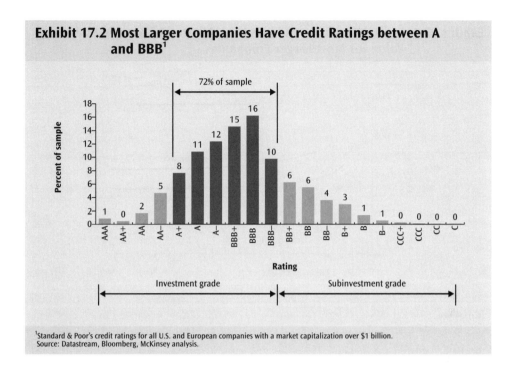

Exhibit 17.2 Most Larger Companies Have Credit Ratings between A and BBB¹

[1]Standard & Poor's credit ratings for all U.S. and European companies with a market capitalization over $1 billion.
Source: Datastream, Bloomberg, McKinsey analysis.

We interpret this distribution of ratings as evidence that for most companies, the range from A+ to BBB– is apparently an effective rating level. As we will see later, it does not mean that all companies have a similar capital structure. Rather, companies with the same credit rating can have very different capital structures across industry sectors because of different business risk.

Within the range from A+ to BBB–, shareholder value does not vary much with a company's capital structure. This is especially true when we compare the impact of credit rating with the impact of key value drivers such as ROIC and growth.

Let's illustrate this with a simple example while focusing on just the tax savings from increased debt financing. Exhibit 17.3 on page 494 shows how the multiple of enterprise value over EBITA for an average company in the S&P 500 would change with the amount of debt financing, as measured by the interest coverage ratio.[18] The EBITA multiple is estimated with the basic value driver formula as presented in Chapter 3, applied using an APV

---

[18] This is the ratio of EBITA to interest expenses, which is widely used by managers and credit raters to measure financial health; see the next section for more details.

Exhibit 17.3 Capital Structure Changes Have Limited Impact on Enterprise Value for Most Larger Companies

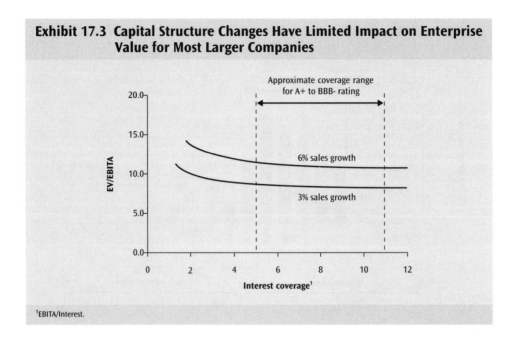

methodology.[19] We assume a long-term ROIC of 14 percent and an unlevered cost of capital of 9 percent—typical scores for a middle-of-the-road S&P 500 company.

As Exhibit 17.3 shows, enterprise value does not change dramatically with the level of debt funding except at very low levels of interest coverage (below 2). But at such low levels of coverage, the company will likely have a credit rating below investment grade, and two factors will make the real value impact of additional debt lower than what follows from this simple model. First, the costs of business erosion and investor conflicts will be-

---

[19] Applying the APV methodology to the value driver formula and discounting the tax shield on interest at the unlevered cost of equity results in the following formula:

$$\text{Value} = \text{NOPLAT} \times \frac{1 - \dfrac{g}{\text{ROIC}}}{k_u - g} + \sum_{t=1}^{\infty} \frac{k_D \times T \times D_t}{\left(1 + k_u\right)^t}$$

where k_u = Unlevered cost of equity
  D = Debt in year t
  k_D = Cost of debt
  T = Tax rate

(All other symbols as defined in Chapter 3.)

If we make the additional assumption that companies finance with debt while maintaining a stable interest coverage ratio, the formula can be simplified as follows:

$$\text{Value} = \text{NOPLAT} \times \frac{\left(1 - \dfrac{g}{\text{ROIC}} + \dfrac{T}{1-T} \times \dfrac{\text{INT}}{\text{EBITA}}\right)}{k_u - g}$$

where EBITA/INT = Target coverage ratio

come significant and offset some of the tax savings. Second, the expected value of any tax savings itself will decline because of the growing probability that the company will not capture these savings in the first place. The real value impact will therefore be even less than predicted by our value driver formula at low coverage ratios, so the true curve would be even flatter than shown here.

Especially when compared with the impact of additional growth (also shown in the exhibit) or ROIC improvements, capital structure is far from a big value booster. In this light, it is therefore not surprising that most companies have a credit rating in the range of A+ to BBB–, roughly corresponding to coverage ratios of 5 to 11 times interest.

Of course, capital structure can make a big difference for companies at the far ends of the interest-coverage spectrum. Companies with strong earnings and cash flows but without any debt probably fail to capture significant value for their shareholders. Well-documented examples include pharmaceutical companies such as American Home Products, which had almost no debt for more than 30 years until 1989. The forgone tax shields on debt amounted to an estimated $1.7 billion over that period.[20] At the other extreme, companies with very high levels of leverage at an interest coverage of 2 and less probably do not render their shareholders a great service either. Such leverage levels are unsustainable and more likely to destroy shareholder value, due to high probability of business erosion, investor conflicts, and ultimately, bankruptcy.

Setting an Effective Capital Structure

Difficult as it may be to determine an optimal capital structure, it is much easier to find an effective structure—that is, one that cannot clearly be improved upon in terms of shareholder value creation because it is somewhere in the relatively flat range of the valuation curves of Exhibits 17.1 and 17.3. To find such an effective structure, you can use several reference points.

Peer group comparison   An industry peer group is a good starting point. The key value trade-offs in designing capital structure as laid out earlier are largely industry specific: growth, return, and asset specificity. If these characteristics are fairly similar across a peer group of companies, market forces will drive these companies toward an effective capital structure. By analyzing what capital structure most companies in the peer group have, you obtain at least some understanding for what a reasonable capital structure could be. Furthermore, the approach also makes sense from a competitive perspective: As long as your capital structure is not too different, you have at least not given away (or gained) any competitive advantage derived

---

[20] See T. Opler, M. Saron, and S. Titman, "Corporate Liability Management: Designing Capital Structure to Create Shareholder Value," *Journal of Applied Corporate Finance*, 10(1) (1997): 21–32.

from capital structure. For example, there is academic evidence that high-leverage companies sometimes fall victim to price wars started by financially stronger competitors.[21]

Credit-rating analysis Peer group comparisons offer meaningless conclusions if many companies in the sector are not at their targeted capital structure. For example, many players in the telecommunications sector had too much debt in the early 2000s as a result of aggressive acquisitions and investments in mobile communication. In that case, it is more interesting to analyze only peers with investment-grade credit ratings and determine what it takes to achieve such a rating. This allows you not only to set a target structure but also to assess how your credit rating would be affected if you deviated from that targeted structure. Since the 1960s, there has been empirical evidence of company credit ratios clustering around industry-specific averages, further indicating that each industry has a different effective capital structure level (see also Chapter 10, Exhibit 10.15).[22]

Cash flow analysis Although external comparisons of capital structure and credit ratings are important, every company will face specific challenges due to particular investment needs, dividend policy, and other considerations. You should therefore carefully analyze future cash inflows and outflows and the capital structure implications. Test a given capital structure under different scenarios to analyze how credit quality will develop over time and what future funding deficits or surpluses to expect. Assess the company's financial *flexibility:* What capital structure will enable you to undertake planned acquisitions or make planned capital expenditures? Also test for financial *robustness:* What levels of risk (e.g., from business or sector downturns) can the company absorb with a given capital structure? Finally, set a capital structure target that accommodates both sufficient flexibility and robustness. Later in this chapter, we will illustrate this approach with a numerical example.

CREDIT RATINGS AND CAPITAL STRUCTURE

Before we can offer guidance on how to set a capital structure target for a specific company, we need to provide further background on credit ratings. Credit-rating estimates are important for three reasons:

1. Ratings are a useful summary indicator of capital structure health; lower ratings reflect higher default probabilities. Exhibit 17.4 shows

---

[21] See, for example, P. Bolton and D. Scharfstein, "A Theory of Predation Based on Agency Problems in Financial Contracting," *American Economic Review,* 80(1) (1990): 93–106.
[22] E. Schwarz and R. Aronson, "Some Surrogate Evidence in Support of the Concept of Optimal Financial Structure," *Journal of Finance,* 22(1) (1967): 10–18.

Exhibit 17.4 Corporate Bond Ratings

percent

Standard & Poor's	Default probability[1]	Moody's	Default probability[2]	
AAA	0.12	Aaa	0.12	
AA	0.33	Aa	0.24	Investment
A	0.75	A	0.54	grade
BBB	3.84	Baa	2.16	
BB	14.45	Ba	11.17	
B	33.02	B	31.99	Subinvestment
CCC	61.35	Caa	60.83	grade
CC		Ca		
C		C		

[1]Percentage defaulting within 5 years based on default rates between 1981–2003.
[2]Percentage defaulting within 5 years based on default rates between 1970–2003.
Source: Standard & Poor's RatingsDirect database, *Statistical Review of Moody's Rating Performance, 1920–2003*, Moody's (2004), McKinsey analysis.

the average default probabilities per credit rating category for Standard & Poor's and Moody's. For example, a capital structure rated B or lower is probably not a wise target because of the very high probability of default.

2. Ratings largely determine the company's access to the debt markets. Below investment-grade BBB ratings, the opportunities for debt funding are much smaller because many investors are barred from investing in sub-investment-grade debt.

3. Ratings are nowadays important elements in the communication to shareholders. Managers should be able to explain whether or not their company can or should maintain its current rating. Since the stock market bubble of the 1990s this has become an important indicator of corporate health for equity investors.

The process of setting a credit rating for a company is elaborate and relies considerably on qualitative assessment of the historical and likely future performance of a company's management and business. Nevertheless, empirical evidence shows that credit ratings are primarily related to two financial indicators:[23]

- *Size* in terms of sales or market capitalization
- *Coverage* in terms of EBITA or EBITDA divided by interest expenses[24]

---

[23] See, for example, J. Pettit, C. Fitt, S. Orlov, and A. Kalsekar, "The New World of Credit Ratings" (UBS research report, September 2004).
[24] Standard & Poor's also uses measures such as FFO (free flow from operations), which differs somewhat from EBITDA but essentially also intends to capture operational cash flow.

Size is especially relevant in its extremes: for example, all companies with AAA ratings are at market capitalizations higher than $50 billion. One explanation for the role of size is the greater likelihood of risk diversification in larger companies. But the relation between size and credit rating is not meaningful for capital structure policy: size is not really controllable by management and has no bearing on the credit health of an individual company. Coverage is much more relevant in this context. Let's first discuss how coverage is related to some other widely used indicators for financial health or risk such as leverage and solvency.

Coverage   A straightforward indicator of a company's ability to comply with its short-term debt service obligations is its interest coverage, defined as follows:

$$\text{Coverage} = \frac{\text{EBITA}}{\text{Interest}} \text{ or } \frac{\text{EBITDA}}{\text{Interest}} \text{ or } \frac{\text{Net Debt}}{\text{EBITDA}}$$

EBITA interest coverage measures how many times a company could pay its interest commitments out of its ongoing operational cash flow if it invested only an amount equal to its annual depreciation charges to keep business running. When expressed as EBITDA to interest, it measures available cash flow before any capital expenditures and taxes. When interest rates are comparable across companies, so-called debt coverage, net debt to EBITDA, is sometimes used instead of interest coverage. Debt coverage also measures the company's ability to service its debt in the short term but is more insightful when companies use large amounts of convertibles or low-interest debt. In terms of straightforward EBIT(D)A interest coverage, their financial health might look very strong. However, when they need to roll over their convertible or low-interest debt into regular debt funding at higher rates, their interest coverage will plummet. Under these circumstances, net debt to EBITDA will be less distorted than EBIT(D)A interest coverage.

Leverage   The traditional measure in the academic literature is leverage in terms of market value, defined as the market value of debt (D) over the market value of debt plus equity (E):

$$\text{Leverage} = \frac{D}{D+E}$$

It measures how much of the company's enterprise value is "claimed" by debt holders and is an important concept for estimating the benefits of tax shields from debt financing. It is therefore also a crucial input in calculating the WACC (see Chapter 10 on capital structure weights).

Leverage, however, suffers from several drawbacks as a way of measuring and targeting a company's capital structure. First, companies could have very low leverage in terms of market value but still be at a high risk of financial distress if their short-term cash flow is low relative to interest payments. High-growth companies are usually at very low levels of leverage, but this does not mean their debt is low risk. A second drawback is that market value can change radically (especially for high-growth, high-multiple companies), making leverage a fast-moving indicator. For example, several European telecom companies, including Royal KPN Telecom and France Telecom, had what appeared to be reasonable levels of debt financing in terms of leverage during the stock market boom of the late nineties. Credit providers appeared willing to provide credit even though the underlying near-term cash flows were not very high relative to debt service obligations. But when the market values plummeted in 2001, leverage for these companies shot up, and financial distress loomed. Thus, it is risky to target a market-value-based measure for capital structure.

This does not mean that leverage and coverage are fundamentally divergent measures. Far from it, they actually measure the same thing but over different time horizons. For ease of explanation, consider a company that has no growth in revenues, profit, or cash flows. For this company, we can express the leverage and coverage as follows:[25]

$$\text{Leverage} = \frac{D}{D+E} = \frac{\text{Int}_{t=1} + \text{PV}\left(\text{Int}_{t=2}\right) + \cdots + \text{PV}\left(\text{Int}_{t\to\infty}\right)}{\text{NOPLAT}_{t=1} + \text{PV}\left(\text{NOPLAT}_{t=2}\right) + \cdots + \text{PV}\left(\text{NOPLAT}_{t\to\infty}\right)}$$

$$\text{Coverage} = \frac{\text{EBITA}_{t=1}}{\text{Int}_{t=1}} = \frac{1}{\left(1-T\right)} \times \frac{\text{NOPLAT}_{t=1}}{\text{Int}_{t=1}}$$

where D = Market value of debt
       E = Market value of equity
       T = Tax rate

The market value of debt captures the present value of all future interest payments, assuming perpetual rollover of debt financing. The enterprise value (E + D) is equal to the present value of future NOPLAT because depreciation equals capital expenditures for a zero-growth company. A leverage ratio therefore measures the company's ability to cover its interest payments over a very long term. The problem is that short-term interest obligations are what mainly get a company into financial distress. Coverage, in contrast, focuses only on the short-term part of the leverage

---

[25] The simplifying no-growth assumption is for illustration purposes only. For a growing company, the same point holds.

definition, keeping in mind that NOPLAT roughly equals EBITA $\times (1 - T)$. Coverage indicates how easily a company can service its debt in the near term.

Both measures are meaningful, and they are complementary. For example, if market leverage were very high in combination with strong current interest coverage, this could indicate the possibility of future difficulties in sustaining current debt levels. This situation applies to single-product companies faced with rapidly eroding margins and cash flows because the product is approaching the end of its life cycle. In spite of very high interest coverage, such companies may not attain high credit ratings and could face limited debt capacity.

Solvency   Book measures of debt over total assets or debt over equity are seldom as meaningful as coverage or leverage. The key reason is that these solvency measures fail to capture the company's ability to comply with debt service requirements in either the short or long term. Market-to-book ratios can vary significantly across sectors and over time, making solvency a poor proxy for long-term debt service ability. The Dutch publishing company Wolters-Kluwer, for example, has had low book equity for years because under Dutch GAAP it had written off all goodwill on acquisitions directly against equity. In spite of very low solvency, with a ratio of equity to total assets below 20 percent, Wolters-Kluwer has been at a credit rating around A, well within investment grade.

Solvency becomes more relevant in times of financial distress, when a company's creditors use it as a rough measure of the available collateral. Higher levels of solvency usually indicate that debt holders stand better chances of recovering their principal and interest due—assuming that asset book values are reasonable approximations of asset liquidation values. However, for capital structure decisions at a going concern, solvency is much less relevant than coverage and leverage measures.

Coverage as key driver of credit ratings   Many models have attempted to explain credit ratings or default probabilities from a company's financial and business characteristics.[26] Based on our own empirical analyses, we find that a limited number of credit ratios explain credit rating fairly well, with interest coverage[27] as the single most significant indicator. Exhibit 17.5 summarizes the results for a sample containing all U.S. and European companies rated by Standard & Poor's (excluding financial institutions). It

---

[26] For an overview, see R. Cantor, "An Introduction to Recent Research on Credit Ratings," *Journal of Banking and Finance*, 28(11) (2004): 2565–2573; and E. Altman, "Financial Ratios, Discriminant Analysis, and the Prediction of Corporate Bankruptcy," *Journal of Finance*, 23(4) (1968): 589–609.

[27] This holds for EBITA as well as EBITDA coverage measures.

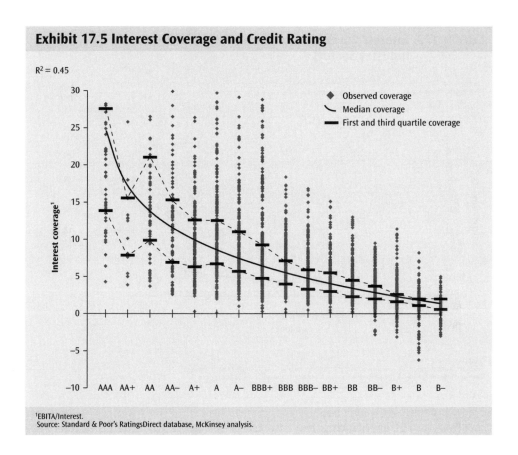

Exhibit 17.5 Interest Coverage and Credit Rating

$R^2 = 0.45$

Interest coverage[1]

- ◆ Observed coverage
- ⌣ Median coverage
- ▬ First and third quartile coverage

AAA AA+ AA AA− A+ A A− BBB+ BBB BBB− BB+ BB BB− B+ B B−

[1] EBITA/Interest.
Source: Standard & Poor's RatingsDirect database, McKinsey analysis.

shows how interest coverage is a key explaining variable for the Standard & Poor's credit ratings, with more than 45 percent of rating differences explained by interest coverage alone.

Analyzing the data further, we also find that coverage for a given credit rating differs by industry in a predictable way. In Exhibit 17.6 on page 502, we show how coverage ratios differ across sectors for a given credit rating. For example, telecom companies will have better credit ratings than steel companies at the same coverage level. To understand why this is the case, we estimated the volatility[28] of EBITDA over the five years preceding the date of the credit rating. For industries with higher volatility of EBITDA, the coverage requirements are higher to attain a given credit rating, as the exhibit shows. This makes sense: For a given level of interest coverage, higher volatility implies a higher probability that a company will lack sufficient cash flow to service its interest commitment in the future. As a result, the credit rating will be lower.

[28] EBITDA volatility is measured here as the average standard deviation of relative annual changes in EBITDA for the largest 25 companies in each sector in terms of market capitalization.

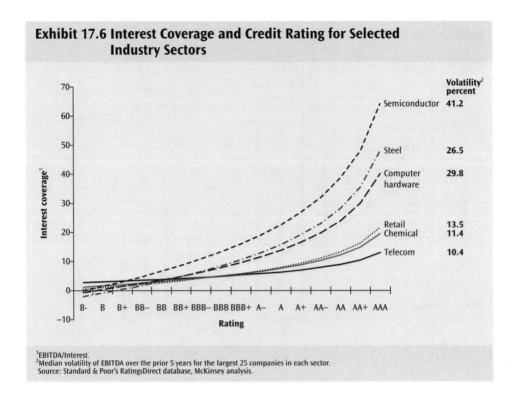

Exhibit 17.6 Interest Coverage and Credit Rating for Selected Industry Sectors

[1]EBITDA/Interest.
[2]Median volatility of EBITDA over the prior 5 years for the largest 25 companies in each sector.
Source: Standard & Poor's RatingsDirect database, McKinsey analysis.

Thus, by differentiating the interest coverage requirements across sectors, it is possible to develop an estimate of the likely credit rating for a given level of operating profit and interest. Obviously, we could further refine the analysis by including more explanatory ratios, such as net debt to EBITDA, free flow from operations (FFO) to interest, solvency, and more. However, these ratios are often highly correlated, so they do not always add explanatory power.

Credit rating and credit spread   The difference between the yields on corporate bonds and risk-free bonds—the *credit spread*—increases with lower credit ratings because the probability of default increases. Exhibit 17.7 plots the cumulative default probabilities over 5 and 10 years and the average credit spreads between 1992 and 2004 against the credit ratings. Notice that credit ratings are not a linear scaling of default probabilities: the difference in default probability between AAA and BBB is much smaller than the difference between a BBB and a B rating. Spreads reflect the increasing default probabilities almost proportionally. However, at the investment-grade benchmarking of BBB, the spread appears to increase more aggressively, although this is less pronounced when excluding the three years immediately following the peak of the bubble in 2000. One explanation is that some institutional investors

Exhibit 17.7 Default Probability and Credit Spread

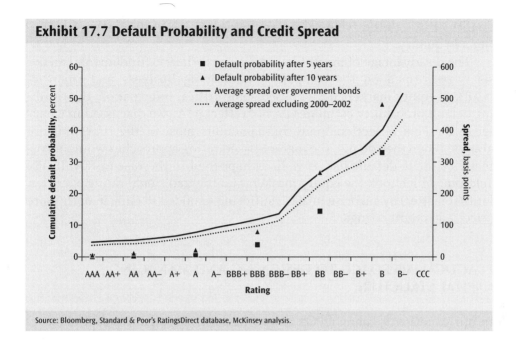

Source: Bloomberg, Standard & Poor's RatingsDirect database, McKinsey analysis.

cannot invest in debt that is below investment grade (BBB–), so the debt market is considerably smaller for below-investment-grade debt, and interest rates are correspondingly higher. Apart from this turning point at the investment grade level, spreads appear to follow changes in default probabilities fairly closely.

Market-based rating approach   Over the past decade, new approaches to credit assessment have been developed based on the notion that equity can be modeled as a call option on the company's enterprise value, with the debt obligations as the exercise price.[29] Using option valuation models and market data on price and volatility of the shares, these approaches estimate the future default probability, that is, the probability that enterprise value will be below the value of debt obligations.[30] The advantage is that all information captured by the equity markets is directly translated into the default estimates. Traditional credit ratings tend to lag changes in a company's performance and outlook because they aim to measure credit

---

[29] This is because equity is a residual claim on the enterprise value after payment of principal and interest for debt. It has value only to the extent that enterprise value exceeds debt commitments. See R. Merton, "On the Pricing of Corporate Debt: The Risk Structure of Interest Rates," *Journal of Finance,* 29 (1974): 449–470; or, for an introduction, R. Brealey and S. Myers, *Principles of Corporate Finance,* 7th ed. (New York: McGraw-Hill, 2003), ch. 24.

[30] See P. Crosbie and J. Bohn, "Modeling Default Risk," Moody's KMV (2003).

quality "through the cycle"[31] and are less sensitive to short-term fluctuations in quality.

The disadvantage of market-based ratings is that no fundamental analysis is performed on the company's underlying business and financial health. If equity markets have missed some critical information, the resulting default probability estimates do not reflect it. As we discussed in Chapter 4, markets reflect company fundamentals most of the time, but not always. When they do not, the market-based rating approaches would incorrectly estimate default risk as well, as happened in the case of Royal KPN Telecom, which took the equity market (and the traditional rating agencies, for that matter) by surprise in 2001, suffering a sudden decline in both share prices and credit ratings.[32]

PRACTICAL APPROACH TO DESIGNING AND MANAGING CAPITAL STRUCTURE

In our experience, many CFOs aim to have their company's capital structure meet criteria such as a specific credit rating, interest coverage, or some other measure of keeping a "safe buffer" of annual cash inflow over fixed charges such as interest payments. Surveys among financial executives also show that they put more emphasis on preserving financial flexibility than on minimizing cost of capital.[33]

Empirical analyses have demonstrated that companies actively manage their capital structure and stay within certain leverage boundaries. Companies are much more likely to issue equity when they are overleveraged relative to this target, and much less likely when they are underleveraged.[34] They make adjustments toward target capital structure with one or two years' delay, rather than immediately, since that would become impractical and costly due to share price volatility and transaction costs.[35] This is also the pattern we would expect to find if companies would target interest coverage: share prices are ultimately driven by future operating earnings and cash flows. If share prices rise and remain there, earnings and cash flows eventually will rise—and that is probably when companies start to increase leverage.

---

[31] See E. Altman and H. Rijken, "How Rating Agencies Achieve Rating Stability," *Journal of Banking and Finance,* 28(11) (2004): 2679–2714.

[32] See Crosbie and Bohn, "Modeling Default Risk," p. 23. (Note 30)

[33] See Graham and Campbell, "How Do CFOs Make Decisions?" (Note 17)

[34] P. Marsh, "The Choice between Equity and Debt: An Empirical Study," *Journal of Finance,* 37(1) (1982): 121–144.

[35] See, for example, M. Leary and M. Roberts, "Do Firms Rebalance Their Capital Structures?" 14th Annual Utah Winter Finance Conference, Tuck Contemporary Corporate Finance Issues III Conference Paper, 2004.

Although leverage and coverage ratios all point in the same direction, interest coverage targets are more appropriate for setting long-term capital structure targets. One reason is that coverage measures credit quality more accurately (see the discussion of leverage and coverage in this chapter). A second reason is that leverage would be a moving target as share prices fluctuate. Finally, coverage can be more readily applied when making long-term capital structure analyses, because it does not require any valuation estimate going forward but simply interest and EBIT(D)A.

In our experience, a straightforward approach is sufficient to develop a long-term capital structure for a company. The approach consists of five steps and is scenario driven. A simple example can illustrate.

Assume a company has sales of €1 billion per year. The company currently has a BBB credit rating and an EBITA-to-interest coverage ratio of 5. It has developed aggressive investment plans for the next six years to boost its sales growth from a current level of 3.5 percent per year to a peak level of 20 percent per year. The investment requirements are accordingly high, amounting to around €340 million in NPPE and working capital until 2010. Furthermore, the company is looking out for interesting acquisition opportunities among its smaller competitors. Its current operating margins at 5 percent of sales will not generate sufficient funds to support such capital expenditures, and new funding is needed. The CFO wants to develop a capital structure that is robust enough that a business downturn will not endanger the company's financial stability, yet flexible enough to allow for a sizable acquisition.

Step 1: Project financing surplus or deficit   The first step is to project the free cash flows resulting from the proposed business plan as well as the financing cash flows resulting from the current capital structure as if unchanged. Assume that any resulting funding deficit or surplus flow is balanced by additional new short-term debt or excess cash, respectively. These projections are shown in Exhibit 17.8 on page 506. It is clear from this chart that the operating cash flows alone cannot support this level of investment. Furthermore, the company has commitments to repay existing debt and to pay out dividends. The cumulative deficit over the next six years amounts to over €280 million. As a working assumption assume that this is to be balanced by new short-term debt.

Step 2: Set target credit rating and ratios   Next, determine what credit rating the company wants to target in the future. Given the need for additional funding, it is probably wise to maintain an investment-grade rating for better access to the capital markets. The CFO wants to aim for a BBB+ rating, which would require an EBITA-to-interest coverage of at least 5 in its industry. In addition to this target, the company should not drop below an interest coverage of 2, even under adverse business conditions, to prevent

Exhibit 17.8 Projections of Financing Surplus (Deficit)

€ million

Cash flow statement	2005	2006	2007	2008	2009	2010
NOPLAT	36	41	49	54	57	60
(Increase) decrease in working capital	(8)	(24)	(36)	(22)	(12)	(13)
(Increase) decrease in net PPE	(15)	(47)	(72)	(43)	(24)	(25)
Free cash flow	13	(30)	(59)	(11)	21	22
Interest expense existing debt[1]	(6)	(4)	(3)	(1)	(0)	–
Debt repayment	(20)	(50)	(20)	(30)	(20)	(10)
Dividends	(10)	(11)	(12)	(13)	(14)	(15)
Cash flow existing financing	(36)	(65)	(35)	(45)	(35)	(25)
Funding surplus (deficit)	**(23)**	**(95)**	**(95)**	**(56)**	**(14)**	**(3)**
Excess cash (increase) decrease	–	–	–	–	–	–
Interest income excess cash[1]	–	–	–	–	–	–
Equity issuance (repayment)	–	–	–	–	–	–
Debt issuance (repayment)	24	101	106	70	29	20
Interest expense new debt[1]	(1)	(6)	(11)	(14)	(16)	(17)
New funding	**23**	**95**	**95**	**56**	**14**	**3**

[1] After-tax.

any financial distress. At 2 times EBITA, the company would still be cash positive after subtracting taxes and interest. For other credit ratios, no targets are set at the moment. If any covenants are in place for existing debt, of course, these requirements also should be observed when setting any target coverage ratios.

Step 3: Develop capital structure for base case scenario   The third step begins by identifying and understanding the key drivers of the financing deficit. The familiar value drivers, growth and return on invested capital, determine uses and sources of *free cash flow from operations*. Higher growth in general leads to greater cash requirements as investments in NPPE and working capital usually go up with growth; higher ROIC leads to lower cash requirements from either higher operating margins over sales or higher turnover of invested capital. (But capital turnover increases have stronger short-term cash impact than margin increases, for the same change in ROIC.) This company's aggressive growth strategy drives a need for cash. Adjusting the growth plans at any time would significantly reduce the cash flow deficit.

In terms of the drivers of *financing cash flow*, the existing debt requires interest and principal payments according to a fixed schedule. Until 2010, all of the company's existing debt needs to be paid down, with a peak repayment of €50 million in 2006. On top of that, the company has established a policy of paying out about 35 percent of profits in shareholder dividends.

With this information, you can develop some initial ideas about the company's future capital structure. Under the base-case projections, the company fails to reach its targeted coverage ratio if the company issues no equity and all funding requirements are met with short-term debt (indicated in Exhibit 17.9 on p. 508). Given the key drivers just described, the company could do one of two things: either reduce its growth plans and capital spending, or issue new capital. Reducing the dividend payout ratio, for example, would have limited effect. Given that equity issuances have high fixed transaction costs, it is probably best to issue a large amount of equity capital in year 1, around €125 million. This will generate more than €100 million of excess cash in 2005, but that will be almost depleted within a year. In this case, the company also has some free debt capacity of around €45 million to €55 million for acquisitions between 2005 and 2010. Exhibit 17.9 plots the interest coverage against requirements under the base case, as well as the free debt capacity for any acquisitions.

Step 4: Test capital structure under downside scenario But how would the company get along if the business were to face a downturn of margins? Would it go bankrupt or get into financial distress? To analyze this, we also constructed a downside scenario in which margins are cut in half, to 2.5 percent of sales, for the next six years. The minimum coverage ratio of 2 is the target for this scenario. Exhibit 17.10 on page 509 summarizes the projections of cash flows and key credit ratios. Of course, the financing deficit and debt will shoot up, and coverage ratios will deteriorate. Nevertheless, thanks to the equity issuance, the company has sufficient reserves to absorb this risk and maintain a coverage ratio just above 2 times interest—even under such an adverse business scenario. Given the opportunities to scale down the growth plans if needed and reduce dividend payout ratios, the company's capital structure seems robust enough. Decreasing the dividend payout ratios could improve the company's cash position, but not by a great amount in this case.

Step 5: Decide on current and future actions After several rounds of testing and adjusting the capital structure plan under both scenarios, you select a final plan. The next step is to decide which elements of the financing plan to carry out now and which to defer to a later stage, when new information is available. In this example, the current decisions under the financing plan would involve the issuance of new equity. All future debt and dividend decisions can be taken in a later stage, when circumstances are fully clear. The cash from the equity issuance will ensure the company has enough funding for at least six years under the base scenario, even allowing for

Exhibit 17.9 Capital Structure Summary for Base Case Scenario

Base case scenario (with equity issue)

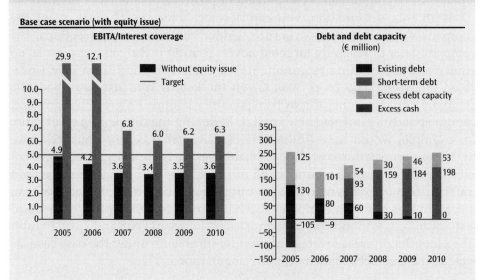

€ million	2005	2006	2007	2008	2009	2010
Balance sheet						
Working capital	158	181	217	239	251	264
Net PPE	315	362	435	478	502	527
Invested capital	**473**	**543**	**652**	**717**	**753**	**791**
(Excess cash)	(105)	(9)	–	–	–	–
Short-term debt	–	–	93	159	184	198
Existing debt	130	80	60	30	10	–
Equity	447	472	499	529	560	592
Investor funds	**473**	**543**	**652**	**717**	**753**	**791**
Cash flow statement						
NOPLAT	36	41	49	54	57	60
Increase working capital	(8)	(24)	(36)	(22)	(12)	(13)
Increase net PPE	(15)	(47)	(72)	(43)	(24)	(25)
Free cash flow	**13**	**(30)**	**(59)**	**(11)**	**21**	**22**
Interest expense existing debt[1]	(6)	(4)	(3)	(1)	0	–
Debt repayment	(20)	(50)	(20)	(30)	(20)	(10)
Dividends	(12)	(13)	(15)	(16)	(17)	(18)
Cash flow existing financing	(38)	(67)	(38)	(47)	(37)	(28)
Funding surplus/deficit	**(25)**	**(97)**	**(97)**	**(58)**	**(16)**	**(6)**
Excess cash (increase) decrease	(105)	96	9	–	–	–
Interest income excess cash[1]	5	0	–	–	–	–
Equity issuance (repayment)	125	–	–	–	–	–
Debt issuance (repayment)	–	–	93	66	25	15
Interest expense new debt[1]	–	–	(4)	(8)	(9)	(9)
New funding	**25**	**97**	**97**	**58**	**16**	**6**

[1] After-tax.

Exhibit 17.10 Capital Structure Summary for Downside Scenario

Downside case scenario (with equity issue)

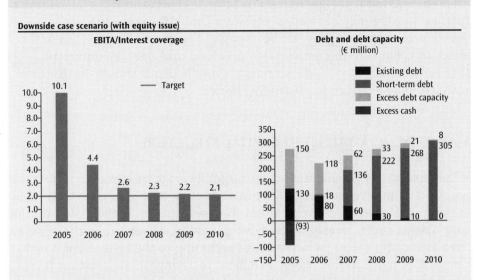

€ million	2005	2006	2007	2008	2009	2010
Balance sheet						
Working capital	158	181	217	239	251	264
Net PPE	315	362	435	478	502	527
Invested capital	**473**	**543**	**652**	**717**	**753**	**791**
(Excess cash)	(93)	–	–	–	–	–
Short-term debt	–	18	136	222	268	305
Existing debt	130	80	60	30	10	–
Equity	435	446	456	466	475	485
Investor funds	**473**	**543**	**652**	**717**	**753**	**791**
Cash flow statement						
NOPLAT	18	21	25	27	28	30
Increase working capital	(8)	(24)	(36)	(22)	(12)	(13)
Increase net PPE	(15)	(47)	(72)	(43)	(24)	(25)
Free cash flow	**(5)**	**(50)**	**(84)**	**(38)**	**(7)**	**(8)**
Interest expense existing debt[1]	(6)	(4)	(3)	(1)	(0)	–
Debt repayment	(20)	(50)	(20)	(30)	(20)	(10)
Dividends	(6)	(6)	(5)	(5)	(5)	(5)
Cash flow existing financing	(32)	(59)	(28)	(37)	(26)	(15)
Funding surplus/deficit	**(36)**	**(110)**	**(112)**	**(75)**	**(33)**	**(23)**
Excess cash (increase) decrease	(93)	93	–	–	–	–
Interest income excess cash[1]	4	–	–	–	–	–
Equity issuance (repayment)	125	–	–	–	–	–
Debt issuance (repayment)	–	18	119	85	46	38
Interest expense new debt[1]	–	(1)	(6)	(11)	(13)	(15)
New funding	**36**	**110**	**112**	**(75)**	**33**	**23**

[1]After-tax.

acquisitions. The company can more easily attract any additional funding after that period if the growth plans have paid off (and if the plans fail, no further funding may be needed anyway). Under the downside scenario, the equity proceeds alone may not be enough to keep a BBB rating but will still allow the company to comply with dividend and debt commitments. Furthermore, in the downside scenario, growth plans should be tempered, which will also reduce the financing deficit.

MAINTAINING A TARGETED CAPITAL STRUCTURE

When companies pursue long-term target leverage or coverage ratios, they will find themselves sooner or later in a situation where they are so far above or below their targeted leverage that they need to adjust their capital structure. For example, leverage may have gradually decreased as the company used free cash flow to pay down debt according to the repayment schedule. Companies must choose when and how to change their existing leverage when they run into funding surpluses or deficits, for example if large investments are needed to pursue business growth or if divestments have generated large excess cash balances.

In these cases, a manager should ensure that the company's capital structure converges toward its long-term target level—but not necessarily completely and immediately. Managers also must take account of transaction costs and signaling effects associated with different ways to adjust the capital structure. As a result of such signaling effects and transaction costs, companies cannot be expected to immediately correct their capital structures to long-term targets. Indeed, recent research has shown that companies adjust their capital structure in a gradual and delayed manner.[36]

Compared with signaling effects, transaction costs are easy to assess. In general, equity issues are more expensive than bond issues, which in turn are more expensive than bank loans. For all categories, there are powerful economies of scale because the costs are largely fixed (see Exhibit 17.11). Thus, from a transaction-cost perspective, equity becomes effective only for larger amounts. For smaller funding amounts, bank loans are the typical solution.

Signaling Effects from Capital Structure Decisions

For listed companies, the complication with capital structure decisions is that they send the capital markets signals about a company's prospects. Investors assume that managers possess more information than investors

---

[36] See Leary and Roberts, "Do Firms Rebalance Their Capital Structures." (Note 35)

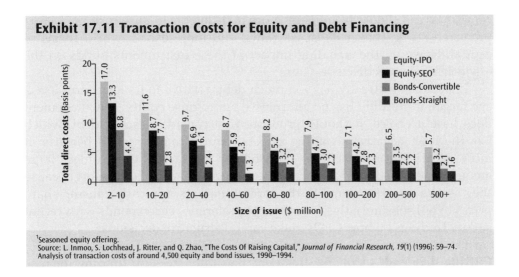

Exhibit 17.11 Transaction Costs for Equity and Debt Financing

[1] Seasoned equity offering.
Source: L. Inmoo, S. Lochhead, J. Ritter, and Q. Zhao, "The Costs Of Raising Capital," *Journal of Financial Research, 19*(1) (1996): 59–74. Analysis of transaction costs of around 4,500 equity and bond issues, 1990–1994.

have about the company's true business and financial outlook. Of course, managers can and do communicate directly with investors, but investors tend to attach less credibility to words than to actions. Therefore, they analyze management's decisions on offerings or repurchases of debt and equity and on dividends for any signals on the company's financial prospects. Managers should be aware of such signals before adjusting capital structure. However, keep in mind that although these signals may lead to short-term price reactions, they do not increase or decrease intrinsic value as such. Managers should ensure that sooner or later they can meet any expectations they have set in the capital market. Signaling excessively rosy prospects will ultimately backfire.

The signaling effects are in addition to the impact any capital structure change may have in itself. For example, cutting dividends not only provides a signal of lower future cash flows but also decreases leverage, thereby reducing tax shields on interest and giving management more slack in discretionary investments. Thus, the impact on share price is even more likely to be negative.

There are some key trade-offs among alternative financing instruments used to resolve funding shortages and surpluses. The trade-offs in handling surpluses and deficits are fairly straightforward in principle. Increasing leverage and returning cash to investors typically meets with positive market reactions. Decreasing leverage and asking investors for more capital typically leads to negative price reactions.

Managing Funding Shortages

Consider three fundamental, alternative ways to resolve funding shortages: cutting dividends, issuing new equity, or issuing new debt. Obviously, companies can choose from many more instruments to raise cash, including preferred stock, convertibles, warrants, and more exotic hybrid forms of capital. However, the signaling impact of these instruments builds on the essential trade-offs discussed here.

If a company already has too much debt, relative to its long-term leverage target, it probably has no alternative but to raise equity. If management does have a choice, it should probably first consider issuing debt, which has the least negative signaling effects. Equity comes second because of more negative price reactions—and higher transaction costs unless large amounts are raised. Dividend cuts are more a measure of last resort because they send a negative signal to the capital markets, typically causing share prices to fall substantially. This order of preference corresponds with recent survey findings on how CFOs make capital structure decisions.[37]

Cutting dividends   Cutting dividends naturally frees up funding for new investments. But the stock market typically interprets dividend reductions as a signal of lower future cash flows. As a result, share prices on average decline around 9 percent on the day a company announces dividend cuts or omissions.[38] Furthermore, some investor groups may count on dividends being paid out every year, and skipping these dividends will force them to liquidate part of their portfolio, leading to unnecessary transaction costs. Unless management has very compelling arguments for withholding dividends to invest in future growth, investors are likely to react negatively to dividend cuts. Some research indeed suggests that companies with more growth opportunities are less severely punished by the stock market.[39] Finally, the amount of funding freed up by cutting dividends is limited, so dividend cuts alone are unlikely to resolve more substantial funding shortages.

Issuing equity   Issuing equity also is likely to lead to a drop in share prices in the short term. Typically, share prices decline by around 3 percent on announcements of seasoned equity offerings.[40] Because investors assume that managers have superior insights into the company's true business and financial outlook, they believe managers will issue equity only if a company's shares are overvalued in the stock market. Therefore, the share price will decrease in the short term on the announcement of an equity issuance, even if it is actually not undervalued.

[37] See Graham and Campbell, "How Do CFOs Make Decisions?" (Note 17)

[38] P. Healey and K. Palepu, "Earnings Information Conveyed by Dividend Initiations and Omissions," *Journal of Financial Economics*, 21(2) (1988): 149–175.

[39] L. Lang and R. Litzenberger, "Dividend Announcements: Cash Flow Signaling versus Free Cash Flow Hypothesis," *Journal of Financial Economics*, 24(1) (1989): 181–192.

[40] See, for example, B. Eckbo, and R. Masulis, "Seasoned Equity Offerings: A Survey," in *Handbooks in Operations Research and Management Science* 9, edited by R. Jarrow, V. Maksimovic, and W. Ziemba (Amsterdam: Elsevier, 1995); and C. Smith, "Investment Banking and the Capital Acquisition Process," *Journal of Financial Economics*, 15(1/2) (1986): 3–29.

Issuing debt   A third way of resolving any funding shortage is issuing debt. There is ample empirical evidence that investors interpret the issuance of new debt much more positively than equity offerings. Because companies commit to fixed future interest payments that can be withheld only at considerable cost, investors see the issuance of debt as a strong signal that future cash flows will be sufficient. Investors also know that debt is more likely to be issued when management perceives a company's share price to be undervalued. As managers are assumed to be better informed on the company's future, share prices typically respond less negatively than when new equity is issued. Empirical research suggests that the price reaction is typically flat.[41]

Managing Funding Surpluses

As for funding deficits, we discuss only three basic alternatives for handling excess cash: dividend increases, share repurchases or extraordinary dividends, and debt repayments. Assuming excess cash is not needed to pay down debt to target levels, managers should probably first consider share repurchases or extraordinary dividends, since these send a favorable signal to capital markets. Voluntary debt repayments do not represent a positive signal, unless the company is close to or in financial distress. Increasing the dividend payout ratio provides the strongest signal. However, this is an attractive measure only if the company can indeed deliver against the investor expectations for higher, ongoing dividends.

The major caveat in returning cash to investors concerns the market's growth expectations for the company in question. High-growth companies could actually face negative reactions if the market interprets returning cash as a signal of lower sustainable growth.

Dividend increases   Companies increasing their dividends generally receive positive market reactions of around 2 percent on the day of announcement.[42] For companies that initiate dividend payments, the impact is even greater.[43] In general, investors interpret dividend increases as good news about the company's long-term outlook for future earnings and cash flows. On average they are right, according to the empirical evidence. Most companies that increase their dividend payout usually do so after strong

---

[41] See, e.g., W. Mikkelson and M. Partch, "Valuation Effects of Security Offerings and the Issuance Process," *Journal of Financial Economics*, 15(1/2) (1986): 31–60; and Smith, "Investment Banking and the Capital Acquisition Process." (Note 40)

[42] See, for example, S. Benartzi, R. Michaely, and R. Thaler, "Do Changes in Dividends Signal the Future or the Past?" *Journal of Finance*, 52(3) (1997): 1007–1034; and J. Aharony and I. Swarey, "Quarterly Dividends and Earnings Announcements and Stockholders," *Journal of Finance*, 35(1) (1980): 1–12.

[43] P. Healey and K. Palepu, "Earnings Information Conveyed by Dividend Initiations and Omissions," *Journal of Financial Economics*, 21(2) (1988): 149–175.

earnings growth and when they are able to maintain these high earnings levels in the year following the dividend increase. Companies that start paying dividends for the first time typically continue to grow their earnings at high rates.

The drawback of increased dividends is that investors interpret this action as a long-term commitment to higher payouts. As noted earlier, the stock market severely penalizes companies for cutting dividends from long-term payout levels. Managers should be confident that future cash flows from operations will be sufficient to pay for capital expenditures as well as higher dividends. In other words, dividend increases are useful to handle structural cash surpluses but much less suited for a one-time surplus payout.

But higher dividends are not necessarily good news: they can also signal that companies have permanently lower future investment opportunities. This could actually lead to declining share prices if the stock market had expected the company to continue to invest strongly in valuable growth opportunities.

Share repurchases   In the 1990s, share repurchases gained notable importance as an alternative way of distributing cash to shareholders. In 1999, for example, share repurchases totaled $181 billion, close to the $216 billion in regular dividend payments for companies listed on the New York Stock Exchange.[44] Even in the wake of the stock market downturn in 2000 major companies in different sectors have continued to repurchase shares on a large scale; examples include Unilever, Marks & Spencer, ExxonMobil, IBM, and Viacom.

Investors typically interpret share repurchases positively for several reasons. First, buying back shares indicates to investors that management believes that the company's shares are undervalued. If shares were overvalued, management should pay down debt instead, to return cash to the capital markets. If management itself buys back shares this effect is reinforced. Second, a share buyback shows that managers are confident future cash flows are strong enough to support future investments and debt commitments. Third, it signals that the company will not spend its excess cash on value destroying investments. Fourth, share buybacks can result in lower taxes for investors than dividend payments in countries where capital gains are taxed at lower rates. In the United States this is the case for most investors, which partly explains the more prominent role of buybacks in the United States than in some European countries. As we pointed out in Chapter 13, most companies' share repurchases lead to an increase in earnings per share (EPS). This is not why markets typically react positively, however.

[44] See J. Pettit, "Is a Share Buyback Right for Your Company?" *Harvard Business Review*, 79(4) (2001): (1) 141–147.

It is the signaling, and not the EPS accretion, that matters. Empirical research shows that share prices on average increase 2 to 3 percent on the day of announcement for "smaller" repurchase programs (i.e., less than 10 percent of shares outstanding are acquired through open-market transactions).[45] For larger but far less frequent repurchase programs, in which usually around 15 percent of shares are bought back through tender offers, price increases are even stronger, at around 16 percent on announcement.[46]

In contrast to dividend increases, share buyback programs are not seen as long-term commitments, so buybacks are more suitable for one-off cash distributions. Sometimes companies have built up very high cash positions because of strong historical earnings combined with decreased investment opportunities. For example, in 2004 Microsoft announced that it would repay a record $75 billion over the next four years in cash to its shareholders, mostly in share repurchases. In other cases companies end up with large cash balances after portfolio divestments, as IBM did in the second half of the 1990s, and they used the cash proceeds to repurchase shares.

As an alternative to share repurchases, a company could declare an extraordinary dividend payout, as Microsoft did in 2004 as part of its cash return program. Microsoft paid out a significant portion in the form of an extraordinary dividend because of its concern that the share repurchase was so massive that it would swamp the liquidity in the market for Microsoft stock. The drawback of extraordinary dividends, compared with share repurchases, is that the dividend forces the cash payout on all shareholders, regardless of their preferences for capital gains or dividends. A share repurchase program at least leaves this decision to the shareholder, who is in the best position to decide whether it would be more beneficial to receive cash or hold on to capital gains.

Again, the risk in share repurchase programs and extraordinary dividends is that companies send a negative or at least ambiguous signal that they have insufficient valuable growth opportunities. An interesting case example is that of Merck, one of the largest pharmaceutical companies worldwide.[47] In 2000, it announced a $10 billion share repurchase, which led to a 15 percent decline in share price in the next four weeks (although the initial price reaction was favorable). Investors apparently assumed that

---

[45] In smaller programs, companies typically buy their own shares at no premium or a limited premium in so-called open-market purchases. Larger programs are often organized in the form of tender offers in which companies announce that they will repurchase a particular amount of shares at a significant premium. See, for example, R. Comment and J. Jarrell, "The Relative Signaling Power of Dutch-Auction and Fixed Price Self-Tender Offers and Open-Market Repurchases," *Journal of Finance*, 46(4) (1991): 1243–1272.

[46] T. Vermaelen, "Common Stock Repurchases and Market Signaling: An Empirical Study," *Journal of Financial Economics*, 9(2) (1981): 138–183.

[47] For this and more examples of share repurchases, see Pettit, "Is a Share Buyback Right for Your Company?" (Note 44)

Merck had been unable to find interesting research and development opportunities and could no longer maintain its long-term earnings growth target of 20 percent.

Debt repayment   The third option to reduce excess cash balances is to repay debt, for example, by buying back corporate bonds in the market. Unless the company needs to pay down debt to recover from financial distress, this typically does not meet with positive stock market reactions. First, it is hard to interpret this as an indication of undervaluation of bonds or debt. Relative to stocks, bonds are less likely to be undervalued unless the company is in financial distress. Thus, buying back bonds is more likely to indicate to investors that management believes stocks are overvalued; otherwise, management should buy back shares. Second, it signals that future cash flows may not be sufficient to support current levels of debt and that management therefore needs to reduce the corporate debt burden now, while it has the cash to do so. Third, as for all cash returns to investors, debt repayments could signal a lack of investment opportunities.

Companies that are highly overleveraged should repay debt or buy back bonds with any excess cash. This advice is consistent with our recommendation that whenever the deviations from long-term target leverage are large, leverage corrections should be made regardless of any signaling effects. Interestingly, for financially distressed companies, buying back bonds can also send a positive signal to the equity markets. For such companies, bond prices go up and down with the enterprise value, just as share prices do. In this situation, a bond buyback could therefore also be a credible signal that management believes the bonds are undervalued (and because in this case bonds are similar to equity, this must also mean that shares are undervalued). For example, when the Swiss-Swedish engineering company ABB announced a €775 million bond buyback in July 2004, its share price increased 4 percent on the day of the announcement. The stock market apparently saw the buyback as further evidence that the company was on a trajectory to recover from an earlier financial crisis.

CREATING VALUE FROM FINANCIAL ENGINEERING

Financial engineering means different things to different people. We define it pragmatically as managing a company's capital structure for maximum shareholder value with financial instruments beyond straight debt and equity. From this perspective, financial engineering represents more than simply setting the most effective leverage or coverage level as we have discussed in this chapter so far. Financial engineering typically involves more complex and sometimes even exotic instruments such as synthetic leasing, mezzanine finance, securitization, commodity-linked debt, commodity and currency derivatives, and balance sheet insurance. We will not discuss precisely what these instruments are or how they are typically applied. Instead, we will focus on the conditions under which financial engineering can create real value for shareholders, as well as some caveats for financial managers.

In general, companies can create much more value for shareholders in their business activities than in financial engineering. As we pointed out in Chapter 4, capital markets typically do a good job of pricing financial instruments, and companies will have difficulty boosting their share price by accessing so-called cheap funding, however complex the funding structures are.

Nevertheless, financial engineering can create shareholder value under specific conditions. This can happen directly through tax savings or lower costs of funding, but also indirectly, for example, by increasing a company's debt capacity so that it can raise funds to capture more value-creating investment opportunities. In the following section we consider three basic forms of financial engineering: transferring company risks to third parties, detaching funding from the company's credit risk, and offering new risk-return combinations in financing.

Derivatives

Derivative instruments—such as forwards, swaps, and options, for example—enable a company to transfer particular risks to third parties that can carry these risks at a lower cost. In most cases, the derivatives companies use involve currency and interest rate swaps.[48] With such swaps, companies convert their floating rate debt into fixed rate debt, and vice versa, or exchange particular currency cash flows into other currency denominations. As a result, companies can reduce their risk of business erosion, lower their cost of funding, and/or increase future tax savings.

McDonald's Corporation used currency and interest swaps to effectively convert the dollar funding of some of its foreign operations to local-currency-denominated debt.[49] Most airlines hedge their fuel costs with derivatives to be less exposed to sudden changes in oil prices. Of course, this does not make airlines immune to prolonged periods of high oil prices because the derivative positions must be renewed at some point in time. But derivatives at least provide the airlines with some time to prepare business measures such as cost cuts or price increases.

[48] See, for example, G. Bodnar, G. Hayt, and R. Marston, "1998 Wharton Survey of Financial Risk Management by U.S. Non-financial Firms," *Financial Management*, 27(4) (1998): 70–91.
[49] See the case description in C. Smithson, C. Smith, and D. Wilford, *Managing Financial Risk: A Guide to Derivative Products, Financial Engineering and Value Maximization* (Burr Ridge, IL: Irwin, 1990): 271–275.

Derivatives can actually create shareholder value when carefully applied in such specific cases. But they are not relevant to all companies. In general, derivatives are useful tools for financial managers when risks are clearly identified, derivative contracts are available at reasonable prices because of liquid markets, and the total risk exposures are so large that they could seriously harm a corporation's health.

Companies should ensure that proper systems and procedures are in place for managing and monitoring any derivative positions. Some high-profile scandals over the past 10 years involving, for example, Metallgesellschaft, Procter & Gamble, and Orange County, California, have underlined the need for such caution.

Off-Balance-Sheet Financing

Off-balance-sheet financing includes a wide range of instruments such as operating leases, synthetic leases, securitization, and project finance. Although the variety of these instruments is huge, they have the common element that companies effectively raise debt funding without carrying the debt on their own balance sheet.

In some cases, a company raises the debt through a separate vehicle[50] that has its own credit rating and credit terms. An example is the large-scale securitization of customer receivables undertaken by Ford Motor Company and General Motors. This securitization has effectively enabled both companies to tap large sums of debt financing that otherwise would have been difficult to obtain at similar terms.

Airlines are heavy users of off-balance-sheet financing in the form of operating leases for their airplanes. Essentially, in this form of funding debt is not just guaranteed by the airline but effectively backed with the plane. Because airplanes are easy to seize and swap among different airlines, they are good collateral for debt funding.

Off-balance-sheet financing can create shareholder value if it enables companies to attract debt funding on terms that would have been impossible to realize for traditional forms of debt. Of course, this assumes that there are enough value-creating investment opportunities for the company (which one may question in the case of the previous airline and automotive examples). This form of funding could make sense for companies that have strong investment opportunities for profitable growth but lack the strong current cash flow required for large amounts of debt funding. Examples are companies that need the funding to start up their business, as in the case of companies building and running gas pipelines,

---

[50] A so-called special-purpose entity (SPE) or, as it is referred to under U.S. GAAP, variable-interest entity (VIE).

toll bridges, or tunnels. They typically use project financing to raise cash for the initial investments; then they pay the interest and principal on the debt to the lender directly from the cash flows from future pipeline revenues.

Some managers find off-balance-sheet financing attractive because it reduces the amount of assets shown in the balance sheet and increases the reported return on assets. That is not a good reason to engage in off-balance-sheet financing. Investors will see through accounting representations, as we discussed in Chapter 4. Furthermore, under the latest U.S. GAAP and IFRS guidelines, many forms of off-balance-sheet financing need to be consolidated and shown in the balance sheet (e.g., via the requirement of full consolidation of special-purpose entities).

Hybrid Financing

Hybrid financing involves forms of funding that share some elements of both equity and debt. Examples are convertible debt and convertible preferred stock. In particular, convertible debt has been widely used in the past decade. The total volume of convertibles issues worldwide amounted to $145 billion in 2003—almost 8 percent of total new debt issuances in that year.[51]

Convertible debt can make sense when investors or lenders differ from managers in their assessment of the company's credit risk.[52] When the discrepancy is great, it may become difficult or even impossible to achieve agreement on the terms of credit. In case of convertible debt, a company's credit risk has less impact on the credit terms. The key reason is that higher credit risk indeed makes the straight-debt component of the convertible less attractive and the warrant component more attractive. Overall, convertible debt is less sensitive to differences in credit risk assessment and may therefore facilitate agreement on credit terms that are attractive to both parties. This also explains why high-growth companies use this instrument much more than other companies; they usually face more uncertainty about their future credit risk.

Do not issue convertible debt because it has a low coupon. The coupon is low because the debt also includes a conversion option. It is a fallacy to think that convertible debt is "cheap" funding. Do not issue convertible debt because it is a way to issue equity against the current share price at some point in the future when share prices will be much higher. That value

---

[51] D. Viazza and D. Aurora, "Global Convertibles to Decelerate from Torrid Pace," *Standard & Poor's Research Report*, March 24, 2004.

[52] See M. Brennan and E. Schwartz, "The Case for Convertibles," *Journal of Applied Corporate Finance*, 1(2) (1988): 55–64.

is already priced into the conversion options. Furthermore, if the company's share price does not increase sufficiently, the convertible debt will not be converted to equity, and the company will end up with interest-bearing debt instead.

SUMMARY

Although a poorly managed capital structure can lead to financial distress and value destruction, capital structure is not a key value driver: For companies whose leverage is already at reasonable levels the potential to add value is limited, especially relative to the impact of improvements in returns on capital and growth. Rather than fine-tuning for the "optimal" capital structure, managers should make sure the company has sufficient financial flexibility to support its strategy while at the same time minimizing the risk of financial distress.

REVIEW QUESTIONS

1. Define optimal capital structure. What is the relationship between optimal capital structure, corporate value, and cost of capital?

2. Academics argue that every corporation has an optimal capital structure. Most firms have a debt position consistent to an S&P financial risk rating between BBB and A. When you evaluate companies, you note that many companies carry essentially no long-term debt and only a minimal short-term debt position in their capital structure (Review the balance sheet of United Microelectronics and Symantec). Provide an explanation as to why well-managed and profitable companies appear to undervalue the benefits associated with an optimal capital structure.

3. How does the concept of an optimal capital structure differ from an effective capital structure?

4. The degree of financial risk is measured and reported by third-party corporations such as Standard & Poor's and Moody's. What factors do these companies evaluate when determining a company's financial risk classification?

5. What is the primary benefit of a company in issuing debt to finance its asset base? What is the primary cost associated with a company's debt position?

6. Identify and quantify the relation between an increase in the debt position of a company and its estimated cost of equity.

7. Outline a process a manager should employ to establish an effective capital structure target.

8. Describe the importance of the pecking order theory for managing the capital structure of a company as it relates to both short-term, tactical financing decisions and long-term, strategic decisions.

18

Investor Communications

Previous chapters in Part Three explored how to measure value and manage a company to create value. The final element of value creation is ensuring that the company's stock market price appropriately reflects its potential for value creation.

CEOs and CFOs spend a large and growing portion of their time on investor communications, yet they are frustrated by the amount of time it absorbs and the nature of their interactions with investors. Executives are obsessed with their company's share price, and worry constantly that it isn't high enough, or that markets don't understand their company sufficiently. They are also puzzled by the emergence of hedge funds, the growing number of analysts working directly for institutional investors, and the increasingly short-term focus of sell-side analysts.

Until recently, companies have approached investor communications in an ad hoc way. Executives receive advice from investor relations consultants, whose background is typically in public relations rather than finance. The academic community has only recently begun to research investor composition and communications. In contrast, a systematic approach to investor communications has two primary benefits. First, it can help align the market price of a company's shares with the company's intrinsic value. That alignment of share price and intrinsic value—and not simply the highest possible share price—should be the objective of investor relations. Second, a systematic approach helps executives communicate with investors more effectively and efficiently.

If a company's stock price exceeds its intrinsic value, it will eventually decline as the company's performance becomes evident to the market. Too high a share price also may encourage managers to support the share price by adopting short-term strategies, such as deferring investments or

Special thanks to Paul Adam, Yuri Maslov, and Jean-Hugues Monier for their support and insights on this chapter.

maintenance costs that will lower long-term value creation. Then, when the share price declines, employee morale suffers, and management must face a concerned board of directors who may not understand why it fell. Conversely, too low a share price has drawbacks, including takeover threats, the unattractiveness of using shares for acquisitions, and possibly demoralized managers and employees.

While the work in understanding investor communications is just beginning, some basic principles can guide companies:

- Investor communication strategy should be grounded in a thoughtful analysis of market value relative to management's careful estimate of intrinsic value. Gaps between intrinsic value and market value are rare, and these gaps often can be readily explained by factors unrelated to communications with investors.

- A company's investment story should be consistent with its underlying strategy and performance. As obvious as this sounds, companies sometimes do not line up their message with their strategy, especially in terms of how they allocate time talking about different business units or strategic initiatives.

- Companies are better off being transparent about performance and the drivers of value (with some exceptions). Transparency includes providing operating measures that the company uses to run its business, as well as financial results.

- Companies can improve investor communications (and sometimes corporate strategies) by understanding their investor base, particularly how it compares with peers and whether it has changed in recent months or years. While there is no evidence that a particular group of investors raises value or lowers volatility, insights from analyzing your shareholders can help you decide how senior executives should spend their time and how to shape your message.

INTRINSIC VALUE VERSUS MARKET VALUE

Senior executives often claim that the stock market undervalues or "doesn't appreciate" their company. They say it not just in public settings, where you would expect them to make that statement, but also in private. If only they had different investors, their argument goes, or if only the investors or analysts better understood their company, then they would have a higher share price. Yet, in some cases, these senior executives have not rigorously developed a perspective on what their company's share price should be. Their belief is based on some high-level analysis of P/E ratios or some comment by an analyst that the shares are undervalued. But any good strategy must begin with an honest assessment of the situation.

A strategy for investor communications must begin with an estimate of the size, if any, of the gap between management's view of the company's intrinsic value and the stock market value. After some thoughtful analysis and probing, we typically find that no significant gap exists, or that the gap can be explained by the company's historical performance relative to its expectations. We will illustrate using two disguised examples, which we call Chemco and PharmaCo.

Chemco Example

Chemco, a large specialty chemicals company, has earned attractive returns on capital, but its product lines are in slow-growth segments, so Chemco's revenue growth has been low. Chemco recently adopted a strategy to buy small companies in faster-growing areas of the industry. The company intends to apply its manufacturing and distribution skills to improve the performance of the acquired companies. The faster-growth segments also have higher returns on capital. Currently, 18 months since the company made its first acquisitions under this strategy, 5 percent of Chemco's revenues are from the fast-growth segments.

Chemco's managers were concerned that its shares' price-to-earnings ratio trailed the P/Es of many companies with which it compared itself. They wondered whether "intangibles," such as the company's old-fashioned name or the small number of analysts covering the industry, were the cause of the low value.

We began to assess the value gap by helping management better understand Chemco's value relative to its peers. First, some of the supposed peers were 100 percent involved in the fast-growth segments, far more than Chemco's 5 percent of revenues from fast-growth segments. Also, some of its peers were going through substantial restructurings, so current earnings were very low. When we segmented Chemco's peers, we found that its earnings multiple was in line with its close peers (see Exhibit 18.1 on p. 526) but behind the companies in the fast-growing segment. A third set of companies had high multiples because of current low earnings due to restructurings. Exhibit 18.1 also shows that Chemco and its closest peers had lower ROICs and much lower growth rates than the other companies. So, from a historical perspective, Chemco's value was aligned with its performance relative to its closest peers.

Next, we reverse engineered the share price of Chemco and its peers. We built a DCF model and estimated the future performance consistent with the current share price. Exhibit 18.2 on page 527 shows that if Chemco grew its revenues at 2 percent per year at its most recent level of margins and capital turnover, its DCF value would equal its current share price. This

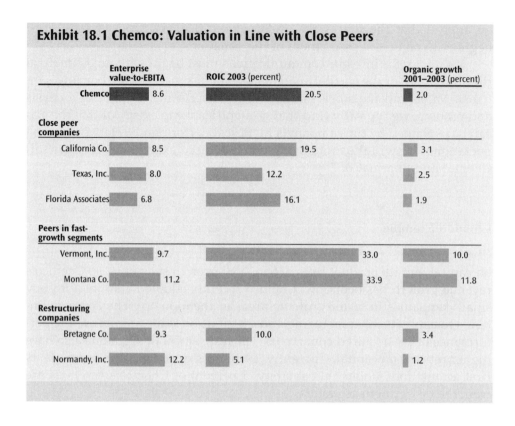

Exhibit 18.1 Chemco: Valuation in Line with Close Peers

	Enterprise value-to-EBITA	ROIC 2003 (percent)	Organic growth 2001–2003 (percent)
Chemco	8.6	20.5	2.0
Close peer companies			
California Co.	8.5	19.5	3.1
Texas, Inc.	8.0	12.2	2.5
Florida Associates	6.8	16.1	1.9
Peers in fast-growth segments			
Vermont, Inc.	9.7	33.0	10.0
Montana Co.	11.2	33.9	11.8
Restructuring companies			
Bretagne Co.	9.3	10.0	3.4
Normandy, Inc.	12.2	5.1	1.2

growth rate was in line with the implicit growth of its closest peers and lower than the companies in the fast-growing segment.

Finally, we used a DCF model to value management's announced growth aspirations. If Chemco achieved its growth aspirations of 6 percent per year, its DCF value would be $19 billion, suggesting a value gap of 36 percent relative to its current equity value of $14 billion. Thus, there was a gap between management's view of Chemco's intrinsic value and its market value. But could better communication close the gap? First, Chemco was valued in line with its closest peers. Second, there was not much evidence that the strategy would succeed. Chemco's managers had been in place for at least five years and had spent most of that time dealing with issues in its core business. The new strategy required Chemco to grow faster than the industry in its core businesses and to successfully acquire and integrate companies in faster-growth product areas, a very difficult task. It is not surprising that the market had adopted a wait-and-see attitude to rewarding Chemco for its new strategy.

PharmaCo Example

PharmaCo makes specialty pharmaceuticals and has been increasing revenues at around 5 percent per year. PharmaCo's managers believed the

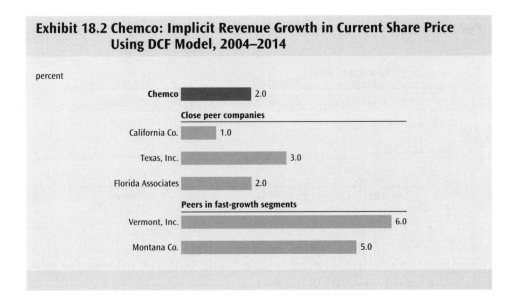

Exhibit 18.2 Chemco: Implicit Revenue Growth in Current Share Price Using DCF Model, 2004–2014

company was not "fairly valued" by the capital market. PharmaCo had a strong product pipeline, with several products coming to market very soon. Management and stock analysts alike expected 23 percent revenue growth for the next three years. Management then expected 13 percent per year for the following 10 years, and also expected to maintain its high margins and ROIC.

The DCF value of PharmaCo's management projections was $65 billion, 60 percent more than its market value of $40 billion. To determine the source of this gap, we also valued PharmaCo's closest peers. We used a DCF model to estimate the long-term growth rates implicit in their share prices. The implied long-term growth rate for PharmaCo was 12 percent per year, while the implied long-term growth rate for its peers, ranged from 2 percent to 6 percent. So the market had already embedded in PharmaCo's share price a growth premium that was substantial relative to its peers, but not as high as PharmaCo hoped. It is doubtful that better communication could close the value gap, given PharmaCo's already high valuation, both in absolute terms (12 percent expected growth) and relative to peers (twice the expected growth of the next best company).

ALIGNMENT OF MESSAGE AND STRATEGY

It is not unusual to see a serious disconnect between a company's value creation strategy and its investor communications. For example, Exhibit 18.3 on page 528 shows an analysis of how MultiBusiness did not align its

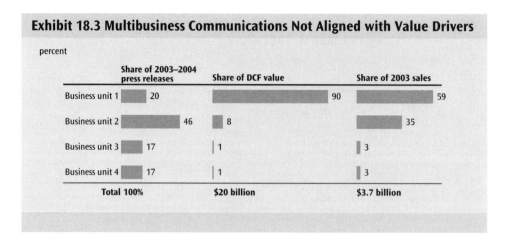

Exhibit 18.3 Multibusiness Communications Not Aligned with Value Drivers

percent

	Share of 2003–2004 press releases	Share of DCF value	Share of 2003 sales
Business unit 1	20	90	59
Business unit 2	46	8	35
Business unit 3	17	1	3
Business unit 4	17	1	3
	Total 100%	$20 billion	$3.7 billion

communications to investors by business unit with the value of the business units. Business Unit (BU) 1 was by far the biggest value creator, responsible for 90 percent of Multi's value. Yet the company devoted only 20 percent of its communications to BU 1.

Effective investor communications should be grounded in a compelling message that lines up with the value management expects to create. The message, or "investment story," should help investors understand what the company stands for, how it differs from other companies, and why the prospects of investing in the company are better than investing in its competitors or even in different industries.

A compelling investment story has three key elements: aspirations, strategy, and evidence. *Aspirations* define what the company wants to accomplish and should be described in financial terms and market terms. For example, a company could define aspirations for revenue growth, profit growth, and returns on capital, as well as market share, product innovation, or customer penetration.

By definition, aspirations should be difficult to achieve, but investors tend to be skeptical about aspirations that are wildly unrealistic, vague, or not grounded in the economics of the industry. For example, companies often have aspirations to increase earnings per share by 10 percent per year (a number that CEOs seem enamored of) for the foreseeable future. Yet our study of a sample of 1,056 companies found that only 16 percent were able to earn 10 percent annual EPS growth 5 years in a row, and only 1 percent earned 10 percent annual EPS growth 10 years in a row. Another problem with an EPS aspiration is that it doesn't differentiate between 10 percent growth driven by share repurchases and expensive acquisitions, on one hand, and an aspiration fueled by organic growth and productivity improvements, on the other hand.

Strategy explains how the company will reach its aspirations. It should explain the company's competitive advantages or unique corporate skills and how those will translate into value creation. Returning to the Chemco example, part of that company's strategy for faster revenue growth was to acquire companies in faster-growing segments. While growth through acquisitions is a strategy, Chemco's investment story didn't explain how its acquisitions would create value, so the story wasn't very compelling. When pushed, Chemco's management explained what the company had accomplished with the smaller, faster-growing acquisitions. They had substantially improved margins and return on capital through application of superior manufacturing techniques that were unique to the industry and through better working capital management. They also integrated the acquired companies' distribution systems into theirs for substantial improvements. Explaining more completely how their acquisition strategy creates value would make a much more compelling investment story.

Evidence helps investors assess whether a company's strategy works to achieve the declared aspiration. Evidence is not necessarily detailed disclosures, but it does include key success stories. A large and highly successful industrial conglomerate had embarked on an ambitious strategy to accelerate organic growth. The company had a distinguished track record of operating excellence and earned exceptional returns on capital, but its focus on ROIC had come at the cost of modest organic growth. The CEO established a number of growth initiatives to change the organization's mind-set toward organic growth. In his communications with the markets, the CEO cited a range of evidence supporting his assertion that organic growth would accelerate, including a large number of recently developed patents in nanotechnology, recent customer successes with a new service model that could be rolled out globally, and success in China at building a strong group of local managers.

HOW MUCH TRANSPARENCY?

Despite the trend toward increasing transparency and disclosure after the corporate scandals beginning in 2000 and the enacting of the Sarbanes-Oxley legislation in the United States and similar reforms in Europe, companies still have tremendous latitude to decide what to disclose. Companies need to decide their strategy for transparency and disclosure: will they drive their industry toward greater transparency, or will they disclose as little as possible?

While legislation and accounting rules continue to require more transparency, much regulated transparency is not that useful because it is too generic. Useful sorts of transparency typically arise more spontaneously within an industry, often responding to explicit demands from investors or the leadership of one or more industry pioneers. For example, in petroleum, the industry has for many years published detailed fact books that describe oil production and reserves by geography, key parameters that investors want to know when valuing petroleum companies. In pharmaceuticals, companies provide detailed information about their product pipelines at every stage of research and development. In these industries, companies that failed to disclose what others disclose would not likely maintain the market's trust. In most industries, however, the level of disclosure and transparency has been less standardized, so management must decide how transparent to be.

Transparency for the Sake of Accurate Valuations

Greater transparency is likely to cause tighter alignment between management's reasonable estimate of intrinsic value and the company's stock price. If investors better understand the drivers of historical and future performance, they can develop more accurate models of the business. For example, in retail, the common practice is to disclose information about the number of stores and same-store sales growth. This information lets investors build models based on these variables and project future revenues accordingly. Without the drivers of value, investors would be forced to extrapolate from historical performance. If investors don't know whether a retailer's sales grew from store growth or sales per store, they have to make their own estimates in modeling the company's performance.

Companies can increase transparency and valuation accuracy by improving their historical financial reporting and, most importantly, by reporting the underlying nonfinancial drivers of performance (referred to in Chapter 13 as business health metrics).

Historical financial reporting   As companies become larger and more complex, it is more difficult to interpret their historical financial performance and forecast their future performance. Larger companies typically have multiple business units, each with different growth, margins, and return on capital. The overall results are often just averages that don't help investors understand the underlying performance of the companies. Investors like to build up the value of the company as the sum of individual components. To help investors understand complex companies, the U.S. GAAP and IFRS require companies to disclose performance by business unit, but companies have significant flexibility in how they report business units.

As investors ask for better segment reporting, some companies are responding. For example, Microsoft reorganized its business unit reporting in 2003 (for its 2002 results) to show more clearly the economics of its key business activities. As Exhibit 18.4 illustrates, before 2002, Microsoft reported three business units: desktop and enterprise software, consumer software and services, and consumer commerce. Many investors argued that this segmentation was not helpful. Along with an internal reorganiza-

Exhibit 18.4 Microsoft®: New Segment Reporting

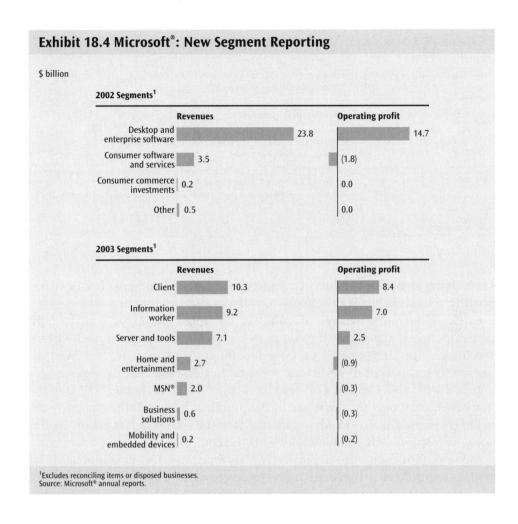

$ billion

2002 Segments[1]

	Revenues	Operating profit
Desktop and enterprise software	23.8	14.7
Consumer software and services	3.5	(1.8)
Consumer commerce investments	0.2	0.0
Other	0.5	0.0

2003 Segments[1]

	Revenues	Operating profit
Client	10.3	8.4
Information worker	9.2	7.0
Server and tools	7.1	2.5
Home and entertainment	2.7	(0.9)
MSN®	2.0	(0.3)
Business solutions	0.6	(0.3)
Mobility and embedded devices	0.2	(0.2)

[1]Excludes reconciling items or disposed businesses.
Source: Microsoft® annual reports.

tion, Microsoft shifted to a presentation along seven business lines that mirror the way the company is managed: client (essentially Windows- and PC-related products), information worker (essentially Microsoft Office), server and tools (products for servers), home and entertainment (mostly Xbox), MSN, business solutions, and mobility-related products. In the new classification, the segments have clearly defined products and competitors. For example, Windows is the operating system for most personal computers and faces a possible long-term threat from Linux. Microsoft Office leads the markets for spreadsheets, word processing, and presentation software. Both Windows and Office have profit margins greater than 75 percent. The Xbox line of computer games competes with Sony and Nintendo and has yet to earn a profit, as the product is young and the market highly competitive. MSN competes with companies like AOL and Google. It, too, has never earned a profit. With this information about the business units, investors can assess the value of each part of Microsoft and more accurately value the company.

Exhibit 18.5 GlaxoSmithKline: Illustration of Disclosures

Historical financial reporting	• Revenue, profit and R&D spending by business unit • Market share by therapeutic area
Current products	• Revenues by key products
Product pipeline	• Extensive description of compounds under development; including development stage
Projections	• Revenue and profit projections by unit • Revenue, prescription, and market share projections for top-selling products

Source: GlaxoSmithKine web site.

Underlying drivers of value   In addition to transparency in financial reporting, investors want to know what drives the financial results. Reporting the underlying drivers of value is the most powerful way to help investors assess the value of a company's shares. As we mentioned earlier, the underlying drivers will vary from company to company, and from industry to industry, but investors want to understand the drivers of revenues, costs, and capital. For revenues, they want to know how big the market is, what new products are in the pipeline, how well the company develops new products, and what market share the company has achieved. For costs, investors want to know how well the company is driving down costs compared with competitors. Similarly, they want to know how much capital will be required to achieve future revenue growth.

Retailers provide some of these answers when they disclose the number of stores and same-store sales growth. When they also report sales per square foot, investors can monitor the impact of changes in store size and configuration. Mobile-telephone companies typically disclose information about their customer base, such as number of subscribers and average revenue per subscriber. In the pharmaceutical industry, Exhibit 18.5 shows some of the disclosure by GlaxoSmithKline (GSK), an industry leader. GSK details its results by therapeutic area (e.g., cardiac drugs versus gastrointestinal drugs), describes drugs in its pipeline, and projects market share and revenues for each major product.

Concerns about Transparency

Many companies dislike transparency. They believe the market is only concerned about smooth growth in earnings per share (EPS), regardless of how companies achieve it. Many managers also believe that transparency reduces their flexibility. They like to be able to use good results from one

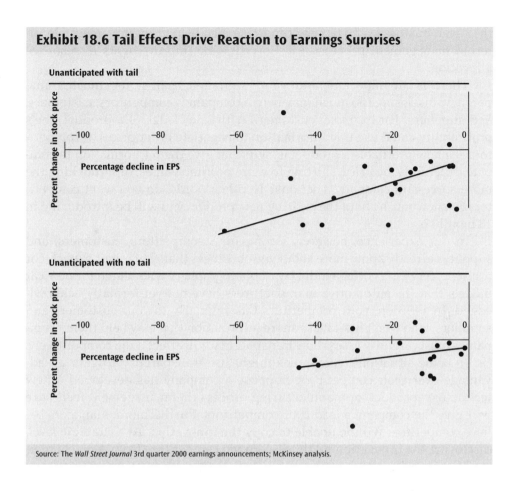

Exhibit 18.6 Tail Effects Drive Reaction to Earnings Surprises

Source: The *Wall Street Journal* 3rd quarter 2000 earnings announcements; McKinsey analysis.

business unit to offset bad results from another, or time asset sales to offset good or bad quarters. But as we showed in Chapter 4, investors are smarter than that, responding to the causes of good or bad results as much as the re-sults themselves. For example, some of our colleagues looked at a sample of companies that did not meet expectations for quarterly earnings. They clas-sified companies by whether or not the problem was likely to persist (did it have a "tail"?). As shown in Exhibit 18.6, the market did not respond blindly to the earnings announcement. The market responded much more mildly when there was evidence that the negative earnings were due to a one-time event, not something that would affect future results.

Companies are getting more comfortable with greater transparency. In-deed, some are embracing it. For example, when Microsoft began reporting along its new business units, it was compelled to disclose how much it had invested through operating losses in Xbox, MSN, and other new products. In a recent interview, John Connors, the company's former CFO, said, "It was surprising how many people within the company didn't really under-stand how intensely analysts, investors and the press would follow each of the seven businesses." The new reporting also helped improvements in internal management processes; it "forced some improvements in resource allocation."[1]

There is an important and valid argument against too much transparency: disclosing too much may help a company's competitors, customers, and suppliers. For example, customers with knowledge of a product line's profitability could use that information to negotiate lower prices. If competitors see how profitable a product is, will that give them information to compete differently, by price, shifting to more profitable lines, or mimicking the more successful company's actions? In other words, do you want competitors to know much about the exciting new product you will be introducing in 18 months?

In our experience, however, a company's competitors, customers, and suppliers already know more about your business than you might expect. For example, there is a cottage industry of photographers who search for new car models that the automotive manufacturers have not yet formally acknowledged. In addition, your competitors talk regularly to your customers and suppliers, who won't hesitate to share information that may help them. Companies must carefully assess how transparency will affect them competitively.

In some situations, companies might use transparency to gain an advantage over their competitors. Suppose a company has developed a new technology, product, or manufacturing process that management feels sure will give the company a lead over competitors. Furthermore, managers believe competitors will be unable to copy the innovation. At a strategic level, disclosing the innovation might discourage competitors from even competing if they believe the company has too great a lead. From an investor's perspective, disclosure of the innovation could increase the company's share price relative to its competitors, thus making it more attractive to potential partners and key employees, and could reduce the price of stock-based acquisitions.

The transition to more transparency can be difficult. Some companies that have not been transparent are pondering whether to change. These are often strongly performing companies with good track records. Over many years, their track record (often steady earnings increases) has permitted them to rebuff investors' demand for more transparency. But, after years of success, growth slows as the business matures or markets become more competitive. In one situation, a large company did not disclose that most of its profits came from aging, low-growth products with a large installed base while its newer high-growth products were far less profitable due to competition and new technologies. In another case, a consumer products company kept its earnings growing by selectively reducing investments in

---

[1] Bertil Chappuis and Timothy Koller, "Finance 2.0: An Interview with Microsoft's CFO," *McKinsey on Finance*, 14 (2005), pp. 7–13.

advertising and promotion. Because of the companies' long histories of success, sudden new transparency would surely cause stock prices to decline. Academic research suggests that when these companies fall, they fall hard.[2] Executives at these companies need to decide whether their current predicament is temporary and short-lived, or whether their days of strong growth and high returns are over. If the latter, they clearly need a quick transition plan. If the former, they need to assess whether they should hold off on transparency and the pain it will cause until they have returned to their growth path.

Earnings Guidance

Should companies provide earnings guidance? Earnings guidance is a relatively recent phenomenon. In the United States, companies began providing guidance only after the SEC issued safe-harbor guidelines in 1995. According to a survey of analysts, earnings guidance is not that important.[3] Indeed, this survey showed that EPS forecasts rank as number 30 in a list of 33 most important aspects of financial disclosure to investors and analysts. There have been no published articles on whether earnings guidance affects the valuation of companies. Recently, however, a number of prominent companies stopped providing guidance. The market's reaction has been mixed. Reviewing some of the key cases, it appears that the market responded negatively to the discontinuance of guidance for companies that otherwise lacked credibility and had unclear strategies and poor disclosures. The market responded positively for companies whose management enjoyed high credibility (as determined by analyst comments) and where the company provided additional business metrics to help investors understand the company's economics.

KNOW YOUR INVESTORS

Does it matter who your investors are? It is not clear whether one investor base is better than another. But understanding the company's investor base can give managers insights that might help them anticipate how the market will react to important events and strategic actions, as well as help managers improve the effectiveness and efficiency of their investor relations activities.

While we often read about managers wanting their company to be perceived a certain way, there is no systematic evidence that one investor base

[2] Douglas J. Skinner and R. G. Sloan, "Earnings Surprises, Growth Expectations, and Stock Returns" (working paper, 2002). See also Linda A. Myers and Douglas J. Skinner, "Earnings Momentum and Earnings Management" (working paper, 2002).

[3] Association for Investment Management and Research, Member Survey of Global Corporate Finance Reporting Quality and Corporate Communication and Disclosure Practices, October 2003 (772 respondents).

is better than another. For example, most companies prefer to be considered "growth" stocks rather than "value" stocks. Growth stocks are defined as having high P/Es relative to value stocks. In our experience, most value stocks have low P/Es because they are mature, slow growers and/or because they earn low returns on capital. Probably, managers can't do anything about this. Companies are constrained by what they are. Likewise, companies with upcoming volatile news will attract investors who like to bet on such news.

Investor Groups and Analysts

In general, managers should devote their communication energy to the investors who matter: those who will affect their share price. In general, these are likely to be large institutional investors.

Retail investors   Our colleagues Kevin Coyne and Jonathan Witter[4] found that, for the most part, retail investors act randomly enough that they rarely create the trading imbalances necessary to move stock prices significantly. But when retail investors act in unison, they can move a company's share price—for example, in response to a major event like an acquisition or CEO change. Similarly, others have found that the share prices of companies with more institutional investors moved faster in response to earnings surprises.[5] More important than the ratio of retail to institutional investors, however, was the investment style of institutional investors.

Sell-side analysts   Traditionally, companies spent the greatest amount of time communicating to sell-side analysts (analysts who work for brokerage firms). One survey suggested that 53 percent of company time was devoted to sell-side analysts.[6] These analysts provide information to investors about their analysis, either selling their research or providing it free in return for trading commissions.

However, the importance of sell-side analysts is diminishing, partly because of the conflict-of-interest scandals early in the decade, but more importantly because institutional investors are learning to analyze companies on their own. There has been a steady increase in the number of analysts who cover stocks in-house, estimated at 5 percent growth per year.[7] In 2003, 60 percent of surveyed asset management companies declared that they plan to add to their in-house research capabilities.[8] Investors are becoming less

---

[4] Kevin Coyne and Jonathan Witter, "Taking the Mystery out of Investor Behavior," *Harvard Business Review* (September 2002).

[5] Edith Hotchkiss and Deon Strickland, "Does Shareholder Composition Matter? Evidence from the Market Reaction to Corporate Earnings Announcements" (working paper, unpublished).

[6] Institutional Investor Research Group, "The European Equities Market Report," March 2004.

[7] Unpublished McKinsey research.

[8] "Global Broker Survey: Putting a Price on Independence," *Global Investor* (September 2003).

trusting of sell-side research because it is still dominated by buy recommendations, although you would expect a rough balance of buy and sell recommendations if analysts were unbiased. According to the Zack's database of analysts' recommendations, in February 2005, of 27,000 ratings the ratio of buy to sell recommendations was 5 to 1 (40 percent buy, 52 percent hold, and 8 percent sell).

Many companies have recognized the declining importance of sell-side analysts. A recent survey by *Institutional Investor* highlighted that the majority of companies plan to increase time allocation to the buy-side analysts working for institutional investors.[9] In recent conversations, some corporate executives have commented that sell-side analysts seem more focused on short-term results while institutional investors (and their analysts) are more likely to ask about longer-term strategic issues. Part of this may be due to the emergence of hedge funds, often the largest clients of the brokerage firms that employ the sell-side analysts. Many hedge fund clients are most interested in short-term news that they can use with their trading strategies.

Hedge funds   Hedge funds are relatively small in absolute terms, but estimates suggest that they accounted for 25 to 30 percent of market turnover in 2002.[10] Additionally, hedge funds are growing fast; their global assets grew at a staggering 26 percent annually between 1990 and 2003.[11] Unfortunately for managers, hedge funds don't disclose their holdings or investment strategies. Not surprisingly, one of the most frustrating investor communication experiences is dealing with hedge funds, often because hedge funds focus on near-term events. As a result, many companies tend to ignore them in their communications as an "alien" type of investor that tends to drive volatility and put downward pressure on stock performance.

However, once a company has diagnosed hedge funds as one of those individual large-mover shareholders that matter (or even once hedge funds cumulatively hold a large proportion of the company's stock), the company needs to better understand these funds' investment motivations and information needs.

Understanding Institutional Investors

Analyzing a company's investor base or identifying potential attractive investors is currently far more art than science. Most of the effort of investor communications rightly focuses on the institutional investors that hold the most shares. In the United States, institutional investors must file information about their portfolios with the SEC every quarter, so they are easy to identify and analyze.

---

[9] "Global Broker Survey: Rethinking the Research Model," *Global Investor* (September 2004).
[10] ITG, Inc., "ITG, Inc. to Acquire Hoenig Group, Inc.," news release, September 27, 2002.
[11] Hedge Fund Research, Inc., "HFR Year End 2003 Industry Report," 2004.

Institutional investors are typically classified by investment style. For example, Thomson Financial examines the portfolios of institutional investors along three dimensions: (1) the portfolio's forward P/E relative to the S&P 500, (2) the indicated dividend yield relative to the S&P 500, and (3) the three- to five-year projected EPS growth rate relative to the S&P 500. Based on this analysis, Thomson identifies a "dominant" style for each investor: momentum, aggressive growth, growth, core growth, growth at a reasonable price (GARP), core value, deep value, income value, yield, or index. However, institutional investors often have multiple funds, under different fund managers. You need to understand the styles of the individual fund managers, not the overall style of the parent group.

The Thomson styles are typical for the investment industry, but their usefulness is still questionable. Take, for example, value investors versus growth investors. At the highest level, growth investors are classified as investors who invest in companies with higher than average P/E ratios (the opposite of value investors). Yet as we showed in Chapter 3, many companies have high P/E ratios because they have high returns on capital, not because they are growing particularly fast.

Instead of classifying investors this way, Coyne and Witter propose comparing investors along two dimensions: their horizon of analysis and the dominant content being analyzed.[12] Along the first dimension, they group investors into four categories:

1. *Fundamental analysts* have the longest horizons and base investment decisions on a comparison between a stock's current price and its estimated intrinsic value based on the company's long-term (five years or more) outlook.

2. *News forecasters* are interested in whether some strategic event will occur within 12 to 18 months and affect the value of the company's shares. They make buy or sell decisions based on predictions of these news events.

3. *Event bettors* have the shortest horizons. They focus on buying or selling ahead of specific news such as earnings predictions or the outcome of an important sale or product announcement.

4. *Passive investors* are typically indexers who hold a company because it is part of an index or sector, or they have a relationship with the company and are unlikely to trade frequently.

Along the dimension of content being analyzed, Coyne and Witter identify three types of investors:

[12] See Coyne and Witter, "Taking the Mystery out of Investor Behavior." (Note 4)

1. *Organization mavens* focus on people issues within the company, particularly changes in top management and their assessment of the quality of management.

2. *Strategy junkies* focus on strategy and operations, asking questions about products and competitive advantages.

3. *Financial addicts* focus on financial measures, such as earnings and margins.

Coyne and Witter's classification leads to 12 combinations. It would be difficult to craft 12 different messages, one for each type of investor, but a company could craft different messages along the dimension most relevant to its situation. For example, a company could craft a long-term strategy message for the fundamental investors and a message around upcoming news for the news forecasters.

Classifying investors helps a company understand how it may be viewed by the market. For example, a company can analyze how its investor base has changed and how it compares with that of peer companies. Exhibit 18.7 shows an analysis of PharmaCo's investors. Currently, PharmaCo has

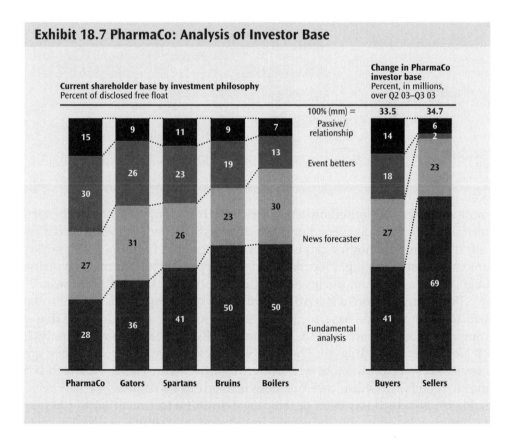

Exhibit 18.7 PharmaCo: Analysis of Investor Base

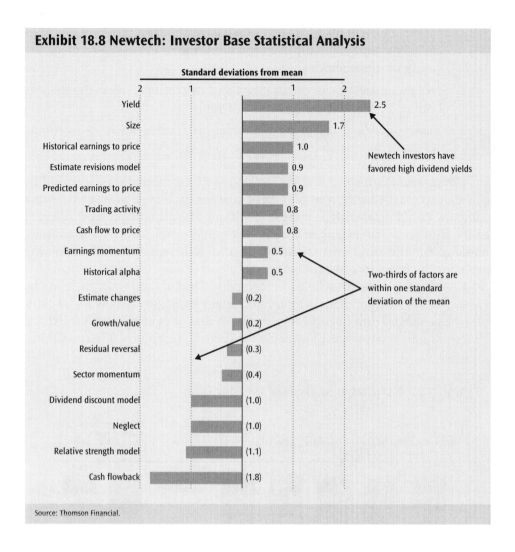

Exhibit 18.8 Newtech: Investor Base Statistical Analysis

Standard deviations from mean

Yield	2.5
Size	1.7
Historical earnings to price	1.0
Estimate revisions model	0.9
Predicted earnings to price	0.9
Trading activity	0.8
Cash flow to price	0.8
Earnings momentum	0.5
Historical alpha	0.5
Estimate changes	(0.2)
Growth/value	(0.2)
Residual reversal	(0.3)
Sector momentum	(0.4)
Dividend discount model	(1.0)
Neglect	(1.0)
Relative strength model	(1.1)
Cash flowback	(1.8)

Newtech investors have favored high dividend yields

Two-thirds of factors are within one standard deviation of the mean

Source: Thomson Financial.

more short-term-oriented investors (event bettors). This skew toward short-term investors has developed only over the last six months, perhaps as a result of PharmaCo moving out of the price range that fundamental analysts are comfortable paying. PharmaCo might expect, then, that once its string of good news dries up, the investor base will shift back to the peer norm.

Thomson also does a statistical analysis of company characteristics relative to their investor base to quantitatively identify unique issues that a company should be attuned to. For example, Exhibit 18.8 shows an analysis of Newtech. According to Thomson's analysis, Newtech's investors are heavily skewed to investors who prefer high dividend yields. Newtech is a mature company whose core business is about to be eclipsed by new technologies. Newtech has been developing a strategy to transition to the new technology, building on its strong brand and marketing skills. The new strategy will require a substantial investment, and Newtech has been considering reducing its dividend to fund its investment. With its investor base analysis, Newtech knows that its core investors may decide to sell when the new strategy is announced. This does not mean Newtech should change its decision, but it should be prepared for a possible sell-off by the dividend-oriented investors and prepare its board for a possible short-term price decline until the new strategy attracts investors with confidence in it.

Which Investors Matter

The analysis in the previous section focuses on classes of investors, rather than individual investors. What matters, of course, are the marginal investors. At any point in time, investors will have a wide range of opinions about the value of a company's shares, varying not just by 10 percent or 20 percent from the current share price, but sometimes by 200 percent or more. The investors with the highest estimates aren't likely to sell soon, just as the investors with the lowest estimate aren't likely to buy soon. The marginal investors are those who would buy if a bit of good news or some new insight into the company convinced them to increase their estimated value relative to the current share price, as well as those who would sell at a hint of bad news. Theoretically, these investors are the ones that matter and should be the focus of management's attention. The problem is that it is hard to identify these investors.

Coyne and Witter looked at the trading behavior for companies in the S&P 500. According to their study, in the quarter following a major announcement by a company, about 70 percent of company-specific changes in stock price (that is, changes that occurred in addition to movements in the sector or market overall) could be explained by the decisions of the 40 to 100 most active investors in the company. These shareholders are not necessarily the largest ones. Some large shareholders are passive, index investors or may be interested in the sector as a whole, rather than the specific company.

To identify key marginal investors, Coyne and Witter suggest the following approach: First, identify the following groups of investors:

- Large investors who have recently made significant purchases of your shares
- Large past investors who have recently bought back into your company
- Small current investors that could increase their holdings substantially or trade very actively
- Potential movers who currently trade in your peers but not you

Next, analyze the trading patterns of these investors. When do they buy/sell? When do they buy/sell your peers? Do they gradually build or reduce positions or move quickly to accumulate or sell shares? How overweight/underweight in your company is their portfolio relative to your peers? You could also (with caution about selective disclosure) interview them to understand their actions, specifically asking what aspects of your company they focus on. For example, in one case, Coyne and Witter found that more than 35 percent of a company's investors valued only two of its divisions.

Once you understand your investors, you will be in a better position to decide how your communications will vary across investors and how to allocate your time to different investors. For example, price-insensitive investors, such as index funds, don't require any specific communications strategy. Fundamental analysts (using Coyne and Witter's terminology) should be targeted with clear descriptions of strategies and key value drivers. News forecasters should be kept up-to-date on near-term events. Finally, you might develop individual account plans for the top 25 to 50 most important (not necessarily largest) investors or potential investors, taking into account their specific investment style, trading practices, and investment objectives.

It is easy to see that if you give "fundamental investors" a clear strategy with evidence, backed up with appropriate transparency, you can narrow the range of value estimates and, therefore, have a stock price that tracks intrinsic value more closely and with less volatility. However, given our current state of knowledge, it is less clear how to communicate with news forecasters or event bettors—and, more importantly, whether doing so makes a difference.

SUMMARY

The issues around investor communications will remain unresolved for some time. Traditionally, there have been two camps: those who believe you can "talk up" your share price and those who believe companies shouldn't spend much time or effort on investor communications because it won't make a difference. Most likely, the answer lies somewhere in the middle. Certainly, investors can more accurately value a company if they have the right information. Also, even if you *can* talk up the stock, it may not be the best thing for the company in the long run.

Regardless of which camp you are in, you can improve the alignment of your company's value with its intrinsic value by applying some of the systematic approaches we have described for understanding your value, understanding your current and potential investors, and communicating with investors. These principles also can help managers use their scarce time for investor communications more efficiently and effectively.

REVIEW QUESTIONS

1. The general consensus among academics is that the capital markets are efficient. If the capital markets are efficient, identify the potential value gained by having management establish an effective investor communications department?

2. Identify and describe the key elements of a well-defined investment story.

3. Compare and contrast intrinsic value to market price. If the capital markets are efficient, what should be the relationship between intrinsic value to market price?

4. Define the term transparency as it relates to corporate investor communications. What is the importance of corporate transparency? Would increased transparency have led the market to different conclusions regarding value for companies involved in recent accounting scandals, such as Adelphia?

5. If transparency is a significant benefit, identify where too much transparency might lead to a reduction in corporate value. Consider in your answer how too much transparency could lead to a decline in a firm's competitive position and enterprise value.

6. What are hedge funds? Why is it important that management understand both the motivation behind and the informational needs of the hedge fund industry?

7. Should the investment story be crafted to the interests of each specific investor group or should there be a consistent investment story that applies to all investors? Explain.

8. Why should managers consider the marginal investor of the company's common equity the main focus of their attention? How might management identify the marginal investor?

Part Four

Advanced Valuation Issues

19

Valuing Multibusiness Companies

Most large companies are in multiple businesses. Some companies are quite diverse; at General Electric, for instance, business units are dedicated to products as varied as jet engines, light bulbs, and consumer appliances. Even companies with a narrower focus, such as consumer products, often compete in multiple segments (Procter & Gamble's beauty products, laundry detergent, pet food, and pharmaceuticals). If each business unit's financial characteristics (growth and return on capital) are significantly different, it is best to analyze and value each unit separately and then sum the parts to estimate the value of the entire company.

But is this process economically sound? Is the value of a diversified business truly the sum of its parts? Over the years, practitioners and academics have debated whether there is a "conglomerate or diversification discount." In other words, does the market value conglomerates at less than the sum of their parts? Unfortunately, the results are incomplete. There is no consensus about whether diversified firms are valued at a discount[1] relative to a portfolio of pure plays in similar businesses. Some argue they may even trade at a premium. Among studies that claim a discount,[2] there is no consensus about whether the discount results from the weaker performance of diversified firms relative to more focused firms, or whether the market values diversified firms lower than focused firms. In our experience, however, whenever we have examined a company valued less than pure-play

Special thanks to S. R. Rajan, who co-wrote this chapter.

[1] P. Berger and E. Ofek, "Diversification's Effect on Firm Value," *Journal of Financial Economics,* 37 (1995): 39–65; and B. Villalonga, "Diversification Discount or Premium? New Evidence from Business Information Tracking Series," *Journal of Finance,* 59(2) (April 2004): 479–506.

[2] A. Schoar, "Effects of Corporate Diversification on Productivity," *Journal of Finance,* 57(6) (2002): 2379–2403; and J. Chevalier, "What Do We Know about Cross-Subsidization? Evidence from the Investment Policies of Merging Firms" (working paper, University of Chicago, July 1999).

peers, it was because the company's business units had lower growth and/or returns on capital relative to pure-play peers. In other words, there was a performance discount, not a diversification or conglomerate discount.

Valuing a multibusiness company by its parts follows the same principles we described in Part Two, with the following unique issues:

- Creating business unit financial statements
- Estimating cost of capital for each business unit
- Valuing each business separately, summing the parts, and interpreting the results

CREATING BUSINESS UNIT FINANCIAL STATEMENTS

To value a company's individual business units, you need income statements, balance sheets, and cash flow statements. Ideally, these financial statements should approximate what the business units would look like if they were stand-alone companies. Creating the financial statements for business units requires consideration of five issues: allocating corporate overhead costs, dealing with intercompany transactions, dealing with intercompany receivables/payables, valuing financial subsidiaries, and dealing with incomplete information when valuing listed companies with limited disclosures.

Corporate Costs

Most multibusiness companies have shared services and corporate overhead, so you need to decide which costs should be allocated and which retained at the corporate level. For services that the corporate center provides, such as payroll, human resources, and accounting, allocate the costs by cost drivers. For example, the aggregate cost of human resource services provided by the corporate parent can be allocated by the number of employees in each business unit. When costs are incurred because the units are part of a larger company (for example, the CEO's compensation or the corporate art collection), you typically should not allocate the costs. They should be retained as a corporate cost center and valued separately for two reasons: First, allocating corporate costs to business units reduces the comparability with pure-play business unit peers that don't incur such costs (most business units have their own chief executives, CFOs, and controllers who are comparable to pure-play competitors). Second, keeping the corporate center as a separate unit reveals how much of a drag it creates on the company value.

Typically, corporate costs for multibusiness-unit firms are 1 to 2 percent of revenue but about 10 to 20 percent of the operating profit. Hence, the negative value contribution of these costs tends to be on the same order of magnitude, or about 10 to 20 percent of the total enterprise value of the firm.

Intercompany Sales

Sometimes business units provide goods and services to one another. To arrive at consolidated corporate results, accountants eliminate the internal revenue and costs to prevent double counting. Only revenue and costs from external sources remain at the consolidated level. Exhibit 19.1 demonstrates how intersegment transactions are accounted for. Unit A provides $100 of widgets to Unit B and recognizes the revenue received and corresponding EBITA. Unit B then installs additional parts on the widgets and resells them to external customers. Assume, however, only 80 percent of the transferred widgets are processed and resold that period. The remaining 20 percent is added to Unit B's inventory at the preprocessing cost ($20). And since the inventoried units have not been sold, they remain on the balance sheet of Unit B. To consolidate the income statement, we eliminate Unit A's internally generated revenue of $100 and the $80 in Unit B's cost of goods sold. The net effect eliminates $20 in gross profit for the consolidated financials. In most situations, this inventory effect is small, because the EBITA impact is driven by the change in inventory, not the ending inventory. In any case, the impact on EBITA does not affect free cash flow, because the EBITA impact is offset by the change in inventory.

When you build and forecast the financial statements for the business units, treat the eliminations as a stand-alone business unit similar to the corporate center. This means as you project individual business unit growth rates, you need to estimate whether intercompany sales will grow as well. The growth rate of intercompany sales can be estimated from the details of how and why these items arise. It is simplest to assume that the eliminations grow at the same rate as the business as a whole. Remember, however, the eliminations are used only to reconcile business unit forecasts

Exhibit 19.1 Intercompany Eliminations with Timing Differences

$	Unit A	Unit B	Eliminations	Consolidated	Comments
External revenues	500	414		914	
Internal revenues	100		(100)	–	Eliminate intercompany revenue
Total revenues	600	414	(100)	914	
COGS	(540)	(290)	80	(750)	Eliminate profit on intercompany sales
Gross profit	60	124	(20)	164	

to the consolidated-enterprise forecasts and do not affect the value of the company or the individual business units.

In addition, to accurately value each business unit, you should record intercompany transfers at the value that would be transacted with third parties. Otherwise, the relative value of the business units will be distorted.

Intercompany Receivables and Payables

Multibusiness companies typically manage cash and debt centrally for all business units. Business units with positive cash flow typically forward all cash generated to the corporate center, sometimes setting up an intercompany receivable from the corporate parent. Units with negative cash flow receive cash from the parent to pay their bills, setting up an intercompany payable to the parent. These intercompany receivables and payables are not like third-party receivables and payables and therefore should not be treated as part of operating working capital. They should be treated like intercompany equity in the calculation of invested capital.

Exhibit 19.2 demonstrates how this is done. The consolidated firm consists of two businesses: the parent (P) and a subsidiary (S). P has invested $25 in S's equity, recorded as an equity investment. (This accounting treatment is for internal reports only; since P entirely owns S, the two companies must consolidate their statements for external reports.) P has also lent $20 to S, which shows up as an intercompany receivable for P and an intercompany payable for S. It would be a mistake to treat this amount as part of the working capital of either P or S. For P, it represents a nonoperating asset that does not generate operating profits, and hence should not be included in P's operating working capital. For S, it represents a financial infusion that is similar to equity, so it is part of S's financing structure but not its working capital. The internal receivable in P's balance sheet should be treated as an equity investment in S, and the internal payable in S's balance sheet should be treated as equity from P.

Failure to correctly handle the intercompany receivables and payables can generate seriously misleading results. In the example, if the intercompany accounts had been treated as working capital instead of equity, the subsidiary's invested capital would have been understated by about 30 percent, leading to an overstatement of ROIC by roughly the same amount.

Financial Subsidiaries

Some firms have financial subsidiaries that provide financing for customers (for example, General Motors Acceptance Corporation [GMAC]) or operate independent financial businesses (GE Capital). Balance sheets of financial businesses are structured differently from those of industrial or service businesses. The assets tend to be financial rather than physical (largely re-

Exhibit 19.2 Intercompany Receivables and Payables

$

Balance sheet	Parent Company P	Subsidiary S	Eliminations	Consolidated
Accounts receivable (external)	100	30	–	130
Accounts receivable (intercompany)	20	–	(20)	–
Other assets	150	50	–	200
Equity investment in S	25	–	(25)	–
Total assets	295	80	(45)	330
Accounts payable (external)	80	15		95
Accounts payable (intercompany)	–	20	(20)	–
Debt	100	20		120
Equity	115	25	(25)	115
Total liabilities and equity	295	80	(45)	330
Invested capital				
Accounts receivable (external)	100	30	–	130
Accounts payable (external)	(80)	(15)	–	(95)
Working capital	20	15	–	35
Other assets	150	50	–	200
Invested capital	**170**	**65**	**–**	**235**
Debt	100	20	–	120
Equity	115	25	(25)	115
Equity equivalent—intercompany payable to P	–	20	(20)	–
Accounts receivable (intercompany)	(20)	–	20	–
Equity investment in S	(25)	–	25	–
Invested capital	**170**	**65**	**–**	**235**

ceivables or loans) and are usually highly leveraged. As we detail in Chapter 25, financial businesses should be valued using cash flow to equity discounted at the cost of equity. Most companies with significant financial subsidiaries provide a separate balance sheet and income statement for those subsidiaries, which can be used to analyze and value the financial subsidiaries separately.

When valuing financial subsidiaries, be careful not to double count the debt of the financial subsidiary in the overall valuation of the company. The equity value of a financial subsidiary is already net of the subsidiary's debt, so when you subtract debt from enterprise value to arrive at the consolidated company's value, subtract only the debt associated with nonfinancial operations. To keep things clean, we usually rework the consolidated company's income statements and balance sheets to treat the financial subsidiary as a nonconsolidated subsidiary. The resulting financial statements contain a single line in the balance sheet representing the net equity of the subsidiary and a single line in the income statement representing the subsidiary's net income.

Valuation with Public Data

If you are valuing a multibusiness company from the outside in, you will not have complete financial statements by business unit. Exhibit 19.3 shows the disclosure typical of U.S. listed companies (IFRS disclosures are similar). Under U.S. GAAP, companies disclose revenues, operating profit (or something similar, such as EBITA), total assets, depreciation, and capital expenditures. You need to convert these items to NOPLAT and invested capital, as shown in Exhibit 19.4.

For the remainder of this chapter we will illustrate the concepts discussed using Personal Products Inc. (PP Inc.), a fictional company with three consumer businesses. PP Inc. has a branded soup unit, a personal care unit, and a food service business. The soup unit produces 40 percent of the company's revenues and more than half the company's profit. It is a shrinking business with intense competition from other soup brands as well as private labels. The personal care division also delivers about 40 percent of the revenues but only a third of the profit. This division's portfolio includes strong but mature brands, with growth equal to GDP growth. The food service business, with a little over 20 percent of the revenues and the remaining profit, has higher growth prospects than the other units, but it operates in an industry that is intensely competitive and fragmented.

NOPLAT To estimate NOPLAT, start with reported EBITA by business unit. Next, allocate income taxes, the pension adjustment, and the operating lease adjustment to each of the business units (for more information on these adjustments, see Chapter 7). To allocate the consolidated-company lease adjustment (if any), estimate the assets leased by each business unit

Exhibit 19.3 Personal Products, Inc.: Business Unit Information Presented in the Annual Report

$ million

	Soup	Personal care	Food service	Eliminations	Corporate	Consolidated
External revenues	2,400	2,200	1,200		–	5,800
Internal revenues	400			(400)		–
Total revenues	2,800	2,200	1,200	(400)	–	5,800
Operating costs	(2,184)	(1,826)	(1,056)	400	(70)	(4,736)
EBITA	616	374	144	–	(70)	1,064
Depreciation (included in operating costs, above)	17	22	12	–	8	59
Capital expenditures	84	77	38			199
Assets	1,200	1,100	540		150	2,990

Exhibit 19.4 Personal Products, Inc.: Estimating Business Unit NOPLAT, Invested Capital, and ROIC

$ million

Income statement	Soup	Personal care	Food service	Eliminations	Corporate	Consolidated	Comments
Revenues	2,800	2,200	1,200	(400)	–	5,800	*From 10-K*
Operating costs	(2,184)	(1,826)	(1,056)	400	(70)	(4,736)	*Plug to match EBITA*
EBITA	616	374	144	–	(70)	1,064	*From 10-K*
Operating taxes	(240)	(146)	(56)	–	27	(415)	*Use rate for whole firm*
NOPLAT	**376**	**228**	**88**	**–**	**(43)**	**649**	

Reconciliation to net income

Net income		564
Interest expense (after tax)		86
Interest income (after tax)		(1)
NOPLAT		**649**

Economic balance sheet and invested capital

	Soup	Personal care	Food service	Eliminations	Corporate	Consolidated	
Total assets	1,200	1,100	540	–	150	2,990	*Given in 10-K*
Goodwill	(150)	(100)	–	–	–	(250)	*From 10-K or recent deals*
Accounts payable	(157)	(143)	(78)	–	–	(378)	*Allocate by revenue*
Wages payable	(62)	(57)	(31)	–	–	(150)	*Allocate by revenue*
Other current liabilities	(41)	(38)	(21)	–	–	(100)	*Allocate by revenue*
Invested capital (excluding goodwill)	**790**	**762**	**410**	**–**	**150**	**2,112**	
Debt						2,000	
Equity						362	
Goodwill						(250)	
Invested capital (excluding goodwill)						**2,112**	
ROIC (percent) (excluding goodwill)	**48**	**30**	**21**			**31**	*NOPLAT/ invested capital*

(often, you must assume leased assets are in the same proportion as purchased assets), and then allocate the consolidated-company lease adjustment by this fraction. We typically allocate the pension adjustment to each business unit by the number of employees. Finally, use the effective overall corporate tax rate for all business units unless you have information to estimate each unit's tax rate. After estimating NOPLAT, reconcile the sum of all business unit NOPLATs to consolidated net income to ensure that all adjustments have been properly made.

Invested capital   To estimate invested capital, start with total assets by business unit, and subtract estimates for nonoperating assets and non-interest-bearing operating liabilities. Nonoperating assets include excess cash, investments in nonconsolidated subsidiaries, pension assets, and deferred tax assets. To measure invested capital excluding goodwill, subtract allocated goodwill by business unit. Frequently, these nonoperating assets are held at the corporate level, not in the business units, so no adjustment is needed. If nonoperating assets are included in the assets of the business units, you may need to do some investigative work to identify them by business unit.

Non-interest-bearing operating liabilities include accounts payable, taxes payable, and accrued expenses. They can be allocated to the business units by either revenue or total assets. Once you have estimated invested capital for the business units and corporate center, reconcile these estimates with the total invested capital derived from the consolidated statements, as shown in Exhibit 19.4. The sum of the invested capital for the business units and corporate center should equal the invested capital calculated from the consolidated financial statements.

ESTIMATE COST OF CAPITAL BY BUSINESS UNIT

Each business unit should be valued at its own cost of capital, because the systematic risk (beta) of operating cash flows and their ability to support debt (that is, the implied capital structure) will differ by business unit. To determine a business unit's cost of capital, we need the unit's target capital structure, its cost of equity (as determined by its beta), and its cost of borrowing (for details on estimating the weighted average cost of capital, see Chapter 10).

Target Capital Structure for Each Business Unit

First, estimate each business unit's target capital structure. We recommend using the median capital structure of publicly traded peers, especially if most peers have similar capital structures. Next, using the debt levels based on industry medians, aggregate the business unit debt to see how the total compares with the company's total target debt level (not necessarily its current level). If the sum of business unit debt differs from the consolidated company's target debt, we typically record the difference as a corporate item, valuing its tax shield separately (or tax cost when the company is more conservatively financed). We do this to minimize differences between the cost of capital and the valuation of the business units relative to their peers.

If the business unit has no comparable peers or if the capital structures of peers are widely different, allocate the consolidated debt across the business units so that each business unit has the same interest coverage ratio (EBITA/interest expense). As we demonstrated in Chapter 17, interest coverage is the single best predictor of credit rating and financial risk. Assigning comparable coverage ratios across business units ensures that they each have roughly the same financial risk and contribution to the company's overall credit risk.

In some cases, one or more business units may have tangible assets that are highly leverageable (for example, real estate, hotels, and airplanes). When this occurs, use tangible assets to apportion debt to these units.

The allocation of debt among business units for legal or internal corporate purposes is generally irrelevant to the economic analysis of the business units. The legal or internal debt is generally driven by tax purposes or is an accident of history (cash-consuming units have lots of debt). These allocations are rarely economically meaningful and should be ignored.

The Cost of Capital by Business Unit

Next, determine the levered beta and cost of equity for each business unit. To determine a business unit's beta, first estimate an unlevered sector median beta (as detailed in Chapter 10). Relever the beta using the same business unit capital structure derived previously. For corporate-center cash flows, use a weighted average of the business unit costs of capital. Exhibit 19.5 summarizes the estimation of cost of capital for PP Inc. While the unlevered betas for PP's business units are in a narrow range (0.7 to 0.9), larger differences in capital structures lead to weighted average costs of capital that range from 8.6 percent for the soup unit to 9.5 percent for the food service unit.

Exhibit 19.5 Personal Products, Inc.: Estimating Business Unit Cost of Capital

	Soup	Personal care	Food service	Corporate	Comments
Estimated unlevered beta	0.7	0.8	0.9	0.8	*Median of peers*
Target debt to capital (percent)	25.0	20.0	15.0	20.0	*Median of peers*
Levered beta	0.9	1.0	1.1	1.0	*At target capital structure*
Cost of debt (percent)	6.0	6.0	6.0	6.0	
Cost of equity (percent)	9.3	9.8	10.3	9.8	
WACC (percent)	7.9	8.6	9.3	8.6	

Risk free rate	5.0%
Inflation	2.8%
Market risk premium	4.8%

When you value a company by summing the business unit values, there is no need to estimate a corporate-wide cost of capital or to reconcile the business unit betas with the corporate beta. The individual business unit betas are more relevant than the corporate beta, which is subject to significant estimation error, especially when the company is widely diversified.

SUM THE PARTS AND INTERPRET RESULTS

The final step in estimating the company's value is to perform a discounted cash flow valuation of each business unit and sum the business unit values. Discount the forecasted free cash flow for each business unit, including an estimate of its continuing value as outlined in Chapter 11.

Value the corporate center cash flows separately as well. We typically project corporate costs to grow at the same rate as the overall company revenues. To determine continuing value, do not use the key value driver formula, as NOPLAT is negative (the corporate cost center has only costs), and ROIC is meaningless. Instead, use a cash flow perpetuity formula. Start with the negative after-tax free cash flow in the first year of the continuing-value period, and assume that it grows in perpetuity at the same growth rate as the overall company.

Add the value of nonoperating assets to the sum of the business unit operating DCF values less the value of the corporate center to figure total enterprise value. From this number, subtract debt and other nonequity claims to obtain the value of equity (see Chapter 11 for more details).

Applying this procedure to the PP Inc. example, Exhibit 19.6 shows the estimated DCF value of each business unit of PP Inc. The equity value derived from the sum-of-parts DCF value is reasonably close to the observed equity value. The resulting enterprise-value-to-forward-EBITA multiples, also shown in the exhibit, reflect the different growth and ROIC characteristics of the units. Soup is growing at 1 percent (shrinking in inflation-adjusted terms) but has the highest ROIC. In spite of the high ROIC, it has the lowest enterprise-value-to-EBITA multiple. Food Service is growing the fastest but has the lowest ROIC. Interestingly, Personal Care has lower growth than Food Service but a higher ROIC. The effect of the higher ROIC overcomes the effect of the lower growth, so its resulting multiple is higher than that for Food Service. As this simple analysis confirms, both ROIC and growth are critical inputs to valuation. Superior growth alone cannot ensure high value unless accompanied by high returns on investment.

Business unit valuation analysis also sets the stage for a comprehensive discussion of management priorities for operational improvement. Returning to the example in Exhibit 19.6, a dollar of revenue growth in the soup unit will add the most value on a relative basis, as it has the highest ROIC (assuming the ROIC on new projects equal its historical ROIC). The incre-

Exhibit 19.6 Summing Business Unit Values

Assumptions	Soup	Personal care	Food service	Corporate
Growth (2005 and after, percent)	1	3	4	3
Operating margins (2005 and after, percent)	22	17	12	
ROIC (2005 and after, percent)	48	30	21	
Invested capital to revenue ratio (percent)	28	35	34	
Enterprise value and multiples				
Estimated DCF enterprise value ($ million)	5,327	3,684	1,351	(873)
Estimated forward EBITA ($ million)	622	385	150	
Enterprise value to EBITA multiple	8.6	9.6	9.0	

Consolidated equity value ($ million)	
Soup	5,327
Personal care	3,684
Food service	1,351
Corporate costs	(873)
Operating enterprise value	9,490
Nonoperating assets	–
Debt and other liabilities	(2,000)
Estimated equity value	7,490
Observed equity value	6,900

mental value from margin improvement or increased capital efficiency in the Food Service unit will have a bigger effect on value than in the other two units.

The valuation of multibusiness-unit firms often leads to interesting insights. In the case of one consumer packaged-goods firm, for example, the core consumer products business represented three-fourths of the revenues and capital invested, with a secondary business representing the remainder. However, the profit margins and return on capital in the secondary business were nearly twice the values for the core business. Consequently, the value creation in the secondary business (total value less capital invested) was similar to that of the core business. A pure top-down view of the firm would not have highlighted this disparity in value creation. The findings had important implications for the relative value of growth and margin improvement in the two businesses and for where management should focus its attention.

Business unit analysis can thus provide striking insights into where value is being created or destroyed within the firm. It offers a road map for reorganizing the portfolio of businesses to create shareholder value.

REVIEW QUESTIONS

1. Identify the differences between an internal estimate of company value and an external estimate of corporate value. Does access to managerial accounting data necessarily lead to better corporate value estimates than relying on publicly available information?

2. Outline a process to identify the target capital structure of a business unit within a multibusiness company.

3. When estimating enterprise value, the firm's cost of capital is a critical driver of value. Explain how both financial and operating risks impact both the company's capital structure and a business unit's target capital structure. What influence do operating and financial synergies have on the component cost estimates of these capital structures?

4. What is meant by the term *conglomerate discount?* If the capital markets are efficient, should a conglomerate discount exist? Assuming that the capital markets are efficient, provide an alternative explanation for the existence of a conglomerate discount.

5. Chapter 19 suggests that business unit valuation might provide managerial benefits, such as a better prioritization both of a manager's time and efforts and of corporate resource allocation. Discuss how business unit valuation might lead to better alignment of corporate priorities with value creation.

6. Identify how intercompany receivables and payables affect the estimation of company value. What steps could a manager take to minimize the impact of intercompany receivables and payables on both business unit value and on corporate value?

7. How should an analyst account for intracompany sales? What impact does intracompany sales have on the valuation of a company?

20

Valuing Flexibility

In valuing companies with the standard DCF approach outlined in Part Two, we did not consider the value of managerial flexibility. Managers react to changes in the economic environment by adjusting their plans and strategies. For example, if a company develops a new product, it may invest to expand this business line. Then, if prices of critical inputs rise, it may scale back production or even terminate the effort. This flexibility represents a certain value, but a single projection or even multiple scenarios for cash flows cannot calculate what that value is.

Corporate-wide valuation models rarely include flexibility. To accurately analyze and model flexibility, you must be able to describe specific decisions managers could take in response to future events, including the cash flow implications of those decisions. Flexibility mostly occurs at the individual business or project level, and concerns decisions related to production, capacity investments, marketing, research and development, and so on. In valuing an entire company, flexibility is relevant only in special cases, such as in the case of companies with a single product, companies in a commodity-based industry, or companies in (or near) distress. For example, to value Internet or biotech companies with a handful of promising new products in development, you could project sales, profit, and investments for the company as a whole that are conditional on the success of product development.[1] Another example is a company that has built its strategy around buying up smaller players and integrating them into a bigger entity, capturing synergies along the way. The first acquisitions may not create value in their own right, but may open opportunities for value creation through further acquisitions.

---

[1] See, for example, E. S. Schwartz and M. Moon, "Rational Pricing of Internet Companies," *Financial Analysts Journal,* 56(3) (2000): 62–75; and D. Kellog and J. Charnes, "Real-Options Valuation for a Biotechnology Company," *Financial Analysts Journal, 56*(3) (2000): 76–84.

Flexibility is typically more relevant in the valuation of individual businesses and projects because it can be more clearly identified, analyzed, and valued in a bottom-up approach. In this chapter, we concentrate on how to value flexibility within the context of project valuation.

When making an investment, companies often have significant flexibility. If an investment project goes poorly, the company may scale it back or abandon it. If it is highly successful, the company may expand or extend it. Furthermore, a company may defer the investment until it resolves uncertainty through market testing. It is important to recognize that flexibility can take many different forms, each of which can represent substantial value.

To capture that value, let us explore two contingent valuation approaches: real-option valuation (ROV), based on formal option-pricing models, and decision tree analysis (DTA). Although they differ on some technical points, both boil down to forecasting, implicitly or explicitly, the future free cash flows contingent on the future states of the world and management decisions, and then discounting these to today's value.

You should learn both the ROV and the DTA approaches, because each has advantages in certain applications. The application of ROV approaches has improved greatly over the past two decades.[2] Real-option valuation is theoretically superior to DTA, and its key concepts (notably, the modeling of managerial flexibility in terms of options) are highly relevant to financial decision making. But ROV is not a cure-all. By definition, it cannot replace traditional discounted cash flow because valuing an option using ROV still requires knowing the value of the underlying assets. Unless the asset has an observable market price, you will have to estimate that value using traditional DCF. Because commodity prices are observable, the ROV approach is especially well suited to decisions in commodity-based businesses, such as investments in oil and gas fields, refining facilities, chemical plants, and power generators.

Valuing flexibility does not always require sophisticated, formal option-pricing models. The DTA approach is an effective alternative for valuing flexibility related to technological risk instead of commodity risk. Furthermore, if you have no reliable estimates on the value and variance of the cash flows underlying the investment decision, there is little justification for using sophisticated ROV approaches. In addition, the DTA approach is more transparent than ROV, which most managers cannot easily decipher.

This chapter is limited to the basic concepts of valuing managerial flexibility and real options. We focus on the following topics:

---

[2] See, for example, E. S. Schwartz and L. Trigeorgis, eds., *Real Options and Investment under Uncertainty: Classical Readings and Recent Contributions* (Cambridge, MA: MIT Press, 2001); T. Copeland and V. Antikarov, *Real Options: A Practitioner's Guide* (New York: Texere, 2003); or L. Trigeorgis, *Real Options: Managerial Flexibility and Strategy in Resource Allocation* (Cambridge, MA: MIT Press, 1996).

- The fundamental concepts behind uncertainty, flexibility, and value: When and why does flexibility have value?

- Classifying flexibility in terms of real options to defer investments, make follow-on investments, and expand, change, or abandon production.

- Comparing DTA and ROV approaches to valuing flexibility and identifying when each approach is most appropriate.

- A four-step approach to analyzing and valuing real options, illustrated with numerical examples using ROV and DTA.

UNCERTAINTY, FLEXIBILITY, AND VALUE

To appreciate the value of flexibility and its key value drivers, consider a simple example:[3] Suppose you are deciding whether to invest $6,000 one year from now to produce and distribute a new pharmaceutical drug already under development. In the upcoming final development stage, the product will undergo clinical tests on patients for one year. The trials will have either of two possible outcomes. If the drug proves to be highly effective, it will generate an annual net cash inflow of $500 into perpetuity. If it is only somewhat effective, however, the annual net cash inflow will be only $100 into perpetuity. These outcomes are equally probable.

Based on this information, the expected future net cash flow is $300, the probability-weighted average of the risky outcomes ($500 and $100). We assume that success in developing the new product and the value of the new product are unrelated to what happens in the overall economy, so this risk is fully diversifiable by the company's investors. Therefore, the cost of capital for this product equals the risk-free rate, say, 5 percent (remember, only nondiversifiable risk requires a premium). Assuming that the company will realize its first year's product sales immediately upon completing the trials and at the end of each year thereafter, the net present value (NPV) of the investment is estimated as follows:

$$\text{NPV} = \frac{-6,000}{1.05} + \sum_{t=1}^{\infty} \frac{300}{(1.05)^t} = 286$$

To apply the NPV approach, we discount the incremental expected project cash flows at the WACC. Any prior development expenses are irrelevant because they are sunk costs. Alternatively, if the project is cancelled, the NPV equals $0. Therefore, management should approve the incremental investment of $6,000.

[3] The example is inspired by A. Dixit and R. Pindyck, *Investment under Uncertainty* (Princeton, NJ: Princeton University Press, 1994), 26.

In this example of the NPV decision rule, undertaking development creates value. But there are more alternatives than deciding *today* whether to invest. Using an approach similar to the scenario approach described in Chapter 11, we can rewrite the previous NPV calculation in terms of the probability-weighted values of the drug, discounted to today:

$$NPV = 0.5 \times \left[\frac{-6,000}{1.05} + \sum_{t=1}^{\infty} \frac{500}{(1.05)^t} \right] + 0.5 \times \left[\frac{-6,000}{1.05} + \sum_{t=1}^{\infty} \frac{100}{(1.05)^t} \right]$$

$$= 0.5(4,286) + 0.5(-3,714) = 286$$

Here, the NPV is the weighted average of two distinct results: a positive NPV of $4,286 following a favorable trial outcome and a negative NPV of −$3,714 for an unfavorable outcome. If the decision to invest can be deferred until trial results are known, the project becomes much more attractive. Specifically, if the drug proves to be less effective, the project can be halted, avoiding the negative NPV. You need invest only if the drug is highly effective, and the annual cash flow of $500 more than compensates for the incremental investment.

This flexibility is essentially an option to defer the investment decision. To value the option, we can use a contingent NPV approach, working from right to left in the payoff tree shown in Exhibit 20.1:

$$NPV = 0.5 \times Max \left[\left(\frac{-6,000}{1.05} + \sum_{t=1}^{\infty} \frac{500}{(1.05)^t} \right), \, 0 \right] + 0.5 \times Max \left[\left(\frac{-6,000}{1.05} + \sum_{t=1}^{\infty} \frac{100}{(1.05)^t} \right), \, 0 \right]$$

$$= 0.5(4,286) + 0.5(0) = 2,143$$

The contingent NPV of $2,143 is considerably higher than the $286 NPV of committing today. Therefore, the best alternative is to defer a decision until

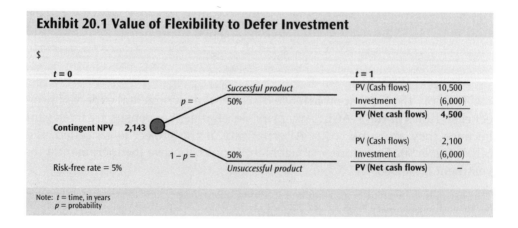

Exhibit 20.1 Value of Flexibility to Defer Investment

$

t = 0			t = 1	
		Successful product	PV (Cash flows)	10,500
	p =	50%	Investment	(6,000)
			PV (Net cash flows)	4,500
Contingent NPV 2,143				
			PV (Cash flows)	2,100
	1 − p =	50%	Investment	(6,000)
Risk-free rate = 5%		*Unsuccessful product*	PV (Net cash flows)	–

Note: *t* = time, in years
      p = probability

the trial outcomes are known. The value of the option to defer investment is the difference between the value of the project with flexibility and its value without flexibility: $2,143 −$286 = $1,857.

Based on this example, we can summarize the distinction between the standard and contingent NPV. The standard NPV is the maximum, decided today, of the expected discounted cash flows or zero:

$$\text{Standard NPV} = \underset{t=0}{\text{Max}} \left[\frac{\text{Expected (Cash Flows)}}{\text{Cost of Capital}}, \; 0 \right]$$

The contingent NPV is the expected value of the maximums, decided when information arrives, of the discounted cash flows in each future state or zero:

$$\text{Contingent NPV} = \text{Expected} \left[\underset{t=0}{\text{Max}} \left(\frac{\text{Cash Flows Contingent on Information}}{\text{Cost of Capital}}, \; 0 \right) \right]$$

These two NPV approaches use information quite differently. Standard NPV forces a decision based on today's expectation of future information, whereas contingent NPV permits the flexibility of making decisions after the information arrives. Unlike standard NPV, it captures the value of flexibility. A project's contingent NPV will always be greater than or equal to its standard NPV.

The value of flexibility is related to the degree of uncertainty and the room for managerial reaction (see Exhibit 20.2 on p. 564). It is greatest when uncertainty is high and managers can react to new information. In contrast, if there is little uncertainty, managers are unlikely to receive new information that would alter future decisions, so flexibility has little value. In addition, if managers cannot act on new information that becomes available, the value of flexibility also is low.

Even if flexibility has value, it may not affect an investment decision. An investment project with a high NPV will be undertaken regardless of new information. The largest impact on decision making occurs when the standard NPV is close to zero, that is, when the decision whether to undertake the project is a close call. Sometimes senior management intuitively overrules standard NPV results and accepts an investment project for "strategic reasons." In these cases, contingent valuation fits better with strategic intuition than with the rigid assumptions of standard NPV approaches.

Drivers of Flexibility

To identify and value flexibility, you must understand what drives its value. Consider what happens if the range of possible annual cash flow outcomes

Exhibit 20.2 When Is Flexibility Valuable?

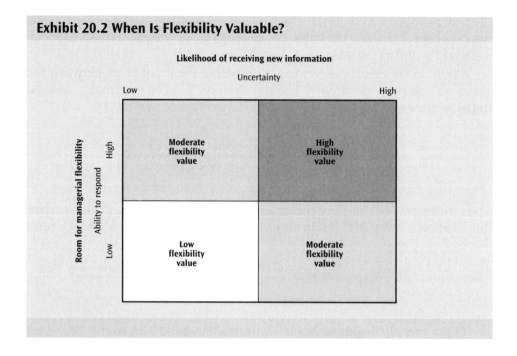

(originally $500 versus $100 per year) increases to $600 versus $0. Since expected cash flows and cost of capital remain unchanged, the standard NPV is the same ($286).[4] However, the contingent NPV increases from its prior level of $2,143 to:

$$\text{NPV} = 0.5 \times \text{Max}\left[\left(\frac{-6,000}{1.05} + \sum_{t=1}^{\infty} \frac{600}{(1.05)^t}\right),\ 0\right] + 0.5 \times \text{Max}\left[\left(\frac{-6,000}{1.05} + \sum_{t=1}^{\infty} \frac{0}{(1.05)^t}\right),\ 0\right]$$

$$= 0.5(6,286) + 0.5(0) = 3,143$$

The contingent NPV of $3,143 is almost 50 percent greater at this higher level of uncertainty. Why? The investment is made only if the drug is highly effective (that is, under a favorable trial outcome), so only the cash flows from the favorable outcome affect the contingent valuation. Since the cash flow projections contingent on the favorable outcome have increased by 20 percent, and the required investment has not changed, the contingent NPV increases very strongly. The value of the deferral option rises from $1,857 to $2,857 (computed as $3,143 − $286).

We can formally derive the key value drivers of real options by making an analogy to financial options and option-pricing theory. In our original example, the deferral option is identical to a call option with an exercise

[4] We assumed that the trial outcome risk is uncorrelated with the overall economy.

Exhibit 20.3 Drivers of Flexibility Value

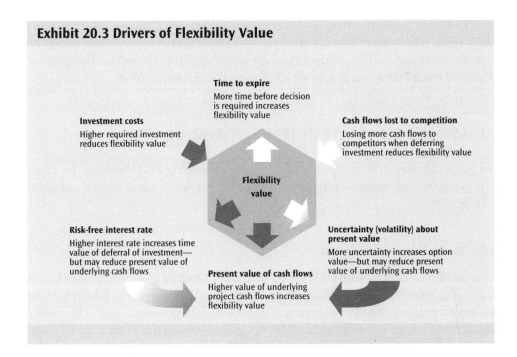

price of $6,000 and a one-year life on an underlying risky asset that has a current value of $6,000 and a variance determined by the cash flow spread of $400 across outcomes. As with financial options, the value of a real option depends on six parameters, summarized in Exhibit 20.3.

These drivers show when flexibility most affects the valuation of a particular investment project. Holding other drivers constant, option value decreases with higher investment costs and more cash flows lost while holding the option. Option value increases with higher value of the underlying asset's cash flows, greater uncertainty, higher interest rates, and a longer lifetime of the option. With higher option values, a standard NPV calculation that ignores flexibility will more seriously underestimate the true NPV.

Be careful how you interpret the impact of value drivers when designing investment strategies to exploit flexibility. The impact described in Exhibit 20.3 holds only when all other value drivers remain constant. In practice, changes in uncertainty and interest rates not only affect the value of the option but will usually change the value of the underlying asset as well. When you assess the impact of these drivers, you need to assess both direct and possible indirect effects. Take the case of higher uncertainty. In our example, we increased the uncertainty of future cash flow without changing its expectation or present value. But, if greater uncertainty lowers the expected level of cash flows or raises the cost of capital, the impact on the value of the option could be negative. The same holds for the impact of an interest rate increase.

Holding the present value of cash inflows constant, higher interest rates only reduce the present value of required investment, thereby increasing the option value. In reality, higher interest rates would also reduce the present value of the underlying asset, which lowers the option's value.

CLASSIFYING FLEXIBILITY IN TERMS OF REAL OPTIONS

To help identify and analyze a company's operating and strategic flexibility, we segment options into four mutually exclusive (but not exhaustive) categories.

Option to Defer Investment

The option to defer an investment is equivalent to a call option on stock. For example, assume a leaseholder of an undeveloped oil reserve has the right to develop the reserve by paying a lease-on-development cost. The lease-holder can defer development until oil prices rise. The expected development cost is equivalent to the exercise price.

Deferring investment is not without cost. The opportunity cost of deferring investment equals the difference between the current net proceeds per barrel of oil produced and the present value per barrel of developed oil reserves. If this opportunity cost is too high, the decision maker may want to exercise the option (e.g., develop the reserve) before its relinquishment date.

Abandonment Option

The option to abandon (or sell) a project, such as the right to abandon a coal mine, is equivalent to a put option on a stock. If a project proceeds poorly, the decision maker may abandon the project and collect the liquidation value. The expected liquidation (or resale) value of the project is equivalent to the exercise price. When the present value of the asset falls below the liquidation value, the act of abandoning (or selling) the project is equivalent to exercising a put. Because the liquidation value of the project sets a lower bound on the project's value, the option to liquidate is valuable. A project that can be liquidated is worth more than a similar project without the possibility of abandonment.

Follow-On (Compound) Options

Technically speaking, follow-on options are options on options (so-called compound options). An example would be phased investments, such as a factory that can be built in stages, each stage contingent on those that precede it. At each decision point, management can continue the project by investing additional funds (an exercise price) or abandon it for whatever it can fetch. Other examples are research and development programs, new-product launches, exploration and development of oil and gas fields, movie sequels, and an acquisition program where the first purchase is thought of as a platform for later acquisitions.

Option to Adjust Production

With an option to adjust production, a company has flexibility in choosing the scale, scope, lifetime, or raw materials for its production processes. Companies can do this in several ways, including the following:

- *Option to expand or contract.* The option to expand the scale of a project is equivalent to a call option on stock. For example, management may choose to build production facilities in such a way that they can be easily expanded if a product is more successful than was anticipated. An option to expand gives management the ability, but not the obligation, to make additional follow-on investments (e.g., to increase the production rate) if the project proceeds well. The option to contract the scale of a project's operation is conceptually equivalent to a put option. Projects should be engineered so that output can be contracted if necessary. The ability to forgo future spending on the project is equivalent to the exercise price of the put.

- *Option to extend or shorten.* Companies that can extend the life of an asset or contract by paying a fixed amount of money (the exercise price) own a valuable option. This is also true if it is possible to shorten the life of an asset or a contract. The option to extend is a call option, and the option to shorten is a put option. Real estate leases often have clauses with an option to extend or shorten the lease.

- *Option to increase or decrease scope.* Scope is the number of activities covered in a project. An option related to scope is the ability to switch among alternative courses of action at a future decision point. Scope is like diversification—it is sometimes preferable to be able, at some exercise cost, to choose among a wide range of alternatives. An option to increase scope is similar to a call.

- *Switching options.* A project whose operation can be switched on and off (or switched between two distinct locations, and so on) is worth more than a similar project without this flexibility. Examples include a flexible manufacturing system that can produce two or more different products, peak-load power generation, and the ability to exit and reenter an industry. The option to switch project locations or choose among raw materials is a portfolio of call and put options. Restarting operations when a project is shut down is equivalent to a call option. Shutting down operations when unfavorable conditions arise is equivalent to a put option. The cost of restarting (or shutting down) operations may be thought of as the exercise price.

METHODS FOR VALUATION OF FLEXIBILITY

There are two methods for contingent valuation: decision tree analysis (DTA) and real option valuation (ROV) using formal option-pricing models. Each method is illustrated with a simple example: the opportunity to invest $105 at the end of one year in a project that has an equal chance of returning either $150 or $50 in cash flow. The risk-free rate, r_f, is 5 percent, and the cost of capital for the project is 10 percent. The present value (PV) of the cash flows as of today is:

$$PV = \frac{0.5(150) + 0.5(50)}{1.10} = 90.9$$

If an investment decision was required immediately, the project would be declined. The standard NPV of the project equals the discounted expected cash flow of $90.9 minus the present value of the investment outlay of $105 next year. Since the level of investment is certain, it should be discounted at the risk-free rate of 5 percent:

$$\text{Standard NPV} = 90.9 - \frac{105}{1.05} = 90.9 - 100 = -9.1$$

The answer changes if management has flexibility to defer the investment decision for one year, allowing it to make the decision after observing next year's cash flow outcome (see Exhibit 20.4). The net cash flows in the favorable state are $150 - $105 = $45. In the unfavorable state, management would decline to invest, accepting net cash flows of $0. We first value this flexibility using an ROV approach.

Real-Option Valuation (ROV)

Option-pricing models use a replicating portfolio to value the project. The basic idea of a replicating portfolio is straightforward: If you can construct a portfolio of priced securities that has the same payouts as an option, the portfolio and option should have the same price. If the securities and the option are traded in an open market, this identity is required; otherwise

Exhibit 20.4 Contingent Payoffs for Investment Project, Twin Security, and Risk-Free Bond

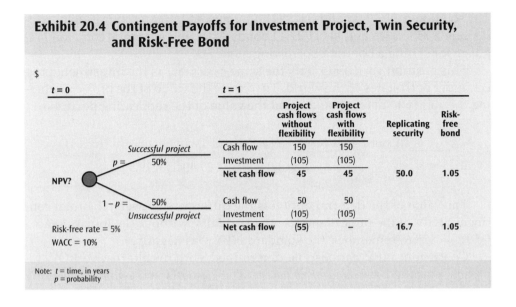

arbitrage profits are possible. The interesting implication is that the ROV approach lets you correctly value complex, contingent cash flow patterns without having to determine the option's expected cash flow and cost of capital.

Returning to our $105 investment project, assume there exists a perfectly correlated security (or commodity) that trades in the market for $30.3 per share.[5] Its payouts ($50.0 and $16.7) equal one-third of the payouts of our project, and its expected return equals the underlying project's cost of capital. This twin security can be used to value the project including an option to defer.[6]

To create a *replicating portfolio,* form a portfolio consisting of N shares of the twin security and B risk-free bonds with a face value of $1. In the favorable state, the twin security pays $50 for each of the N shares, and each bond pays its face value plus interest, or $(1 + r_f)$. Together, these payouts must equal $45. Applying a similar construction to the unfavorable state, we can write two equations with two unknowns:

$$50.0N + 1.05B = 45$$

$$16.7N + 1.05B = 0$$

[5] You could also use the twin security to value the investment project without flexibility by means of a replicating portfolio. Because the twin security's cash flows are always exactly one-third of the project cash flows, the project without flexibility should be worth three times as much as the twin security, or 90.9 (= 3 × 30.3). The twin security is a basic concept that is implicitly used in standard DCF as well; you derive the beta of a project by identifying a highly correlated, traded security and use that security's beta as input for the cost of capital in the DCF valuation.

[6] If the project itself would be traded, you would not need a twin security but would construct a replicating portfolio with the traded value of the project itself.

The solution is $N = 1.35$ and $B = -\$21.43$. Thus, to build a replicating portfolio, buy 1.35 shares and short 21.43 bonds (shorting a bond is common language for selling a bond, or borrowing money).

This position pays off exactly the same cash flow as the investment project under both states of the world. Therefore, the value of the project including the ability to defer should equal the value of the replicating portfolio:

$$\text{Contingent NPV} = (N \times \text{Price of Twin Security}) - (B \times 1)$$

$$= 1.35(30.3) - 21.43(1) = 19.5$$

The value of the deferral option is the difference between the total contingent NPV of the project and its standard NPV without flexibility: $19.5 - (-\$9.1) = \$28.6$ (remember, the standard NPV was negative).

Contingent NPV can also be determined with an alternative ROV approach, so-called *risk-neutral valuation*. The name is somewhat misleading because a risk-neutral valuation does adjust for risk, but as part of the scenario probabilities rather than the discount rate. To value an option, we weight the future cash flows by risk-adjusted (or so-called risk-neutral) probabilities instead of the actual scenario probabilities. The probability-weighted average cash flow is then discounted by the risk-free rate to determine current value. The risk-neutral probability of the favorable state, p^*, is defined as:

$$p^* = \frac{1 + r_f - d}{u - d} = 0.45$$

where

$$u = \frac{\text{FV(Favorable State)}}{\text{PV}} = \frac{50.0}{30.3} = 1.65$$

$$d = \frac{\text{FV(Unfavorable State)}}{\text{PV}} = \frac{16.7}{30.3} = 0.55$$

These probabilities implicitly capture the risk premium for investments perfectly correlated with the twin security. We discount the future cash flows weighted by these risk-adjusted probabilities at the risk-free rate of 5 percent, arriving at exactly the same value determined using the replicating portfolio:

$$\text{Contingent NPV} = \frac{0.45(45) + 0.55(0)}{1.05} = 19.5$$

It is no coincidence that the replicating portfolio and risk-neutral valuation lead to the same result. They are mathematically equivalent, and both rely on the price of the twin security to derive the value of an investment project with an option to defer.

VALUATION BASED ON DECISION TREE ANALYSIS

A second method for valuing a project with flexibility is to use decision tree analysis (DTA). This involves discounting the contingent future cash flows at the project's cost of capital. This leads to the right answer in principle, but only if we can determine the *correct* cost of capital for a project with contingent cash flows. We *cannot* simply use the cost of capital from the stand-alone project without flexibility, because the contingent cash flows have a very different risk profile. For example, if we value the project including flexibility using a cost of capital of 10 percent, the DTA results would be too high:

$$\text{Contingent NPV} = \frac{0.5(45) + 0.5(0)}{1.10} = 20.5$$

If we discount the cash flows at the 10 percent cost of capital but the investment at the risk-free rate of 5 percent, the DTA valuation would be too low:[7]

$$\text{Contingent NPV} = 0.5\left[\frac{150}{1.10} - \frac{105}{1.05}\right] + 0.5(0) = 18.2 \qquad (20.1)$$

We can correctly estimate the appropriate cost of capital for the contingent cash flows using the preceding ROV results. Based on the ROV results, the project with the option is worth $19.5 and has an equal chance of paying off $45 or $0. Thus, the implied risk-adjusted discount rate for the project with the option is 15.5 percent, significantly above the underlying project's 10 percent cost of capital.[8] This occurs because the option is far more risky than the project itself: It has a present value of $19.5 with equal chances of a 131 percent increase or a 100 percent decrease. Conversely, the underlying

---

[7] This DTA approach leads to the correct value of flexibility only if the underlying risk is too small to influence the future investment decision (i.e., if the project value would exceed the investment requirements even in the unfavorable state).

[8] In this simplified example, there is one value for the cost of capital. In general, the cost of capital for the contingent cash flows is not constant. It changes with the risk of the option across time and states of the world.

project has a present value of $90.9 and a fifty-fifty chance of rising to $150 (a 65 percent increase) or falling to $50 (a 45 percent decrease).

Comparing ROV and DTA Approaches

As summarized in Exhibit 20.5, the standard NPV approach undervalues the project. The ROV approach generates a correct value because it captures the value of flexibility by using a replicating portfolio or risk-neutral valuation. The DTA approach could lead to the same result and is quite close in this example. Unfortunately, the DTA results could be much further off, since in most cases there is no way to properly determine the cost of capital for the contingent cash flows other than using ROV.

This example, however, does not mean that ROV is the single best approach to valuation of managerial flexibility. The stylized example did not take into account two important aspects of real-life strategic decisions: the type of underlying risk and the availability of data on the value and variance of the underlying asset. Exhibit 20.6 describes when each method is most suitable. ROV works best when the future cash flows are closely linked to traded commodities, securities, or currencies. Not surprisingly, real-option valuations are most often used for commodity-linked invest-

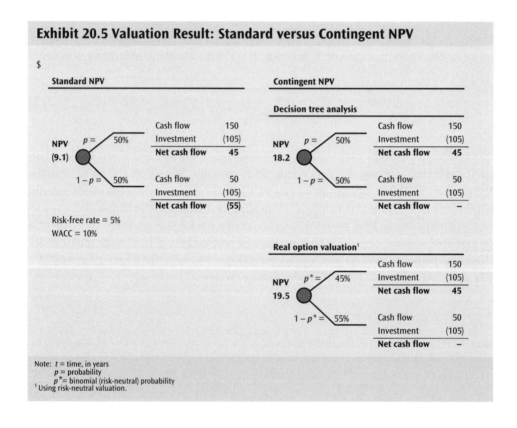

Exhibit 20.5 Valuation Result: Standard versus Contingent NPV

Note: t = time, in years
p = probability
p^* = binomial (risk-neutral) probability
[1] Using risk-neutral valuation.

Exhibit 20.6 Application Opportunities for ROV versus DTA

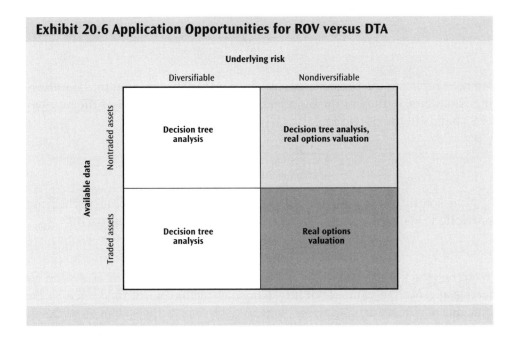

ments, such as in the mining and oil industry. In most other cases, we recommend the more straightforward DTA approach because (most of) the underlying risk is diversifiable or because only rough estimates are available for required inputs such as the underlying asset value and variance.

Underlying risk: Diversifiable versus nondiversifiable   In the pharmaceutical drug example at the beginning of the chapter, we did not use an option-pricing model to value the investment, but instead chose a simple DTA approach. Did we make a mistake? No, the DTA results were correct because we used the correct cost of capital. If the risk driving the cash flow uncertainty is uncorrelated with the market (and thus fully diversifiable), the cost of capital for the contingent cash flows is the same as for the underlying product. In the example, the underlying risk is purely technological-development risk, so we were able to use the cost of capital for the fully developed drug—in this case, the risk-free rate.

To demonstrate this, we use ROV to value the drug's deferral option with a replicating portfolio. Assume a twin security exists whose payoffs are perfectly correlated with the outcome of the drug trial, generating $52.5 when the outcome is favorable and $10.5 when it is unfavorable. Because its cash flows are driven by technological risk only, the security's market beta is zero, and its present value must be:

$$PV = \frac{0.5(52.5) + 0.5(10.5)}{1.05} = 30$$

We next replicate the project's payoffs by finding the solution to the following equations, with N as the number of twin securities and B as the number of $1 bonds in the portfolio:

$$52.5N + 1.05B = 4{,}500$$

$$10.5N + 1.05B = 0$$

The solution is $N = 107.1$ and $B = -1{,}071.4$, so the value of the replicating portfolio leads to exactly the same result as with the DTA approach:[9]

$$107.1(30) - 1{,}071.4(1) = 2{,}143$$

When the key *underlying risk is diversifiable*, a straightforward DTA is an effective approach to value flexibility. Consider technological risks such as the outcome of clinical drug trials, geological risks such as the size of an undeveloped oil field, or even some forms of marketing risk such as consumer acceptance of a new product. These risks are diversifiable, because the correlation of the outcome with overall economic activity is low. And these risks can be far more important for evaluating future investment decisions than the nondiversifiable risk as measured by the beta of the underlying asset (e.g., a successful drug or developed oil field). For example, the driver of the investment decision in drug development is whether the drug passes the trials (technological risk), not whether the drug—once successfully developed—is worth more or less depending on general economic conditions (beta risk).

In this case, estimate the value of the project including flexibility by discounting the underlying asset's future cash flows and the investment requirement in each state of the world at their respective costs of capital, as in equation 20.1. In the earlier example, we assumed the completed drug had a zero beta, so we used the risk-free rate. In reality, the underlying asset is more likely to have a nonzero beta. We can still apply DTA if the contingent invesment decisions are not driven by this beta risk but by diversifiable risk (e.g., the outcome of clinical trials). Then discount the asset's cash flows at the appropriate WACC and the investment cash flows at the risk-free rate in each state of the world.[10]

If the *underlying risk is not diversifiable* and therefore priced in the financial markets, the DTA approach is more difficult to apply because it is unclear how to estimate the cost of capital correctly. In this case, only ROV leads to the theoretically correct valuation. Sometimes a project's cash

---

[9] See also Dixit and Pindyck, *Investment under Uncertainty* (see note 3), pp. 30–32, for a similar proof.
[10] If nondiversifiable (beta) risk does not make a difference in the investment decision, the DTA approach leads to the same value as an ROV approach (see also note 7).

flows are clearly correlated with commodity prices, such as in mining, the oil industry, or power generation. The key underlying risk for an investment decision is then often commodity price-related and not diversifiable. In this case, use the ROV approach with the commodity as a twin security to correctly value the project.

Data availability: Traded versus untraded assets The results of an ROV (and DTA) valuation critically depend on well-grounded estimates for the value and the variance of the underlying asset.

If the estimate for the *underlying asset value* is inaccurate, the flexibility value will also be inaccurate. Returning to our first example, if we misestimate the future cash flows generated by a highly effective drug, the value of the option to defer will be inaccurate. In this simple example, we assumed a no-growth cash flow perpetuity. In practice, you would have to estimate the value with a full-fledged DCF model projecting sales growth, operating margins, capital turnovers, and so on. All ROV (and DTA) approaches build on this valuation of the underlying asset.

A similar argument holds for estimates of the *variance* of the underlying asset's cash flows (called volatility in the option-pricing literature). Volatility can have a great impact on value because real options typically have long lifetimes and are often "at the money" or close to it,[11] meaning the decision of whether to undertake the project is a close call.[12]

To illustrate the impact of volatility on such options, consider the value of a 10-year, at-the-money call option on a dividend-paying stock. Assume the risk-free rate is 5 percent, the dividend yield is 2.5 percent, and the current price for the underlying stock is $100. The value of the call option would be $27 based on a volatility of 20 percent and $35 for a volatility of 30 percent—a increase in value of almost 30 percent.[13] Likewise, in the drug development example, changes in variance significantly affect the option's value. Still, for many managers and practitioners, volatility remains an abstract concept: How do you reasonably estimate the range of cash flow outcomes[14] from the sale of a product that has yet to be released?

Sometimes the underlying asset value and variance can be derived from traded assets. Examples include options to shut down gas-fueled power generation, abandon a copper mine, or defer production of an oil field. In such cases, because you can estimate the key inputs with reasonable accuracy, ROV should be more accurate than DTA. Even then, accurately estimating

---

[11] It follows from option-pricing theory that the sensitivity of option value to changes in variance (referred to as vega) increases as the option's lifetime increases and as the option is closer to the money. An option is at the money if its exercise price equals the value of the underlying asset.

[12] If the investment decision were a clear go or no-go, there would be little value in flexibility in the first place, and no need to consider the option value.

[13] The results were obtained with a Black-Scholes option-pricing model. See, for example, R. Brealey and S. Myers, *Principles of Corporate Finance*, 7th ed. (New York: McGraw-Hill, 2003), ch. 21.

[14] The range needs to include the associated probabilities to provide a variance estimate.

underlying value and variance is not straightforward. Although short-term volatility can be measured using commodity prices, it is the long-term volatility that is important for real options (because they have long life-times). In fact, short-term volatility can be misleading. For example, the current volatility of spot prices for crude oil is not meaningful for the valuation of a long-term, oil-related option. Extrapolating high short-term volatility would suggest future oil prices that are unrealistically high or low.

When estimates for the underlying asset valuation and variance (volatility) cannot be derived from traded assets and are largely judgmental, a DTA approach is more appropriate. It is more straightforward and transparent to decision makers than the ROV approach. Transparency is especially important when critical valuation assumptions require the decision maker's judgment. DTA captures the essence of flexibility value, and the theoretical advantage of ROV is less important if required inputs are unavailable.

FOUR-STEP PROCESS FOR VALUING FLEXIBILITY

To value flexibility, use the four-step process illustrated in Exhibit 20.7. In Step 1, conduct a valuation of the investment project without flexibility, using a traditional discounted cash flow model. In Step 2, expand the DCF model into an event tree, mapping how the value of the project evolves over time, using unadjusted probabilities and the weighted average cost of capi-

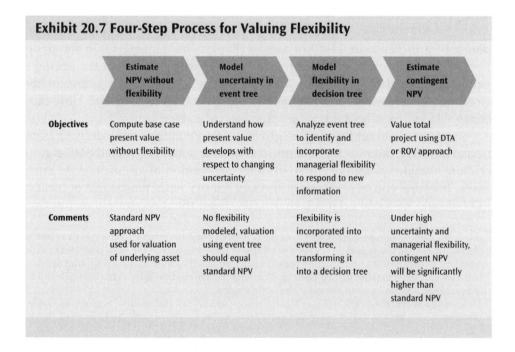

Exhibit 20.7 Four-Step Process for Valuing Flexibility

	Estimate NPV without flexibility	Model uncertainty in event tree	Model flexibility in decision tree	Estimate contingent NPV
Objectives	Compute base case present value without flexibility	Understand how present value develops with respect to changing uncertainty	Analyze event tree to identify and incorporate managerial flexibility to respond to new information	Value total project using DTA or ROV approach
Comments	Standard NPV approach used for valuation of underlying asset	No flexibility modeled, valuation using event tree should equal standard NPV	Flexibility is incorporated into event tree, transforming it into a decision tree	Under high uncertainty and managerial flexibility, contingent NPV will be significantly higher than standard NPV

tal. At this stage, the model does not include flexibility, so the present value of the project, based on the event tree, should equal the standard DCF value from the first step.

In Step 3, turn the event tree into a decision tree by identifying the types of managerial flexibility that are available. Build the flexibility into the nodes of the tree. Multiple sources of flexibility are possible at a single decision node, such as the option to abandon and expand, but it is important to have clear priorities among them. Be careful in establishing the sequence of decisions regarding flexibility, especially when the decision tree has compound options.

Finally, Step 4 requires recognizing how the exercise of flexibility alters the project's risk characteristics. If (most of) the risk driving the contingent cash flows is fully diversifiable, you need no special modeling and can use DTA, discounting investment cash flows at the risk-free rate and the underlying project's cash flows at the weighted average cost of capital, as in the pharmaceutical example in the next section. If the risk is (mostly) nondiversifiable and priced in the market, the appropriate risk-adjusted discount rate for the project's cash flows is no longer the weighted average cost of capital used in Step 1. In that case, use an ROV approach for the project with flexibility, using a replicating portfolio or risk-neutral valuation.

REAL-OPTIONS VALUATION: NUMERICAL EXAMPLE

Using the four-step process, we illustrate the ROV approach with a straightforward binomial lattice. The results are identical to alternative option-pricing models that use more complicated mathematics such as stochastic calculus.

Step 1: Estimate present value without flexibility Assume that an investment project generates cash flows whose present value (PV) equals $100, volatility is 15 percent per year,[15] and expected rate of return (R_k) equals 8 percent per year. The risk-free rate is 5 percent per year, and the cash outflow necessary to undertake the project, if we invest in it immediately, is $105. Thus, the standard NPV is –$5, and we would not undertake the project if we had to commit today.

Step 2: Model uncertainty using event tree The lattice that models the potential values of the underlying risky asset is called an event tree. It contains no decision nodes and simply models the evolution of the underlying asset. To model changes in the value of the project, we can choose either of two event trees: geometric or arithmetic. A geometric tree determines the asset value in the next node by multiplying the value in the previous node

---

[15] The standard deviation of the rate of change of the factory value.

Exhibit 20.8 Event Tree: Factory without Flexibility

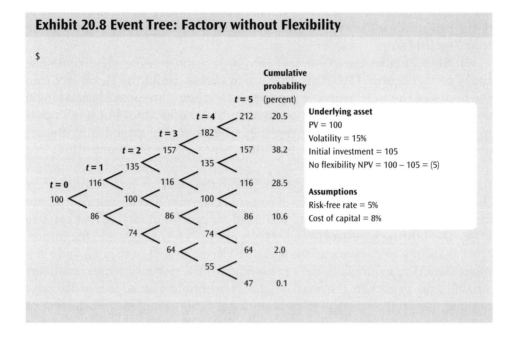

by a factor. The geometric tree has no upper bound, but is bounded below by zero. An arithmetic tree determines the next node by adding (or subtracting) a value to the previous node. We prefer the geometric event tree because its value cannot fall below zero.

Exhibit 20.8 illustrates potential values the project might take for each of next five years. Defining T as the number of years per upward movement and σ as the annualized volatility of the underlying project value, we can determine the up-and-down movements by using the following formulas:[16]

$$\text{Up Movement} = u = e^{\sigma\sqrt{T}}$$

$$\text{Down Movement} = d = \frac{1}{u}$$

Substitute numerical values into these formulas:

$$u = e^{0.15\sqrt{1}} = 1.1618$$

$$d = \frac{1}{1.1618} = 0.8607$$

[16] J. Cox, M. Rubinstein, and S. Ross, "Option Pricing: A Simplified Approach," *Journal of Financial Economics*, 7(3) (1979): 229–263.

Based on traditional DCF using an 8 percent cost of capital, the probability of an up movement is 72.82 percent, and the probability of a down movement is 27.18 percent.[17] As can be verified, the present value of any branch in the event tree equals the expected payout discounted at the 8 percent cost of capital. Let's take the uppermost branch in the fifth time period. Its present value is:

$$PV_{t=4} = \frac{E\left(PV_{t=5}\right)}{\left(1+R_k\right)} = \frac{\left(0.7282 \times 211.7 + 0.2718 \times 156.8\right)}{\left(1.08\right)} = 182.2$$

A similar calculation will produce any of the values in the event tree, resulting in a PV of the project of $100 at $t = 0$. That present value equals the result in Step 1, so we know the tree is correct.

Step 3: Model flexibility using decision tree   When we add decision points to an event tree, it becomes a decision tree. Suppose the factory can be expanded for an additional $15. The expansion increases the factory's value at that node by 20 percent. The option can be exercised at any time during the next five years.

Exhibit 20.9 on page 580 shows the resulting decision tree. To find the payouts at a given point on the tree, start with the final branches and work backward through time. Consider the uppermost branch in period 5. On the upward limb, the payout absent expansion would be 211.7, but with expansion, it is $1.20 \times 211.7 - 15 = 239.0$. Since the value with expansion is higher, we would decide to expand. On the lower limb of that same node, the payout with expansion is $1.20 \times 156.8 - 15 = 173.2$, versus 156.8 without expansion, so again we would expand.

Step 4: Estimate value of flexibility   To determine the value of the project with the flexibility to expand, we work backward through the decision tree, using the replicating portfolio method at each node. For the node highlighted in Exhibit 20.9, we can replicate the payoffs from the option to expand using a portfolio of N units of the underlying project[18] and B units of $1 risk-free bonds:

$$116.2N + 1.05B = 124.4$$

$$86.1N + 1.05B = 88.3$$

---

[17] The formula for estimating the upward probability is:

$$\frac{\left(\left[1+R_k\right]^T - d\right)}{\left(u-d\right)} = \frac{\left([1+8\%]^1 - 0.8607\right)}{\left(1.1618 - 0.8607\right)} = 0.7282$$

See note 16.

[18] If the project itself is not traded but a traded twin security exists, we could construct the portfolio in a similar way with units of the twin security and risk-free bonds.

Exhibit 20.9 Decision Tree: Option to Expand Factory

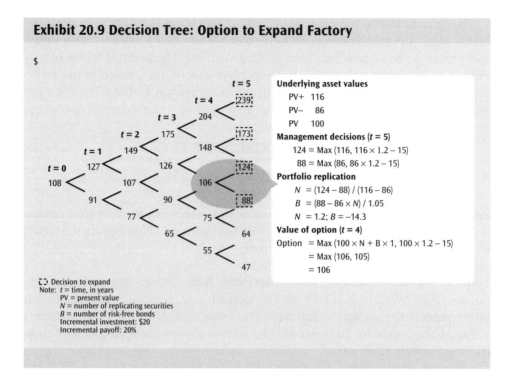

$

Note: t = time, in years
PV = present value
N = number of replicating securities
B = number of risk-free bonds
Incremental investment: $20
Incremental payoff: 20%

Decision to expand

Solving the equations, we find that $N = 1.2$, and $B = -14.3$. Therefore, a replicating portfolio consists of 1.2 units of the project without flexibility (at that node, valued at $100), plus a short position of 14.3 bonds worth $1. As shown in Exhibit 20.9, the value of the option is then:

$$PV = 100N + 1B = 105.7$$

Working backward from right to left, node by node, we obtain a present value of $108.4 for a project that has an option to expand. As a result, the net present value of the project increases from −$5.0 to $3.4, so the option itself is worth $8.4.

If instead, management had the option to abandon the factory at any node for a fixed liquidation value of $100, the valuation would be as shown in Exhibit 20.10. Again, work from right to left through the decision tree. For the highlighted node, the value of the underlying factory is $116.2 in the upward branch and $86.1 in the downward branch. Given the ability to do so, the company would abandon the project for $100 in the downward branch, so the payoffs in the decision tree are $116.2 in the upward and $100 in the downward branch. Using risk-neutral valuation this time, the abandonment option can be valued in this node at $104.9 as shown in Exhibit 20.10 (the exact same result a replicating portfolio would have generated).

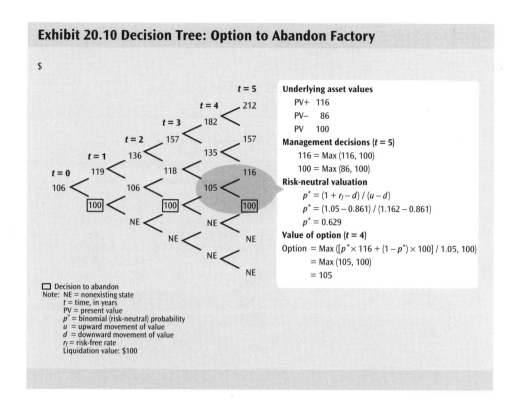

Exhibit 20.10 Decision Tree: Option to Abandon Factory

$

					$t = 5$
				$t = 4$	212
			$t = 3$	182	
		$t = 2$	157		157
	$t = 1$	136		135	
$t = 0$	119		118		116
106		106		105	
	100		100		100
		NE		NE	
			NE		NE
				NE	
					NE

Underlying asset values
  PV+ 116
  PV−   86
  PV   100
Management decisions ($t = 5$)
  116 = Max (116, 100)
  100 = Max (86, 100)
Risk-neutral valuation
  $p^* = (1 + r_f - d) / (u - d)$
  $p^* = (1.05 - 0.861) / (1.162 - 0.861)$
  $p^* = 0.629$
Value of option ($t = 4$)
  Option = Max ([$p^* \times 116 + (1 - p^*) \times 100$] / 1.05, 100)
       = Max (105, 100)
       = 105

□ Decision to abandon
Note: NE = nonexisting state
  t = time, in years
  PV = present value
  p^* = binomial (risk-neutral) probability
  u = upward movement of value
  d = downward movement of value
  r_f = risk-free rate
  Liquidation value: $100

Working backward through time, the value for a factory with the ability to abandon is $106.4.

Multiple sources of flexibility can be combined within a single decision tree, as illustrated in Exhibit 20.11 on page 582 using risk-neutral valuation. The value of the project including the options to abandon and expand would be $113.5, rather than $100.0, its stand-alone value without flexibility. With these options, the correct decision would be to accept the project. Note that the value of the combined expansion-abandonment flexibility, $13.5, is less than the sum of the individual flexibility values ($8.4 + $6.4 = $14.8) but greater than either of them individually. The values of both options are not additive because they interact in complex ways (for example, you cannot expand the factory once you have abandoned it).

Real-Options Valuation and Decision Tree Analysis: A Numerical Example

In our next example, we show how to use a DTA or ROV approach for the valuation of a research and development project. Assume a company needs to decide on whether to develop a new pharmaceutical drug. In our simplified

Exhibit 20.11 Decision Tree: Option to Expand or Abandon Factory

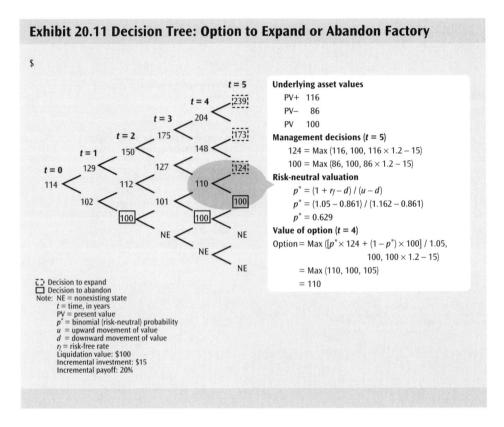

example,[19] the first step in development is a research phase of three years, in which the most promising chemical compounds are selected. The probability of success in the research phase is estimated at 15 percent. This is followed by a three-year testing phase, during which the compounds are tested in laboratory and clinical settings. The chance of successfully completing the testing phase is 40 percent. If there are successful results, the drug can be released in the market. On failure in any phase, the company terminates development, and the product dies worthless.

Step 1: Estimate present value without flexibility   If the development process is successful, the drug will have great value. Margins in the pharmaceutical industry are high, because drugs are protected against competition through patents. If marketed today, a successful drug would generate annual sales of $1,950 million and a 45 percent EBITDA margin on sales for the next 10 years until patent expiration. (Because prices drastically decline after a patent expires, we do not count proceeds beyond that time.) Assum-

---

[19] Pharmaceutical research and development are much more complex and consist of more phases than shown in this example. For a more extensive example of valuing flexibility in pharmaceutical research and development, see D. Kellog and J. Charnes, "Real-Options Valuation for a Biotechnology Company." (Note 1)

ing a 30 percent tax rate and a 7 percent cost of capital, a marketable drug's present value as of today would be $4,314 million. However, the odds of successful development are small. The cumulative probability of success over the research and testing phase is only 6 percent (0.15×0.40). The present value of a drug that still needs to be developed and tested therefore amounts to $259 million ($0.06 \times \$4,314$ million).

The investments needed to develop, test, and market a drug are high: $100 million in the research phase, $250 million in the testing phase, and $150 million in marketing. If we had to commit today to all three investments, we should not proceed because the NPV is negative:

$$\text{Standard NPV} = \text{PV(Expected Cash Flows)} - \text{PV (Investments)}$$

$$= 259 - 100 - \frac{250}{(1.05)^3} - \frac{150}{(1.05)^6} = -169$$

If management has the ability to abandon the project, however, the contingent NPV is significantly higher. To see this, we estimate the contingent NPV with a straightforward DTA approach and then with the more sophisticated ROV approach.

Step 2 (DTA): Model uncertainty using event tree   In this development project, the source of risk that drives the contingent cash flows is the technological risk around the research and testing outcomes. We can model this uncertainty using a straightforward event tree (see Exhibit 20.12 on p. 584). Note that the tree shows all cash inflows and outflows at values discounted to today. For example, the expected value of a marketable drug after six years is shown at its present value as of today ($t = 0$) of $4,314 million (the expected value after six years equals $4,314 compounded at 7 percent: $6,475). Since the investment outlays are certain, they are discounted at the risk-free rate of 5 percent.[20]

Step 3 (DTA): Model flexibility using decision tree   We next include the decision flexibility in the tree, working from right to left (see Exhibit 20.13 on p. 584). At the end of the testing phase, you have the option to invest $150 million in marketing, which equals $112 million in today's dollars. You should invest only if testing has produced a marketable product, so the project's value at that point is Max[$(4,314 - 112), 0] = \$4,202$ million. At the end of the research phase, you have the option to proceed with the testing phase. If the research phase fails, there is no point in proceeding, and if it is successful, you will proceed to testing only if the payoffs justify the incremental investment of $250 million (or $216 million discounted to today at the risk-free rate).

[20] The assumption to discount investment outlays at the risk-free rate is also implicitly made in the ROV approach later in this section.

Exhibit 20.12 Event Tree: Research and Development Option with Technological Risk

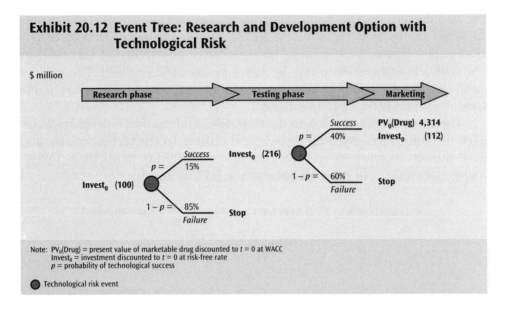

Step 4 (DTA): Estimate value of flexibility Because the technological risk is fully diversifiable, we apply a DTA approach for the valuation of flexibility. The value of the option to proceed at the end of the research phase is calculated as follows:

$$PV(\text{Option}) = \text{Max}[PV(\text{Testing}) - \text{Inv}(\text{Testing}), 0]$$

In this equation, PV(Testing) is the present value of proceeding with testing, which equals the probability-weighted future payoffs:

Exhibit 20.13 Decision Tree: Research and Development Option with Technological Risk

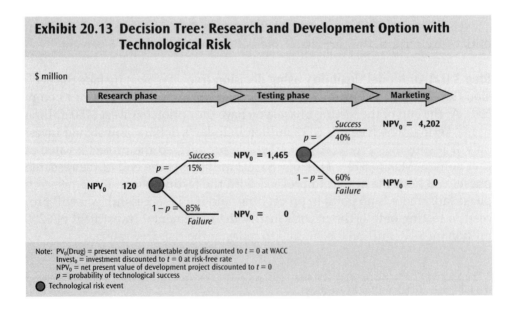

$$PV(Testing) = 0.40(4,202) + 0.60(0) = 1,681$$

Inv(Testing), the investment requirement for the testing phase, equals $250 million or $216 million discounted to $t = 0$. Substituting, we can find the present value of the development project prior to the testing phase:

$$PV(Option) = Max\ [(1,681 - 216), 0] = 1,465$$

These amounts need not be discounted further because they already represent present value as of $t = 0$. Working farther from right to left in the tree, we find the contingent NPV for the entire development project prior to the research phase:

$$PV(Option) = Max[PV(Research) - Inv(Research), 0]$$
$$= Max[0.15(1,465) + 0.85(0) - 100, 0] = \$120\ million$$

This value is significantly higher than the standard NPV of –$169 million.

ROV approach: Technological and commercial risk   Our analysis thus far did not include the other source of uncertainty in the development project: the commercial risk around the future cash flow potential of the successfully developed and marketed drug. ROV is necessary to handle both technological and commercial risk. Step 1 is identical to the DTA approach.

Step 2 (ROV): Model uncertainty using event tree   We can model both risks in a combined event tree (see Exhibit 20.14 on p. 586). In contrast to the event tree in the DTA approach, the amounts in this tree do not represent present values but future values that will need to be discounted when we solve for the value of the option. For simplicity, we have chosen a one-step binomial lattice to describe the evolution of the drug value over each three-year period.[21] Assuming an annual volatility of 15 percent, we can derive the upward and downward movements, u and d, as follows:[22]

$$u = e^{\sigma\sqrt{T}} = e^{0.15\sqrt{3}} = 1.30$$

$$d = \frac{1}{u} = \frac{1}{1.30} = 0.77$$

---

[21] With more nodes, the tree quickly becomes too complex to show in an exhibit because it does not converge in the technological risk. We also did the analysis with 10 nodes, but that did not affect the results for this particular example.
[22] See note 16.

Exhibit 20.14 Event Tree: Research and Development Option with Technological and Commercial Risk

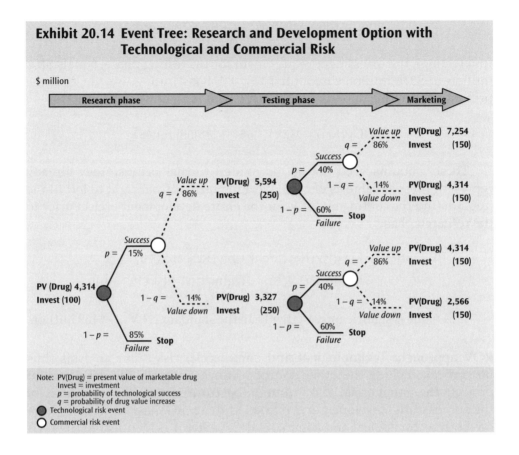

Note: PV(Drug) = present value of marketable drug
　　　 Invest = investment
　　　 p = probability of technological success
　　　 q = probability of drug value increase
　　⬤ Technological risk event
　　◯ Commercial risk event

The probability of an upward movement is 86 percent, and the probability of a downward movement is 14 percent.[23] The value of a marketable drug at the start of the research phase is $4,314 million. At the end of the research phase, there are three possible outcomes: failure leading to a drug value of zero, success combined with an increase in the value of a marketable drug to $5,594 million, and success combined with a decrease in the value of a marketable drug to $3,327 million. Following the same logic, there are six possible outcomes after the testing phase.

Step 3 (ROV): Model flexibility using decision tree   The logic underlying the decision tree including commercial risk (see Exhibit 20.15) is the same as under the DTA approach. For example, the payoff at the end of the testing

[23] The formula for estimating the upward probability is:

$$\frac{\left(\left[1+R_k]^T\right]-d\right)}{(u-d)} = \frac{\left(1.07^3 - 0.77\right)}{(1.30 - 0.77)} = 0.86$$

R_k is the expected return on the asset. See also note 16.

Exhibit 20.15 Decision Tree: Research and Development Option with Technological and Commercial Risk

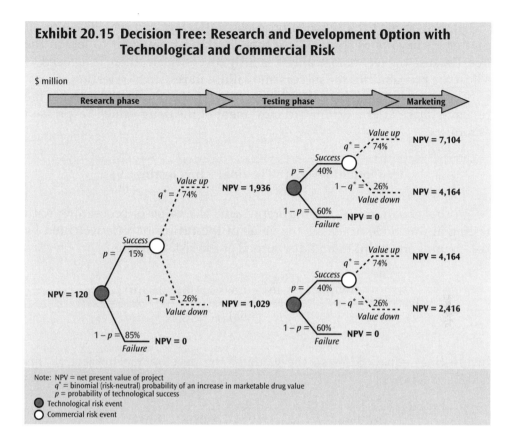

$ million

Note: NPV = net present value of project
  q^* = binomial (risk-neutral) probability of an increase in marketable drug value
  p = probability of technological success
● Technological risk event
○ Commercial risk event

phase in the top branch equals Max[(7,254 − 150), 0] = 7,104. The primary difference is that in the ROV version of the tree, we recognize the ability to abandon development if the value of a marketable drug drops too much.

Step 4 (ROV): Estimate value of flexibility The commercial risk around the drug's future cash flows is not diversifiable,[24] so we need to use an ROV approach to include it in our valuation. In this example, we use risk-neutral valuation. Therefore, we risk-adjust all probabilities of the upward and downward movements for the drug's value:

$$p^* = \frac{\left(\left[1+r_f\right]^T - d\right)}{(u-d)} = \frac{\left(1.05^3 - 0.77\right)}{(1.30 - 0.77)} = 0.74$$

---

[24] Recall that we assumed the cost of capital for a marketed drug was 7 percent. Given our assumption for a risk-free rate of 5 percent, its beta must be different from zero.

Having applied the risk-neutral probabilities, we can now discount all contingent payoffs at the risk-free rate, working from right to left in the tree. Because the technological risk is fully diversifiable, there is no need to adjust the probabilities for success and failure in research or testing.

For example, from Exhibit 20.15, the value of the option at the end of the research phase after a downward movement of the drug value is expressed as follows:

$$PV(Option) = Max[PV(Testing) - Inv(Testing), 0]$$

In this equation, PV(Testing) represents the value of proceeding with testing at this node. It equals the value of the future payoffs weighted by risk-neutral probabilities and discounted at the risk-free rate:

$$PV(Testing) = \frac{\left[0.40\left(0.74 \times 4,164 + 0.26 \times 2,416\right) + 0.60\left(0\right)\right]}{\left(1.05\right)^3} = 1,279$$

Inv(Testing) equals $250, so the value of the development project at this node is as follows:

$$PV(Option) = Max[(1,279 - 250), 0] = 1,029$$

We can solve for the other nodes in the same way. Working backward through the tree, we estimate the contingent NPV at $120 million, the same result we obtained in the DTA approach without commercial risk.

This is not surprising. A closer look at the decision tree reveals that the uncertainty around the future marketable drug value is not significant enough to influence any of the decisions in the development process. In this example, the commercial risk makes no difference, even if we assume higher volatility, such as 50 percent; an amount which exceeds the volatility of many high-tech stocks. As we noted earlier, when nondiversifiable risk (the drug's commercial risk as measured by its beta) does not influence investment decisions, the DTA and ROV results are equivalent.

Moreover, in real situations the key uncertainty in drug development is whether the drug proves to be an effective disease treatment without serious side effects. The commercial risk is far less relevant, because a truly effective drug almost always generates attractive margins. The example illustrates that in such cases, it is more practical to focus on the technological risk entirely, using a DTA approach. Explicitly modeling the nondiversifiable (e.g., commercial) risk requires an ROV approach that is more complex and may not even affect the valuation results.

In general, when faced with multiple sources of underlying risk, carefully assess whether all these possible risks are important or whether one dominates all others. Sometimes you can focus the valuation approach on just one or two sources of uncertainty and greatly simplify the analysis.

SUMMARY

Managerial flexibility can substantially alter the value of a business because it lets managers defer or change investment decisions as the business develops. Rigid use of standard DCF analysis fails to account for such flexibility in business decisions. Flexibility comes in many forms, such as the option to defer, expand, contract, abandon, or switch projects on and off; we have illustrated only a few applications in this chapter. Contingent-NPV analysis, in the form of decision tree analysis (DTA) or real options valuation models (ROV), correctly captures the value of flexibility. Although the ROV approach is theoretically superior to DTA, its application is more complex, so ROV is often limited to the valuation of flexibility in commodity-based industries (where commodity prices are measurable). In most other cases, a careful DTA approach delivers results that are reasonably solid and have the potential to provide more valuable insights.

REVIEW QUESTIONS

1. Present the general decision rule for NPV. If a project has NPV = 0, should a manager accept the project?

2. Define *contingent* NPV. Outline and explain the differences between standard and contingent NPV.

3. Identify the value drivers embedded in a *real option* and how they might interact.

4. Describe the DTA and ROV valuation models. How do these models differ from the standard NPV model?

5. When and under what circumstances should a manager apply a standard, DTA or ROV approach to valuation?

6. Outline the four-step process for valuing flexibility.

7. It is often argued that the two most important real options available to a manager evaluating investment decisions are the option to defer an investment decision and the option to abandon an investment decision. Explain the significance of these two options. How could the Black-Scholes model provide insight into these decisions?

8. Consider the project described in Exhibit 20.4 again. One could argue that the flexibility to defer the investment decision until the trial results are known reduces risk because the adverse outcome of a $55 loss can be avoided. But we know that to correctly value the flexibility in a DTA approach, we need to use a discount rate of 15.5 percent, which is above the 10 percent cost of capital for the project without flexibility. How can lower risk lead to a higher discount rate? Explain.

21

Cross-Border Valuation

To value companies outside your home country, follow the same principles and methods that we presented in Part Two. However, some issues need special attention:

- International accounting differences
- International taxation
- Translation of foreign-currency financial statements
- Forecasting cash flows in foreign and domestic currency
- Estimating the cost of capital in foreign currency
- Incorporating foreign-currency risk in valuations

In this chapter, we highlight each of these issues in terms of the steps that require special analyses. Throughout the chapter, "domestic currency" means the home currency of the person who is doing the valuation, and "foreign currency" refers to the currency of the foreign entity to be valued.

INTERNATIONAL ACCOUNTING DIFFERENCES

International accounting differences are rapidly becoming less of an issue, for two reasons. First, as of 2005, most major countries in Europe and Asia have harmonized their accounting practices by adopting International Financial Reporting Standards (IFRS).[1] Most other countries are expected

---

[1] IFRS includes previous International Accounting Standards (IAS) and recently introduced standards. Within the European Union, there is a temporary exception until 2007 for companies that are traded in the United States and use U.S. GAAP, as well as for companies that have issued public debt.

to adopt either IFRS or U.S. GAAP to facilitate international comparisons and transparency for investors and analysts.

Second, IFRS and U.S. GAAP, which are now by far the two most common sets of accounting standards, have converged over recent years. In 2002, the International Accounting Standards Board (IASB), which sets the standards for IFRS, and its U.S. counterpart, the Financial Accounting Standards Board (FASB), agreed on a joint short-term convergence project, as well as ongoing coordination. These efforts have led to various amendments to existing standards in both IFRS and U.S. GAAP, as well as the introduction of new standards to make the sets of guidelines more comparable.

With the recent revision of IFRS becoming effective at the beginning of 2005, the major differences between IFRS and U.S. GAAP have disappeared. However, when analyzing longer-term historical performance, you may find that former differences still have an impact because companies usually provide only a few years of results based on similar accounting principles for comparison purposes.

In Chapter 7, we described how to reorganize a company's financial statements to estimate NOPLAT, invested capital, and free cash flow. If you follow the recommendations in Chapter 7, you will get similar results regardless of the accounting principles used to prepare the financial statements. For example, the way we treat goodwill and its amortization in NOPLAT and invested capital makes our concepts insensitive to whether companies actually amortize goodwill. However, to make the proper adjustments, you need to understand how the company accounted for goodwill.

In the remainder of this section, we briefly describe the key differences between the two major sets of accounting standards. The summary in Exhibit 21.1 compares IFRS and U.S. GAAP across the major items from the income statement and balance sheet.

Consolidation

Under both U.S. GAAP and IFRS, consolidation is determined by effective control: if parent companies effectively control subsidiaries, these must be consolidated. Under IFRS, what determines control is the substance of the parent-subsidiary relationship, not necessarily the actual ownership or voting interest. U.S. GAAP typically assumes effective control when a parent has the majority of voting rights, either directly or indirectly. However, there are two exceptions. Accounting Research Bulletin (ARB) 51 indicates that a majority voting interest does not lead to consolidation if there is significant doubt about the parent's ability to control the subsidiary. It also states that, in certain situations, control is achieved through arrangements that do not involve voting stakes, so-called Variable Interest Entities (VIEs).

Exhibit 21.1 Key Differences between IFRS and U.S. GAAP

Principles

Consolidation	• Consolidation requirements determined by majority of voting rights under U.S. GAAP and based on control by parent under IFRS, which encompasses a broader set of assessment criteria • Joint ventures accounted for by proportional consolidation or equity method under IFRS and by equity method under U.S. GAAP
Translation	• Statements of subsidiaries in hyperinflation economies based on temporal method under U.S. GAAP and using current method with inflation adjustments under IFRS

Income statement

Revenue recognition	• Differences only in industry-specific situations (for example, license revenues in pharmaceutical industry)
Employee stock options	• Expensed at fair value in income statement under IFRS as of January 2005 and under U.S. GAAP planned as of December 2005

Balance sheet assets

Inventory	• U.S. GAAP allows LIFO approach for recording inventory, IFRS does not
Tangible fixed assets	• Upward revaluation allowed under IFRS, not under U.S. GAAP • Capitalization of interest costs for self-constructed assets allowed under U.S. GAAP, not under IFRS
Leases	• Differences mainly in lease classification—based on quantitative criteria under U.S. GAAP—based on broader set of (partly) judgmental criteria under IFRS
Goodwill and acquired intangible assets	• In-process R&D expensed under U.S. GAAP—recognized as goodwill or intangible asset under IFRS • Revaluation of acquired intangibles allowed under IFRS—not under U.S. GAAP
Other intangible assets	• Under U.S. GAAP, research and development expenses cannot be capitalized, with exception of some software and website development costs—under IFRS, research costs are expensed and development costs can be capitalized under specific conditions
Impairment of goodwill and long-lived assets	• Under IFRS, goodwill is tested for impairment before other assets—under U.S. GAAP, individual assets are tested for impairment before goodwill impairment • Reversal of impairment on long-lived assets allowed under IFRS in special conditions
Financial assets	• Broadly similar, with minor differences (for example, unlisted equity investments "available for sale" are carried at historical costs under U.S. GAAP—at fair value under IFRS)
Derivatives and hedge accounting	• Similar principles with hedge accounting possible under both standards

Balance sheet liabilities

Provisions—general	• Similar guidelines, but U.S. GAAP includes various standards for specific provisions • U.S. GAAP requires recognition of low-end of range of possible outcomes, while IFRS requires mid-range amount
Pensions	• IFRS immediately recognizes additional expenditures due to plan amendments—U.S. GAAP recognizes these over remaining employment period • U.S. GAAP may require an additional minimum pension liability under specific conditions

In situations involving VIEs, the investor that absorbs the majority of the economic gains or losses is required to consolidate.

Consolidation requirements for joint ventures differ. For cases of joint control (situations where a contractual obligation exists to share control), IFRS allows either proportional consolidation or application of the equity method. U.S. GAAP allows only the application of the equity method, except in specific circumstances.

Translation

Both U.S. GAAP and IFRS apply the *current method* for the translation of financial statements of subsidiaries in moderate-inflation countries into the currency of the parent company. For financial statements in hyperinflationary currencies, U.S. GAAP requires the so-called *temporal method*, but IFRS requires an *inflation-adjusted current method*. All methods are discussed in more detail later in this chapter.

Revenue Recognition

General criteria for revenue recognition are similar, but U.S. GAAP has more detailed guidelines for specific situations. An example of a difference is for up-front payments related to revenue agreements, such as licensing agreements between pharmaceutical companies. Pharmaceutical companies often license peer companies to market a particular product in a specific country. Such licensing agreements may include an initial payment up front, which is immediately recognized as revenue under IFRS if it is neither refundable nor conditional on future events. However, U.S. GAAP requires booking the initial payment as deferred income on the balance sheet, recognizing the payment as revenue over the license period.

Employee Stock Options and Other Share-Based Payments

Both IFRS and U.S. GAAP require that the fair value of stock options granted be recorded as a cost in the income statement (under U.S. GAAP planned as of December 2005). Both standards require that the fair value of the stock options be estimated with option-pricing models (e.g., Black-Scholes or a binomial model), but neither standard requires a specific method. U.S. GAAP already required the disclosure of the fair value of granted stock options in the footnotes, and 115 companies in the S&P 500 had voluntarily adopted the newly proposed standard to expense stock options in 2004. However, for non-U.S. companies, the disclosure requirements for employee stock options are entirely new, creating a difference with historical accounts.

Inventory

The book value of inventory can be based on different methodologies: FIFO, LIFO, or a weighted-average approach. IFRS does not allow a LIFO approach, but U.S. GAAP does. IFRS allows reversal of previous write-downs in the inventory, if the value of inventory has increased. U.S. GAAP does not allow reversals.

Tangible Fixed Assets

Under both IFRS and U.S. GAAP, the asset account for property, plant, and equipment is usually recorded at historical cost net of accumulated depreciation. Both sets of standards may require a one-off reduction in the book value (see impairment of long-lived assets later in this chapter) if the fair value of the asset is less than the balance sheet value. However, IFRS also allows (upward) revaluation of the assets, which is prohibited under U.S. GAAP. Not all European countries previously allowed revaluation of tangible fixed assets under local GAAP.

Another difference exists for interest costs associated with self-constructed assets. These costs can be capitalized under U.S. GAAP but must be expensed under IFRS.

Leases

The requirements for classification of leases into operating or capital/finance leases are conceptually similar under both accounting standards. For example, a relatively long lease term and a high present value of the minimum lease payments relative to the asset's fair value are indicators of a finance lease under both IFRS and U.S. GAAP. However, in contrast to IFRS, U.S. GAAP stipulates specific criteria such as a lease term of 75 percent or more of the asset's economic life and a present value of lease payments of at least 90 percent of the asset's fair value. As discussed in Chapter 7, off-balance-sheet operating leases need to be adjusted by including the capitalized value in invested capital. Differences in accounting should therefore have a minimal impact on the adjusted figures and the valuation results.

Goodwill and Acquired Intangible Assets

Accounting for business combinations (i.e., mergers and acquisitions) has changed drastically under both U.S. GAAP and IFRS. Pooling of interest has not been allowed under U.S. GAAP since 2001, and merger accounting, the international standards equivalent, was already severely restricted and is now completely abolished as of 2005. Both U.S. GAAP and IFRS currently allow only the purchase method for accounting of business combinations. Any resulting goodwill from a transaction must be capitalized and will not be amortized over a fixed time period. Instead, companies must assess annually whether impairment of the book value of the goodwill is required (see under impairment later in this section). This was introduced under U.S. GAAP in 2001. Outside the United States, the treatment of goodwill varied widely until the introduction of IFRS in 2005. In most countries, companies were required to amortize goodwill. Some countries had already adopted IFRS for goodwill accounting so that no goodwill was amortized. In a few countries, such as the Netherlands, goodwill could be written off directly against equity in the year of the acquisition. Therefore, long-term historical analysis still requires careful analysis and interpretation of reported goodwill.

Both standards allow recognition of acquired intangible assets on the balance sheet if the intangibles are identifiable so that they can be distinguished from goodwill. Generally this will yield similar results under IFRS and U.S. GAAP, but sometimes differences could occur. A key difference between U.S. GAAP and IFRS exists in the treatment of acquired in-process R&D, which can be capitalized as goodwill or an acquired intangible asset under IFRS but is usually expensed under U.S. GAAP. Both standards will amortize acquired intangible assets with a definite life, with indefinite-life assets being subject to impairment (discussed later in this section). Furthermore, IFRS allows for (upward) revaluation of intangibles, which is not possible under U.S. GAAP.

Other Intangible Assets

The accounting treatment of intangible assets, such as patents, copyrights, and customer lists, depends on how these assets were obtained. Intangible assets that were acquired from other companies (e.g., licenses or purchased customer lists) should be capitalized at historical cost and amortized over their economic lifetime under both IFRS and U.S. GAAP. Internally generated intangible assets (e.g., brands, mastheads, publishing titles, and own customer lists) cannot be capitalized. Under U.S. GAAP, only development costs for software and Web sites that meet specific criteria can be capitalized. All other R&D expenditures must be expensed. Under IFRS, research costs must be expensed. Development costs for intangible assets can be capitalized only under stringent conditions.

Impairment of Goodwill and Long-Lived Assets

As mentioned, goodwill on acquisitions is no longer amortized under U.S. GAAP and IFRS. Instead, an annual impairment test is required for goodwill. This means companies have to determine whether the current economic value of an acquired company is no less than the book value of its net assets plus goodwill (i.e., the original transaction price if no prior impairment has occurred). Although the principle is similar, the impact of an impairment on the financial statements can differ under IFRS and U.S. GAAP. IFRS requires a reduction in goodwill before any other assets are impaired (on a pro rata basis for any remaining amount left), whereas U.S. GAAP first requires assessment and reduction of individual assets before any goodwill is impaired.

Impairment is not limited to goodwill but can also apply to other long-lived assets, both tangible (e.g., net property, plant, and equipment) and intangible. IFRS and U.S. GAAP may use somewhat different approaches to determine whether an impairment is required, but under both standards, the estimated fair value of the asset is compared with its current book value. Any impairment will be recognized in the income statement. IFRS allows reversal of the impairment if economic conditions have changed; such a reversal is prohibited under U.S. GAAP.

Financial Assets

Both IFRS and U.S. GAAP require initial recording of financial assets at fair value, with subsequent treatment depending on the classification of the asset. Assets are classified as either "held-to-maturity," "trading," or "available for sale." This classification determines whether the book value is market based ("available for sale" and "trading") or based on historical costs net of accrued amortization ("held-to-maturity"). Prior to the introduction of IFRS, many non-U.S. companies did not report financial assets at their fair value.

The differences between IFRS and U.S. GAAP are minor. For example, in the case of unlisted equity investments classified as "available for sale," U.S. GAAP requires the use of historical cost, whereas IFRS requires a fair-value measurement.

Derivatives and Hedge Accounting

Both IFRS and U.S. GAAP require that derivatives be treated as financial assets and included on the balance sheet at fair value. This requirement also holds for so-called embedded derivatives—derivative components of non-derivative contracts. The embedded derivatives need to be stripped from their host contracts and reported separately on the balance sheet. Before converting to IFRS, few non-U.S. companies followed this practice. Under both standards, companies can use *hedge accounting* to avoid the profit-and-loss impact of changes in the fair value of the derivative instruments. However, hedge accounting can be applied only under specific conditions. A key condition is that the hedge is "effective," meaning a change in the value of the asset or liability that is hedged is indeed offset by an opposite change in the value of the derivative. The exact measures for hedge effectiveness differ somewhat between the two standards.

Provisions

U.S. GAAP and IFRS are broadly similar in their treatment of provisions in terms of recognition requirements and their prohibition of the use of provisions to cover future operating losses. With IFRS being in line with U.S. GAAP, the use of provisions has become much more restrictive for many non-U.S. companies than before. Due to minor differences in formulating probability requirements for recognizing provisions, timing between U.S. GAAP and IFRS can be somewhat different. In addition, U.S. GAAP requires the use of the low end of a range of possible liabilities, whereas IFRS requires midpoint estimates.

For restructuring provisions, IFRS requires recognition when a company is "demonstrably committed" to the restructuring because of either a legal or a constructive obligation (e.g., it has started to implement a plan already). Under U.S. GAAP, a restructuring provision must meet the definition of a liability, so there must be a high likelihood that the plan will not change and/or that the company will not withdraw the plan.

Pensions and Other Postemployment Benefits

Both U.S. GAAP and IFRS require the recognition of a provision or liability for retirement-related benefits where the company carries the risk (e.g., because of guaranteed payments). This requirement typically holds for defined-benefit pension plans, as well as medical benefits in the United States. Both standards use similar approaches in establishing the retirement-related liability and expense. Changes in actuarial assumptions affect the value of retirement-related assets and liabilities. Both standards require recognition in the income statement only if the cumulative gains or losses exceed a certain range.

There are some differences. IFRS immediately recognizes additional expenses due to plan amendments, whereas U.S. GAAP amortizes these costs over the remaining employment period. In addition, U.S. GAAP requires an additional minimum pension liability if the accumulated benefit obligation (based on current or past compensation levels) exceeds the fair value of the plan assets. Finally, proposals are being discussed under IFRS to have all actuarial gains and losses run through the income statement without the application of the range mentioned earlier.

The impact of accounting for retirement-related liabilities under IFRS on European companies will differ from country to country. In some European countries (including Belgium and Sweden) the government, rather than the company, provides for pensions. For companies in these countries, the new accounting rules for retirement-related liabilities have limited impact. In other countries, including Germany, companies are not required to have funded pension plans. In those cases, the balance sheet typically already reflects an actuarial value of the liability, but under IFRS this value will be measured differently. In other countries, such as the Netherlands, companies are required to have funded pension plans. In these cases, the liability on the balance sheet used to reflect only the outstanding obligation to the pension fund (e.g., for underfunding). From 2005 onward, European companies have to report a net liability or asset based on the fair value of the plan assets and liabilities, similar to the way U.S. companies report on their pension plans (although the recognition of any gains or losses in the income statement is somewhat different, as described earlier).

INTERNATIONAL TAXATION

Taxation of corporate income and profit distributions differs across countries. Even so, for the purpose of analyzing historical financial performance, we can ignore most of these differences. By ignoring taxation and comparing pretax performance, we can generate the desired insights into the company's true economic performance. However, for valuation purposes, a proper understanding of the tax situation is crucial. All tax benefits and expenses represent a certain value or claim and need to be included in the stand-alone valuation of the entity.

To address international differences in taxation, you need to answer a few key questions:

- What are the relevant tax rate and taxable income?
- Can fiscal grouping be applied to offset profits and losses of different entities?
- What are the relevant cross-border taxation issues?
- How does taxation affect shareholders in different countries?

Relevant Tax Rate and Taxable Income

To estimate taxes on projected future income, you need to understand what the relevant tax rate is and what amount of profit is actually taxable. Some countries have one corporate tax rate. In others, including the United States, there is a federal tax rate and a state tax rate. Some countries have special surtaxes that increase the average tax rate for companies. In addition, some profit that is taxed in one country may not be taxable in another.

For example, for companies in the Netherlands profits from nonconsolidated subsidiaries are tax-exempt if the parent company has an equity stake of more than 20 percent.

Fiscal Grouping

Many countries offer the possibility of fiscal grouping—that is, preparing consolidated tax filings for a group of companies that are directly or indirectly owned by the same parent company (ownership level requirements differ by country). If a specific company in the group generates a profit, it can offset that profit against losses from other group companies, or vice versa. The amount of taxes that a company would pay on a stand-alone basis can therefore differ from what it actually pays as part of a fiscal group. Although many countries allow consolidated taxation for a group of resident companies, this is, in general, not possible for a group of companies in different jurisdictions. In the case of mergers and acquisitions, fiscal grouping can be important. For example, if fiscal grouping is not possible between the acquirer and the target company, any tax loss carry-forwards in the target need to be earned back through future profits of the target company itself, and the acquirer will not have the benefit of directly offsetting these losses against its own taxable income.

Cross-Border Taxation

Even if an international group of companies is not able to achieve a consolidated tax status, cross-border taxation does not necessarily cause profits to be fully taxed multiple times. Relief may come through tax exemptions, tax credits, and tax treaties. When exemptions apply, profits from foreign subsidiaries that were already taxed abroad are exempt from domestic taxation for the parent. The European Parent-Subsidiary Directive prohibits European Union member states from taxing profits distributed by a subsidiary from another member state. Also, the directive makes profit distributions exempt from withholding taxes in the member state of the subsidiary. In other cases, countries provide tax credits to avoid double taxation. Finally, bilateral tax treaties can reduce or even eliminate withholding taxes on dividend, interest, or royalty payments.

Consider Exhibit 21.2, a simplified case of tax credits for a U.S.-based company. The assumed local tax rates are 34 percent on U.S. income, 20 percent on income in country X, and 60 percent on income in country Y. U.S. taxes are computed as 34 percent of consolidated pretax income less foreign tax credits that may not exceed 34 percent of foreign income. Whenever foreign tax credits reach the maximum allowable under U.S. law, as in the top half of Exhibit 21.2, consolidated taxes paid equal the total of local taxes,

Exhibit 21.2 Tax Calculation for a US Company with and without Foreign Tax Credits

1. With excess foreign tax credits

	U.S.	Country X	Country Y	Group
Pretax income	1,000	200	300	1,500
Local tax rate	34%	20%	60%	–
Local taxes	340	40	180	
U.S. tax rate				34%
Preliminary U.S. taxes				510
Foreign tax credits[1]				(170)
Net U.S. taxes				340
Foreign taxes				220
Consolidated income taxes				560
Total local taxes				(560)
Corporate tax penalty				0

2. Without excess foreign tax credits

	U.S.	Country X	Country Y	Group
Pretax income	1,000	400	100	1,500
Local tax rate	34%	20%	60%	–
Local taxes	340	80	60	
U.S. tax rate				34%
Preliminary U.S. taxes				510
Foreign tax credits[1]				(140)
Net U.S. taxes				370
Foreign taxes				140
Consolidated income taxes				510
Total local taxes				(480)
Corporate tax penalty				30

[1]Foreign tax credit is the foreign taxes paid or the foreign income times U.S. tax rate, whichever is lower.

and no corporate tax penalty is levied. When tax credits are below the maximum allowable, as in the bottom half of Exhibit 21.2, consolidated taxes exceed the total of local taxes, and a U.S. corporate tax penalty is levied. In effect, the U.S. Tax Code may raise the effective tax rate for subsidiaries located in lower-tax countries.

The effective tax rate for a subsidiary in a foreign country may not be its domestic statutory rate, because, given the specific circumstances, it may depend on the parent company's tax rate. In the second scenario in Exhibit 21.2, the U.S. Tax Code has raised the average effective tax rate to the parent company on income in country X from 20 percent to $(30 + 80)/400 = 27.5$ percent. The marginal effective tax rate on country X income is 34 percent, the U.S. tax rate. If the parent expected this situation to persist, it might be better off selling company X to an owner from country X. Note that these examples are simplified. Any tax credit or penalty is settled only upon repatriation of foreign profits to the United States, which is why U.S. corporations have significant profits locked up in foreign entities. The U.S. government has therefore created a special tax facility for efficient repatriation of foreign profits in 2004 and 2005.

Taxation of Shareholders in Different Countries

Differences in taxation of dividends and capital gains have an impact on the effective taxes paid by shareholders. If shareholders pay taxes on dividends received, the dividends are effectively taxed twice: first by corporate income tax, and second by personal income tax on the dividends. Many countries have integrated corporate and personal tax systems to eliminate some or all of the double taxation on dividends to shareholders. Mechanisms to reduce double taxation may affect companies' value.

Some countries use a dividend imputation system that gives shareholders a tax credit for some or all of the corporate taxes that the company has already paid. Dividend imputation effectively increases cash flow to shareholders by decreasing the amount of taxes received by the government. This cash flow may take the form of a tax reduction or of a tax refund, depending on the shareholder's overall tax liability. Exhibit 21.3 shows the calculation of tax credits under the United Kingdom's dividend imputation system and the

Exhibit 21.3 How Dividend Imputation Works

	Classic (double taxation)	Dividend imputation	
Corporate tax rate	30.0%	30.0%	
Tax credit (rate on net dividend)	0.0%	11.0%	
Dividend payout ratio	40.0%	40.0%	
Shareholder tax rate	33.0%	33.0%	
Company cash flow			
Earnings before taxes	100.0	100.0	
Corporate taxes	(30.0)	(30.0)	
Net income	70.0	70.0	
Cash dividend paid	28.0	28.0	
Shareholder taxation			
Shareholder tax base[1]	28.0	31.1	(=28.0 × 1.11)
Shareholder taxes	(9.2)	(10.2)	(=31.1 × 0.33)
Tax credit	–	3.1	(=28.0 × 0.11)
Taxes (paid) received	(9.2)	(7.1)	
Shareholder cash flows			
Cash dividend received	28.0	28.0	
Taxes (paid) received	(9.2)	(7.1)	
Net cash to investor	18.8	20.9	

[1]Actual cash dividend grossed up by the tax credit rate under the dividend imputation system.

resulting differences in net cash flows to investors. Under the classic system, with double taxation, shareholders pay 33 percent tax on the cash dividends received, versus 25 percent under the imputation system.

Most imputation systems provide only partial imputation of taxes paid, and the net impact is relatively small, as the example of the U.K. system shows (because the tax credit is only 11 percent). Therefore, in practice, there is often no need for any adjustment to the cash flows or the discount rate to capture the imputation impact in the valuation. More importantly, many shareholders will not even benefit from the imputation system. For the majority of companies, the shareholder base is diverse in terms of foreign and domestic shareholders as well as institutional and retail investors. Dividend imputation matters less for share prices if the price-setting investors are institutional investors or foreign investors who do not benefit from the dividend tax credit.

TRANSLATION OF FOREIGN-CURRENCY FINANCIAL STATEMENTS

Analyzing the historical performance of foreign subsidiaries is best done in the currency of that subsidiary to avoid distortion from currency translation. But in many cases this is not possible because the subsidiary's statements are translated in the parent's currency and included (or consolidated) in the parent's accounts. For example, an English subsidiary of a European corporate group would always prepare financial statements in British pounds. When the European parent company prepares its financial statements, it translates the British pound statements of the English subsidiary at the current euro-pound exchange rate. If the exchange rate fluctuates from year to year, the European parent company reports the same asset at a different euro amount each year, even if the asset's value in pounds sterling has not changed. The statements of the English subsidiary in the parent's reporting currency would suggest a cash expenditure because of the change in asset value, even though no cash has been spent and the change is solely due to a change in exchange rate. Therefore, following the guidelines from Chapter 7, a correction to the cash flow is needed that is equal to the gains/losses from currency translation.

Overseeing U.S. GAAP and IFRS, there are three approaches to translating the financial statements of foreign subsidiaries into the parent company's currency. Exhibit 21.4 on page 604 shows the approaches used under U.S. GAAP and IFRS for so-called moderate-inflation countries and hyper-inflationary countries: the current method, temporal method, and inflation-adjusted current method.

For subsidiaries in moderate-inflation countries, translation of the financial statements into the currency of the parent company is fairly straightforward. Both U.S. GAAP and IFRS apply the so-called current method. All balance sheet items except equity are translated at the year-end

Exhibit 21.4 Currency Translation Approaches

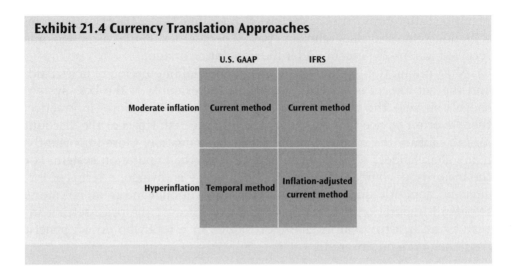

exchange rate. Translation gains and losses on the balance sheet are recognized in the equity account and do not affect net income. The average exchange rate for the period is used for translating the income statement.

In the case of hyperinflationary economies, IFRS and U.S. GAAP differ in terms of when hyperinflation is assumed, whether statements are adjusted for inflation, and what approach is used to translate the financial statements. U.S. GAAP defines hyperinflation as cumulative inflation over three years of approximately 100 percent or more. IFRS states that this is one indication but also suggests considering other factors such as local investor preference to keep wealth in nonmonetary assets or stable foreign currency.

U.S. GAAP requires the so-called temporal method for translating the financial statements in hyperinflationary currencies. All items in the financial statements are translated at the exchange rate at transaction date. This means historical exchange rates for items carried at historical cost, current exchange rates for monetary items, and year-average or other specific exchange rates for other balance sheet items and the income statement. Any resulting currency gains or losses are reported on the income statement of the parent.

Under IFRS, the translation approach for subsidiaries in hyperinflationary countries is similar to that for moderate-inflation countries. The key difference is that before translation, IFRS requires the hyperinflationary statements to be restated to current (foreign) currency units based on a general price index. All items except some monetary items are restated for the estimated impact of inflation. This generally requires judgment and will also depend on specific agreements and contracts (e.g., debt financing may or may not be linked to an index). The restatement results in a gain or loss on the subsidiary's income statement. Because the full statements are restated at current (year-end) foreign currency units, the year-end exchange rate is

Exhibit 21.5 Currency Translation

| | Local currency | Current method | | Temporal method | | Inflation-adjusted currency method | | |
		Foreign exchange rate	US $	Foreign exchange rate	US $	Adjusted	Foreign exchange rate	US $
Balance sheet								
Cash and receivables	100	0.85	85	0.85	85	100	0.85	85
Inventory	300	0.85	255	0.90	270	321	0.85	273
Net fixed assets	600	0.85	510	0.95	570	684	0.85	581
	1,000		850		925	1,105		939
Current liabilities	265	0.85	225	0.85	225	265	0.85	225
Long-term debt	600	0.85	510	0.85	510	684	0.85	581
Equity								
Common stock	100	0.95	95	0.95	95	100	0.95	95
Retained earnings	35		32		95	56		48
Foreign currency adjustment			(12)					(10)
	1,000		850		925	1,105		939
Income statement								
Revenue	150	0.90	135	0.90	135	161	0.85	137
Cost of goods sold	(70)	0.90	(63)	0.93	(65)	(75)	0.85	(64)
Depreciation	(20)	0.90	(18)	0.95	(19)	(23)	0.85	(20)
Other expenses, net	(10)	0.90	(9)	0.90	(9)	(11)	0.85	(9)
Foreign exchange gain/(loss)					66	20[1]	0.85	17
Income before taxes	50		45		108	72		61
Income taxes	(15)	0.90	(13)	0.90	(13)	(16)	0.85	(13)
Net income	35		32		95	56		48

[1]Gain from restatement.

used to translate both the balance sheet and the income statement. Any translation effects will be included in the equity account of the parent.

Exhibit 21.5 shows an example of currency translation under the three approaches. In this example, the exchange rate has changed from 0.95 at the beginning of the year to 0.85 at the end of the year, consistent with 14 percent inflation in the foreign country during the year and U.S. inflation of 2 percent. The average exchange rate for the year is 0.90. As the exhibit illustrates, the three approaches can result in significantly different amounts for net income and equity in the parent company's currency.

FORECASTING CASH FLOWS IN FOREIGN AND DOMESTIC CURRENCY

To value a company with international operations, first forecast the components of cash flow in their most *relevant* currency. This means forecasting the British pound cash flows in British pounds, the Swiss franc cash flows

Exhibit 21.6 Consistent Monetary Assumptions for Cost of Capital Estimates and Cash Flow Projections

Domestic inflation and interest rates	Year 1	2	3	4	5	
Term structure estimates (percent)						
Nominal risk-free rate	15.4	13.8	12.6	11.5	10.4	Use nominal risk-free rate plus risk premium in domestic cost of capital estimates
Inflation rate	12.0	10.5	9.3	8.2	7.2	
Real risk-free rate	3.0	3.0	3.0	3.0	3.0	
Annual estimates (percent)						
Nominal risk-free rate	15.4	12.3	10.2	8.2	6.1	Use annual inflation rates when forecasting domestic company results and cash flows
Inflation rate	12.0	9.0	7.0	5.0	3.0	
Real risk-free rate	3.0	3.0	3.0	3.0	3.0	

International foreign exchange rates						
Foreign exchange rate estimates						
Forward foreign exchange rate	0.92	0.86	0.81	0.78	0.76	Use forward foreign exchange rates for conversion of future domestic and foreign cash flows
Spot foreign exchange rate 1.00						

Foreign inflation and interest rates						
Term structure estimates (percent)						
Nominal risk-free rate	9.2	8.7	8.3	8.0	7.6	Use nominal risk-free rate plus risk premium in foreign cost of capital estimates
Inflation rate	6.0	5.5	5.2	4.9	4.5	
Real risk-free rate	3.0	3.0	3.0	3.0	3.0	
Annual estimates (percent)						
Nominal risk-free rate	9.2	8.2	7.6	7.1	6.1	Use annual inflation rates when forecasting foreign company results and cash flows
Inflation rate	6.0	5.0	4.5	4.0	3.0	
Real risk-free rate	3.0	3.0	3.0	3.0	3.0	

in Swiss francs, and so on, before combining them into a set of financials for the entire company. In practice, this is an iterative process: You cannot forecast the individual line items without considering how they affect the other line items in the forecast. You need a coherent, integrated forecast that reflects the competitive dynamics of the business operations.

The assumptions underlying your forecasts of financial results in domestic or foreign currency and cost of capital must all be consistent. Exhibit 21.6 shows how some fundamental monetary assumptions should be defined in a consistent way to avoid any biases in the valuation results.

For domestic-currency projections, work from a single set of monetary assumptions for annual inflation and risk-free real interest rates, which together define the term structure of nominal interest rates. Whenever possible, base the interest rate assumptions on market quotes. All cash flow projections and cost-of-capital estimates in domestic currency should be based on this single set of monetary assumptions to avoid inconsistencies in the valuation. For example, if future inflation rates underlying sales forecasts are around 10 percent per year but the cost of capital estimates are built on long-term interest rates that reflect inflation declining toward 5 percent, the resulting DCF value will be too high.

Foreign-currency projections require a similar set of assumptions. Given the domestic and foreign sets of monetary assumptions, the forward exchange rates between both currencies are set (see the following discussion). To ensure consistent valuation results, always use these forward exchange rates when converting future cash flows from one currency into another. If market quotes are available for longer-term forward exchange rates, test your assumptions against them. If there are significant deviations, it probably means that your assumptions for the domestic or foreign inflation or interest rate do not reflect market expectations and should be revised.

A company valuation should always lead to the same result regardless of the currency or mix of currencies in which cash flows are projected. Use one of the following two methods for forecasting and discounting foreign currency cash flows:

1. *Spot-rate method:* Project foreign cash flows in foreign currency, and discount these at the foreign cost of capital. Then convert the present value of the cash flows into domestic currency, using the spot exchange rate.

2. *Forward-rate method:* Project foreign cash flows in foreign currency, and convert these into domestic currency using the forward exchange rates. Then discount the converted cash flows at the cost of capital in domestic currency.

We first illustrate both methods with a simple example (see Exhibit 21.7 on p. 608). Assume a German company generates significant risk-free cash flows in Switzerland. Using the spot-rate method, simply project cash flows in Swiss francs and discount them at the Swiss risk-free interest rate. The resulting present value is CHF 568. Converting this value at the spot exchange rate of 1.533 Swiss francs per euro results in €366.

The forward-rate method is more complex. The projected cash flows in Swiss francs should be converted to euros on a year-by-year basis using forward rates and then discounted at the euro risk-free rate. As a practical matter, for most currencies, forward exchange rates are not available beyond 18 months. This means that you need to estimate synthetic forward exchange rates by using interest rate parity.

The interest-rate-parity theory is based on the idea that changes in foreign exchange rates are related to the ratio of expected inflation rates between two countries. Exhibit 21.8 on page 609 plots the relationship between domestic inflation and domestic interest rates for 38 countries from

Exhibit 21.7 Spot-Rate and Forward-Rate Method for Foreign Cash Flows

	Year 0	1	2	3	4	5
Interest rates						
r^F—Swiss sovereign interest rate (percent)		0.9	1.5	2.2	2.4	2.9
r^D—Euro sovereign interest rate (percent)		2.3	2.9	3.4	3.9	4.2
$(1+r^F)/(1+r^D)$		0.9863	0.9730	0.9656	0.9435	0.9392
Exchange rates						
X_0—spot rate CHF/€	1.553					
X_t—estimated forward rate CHF/€		1.532	1.511	1.500	1.465	1.459
1. Spot rate method						
Cash flow in CHF	105.0	110.3	115.8	121.6	127.6	134.0
Discount factor from r^F		0.991	0.971	0.937	0.909	0.867
Present value in CHF		109.3	112.4	113.9	116.1	116.2
Sum of cash flow in CHF	567.7					
Sum of cash flow in €	365.6					
2. Forward rate method						
Cash flow in €		72.0	76.6	81.1	87.1	91.9
Discount factor from r^D		0.978	0.944	0.905	0.858	0.814
Present value in €		70.4	72.4	73.3	74.7	74.8
Sum of cash flows in €	365.6					

Note: CHF = Swiss franc.

1995 to 2004. The exhibit shows that inflation differences explain most of the difference in nominal interest rates.

Across countries, the interest-rate-parity theory is expressed as follows. The forward foreign exchange rate in year t, X_t, is equal to the current spot rate, X_0, multiplied by the ratio of nominal interest rates in the two countries over the forecast interval, t:

$$X_t = X_0 \times \left[\frac{1 + r^F}{1 + r^D} \right]^t$$

where r^F = Interest rate in foreign currency
    r^D = Interest rate in domestic currency

To illustrate the theory for a single year, suppose that the German company can borrow one-year money in Switzerland at a 0.9 percent nominal interest rate, r^F, while the borrowing rate in euros, r^D, is 2.3 percent. The spot exchange rate, X_0, is 1.553 Swiss francs per euro, and the one-year forward

Exhibit 21.8 Relationship between Inflation and Interest Rates

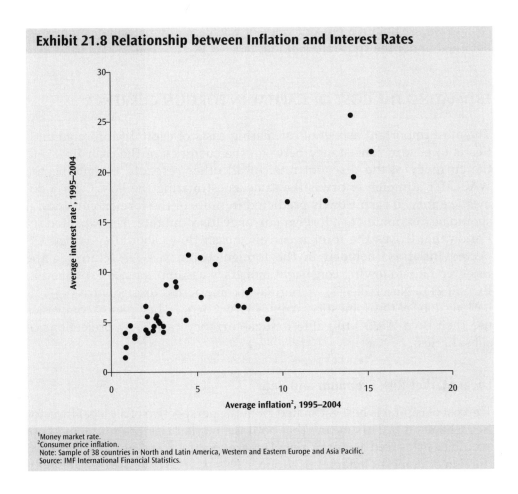

¹Money market rate.
²Consumer price inflation.
Note: Sample of 38 countries in North and Latin America, Western and Eastern Europe and Asia Pacific.
Source: IMF International Financial Statistics.

rate, X_1, is 1.532 Swiss francs per euro. We can use interest rate parity to estimate the equivalent euro borrowing rate for a 0.9 percent borrowing rate in Switzerland:

$$\left(1 + r^{D}\right) = \frac{X_0}{X_t} \times (1 + r^{F}) = \left(\frac{1.553}{1.532}\right) \times (1.009) = 1.023$$

No practical difference exists between borrowing in euros at 2.3 percent or in Swiss francs at 0.9 percent. The foreign borrowing rate, when converted to a domestic equivalent rate, is usually close to the domestic rate (unless there are tax implications).

We can use interest rate parity to estimate forward exchange rates by multiplying the ratio of nominal interest rates by the current spot rate. The Swiss franc cash flows are converted to euro cash flows by using the forward exchange rates. Using the euro interest rates to discount the converted cash flows, we obtain a present value of €366, exactly the same value as we obtained under the spot-rate method.

ESTIMATING THE COST OF CAPITAL IN FOREIGN CURRENCY

The most important aspect of estimating costs of capital for foreign entities is to ensure consistency between the currency of the cash flow and the currency of the discount rate. In all other respects, estimating the WACC for a foreign entity is the same as estimating the WACC for a domestic entity. If cash flow is predicted in units of the foreign currency, it should be discounted at a foreign-currency discount rate. The expected inflation that drives the foreign-currency cash flows should equal the expected inflation included in the foreign-currency WACC through the risk-free rate, following consistent monetary assumptions as explained in Exhibit 21.6. Nevertheless, we regularly come across foreign-currency valuations done at the domestic-currency WACC (e.g., when parent companies use their own WACC to value foreign-currency cash flow projections of subsidiaries).

Local Market Risk Premium and Beta

The cost of capital is best estimated from the perspective of a global investor (see Chapter 10). This means that both the market risk premium and beta should be measured against a global market portfolio and not against a local (foreign or domestic) market portfolio.

Our reasoning is based on the globalization of capital markets. A considerable share of all equity trades is international. These global traders, primarily large institutional investors, draw their capital from and invest it all over the world. If expected premiums were significantly different across countries (on a risk-adjusted basis), you would expect to see significant flows to countries with higher-than-average premiums and away from lower-than-average premiums. That is difficult to argue. In theory, such a movement would also tend to re-equalize premiums.

Application of a global market risk premium also makes intuitive sense. Consider the consumer goods companies Procter & Gamble and Unilever. Both sell their household products globally with roughly the same geographic spread. The shares of both are traded in the United States and Europe. The primary difference is that Procter & Gamble is domiciled in the United States, and Unilever is domiciled in the United Kingdom and the Netherlands. With similar investor bases, it would be odd if the two companies had different costs of capital.

Given this reasoning, how do we account for different realized premiums? Exhibit 21.9 compares the realized premiums on stock market indexes

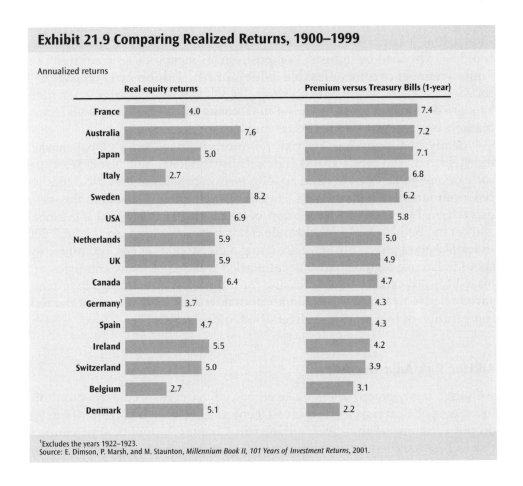

Exhibit 21.9 Comparing Realized Returns, 1900–1999

Annualized returns

	Real equity returns	Premium versus Treasury Bills (1-year)
France	4.0	7.4
Australia	7.6	7.2
Japan	5.0	7.1
Italy	2.7	6.8
Sweden	8.2	6.2
USA	6.9	5.8
Netherlands	5.9	5.0
UK	5.9	4.9
Canada	6.4	4.7
Germany[1]	3.7	4.3
Spain	4.7	4.3
Ireland	5.5	4.2
Switzerland	5.0	3.9
Belgium	2.7	3.1
Denmark	5.1	2.2

[1]Excludes the years 1922–1923.
Source: E. Dimson, P. Marsh, and M. Staunton, *Millennium Book II, 101 Years of Investment Returns*, 2001.

with government bond returns for a number of countries. These numbers are from Dimson, Marsh, and Staunton's analysis of long-term average returns on equities, corporate bonds, and short-term government bonds.[2]

Realized returns vary considerably depending on the time period over which they are measured. Exhibit 21.9 shows that even for a 100-year period, realized returns can still vary a lot. One driver is the difference in economic development over the last century for the countries listed. Furthermore, some of the markets may have shown limited integration with international capital markets in the past, depending on the major companies traded on each of the exchanges. Therefore, the historical data may not properly represent the current situation. More important is the argument that these market indexes do not represent large, diversified portfolios. In particular, the key stock market indexes in the majority of European countries typically include only 25 to 40 companies but account

[2] E. Dimson, P. Marsh, and M. Staunton, *Millennium Book II: 101 Years of Investment Returns* (ABN AMRO and London Business School, 2001).

for the majority of total capitalization of the stock market. Research has shown that a large fraction of the returns on European market indexes could be explained by industry composition, as most indexes consisted of a limited number of companies (see Exhibit 21.10).[3] Exhibit 21.11 on page 614 shows some more recent data on several stock markets: Smaller stock markets are dominated more by individual stocks and sectors, whereas larger markets and the S&P 500 Index are much more diversified.

Ideally, the global market risk premium is based on a global market index such as the MSCI World Index. Unfortunately, global indexes typically do not go far back in time, so long-term estimates of historical market risk premiums are not available. Therefore, we typically resort to the well-diversified U.S. market. Correlation between the S&P 500 and the global market index (e.g., MSCI World Index) has been very high, so the S&P 500 Index is a good proxy. Since we are using a global market risk premium, we should also use a global beta. Local market indexes of many countries are biased toward certain companies and/or industries. Therefore, a beta measured relative to a local market index does not necessarily represent the risk contribution of that stock to a diversified, global portfolio.

Ad Hoc Risk Adjustments

Although many practitioners make ad hoc adjustments to the discount rate to reflect political risk, foreign-investment risk, or foreign-currency risk, we do not recommend this. As explained in Chapter 22, political or country risk is best handled by adjusting expected cash flows, weighting them by the probability of various scenarios. Foreign-currency risk and foreign-investment risk are already captured in the spot and forward exchange rates. As we will discuss in the following section, there is no need for an additional risk premium for currency risk.

INCORPORATING FOREIGN-CURRENCY RISK IN VALUATIONS

Many executives are concerned about foreign-currency risk when it comes to valuing foreign entities. Some even turn to hedging strategies with derivative instruments to try to manage their exposure to currency risk from specific transactions or perhaps entire foreign business operations. To what extent should executives be concerned about currency risk, and how important is it in valuing foreign entities?

---

[3] R. Roll, "Industrial Structure and the Comparative Behavior of International Stock Market Indexes," *Journal of Finance*, 47(1) (1992): 3–42.

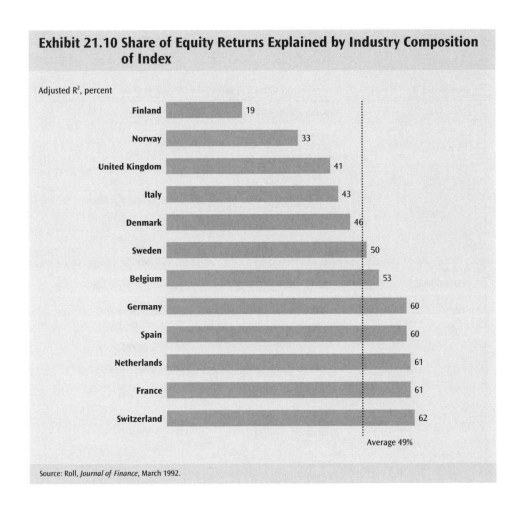

Exhibit 21.10 Share of Equity Returns Explained by Industry Composition of Index

Adjusted R², percent

Finland	19
Norway	33
United Kingdom	41
Italy	43
Denmark	46
Sweden	50
Belgium	53
Germany	60
Spain	60
Netherlands	61
France	61
Switzerland	62

Average 49%

Source: Roll, *Journal of Finance*, March 1992.

No Currency Risk Premium in Weighted Average Cost of Capital

We do not support the inclusion of an additional risk premium in the discount rate to cover for perceived currency risk. If there is a currency risk premium, it is already included in the spot and forward exchange rates that we use to translate currencies. To what extent financial markets actually "price" currency risk in spot and forward exchange rates is still an open debate in academia.[4] But these risk premiums—if any—are likely to be small.[5] This should not come as a surprise. Basic finance theory tells us that there is no value in a company managing currency risk for its shareholders if the shareholders themselves can achieve this by simply diversifying their

---

[4] See, for example, B. Solnik, *International Investments*, 4th ed. (Reading, MA: Addison-Wesley, 1999), ch. 5.
[5] P. Sercu and R. Uppal, *International Financial Markets and the Firm*, (Cincinnati, OH: South-Western, 1995), ch. 14.

Exhibit 21.11 Comparing Stock Market Concentration

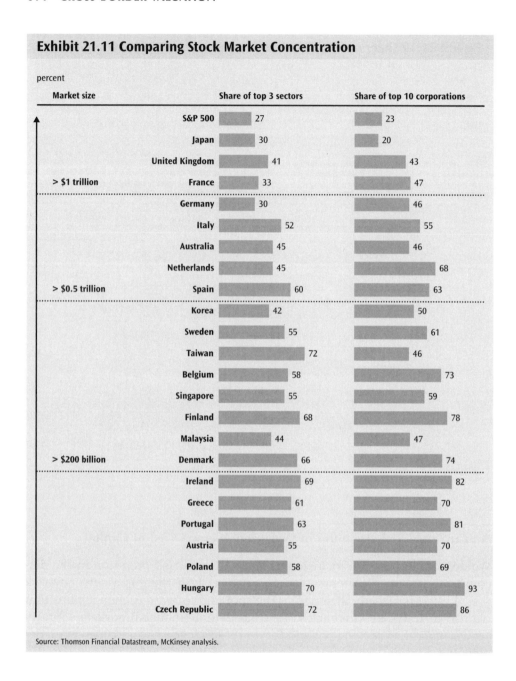

percent

Market size	Share of top 3 sectors	Share of top 10 corporations
S&P 500	27	23
Japan	30	20
United Kingdom	41	43
> $1 trillion — France	33	47
Germany	30	46
Italy	52	55
Australia	45	46
Netherlands	45	68
> $0.5 trillion — Spain	60	63
Korea	42	50
Sweden	55	61
Taiwan	72	46
Belgium	58	73
Singapore	55	59
Finland	68	78
Malaysia	44	47
> $200 billion — Denmark	66	74
Ireland	69	82
Greece	61	70
Portugal	63	81
Austria	55	70
Poland	58	69
Hungary	70	93
Czech Republic	72	86

Source: Thomson Financial Datastream, McKinsey analysis.

portfolio. There are indications that currency risk is indeed to a large extent diversifiable; Exhibit 21.12 provides an example.

Keep in mind that nominal currency risk is irrelevant if exchange rates immediately adjust to differences in inflation rates. The only relevant currency risk is real currency risk as measured by changes in relative purchas-

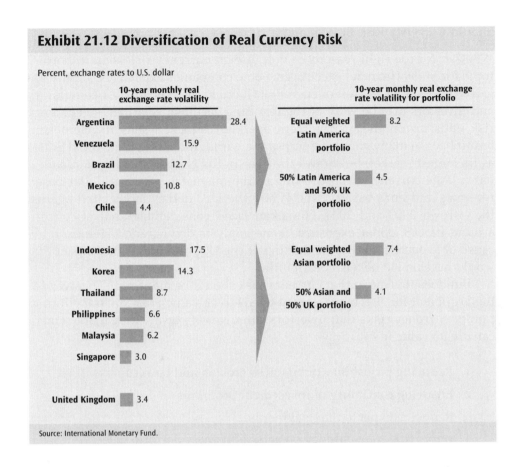

Exhibit 21.12 Diversification of Real Currency Risk

Percent, exchange rates to U.S. dollar

ing power parity. Analysis of purchasing power parity indicates that currencies indeed revert to parity levels but not immediately. Short-term deviations from purchasing power parity levels can be significant, and have the potential to leave corporations exposed to currency risk in real terms. However, shareholders are typically in a good position to diversify the real currency risk. Exhibit 21.12 shows the monthly volatility of real exchange rates for a selection of Latin American and Asian currencies, as well as the British pound. Although some of these currencies have a high volatility, a regional portfolio already eliminates a lot of real currency risk, as shown by its lower volatility. Combining a developing-markets portfolio with British pounds diversifies the risk even further. If real currency risk is mostly diversifiable for shareholders, there should not be a currency risk premium of any significance in the company's cost of capital either.

However, suppose a company's total exposure to currency risk is at such a level that it could result in financial distress. In that case, currency risk does become relevant for shareholder value creation because it could trigger losses that shareholders cannot diversify away.

Should Currency Risk Be Managed?

Whether for the right reasons or not, foreign-currency risk is an important topic for many financial executives. Some companies experience significant gains or losses as a result of currency fluctuations. The analyst community and investors may be wary of the resulting earnings volatility, so currency risk ends up on the management agenda. Heineken sells its Heineken-brand beer in many countries across the world, including the United States as its largest market, but brews the beer in the Netherlands. As a result, it has a large currency exposure due to the mismatch between dollar-based revenues and euro-based costs. When the U.S. dollar depreciated against the euro in 2003 and 2004, Heineken faced considerable analyst concern around its U.S. dollar exposure. Some analysts downgraded Heineken because of expected further weakening of the U.S. dollar and the impact that would have on Heineken's profitability.

But does this mean that currency risk should be managed? The overriding argument for risk management needs to be value creation, not elimination of currency risks that investors can diversify away. Risk management can create value in four ways:

1. Reducing probability of business erosion and bankruptcy
2. Ensuring continuity of investment programs
3. Reducing expected tax payments
4. Improving transparency on actual business performance

We believe that most of the value creation potential lies in the first two sources. We already discussed the importance of the risk of business erosion and bankruptcy in Chapter 17. Ensuring continuity of investment programs is especially important for companies with significant growth opportunities that could be lost if critical investments are deferred or canceled in case of funding shortages due to currency losses.

The opportunity to reduce expected tax payments is probably limited. For example, when a corporation incurs losses due to currency fluctuations, in most countries it does not receive an immediate tax refund. Instead, it may offset future taxable profits against the current loss via a so-called tax loss carryforward. If risk management can smooth the corporation's earnings over the years and prevent these from turning negative, the corporation can avoid the loss of time value related to the tax loss carryforward. However, this applies mainly to companies whose earnings indeed turn negative due to currency fluctuations, and it only reduces the time value lost.

The real benefits from improving transparency are difficult to assess. On one hand, risk management can reduce currency-driven fluctuations in corporate results and thereby help to provide a better perspective on the company's true economic performance. On the other hand, such transparency can also be achieved by internal and external reporting of results in constant currency rates (as some international companies do) without incurring the costs of risk management programs.

Economic versus Accounting Exposure

For currency risk management to create value, it needs to address the company's economic exposure, not its accounting exposure. The impact of currency fluctuations on the balance sheet and income statement is not very relevant in itself because these do not necessarily reflect a company's true economics. It is much more important to understand economic exposure, that is, how currency risk affects a company's current and future cash flows, and whether this could lead to loss of investment opportunities, business erosion, or even bankruptcy. Corporations with international operations typically face three sources of economic exposure to currency risk:

1. Competitive exposure from currency mismatches of revenue and cost base. For example, a European company with a local cost base but mainly sales in the United States would face competitive pressure if the euro were to appreciate. It might not be able to increase the price in U.S. dollars, so its margin would deteriorate.

2. Transaction exposure from time lags and fixed prices in contractual arrangements and other business transactions. For example, if a company agrees to a purchase price for raw materials that is fixed in foreign currency, but settles the transaction a month later, it faces a loss if the foreign currency appreciates.

3. Portfolio exposure from conversion of foreign subsidiary cash flows into domestic-currency cash flows. Even if foreign operations are sourcing locally and are funded locally, they can still lead to currency exposure for the parent, because the value of the net cash flows as measured in the parent's currency will fluctuate with the exchange rate.

Competitive exposure is what matters most for the continuity of investment programs and financial health of a company. A significant currency mismatch between cash inflows and outflows can change the short-term economics of the business and even lead a company into financial distress. Given the size and uncertainty[6] of this type of exposure, hedging with financial instruments does not offer a solution for the long term. The most common strategy is to fix the underlying currency mismatch by shifting the

---

[6] The size of the competitive exposure is difficult to predict because it depends on the level of future business activity.

cost base. This is what several Japanese and European automotive and equipment manufacturers, including Toyota, BMW, and Daimler-Benz, did in the 1980s when the yen and Deutsche mark appreciated strongly against the U.S. dollar. As discussed earlier, Heineken has a significant competitive exposure that leads to lower cash flows if the U.S. dollar depreciates. Such exposure can only be hedged with financial instruments over the short term and at considerable costs. Branding considerations probably make Heineken unwilling to shift beer production to the United States. Although it cannot reduce the risk, Heineken can absorb it because of its conservative capital structure. The U.S. dollar is unlikely to lead to financial distress for Heineken. Nevertheless, the competitive exposure means that Heineken's cash flow and share price will remain sensitive to fluctuations in the exchange rate of U.S. dollars to euros.

Transaction exposure is typically too small to be relevant as a potential source of interruption of investment programs or business erosion, unless there is exposure on, for example, major investment outlays or specific commitments. In most cases, transaction exposure can be hedged with financial instruments or handled through contractual arrangements, if needed.

Portfolio exposure is also unlikely to lead to reduction of investments or to business erosion. As long as a company's debt is roughly in line with the currencies in which it generates cash flows, portfolio exposure cannot turn cash flows negative. In addition, different shareholders may have different perspectives on portfolio exposure. For example, if a European company acquires a U.S. subsidiary, it increases its U.S. dollar portfolio exposure. For its U.S. shareholders, this actually reduces their euro currency risk, whereas its European shareholders incur additional dollar risk. Therefore, this type of exposure typically does not call for hedging.

Ideally, you should analyze the impact of different exchange rate scenarios on the investment opportunities of the company and the company's ability to service its debt payments. Note that cash flow volatility in itself is not what counts; equally volatile cash flow patterns can have completely different risk management implications. Understand how cash flow volatility due to currency risk could affect the company's ability to fund future capital expenditures, pay taxes, service its interest payments, and return cash to shareholders. If insufficient cash flow leads to deferral or cancellation of capital expenditures, this could undermine the company's growth and competitive position. Inability to fulfill debt servicing on an ongoing basis will obviously mean bankruptcy. In Exhibit 21.13, the first cash flow pattern (EBITDA Profile 1) does not necessarily require risk management, because it does not affect the company's ongoing ability to fund growth and return cash to its investors. The second cash flow pattern (EBITDA Profile 2), in contrast, does significantly affect the company's investment program, so it may benefit from an active risk management strategy. The appropriate strategy to reduce the company's currency risk depends on whether the

Exhibit 21.13 Impact of Cash Flow Volatility

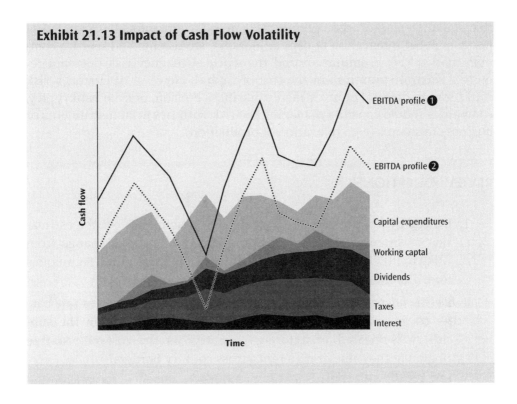

risk results from competitive, transaction, or portfolio exposure. As we have argued, competitive exposure is usually the most important source of currency risk—and also the most difficult one to manage.

SUMMARY

A number of difficult issues arise in the valuation of foreign companies or domestic companies with foreign operations. It is important to consider different accounting standards and tax systems, consistent assumptions underlying cash flow forecasts and discount rates, and the effect of currency risk on value. Still, in the end, the way you apply the DCF valuation approach to foreign companies is the same as for domestic companies. You need to understand and reflect local accounting and taxation in your analysis, but the adjustments are straightforward. The dominant positions of IFRS and U.S. GAAP will strongly reduce issues related to international accounting differences. Cash flows for foreign business can be projected in foreign or domestic currency as long as you consistently apply the spot-rate or forward-rate method. The approach to estimating cost of capital also is the same around the world, although estimation of some of the parameters (particularly market risk premium) can be controversial. Considering today's global integration of capital markets, we recommend using a common market risk premium around the world. Currency risk does not require a separate premium in the cost of capital. However, if currency risk could lead to deferral of investments, business erosion, or even bankruptcy, companies should consider managing the risk with financial instruments or business measures (e.g., relocation of production).

REVIEW QUESTIONS

1. Do the differences between accounting practices affect the estimation of an entity's value (for example, would either a change from LIFO to FIFO or would the use of alternative depreciation techniques for different asset classes affect enterprise value)? Explain.

2. Define *interest rate parity*. What is the significance of interest rate parity to an analyst forecasting a subsidiary's value, when the subsidiary is located in a foreign country? Is the cost of risk-free financing the same or different across country borders?

3. U.S. GAAP and IFRS accounting standards appear to be converging. If this is the case, why does a manager need to understand the historical differences between these standards?

4. Define and give two examples of an *intangible asset*. Identify the accounting treatments for acquired versus internally generated intangible assets.

5. In a cross-border acquisition, an analyst must consider the impact of taxes when estimating relevant cash flows. Identify four differences an analysis must account for in the estimation of risk and cash flows.

6. Discuss the differences between the current, temporal, and inflation-adjusted current methods to translate the financial statements of acquisitions or divisions located in moderately and hyperinflationary economic environments.

7. What impact does the globalization of capital markets have on a manager's estimate of an appropriate cost of capital used to estimate the value of a subsidiary headquartered in a foreign country?

22

Valuation in
Emerging Markets

The emerging economies in Asia and South America will experience strong growth over the next decades; many analysts see China and India moving into the ranks of the world's largest economies.[1] This sometimes spectacular economic development will produce many situations requiring sound analysis and valuation. In the rising number of privatizations, joint ventures, mergers and acquisitions, local financial parties such as banks and capital markets will display growing sophistication. Institutional investors will also continue to diversify their portfolios, adding international holdings in emerging-market stocks.

In this chapter we focus on issues that arise in financial analysis and valuation of businesses in emerging markets. Valuation is much more difficult in these environments because of risks and obstacles to businesses, including great macroeconomic uncertainty, illiquid capital markets, controls on the flow of capital into and out of the country, less-rigorous accounting standards and disclosure levels, and high levels of political risk. Academics, investment bankers, and industry practitioners have yet to agree on how to address these challenges. Methods vary considerably and practitioners often make arbitrary adjustments based on intuition and limited empirical evidence.

With agreement lacking and emerging-market valuations so complex, we recommend a triangulation approach—comparing estimates of the value from three methods. First, we use discounted cash flows with

Special thanks to our colleagues William Jones and Gustavo Wigman, who contributed to this chapter.
[1] See, for example, D. Wilson and R. Purushothaman, "Dreaming with BRICs: The Path to 2050" (Global Economics paper no. 99, Goldman Sachs & Co., October 2003).

probability-weighted scenarios that explicitly model the risks the business faces. Then we compare the value obtained from this approach with the results of two secondary approaches: a DCF approach with a country risk premium built into the cost of capital, and a valuation based on comparable trading and transaction multiples.

The basics of estimating a DCF value are the same in emerging markets as elsewhere. Therefore, we focus on complications specific to emerging-market valuations:

- Handling foreign exchange rates, inflation, and interest rate gaps with developed markets consistently when making financial projections
- Factoring inflation into historical financial analysis and cash flow projections
- Incorporating special emerging-market risks consistently in the valuation
- Estimating the cost of capital in emerging markets
- Using market-based references such as trading multiples and transaction multiples when interpreting and calibrating valuation results

We will apply our valuation approach in this chapter to ConsuCo, a leading Brazilian manufacturer of consumer goods.[2]

EXCHANGE RATES, INFLATION, AND INTEREST RATE GAPS

Because exchange rates, inflation, and interest rates can fluctuate wildly from year to year in emerging markets, assumptions underlying estimates of future financial results in domestic or foreign currency and cost of capital must be consistent. In Chapter 21 we discussed how some fundamental monetary assumptions should be defined consistently to avoid any biases in the valuation results. This becomes even more important when you value companies in emerging markets.

The components of the cash flows of emerging-market companies are often denominated in several currencies. Consider an oil exporter. Its revenues are determined by the dollar price of oil, while many of its costs (labor and domestic purchases) are determined by the domestic currency. If foreign-exchange rates would perfectly reflect inflation differentials—so that purchasing power parity would hold—the company's operating margins and cash flows in real terms would be unaffected. In that case, changes in exchange rates would be irrelevant for valuation purposes.

However, at least in the short run, this does not always hold, because in emerging markets, exchange rates move far and fast. For example, in Argentina at the end of 2001, the exchange rate rose from 1.0 peso per U.S. dollar to nearly 1.9 pesos per U.S. dollar in 15 days, and to 3.1 in less than 4

---

[2] This case illustration is a disguised example.

Exhibit 22.1 Brazilian PPP-Adjusted Dollar Exchange Rates

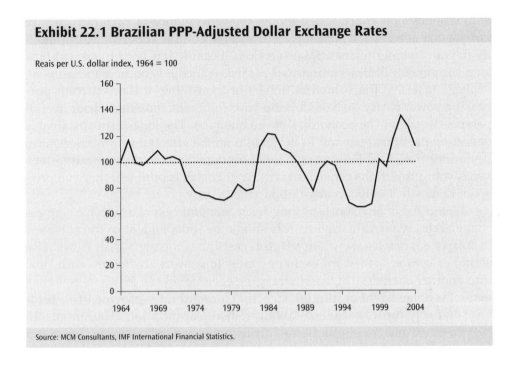

Reais per U.S. dollar index, 1964 = 100

Source: MCM Consultants, IMF International Financial Statistics.

months. During a period of just a couple of weeks in 1999, Brazil's currency, the Real, weakened by more than 50 percent relative to the U.S. dollar.

When estimating the impact of exchange rate movements on cash flow forecasts, keep in mind that evidence shows that, over the long run, purchasing power parity does hold,[3] even between emerging and developed economies. In other words, exchange rates ultimately do adjust for differences in inflation between countries. For example, if you held $100 million of Brazilian currency in 1964, by 2004 it would have been practically worthless in U.S. dollars. Yet, if we adjust for purchasing power, the value of the currency didn't change very much, as Exhibit 22.1 shows. In other words, suppose that, instead of holding $100 million of Brazilian currency, you held $100 million of assets in Brazil whose value increased with inflation. In 2004, your assets would have been worth about $90 million (in real terms). Therefore, when you perform valuations, your best assumption is that purchasing power parity holds in the long term; any other approach implies taking a bet on future real exchange rate movements.

Nevertheless, as Exhibit 22.1 also shows, exchange rates can deviate from purchasing power parity (PPP) by as much as 20 percent to 30 percent for several years (keeping in mind that PPP-adjusted exchange rates are difficult to estimate). Therefore, before making financial projections, assess whether the current exchange rate is over- or undervalued on a PPP basis

[3] For a recent overview, see Alan M. Taylor and Mark Peter Taylor, "The Purchasing Power Parity Debate" (CEPR discussion paper no. 4495, 2004).

and, if so, by how much. Then model the convergence of currency rates to purchasing power parity, and reflect its impact on the company's profitability in your long-term financial projections. Because it is hard to predict how long the current PPP deviation will persist, you could conduct a sensitivity analysis to assess the valuation impact of the timing of the return to purchasing power parity. As you develop your forecasts, remember your overall perspective about the economics of the business. The long-term sustainable operating profit margin and ROIC should not be affected by any short-term deviations from PPP. Relying on a set of fundamental monetary assumptions keeps your projections consistent with your cost of capital whether you project in domestic, foreign, real, or nominal currency.

Regardless of any short- or long-term economic exposure to varying exchange rates, your valuation results should be independent of the currency or mix of currencies in which you forecast the company's cash flows. Use actual or synthetic forward exchange rates to convert any future cash flow into another currency. In many emerging economies, the forward-exchange market is nonexistent or illiquid, so actual forward rates provide little guidance on likely future exchange rate movements or inflation differentials. In that case, estimate a synthetic forward rate from your assumptions about future inflation and interest rates for the currencies concerned (see Chapter 21 for details).

FACTORING INFLATION INTO HISTORICAL ANALYSIS AND FORECASTS

Even with consistent assumptions about inflation, interest rates, and foreign exchange rates, sound analysis and forecasting of the financial performance of emerging-market companies remains challenging. Inflation distorts the financial statements, so it is hard to make year-to-year historical comparisons, perform ratio analysis, or forecast performance.

For companies operating in high-inflation environments, historical analysis and forecasting should be carried out in both nominal and real (constant currency) terms whenever possible. As we will explain, nominal indicators are sometimes not meaningful (e.g., for capital turnover), and in other cases, real indicators are problematic (e.g., to determine corporate income taxes). Proper valuation requires insights from both nominal- and real-terms historical analyses. Financial projections can be made in real or nominal terms or both; properly done projections should yield an identical value.

Historical Analysis

Accounting conventions in emerging markets often differ substantially from those of developed markets, so a company's economics may be difficult to understand. Furthermore, in many countries, complicated tax credits and adjustments make cash taxes harder to estimate than in developed markets. For example, Brazil has made large and frequent changes to its tax code. Brazil eliminated inflation accounting and reduced the corporate tax rate to 30.5 percent in 1996, and in 1997 disallowed the deductibility of the social contribution tax, effectively increasing the tax rate to 33 percent. To make up for the loss of the tax shields that inflation accounting had generated, Brazil's government allowed companies to deduct deemed interest on equity net of a withholding tax of 15 percent.

Large accounting and tax differences are frequently eliminated when the income statement and the balance sheet are brought together in the cash flow calculation, following the guidelines set out in Chapter 7. Still, before starting a valuation, you need to understand these differences. Unfortunately, the differences across emerging markets are too complex and varied for a detailed discussion in this chapter. Instead, we highlight the most common issues involving the impact of high inflation on your historical analysis.

In countries experiencing extreme inflation (more than 25 percent per year), companies often report in year-end currency. In the income statement, items such as revenues and costs that were booked throughout the year are restated at year-end purchasing power. Otherwise, the addition of these items would not be meaningful. The balance sheet usually has adjustments to fixed assets, inventory, and equity; the accounts payable and receivable are already in year-end terms.

In most countries, however, financial statements are not adjusted to reflect the effects of inflation. If inflation is high, this leads to distortions in the balance sheet and income statement. In the balance sheet, so-called nonmonetary assets, such as inventories and property, plant, and equipment, are shown at values far below current replacement value if they are long-lived assets. In the income statement, depreciation charges are too low relative to current replacement costs. Sales and costs in December and January of the same year are typically added as if they represent the same purchasing power.

As a result, many financial indicators typically used in historical analyses can be distorted when calculated directly from the financial statements. In emerging markets, companies often index their internal management accounts to overcome these issues. If they do not, or if you are doing an outside-in analysis, at least correct for the following distortions:

- Growth is overstated in times of inflation, so restate it in real terms by deflating with an annual inflation index if sales are evenly spread across the year. If sales are not spread evenly, use quarterly or monthly inflation indexes to deflate the sales in each corresponding interval.

- Capital turnover is typically overstated because operating assets are carried at historical costs. You can approximate the current costs of long-lived assets by adjusting their reported value with an inflation index for their estimated average lifetime. Or consider developing ratios of real sales relative to physical capacity indicators appropriate for the sector—for example, sales per square meter in consumer retail. Inventory levels also need restating if turnover is low and inflation is very high.

- Operating margins (operating profit over sales) can be overstated because of too-low depreciation and large holding gains on slow-moving inventories. Corrections for depreciation charges follow from adjustments to property, plant, and equipment. You can estimate cash operating expenses at current-cost basis by inflating the reported costs for the average time held in inventory. Alternatively, use historical EBITDA-to-sales ratios to assess the company's performance relative to peers; these ratios at least do not suffer from any depreciation-induced bias.

- Use caution in interpreting credit ratios and other indicators of capital structure health. Distortions are especially significant in solvency ratios such as debt to equity or total assets, because long-lived assets are understated relative to replacement costs, and floating-rate debt is at current currency units. As we advised in Chapter 17, use coverage ratios such as EBITDA to interest expense.[4] These are less exposed to accounting distortions because depreciation has no impact and debt financing in emerging markets is mostly at floating interest rates or in foreign currency.

Financial Projections in Real and Nominal Terms

When you make financial projections of income statements and balance sheets under high inflation for a valuation, keep in mind that accounting adjustments cannot affect free cash flow. Thus, for valuation purposes, we project financial statements without any accounting adjustments for inflation. The projections can be made in nominal or real terms. Exhibit 22.2 summarizes the major advantages and shortcomings of each approach.

Neither approach is perfect, so use elements of both to prepare consistent financial projections. Specifically, when projecting in real terms, it is often difficult to calculate taxes correctly, as taxes are often calculated based on nominal financial statements. Furthermore, you need to explicitly project the cash flow effects of working capital changes because these do not automatically follow from the annual change in working capital. The

---

[4] Distortions occur in the ratio of EBITA to interest coverage if operating profit is overstated due to low depreciation charges and low costs of procured materials.

Exhibit 22.2 Combining Real and Nominal Approaches to Financial Modeling

Estimates	Modeling approach		Preferred application
	Real	Nominal	
Operational performance			
Sales	✓	✓	
EBITDA	✓	✓	
EBITA	✓	–	
Capital expenditures	✓	–	
Investments in working capital	✓[1]	✓	
Income taxes	–	✓	
Financial statements	✓[2]	✓	
Continuing value	✓[1]	✓	

[1] If inflation impact on investments in working capital is explicitly included.
[2] If inflation corrections are separately modeled and included in income statement and balance sheet.

main downside of using nominal cash flows is that future capital expenditures are difficult to project because the typically stable relationship between revenues and fixed assets does not hold under high inflation. As a result, depreciation charges and EBITA also are difficult to project.

Five-Step Approach to Combined Nominal and Real-Terms Financial Projections

We illustrate below how to combine both nominal and real forecasts in a DCF valuation. In this example, the company's revenues grow at 2 percent in real terms, and the annual inflation rate is 20 percent in the first forecasted year and 10 percent thereafter (see Exhibit 22.3 on p. 628). To simplify, we assumed that all cash flows occur at the end of the year. Under extreme inflation levels, this assumption could distort financial projections because the cash flows that accumulate throughout the year are subject to different inflation rates. In that case, split the year into quarterly or even monthly intervals, project cash flows for each interval, and discount the cash flows at the appropriate discount rate for that interval.

In practice, many more issues around financial projections arise in emerging-market valuations than in this simplified example. Nevertheless, it shows how to address some key issues when developing a cash flow forecast under high inflation, by means of the following step-by-step approach, leading to the real and nominal valuation results shown in Exhibit 22.4 on page 629.

Step 1: Forecast operating performance in real terms   To the extent possible, convert historical nominal balance sheets and income statements into

Exhibit 22.3 DCF under Inflation: Key Assumptions

Operations	Year 1	Forecasts 2	3	4	5	25
Real growth rate (percent)	2	2	2	2	2	
Real revenues	1,000	1,020	1,040	1,061	1,082	1,608
Real EBITDA	300	306	312	318	325	483
Net working capital/revenues (percent)	20	20	20	20	20	20
Real net PPE/real revenues (percent)	40	40	40	40	40	40
Lifetime of net PPE	5					
Other						
Inflation rate (percent)		20	10	10	10	10
Inflation index	1.00	1.20	1.32	1.45	1.60	10.75
Tax rate (percent)	35	35	35	35	35	35
Real WACC (percent)		8.0	8.0	8.0	8.0	8.0
Nominal WACC (percent)		29.6	18.8	18.8	18.8	18.8

Note: Adjusted formula for real-terms continuing value.

real terms (usually at the current year's currency value). At a minimum, make a real-terms approximation of the historical development of the key value drivers: growth and return on capital and the underlying capital turnover and EBITA margin, so you can understand the true economics of the business. With these approximations, forecast the operating performance of the business in real terms:

- Project future revenues and cash expenses to obtain EBITDA forecasts.[5]
- Estimate property, plant, and equipment (PPE) and capital expenditures from your assumptions on real-terms capital turnover.
- Working capital follows from projected revenues and assumptions on days of working capital required.
- From projected net PPE and assumptions on the lifetime of the assets, derive the annual depreciation to estimate real-terms EBITA.

Step 2: Build financial statements in nominal terms   Nominal projections can be readily derived by converting the real operating projections into nominal terms (note that these projections do not include any monetary adjustments as under, for example, inflation accounting):

- Project nominal revenues, cash expenses, EBITDA, and capital expenditures by multiplying their real-terms equivalents by the inflation index for the year.

---

[5] This step assumes that all expenses included in EBITDA are cash costs.

Exhibit 22.4 DCF under Inflation: Real and Nominal Models

	Real projections						Nominal projections					
NOPLAT	Year 1	2	3	4	5	25	Year 1	2	3	4	5	25
Revenues	1,000	1,020	1,040	1,061	1,082	1,608	1,000	1,224	1,373	1,541	1,729	17,283
EBITDA	300	306	312	318	325	483	300	367	412	462	519	5,185
Depreciation	(80)	(80)	(82)	(83)	(85)	(126)	(80)	(80)	(85)	(92)	(100)	(926)
EBITA	220	226	231	235	240	356	220	287	327	370	419	4,259
Taxes	(77)	(84)	(87)	(89)	(92)	(139)	(77)	(101)	(114)	(130)	(147)	(1,491)
NOPLAT	143	142	144	146	148	218	143	187	212	241	272	2,768
Free cash flow												
NOPLAT	143	142	144	146	148	218	143	187	212	241	272	2,768
Depreciation	80	80	82	83	85	126	80	80	85	92	100	926
Capital expenditures	(80)	(88)	(90)	(92)	(93)	(139)	(80)	(106)	(118)	(133)	(149)	(1,491)
Investment in net working capital		(37)	(23)	(23)	(24)	(35)		(45)	(30)	(34)	(38)	(376)
Free cash flow	143	97	113	114	116	170	143	116	149	166	185	1,827
Invested capital												
Net PPE (beginning of year)	400	400	408	416	424	631	400	400	426	459	500	4,631
Depreciation	(80)	(80)	(82)	(83)	(85)	(126)	(80)	(80)	(85)	(92)	(100)	(926)
Capital expenditures	80	88	90	92	93	139	80	106	118	133	149	1,491
Net PPE (end of year)	400	408	416	424	433	643	400	426	459	500	549	5,196
Net working capital	200	204	208	212	216	322	200	245	275	308	346	3,457
Invested capital	600	612	624	637	649	965	600	670	734	808	895	8,653
Ratios (percent)												
Net PPE/revenues		40	40	40	40	40		35	33	32	32	30
Net working capital/revenues		20	20	20	20	20		20	20	20	20	20
ROIC		24	24	23	23	23		31	32	33	34	36
Free cash flow growth rate		17	1	1	1	2		28	11	12	12	12
DCF valuation												
Free cash flow		97	113	114	116	170		116	149	166	185	1,827
Continuing value (value driver formula)[1]						2,891						31,063
Continuing value (cash flow perpetuity formula)						2,891						31,064
Present value factor		0.93	0.86	0.79	0.74	0.16		0.77	0.65	0.55	0.46	0.01
DCF value	1,795						1,795					

[1]Adjusted formula for real-terms continuing value.

- Estimate net property, plant, and equipment on a year-by-year basis from the prior-year balance plus nominal capital expenditures minus nominal depreciation (which is estimated as a percentage of net PPE according to the estimated lifetime).
- Working capital follows from revenues and days of working capital required.
- Subtract the depreciation charges from EBITDA to obtain nominal EBITA.
- Calculate income taxes on nominal EBITA without inflation corrections. (Always check the local tax rules for the reasonableness of this assumption.)

In contrast to the real-terms projections, the capital turnover is now increasing over time because nominal net PPE grows slower than revenues in a high-inflation environment. In this example, we did not build a complete balance sheet and income statement. That would require the following additional steps:

- Forecast interest expense and other nonoperating income statement items in nominal terms (based on the prior year's balance sheet).
- Equity should equal last year's equity plus earnings, less dividends, plus or minus any share issues or repurchases.
- Finally, balance the balance sheet with debt or marketable securities.[6]

Step 3: Build financial statements in real terms   Most of the operating items for the real-terms income statement and balance sheet were already estimated in step 1. Now also include the real-terms taxes on EBITA by deflating the nominal taxes as estimated in step 2. For full financial statements, use the inflation index to convert debt, marketable securities, interest expense, income taxes, and nonoperating terms from the nominal statements into real terms. The real-terms equity account is a plug to balance the balance sheet. To make sure you have done this correctly, be sure the real equity account equals last year's equity plus earnings, less dividends, plus or minus share issues or repurchases, and plus or minus inflationary gains or losses on the monetary assets (such as cash, receivables, payables, and debt).

Step 4: Forecast the future free cash flows in real and nominal terms from the projected income statements and balance sheets   Follow the general approach described in Chapter 7. The only difference is that the real-terms

---

[6] As noted, these projections are made for valuation purposes and not necessarily in accordance with local or international accounting standards prescribing any inflation or monetary corrections for particular groups of assets and liabilities. Free cash flows are not affected by such adjustments.

investment in net working capital (NWC^R) is equal to the increase in working capital plus a monetary loss due to inflation:[7]

$$\text{Investment in NWC}_t = \text{Increase in NWC}_t^R + \text{NWC}_{t-1}^R \left[1 - \frac{\text{IX}_{t-1}}{\text{IX}_t}\right]$$

where IX_t is the inflation index for the year t.

To check for consistency, use the inflation index to convert the free cash flows from the nominal projections to real terms. These should equal the free cash flows from the real-terms projections in each year.

Step 5: Estimate DCF value in real and nominal terms   When discounting real and nominal cash flows under high inflation, you must address three key issues:

1. Ensure that the WACC estimates in real terms (WACC^R) and nominal terms (WACC^N) are defined consistently with the inflation assumptions in each year:

$$\left(1 + \text{WACC}_t^N\right) = \left(1 + \text{WACC}_t^R\right) \times \left(1 + \text{Inflation}_t\right)$$

   Later in this chapter, we will discuss how to estimate WACC for companies in emerging markets.

2. The value-driver formula as presented in Chapter 9 should be adjusted when estimating continuing value in real terms. The returns on capital in real-terms projections overestimate the economic returns in the case of positive net working capital. The free cash flow in real terms differs from the cash flow implied by the value driver formula by an amount equal to the annual monetary loss on net working capital:

$$\text{FCF}_t^R = \left(1 - \frac{g_t^R}{\text{ROIC}_t^R}\right) \times \text{NOPLAT}_t^R - \text{NWC}_{t-1}^R \left(1 - \frac{\text{IX}_{t-1}}{\text{IX}_t}\right)$$

   The real-terms value driver formula is adjusted for this monetary loss, reflecting the perpetuity assumptions for inflation (i) and the ratio of net working capital to invested capital (NWC^R/IC^R):

---

[7] Even for assets held at constant levels in real-terms balance sheets, replacement investments are required at increasing prices in an inflationary environment. These replacement investments represent a cash outflow, also in real terms, but do not show up from real-terms balance sheet differences from year to year. In contrast, the nominal investment cash flow does follow from the nominal balance sheet differences from year to year.

$$CV^R = \frac{\left(1 - \dfrac{G^R}{ROIC^R}\right) NOPLAT^R}{WACC^R - g^R}$$

where

$$G^R = g^R - \left[\frac{NWC^R}{IC^R} \times \left(\frac{i}{1+i}\right)\right]$$

The resulting continuing-value estimate is the same as that obtained from a free cash flow perpetuity formula. After indexing for inflation, it also equals the continuing-value estimates derived from nominal projections.

3. When using the continuing-value formulas, make sure the explicit forecast period is long enough for the model to reach a steady state with constant growth rates of free cash flow. Because of the way inflation affects capital expenditures and depreciation, you need a much longer horizon than for valuations with no or low inflation.

ConsuCo Case Example: Inflation Adjustments

Let's explore how to handle inflation and accounting issues in the financial analysis and valuation of ConsuCo.

Historical analysis In analyzing ConsuCo's historical financial statements, we made adjustments in two areas. First, following the approach in Chapter 7, we rearranged the balance sheet and the income statements to get the statements for NOPLAT, invested capital, and free cash flow. Chapter 7 discusses adjustments needed for financial statements according to U.S. GAAP or IFRS, but the ConsuCo statements follow Brazilian GAAP, so we had to make some additional adjustments. Most of these were relatively minor. The largest involved the consolidation of a securitization vehicle, for which only the net asset position is shown under Brazilian GAAP.

Second, we estimated some key financial ratios on an approximate real-terms basis. Although annual inflation in Brazil has been moderate since 1997 at levels between 5 and 10 percent, ratios such as operating margin and capital turnover are likely to be biased when directly calculated from the financial statements. Therefore, we looked at trends in cash operating margins (EBITDA over sales). In addition, we estimated the sales revenues in real terms per unit of production capacity over time to better understand the development of real-terms capital turnover.

Exhibit 22.5 ConsuCo: Key Historical Financial Indicators

percent

Nominal indicators	1998	1999	2000	2001	2002	2003
Sales growth	41	32	31	6	17	14
Adjusted EBITA/sales	3.5	4.6	5.7	5.3	5.3	6.9
NOPLAT/sales	2.9	3.3	4.8	4.5	3.9	5.3
Invested capital (excluding goodwill)/sales	35.2	34.8	57.0	64.9	62.4	64.5
Invested capital (including goodwill)/sales	42.3	40.3	61.9	74.7	71.7	72.9
ROIC (excluding goodwill)	8.3	9.5	8.4	6.9	6.2	8.2
ROIC (including goodwill)	6.9	8.2	7.7	6.0	5.4	7.3
Approximate real indicators						
Sales growth (inflation-adjusted)	32	24	23	(2)	9	5
EBITDA/sales	5.7	6.7	7.2	7.6	7.5	9.2
Sales/capacity[1]	8.7	7.9	7.0	6.4	6.3	6.2

[1] In inflation-adjusted Reais million per capacity unit.

The results are reflected in Exhibit 22.5. Between 1998 and 2003, ConsuCo's sales grew significantly in real terms at around 15 percent per year, largely driven by acquisitions. But growth has slowed considerably since 2000. Cash operating margins improved significantly, from 5.7 percent in 1998 to 9.2 percent in 2003. In real terms, annual sales per unit of production capacity have been fairly stable since 2000 at around 6.0 to 6.5 million Reais, as have nominal turnover levels for invested capital (excluding goodwill).

Financial projections Based on the findings from the historical analysis and analyst consensus forecasts as of July 2004, we made the operating and financial forecasts summarized in Exhibit 22.6 on page 634 in real and nominal terms. We assumed that no major economic crisis will materialize in Brazil.

ConsuCo is investing heavily for future growth. Real-terms sales growth is projected to peak at 8 percent in 2005 and then gradually decline over the next four years to around 3 percent, close to Brazil's long-term expected real GDP growth. Cash margins will continue to rise to 9.7 percent in 2005 and stay at that level in perpetuity. Tougher competition will create downward pressure on margins, but the company's improvements in selling, general and administrative expenses compensate for this.

Capacity requirements are derived from sales forecasts in real terms, assuming sales productivity of 6.2 millon Reais per unit of capacity. Capital expenditures for maintenance are estimated in real terms as a percentage of projected total capacity and expenditures for capacity expansion are projected at around 2.3 million Reais per unit. The future development of net PPE in real terms is derived from the capital expenditure projections.

The resulting ROIC (excluding goodwill) in real terms for ConsuCo decreases from its current value of around 7.6 percent to around 6.6 percent in

Exhibit 22.6 ConsuCo: Summary Financial Projections, Base Case

Reais million, percent

	2004	2005	2006	2007	2008	2009	2014	2019
Operating projections								
Sales growth (real, percent)	7.0	8.0	7.0	6.0	5.0	3.0	3.0	3.0
EBITDA/sales (percent)	9.5	9.7	9.7	9.7	9.7	9.7	9.7	9.7
EBITDA (real terms, percent)	2,201	2,427	2,597	2,753	2,890	2,977	3,451	4,001
Sales/capacity[1]	6.2	6.2	6.2	6.2	6.2	6.2	6.2	6.2
Capacity units	3,757	4,058	4,342	4,602	4,832	4,977	5,770	6,689
Capital expenditures (expansion)[2]	558	682	645	591	522	329	382	442
Capital expenditures (maintenance)[2]	663	709	766	819	869	912	1,057	1,226
Real projections								
Sales	23,126	24,976	26,724	28,327	29,744	30,636	35,516	41,172
Adjusted EBITA/sales (percent)	7.2	7.4	7.5	7.5	7.6	7.6	7.7	7.8
NOPLAT/sales (percent)	4.8	4.8	4.7	4.6	4.5	4.4	4.2	4.1
Invested capital (excluding goodwill)/ sales (percent)	70.2	69.3	68.6	68.0	67.6	67.2	65.9	65.0
ROIC (excluding goodwill, percent)	7.6	7.6	7.4	7.3	7.2	7.0	6.7	6.6
Nominal projections								
Sales	24,778	28,258	31,721	35,164	38,558	41,474	59,717	85,984
Adjusted EBITA/sales (percent)	6.9	7.0	7.0	7.0	6.9	6.9	6.8	6.8
NOPLAT/sales (percent)	5.0	5.2	5.2	5.2	5.2	5.1	5.1	5.1
Invested capital (excluding goodwill)/ sales (percent)	60.0	58.3	57.2	56.3	55.5	54.7	52.2	51.0
ROIC (excluding goodwill, percent)	8.4	8.9	9.0	9.2	9.3	9.3	9.8	10.1

[1]In inflation-adjusted Reais million per capacity unit.
[2]In inflation-adjusted Reais million.

the continuing value period. In contrast, the ROIC in nominal terms increases from 8.4 to around 10.1 percent because of the inflation impact on capital turnover.

INCORPORATING EMERGING-MARKET RISKS IN THE VALUATION

The major distinction between valuing companies in developed markets and emerging markets is the increased level of risk. Not only must you account for risks related to the company's strategy, market position, and industry dynamics, as you would in a developed market, you must also deal with the risks caused by greater volatility in the capital markets and in the macroeconomic and political environments.

There is no consensus on how to reflect this higher level of risk in a DCF valuation. The most common approach is to add a country risk premium to the discount rate. The alternative is to model risks explicitly in the cash flow projections in what we call the *scenario DCF approach*. Both methodologies, if correctly and consistently applied, lead to the same result. We show this in the following example of an investment in two identical production plants, one in Europe and the other in an emerging economy (see Exhibit 22.7 on p. 636). However, the scenario DCF approach is analytically more robust and better shows the impact of emerging-market risks on value.

Scenario DCF Approach

The scenario DCF approach simulates alternative trajectories for future cash flows. At a minimum, model two scenarios: One should assume that cash flow develops according to conditions reflecting business as usual (i.e., without major economic distress). The second should reflect cash flows assuming that any emerging-market risks materialize.

In the example, the cash flows for the European plant grow steadily at 3 percent per year into perpetuity. For the plant in the emerging market, the cash flow growth is the same under a business-as-usual scenario, but there is a 25 percent probability of economic distress resulting in a cash flow that is 55 percent lower into perpetuity. The emerging-market risk is taken into account, not in the cost of capital, but in the lower expected value of future cash flows from weighting both scenarios at the assumed probabilities. The resulting value of the emerging-market plant (€1,917) is clearly below the value of its European sister plant (€2,222), using a WACC of 7.5 percent.

We assumed for simplicity that if adverse economic conditions develop in the emerging market, they will do so in the first year of the plant's operation. In reality, of course, the investment will face a probability of domestic economic distress in each year of its lifetime. Modeling risk over time would require more complex calculations yet would not change the basic results. We also assumed that in a local crisis, the emerging-market business would face significantly lower cash flows but not wind up entirely worthless.

Country Risk Premium DCF Approach

The second approach is to add a country risk premium to the cost of capital for comparable investments in developed markets. We then apply the resulting discount rate to the cash flow projections following a business-as-usual scenario. The key drawback is that there is no objective way to establish the country risk premium. For our two-plant example, we can derive in hindsight what the premium should be to obtain the same result as under the scenario DCF approach. For us to arrive at a value of €1,917 for the emerging-market plant, the discount rate for the business-as-usual projections would have to be 8.2 percent, which translates to a country risk premium of 0.7 percent.

On occasion, practitioners make the mistake of adding the country risk premium to the cost of capital to discount the *expected* value of future cash

Exhibit 22.7 Scenario DCF versus Country Risk Premium DCF

Net present value for identical facilities in …

… a European market

Scenario approach

Cash flows in perpetuity[1]

Probability		Year 1	2	3	4…
100%	"As usual"	100	103	106	109
0%	"Distressed"				

Cost of capital — 7.5%

Net present value — 2,222

Country risk premium approach

Cash flows in perpetuity[1]

	Year 1	2	3	4…
"As usual"	100	103	106	109

Cost of capital — 7.5%

Net present value — 2,222

… an emerging market

Scenario approach

Cash flows in perpetuity[2]

Probability		Year 1	2	3	4…
75%	"As usual"	100	103	106	109
25%	"Distressed"	45	46	48	49
	Expected cash flows	86	89	92	94

Cost of capital — 7.5%

Net present value — 1,917 → **86% of European NPV**

Country risk premium approach

Cash flows in perpetuity[2]

	Year 1	2	3	4…
"As usual"	100	103	106	109

Cost of capital — 7.5%
Country risk premium — 0.7%
Adjusted cost of capital — 8.2%

Net present value — 1,917 → **86% of European NPV**

[1] Assuming perpetuity cash flow growth of 3%.
[2] Assuming perpetuity cash flow growth of 3% and recovery under distress of 45% of cash flows "as usual."

flows rather than to the "promised" cash flows of a business-as-usual scenario. The resulting value is too low because the probability of a crisis is accounted for twice.[8]

Scenario DCF as Prime Valuation Approach

Some surveys show that managers generally adjust for emerging-market risks by adding a risk premium to the discount rate.[9] Nonetheless, we recommend the scenario DCF approach. It provides a more solid analytical foundation and a more robust understanding of the value than incorporating country risks in the discount rate.

One reason is that most country risks, including expropriation, devaluation, and war, are largely diversifiable (though not entirely, as the economic crisis in 1998 demonstrated). Consider the international consumer goods player illustrated in Exhibit 22.8 on page 638. Its returns on capital were highly volatile for individual emerging markets, but taken together, these markets were hardly more volatile than developed markets; the corporate portfolio diversified away most of the risks. Finance theory clearly indicates that the cost of capital should not reflect risk that can be diversified. This does not mean that diversifiable risk is irrelevant for a valuation: the possibility of adverse future events will affect the level of expected cash flows, as in the example in Exhibit 22.7. But once this has been incorporated in the forecast for cash flows, there is no need for an additional markup of the cost of capital if the risk is diversifiable.

Another argument against a country risk premium is that many country risks apply unequally to companies in a given country. For example, banks are more likely to be affected than retailers. Some companies (raw-materials exporters) might benefit from a currency devaluation, while others (raw-materials importers) will be damaged. For the consumer goods company in Exhibit 22.8, economic crises had only a short-term impact on sales and profit as measured in stable currency. In most cases, after a year or two, sales and profits roughly regained their original growth trajectories. Applying the same risk premium to all companies in an emerging market could overstate the risk for some businesses and understate it for others.

Furthermore, there is no systematic method to calculate a country risk premium. In our example, we could reengineer this premium because the true value of the plant was already known from the scenario approach. In practice, the country risk premium is sometimes set at the spread of the

---

[8] This is analogous to the error made by discounting the expected coupon and principal payments on a corporate bond at the promised yield (i.e., the yield to maturity) instead of the expected yield (i.e., the cost of debt).
[9] T. Keck, E. Levengood, and A. Longfield, "Using Discounted Cash Flow Analysis in an International Setting: A Survey of Issues in Modeling the Cost of Capital," *Journal of Applied Corporate Finance*, 11(3) (1998).

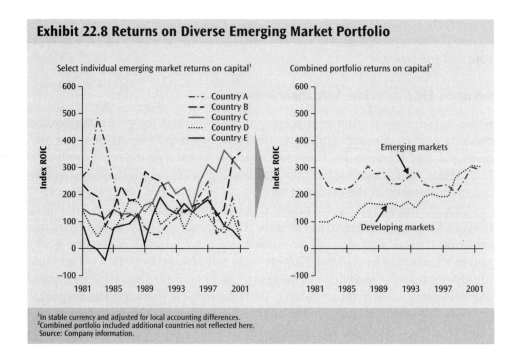

Exhibit 22.8 Returns on Diverse Emerging Market Portfolio

Select individual emerging market returns on capital[1]

Combined portfolio returns on capital[2]

[1] In stable currency and adjusted for local accounting differences.
[2] Combined portfolio included additional countries not reflected here.
Source: Company information.

local government debt rate[10] denominated in U.S. dollars and a U.S. government bond of similar maturity. However, that is reasonable only if the returns on local government debt are highly correlated with returns on corporate investments.

Finally, when managers have to discuss emerging-market risks and their effect on cash flow in scenarios, they gain more insights than they would get from a "black box" addition to the discount rate. By identifying specific factors with a large impact on value, managers can plan to mitigate these risks. Furthermore, managers easily underestimate the impact of even a small country risk premium in the discount rate: In the example of Exhibit 22.8, setting a country risk premium to 3 percent would be equivalent to assuming a 70 percent probability of economic distress.

Constructing Cash Flow Scenarios and Probabilities

To use the scenario DCF approach, construct at least two scenarios. The base case, or business-as-usual scenario, describes how the business will per-

[10] This is also a promised yield rather than an expected yield on government bonds, further underlining the point that the cost of capital based on country risk premium should not be applied to expected cash flows, but to "promised" cash flows (those following a business-as-usual scenario in which no country risk materializes).

form if no major crises occur. The downside scenario describes the financial results if a major crisis does occur.

For both scenarios, start by projecting the macroeconomic environment because this influences industry and company performance. The major macroeconomic variables to forecast are GDP growth, inflation rates, foreign-exchange rates, and interest rates. These items must be linked in a way that reflects economic realities and should be included in the basic set of monetary assumptions underlying your valuation. For instance, when constructing a downside scenario with high inflation, make sure that the same inflation rates underlie the financial projections and cost of capital estimates for the company to be valued. Foreign-exchange rates should also reflect this inflation in the long run because of purchasing power parity.

Given the assumptions for macroeconomic performance, construct the industry scenarios basically in the same way as in developed markets. The major difference is in the greater uncertainty involved in modeling outcomes under severe crises for which there may be no precedent.

While estimating probabilities for the cash flow scenarios is ultimately a matter of management judgment, there are indicators of reasonable probabilities. Historical data on previous crises can give some indication of frequency and severity of country risk and the time required for recovery. Analyzing the changes in GDP of 20 emerging economies over the past 20 years, we found that these economies had experienced economic distress about once every five years (a real-terms GDP decline of more than 5 percent). This would suggest a 20 percent probability for a downside scenario.

Another source of information for estimating probabilities is prospective data from current government bond prices.[11] Recent academic research suggests that government default probabilities five years into the future in emerging markets such as Argentina, were around 30 percent in nondistress years.[12]

ConsuCo Case Example: Cash Flow Scenarios and Probabilities

Returning to the ConsuCo example, we already constructed a business-as-usual scenario in the previous section. For a downward scenario, we analyzed ConsuCo's performance under more adverse economic conditions in the past. Brazil has experienced several severe economic and monetary downturns, including an inflation rate that surpassed 2,000 percent in 1993. Judging by its key financial indicators, such as EBITDA to sales and real-terms sales growth, the impact on ConsuCo's business performance was

[11] See, for example, D. Duffie and K. Singleton, "Modeling Term Structures of Defaultable Bonds," *Review of Financial Studies* 12 (1999): 687–720; and R. Merton, "On the Pricing of Corporate Debt: The Risk Structure of Interest Rates," *Journal of Finance*, 29(2) (1974): 449–470.
[12] See J. Merrick, "Crisis Dynamics of Implied Default Recovery Ratios: Evidence from Russia and Argentina," *Journal of Banking and Finance*, 25(10) (2001): 1921–1939.

Exhibit 22.9 ConsuCo: ROIC in Downside Scenario versus Base Case

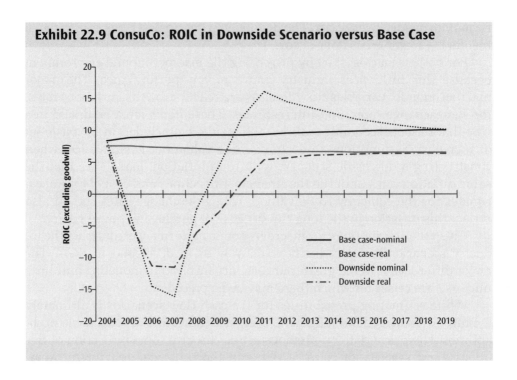

significant. ConsuCo's cash operating margin was negative for four years, at around −10 to −5 percent, and then recovered to its normal levels. In the same period, sales in real terms declined by 10 to 15 percent per year but grew sharply after the crisis. For the downside scenario projections, we assumed similar negative cash margins and real-terms sales decline for up to five years, followed by a gradual return to the long-term margins and growth assumed under the business-as-usual scenario. Exhibit 22.9 compares the nominal and real returns on invested capital under both scenarios: In the downside scenario, the returns plummet and then increase as the recovery starts. After 2010, the nominal returns even surpass those in the base case as the extreme inflation levels push up the capital turnovers. Of course, the nominal returns are artificially high, as a comparison with the real returns shows. The DCF value under the downside scenario will turn out to be only half of the base-case value. We estimated the probability of this downside scenario at 25 to 35 percent.

ESTIMATING COST OF CAPITAL IN EMERGING MARKETS

Calculating the cost of capital in any country can be challenging, but for emerging markets, the challenge is an order of magnitude higher. In this section, we provide our fundamental assumptions, background on the important issues, and a practical way to estimate the components of the cost of capital.

Fundamental Assumptions

Our analysis adopts the perspective of a global investor—either a multi-national company or an international investor with a diversified portfolio. Of course, many emerging markets are not well integrated with the global market, and local investors may face barriers to investing outside their home market. As a result, local investors cannot always hold well-diversified portfolios, and their cost of capital may be considerably different from that of a global investor. Unfortunately, there is no established framework for estimating the capital cost for local investors. Furthermore, as long as international investors have access to local investment opportunities, local prices will be based on an international cost of capital. Finally, according to empirical research, emerging markets have become increasingly integrated into global capital markets.[13] We believe that this trend will continue and that most countries will gradually reduce foreign-investment restrictions for local investors in the long run.

Another assumption is that most country risks are diversifiable from the perspective of the global investor. We therefore need no additional risk premiums in the cost of capital for the risks encountered in emerging markets when discounting expected cash flows. Of course, if you choose to discount the cash flow from the business-as-usual scenario only, you should add a country risk premium.

Given these assumptions, the cost of capital in emerging markets should generally be close to a global cost of capital adjusted for local inflation and capital structure. It is also useful to keep some general guidelines in mind:

- *Use the CAPM to estimate the cost of equity in emerging markets.* The CAPM may be a less robust model for the less-integrated emerging markets, but there is no better alternative model today. Furthermore, we believe it will become a better predictor of equity returns worldwide as markets continue to become more integrated.

- *There is no one "right" answer, so be pragmatic.* In emerging markets, there are often significant information and data gaps (e.g., for estimating betas or the risk-free rate in local currency). Be flexible as you assemble the available information piece by piece to build the cost of capital, and triangulate your results with country risk premium approaches and multiples.

---

[13] See, for example, C. Harvey, "The Drivers of Expected Returns in International Markets," *Emerging Markets Quarterly* (Fall 2000): 1–17.

- *Be sure monetary assumptions are consistent.* Ground your model in a common set of monetary assumptions to ensure that the cash flow forecasts and discount rate are consistent. If you are using local nominal cash flows, the cost of capital must reflect the local inflation rate that is embedded in the cash flows. For real-terms cash flows, subtract inflation from the nominal cost of capital.

- *Allow for changes in cost of capital.* The cost of capital in an emerging-market valuation may change, based on evolving inflation expectations, changes in a company's capital structure and cost of debt, or foreseeable reforms in the tax system. For example, for valuations in Argentina during the economic and monetary crisis of 2002, the short-term inflation rate of 30 percent could not be considered a reasonable basis for a long-term cost of capital estimate because such a crisis could not be expected to last forever.[14] In such cases, estimate the cost of capital on a year-by-year basis, following the underlying set of basic monetary assumptions.

- *Don't mix approaches.* Use the cost of capital to discount the cash flows in a probability-weighted scenario approach. Do not add any risk premium, because you would be double-counting risk. If you are discounting only future cash flows in a business-as-usual scenario, add a risk premium to the discount rate.

Estimating the Cost of Equity

To estimate the components of the cost of equity, use the standard CAPM model described in Chapter 10.

Risk-free rate   In emerging markets, the risk-free rate is harder to estimate from government bonds than in developed markets. Three main problems arise. First, most of the government debt in emerging markets is not, in fact, risk free: The ratings on much of this debt are often well below investment grade. Second, it is difficult to find long-term government bonds that are actively traded with sufficient liquidity. Finally, the long-term debt that is traded is often in U.S. dollars, a European currency, or the Japanese yen, so it is not appropriate for discounting local nominal cash flows.

Our recommendation is to follow a very straightforward approach. Start with a risk-free rate based on the 10-year U.S. government bond yield, as in developed markets. Add to this the projected difference over time between U.S. and local inflation to develop a nominal risk-free rate in local cur-

---

[14] Annual consumer price inflation came down to around 5 percent in Argentina in 2004.

Exhibit 22.10 ConsuCo: Estimating Beta

Peers	Unlevered betas			
	Bloomberg[1]	Barra	Adjusted[2]	Average
ConsuCo	0.733	1.343	0.748	1.038
PeerCo 1	0.664	0.712	0.782	0.688
PeerCo 2	0.589	0.407	0.846	0.498
PeerCo 3	0.795	0.693	1.232	0.744
PeerCo 4	0.492	0.236	0.346	0.364
PeerCo 5	0.475	0.749	0.439	0.612
PeerCo 6	0.480	0.231	0.381	0.356
PeerCo 7	0.294	0.198	0.271	0.246
PeerCo 8	0.278	0.361	0.386	0.319
PeerCo 9	0.418	0.384	0.641	0.401
PeerCo 10	0.820	0.635	0.803	0.728
PeerCo 11	0.649	0.688	0.625	0.669
Average	0.557	0.553	0.625	0.555
Median	0.541	0.521	0.633	0.531

[1] Against FT World Index on a weekly basis over past 2 years.
[2] Adjusted for the high-tech boom (see chapter 10).
Source: Bloomberg, Barra, Datastream, McKinsey analysis.

rency.[15] Sometimes you can derive this inflation differential from the spread between local government bond yields denominated in local currency versus U.S. dollars.[16]

Beta Sometimes practitioners calculate beta relative to the local market index. This is not only inconsistent from the perspective of a global investor, but also potentially distorted by the fact that the index in an emerging market will rarely be representative of a diversified economy. Instead, estimate industry betas relative to a well-diversified or global market index as recommended in Chapter 10. Since equity markets in emerging economies are often small, with liquidity concentrated in a few stocks, it may be hard to find a representative sample of publicly traded local companies to estimate an industry beta. In that case, derive an industry beta from international comparables that operate in the same or a similar sector. The implicit assumption is that the fundamental drivers of systematic risk will be similar in emerging and developed markets.

For ConsuCo, we used three sources for estimates of beta in an international peer group: Bloomberg betas calculated against the FT World Index, Barra betas, and betas adjusted for the high-tech boom (see Chapter 10 for more details). Note that the unlevered beta estimates are similar for industry peers, with some exceptions, as shown in Exhibit 22.10. Overall,

[15] In this way, we do not model the U.S. term structure of interest rates. Technically, this should be included as well, but it will not make a large difference in the valuation.
[16] Technically, this is correct only if the emerging-market bonds are relatively low risk, as for example for Chile and South Korea.

Exhibit 22.11 ConsuCo: Estimating the Nominal Cost of Equity

	2004	2005	2006	2007	2008	2009	2014	2019
United States								
Inflation (percent)	2.0	2.0	2.0	2.0	2.0	2.0	2.0	2.0
Risk-free interest rate (percent)	4.6	4.6	4.6	4.6	4.6	4.6	4.6	4.6
Brazil								
Inflation (IPCA, percent)	7.1	5.6	4.9	4.6	4.4	4.4	4.4	4.4
Risk-free interest rate (percent)[1]	9.8	8.2	7.5	7.2	7.0	7.0	7.0	7.0
Relevered beta	0.8	0.8	0.8	0.8	0.8	0.8	0.8	0.8
Market risk premium (percent)	5.0	5.0	5.0	5.0	5.0	5.0	5.0	5.0
Cost of equity (percent)	14.0	12.4	11.7	11.3	11.1	11.1	11.1	11.1

[1]Brazilian risk-free rate estimated as: (1 + U.S. risk free rate) × (1 + Brazilian inflation) ÷ (1 + U.S. inflation) − 1.
Source: Banco Central do Brasil, Bloomberg, EIU Viewswire, McKinsey analysis.

our estimate for the unlevered industry beta is 0.55, translating into an equity beta for ConsuCo of 0.8 (given a debt-to-capital target weight of 0.3, as discussed later).

Market risk premium   As discussed in Chapter 21, excess returns of local equity markets over local bond returns are not a good proxy for the market risk premium. This holds even more so for emerging markets given the lack of diversification in the local equity market. Furthermore, the quality and length of available data on equity and bond market returns are usually unsuitable for making long-term estimates. To use a market risk premium that is consistent with the perspective of a global investor, use a global estimate (as discussed in Chapter 10) of 4.5 to 5.5 percent.

In Exhibit 22.11, we summarize the nominal cost of equity calculation for ConsuCo. In the base case, we have assumed a decreasing rate of inflation for the Brazilian economy from 7.1 percent in 2004 to 4.4 percent in 2008 and beyond. This is also reflected in the cost of capital estimates going forward. For the downside scenario, inflation projections follow a different trajectory, and the cost of capital for this scenario is adjusted accordingly.

Estimating the After-Tax Cost of Debt

In most emerging economies, there are no liquid markets for corporate bonds, so little or no market information is available to estimate the cost of debt. However, from an international investor's perspective, the cost of debt in local currency should simply equal the sum of the dollar (or euro) risk-free rate, the systematic part of the credit spread,[17] and the inflation differ-

[17] See Chapter 10 for more on the systematic part of the credit spread.

Exhibit 22.12 ConsuCo: Estimating the Nominal Cost of Debt

percent

	2004	2005	2006	2007	2008	2009	2014	2019
Risk-free interest rate	9.8	8.2	7.5	7.2	7.0	7.0	7.0	7.0
BBB credit spread	1.2	1.2	1.2	1.2	1.2	1.2	1.2	1.2
Systematic credit spread for B+	0.5	0.5	0.5	0.5	0.5	0.5	0.5	0.5
Cost of debt	11.5	9.9	9.2	8.9	8.8	8.8	8.8	8.8
Tax rate	34	34	34	34	34	34	34	34
After-tax cost of debt	7.6	6.6	6.1	5.9	5.8	5.8	5.8	5.8

Source: Standard & Poor's, McKinsey analysis.

ential between local currency and dollars (or euros). Most of the country risk can be diversified away in a global bond portfolio. Therefore, the systematic part of the default risk is probably no larger than that of companies in international markets, and the cost of debt should not include a separate country risk premium (see Chapter 10 for details on the systematic part of credit spread). This explains why the funding costs of multinationals with extensive emerging-market portfolios, companies including Coca-Cola and Colgate-Palmolive, have a cost of debt no higher than their mainly U.S.-focused competitors.

Returning to the ConsuCo example, we calculated the cost of debt in Brazilian Reais. ConsuCo does not have its own credit rating, but based on its EBITDA coverage ratios versus rated peers, we estimated that ConsuCo would probably have a B to B+ rating. ConsuCo's cost of debt can be estimated as the sum of the risk-free rate in Brazilian Reais plus the systematic credit spread for a U.S. corporate bond rated B+ versus the U.S. government bond yield as shown in Exhibit 22.12. Of course, the inflation assumptions underlying the estimates for cost of debt should be consistent with those for the base-case and downside scenarios.

Remember that ConsuCo's cost of debt is significantly lower than the interest rate it is currently paying because the latter represents the promised yield, not the expected yield.

The marginal tax rate in emerging markets can be very different from the effective tax rate, which often includes investment tax credits, export tax credits, taxes, equity or dividend credits, and operating loss credits. Many of these do not provide a tax shield on interest expense. Only taxes that apply to interest expense should be used in the WACC estimate. Other taxes or credits should be modeled directly in the cash flows. For ConsuCo, we used the Brazilian corporate income tax rate of 25 percent plus social contribution tax of 9 percent.

Estimating WACC

Given the estimates for cost of equity and after-tax cost of debt, we need debt and equity weights to derive an estimate of the weighted average cost of capital. In emerging markets, many companies have unusual capital structures compared with their international peers. One reason is, of course, the country risk. The possibility of macroeconomic distress makes companies more conservative in setting their leverage. Another reason could be anomalies in the local debt or equity markets. In the long run, when the anomalies are corrected, the companies should expect to converge to a capital structure similar to that of their global competitors. You could forecast explicitly how the company evolves to a capital structure that is more similar to global standards. In that case, you should consider using the APV approach discussed in Chapter 5.

For the ConsuCo case, we kept the capital structure going forward at its long-term historical levels, with leverage somewhat below the peer group average at a ratio of debt to enterprise value of 0.3. Exhibit 22.13 summarizes the WACC estimates for both the base case and downside scenario in nominal terms. Note how the extreme inflation assumption underlying the downside scenario leads to a radically higher cost of capital in the crisis years until 2009.

Estimating the Country Risk Premium

If you are discounting business-as-usual cash flows instead of expected cash flows, you should add a country risk premium to the WACC. There is no agreed-upon approach to estimating this premium, but we have some advice.

Do not simply use the sovereign risk premium   The long-term sovereign risk premium equals the difference between a long-term (e.g., 10-year) U.S.

Exhibit 22.13 ConsuCo: Estimating Nominal WACC for ConsuCo

	2004	2005	2006	2007	2008	2009	2014	2019
Base case								
After-tax cost of debt (percent)	7.6	6.6	6.1	5.9	5.8	5.8	5.8	5.8
Cost of equity (percent)	14.0	12.4	11.7	11.3	11.1	11.1	11.1	11.1
Debt/enterprise value	0.3	0.3	0.3	0.3	0.3	0.3	0.3	0.3
WACC (percent)	12.0	10.5	9.9	9.5	9.4	9.4	9.4	9.4
Downside								
After-tax cost of debt (percent)	7.6	37.1	105.9	37.1	19.9	6.2	5.8	5.8
Cost of equity (percent)	14.0	59.6	166.0	59.6	33.0	11.7	11.1	11.1
Debt/enterprise value	0.3	0.3	0.3	0.3	0.3	0.3	0.3	0.3
WACC (percent)	12.0	52.3	146.5	52.3	28.8	9.9	9.4	9.4

government bond yield and a dollar-denominated local bond's stripped yield[18] with the same maturity. This difference will reasonably approximate the country risk premium only if the cash flows of the corporation being valued move closely in line with the payments on government bonds. This is not necessarily the case. In the consumer goods or raw-materials sector, for example, cash flows have low correlation with local government bond payments and lower volatility.

Understand estimates from different sources   Estimates for country risk premiums from different sources usually fall in a very wide range because analysts use different methods.[19] But they frequently compensate for high estimates of country risk premiums by making aggressive estimates for growth and return forecasts.

An example is the valuation of a large Brazilian chemicals company that we undertook in 2002. Using a local WACC of 10 percent, we reached an enterprise value of 4.0 to 4.5 times EBITDA. A second advisor was also asked to value the company and came to a very similar valuation result—an EBITDA multiple of around 4.5—in spite of using a very high country risk premium of 11 percent on top of the WACC. The result was similar because the second advisor made performance assumptions that were extremely aggressive: real sales growth of almost 10 percent per year and a ROIC increasing to 46 percent in the long term. Such long-term performance assumptions are unrealistic for a commodity-based, competitive industry such as chemicals.

Be careful to avoid setting the country risk premium too high   Make sure you understand the economic implications of a high country risk premium. We believe that a country risk premium for Brazil is far below the premiums of 5 percent and higher that analysts typically use.

One reason is that current valuations in the stock market do not support the discount rates implied by higher risk premiums. We estimated the trading multiples of enterprise value to the 2004 forecasted EBITA for the 30 largest Brazilian companies in terms of market capitalization. The median value for the multiple was 7.4 in October 2004. We estimated the implied WACC by means of a DCF valuation. We set the future long-term return on invested capital at 11 percent, approximately equal to the median historical ROIC for these companies over the past five or six years (a period after Brazil brought inflation under control, so it is indicative of a business-as-usual scenario). Assuming future long-term inflation at 4.4 percent and

---

[18] Some emerging markets' country debt is partially guaranteed by international institutions or backed by U.S. Treasury bonds. For these bonds, you need to estimate the yield on the nonguaranteed part of the bond, the "stripped" yield. Stripped yields are available from bond data suppliers.
[19] For an overview, see, for example, L. Pereiro, *Valuation of Companies in Emerging Markets: A Practical Approach* (New York: Wiley, 2002), 118.

real growth at 3.0 percent for the Brazilian economy as a whole, the WACC for the Brazilian market implied by the EBITA multiple of 7.4 is around 10.3 percent. The WACC estimated with the CAPM method previously described is around 9.8 percent.[20] This would imply a country risk premium for Brazil of around 0.5 percent. Of course, this is not a precise estimate; as the Brazilian market goes up and down, the implied WACC and country risk premium would change as well. But it does suggest a country risk premium that is far below the 5 percent that many analysts currently use.

The other reason for such a low country risk premium is that historical returns in the Brazilian stock market do not support a high premium. The average real-terms return on the Brazilian stock market over the past 10 years is 3.8 percent per year. Let's take this period as a proxy for a business-as-usual scenario: real GPD grew by around 2 percent per year on average, and inflation was moderate at around 9 percent annually. At a country risk premium of 5 percent, the expected return on a stock with a beta equal to one under a business-as-usual scenario should be around 12 percent in real terms,[21] which is far above these historical returns.

CALCULATING AND INTERPRETING RESULTS

Given the estimates for cash flow and the cost of capital, we can discount the free cash flows for ConsuCo under the base-case and downside scenarios. The resulting present values of operations are shown in Exhibit 22.14. Under each scenario, the valuation results are exactly the same for the nominal and real projections. The next step is to weight the valuation results by the scenario probabilities and derive the present value of operations. Finally, add the market value of the nonoperating assets and subtract the financial claims to get at the estimated equity value. The estimated value obtained for ConsuCo is 188 to 206 Reais per share, given a probability of economic distress of 25 to 35 percent.

ConsuCo's share price, like the Brazilian stock market in general, has been extremely volatile over recent years, as shown in Exhibit 22.15 on page 650. Thus, you need to be careful in comparing the valuation outcome of 188 to 206 Reais per share with the current (December 2004) share price of 230 Reais. Just four months earlier, the price was 150 Reais. At the beginning of that year it traded for 270 Reais.

Of course, in emerging markets share prices are not always reliable references for intrinsic value, for several reasons. First, free float is often limited, with large equity stakes in the hands of a small group of owners, leaving

---

[20] Based on a real risk-free rate of 2 percent, long-term inflation of 4.4 percent, a market risk premium of 5.0 percent, cost of debt of 7.6 percent, and a debt-to-capital ratio of 0.25.

[21] Assuming a real risk-free rate of 2 percent and a market risk premium of 5 percent.

Exhibit 22.14 ConsuCo: Scenario DCF Valuation

Reais million, percent

		2004	2005	2006	2007	2008	2009	2014	2019
Base case									
Nominal projections									
Free cash flow		331	(161)	(14)	166	379	833	1,065	1,491
WACC (percent)		12.0	10.5	9.9	9.5	9.4	9.4	9.4	9.4
Real projections									
Free cash flow		309	(143)	(12)	134	293	615	633	714
WACC (percent)		4.5	4.6	4.7	4.7	4.7	4.7	4.7	4.7
Downside									
Nominal projections									
Free cash flow		135	(2,817)	(11,192)	(11,205)	(10,491)	(4,039)	(3,851)	8,004
WACC (percent)		12.0	52.3	146.5	52.3	28.8	9.9	9.4	9.4
Real projections									
Free cash flow		126	(1,753)	(2,786)	(1,859)	(1,392)	(511)	(392)	656
WACC (percent)		4.5	1.5	(1.4)	1.5	3.0	4.7	4.7	4.7

$1 - p^1 = 75\%$
(65%)

DCF value	**24,459**
Nonoperating assets	3,010
Debt and debt equivalents	(11,097)
Equity value	**16,372**
Value per share (Reais)	**253**

$p^1 = 25\%$
(35%)

DCF value	**12,427**
Nonoperating assets	3,010
Debt and debt equivalents	(11,097)
Equity value	**4,340**
Value per share (Reais)	**67**

Value
per
share
(Reais)

206
(188)

[1] p = probability of economic distress.

649

Exhibit 22.15 ConsuCo: Historical Share Price Development

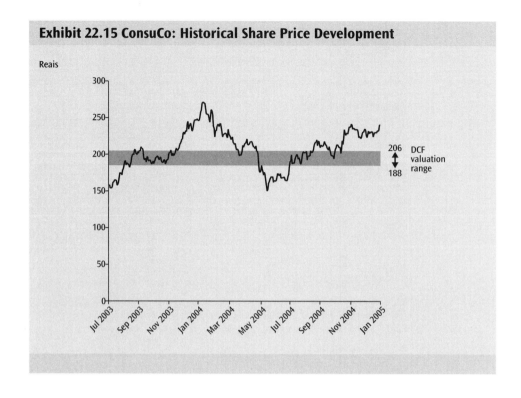

public shareholders with little or no influence. As a result, the share price in the market could well be below intrinsic value, as estimated from a DCF analysis. Also, liquidity in emerging-markets stocks is often much lower than in developed markets. Share prices may not fully reflect intrinsic value because not all information is incorporated in the market value. Finally, share prices in emerging markets are often much more volatile than in developed markets. The share price on any particular day could therefore be off from intrinsic value.

ConsuCo has a primary listing on the Brazilian stock exchange. Turnover in the stock, as measured by the number of days to trade the free float, is around 130 days, not too far above typical levels of around 100 days in the United States and Europe. Still, because of the share price volatility, triangulation of the DCF results with multiples and a country risk premium approach is important.

Triangulating with Multiples and Country Risk Premium Approach

For triangulation with multiples, we apply Chapter 12's guidance on how to do a best-practice multiples analysis to check valuation results. For the ConsuCo example, we compared the implied multiples of enterprise value over EBITDA with those of peer companies across the world. All multiples are forward-looking multiples over EBITDA as expected for 2005, based on ana-

Exhibit 22.16 ConsuCo: Multiples Analysis versus Peers

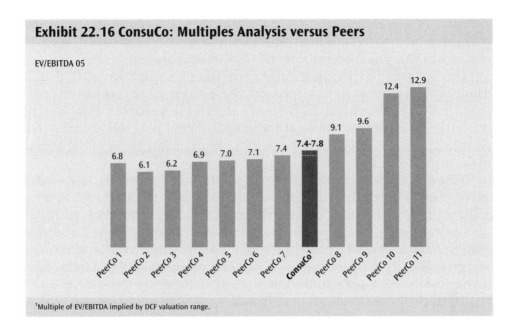

EV/EBITDA 05

[Bar chart values, left to right:]
PeerCo 1: 6.8
PeerCo 2: 6.1
PeerCo 3: 6.2
PeerCo 4: 6.9
PeerCo 5: 7.0
PeerCo 6: 7.1
PeerCo 7: 7.4
ConsuCo[1]: 7.4-7.8
PeerCo 8: 9.1
PeerCo 9: 9.6
PeerCo 10: 12.4
PeerCo 11: 12.9

[1]Multiple of EV/EBITDA implied by DCF valuation range.

lyst consensus forecasts. As Exhibit 22.16 illustrates, the implied multiple from our ConsuCo valuation is quite similar to most of its peers, at around seven times EBITDA. Apparently, the fact that ConsuCo is domiciled in Brazil does not matter much for the relative pricing of its stock. This is another indication that any country risk premium for ConsuCo should be very small. Using the average multiple for the peer group of 8.3, the value of ConsuCo would end up at 228 Reais, as shown in Exhibit 22.17. Note that this is

Exhibit 22.17 ConsuCo: Valuation Summary

Reais, million

	Scenario DCF valuation[1] low	Scenario DCF valuation[1] high	Average multiple valuation	Median multiple valuation	Country risk premium DCF valuation
EBITDA multiple			8.3	7.1	
EBITDA 2005			2,746	2,746	
DCF value	20,248	21,451	22,841	19,496	18,933
Nonoperating assets	3,010	3,010	3,010	3,010	3,010
Debt and debt equivalents	(11,097)	(11,097)	(11,097)	(11,097)	(11,097)
Equity value	12,161	13,364	14,754	11,409	10,846
Number of shares (million)	65	65	65	65	65
Value per share	188	206	228	176	167

[1]Shown are the probability-weighted values.

probably an aggressive estimate, given that there are some outliers in the peer group with extremely high multiples. Using the median multiple of 7.1 would lead to a valuation estimate of 176 Reais per share.

The last part of the triangulation consists of a valuation of ConsuCo using a country risk premium approach. We estimated the country risk premium for Brazil at around 0.5 percent earlier in this chapter. Discounting the business-as-usual scenario at the cost of capital plus this country risk premium leads to a value per share of 167 Reais, below the result obtained in the scenario DCF approach.

Note that a risk premium of 5 percent (as typically used in Brazil) would either result in unrealistically low valuations relative to current share price and peer group multiples, or require an unrealistic, bullish forecast of future performance with returns on capital of at least 15 percent and real growth rates of at least 6 percent for many years. Given long-term returns and growth in its industry and the historical performance of ConsuCo, even taking just the good years into account, such forecasts are unreasonable.

Given the inherent uncertainty in valuing emerging-market companies, it is best to use an explicit value range instead of a point estimate. For ConsuCo, we summarize the valuation findings in Exhibit 22.17. Based on the DCF valuation and multiples comparison, we end up with a range of about 175 to 205 Reais per share, depending on the exact scenario and probability assumptions, compared with a 12-month share price range of 150 to 270 Reais per share.

SUMMARY

To value companies in emerging markets, we use concepts similar to the ones applied to developed markets. However, the application of these concepts can be somewhat different. Inflation, which is often high in emerging markets, is factored into the cash flow projections by combining insights from both real and nominal financial analyses. Emerging market risks such as macroeconomic or political crises can be incorporated following the scenario DCF approach by developing alternative scenarios for future cash flows, discounting the cash flows at the cost of capital without country risk premium, and then weighting the DCF values by the scenario probabilities. The cost of capital estimates for emerging markets build on the assumption of a global risk-free rate, market risk premium and beta, following guidelines similar to those used for developed markets. Since the value of companies in emerging markets is often more volatile than in developed markets, we recommend triangulating the scenario DCF results with a country risk premium DCF and a multiples-based valuation.

REVIEW QUESTIONS

1. Identify and describe three adjustments to the enterprise DCF and economic profit models when attempting to establish the value of a company located in an emerging market.

2. Define *purchasing power parity.* What is the importance of purchasing power parity to an analyst attempting to establish value for a company located in an emerging market?

3. Describe the impact of high inflation on the financial statements of a company headquartered in an emerging market. What unique challenges does inflation present to an analyst?

4. Describe the five-step approach managers should employ to combine nominal and real forecasts.

5. Identify four risks associated with emerging markets that impact enterprise DCF valuation. How should these risks be treated within the enterprise DCF model?

6. Describe the benefits of a scenario DCF valuation model. What factors should be considered when constructing scenario parameters?

7. You are computing the value of a firm headquartered in an emerging market. Identify the factors unique to an emerging market that need to be evaluated when estimating the cost of equity via the CAPM.

8. Why must a manager construct both real and nominal corporate forecasts? Illustrate the effects of depreciation and taxation on forecasting by paying special attention to high, low, and crash inflation scenarios. Draw a flow chart that details a method for forecasting financial variables.

9. Catalogue emerging market risks with examples of effects on valuation components. Discuss the merits of including risk adjustments in cash flow or in discount rates.

23

Valuing High-Growth
Companies

In the late 1990s, Internet entrepreneurs quickly transformed business
ideas into billion-dollar valuations that seemed to defy common wisdom
about profits, cash flows, and valuation multiples. As we learned from the
rise and fall of Internet stocks, valuing high-growth, high-uncertainty
companies is a challenge; some practitioners have even described it as
hopeless.

The valuation principles in this book work well even for high-growth
companies.[1] The best way to value high-growth companies (those whose organic revenue growth exceeds 15 percent annually) is with a classic DCF
valuation, buttressed by microeconomic fundamentals and probability-
weighted scenarios. Although scenario-based DCF may sound suspiciously
retro, it works where other methods fail, since the elements of economics
and finance apply even in uncharted territory. Nevertheless, while scenario-
based DCF techniques can help bound and quantify uncertainty, they will
not make it disappear. High-growth companies have volatile stock prices for
sound and logical reasons.

DCF ANALYSIS WHEN THERE IS NO CASH FLOW

When Internet stocks peaked in early 2000, the most common critique
about valuation was that market values appeared to increase as losses grew

---

[1] In this chapter, we analyze companies that are growing quickly through new products, new
technologies, and a rapidly growing end-product market. Companies that generate above-
normal revenue growth through acquisitions, currency fluctuations, and accounting changes
are analyzed in Chapter 7.

larger. The perceived correlation between ever-higher stock prices and ever-higher losses became a rich source of jokes for cartoonists and stand-up comedians, even though the phenomenon is consistent with economic principles.

Losses and value rise at the same time because today's supernormal growth often requires large investments that companies expense through the income statement, instead of capitalizing them on the balance sheet. For instance, many Internet-related start-ups experienced annual growth rates exceeding 100 percent. Fueling this growth required significant investment. Yet Internet and other technology-related companies typically do not invest in physical assets that are capitalized, such as physical equipment and factories. These start-ups invest primarily in customer acquisition, through advertising and direct mail. That spending must be expensed through the income statement. With limited exceptions, research and development also must be expensed in the current period.[2] Because these companies expensed, rather than capitalized, their investments, significant losses replaced growing balance sheets. Analysts were skeptical of companies with only moderate losses and asked, "Are they investing enough to win?"

High growth and accounting losses make discounted cash flow valuation challenging. Even so, DCF remains the best method. Alternatives, such as price-earnings multiples, generate extremely imprecise results (earnings are highly volatile), often cannot be used (when earnings are negative), and provide little insight about what drives the company's valuation. More important, these shorthand methods cannot account for the uniqueness of each company in a fast-changing environment. Another alternative—real options—is promising, but current implementation techniques still require estimates of the long-term revenue growth rate, long-term volatility of revenue growth, and profit margins—the same requirements as for discounted cash flow.[3]

Since DCF remains our preferred method, why dedicate a chapter to high-growth companies? Although the components of valuation are the same, their order and emphasis differ from the traditional process for established companies. Instead of starting by analyzing historical performance, we start by examining the expected long-term development of the company's markets and then work backwards. In addition, since long-term projections are highly uncertain, always create multiple scenarios.

---

[2] FASB Statement No. 86 allows certain development costs of computer software to be capitalized, once the software is technologically feasible.

[3] Schwartz and Moon value Amazon.com using real options. To generate a real options valuation, however, they estimate that long-term mean revenue growth equals 6 percent, revenue growth volatility equals 10 percent, and COGS margins equal 75 percent of revenues. Eduardo Schwartz and Mark Moon, "Rational Pricing of Internet Companies," *Financial Analysts Journal*, 56(3) (2000): 62–75.

Each scenario details how the market might develop under different conditions. The DCF approach cannot eliminate the need to make difficult forecasts, but it coherently addresses the problems of ultrahigh growth rates and uncertainty.

THE VALUATION PROCESS

For the valuation of an established company, the first step is to analyze historical performance. But in the case of a high-growth company, historical financial results provide limited clues about future prospects. Therefore, begin with the future, not with the past. Focus on sizing the future market, predicting the level of profitability, and estimating the investments necessary to achieve success. To do this, choose a point well into the future, at a time when financial performance is likely to stabilize, and begin forecasting.

Once you have developed a forecast such that the company's economics are stable, work backward to link it to current performance. Current performance is likely to commingle investments and expenses, so when possible, capitalize hidden investments (even those expensed under traditional accounting rules). This is challenging, as the distinction between investment and expense is often unobservable and usually subjective.

Given the uncertainty associated with high-growth companies, do not rely on a single long-term forecast. Describe the market's development in terms of multiple scenarios including total size, ease of competitive entry, and so on. When you build a comprehensive scenario, be sure all forecasts, including revenue growth, profitability margins, and required investment, are consistent with the underlying assumptions of the particular scenario.

Finally, apply probabilistic weights to each scenario. The weights must be consistent with long-term historical evidence on corporate growth. As we saw during the Internet run-up, valuations that rely too heavily on unrealistic assessments can lead to overestimates of value and strategic errors.

To a certain extent, the concepts behind probability-weighted scenarios are similar to those for real options valuation. By using a few well-developed scenarios instead of the more complicated modeling associated with real options, we can highlight the economic issues driving a company's value (which complex models often hide). In addition, real option valuation relies on tracking portfolios to replicate the company's cash flows. But what is the proper tracking portfolio for a new concept in uncharted territory? Real options valuation has potential but is still of limited applicability (for more on real options valuation, see Chapter 20).

Start from the Future

When valuing high-growth companies, start by thinking about what the industry and company might look like as the company evolves from its current high-growth, uncertain condition to a sustainable, moderate growth state in the future. Then interpolate back to current performance. The future state should be defined and bounded by measures of operating performance, such as penetration rates, average revenue per customer, and sustainable gross margins. Next, determine how long hyper growth will continue before stabilizing to normal levels. Since most high-growth companies are start-ups, stable economics probably lie at least 10 to 15 years in the future.

To demonstrate the specifics of the process, let's examine Internet retailer Amazon.com. Amazon's revenues grew from $150 million in 1997 to nearly $7 billion in 2004. To put this extraordinary growth in perspective, compare it with the first seven years' revenues of four other high-growth, successful companies: Dell, Home Depot, Microsoft, and Wal-Mart (see Exhibit 23.1). Whereas Amazon.com reached $6.9 billion in seven years, Dell grew to annual revenue of $3.3 billion, Home Depot grew to $3.0 billion, Microsoft to $2.9 billion, and Wal-Mart to only $1.5 billion over the same number of years.

Amazon's ability to enter and lead categories is unprecedented, in both the off-line and the online worlds. In 1998, the company took just three months to banish CDnow to second place among online purveyors of music.

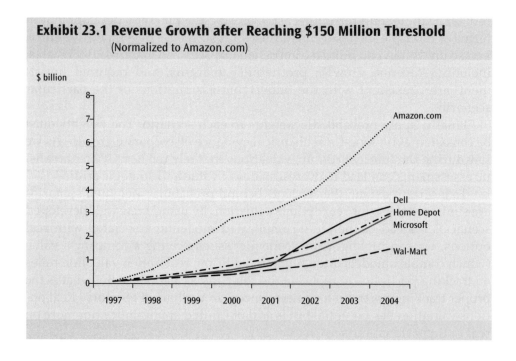

Exhibit 23.1 Revenue Growth after Reaching $150 Million Threshold
(Normalized to Amazon.com)

Exhibit 23.2   North American Media Sales

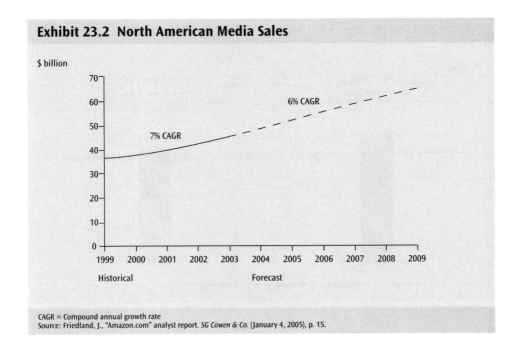

CAGR = Compound annual growth rate
Source: Friedland, J., "Amazon.com" analyst report. *SG Cowen & Co.* (January 4, 2005), p. 15.

In early 1999, it assumed the leadership position among online sellers of videos in 45 days; later that year, it became the leading online seller of consumer electronics in only 10 days. More recently, the company has expanded through fee-driven services: Marketplace for small businesses and Merchants@ for large, branded businesses.

But can this revenue growth continue? To answer this question, forecast how each of Amazon's retail product markets will grow, how much of each product market will be captured by Internet retailers, and what share of online purchases Amazon.com is likely to control. Exhibit 23.2 presents a forecast of North American media sales estimated by the investment banking firm SG Cowen.[4] The forecast was created by aggregating separate forecasts of media's major subsegments: books, videos, CDs, and DVDs. In the case of books, growth is slow and steady, with little uncertainty. Simple extrapolation suffices. In contrast, DVD players are somewhat new, so the market for DVDs is still developing. To forecast DVD sales, the analysts estimated DVD player penetration rates and combined the estimate for player penetration with average household expenditures for homes with and without DVD players.

Once a base forecast is developed for each product category, assess online penetration rates. To do this, SG Cowen relied on consumer surveys for each product category. For example, 26 percent of respondents expected to increase online purchases of media, whereas only 14 percent planned to

[4] Jim Leeland, "Amazon.com: Expect Increasing ROIC to Drive Long-Term Value," SG Cowen & Co., San Francisco, January 4, 2005.

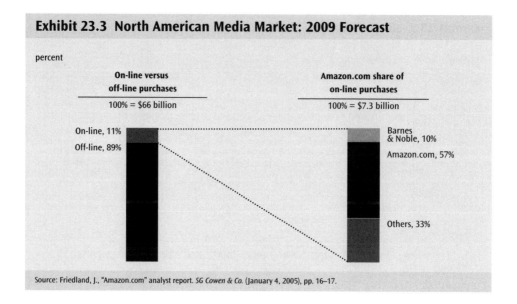

Exhibit 23.3 North American Media Market: 2009 Forecast

percent

On-line versus off-line purchases
100% = $66 billion

On-line, 11%
Off-line, 89%

Amazon.com share of on-line purchases
100% = $7.3 billion

Barnes & Noble, 10%
Amazon.com, 57%
Others, 33%

Source: Friedland, J., "Amazon.com" analyst report. *SG Cowen & Co.* (January 4, 2005), pp. 16–17.

increase online purchases of kitchen supplies and cookware. Based on this analysis, SG Cowen forecasts online penetration of media to grow from 8 percent in 2004 to 11 percent in 2009 (see Exhibit 23.3).

Finally, forecast Amazon.com's share of the online market. In 2004, Amazon.com led the market for online media sales with a 64 percent market share. At a distant second, with only 11 percent of the market, was Barnes & Noble. But even in its leading position, Amazon.com has lost share to competitors (its market share of online media dropped from 78 percent in 1999 to 64 percent in 2004). Predicting that the share will continue to drop, SG Cowen estimates Amazon.com's market share at 57 percent in 2009. By applying this share to the size of the market, SG Cowen projects North American media revenue of $4.3 billion. Using a similar analysis for Amazon.com's other products, as well as the company's international sales, leads to a base estimate of $19 billion in 2009.[5]

With a revenue forecast in hand, next forecast long-term ROIC. For Amazon.com, this requires an assessment of the improved efficiency of Internet retailers versus traditional bricks-and-mortar companies as well as the strength of competitive barriers to entry. Internet retailers have certain operational advantages, but can they protect those advantages? Or will Internet companies pass them to consumers in the form of lower prices?

To start our analysis (and ground it in actual data), we examined the ROIC characteristics of five retailers: Barnes & Noble, Best Buy, Dell, Lands' End, and Wal-Mart. Barnes & Noble is a traditional media retailer, with a

---

[5] Ideally, we would prefer longer-dated estimates, given Amazon.com's rapidly changing business. For pragmatic reasons, we start with assessments generated by others.

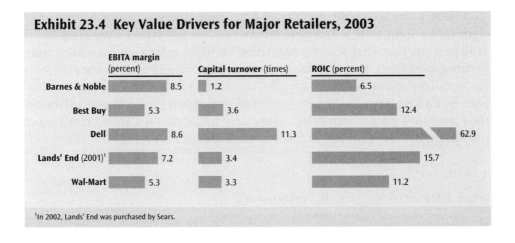

Exhibit 23.4 Key Value Drivers for Major Retailers, 2003

	EBITA margin (percent)	Capital turnover (times)	ROIC (percent)
Barnes & Noble	8.5	1.2	6.5
Best Buy	5.3	3.6	12.4
Dell	8.6	11.3	62.9
Lands' End (2001)[1]	7.2	3.4	15.7
Wal-Mart	5.3	3.3	11.2

[1] In 2002, Lands' End was purchased by Sears.

focus on books and music. Best Buy sells mostly electronics but also carries an extensive selection of music, videos, and DVDs. Dell is a manufacturer and online retailer of personal computers. Before being purchased by Sears in 2002, Lands' End was an independent retailer, primarily selling through mail order. Wal-Mart, the largest retailer in the world, sells a wide selection of consumer goods. Exhibit 23.4 presents a breakdown of pretax operating margins, capital turnover, and ROIC for each company.[6] Profit margin is quite tight across companies, varying between 5.3 percent and 8.6 percent. Capital turnover, however, varies greatly. Barnes & Noble generates little more than $1 in revenue for each dollar in invested capital, whereas Best Buy, Lands' End, and Wal-Mart all generate approximately $3.50 in revenue per dollar of invested capital. Dell, using a build-to-order manufacturing process and no retail stores, generates $11.30 in revenue for every dollar of invested capital.

But given that Dell is an online retailer *and* manufacturer, is the company's capital turnover even relevant for valuing Amazon.com? For guidance on this question, we compared Amazon's current inventory holding period with that of the other retailers. Amazon's inventory holding period averages 17 days, whereas Best Buy and Wal-Mart average near 35 days. Dell averages only six days in inventory. If the difference in current inventory turns is a good predictor of future invested capital turnover, Amazon's long-term capital turnover should lie between that of Dell and traditional retailers. Perhaps eight times is appropriate.[7]

---

[6] All three ratios have been adjusted for operating leases.

[7] Given the uncertainty surrounding any forecast, we use a back-of-the-envelope calculation for capital turns. A more rigorous approach would consider systematic differences between traditional retailers and online retailers. For example, how would capital turnover change for a traditional retailer if we eliminated net property, plant, and equipment related to stores but not warehouses?

Using a pretax profit margin of 8 percent times a capital turnover of eight times along with a 37.5 percent tax rate, we estimate a long-term ROIC at 40 percent. But what about competition? If ROIC is so high, shouldn't competitors steal share and eventually force prices down? For Amazon.com, this is a serious concern and probably the largest threat to the company's valuation. But a long-term return on capital of 40 percent probably overestimates the company's cumulative ROIC, especially if early losses are reclassified as investments. We examine this issue in the next section.

Work Backward to Current Performance

Having completed a forecast for total market size, market share, and return on invested capital, reconnect the long-term forecast back to current performance. To do this, we have to assess the speed of transition from current performance to future long-term performance. Estimates must be consistent with economic principles and industry characteristics. For instance, from the perspective of operating margin, how long will fixed costs dominate variable costs, resulting in low margins? Concerning capital turnover, what scale is required before revenues rise faster than capital? As scale is reached, will competition drive down prices? Often, there are more questions than answers.

One way to estimate the speed of transition is to look historically. Consider Amazon's improvement in operating margin between 1999 and 2003. In 1999, Amazon.com earned a negative EBITA margin of −23.4 percent. Over the next two years, margins increased by approximately 11 percentage points per year, to −1.6 percent. Then margin improvement dramatically slowed. In 2002, margin improvement declined to only 4.4 percentage points, and by 2003, margin improvement was only 2.2 percentage points. Assuming that this trend of margin improvements continuing to decline by a little less than half endures, the EBITA margin will reach 8 percent by 2009, consistent with our point forecast from the previous section (see Exhibit 23.5).

Historical financial performance for high-growth companies is often misleading, because long-term investments for today's high-growth companies tend to be intangible. Under current accounting rules, these investments must be expensed. Therefore, both early accounting profits and invested capital will be understated. We illustrate this by continuing our examination of Amazon.com. By year-end 2003, the company had an accumulated deficit of $3.0 billion, even though revenues and gross profits had grown steadily. How could this occur? Marketing- and technology-related expenses significantly outweighed gross profits. In the years between 1999 and 2003, Amazon.com expensed $742 million in marketing and $1.1 billion in technology development. In 1999, Amazon's marketing expense was

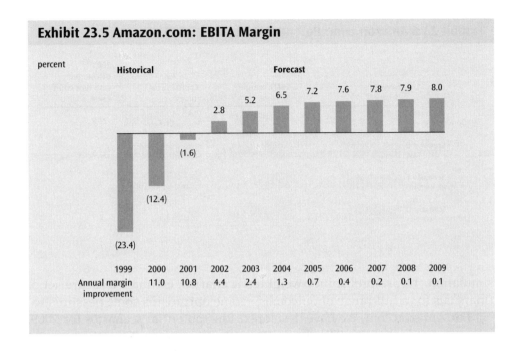

Exhibit 23.5 Amazon.com: EBITA Margin

percent

Historical   Forecast

	1999	2000	2001	2002	2003	2004	2005	2006	2007	2008	2009
Annual margin improvement		11.0	10.8	4.4	2.4	1.3	0.7	0.4	0.2	0.1	0.1

10 percent of revenue. In contrast, Best Buy spends about 2 percent of revenue for advertising. One might argue that the 8 percent differential is more appropriately classified as a brand-building activity, not a short-term revenue driver.

In the previous section, we used the performance of mature retailers to generate a long-term estimate of ROIC for Amazon.com at 40 percent. This ROIC, however, overstates the potential return on capital for new entrants, because it ignores historically expensed investment.[8] In niche areas, competitors probably will enter. But on a broad base, other online retailers may hesitate to compete directly with Amazon.com because of the heavy required investments in technology and brand building. Competitors may doubt that the potential profits justifies the incremental billions required.

Develop Scenarios

A simple and straightforward way to deal with uncertainty associated with high-growth companies is to use probability-weighted scenarios. Using just a few scenarios makes critical assumptions and interactions more transparent than other modeling approaches, such as real options and Monte Carlo

---

[8] The way a company classifies advertising will not affect cash flow. The money has been spent regardless. But reclassifying certain expenditures as investments will lower ROIC in future years.

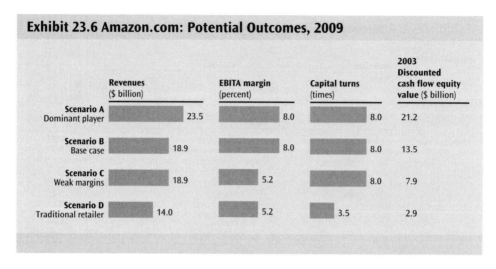

Exhibit 23.6 Amazon.com: Potential Outcomes, 2009

	Revenues ($ billion)	EBITA margin (percent)	Capital turns (times)	2003 Discounted cash flow equity value ($ billion)
Scenario A Dominant player	23.5	8.0	8.0	21.2
Scenario B Base case	18.9	8.0	8.0	13.5
Scenario C Weak margins	18.9	5.2	8.0	7.9
Scenario D Traditional retailer	14.0	5.2	3.5	2.9

simulation. To use probability-weighted scenarios, estimate a future set of financials for a full range of outcomes—some optimistic, some pessimistic.

For Amazon.com, we have developed four potential scenarios for 2009, summarized in Exhibit 23.6. In Scenario A, we assume Amazon.com succeeds on all fronts. The company is able to generate $23.5 billion in revenues by 2009, its pretax operating margin rises to 8 percent (the high end of our retail sample), and its capital turnover stabilizes at eight times (between traditional retailers and Dell). This assessment leads to an estimated equity valuation of $21.2 billion.

In Scenario B, our base scenario, revenues grow to $18.9 billion in 2009, pretax margins rise to 8 percent, and capital turns equal eight times. In the second scenario, Amazon.com has an estimated equity value equal to $13.5 billion.

In Scenario C, we assume Amazon.com can generate $18.9 billion in revenue by 2009 but operating margins remain at the 2003 level of 5.2 percent. Again, capital turns equal eight times. In Scenario C, Amazon.com's estimated equity valuation equals $7.9 billion.

Scenario D assumes that Amazon.com generates only $14.0 billion in revenue by 2009 and that margins and turns are consistent with traditional retailers. In Scenario D, online retailing mimics most other industries, with many competitors in each field. This competition transfers most of the value for going online to consumers. Assuming margins remain at 5.2 percent and capital turns equal just 3.5 times, Amazon.com has an equity value of only $2.9 billion.

Because Amazon.com's resulting equity value in Scenario D is much lower than the company's current market value, it is necessary to separately value the company's debt. After further analysis, it appears that book value suffices even in Scenario D because Amazon.com's net debt (total debt minus excess cash) is quite low. Had this not been the case, there is a good chance Amazon.com's debt value would have been lower than book because of a higher probability of default. You must take this into consideration when determining equity value in pessimistic scenarios (for more on scenario analysis and its impact on financial claims, see Chapter 11).

Besides using scenarios to prepare our valuation, we can use scenario analysis to determine the value impact of changes in individual drivers. If we move from Scenario A to Scenario B, expected revenue growth drops from a six-year compounded rate of 28.4 percent to 23.7 percent, and estimated equity value drops $7.6 billion (a drop of 36 percent). If we move from Scenario B to Scenario C, long-term operating margins drop from 8.0 percent to 5.2 percent, and estimated equity value drops $5.6 billion (a decline of 42 percent).

Weight Scenarios Consistently with Historical Evidence

During the Internet boom, rising stock prices were hard to ignore. When Internet stocks reached their peak, economic reality seemed to conflict with widely accepted beliefs in efficient markets. Following the dramatic fall, however, economic reality once again appears to have triumphed. As a result, today we believe more than ever that probabilistic weightings and their resulting valuations must be consistent with economic evidence on long-term corporate performance.

To derive current equity value for Amazon.com, we weight the potential equity value from each scenario by its estimated likelihood of occurrence. Exhibit 23.7 lists the potential equity value and the probability of occurrence for each scenario. To estimate the company's current equity value, sum across each scenario's contribution. Based on our probability assessments, we estimate Amazon.com's equity value at $12.9 billion. During 2004, the company's equity value was volatile, trading between $14 billion and $22 billion (in December 2004, Amazon.com was trading near $18 billion).

Exhibit 23.7 Amazon.com: Expected Value

	2003 Discounted cash flow equity value ($ billion)	×	Probability (percent)	=	Contribution to equity value ($ billion)
Scenario A	21.2		20		4.2
Scenario B	13.5		50		6.8
Scenario C	7.9		20		1.6
Scenario D	2.9		10		0.3
			100		12.9
		Shares (billion)			0.403
		Equity share value ($)			31.9

Scenario probabilities are unobservable and highly subjective. As a result, the final valuation will be quite sensitive to probability weightings. Thus, any set of forecasts built on fundamental economic analysis (such as market size, market share, and competitor margins) should be calibrated against the historical performance of other high-growth companies. Otherwise, assigning too high a weighting to an implausible scenario could make the valuation too high (or too low if you are overly conservative).

To further assess which scenario is most plausible, we compare Amazon.com's recent revenue growth with the historical performance of other high-growth companies. Earlier in this chapter, we plotted Amazon's revenue growth versus four other remarkably successful growth companies: Dell, Home Depot, Microsoft, and Wal-Mart (see Exhibit 23.1). Amazon's growth was unparalleled. In the seven years after reaching $150 million in revenues, Amazon.com grew at nearly twice the speed of other highfliers. Such growth might lead an observer to believe Amazon.com could easily reach $50 billion by 2009.

But Exhibit 23.1 is misleading. Once Amazon.com reached $4 billion, the company's supernormal revenue growth normalized. Amazon's revenue growth now tracks that of Home Depot, Microsoft, and Wal-Mart quite closely, as shown in Exhibit 23.8. Apparently, the growth Amazon.com exhibited during its first few years has been tamed by its large size, and the

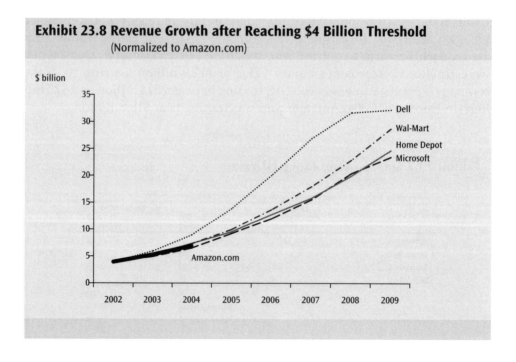

Exhibit 23.8 Revenue Growth after Reaching $4 Billion Threshold
(Normalized to Amazon.com)

company now significantly trails Dell's rate of growth over the same life cycle period. Based on this simple analysis, any assessments of revenues growing beyond $30 billion by 2009 are inconsistent with historical evidence. Even to generate $23.5 billion by 2009 (our most optimistic scenario), Amazon.com must outpace Microsoft, arguably one of the most successful companies in history. It could happen, but the feat is far from certain.

VALUING AMAZON.COM: THEN AND NOW

In the previous edition of this book (published in early 2000), we applied the preceding techniques to value Amazon.com. At the time, Internet valuations were at their peak, Amazon.com was growing at 168 percent a year, and the company was losing nearly $2 million a day. Needless to say, Amazon.com's future was unclear, and creating meaningful scenarios was extremely challenging. Nonetheless, we stepped through a careful analysis of Amazon's potential markets, estimated the company's potential share, and analyzed the margins for traditional retailers. Exhibit 23.9 summarizes the forecast scenarios we prepared for the 2000 edition.

A comparison of these numbers with our current set of forecast scenarios in Exhibit 23.6 shows that performance estimates were dramatically higher in 1999 than the levels we now estimate. At that time, the Internet was uncharted water and anything seemed possible. Unrealistic assessments were required to justify the marketplace's exuberant valuations. As time has passed, however, only the previous edition's worst scenario has been consistent with actual performance. Based on these financial results,

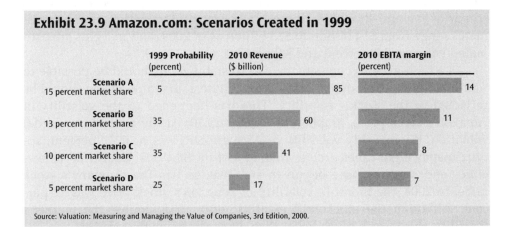

Exhibit 23.9 Amazon.com: Scenarios Created in 1999

	1999 Probability (percent)	2010 Revenue ($ billion)	2010 EBITA margin (percent)
Scenario A 15 percent market share	5	85	14
Scenario B 13 percent market share	35	60	11
Scenario C 10 percent market share	35	41	8
Scenario D 5 percent market share	25	17	7

Source: Valuation: Measuring and Managing the Value of Companies, 3rd Edition, 2000.

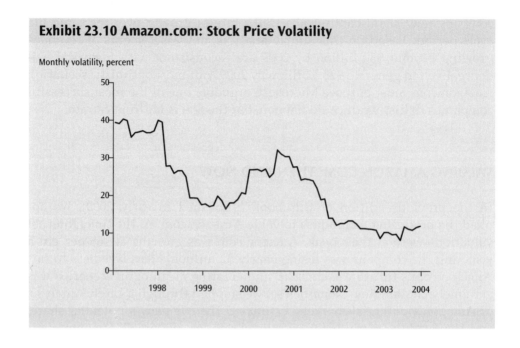

Exhibit 23.10 Amazon.com: Stock Price Volatility

it is not surprising that Internet market capitalizations dropped precipitously in 2001 and 2002.

A second difference between the two valuations comes into view by examining the range of variability across scenarios. In 1999, little historical data existed for either Amazon.com or the industry as a whole. To capture this uncertainty, our estimates of projected revenue ranged from $17 billion to $85 billion, and margins ranged from 7 percent to 14 percent. For our more recent valuation, we have five additional years of data (more than doubling the number of historical observations), revenue growth rates have declined to traditional levels, and the company is now profitable. Thus, scenarios can and should be tighter. In our current valuation, revenue estimates range from $14 billion to $23 billion as of 2009, and margins are estimated between 5.2 percent and 8.0 percent.

As a high-growth company begins to stabilize, it should be possible to tighten the range of potential outcomes. These gains in precision should be reflected in the stock's volatility. This has happened to the volatility of Amazon's stock price, graphed in Exhibit 23.10. At the time of our initial valuation, the monthly volatility of Amazon.com was near 40 percent, approximately eight times greater than that of the S&P 500. Over time, as revenues and margins have begun to stabilize, so has the company's stock price. In 2004, the monthly volatility of Amazon's stock price was 12 percent. Although the stock still exhibits more than double the market's volatility, this level is much lower than when the stock first traded.

UNCERTAINTY IS HERE TO STAY

By adapting the DCF approach, we can generate reasonable valuations for seemingly unreasonable businesses. But investors and companies entering fast-growth markets like those related to the Internet should expect to face huge uncertainties. To see this, look at what could happen under our four scenarios to an investor who holds a share of Amazon.com stock for 10 years after buying it in 2004. To facilitate the calculation, we assume the investor gradually learns about the most likely scenario.

If Scenario A plays out, the investor will earn a 13 percent annual return, and as of 2004, the market will seem to have undervalued Amazon.com. An annual return of 13 percent may not seem very high, but recall that much of Amazon's potential success is already incorporated into the company's stock price. If Scenario D plays out, the investor will lose about 8 percent a year, and it will appear that the company was substantially overvalued in 2004. In fact, our worst scenario forecasted in the 2000 edition has been playing out. An investor who purchased Amazon.com after reading that edition has lost nearly 7 percent annually (31 percent cumulatively). Going forward, these high or low potential returns should not be interpreted as implying that the current share price was irrational; they merely reflect uncertainty about the future.

A great deal of this uncertainty is associated with the problem of identifying the eventual winner in a large competitive field: Not even in the world of high-tech initial public offerings can every company become the next Microsoft. History shows that a few players will win big, while the vast majority will toil away amid obscurity and worthless options. It is difficult to predict which companies will prosper and which will not. Neither investors nor companies can eliminate this uncertainty, and that is why advisors tell investors to diversify their portfolios—and why companies do not pay cash when acquiring young, high-growth firms.

SUMMARY

The emergence of the Internet and related technologies created impressive value for select entrepreneurs at the end of the twentieth century. It also raised questions about the sanity of a stock market that appeared to assign higher value to companies the more their losses mounted. But as this chapter demonstrates, the DCF approach remains an essential tool for understanding the value of high-growth companies. You must make some adaptations when valuing these companies: starting from the future rather than the present when making your forecast, thinking in terms of probabilities, and understanding the economics of the business model compared with peers. Though you cannot reduce these companies' volatility, at the very least you can understand it.

REVIEW QUESTIONS

1. Explain how the process of valuing a high-growth company differs from valuing an established company? In what way would valuing a high-growth firm be similar to valuing an established firm that has recently hired a new chief executive officer?

2. How could scenario analysis be employed to gain a better understanding of the value drivers embedded in a high-growth firm?

3. Identify the key issues an analyst should consider when valuing start-up companies. How might an analyst resolve these issues?

4. Discuss the similarities and differences of business-to-consumer to business-to-business valuations in terms of value drivers, controlling growth, and economic scenarios.

24

Valuing Cyclical Companies

A cyclical company is one whose earnings demonstrate a repeating pattern of significant increases and decreases. The earnings of such companies, including those in the steel, airline, paper, and chemical industries, fluctuate because of large changes in the prices of their products. In the airline industry, earnings cyclicality is linked to broader macroeconomic trends. In the paper industry, cyclicality is largely driven by industry factors, typically related to capacity. Volatile earnings introduce additional complexity into the valuation of these cyclical companies. For example, historical performance must be assessed in context of the cycle. A decline in recent performance does not necessarily indicate a long-term negative trend, but rather a shift to a different part of the cycle.

In this chapter, we explore the valuation dynamics particular to cyclical companies. We start with an examination of how the share prices of cyclical companies behave. This leads to a suggested approach to valuing these companies, as well as possible implications for managers.

SHARE PRICE BEHAVIOR

The share prices of companies with cyclical earnings tend to be more volatile than those of less cyclical companies. Is this consistent with the DCF valuation approach? At first glance, theory and reality diverge.

When Theory and Reality Conflict

Let's explore the theory. Suppose that you were using the DCF approach to value a cyclical company and you had perfect foresight about the industry

This chapter is partially based on an analysis for a dissertation, "Underestimating Change," (Rotterdam: Erasmus University, August 1999), by Marco De Heer, under the supervision of one of the coauthors.

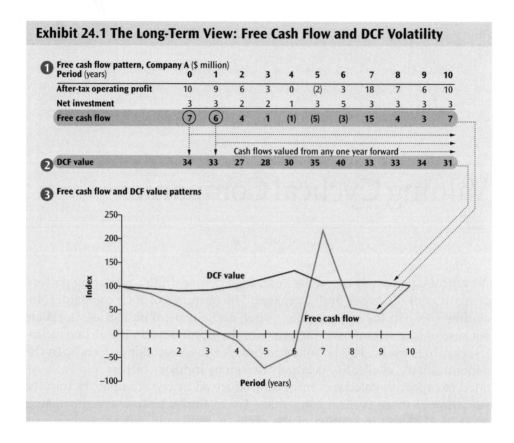

Exhibit 24.1 The Long-Term View: Free Cash Flow and DCF Volatility

1 Free cash flow pattern, Company A ($ million)

Period (years)	0	1	2	3	4	5	6	7	8	9	10
After-tax operating profit	10	9	6	3	0	(2)	3	18	7	6	10
Net investment	3	3	2	2	1	3	5	3	3	3	3
Free cash flow	(7)	(6)	4	1	(1)	(5)	(3)	15	4	3	7

Cash flows valued from any one year forward

2
DCF value		34	33	27	28	30	35	40	33	33	34	31

3 Free cash flow and DCF value patterns

cycle. Would the company's value and earnings behave similarly? No, the DCF value would exhibit much lower volatility than the earnings or cash flows. DCF reduces future expected cash flows to a single value. As a result, any single year is unimportant. For a cyclical company, the high cash flows cancel out the low cash flows. Only the long-term trend really matters.

An example can clarify. The business cycle of Company A is 10 years. Exhibit 24.1, Part 1, shows the company's hypothetical cash flow pattern. It is highly volatile, containing both positive and negative cash flows. Discounting the future free cash flows at 10 percent produces the succession of DCF values in Exhibit 24.1, Part 2.

Exhibit 24.1, Part 3, compares the cash flows and DCF values (the values are indexed for comparability). It shows that the DCF value is far less volatile than the underlying cash flow. In fact, the value displays almost no volatility because no single year's performance has a significant impact on the value of the company.

In the real world, the share prices of cyclical companies are less stable. Exhibit 24.2 shows the earnings and share values (indexed) for 15 companies with a four-year cycle. The share prices are more volatile than the DCF approach would predict—suggesting that theory and reality conflict.

Exhibit 24.2 Share Prices and EPS for 15 Cyclical Companies

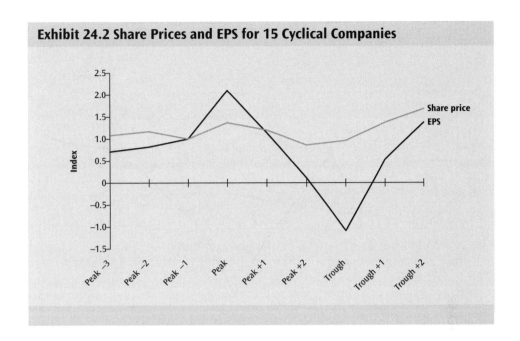

Are Earnings Forecasts the Culprit?

How can we reconcile this divergence? We examined equity analysts' consensus earnings forecasts for cyclical companies to see if they provided any clues to the volatile stock prices of these companies.

What we found surprised us. Consensus earnings forecasts for cyclical companies appeared to ignore cyclicality entirely. The forecasts invariably showed an upward-sloping trend, whether the companies were at the peak or trough of the cycle. What appeared was not that the DCF model was inconsistent with the facts, but that the earnings and cash flow projections of the market (assuming the market followed the analysts' consensus) were to blame.

The conclusion was based on an analysis of 36 U.S. cyclical companies during 1985 to 1997. We divided them into groups with similar cycles (e.g., three, four, or five years from peak to trough) and calculated scaled average earnings and earnings forecasts. We then compared actual earnings with consensus earnings forecasts over the cycle.[1]

Exhibit 24.3 on page 674 plots the actual earnings and consensus earnings forecasts for the set of 15 companies with four-year cycles in primary metals and manufacturing transportation equipment. The consensus forecasts do not predict the earnings cycle at all. In fact, except for the "next-year

---

[1] Note that we have already adjusted downward the normal positive bias of analyst forecasts to focus on just the cyclicality issue. V. K. Chopra, "Why So Much Error in Analysts' Earnings Forecasts?" *Financial Analysts Journal* (November/December 1998): 35–42.

Exhibit 24.3 Actual EPS and Consensus EPS Forecasts for 15 Cyclical Companies

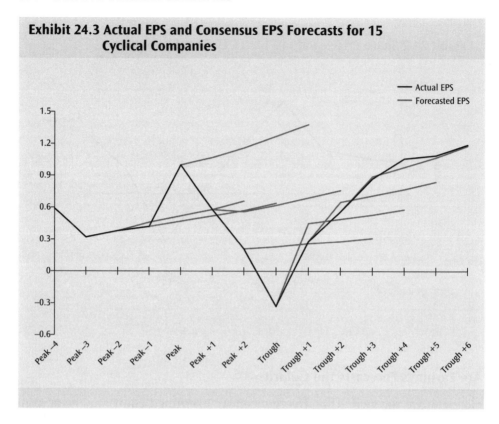

forecasts" in the years following the trough, the earnings per share are forecast to follow an upward-sloping path with no future variation. You might say that the forecast does not even acknowledge the existence of a cycle.[2]

One explanation could be that equity analysts have incentives to avoid predicting the earnings cycle, particularly the down part. Academic research has shown that earnings forecasts have a general positive bias that is sometimes attributed to the incentives facing equity analysts at investment banks.[3]

Pessimistic earnings forecasts may damage relations between an analyst's employer—an investment bank—and a particular company. In addition, companies that are the target of negative commentary might cut off an analyst's access to management. From this evidence, we could conclude that

---

[2] Similar results were found for companies with three- and five-year cycles.

[3] The following articles discuss this hypothesis: M. R. Clayman and R. A. Schwartz, "Falling in Love Again—Analysts' Estimates and Reality," *Financial Analysts Journal* (September/October 1994): 66–68; J. Francis, and D. Philbrick, "Analysts' Decisions as Products of a Multi-Task Environment," *Journal of Accounting Research*, 31(2) (Autumn 1993): 216–230; K. Schipper, "Commentary on Analysts' Forecasts," *Accounting Horizons* (December 1991): 105–121; B. Trueman, "On the Incentives for Security Analysts to Revise Their Earnings Forecasts," *Contemporary Accounting Research*, 7(1): 203–222.

analysts as a group are unable or unwilling to predict the cycle for these companies. If the market followed analyst forecasts, that behavior could account for the high volatility of cyclical companies' share prices.

The Market Appears Smarter Than the Consensus Forecast

We know that cycles are hard to predict, particularly their inflection points. So it is not surprising that the market does not get it exactly right. However, we would be disappointed if the stock market entirely missed the cycle as the consensus earnings analysis suggests. To address this issue, we returned to the question of how the market should behave. Should it be able to predict the cycle and therefore exhibit little share price volatility? That would probably be asking too much. At any point, the company or industry could break out of its cycle and move to one that is higher or lower, as illustrated in Exhibit 24.4.

Suppose you are valuing a company that seems to be at a peak in its earnings cycle. Based on past cycles, you expect the industry to turn down soon. However, there are signs that the industry is about to break out of the old cycle. A reasonable valuation approach would be to build two scenarios and weight their values. Suppose you assumed, with a 50 percent probability, that the cycle will follow the past and that the industry will turn down in the next year or so. The second scenario, also with 50 percent probability,

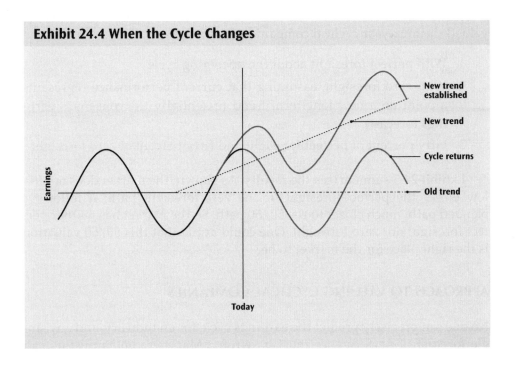

Exhibit 24.4 When the Cycle Changes

New trend established

New trend

Cycle returns

Old trend

Earnings

Today

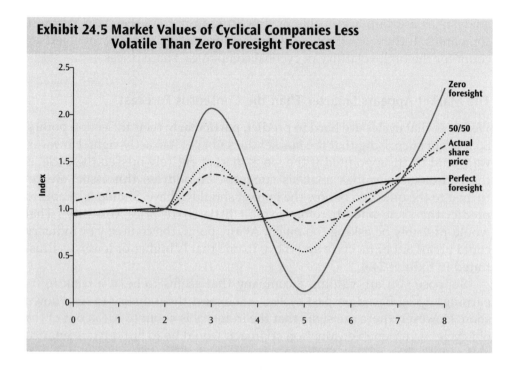

Exhibit 24.5 Market Values of Cyclical Companies Less Volatile Than Zero Foresight Forecast

would be that the industry will break out of the cycle and follow a new long-term trend based on current improved performance. The value of the company would then be the weighted average of these two values.

We found evidence that this is in fact the way the market behaves. We valued the four-year cyclical companies three ways:

1. With perfect foresight about the upcoming cycle
2. With zero foresight, assuming that current performance represents a point on a new long-term trend (essentially the consensus earnings forecast)
3. Fifty percent of perfect foresight and fifty percent of zero foresight

Exhibit 24.5 summarizes the results. As shown, the market does not follow either the perfect-foresight or the zero-foresight path; it follows a blended path, much closer to the 50/50 path. So the market has neither perfect foresight nor zero foresight. One could argue that this 50/50 valuation is the right place for the market to be.

APPROACH TO VALUING CYCLICAL COMPANIES

No one can precisely predict the earnings cycle for an industry, and any single forecast of performance must be wrong. Managers and investors can benefit from following explicitly the multiple-scenario probabilistic approach to valuing cyclical companies outlined earlier, similar to the approach we used in the Heineken case in Chapter 11 and the high-growth company valuation in Chapter 23. The probabilistic approach avoids the traps of a single forecast and allows the exploration of a wider range of outcomes and their implications.

Here is a two-scenario approach for valuing cyclical companies (of course, you could always have more than two scenarios):

1. Construct and value the "normal cycle" scenario, using information about past cycles. Pay particular attention to the long-term trend lines of operating profits, cash flow, and ROIC because they will have the largest impact on the valuation. Make sure the continuing value is based on a normalized level of profits (i.e., a point on the company's long-term cash flow trend line), not a peak or trough.

2. Construct and value a new trend-line scenario based on the recent performance of the company. Once again, focus primarily on the long-term trend line, because it will have the largest impact on value. Do not worry too much about modeling future cyclicality (although future cyclicality will be important for financial solvency).

3. Develop the economic rationale for each of the two scenarios, considering factors such as demand growth, companies entering or exiting the industry, and technology changes that will affect the supply and demand balance.

4. Assign probabilities to the scenarios, and calculate a weighted value of the scenarios. Use the economic rationale and its likelihood to estimate the weights assigned to each scenario.

This approach provides an estimate of the value as well as scenarios that put boundaries on the valuation. Managers can use these boundaries to improve their strategy and respond to signals about which scenario is likely to occur.

IMPLICATIONS FOR MANAGING CYCLICAL COMPANIES

Is there anything managers can do to reduce or take advantage of the cyclicality of their industry? Evidence suggests that, in many cyclical industries, the companies themselves are what drives cyclicality. Exhibit 24.6 on page 678 shows the return on capital and net investment in commodity chemicals from 1980 to 2001. The chart shows that, collectively, commodity chemical companies invest large amounts when prices and returns are high. Since capacity comes on line in very large chunks, however, utilization

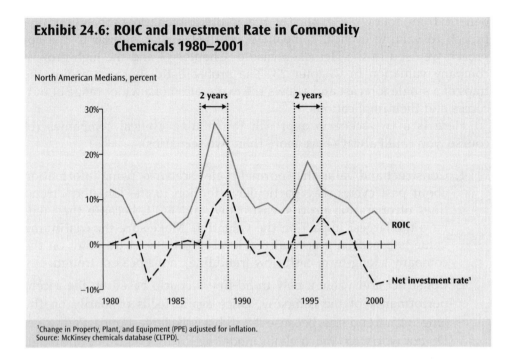

Exhibit 24.6: ROIC and Investment Rate in Commodity Chemicals 1980–2001

North American Medians, percent

[1] Change in Property, Plant, and Equipment (PPE) adjusted for inflation.
Source: McKinsey chemicals database (CLTPD).

plunges, and this places downward pressure on prices and returns on capital. The cyclical investment in capacity is the driver of the cyclical profitability. Fluctuations in demand from customers do not cause cyclicality in profits. Producer supply does.

Managers who have detailed information about their product markets should be able to do a better job than the financial market in figuring out the cycle and then take appropriate actions. We can only speculate why they do not do so. Still, based on conversations with these executives, we believe that the herding behavior is caused by three factors: First, it is easier to invest when prices are high because that is when cash is available. Second, it is easier to get approval from boards of directors to invest when profits are high. Finally, executives are concerned about their rivals growing faster than themselves (investments are a way to maintain market share).

This behavior also sends confusing signals to the stock market. Expanding when prices are high tells the financial market that the future looks great (often just before the cycle turns down). Signaling pessimism just before an upturn also confuses the market. Perhaps it should be no surprise that the stock market has difficulty valuing cyclical companies.

How could managers exploit their superior knowledge of the cycle? The most obvious action would be to time capital spending better. Companies could also pursue financial strategies, such as issuing shares at the peak of the cycle or repurchasing shares at the cycle's trough. The most aggressive managers could take this one step further by adopting a trading approach,

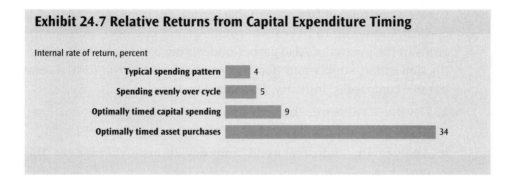

Exhibit 24.7 Relative Returns from Capital Expenditure Timing

Internal rate of return, percent

Typical spending pattern	4
Spending evenly over cycle	5
Optimally timed capital spending	9
Optimally timed asset purchases	34

making acquisitions at the bottom of the cycle and selling assets at the top. Exhibit 24.7 shows the results of a simulation of optimal cycle timing. The typical company's returns on investment could increase substantially.

Can companies really behave this way and invest against the cycle? It is actually very difficult for a company to take the contrarian view. The CEO must convince the board and the company's bankers to expand when the industry outlook is gloomy and competitors are retrenching. In addition, the CEO has to hold back while competitors build at the top of the cycle. Breaking out of the cycle may be possible, but it is the rare CEO who can do it.

SUMMARY

At first glance, the share prices of cyclical companies appear too volatile to be consistent with the DCF valuation approach. In this chapter, however, we have seen that share price volatility can be explained by the uncertainty surrounding the industry cycle. Using scenarios and probabilities, managers and investors can take a systematic DCF approach to valuing and analyzing cyclical companies.

REVIEW QUESTIONS

1. What are the characteristics of a cyclical company? How does the valuation of a cyclical company differ from the valuation of a noncyclical company? Compare and contrast the differences of evaluating firms in the electric generation industry compared to firms in the automotive manufacturing industry.

2. Why should a manager apply a multi-scenario approach to value cyclical companies as opposed to the single-forecast approach normally associated with enterprise DCF and economic profit valuation models?

3. Create a portfolio of five comparable companies in an industry that is cyclical. Gather up to 10 years of financial and operating data for the firms in the portfolio. Also gather underlying commodity price, production index, supply and demand market information for the comparable companies' industry. Use this data to:

   a. Develop a value tree that explains return on invested capital down to the profit margin layer of analysis for each year.

   b. Analyze the industry trend and deviations exhibited in this portfolio.

   c. Analyze movements in underlying commodity prices and production.

   d. Correlate industry value driver movements with underlying industry supply and demand dynamics.

4. Collect monthly share prices for the portfolio and use this data to:

   a. Create an equity book value weighted index of value and analyze the cyclical character of the share prices.

   b. Correlate the value tree movements year-to-year to the cyclical dynamics of the underlying industry.

   c. Develop three potential scenarios along which cyclical factors change over a short-term forecasting horizon.

   d. Develop three potential scenarios to extrapolate the movement of cyclical factors in the long term.

25

Valuing Financial
Institutions

In this chapter we provide an overview of valuing financial institutions—
banks and insurance companies. These are some of the most complex companies to value, especially from the outside in. Outside analysts always lack
some critical information about these companies' economics (such as asset-
liability mismatch and credit losses for banks), so they must rely on rough
estimates and judgment about the accuracy of management's accounting
decisions. Moreover, due to the nature of their operating model, these companies are highly levered. That makes valuations extremely sensitive to
even small changes in key drivers.

We will highlight some of the primary issues you may encounter when
valuing financial institutions. Our basic approach to valuing industrial companies, described earlier in this book, will serve as a foundation from which
we can focus on areas where the valuation process for financial companies
differs. First we describe why you should use the equity cash flow approach
for valuing these companies. Then we provide details on how to put this approach into practice. Finally we discuss, in turn, specific issues relating to
banks and insurance companies, including some of the methods and metrics
that internal analysts use to better assess their performance and value.

EQUITY CASH FLOW APPROACH

Throughout most of this book, we detail the enterprise DCF approach to
valuation, which we use for nonfinancial companies in cases where operating decisions and financing decisions are separate. For financial companies,

Special thanks to Susan Nolen Foushee who cowrote this chapter.

however, we cannot value operations separately from interest income and expense, since these are important components of their income. Another distinction involves our concept of invested capital, which focuses on a company's operating assets and is indifferent, within bounds, to how those assets are financed. However, financing decisions (the choice of leverage, for example) are at the core of how banks and insurers generate earnings. Therefore, to value financial institutions you should use the equity cash flow method rather than the enterprise DCF method. (See Chapter 5 for a comparison of these methods.)

Calculating Equity Cash Flow

We can derive equity cash flow from two starting points. First, equity cash flow is driven by net income minus the earnings retained in the business:

Equity Cash Flow = Net Income − Increase in Equity + Other Comprehensive Income

(Net income itself is driven by the revenues and expenses of the company; in the following sections on banks and insurers, we discuss these items in more detail.)

We start with net income because it represents the earnings theoretically available to shareholders after the company has paid all expenses, including those to debt holders. However, net income by itself is not cash flow. As a financial institution grows, it will need to increase its equity; otherwise, its debt/equity ratio would rise, which might cause regulators and customers to worry about the company's solvency. Increases in equity reduce equity cash flow, because they mean the company is setting aside earnings that could otherwise be paid out to shareholders. Finally, we add back other comprehensive income, which under U.S. GAAP consists of several noncash items that are added to or subtracted from the equity account.[1] Adjusting for other comprehensive income cancels out this noncash adjustment to equity.

Another way to calculate equity cash flow is as the sum of all cash paid to or received from shareholders, including dividends, share repurchases, and new share issuances. Exhibit 25.1 shows a sample equity cash flow calculation for a bank. We calculate equity cash flow according to the previous formula, and then cross-check our result by summing all the various payments made to or by holders of common and preferred shares. Both calculations arrive at the same result.

In addition to these two relatively simple approaches, you can calculate equity cash flow from the changes in all the balance sheet accounts. For example, equity cash flow for a bank equals net income plus the increase in

---

[1] The main items included in "other comprehensive income" are net unrealized gains and losses on certain equity and debt investments, net unrealized gains and losses on hedging activities, adjustments to the minimum pension liability, and foreign-currency translation items.

Exhibit 25.1 ABC Bank: Equity Cash Flow

$ million

Equity cash flow	2002	2003
Net income	1,678	1,823
Other comprehensive income	66	(11)
Increase in equity	(913)	(1,221)
Equity cash flow	**831**	**592**
Check of equity cash flow		
Net buyback (issuance) of common stock	249	(77)
Net buyback (issuance) of preferred stock	(61)	(44)
Common dividends	551	744
Other changes in equity	92	(30)
Equity cash flow	**831**	**592**

deposits and reserves, less the increase in loans and investments, and so on. The result will be identical to the two simpler approaches, and it highlights changes in the company's asset or liability composition.

People often equate the equity cash flow method with discounting dividends. In a simplified world, dividends are indeed the same as equity cash flow. However, real-world companies are generally more complex. In the example shown in Exhibit 25.1 dividends are the largest component of cash flow. But other items, such as share buybacks and issuances, still have a material impact.

Understanding a Company's Equity Needs

Forecasting future equity cash flows is more complex than the historical calculation discussed earlier. The reason is that as a financial institution grows and increases its net income, it will need to increase its equity. But how much equity will it need? In this area our perspective may differ, depending on whether you are doing a valuation inside or outside the institution.

The crux of the issue is this: Financial institutions are highly levered because of the nature of their business—taking money from depositors or policyholders, then lending it out and/or placing it into investments. Fundamentally, much of these institutions' business involves risking other people's money. Regulators (and prudent managers) will want to make sure that the company also puts some of its owners' money at risk by financing some of its activities with equity, and that companies do not achieve high returns simply by operating at unsustainably high levels of leverage.

Risk capital versus book equity From the perspective of regulators and risk management, the amount of equity a financial institution should have depends on the risks in its portfolio. The 1988 Basel I accord established rules for banks regarding how much capital they must hold based on their level of risk-weighted assets (RWAs). These RWAs were defined as a bank's loan portfolio weighted by the riskiness of different classes of borrowers. The same accord also specified how much of the capital had to consist of straightforward shareholders' equity, and how much could consist of other forms of financing, such as complex subordinated debt instruments. More recently, the Basel II accords (already adopted in Europe and under process of adoption in the United States) provide banks more flexibility in using internal risk models to assess their capital needs. However, Basel II maintains the general principle that capital should be related to risk (and may lead to major revisions of capital needs per product type). Similarly, insurers operate under national regulations regarding solvency that seek to make sure they have enough capital to meet their risks.

Banks and insurers make internal calculations of the *risk capital* required to operate prudently. (Note that the amount of risk capital a financial institution believes it needs to hold may be less than that required by regulators and, indeed, less than the total equity on its books.) In this context, when you analyze financial institutions, you will often hear term like *RAROC* (risk-adjusted return on capital) or *RORAC* (return on risk-adjusted capital). These concepts are used in most modern performance management systems to evaluate the economic performance of business units within a bank or insurance company.

From an external perspective, we are unlikely to know a financial institution's risk capital per business unit. Indeed, we may not know whether a bank or insurer overall has excess (or insufficient) risk capital. Therefore, when valuing an entire bank or insurance company from the outside in, we make the assumption that the amount of risk capital employed by the company is essentially equal to the book value of its equity.

Forecasting equity cash flows   When we use book equity, how do we forecast how much equity a company will need? For industrial companies, the key drivers of value are growth and return on capital (relative to the cost of capital). For financial companies, the key drivers are growth and return on equity. At a high level, we can say that growth and ROE drive equity cash flow.

To forecast equity cash flow, begin by forecasting the company's income statement and balance sheet. We typically forecast equity in relation to other balance sheet items, such as total assets. The equity cash flow then flows from these statements. (You can either explicitly estimate the dividends as part of this forecast or simply forecast overall equity cash flow.) This approach ensures that you understand how the income statement, balance sheet, cash flows, and return on equity interact and drive the value of the company. If you make an explicit forecast of dividends and then solve

Exhibit 25.2 ABC Bank: Check of Equity Cash Flow

$ million

Net income	1,678	1,823
Other comprehensive income	66	(11)
Change in assets		
Cash	(251)	669
Federal funds/repos	(189)	126
Investments	(3,032)	4,791
Net loans	(5,859)	(17,801)
Property, plant and equipment	(41)	45
Goodwill	(66)	(182)
Other assets	(2,805)	999
Total change in assets	**(12,244)**	**(11,353)**
Change in liabilities		
Deposits	8,721	9,003
Short-term debt	(1,275)	(2,584)
Other liabilities	584	(1,087)
Long-term debt	3,301	4,801
Total change in liabilities	**11,330**	**10,133**
Equity cash flow	**831**	**592**

for the rest of the balance sheet, you may inadvertently change the company's capital structure, leading to excess capital or excessive leverage.

From a pure accounting perspective, you can calculate changes in equity by considering overall changes in the balance sheet. In the course of its operations, a financial institution will increase or decrease both its assets and its liabilities. For example, a bank's loans, securities holdings, deposits, and debt will all change over the course of a year. Because the balance sheet must balance, you can infer the changes in equity from the changes in assets and liabilities. By itself this perspective is not particularly insightful, but it is useful as a check when you build cash flow forecasts. Exhibit 25.2 provides an example using the same financials as the previous exhibit.

Accounting issues that may affect your calculations   Goodwill is an important accounting issue in the valuation of financial institutions. Just as with industrial companies, calculate ROE before and after goodwill to understand the underlying economics of the company versus its performance as an acquirer. To estimate ROE without goodwill, add any goodwill amortization to net income for the numerator. Subtract goodwill from equity for the denominator. Exhibit 25.3 on page 686 shows how great an impact goodwill can have on ROE. Insurer A buys Insurer B for a $7.5 billion premium

Exhibit 25.3 Impact of Goodwill on ROE

$ million, percent

	Insurer A	Insurer B	Acquisition impact	Interim pro forma
Net income	519	627	–	1,145
Tangible assets	6,878	8,498	–	15,376
Goodwill	2,455	2,193	7,513	12,161
Total assets	9,333	10,691	7,513	27,538
Miscellaneous liabilities	3,960	5,876	–	9,836
Debt	1,115	830	–	1,945
Equity	4,258	3,985	7,513	15,757
Total liabilities and equity	9,333	10,691	7,513	27,538
Equity excluding goodwill	1,803	1,792		3,595
RoE including goodwill	12%	16%		7%
RoE excluding goodwill	29%	35%		32%

over book value. With goodwill, the combined company's ROE is only 7 percent. Without goodwill, its ROE is 32 percent. Both perspectives are useful: The ROE without goodwill is a better indicator of the likely incremental ROE that will drive the insurer's equity cash flow and value. The ROE with goodwill indicates how much the acquiring insurer's performance must improve to compensate for the acquisition premium.

Stock options may be an important issue as well, as they may affect both the company's margin and its overall valuation. As we explained in Part Two, you should adjust a company's expenses to reflect the cost of issuing employee stock options if the company does not explicitly do so already. You should also add the value of current and forecasted future stock options to the firm's overall equity value.

You may need to make other adjustments to ROE, including adjustments for pension accounting. While these adjustments will not affect cash flow, they may provide insights into the underlying economics of the business.

Other Issues in the Equity Cash Flow Method

When using the equity cash flow method, you also need to modify the continuing-value formula and the estimation of economic profit. In doing so, remember to use the cost of equity instead of the overall weighted average cost of capital. For continuing value, we recommend using a value driver formula:

$$CV = \frac{NI \times \left(1 - \frac{g}{RONE}\right)}{(k_e - g)}$$

where CV = Continuing value

NI = Net income in the first year after the explicit forecast ends

g = Net income growth in the continuing-value period

RONE = Incremental return on new equity in the continuing-value period

k_e = Cost of equity

This formula is analogous to the value driver formula used in Chapter 9 on continuing value.

Keep in mind two important considerations when you apply this formula. First you should adjust net income by adding back goodwill amortization (similar to the way NOPLAT is calculated before goodwill amortization). Second you should compare the return on incremental equity for the continuing value with ROE before goodwill. In other words, if you believe that the return on incremental equity should equal the ROE in the explicit forecast period, use the ROE before goodwill as a proxy for the bank's underlying economics.

For guidance on calculating the cost of equity, see Chapter 10 on the cost of capital. We do not recommend adjusting betas for different leverage levels for financial institutions.[2]

As with industrial companies, we can make good use of an economic profit calculation to understand whether a financial institution is creating or destroying value in any given year. We can calculate it in two ways:

$$\text{Economic Profit} = \text{Equity} \times (\text{ROE} - k_e)$$

or

$$\text{Economic Profit} = \text{Net Income} - (\text{Equity} \times k_e)$$

Just as you can value a nonfinancial company by discounting economic profit, you can also value a financial institution by discounting its economic profit, using (and discounting back) an appropriate continuing-value formula, and adding the starting equity.

---

[2] Unpublished research by McKinsey & Company also suggests that, in fact, banks' asset-liability mismatch, more than their leverage, affects the volatility of their returns.

SPECIFIC ISSUES IN VALUING BANKS

When you apply the equity cash flow approach to valuing banks, there are several issues to watch out for. This section describes some basic aspects of bank economics, discusses issues encountered in valuing banks either outside-in or inside-out, and provides an example of a bank valuation.

Basic Bank Economics

Banks make money in several ways, including lending activities and fees for services rendered. The most important income categories are net interest income and fee (or noninterest) income.

Net interest income is the difference between the interest income a bank earns from lending and the interest expense it pays to borrow funds. This seemingly straightforward item actually contains two separate components: One is a true customer spread—lending out funds at a higher rate of interest than the bank pays—which is value-creating. The other component is maturity mismatch income, which arises when a bank's assets have a different duration than its liabilities have, and the bank earns a spread from being on different parts of the yield curve. Mismatch profits are difficult to sustain and are typically not value-creating when the risk of taking positions on their yield curve is taken into account. (With perfect information, you would remove mismatch profits from forecasts of net interest income, but this information is difficult to obtain.)

Often analysts will speak of the "income" or the "spread" model for calculating net interest income. The two methods are actually equivalent. The income method (shown in Exhibit 25.4, for a hypothetical bank) subtracts interest expense from interest income, then subtracts other expenses and

Exhibit 25.4 XYZ Bank: Income Model

$ million

Balance sheet		Income statement	
Assets			
Cash	120	Interest income (12% × 933)	112
Loans	933	Interest expense (5% × $1,000)	(50)
Total assets	1,053	Other expenses	(48)
		Net profit before tax	14
Liabilities		Taxes at 40 percent	(6)
Deposits	1,000	Net income	8
Equity	53		
Total liabilities and equities	1,053		

Exhibit 25.5 XYZ Bank: Spread Model

$ million

Definition	Calculation	
(Spread on loans) × (loan balance)	(12% − 8%) × ($933)	37
+ (Spread on deposits) × (deposit balance)	+ (8% − 5%) × ($1,000)	30
+ (Equity credit rate) × (equity)	+ (8%) × ($53)	4
− (Opportunity cost) × (cash)	− (8%) × ($120)	(10)
− Expenses		(48)
= Net profit before tax		14
− Taxes at 40%		(6)
Net income		**8**

taxes as well and arrives at net income of $8 million. The spread method (in Exhibit 25.5) arrives at the same answer but along the way shows where the bank earns its profits (lending versus deposit taking). In this example, assume that the funds provided by the deposit-taking activities of the bank (which pays customers 5 percent) are lent to the wholesale bank at an opportunity cost of 8 percent; the wholesale bank then lends them to customers at an external rate of 12 percent. The bank earns a spread of 4 percent on its loans, generating $37 million of income. It earns a spread of 3 percent on its deposits for $30 million of income. However, its nonearning cash held as a cushion against risk has an opportunity cost of $10 million. Finally, its equity balance doesn't have any accounting cost (though it does have an opportunity cost), generating $4 million of income. After we deduct operating expenses, net income is $8 million, the same as with the income method. The income method is easier to use outside-in, while the spread method can be helpful for determining true value creation by different parts of the bank.

Fee income is revenue from services provided to customers, whether in retail banking, private banking services, M&A, or asset management. Fee income is usually easier to understand than net interest income, as it is financing independent.

Banks may also derive income from other financial activities, such as proprietary trading or taking capital gains on their securities portfolio. These sources of income are often highly volatile.

On the cost side, two cost categories are significant. One major cost is the provision for loan losses. Clearly, an important value driver for any bank is how many of its loans are repaid on a timely basis. However, it is difficult for an outsider to really understand the quality of a bank's loan portfolio; at best you can only make estimates of future loan losses. The other major cost category is noninterest expenses, which include selling, general, and administrative expenses. These costs are typically easier to understand and forecast from the outside in.

On the balance sheet, banks' major assets are typically their loan portfolio and their portfolio of securities and cash. Usually, fixed assets and working capital are only a small portion of the balance sheet total. The major liabilities are usually deposits, debt, and equities.

Valuing Banks from the Outside In

In building a cash flow model of a bank from the outside in, we must make several simplifications. We cannot truly understand the contribution of mismatch profits to overall net interest income, the quality of the loan portfolio, or whether the company has excess equity. However, given these shortcomings, we can still use an equity cash flow model to understand a company's economics and prospects.

We have created a disguised example based on a major U.S. retail bank, which we'll call Big Bank. Our goal is to illustrate the various steps in the estimation of a bank's value, not to create a highly detailed forecast (although our model does closely approximate the market capitalization of Big Bank as of the time of writing). We have created a full income statement and balance sheet, along with an abbreviated schedule of changes in shareholders' equity, which then lead to the equity cash flow. We have also used publicly available Federal Deposit Insurance Corporation (FDIC) information about risk-weighted assets and Tier 1 capital (equity and other capital that provides the most cushion for depositors and creditors) so that we can incorporate some estimates of capital adequacy.

Looking at Big Bank's historical performance, we see that over the past several years it has generally done well. Revenues increased by 16 percent and net income grew by 35 percent per year from 2001 to 2003. Expense control may be an issue, as the efficiency ratio (the ratio of noninterest expense to total revenue) has risen over the past few years from 58 percent to 60 percent. Nonetheless, Big Bank has been creating value vigorously; its return on equity (including goodwill) in 2003 was 19 percent, well above its 8.4 percent cost of equity. Its ROE, excluding goodwill, was even higher, at 28 percent. (Our hypothesis is that Big Bank is holding little, if any, excess risk capital, so we believe these ROE numbers are an accurate reflection of the bank's underlying operating performance.)

Exhibits 25.6 to 25.8 provide our forecast for Big Bank. On a high level, our approach is as follows:

- For income statement items (see Exhibit 25.6), we estimate interest income and interest expense by forecasting margins on future amounts of loans and deposits. We also forecast future levels of loan

Exhibit 25.6 Big Bank: Historical and Forecast Income Statement

$ million

	Historical			Forecast										2014 (CV)
	2001	2002	2003	2004	2005	2006	2007	2008	2009	2010	2011	2012	2013	
Interest on loans	8,222	7,674	8,198	8,453	8,741	9,039	9,349	9,670	10,002	10,347	10,704	11,075	11,459	11,858
Interest on investments held for sale	2,621	3,015	3,061	3,054	3,158	3,265	3,377	3,493	3,613	3,738	3,867	4,001	4,140	4,284
Other interest income	167	169	164	168	173	179	184	190	195	201	207	213	220	226
Total interest income	**11,010**	**10,858**	**11,422**	**11,675**	**12,072**	**12,483**	**12,910**	**13,352**	**13,811**	**14,286**	**14,778**	**15,289**	**15,818**	**16,367**
Interest on deposits	(2,090)	(1,129)	(949)	(1,150)	(1,196)	(1,244)	(1,294)	(1,346)	(1,399)	(1,455)	(1,514)	(1,574)	(1,637)	(1,703)
Interest on short-term borrowings	(749)	(315)	(189)	(140)	(184)	(190)	(197)	(203)	(210)	(218)	(225)	(233)	(241)	(249)
Interest on long-term debt	(1,126)	(895)	(868)	(1,100)	(1,100)	(1,133)	(1,184)	(1,234)	(1,287)	(1,342)	(1,398)	(1,457)	(1,518)	(1,581)
Total interest expense	**(3,965)**	**(2,339)**	**(2,006)**	**(2,390)**	**(2,481)**	**(2,568)**	**(2,674)**	**(2,783)**	**(2,897)**	**(3,015)**	**(3,137)**	**(3,264)**	**(3,396)**	**(3,533)**
Net interest income	7,045	8,519	9,416	9,285	9,591	9,916	10,236	10,569	10,914	11,271	11,641	12,025	12,422	12,834
Provision for loan losses	(1,016)	(991)	(1,013)	(1,112)	(1,150)	(1,189)	(1,230)	(1,272)	(1,316)	(1,361)	(1,409)	(1,457)	(1,508)	(1,560)
Net interest income after provision for loan losses	**6,029**	**7,529**	**8,403**	**8,172**	**8,441**	**8,726**	**9,005**	**9,297**	**9,597**	**9,910**	**10,233**	**10,568**	**10,914**	**11,274**
Fee income	6,016	6,354	7,249	7,503	7,765	8,037	8,318	8,609	8,911	9,223	9,545	9,879	10,225	10,583
Capital gains (losses)	(719)	(20)	35	-										
Total noninterest income	**5,297**	**6,334**	**7,284**	**7,503**	**7,765**	**8,037**	**8,318**	**8,609**	**8,911**	**9,223**	**9,545**	**9,879**	**10,225**	**10,583**
Total noninterest expense	(8,114)	(8,654)	(10,112)	(10,165)	(10,509)	(10,871)	(11,234)	(11,613)	(12,004)	(12,409)	(12,829)	(13,263)	(13,713)	(14,179)
Net income before income taxes	**3,212**	**5,209**	**5,575**	**5,510**	**5,697**	**5,893**	**6,089**	**6,293**	**6,504**	**6,723**	**6,949**	**7,184**	**7,426**	**7,678**
Income taxes	(1,205)	(1,849)	(1,926)	(1,929)	(1,994)	(2,062)	(2,131)	(2,203)	(2,277)	(2,353)	(2,432)	(2,514)	(2,599)	(2,687)
Net income before preferred dividends	**2,007**	**3,359**	**3,648**	**3,582**	**3,703**	**3,830**	**3,958**	**4,091**	**4,228**	**4,370**	**4,517**	**4,669**	**4,827**	**4,990**
Preferred dividends	(8)	(2)	(2)	(2)	(2)	(2)	(2)	(2)	(2)	(2)	(2)	(2)	(2)	(2)
Net income applicable to common stock	**1,999**	**3,357**	**3,647**	**3,580**	**3,701**	**3,829**	**3,956**	**4,089**	**4,226**	**4,368**	**4,515**	**4,668**	**4,825**	**4,989**
Dividends paid to common stock	(1,006)	(1,102)	(1,486)	(2,445)	(3,180)	(3,288)	(3,396)	(3,508)	(3,624)	(3,744)	(3,868)	(3,996)	(4,129)	(4,267)
Memo: total revenue	**12,342**	**14,853**	**16,700**	**16,787**	**17,356**	**17,953**	**18,554**	**19,179**	**19,824**	**20,494**	**21,186**	**21,904**	**22,647**	**23,417**

loss provisions, non-interest expense, and income taxes on a percentage basis (of loans, revenues, and pretax income, respectively). We forecast future capital gains—which relate to the bank's relatively small trading portfolio of securities held for sale—at zero, because they are immaterial. If the bank relied on its trading portfolio for a significant portion of income, we would need to estimate the returns on its trading activities.

- On the balance sheet (see Exhibit 25.7), we use our forecast of deposit growth as a driver; then we forecast the ratio of loans to deposits based on historical performance. We then relate other accounts on the asset side of the balance sheet (except excess cash) to either loans or deposits.

- On the liability side, we forecast a stable capital structure, so we have chosen to forecast the required level of equity each year through a rough estimate of the ratio of risk-weighted assets to Tier 1 capital (using numbers from the FDIC), as detailed in Exhibit 25.8 on page 694. Going forward, using the historical ratio of risk-weighted assets to total loans, we forecast the amount of risk-weighted assets. We then set the ratio of Tier 1 capital to risk-weighted assets at 8 percent (the regulatory minimum) to derive the needed amount of Tier 1 capital. Adding goodwill to the required Tier 1 capital then gives us the required amount of total shareholders' equity. We balance each year's statement of changes in equity by adjusting payouts to or from shareholders, in the form of dividends, share buybacks, or share issuances. Given the level of equity and assets for each year, we can balance the balance sheet each year either by adding debt or by adding excess cash.

- To check on how plausible our forecasts are, we calculate a number of output ratios, shown in Exhibit 25.9 on page 695. These include growth in revenues and net income, ratios between different balance sheet items, and returns on assets and equity. For example, in this particular model the forecast for ROE including goodwill is 17 percent to 18 percent, and ROE excluding goodwill is about 24 percent, which is in line with recent past performance. Revenues and net income grow at 3.4 percent, which is lower than some previous years' performance but in line with our hypothesis that Big Bank's organic growth will lag nominal GDP growth of 4.5 percent to 5.0 percent.

- To complete the valuation, as shown in Exhibit 25.10 on page 696, we compute equity cash flows and a continuing value using the formula described earlier in this chapter. Then, using our CAPM-derived cost of equity of 8.4 percent, we discount the cash flows and the continuing value to arrive at an equity value for the company.

Exhibit 25.7 Big Bank: Historical and Forecast Balance Sheet

$ million	Historical 2001	2002	2003	Forecast 2004	2005	2006	2007	2008	2009	2010	2011	2012	2013	2014
Assets														
Cash and due from banks	9,981	10,482	9,145	11,014	11,389	11,778	12,181	12,599	13,033	13,482	13,948	14,431	14,931	15,450
Excess marketable securities				390										
Federal funds sold and repos	1,488	1,867	1,615	1,936	2,002	2,071	2,142	2,215	2,291	2,370	2,452	2,537	2,625	2,716
Investments held for sale	44,387	50,451	40,869	50,892	52,626	54,424	56,287	58,218	60,220	62,296	64,448	66,679	68,993	71,392
Loans	101,470	113,222	148,866	143,025	147,898	152,949	158,185	163,613	169,239	175,073	181,120	187,391	193,893	200,636
Allowance for loan losses	(2,212)	(2,246)	(2,289)	(2,145)	(2,218)	(2,294)	(2,373)	(2,454)	(2,539)	(2,626)	(2,717)	(2,811)	(2,908)	(3,010)
Net loans	99,258	110,976	146,578	140,880	145,680	150,655	155,812	161,158	166,701	172,446	178,404	184,580	190,985	197,626
Premises and equipment, net	2,088	2,169	2,079	2,355	2,329	2,463	2,519	2,620	2,703	2,800	2,894	2,996	3,099	3,207
Goodwill	5,604	5,737	6,101	6,101	6,101	6,101	6,101	6,101	6,101	6,101	6,101	6,101	6,101	6,101
Other assets	18,117	23,728	21,731	25,233	26,092	26,984	27,907	28,865	29,857	30,887	31,954	33,060	34,207	35,396
Total assets	**180,923**	**205,410**	**228,116**	**238,801**	**246,220**	**254,475**	**262,949**	**271,776**	**280,905**	**290,381**	**300,200**	**310,383**	**320,940**	**331,888**
Liabilities														
Noninterest-bearing deposits	38,448	43,585	43,757	44,632	45,525	46,435	47,364	48,311	49,278	50,263	51,268	52,294	53,340	54,406
Interest-bearing deposits	71,708	84,013	101,847	105,921	110,158	114,564	119,147	123,913	128,869	134,024	139,385	144,960	150,759	156,789
Total deposits	**110,156**	**127,598**	**145,604**	**150,553**	**155,683**	**160,999**	**166,511**	**172,224**	**178,147**	**184,287**	**190,653**	**197,254**	**204,098**	**211,195**
Short-term borrowings	22,225	19,674	14,505	19,106	19,757	20,432	21,131	21,856	22,608	23,387	24,195	25,033	25,901	26,802
Accrued expenses and other liabilities	9,869	10,771	10,295	10,295	10,295	10,295	10,295	10,295	10,295	10,295	10,295	10,295	10,295	10,295
Existing long-term debt	22,664	29,532	37,436	37,436	37,436	37,436	37,436	37,436	37,436	37,436	37,436	37,436	37,436	37,436
Additional long-term debt					1,117	2,840	4,543	6,351	8,203	10,135	12,132	14,206	16,354	18,583
Total liabilities	**54,758**	**59,978**	**62,236**	**66,837**	**68,605**	**71,003**	**73,405**	**75,938**	**78,542**	**81,253**	**84,058**	**86,970**	**89,987**	**93,116**
Shareholders' equity														
Preferred stock	128	148	126	126	126	126	126	126	126	126	126	126	126	126
Common stock	1,702	1,702	1,702	1,702	1,702	1,702	1,702	1,702	1,702	1,702	1,702	1,702	1,702	1,702
Additional paid-in capital	5,551	5,587	5,672	5,672	5,672	5,672	5,672	5,672	5,672	5,672	5,672	5,672	5,672	5,672
Retained earnings	9,415	11,385	13,436	14,571	15,093	15,633	16,194	16,775	17,377	18,001	18,649	19,320	20,016	20,738
Treasury stock	(1,139)	(1,450)	(1,078)	(1,078)	(1,078)	(1,078)	(1,078)	(1,078)	(1,078)	(1,078)	(1,078)	(1,078)	(1,078)	(1,078)
Cumulative other comprehensive income	442	574	552	552	552	552	552	552	552	552	552	552	552	552
Other equity accounts	(91)	(112)	(135)	(135)	(135)	(135)	(135)	(135)	(135)	(135)	(135)	(135)	(135)	(135)
Total shareholders' equity	**16,008**	**17,835**	**20,276**	**21,410**	**21,932**	**22,473**	**23,033**	**23,614**	**24,216**	**24,841**	**25,488**	**26,159**	**26,855**	**27,577**
Total liabilities and stockholders' equity	**180,923**	**205,410**	**228,116**	**238,801**	**246,220**	**254,475**	**262,949**	**271,776**	**280,905**	**290,381**	**300,200**	**310,383**	**320,940**	**331,888**

693

Exhibit 25.8 Big Bank: Changes in Equity

$ million	Historical 2001	2002	2003	Forecast 2004	2005	2006	2007	2008	2009	2010	2011	2012	2013	2014 (CV)
Estimate of risk-weighted assets														
Total risk-weighted assets	145,251	166,401	179,589	191,373	197,893	204,651	211,657	218,919	226,448	234,253	242,345	250,735	259,435	268,457
Total risk-weighted assets/total loans (percent)		147	121	134	134	134	134	134	134	134	134	134	134	134
Estimate of tier 1 capital														
Estimated tier 1 capital/total risk-weighted assets (percent)	7.2	7.3	7.9	8.0	8.0	8.0	8.0	8.0	8.0	8.0	8.0	8.0	8.0	8.0
Total shareholders' equity (prior to any new share issuance)	16,008	17,835	20,276											
Goodwill	(5,604)	(5,737)	(6,101)											
Rough estimate tier 1 capital	10,404	12,098	14,175											
Reported tier 1 capital	10,734	12,654	15,120											
Difference	329	556	945											
Forecast tier 1 capital				15,310	15,831	16,372	16,933	17,514	18,116	18,740	19,388	20,059	20,755	21,477
Goodwill				6,101	6,101	6,101	6,101	6,101	6,101	6,101	6,101	6,101	6,101	6,101
Implied total shareholders' equity				21,410	21,932	22,473	23,033	23,614	24,216	24,841	25,488	26,159	26,855	27,577
Forecast changes in equity														
End-of-year equity implied by target tier 1 ratio				21,410	21,932	22,473	23,033	23,614	24,216	24,841	25,488	26,159	26,855	27,577
Components of equity other than retained earnings				(6,839)	(6,839)	(6,839)	(6,839)	(6,839)	(6,839)	(6,839)	(6,839)	(6,839)	(6,839)	(6,839)
Forecast end-of-year retained earnings				14,571	15,093	15,633	16,194	16,775	17,377	18,001	18,649	19,320	20,016	20,738
Start of year retained earnings		9,415	11,385	13,436	14,571	15,093	15,633	16,194	16,775	17,377	18,001	18,649	19,320	20,016
Net income before preferred dividends		3,359	3,648	3,582	3,703	3,830	3,958	4,091	4,228	4,370	4,517	4,669	4,827	4,990
Preferred dividends		(2)	(2)	(2)	(2)	(2)	(2)	(2)	(2)	(2)	(2)	(2)	(2)	(2)
Common dividends		(1,102)	(1,486)	(2,445)	(3,180)	(3,288)	(3,396)	(3,508)	(3,624)	(3,744)	(3,868)	(3,996)	(4,129)	(4,267)
Other (share issuances or repurchases)		(167)	(64)											
End of year retained earnings		11,385	13,436	14,571	15,093	15,633	16,194	16,775	17,377	18,001	18,649	19,320	20,016	20,738

Exhibit 25.9 Big Bank: Output Ratios

percent

	Historical 2002	2003	Forecast 2004	2005	2006	2007	2008	2009	2010	2011	2012	2013	2014 (CV)
Growth in total revenue	20.3	12.4	0.5	3.4	3.4	3.3	3.4	3.4	3.4	3.4	3.4	3.4	3.4
Growth in net income	67.4	8.6	(1.8)	3.4	3.4	3.3	3.4	3.4	3.4	3.4	3.4	3.4	3.4
Noninterest income/revenue	42.8	43.4	44.7	44.7	44.8	44.8	44.9	44.9	45.0	45.1	45.1	45.1	45.2
Loans/assets	55.1	65.3	59.9	60.1	60.1	60.2	60.2	60.2	60.3	60.3	60.4	60.4	60.5
Deposits/liabilities	212.7	234.0	225.3	226.9	226.8	226.8	226.8	226.8	226.8	226.8	226.8	226.8	226.8
Debt/equity (book)	275.9	256.2	264.1	260.8	257.5	254.3	251.1	247.9	244.9	241.8	238.8	235.8	232.9
Equity/total assets	8.7	8.9	9.0	8.9	8.8	8.8	8.7	8.6	8.6	8.5	8.4	8.4	8.3
Common dividends as a percent of net income	32.8	40.7	68.3	85.9	85.8	85.8	85.8	85.7	85.7	85.6	85.6	85.5	85.5
Return on average assets		1.7	1.5	1.5	1.5	1.5	1.5	1.5	1.5	1.5	1.5	1.5	1.5
Return on average equity (including goodwill)		19.1	17.2	17.1	17.2	17.4	17.5	17.7	17.8	17.9	18.1	18.2	18.3
Return on average equity (excluding goodwill)		27.8	24.3	23.8	23.8	23.8	23.7	23.7	23.7	23.7	23.7	23.6	23.6

Exhibit 25.10 Big Bank: Cash Flows and Valuation

$ million

	Forecast 2004	2005	2006	2007	2008	2009	2010	2011	2012	2013
Equity cash flow										
Net income after preferred dividends	3,580	3,701	3,829	3,956	4,089	4,226	4,368	4,515	4,668	4,825
Other comprehensive income	–	–	–	–	–	–	–	–	–	–
Changes in equity	(1,135)	(522)	(541)	(560)	(581)	(602)	(624)	(647)	(671)	(696)
Equity cash flow	2,445	3,180	3,288	3,396	3,508	3,624	3,744	3,868	3,996	4,129
Check of equity cash flow										
Common dividends	2,445	3,180	3,288	3,396	3,508	3,624	3,744	3,868	3,996	4,129
Share repurchases (or issuances)	–	–	–	–	–	–	–	–	–	–
Check of equity cash flow	2,445	3,180	3,288	3,396	3,508	3,624	3,744	3,868	3,996	4,129

Year	Equity cash flow	Discount factor (8.4%)	Discounted cash flow
2004	2,445	0.923	2,256
2005	3,180	0.851	2,706
2006	3,288	0.785	2,581
2007	3,396	0.724	2,459
2008	3,508	0.668	2,344
2009	3,624	0.616	2,233
2010	3,744	0.569	2,129
2011	3,868	0.525	2,029
2012	3,996	0.484	1,934
2013	4,129	0.446	1,843
Continuing value[1]	87,557	0.446	39,084
Equity value			**61,598**

[1]Continuing value assumptions: growth = 3.5%, return in incremental equity = 25%.

- Finally, to check our overall valuation, we also calculate an annual economic profit forecast and economic profit continuing value. Discounting these items to the present and adding the initial level of equity, we arrive at the same value as our equity cash flow model.

Our main finding from this analysis is that a forecast that estimates top-line revenue growing at somewhat less than nominal GDP growth and that maintains (or slightly raises) the overall return on equity of Big Bank can explain Big Bank's market capitalization today. Our valuation gives us a forward price-to-earnings multiple of 17.1 and market value-to-equity book value of 3.0, which are both higher than peers as of this writing. These multiples reflect the higher than average spread that Big Bank earns versus its cost of equity.

Valuing Banks from the Inside

A valuation with inside information about a bank can be much more detailed. In particular, we can understand two aspects of the bank better: the true value creation in its lending and borrowing activities (and thus the mismatch profit, if any), and the contribution of each of the bank's businesses to value creation.

To understand true value creation in lending, consider the bank as consisting of a retail bank, a wholesale bank, and a treasury (see Exhibit 25.11). The retail bank collects deposits, which provide funds that it can in turn lend to the treasury. The treasury lends funds to the wholesale bank, which in turn lends them to external customers. Conceptualizing these funds transfers as a series of internal loans requires us to set a transfer price at each step of the way, which is important in understanding the true profitability of each unit.

Exhibit 25.11 Business Unit Structure of Banks

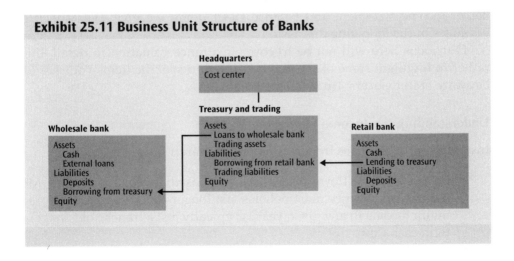

More broadly, an insider's view of the bank helps us understand which business units create and which destroy value. The crucial prerequisite is the allocation of risk capital per business, which very few companies publish. With this information, we can understand RAROC, or the ratio of net profit to economic capital in any given business unit, the key metric used by many banks today to assess their performance.

Risk capital information can also help us determine whether the bank as a whole has excess capital. In such cases, we typically adjust the year 1 cash flows such that the bank will pay out the excess.

SPECIFIC ISSUES FOR INSURANCE COMPANIES

Like banks, insurance companies are among the most challenging companies to value. While the three main types of insurance companies—life, property and casualty, and reinsurance—differ in the kinds of risk they insure, they share certain complexities for financial analysis.

As with banks, understanding the insurance business depends on properly assessing risk. From the outside looking in, it is difficult to know how much capital an insurer needs to hold in order to ensure that it can meet unexpected claims. Insurers themselves employ actuaries and risk management experts, while ratings agencies and regulators provide outside scrutiny. As a financial analyst looking in from outside, you will likely have only imperfect information about an insurer's capital.

Another source of complexity more specific to insurers is that insurers' cash flows extend over long periods of time. As a result it can be difficult to match revenues and expenses to understand a company's true profitability. To deal with this issue, the insurance industry in the United States uses two different accounting methods: GAAP, which is used for reporting to the SEC, and statutory accounting, which is used for reporting to state insurance regulators. As a result, there are differences in the treatment of a number of income statement and balance sheet items; we give some specific examples in the following discussion.

Our focus here will not be to cover insurance valuation in detail, but rather to highlight some of the major issues and specific items you should be aware of in insurers' financial statements.

Understanding the Income Statement

Insurers derive revenues from a number of different sources:

- *Premium income* flows from the payments that customers make for their policies. Since most policies last longer than one year, the premium income in any given year is typically just a tranche of a longer-term cash flow.

- There is a time lag between when customers pay premiums and when insurers must pay out any benefits and claims. During this period, insurers invest the funds received from their customers and derive *investment income* in the form of interest or dividends. Like banking, insurance is essentially a "spread" business, where the insurer seeks to earn profits from the spread between investment returns and its sources of funding.

- Insurers can also *realize capital gains* (or losses) on their investment portfolio. In terms of the company's fundamental economics, it should make no difference whether the company realizes these gains (or losses) in any given year (with the exception of possible tax consequences). However, this decision can significantly affect a company's reported net income in any given year.

- Finally, many life insurers aspire to sell customers a broader range of investment products. When they sell these products, they derive *fee income* (for example, asset management fees on mutual funds or similar products).

On the cost side, insurers have several industry-specific items you should be aware of, as well as operating costs similar to those of any company:

- One unique item is the *cost of reinsurance,* which occurs when an insurer transfers the underlying risk of a policy to a reinsurer. Insurers generally net this cost against premiums rather than report it as a separate item.

- *Benefits and claims* are typically a very large expense. Depending on the type of product sold, these items may be labeled as "benefits and claims," "interest credited to policyholders," "dividends payable to policyholders," or similar items. In property and casualty insurance, the ratio of benefits and claims to premiums is called the loss ratio.

- *Commissions and other policy acquisition costs* are the costs incurred to sell policies to customers. Commissions are typically paid when the policy is sold, even though the policy is expected to generate premiums for several years, creating an accounting dilemma about when to record commissions incurred as an expense. The two accounting systems used for insurers in the United States take different approaches to these questions, based on their underlying goals:

  —GAAP accounting seeks to match revenues and expenses as closely as possible over time. Since an insurance policy is likely to bring in premium income over multiple years, GAAP states that the costs associated with selling the policy to the customer in the first place should be spread over the expected life of the policy.

Thus, companies capitalize these costs and put them on their balance sheet as an asset called "deferred (policy) acquisition costs" (sometimes shortened to "DAC asset"). In each subsequent year, companies recognize an expense called "amortization of deferred (policy) acquisition costs," which represents each year's tranche of the costs associated with the premiums recognized that year, and the DAC asset is reduced accordingly. Unlike goodwill amortization, the amortization of deferred policy acquisition costs represents a real economic expense for the insurance company, where the cash costs of commissions and so on, are spread over time.

—Because statutory accounting has different overriding principles than GAAP accounting, it treats DAC costs differently. Statutory accounting focuses on the financial strength of an insurer and its policyholders. Thus, it tends to treat many items on a cash basis, in contrast to the accrual basis of GAAP accounting. In particular, statutory accounting requires that an insurer expense all its commission costs in the year that they are incurred, and does not allow companies to create a DAC asset.

- Insurance companies also incur other expenses typical of any company, such as selling, general, and administrative expenses.

Insurers refer to the ratio of total costs (including benefits or claims and all operating expenses) to premium revenues as the combined ratio. The combined ratio for many insurance companies exceeds 100 (all costs exceed premiums). These insurance companies stay in business and earn returns on equity by investing the premiums they receive to make up for their underwriting losses. The best-performing insurers, however, try to maintain discipline in their underwriting performance.

Understanding the Balance Sheet

The asset side of an insurance company's balance sheet is typically weighted heavily to a few items:

- *Investments* predominate on the asset side of an insurance company balance sheet. Companies typically provide a breakdown of the kind of assets they invest in (fixed income, equity, or alternatives). Under GAAP accounting, equity and debt securities are both on the balance sheet at fair value; under statutory accounting, debt securities and preferred stock that the insurer intends to hold to maturity are carried on the balance at historical cost (plus amortization or any premium or discount to face value).

- Another large asset on the books of many life insurers is called "separate account" assets. These represent funds entrusted to the insurance company to invest on behalf of their customers (for instance, in mutual funds). These assets are exactly counterbalanced by separate account liabilities, as the insurer has no claim on the underlying assets.

- Under GAAP accounting, insurers may have a *deferred policy acquisition cost asset,* as described with the income statement items.

- Insurers also may have a number of "typical" assets on their books, such as working capital, fixed assets, and goodwill. However, even here, GAAP and statutory accounting may vary. Statutory accounting requires that certain kinds of assets (such as furniture and equipment) be written off against surplus. This treatment is in line with the general conservatism of statutory accounting; it treats these purchases as cash expenses, not as longer-term investments for the company.

The liability side of the balance sheet has a number of items to note as well:

- The largest liability for any insurer is its *reserves.* These represent the present value of expected benefits and claims to be paid out (less the present value of expected premiums for life insurers). Insurers use actuarial guidelines to estimate the size of reserves, taking into account such factors as underlying customer risks, persistence (rate of renewals), investment returns, and inflation. Companies must use a certain amount of judgment in estimating their reserves, and publicly traded companies' shares often react negatively when insurers announce that they must increase reserves, an action taken as a sign that management previously lacked caution. Also, reserve requirements under statutory accounting generally are more stringent than those under GAAP accounting.

- Insurers also have *debt and equity financing.* Debt is straightforward, as the balance sheet amounts and related notes are generally self-explanatory. Equity, however, can be somewhat more complicated. As for banks, under GAAP accounting, equity can be affected by pension accounting, foreign-currency translation, and other items. Under statutory accounting, equity reported on the balance sheet (generally referred to as surplus) may be very different from the equity reported under GAAP, as this account is affected by various differences in accounting policies (for example, differences in valuing fixed income investments, recognition of policy acquisition costs, and acquisition of fixed assets).

Implications for Valuation

Despite the inherent complexities of insurance companies and the long list of accounting issues, it is still possible to do an informative valuation of an insurer. We have prepared a disguised example of a large U.S. life insurance company, which we refer to as Acme, as captured in Exhibits 25.12 to 25.16. We used the following approach:

- For the income statement (see Exhibit 25.12), we forecast growth in premium and fee income as our main drivers. Investment income is based on growth in investments (as detailed in the discussion of the balance sheet that follows) and a forecast investment yield. For Acme, we estimate that over the long run, the growth in each of these items will be 4.5 percent (within the range of nominal GDP growth forecasts in the United States).

- On the expense side, we forecast benefits and claims as a percentage of premium and fee income equal to 130 percent, thus keeping the overall profitability stable. We also forecast stable rates of additions to and amortization of deferred acquisition costs.

- For the balance sheet (see Exhibit 25.13 on p. 704), we project that investments will grow in line with overall premium and fee income, and that reserves in turn will grow in line with investments. This last assumption is a simplification, because the actual sensitivity of reserves to premiums may be low, depending on the life span (also known as the "tail") of the business; however, this is our best outside-in assumption. In Exhibit 25.14 on page 705, we balance the balance sheet by assuming a target level of equity to assets (to approximate solvency) and then solving the statement of changes in equity accordingly, with dividends, share buybacks, or issuances as a plug.

The resulting return on equity for Acme is 10.5 percent including goodwill and 11.5 percent excluding goodwill (see Exhibit 25.15 on p. 706). These returns on equity are in line with our hypothesis that Acme's economics are unlikely to change over the forecast period.

While Acme has reasonable growth, its return on equity is disappointing as it is close to Acme's 10.5 percent cost of equity. This indicates that Acme is not generating much value for its shareholders.

To forecast the cash flow (see Exhibit 25.16 on p. 707), we use our general formula: Net Income + Other Comprehensive Income − Changes in Equity. The other comprehensive income is especially important here, as it captures the company's unrealized capital gains. From an economic perspective, capital gains (or losses) are a cash flow item, whether or not they are realized. However, since U.S. accounting strictly segregates realized

Exhibit 25.12 Acme Insurance: Income Statement

$ million

| | Historical | | | Forecast | | | | | | | | | |
	2001	2002	2003	2004	2005	2006	2007	2008	2009	2010	2011	2012	2013	2014
Fee income	2,344	2,365	2,592	2,708	2,830	2,957	3,091	3,230	3,375	3,527	3,686	3,851	4,025	4,206
Premium income	578	695	980	1,024	1,070	1,119	1,169	1,222	1,277	1,334	1,394	1,457	1,522	1,591
Net investment income	3,995	4,413	5,137	5,336	5,576	5,827	6,089	6,363	6,650	6,949	7,262	7,589	7,930	8,287
Net realized gains (losses)	(30)	(203)	(196)	–	–	–	–	–	–	–	–	–	–	–
Other	176	291	538	563	588	614	642	671	701	733	766	800	836	874
Total revenues	**7,062**	**7,562**	**9,051**	**9,631**	**10,065**	**10,518**	**10,991**	**11,486**	**12,003**	**12,543**	**13,107**	**13,697**	**14,313**	**14,957**
Benefits and claims	(3,612)	(3,942)	(4,719)	(4,870)	(5,089)	(5,318)	(5,557)	(5,807)	(6,069)	(6,342)	(6,627)	(6,925)	(7,237)	(7,563)
Interest expense	(126)	(177)	(221)	(297)	(299)	(300)	(302)	(304)	(305)	(307)	(309)	(311)	(312)	(314)
Amortization of deferred acquisitions costs (DAC)	(801)	(1,560)	(919)	(1,011)	(1,100)	(1,188)	(1,274)	(1,361)	(1,447)	(1,534)	(1,621)	(1,711)	(1,802)	(1,895)
Other operating expenses	(1,217)	(1,541)	(1,895)	(1,926)	(2,013)	(2,104)	(2,198)	(2,297)	(2,401)	(2,509)	(2,621)	(2,739)	(2,863)	(2,991)
Total benefits and expenses	**(5,755)**	**(7,220)**	**(7,754)**	**(8,104)**	**(8,501)**	**(8,910)**	**(9,332)**	**(9,769)**	**(10,221)**	**(10,691)**	**(11,179)**	**(11,686)**	**(12,214)**	**(12,764)**
Income from continuing operations before tax	1,307	342	1,298	1,528	1,564	1,608	1,659	1,717	1,781	1,852	1,929	2,011	2,099	2,194
Income tax	(331)	17	(275)	(382)	(391)	(402)	(415)	(429)	(445)	(463)	(482)	(503)	(525)	(548)
Income from continuing operations after tax	976	359	1,023	1,146	1,173	1,206	1,244	1,288	1,336	1,389	1,446	1,508	1,575	1,645
Nonrecurring items	(26)	8	(1)	–	–	–	–	–	–	–	–	–	–	–
Net income	**949**	**367**	**1,022**	**1,146**	**1,173**	**1,206**	**1,244**	**1,288**	**1,336**	**1,389**	**1,446**	**1,508**	**1,575**	**1,645**

Exhibit 25.13 Acme Insurance: Balance Sheet

$ million

| | Historical | | Forecast | | | | | | | | | | |
	2002	2003	2004	2005	2006	2007	2008	2009	2010	2011	2012	2013	2014
Investments	90,005	99,215	106,723	111,526	116,545	121,789	127,270	132,997	138,982	145,236	151,771	158,601	165,738
Deferred policy acquisition costs	6,962	7,659	8,336	9,001	9,656	10,309	10,962	11,619	12,284	12,961	13,651	14,359	15,086
Goodwill	1,054	1,056	1,056	1,056	1,056	1,056	1,056	1,056	1,056	1,056	1,056	1,056	1,056
Other assets	4,658	6,074	6,463	6,754	7,058	7,376	7,708	8,054	8,417	8,796	9,191	9,605	10,037
Separate account assets	115,801	140,156	144,361	148,692	153,153	157,747	162,480	167,354	172,375	177,546	182,872	188,359	194,009
Total assets	**218,479**	**254,160**	**266,940**	**277,028**	**287,468**	**298,277**	**309,475**	**321,080**	**333,113**	**345,594**	**358,542**	**371,979**	**385,926**
Policy reserves	83,431	91,973	98,934	103,386	108,038	112,900	117,980	123,290	128,838	134,635	140,694	147,025	153,641
Short-term debt	6	472	496	515	534	554	575	597	619	642	666	691	717
Existing long-term debt	2,754	3,233	3,233	3,233	3,233	3,233	3,233	3,233	3,233	3,233	3,233	3,233	3,233
Additional long-term debt			182	660	1,125	1,582	2,035	2,487	2,943	3,404	3,873	4,353	4,847
Other liabilities	7,576	8,315	8,847	9,245	9,661	10,096	10,551	11,025	11,522	12,040	12,582	13,148	13,740
Liabilities related to separate accounts	115,801	140,156	144,361	148,692	153,153	157,747	162,480	167,354	172,375	177,546	182,872	188,359	194,009
Total liabilities	**209,569**	**244,149**	**256,053**	**265,730**	**275,744**	**286,112**	**296,853**	**307,986**	**319,528**	**331,500**	**343,920**	**356,809**	**370,187**
Shareholders' equity	8,910	10,011	10,887	11,298	11,724	12,165	12,621	13,095	13,585	14,094	14,622	15,170	15,739
Total liabilities and equity	**218,479**	**254,160**	**266,940**	**277,028**	**287,468**	**298,277**	**309,475**	**321,080**	**333,113**	**345,594**	**358,542**	**371,979**	**385,926**

Exhibit 25.14 Acme Insurance: Changes in Equity

$ million

	Historical 2001	2002	2003	Forecast 2004	2005	2006	2007	2008	2009	2010	2011	2012	2013	2014
Target end-of-year equity (based on equity/assets ratio)				10,887	11,298	11,724	12,165	12,621	13,095	13,585	14,094	14,622	15,170	15,739
Start-of-year equity				(10,011)	(10,887)	(11,298)	(11,724)	(12,165)	(12,621)	(13,095)	(13,585)	(14,094)	(14,622)	(15,170)
Forecast change in equity				**876**	**411**	**426**	**441**	**457**	**473**	**491**	**509**	**528**	**548**	**569**
Net income	949	332	915	1,146	1,173	1,206	1,244	1,288	1,336	1,389	1,446	1,508	1,575	1,645
Net unrealized gains (losses) on securities	226	430	305	328	343	358	374	391	409	427	446	466	487	509
Other comprehensive income	(23)	25	(64)	—	—	—	—	—	—	—	—	—	—	—
Total comprehensive income	1,152	787	1,156	1,474	1,515	1,564	1,619	1,679	1,745	1,816	1,893	1,974	2,062	2,154
Dividends	(142)	(162)	(181)	(205)	(231)	(261)	(295)	(333)	(376)	(424)	(479)	(541)	(611)	(690)
Share issuance (buyback/plug)		1,936	—	(393)	(873)	(877)	(883)	(889)	(895)	(901)	(904)	(905)	(903)	(896)
Other	16	(260)	20	—	—	—	—	—	—	—	—	—	—	—
Total change in equity	**1,025**	**2,300**	**994**	**876**	**411**	**426**	**441**	**457**	**473**	**491**	**509**	**528**	**548**	**569**

Exhibit 25.15 Acme Insurance: Output Ratios

percent

	Historical 2002	2003	Forecast 2004	2005	2006	2007	2008	2009	2010	2011	2012	2013	2014
Growth in revenues	7.1	19.7	6.4	4.5	4.5	4.5	4.5	4.5	4.5	4.5	4.5	4.5	4.5
Growth in benefits and claims	9.2	19.7	3.2	4.5	4.5	4.5	4.5	4.5	4.5	4.5	4.5	4.5	4.5
Growth in net income	(61.4)	178.7	12.1	2.4	2.8	3.2	3.5	3.7	4.0	4.1	4.3	4.4	4.5
Net income margin	4.8	11.3	11.9	11.7	11.5	11.3	11.2	11.1	11.1	11.0	11.0	11.0	11.0
Equity/revenues	117.8	110.6	113.0	112.3	111.5	110.7	109.9	109.1	108.3	107.5	106.8	106.0	105.2
Return on average equity (including goodwill)		10.8	11.0	10.6	10.5	10.4	10.4	10.4	10.4	10.5	10.5	10.6	10.6
Return on average equity (excluding goodwill)		12.2	12.2	11.7	11.5	11.4	11.4	11.3	11.3	11.3	11.3	11.4	11.4
Total investment yield (investment income, realized and unrealized gains)	5.2	5.3	5.3	5.3	5.3	5.3	5.3	5.3	5.3	5.3	5.3	5.3	5.3

Exhibit 25.16 Acme Insurance: Cash Flows

$ million

	Historical 2002	2003	Forecast 2004	2005	2006	2007	2008	2009	2010	2011	2012	2013	2014
Net income	367	1,022	1,146	1,173	1,206	1,244	1,288	1,336	1,389	1,446	1,508	1,575	1,645
Net unrealized gains (losses) on securities	430	305	328	343	358	374	391	409	427	446	466	487	509
Other comprehensive income	25	(64)	–	–	–	–	–	–	–	–	–	–	–
Change in equity	(2,300)	(994)	(876)	(411)	(426)	(441)	(457)	(473)	(491)	(509)	(528)	(548)	(569)
Equity cash flow	(1,478)	268	597	1,104	1,138	1,178	1,222	1,271	1,325	1,384	1,446	1,514	1,586
Check of equity cash flow													
Dividends			205	231	261	295	333	376	424	479	541	611	690
Share repurchases			393	873	877	883	889	895	901	904	905	903	896
Other			–	–	–	–	–	–	–	–	–	–	–
Equity cash flow			597	1,104	1,138	1,178	1,222	1,271	1,325	1,384	1,446	1,514	1,586

Year	Equity cash flow	Discount factor (10.5%)	Discounted cash flow
2004	597	0.905	541
2005	1,104	0.819	904
2006	1,138	0.741	844
2007	1,178	0.671	790
2008	1,222	0.607	742
2009	1,271	0.549	698
2010	1,325	0.497	659
2011	1,384	0.450	622
2012	1,446	0.407	589
2013	1,514	0.368	558
Continuing value[1]	21,091	0.368	7,771
Equity value			14,714

[1]Continuing value assumptions: growth = 4.0%, return in incremental equity = 11%.

from unrealized gains, we need to include the other comprehensive income items in order to better reflect Acme's economics.

Our $14.6 billion DCF value for Acme is within 10 percent of its actual market value at the time of writing. Its 12.8 forward price-to-earnings ratio is generally in line with peers, as is its implied 1.3 market-to-book ratio. However, Acme's valuation is highly dependent on its ability to invest successfully and create an ongoing stream of capital gains, without which the company would barely create value.

Valuing Insurance Companies from the Inside

If we were to value an insurance company from the inside, we would seek to take the valuation to a greater level of detail on a number of dimensions:

- For a life insurer, we would try to understand its embedded value. This concept—widely used and published in Europe—aims to communicate the value of the insurer's current book of business. It is defined as the present value of the future cash flow from business in force (that is, already-written business) plus the book value of shareholders' equity. Because embedded value incorporates a calculation of NPV, it avoids many of the timing issues inherent in year-on-year profitability calculations. Analysts use embedded value in many contexts, such as calculating multiples and understanding how much of a company's market value comes from existing versus future business.

- For any kind of insurer, we would try to gain a more detailed sense of the company's overall solvency position and whether or not the business has capital above its economic needs and regulatory requirements. If it does, we could incorporate in our valuation scenarios where the company either deploys the excess capital in new businesses or distributes it to shareholders.

- We would also differentiate various lines of business for the company, using internal information about the economic capital in each business. This would most likely include separate valuations of the underwriting functions (and, if possible, a separate valuation of the investment function) to help management understand where value was truly being created, as well as valuations of the separate product lines.

- If possible, we would explicitly model the "run-off triangle" (the expected claims payout per year) per product line. That model would capture the expected claims on existing and future business for each forecast year and give a better sense of profitability by product and by time period.

These more detailed analyses, available only when working with internal data, would give us much greater insight into the value creation of each business unit and/or product of the company in question.

SUMMARY

Valuing financial institutions is difficult. We need extensive inside information before we can truly understand what risks are in the portfolio of a bank or insurer, or where the value is created in their different businesses. Nonetheless, correctly applying the equity cash flow method can help analysts understand a financial institution's performance and its value.

REVIEW QUESTIONS

1. Why should an analyst compute the value of a financial institution by employing the equity cash flow method when the enterprise DCF and economic profit models have been stressed throughout the text?

2. Identify the value drivers embedded in the equity cash flow model. How do the equity cash flow drivers differ from the drivers of the enterprise DCF and the economic profit models?

3. Define duration. Why is duration important both for understanding a financial institution's risk and for analyzing performance?

4. Compare the typical duration of a commercial bank's asset structure to its liability structure. What does the relationship between these two duration measurements suggest to the analyst?

5. Compare the typical duration of a life insurance company's asset structure to its liability structure. What does the relationship between these two duration measurements suggest to the analyst?

6. What are deferred acquisition costs? How are deferred acquisition costs computed? Should deferred acquisition costs be treated the same way that amortization costs are treated in the firm's accounting statements? Should deferred acquisition costs be treated the same way as amortization costs in the computation of enterprise value?

7. Statutory accounting standards differ from GAAP standards for the valuation of many account items. Identify and discuss the importance of two differences between these standards. Would differences between the two standards, with respect to asset valuation and expense recognition, lead to significant differences between a

corporate insider's estimate of value and an external analyst's estimate of corporate value?

8. Define the term *reserves* as it relates to a life insurance company's liability section of the balance sheet. In what way is a life insurance company's reserve position similar to a company's accumulated pension obligation?

9. The following is a very simplified version of Neighborhood Bank System's balance sheet, income statement, and average rates for 2005. Value Neighborhood Bank System, Inc., using the equity cash flow method. Depreciation is $1.434 million for 2005. Neighborhood Bank System, Inc.'s equity beta is 1.20.

Income Statement

	2005	
	Amount	Rate
Interest income	66.919	8.11%
– Interest expense	(25.221)	3.52%
Net interest income	41.698	4.59%
+ Other income	5.120	
– Other expenses	(26.498)	
Net profit before tax	20.320	
– Taxes	(7.721)	38.00%
Net income	12.598	

Balance Sheet

	2005	
	Amount	Rate
Cash reserves	32.411	
Investment securities	378.520	6.93%
Net loans	446.135	9.12%
Net premises, other assets	25.526	
Less: provision for credit losses	(6.281)	
TOTAL ASSETS	876.311	
Interest-bearing deposits	552.892	3.29%
Noninterest-bearing deposits	98.587	
Other short-term liabilities	6.102	
Federal funds purchased	57.300	4.00%
Term borrowings	05.550	4.49%
LIABILITIES	820.431	
SHAREHOLDERS' EQUITY	55.880	13.48%
TOTAL	876.311	

Economic Profit and the
Key Value Driver Formula

In Chapter 3, we convert the growing cash flow perpetuity:

$$V = \frac{FCF_1}{WACC - g}$$

into the key value driver formula:

$$V = \frac{NOPLAT_1 \left(1 - \dfrac{g}{ROIC}\right)}{WACC - g}$$

This representation of value can be rearranged further into a formula based on economic profit. We do this to demonstrate that discounted cash flow is also equivalent to the current book value of invested capital plus the present value of economic profit. A more general (and more technical proof) on their equivalence is provided in Appendix B.

To convert the key value driver formula into a formula based on economic profit, we use the definition of ROIC as NOPLAT divided by invested capital to restate NOPLAT as the product of invested capital (IC) and ROIC:

$$V = \frac{IC_0 \times (ROIC) \times \left(1 - \dfrac{g}{ROIC}\right)}{WACC - g}$$

where IC_0 = Current invested capital

ROIC = NOPLAT/beginning-of-year invested capital

g = Growth in NOPLAT and cash flow

WACC = Weighted average cost of capital

Next, simplify by distributing ROIC in the numerator:

$$V = IC_0 \times \frac{ROIC - g}{WACC - g}$$

This equation more clearly shows two requirements for using the key value driver formula: Both WACC and ROIC must be greater than the growth rate in cash flow. If WACC is less than the growth rate, cash flows grow faster than they can be discounted, and value approaches infinity (perpetuity-based formulas should never be used to value cash flows whose growth rates exceed WACC). Alternatively, if ROIC is less than the growth rate, cash flows are negative, producing a negative value. In actuality, this situation is unlikely; investors would not finance a company that is never expected to return positive cash flow.

To complete the transformation to economic profit, we next add and subtract WACC in the numerator:

$$V = IC_0 \times \frac{ROIC - WACC + WACC - g}{WACC - g}$$

We separate the fraction into two components and then simplify:

$$V = IC_0 \times \frac{ROIC - WACC}{WACC - g} + IC_0 \times \frac{WACC - g}{WACC - g}$$

$$= IC_0 + \frac{IC_0 \times (ROIC - WACC)}{WACC - g}$$

Economic profit is defined as invested capital times the difference of ROIC minus WACC. Substituting this definition into the previous equation leads to our final equation:

$$V = IC_0 + \frac{Economic\ Profit_1}{WACC - g}$$

According to this formula, a company's enterprise value equals the book value of its invested capital plus the present value of all future economic profits (the final term is a growing perpetuity of economic profits). Note that if expected economic profits are zero going forward, the value of a company equals its book value. In addition, if economic profits are expected to be less than zero in the future, then enterprise value should trade at less than the book value of invested capital—an occurrence observed in practice.

Discounted Economic Profit Equals Discounted Free Cash Flow

In this appendix, we provide a generalized proof of the equivalence between discounted cash flow and discounted economic profit. A less technical but specialized proof of equivalence is demonstrated using the key value driver formula in Appendix A. To prove equivalence, start by computing the present value of a periodic stream of cash flow:

$$V = \sum_{t=1}^{\infty} \frac{\text{FCF}_t}{(1 + \text{WACC})^t}$$

where FCF_t = Free cash flow in year t
  WACC = Weighted average cost of capital

Next add and subtract the cumulative sum of all future amounts of invested capital (IC):

$$V = \sum_{t=0}^{\infty} \frac{\text{IC}_t}{(1 + \text{WACC})^t} - \sum_{t=0}^{\infty} \frac{\text{IC}_t}{(1 + \text{WACC})^t} + \sum_{t=1}^{\infty} \frac{\text{FCF}}{(1 + \text{WACC})^t}$$

where IC_t = Invested capital for year t

Next, adjust the previous equation slightly. First, strip invested capital at time zero from the first cumulative sum. Next, convert the second cumulative sum to $t = 1$ to infinity, changing each each t inside the second cumulative sum to $t - 1$. This new representation is identical to the original representation, but will allow us to cancel terms later. The new representation equals:

$$V = IC_0 + \sum_{t=1}^{\infty} \frac{IC_t}{(1+WACC)^t} - \sum_{t=1}^{\infty} \frac{IC_{t-1}}{(1+WACC)^{t-1}} + \sum_{t=1}^{\infty} \frac{FCF}{(1+WACC)^t}$$

Multiply the second cumulative sum by $(1+WACC)/(1+WACC)$. This action converts the exponent $t-1$ in the denominator of the cumulative sum to t. We also substitute for free cash flow in the third cumulative sum, using its definition, NOPLAT less the increase of invested capital:

$$V = IC_0 + \sum_{t=1}^{\infty} \frac{IC_t}{(1+WACC)^t} - \sum_{t=1}^{\infty} \frac{(1+WACC)IC_{t-1}}{(1+WACC)^t} + \sum_{t=1}^{\infty} \frac{NOPLAT - (IC_t - IC_{t-1})}{(1+WACC)^t}$$

Because there is now a consistent denominator across all three cumulative sums, combine the final three terms into a single cumulative sum:

$$V = IC_0 + \sum_{t=1}^{\infty} \frac{IC_t - (1+WACC)IC_{t-1} + NOPLAT - IC_t + IC_{t-1}}{(1+WACC)^t}$$

In the second term of the numerator, we distribute $(1+WACC)\,IC_{t-1}$ into its two components, IC_{t-1} and $WACC(IC_{t-1})$:

$$V = IC_0 + \sum_{t=1}^{\infty} \frac{IC_t - IC_{t-1} - WACC(IC_{t-1}) + NOPLAT - IC_t + IC_{t-1}}{(1+WACC)^t}$$

Simplify by collecting terms:

$$V = IC_0 + \sum_{t=1}^{\infty} \frac{NOPLAT - WACC(IC_{t-1})}{(1+WACC)^t}$$

The numerator is the definition of economic profit; therefore, the result is a valuation based on economic profit:

$$V = IC_0 + \sum_{t=1}^{\infty} \frac{Economic\ Profit_t}{(1+WACC)^t}$$

The enterprise value of a company equals the book value of its invested capital plus the present value of all future economic profits. To calculate the value correctly, you must calculate economic profit using last year's (i.e., the beginning-of-year) invested capital.

The interdependence of invested capital, economic profit, and free cash flow is not surprising. Think of discounted cash flow this way: A portion of future cash flows is required to cover the required return for the investor's capital. The remaining cash flow is either used to grow invested capital (to generate additional future cash flows) or returned to investors as an extra "bonus." This bonus, of course, is valuable, so investors desire (and are willing to pay a premium for) cash flows above the amount required. Subsequently, companies with positive economic profits will trade at a premium to the book value of invested capital.

Adjusted Present Value
Equals Discounted
Free Cash Flow

In Chapter 5, we numerically demonstrate the equivalence of enterprise DCF, adjusted present value, and the cash-flow-to-equity valuation when leverage (as measured by the market-based debt-to-equity ratio) is constant. In this appendix, we demonstrate their equivalence algebraically. To simplify the analysis, we assume cash flows for debt and equity are constant. This way we can use zero-growth perpetuities to analyze the relation between methods.[1]

ENTERPRISE DISCOUNTED CASH FLOW

Enterprise value equals the market value of debt plus the market value of equity:

$$V = D + E$$

Next, multiply the right side of the equation by a complex fraction equivalent to 1. Over the next few steps, the fraction's denominator will be converted into the weighted average cost of capital. We will show later that the numerator equals free cash flow.

$$V = (D + E) \times \left(\frac{CF_d(1 - T_m) + CF_e}{CF_d(1 - T_m) + CF_e} \right)$$

---

[1] For an analysis that applies to more complex situations (i.e., when cash flows can follow any pattern), see J. A. Miles and J. R. Ezzell, "The Weighted Average Cost of Capital, Perfect Capital Markets, and Project Life: A Clarification," *Journal of Financial and Quantitative Analysis*, 15 (1980): 719–730 (for a discussion of enterprise DCF and WACC); and S. C. Myers, "Interactions of Corporate Financing and Investment Decisions: Implications for Capital Budgeting," *Journal of Finance*, 29 (1974): 1–25 (for a discussion of adjusted present value).

where CF$_d$ = Cash flow to debt holders

$\quad$ T_m = Marginal tax rate

$\quad$ CF$_e$ = Cash flow to equity holders

Since cash flow to debt holders is constant, we use a perpetuity to value the debt:

$$D = \frac{CF_d}{k_d}$$

where k_d = Cost of debt

Rearranging this equation to solve for cash flow leads to:

$$CF_d = D \times k_d$$

The same holds true for equity cash flows: CF$_e$ = $E \times k_e$. Substitute these two expressions into the denominator of the value expression:

$$V = (D + E) \times \left(\frac{CF_d(1 - T_m) + CF_e}{D(k_d)(1 - T_m) + E(k_e)} \right)$$

Next, divide the numerator and denominator by $(D + E)$. This will eliminate the first $(D + E)$ expression and place it in the denominator as a divisor. Distributing the term across the denominator leads to:

$$V = \frac{CF_d(1 - T_m) + CF_e}{\dfrac{D}{D + E}(k_d)(1 - T_m) + \dfrac{E}{D + E}(k_e)}$$

$\quad$ The expression in the denominator is the weighted average cost of capital (WACC). Therefore, the equation can be rewritten as:

$$V = \frac{CF_d(1 - T_m) + CF_e}{WACC}$$

such that

$$WACC = \frac{D}{D + E}(k_d)(1 - T_m) + \frac{E}{D + E}(k_e)$$

Note how the after-tax cost of debt and the cost of equity are weighted by each security's *market* weight to enterprise value. This is why market-based values, and not book values, should be used to build the cost of capital.

$\quad$ Next, we focus on the numerator. Assuming only interest is paid out (and that debt is constant and principal payments are rolled over), cash flow to debt holders equals interest paid. This allows us to substitute Interest for CF$_d$. Cash flow to equity (CF$_e$) equals EBIT – Interest – Taxes – Net investment + Increase in debt. Since debt is constant, the last term in cash flow to equity is zero. Substitute the expressions for CF$_d$ and CF$_e$ into the previous equation:

$$V = \frac{\text{Interest}(1 - T_m) + \text{EBIT} - \text{Interest} - \text{Taxes} - \text{Net Investment}}{\text{WACC}}$$

Next, distribute the after-tax interest expression into its two components:

$$V = \frac{\text{Interest} - T_m(\text{Interest}) + \text{EBIT} - \text{Interest} - \text{Taxes} - \text{Net Investment}}{\text{WACC}}$$

Simplify by canceling and rearranging terms. We now have free cash flow in the numerator:

$$V = \frac{\text{EBIT} - (\text{Taxes} + T_m[\text{Interest}]) - \text{Net Investment}}{\text{WACC}}$$

Since NOPLAT is defined as EBIT less all-equity taxes, we can further simplify the equation:[2]

$$V = \frac{\text{NOPLAT} - \text{Net Investment}}{\text{WACC}} = \frac{\text{Free Cash Flow}}{\text{WACC}}$$

This is why free cash flow should be discounted at the weighted average cost of capital to determine enterprise value. Remember, however, that you can only use a constant WACC over time when leverage is expected to remain constant (i.e., debt grows as the business grows). This restriction was implicitly imposed by using securities with constant cash flows.[3]

ADJUSTED PRESENT VALUE

To determine enterprise value using adjusted present value, once again start with $V = D + E$ and multiply by a fraction equal to 1. This time, however, do not include the marginal tax rate in the fraction:

$$V = (D + E) \times \left(\frac{\text{CF}_d + \text{CF}_e}{\text{CF}_d + \text{CF}_e} \right)$$

Following the same process as before, convert each cash flow in the denominator to its present value times its expected return, and divide the fraction by $(D + E)/(D + E)$:

$$V = \frac{\text{CF}_d + \text{CF}_e}{\dfrac{D}{D+E}(k_d) + \dfrac{E}{D+E}(k_e)}$$

[2] All-equity taxes are the hypothetical taxes computed as if the company were financed entirely with equity. They equal reported taxes plus the interest tax shield.
[3] To see this restriction applied in a more general setting, see Miles and Ezzell, "The Weighted Average Cost of Capital," note 1.

In Appendix D, we show that if the company's interest tax shields have the same risk as the company's operating assets (as we would expect when the company maintains a constant capital structure), the fraction's denominator equals k_u, the unlevered cost of equity. Make this substitution into the previous equation:

$$V = \frac{CF_d + CF_e}{k_u}$$

Next, we focus on the numerator, substituting the definitions of cash flow to debt and cash flow to equity as we did for enterprise DCF:

$$V = \frac{\text{Interest} + \text{EBIT} - \text{Interest} - \text{Taxes} - \text{Net Investment}}{k_u}$$

In this equation, the two interest terms cancel, so we simplify by canceling these two terms. We next insert $T_m(\text{Interest}) - T_m(\text{Interest})$ into the numerator of the expression:

$$V = \frac{\text{EBIT} - \text{Taxes} + T_m(\text{Interest}) - T_m(\text{Interest}) - \text{Net Investment}}{k_u}$$

Next, aggregate reported taxes and the negative expression for $T_m(\text{Interest})$ into all-equity taxes. Move the positive expression for $T_m(\text{Interest})$ into a separate fraction:

$$V = \frac{\text{EBIT} - (\text{Taxes} + T_m[\text{Interest}]) - \text{Net Investment}}{k_u} + \frac{T_m(\text{Interest})}{k_u}$$

At this point, we once again have free cash flow in the numerator of the first fraction. The second fraction equals the present value of the interest tax shield. Thus, enterprise value equals free cash flow discounted by the unlevered cost of equity plus the present value of the interest tax shield:

$$V = \frac{\text{Free Cash Flow}}{k_u} + \text{PV(Interest Tax Shield)}$$

This expression is commonly referred to as adjusted present value.

In this simple proof, we assumed tax shields should be discounted at the unlevered cost of equity. This need not be the case. Some financial analysts discount expected interest tax shields at the cost of debt. If you do this, however, free cash flow discounted at the traditional WACC (defined earlier) and adjusted present value will lead to different valuations. In this case, WACC must be adjusted to reflect the alternative assumption concerning the risk of tax shields.

Levering and Unlevering
the Cost of Equity

In Chapter 5, we introduced adjusted present value (APV). To apply APV, first discount free cash flow at the unlevered cost of equity. Then add the present value of any financing side effects, such as the interest tax shield, to this value to determine enterprise value. One key input for APV is the unlevered cost of equity. In this appendix, we derive various formulas that can be used to compute the unlevered cost of equity under different assumptions.

Chapter 10 introduced a second application for the unlevered cost of equity. To determine the cost of equity for use in a company's cost of capital, we did not use raw regression results (because of estimation error). Instead, we relied on an unlevered *industry* beta that was relevered to the company's target capital structure. To build an unlevered industry beta, we use techniques identical to the unlevered cost of equity. We discuss both in this appendix.

UNLEVERED COST OF EQUITY

Franco Modigliani and Merton Miller postulated that the market value of a company's economic assets, such as operating assets (V_u) and tax shields (V_{txa}), should equal the market value of its financial claims, such as debt (D) and equity (E):

$$V_u + V_{txa} = \text{Enterprise Value} = D + E \tag{1}$$

A second result of Modigliani and Miller's work is that the total risk of the company's economic assets, operating and financial, must equal the total risk of the financial claims against those assets:

$$\frac{V_u}{V_u + V_{txa}}(k_u) + \frac{V_{txa}}{V_u + V_{txa}}(k_{txa}) = \frac{D}{D+E}(k_d) + \frac{E}{D+E}(k_e) \tag{2}$$

where k_u = Unlevered cost of equity

k_{txa} = Cost of capital for the company's interest tax shields

k_d = Cost of debt

k_e = Cost of equity

The four terms in this equation represent operating assets, tax assets, debt, and equity, respectively.

Since k_u is unobservable, we must solve for it, using the equation's other inputs. The required return on tax shields, k_{txa}, is also unobservable. With two unknowns and only one equation, we must therefore impose additional restrictions to solve for k_u. If debt is a constant proportion of enterprise value (i.e., debt grows as the business grows), k_{txa} should equal k_u. Imposing this restriction leads to:

$$\frac{V_u}{V_u + V_{txa}}(k_u) + \frac{V_{txa}}{V_u + V_{txa}}(k_u) = \frac{D}{D+E}(k_d) + \frac{E}{D+E}(k_e)$$

Combining terms on the left side generates an equation for the unlevered cost of equity when debt is a constant proportion of enterprise value:

$$k_u = \frac{D}{D+E}(k_d) + \frac{E}{D+E}(k_e) \tag{3}$$

Unlevered Cost of Equity When k_{txa} Equals k_d

Some financial analysts model the required return on interest tax shields equal to the cost of debt. In this case, equation 2 can be expressed as follows:

$$\frac{V_u}{V_u + V_{txa}}(k_u) + \frac{V_{txa}}{V_u + V_{txa}}(k_d) = \frac{D}{D+E}(k_d) + \frac{E}{D+E}(k_e)$$

To solve for k_u, multiply both sides by enterprise value:

$$V_u k_u + V_{txa} k_d = D k_d + E k_e$$

and move $V_{txa} k_d$ to the right side of the equation:

$$V_u k_u = (D - V_{txa}) k_d + E k_e$$

To eliminate V_u from the left side of the equation, we rearrange equation 1 to $V_u = D - V_{txa} + E$ and divide both sides by this value:

$$k_u = \frac{D - V_{txa}}{D - V_{txa} + E}(k_d) + \frac{E}{D - V_{txa} + E}(k_e) \tag{4}$$

Exhibit D.1 The Unlevered Cost of Equity

	Dollar level of debt fluctuates	Dollar level of debt is constant
Tax shields have the same risk as operating assets $k_{txa} = k_u$	$k_u = \dfrac{D}{D+E}k_d + \dfrac{E}{D+E}k_e$	$k_u = \dfrac{D}{D+E}k_d + \dfrac{E}{D+E}k_e$
Tax shields have the same risk as debt $k_{txa} = k_d$	$k_u = \dfrac{D-V_{txa}}{D-V_{txa}+E}k_d + \dfrac{E}{D-V_{txa}+E}k_e$	$k_u = \dfrac{D\left(1-T_m\right)}{D\left(1-T_m\right)+E}k_d + \dfrac{E}{D\left(1-T_m\right)+E}k_e$

Note: k_e = cost of equity
k_d = cost of debt
k_u = unlevered cost of equity
k_{txa} = cost of capital for tax shields
T_m = marginal tax rate
D = market value of debt
E = market value of equity
V_{txa} = present value of tax shields

Equation 4 mirrors equation 2 closely. It differs from equation 2 only in that the market value of debt is reduced by the present value of expected tax shields.

Exhibit D.1 summarizes the four methods to estimate the unlevered cost of equity. The two formulas in the top row assume that the risk associated with interest tax shields equals the risk of operations. When this is true, whether debt is constant or expected to change, the formula remains the same. The bottom-row formulas assume that the risk of interest tax shields equals the risk of debt. On the left, future debt can take on any value. On the right, an additional restriction is imposed that debt (in dollars) remains constant.

LEVERED COST OF EQUITY

In certain situations, you will have already estimated the unlevered cost of equity and need to relever the cost of equity to a new target structure. In this case, use equation 2 to solve for the levered cost of equity, k_e:

$$\frac{V_u}{V_u + V_{txa}}\left(k_u\right) + \frac{V_{txa}}{V_u + V_{txa}}\left(k_{txa}\right) = \frac{D}{D+E}\left(k_d\right) + \frac{E}{D+E}\left(k_e\right)$$

Multiply both sides by enterprise value:

$$V_u\left(k_u\right) + V_{txa}\left(k_{txa}\right) = D\left(k_d\right) + E\left(k_e\right)$$

Next, move $D(k_d)$ to the opposite side of the equation and divide the entire equation by the market value of equity, E:

$$k_e = \frac{V_u}{E}(k_u) - \frac{D}{E}(k_d) + \frac{V_{txa}}{E}(k_{txa})$$

To eliminate V_u from the left side of the equation, rearrange equation 1 to $V_u = D - V_{txa} + E$, and use this identity to replace V_u:

$$k_e = \frac{D - V_{txa} + E}{E}(k_u) - \frac{D}{E}(k_d) + \frac{V_{txa}}{E}(k_{txa})$$

Distribute the first fraction into its component parts:

$$k_e = k_u - \frac{V_{txa}}{E}(k_u) + \frac{D}{E}(k_u) - \frac{D}{E}(k_d) + \frac{V_{txa}}{E}(k_{txa}) \tag{5}$$

and consolidate terms. This leads to the general equation for the cost of equity.

$$k_e = k_u + \frac{D}{E}(k_u - k_d) - \frac{V_{txa}}{E}(k_u - k_{txa}) \tag{6}$$

If debt is a constant proportion of enterprise value (i.e., debt grows as the business grows), k_u will equal k_{txa}, and the final term drops out:

$$k_e = k_u + \frac{D}{E}(k_u - k_d)$$

Levered Cost of Equity When k_{txa} Equals k_d

The same analysis can be repeated under the assumption that the risk of interest tax shields equals the risk of debt. Rather than repeat the first few steps, we start with equation 5:

$$k_e = k_u - \frac{V_{txa}}{E}(k_u) + \frac{D}{E}(k_u) - \frac{D}{E}(k_d) + \frac{V_{txa}}{E}(k_{txa})$$

To solve for k_e, we replace k_{txa} with k_d:

$$k_e = k_u - \frac{V_{txa}}{E}(k_u) + \frac{D}{E}(k_u) - \frac{D}{E}(k_d) + \frac{V_{txa}}{E}(k_d)$$

and consolidate like terms:

$$k_e = k_u + \frac{D - V_{txa}}{E}(k_u) - \frac{D - V_{txa}}{E}(k_d)$$

Finally, we further simplify the equation by once again combining like terms:

$$k_e = k_u + \frac{D - V_{txa}}{E}(k_u - k_d)$$

We now have the levered cost of equity for a company whose debt can take any value but whose interest tax shields have the same risk as the company's debt.

Exhibit D.2 summarizes the formulas that can be used to estimate the levered cost of equity. The top row in the exhibit contains formulas that assume k_{txa} equals k_u. The bottom row contains formulas that assume k_{txa} equals k_d. The formulas on the left side are flexible enough to handle any future capital structure but require valuing the tax shields separately. The formulas on the right side assume the dollar level of debt is fixed over time.

LEVERED BETA

Similar to the cost of capital, the weighted average beta of a company's assets, both operating and financial, must equal the weighted average beta of its financial claims:

$$\frac{V_u}{V_u + V_{txa}}(\beta_u) + \frac{V_{txa}}{V_u + V_{txa}}(\beta_{txa}) = \frac{D}{D + E}(\beta_d) + \frac{E}{D + E}(\beta_e)$$

Exhibit D.2 The Levered Cost of Equity

	Dollar level of debt fluctuates	Dollar level of debt is constant
Tax shields have the same risk as operating assets $k_{txa} = k_u$	$k_e = k_u + \frac{D}{E}(k_u - k_d)$	$k_e = k_u + \frac{D}{E}(k_u - k_d)$
Tax shields have the same risk as debt $k_{txa} = k_d$	$k_e = k_u + \frac{D - V_{txa}}{E}(k_u - k_d)$	$k_e = k_u + (1 - T_m)\frac{D}{E}(k_u - k_d)$

Note: k_e = cost of equity
k_d = cost of debt
k_u = unlevered cost of equity
k_{txa} = cost of capital for tax shields
T_m = marginal tax rate
D = market value of debt
E = market value of equity
V_{txa} = present value of tax shields

Exhibit D.3 Levered Beta

	Dollar level of debt fluctuates	Dollar level of debt is constant and debt is risky	Dollar level of debt is constant and debt is risk free[1]
Tax shields have the same risk as operating assets $\beta_{txa} = \beta_u$	$\beta_e = \beta_u + \dfrac{D}{E}\left(\beta_u - \beta_d\right)$	$\beta_e = \beta_u + \dfrac{D}{E}\left(\beta_u - \beta_d\right)$	$\beta_e = \left(1 + \dfrac{D}{E}\right)\beta_u$
Tax shields have the same risk as debt $\beta_{txa} = \beta_d$	$\beta_e = \beta_u + \dfrac{D - V_{txa}}{E}\left(\beta_u - \beta_d\right)$	$\beta_e = \beta_u + \left(1 - T_m\right)\dfrac{D}{E}\left(\beta_u - \beta_d\right)$	$\beta_e = \left(1 + \left(1 - T_m\right)\dfrac{D}{E}\right)\beta_u$

Note: β_e = cost of equity
β_d = cost of debt
β_u = unlevered cost of equity
β_{txa} = cost of capital for tax shields
T_m = marginal tax rate
D = market value of debt
E = market value of equity
V_{txa} = present value of tax shields

[1]When $\beta_{txa} = \beta_u$, the resulting formula holds for all debt patterns, not just constant debt.

Since the form of this equation is identical to the cost of capital, we can rearrange the formula using the same process as previously described. Rather than repeat the analysis, we provide a summary of levered beta in Exhibit D.3. As expected, the first two columns are identical in form to Exhibit D.2, except that the beta (β) replaces the cost of capital (k).

By using beta, we can make one additional simplification. If debt is risk free, the beta of debt is 0, and β_d drops out. This allows us to convert the following general equation (when β_{txa} equals β_u):

$$\beta_e = \beta_u + \frac{D}{E}(\beta_u - \beta_d)$$

into the following:

$$\beta_e = \left(1 + \frac{D}{E}\right)\beta_u$$

This last equation is an often-applied formula for levering (and unlevering) beta when the risk of interest tax shields equals the risk of operating assets *and* the company's debt is risk free. For investment grade companies, debt is near risk free, so any errors using this formula will be small. If the company is highly leveraged, however, errors can be large. In this situation, estimate the beta of debt, and use the more general version of the formula.

Leverage and the Price-Earnings Multiple

This appendix demonstrates that the P/E ratio of a levered company depends on its unlevered (all-equity) P/E ratio, its cost of debt, and its leverage ratio. When the unlevered P/E ratio is less than $1/k_d$ (where k_d equals the cost of debt), the P/E ratio falls as leverage rises. Conversely, when the unlevered P/E is greater than $1/k_d$, the P/E ratio rises with increased leverage.

In this proof we assume the company faces no taxes and no distress costs. We do this to avoid modeling the complex relationship between debt-to-value and enterprise value. Instead, our goal is to show that there is a systematic relation between debt-to-value and the price-earnings ratio.

STEP 1

To build the relation between P/Es and leverage, start with the definition of an unlevered P/E ratio (PE_u). When the company is entirely financed with equity, its enterprise value equals its equity value, and its NOPLAT equals its net income:

$$PE_u = \frac{V_{ENT}}{NOPLAT_{t+1}}$$

This equation can be rearranged to solve for the enterprise value, which we will use in the next step:

$$V_{ENT} = NOPLAT_{t+1} \times PE_u \qquad (1)$$

STEP 2

Next, we define net income as a function of NOPLAT. For a company with leverage, net income equals NOPLAT less interest payments. The amount of interest equals

725

the cost of debt times the amount of debt, which can be defined by multiplying enterprise value by the debt-to-value ratio:

$$NI_{t+1} = \text{NOPLAT}_{t+1} - V_{\text{ENT}} \left(\frac{D}{V} \right) k_d$$

At this point, we substitute equation 1 for the enterprise value,

$$NI_{t+1} = \text{NOPLAT}_{t+1} - \text{NOPLAT}_{t+1} \left(PE_u \right) \left(\frac{D}{V} \right) k_d$$

and factor NOPLAT into a single term:

$$NI_{t+1} = \text{NOPLAT}_{t+1} \left(1 - (PE_u) \left(\frac{D}{V} \right) k_d \right) \qquad (2)$$

STEP 3

At this point, we are ready to solve for the company's price-to-earnings ratio. Since price-to-earnings is based on equity values, we first convert enterprise value to equity value. To do this, we once again start with equation 1:

$$V_{\text{ENT}} = \text{NOPLAT}_{t+1} \times PE_u$$

This time, however, we focus on the value of equity. Thus, to convert enterprise value into equity value, we multiply both sides by 1 minus the debt-to-value ratio (which equals the equity-to-value ratio):

$$V_{\text{ENT}} \left(1 - \frac{D}{V} \right) = \text{NOPLAT}_{t+1} \times PE_u \times \left(1 - \frac{D}{V} \right)$$

Next, we use equation 2 to eliminate NOPLAT:

$$E = \frac{NI_{t+1} \times PE_u \times \left(1 - \dfrac{D}{V} \right)}{1 - \left(PE_u \right) \left(\dfrac{D}{V} \right) k_d}$$

Dividing both sides by net income results in the levered P/E ratio:

$$\frac{E}{NI_{t+1}} = \frac{PE_u - PE_u \left(\dfrac{D}{V} \right)}{1 - \left(PE_u \right) \left(\dfrac{D}{V} \right) k_d}$$

At this point, we have a relation between equity value and net income, which depends on the unlevered P/E, the debt-to-value ratio, and the cost of debt. Debt to value, however, is in both the numerator and the denominator, so it is difficult to distinguish how leverage affects the levered P/E ratio. To eliminate the debt-to-value ratio in the numerator, we use a few algebraic tricks. First, we multiply both the numerator and denominator by k_d:

$$\frac{E}{NI_{t+1}} = \frac{PE_u k_d - PE_u \left(\frac{D}{V}\right) k_d}{k_d \left(1 - (PE_u)\left(\frac{D}{V}\right) k_d\right)}$$

Next, we subtract and add 1 (a net difference of 0) in the numerator:

$$\frac{E}{NI_{t+1}} = \frac{\left(PE_u k_d - 1\right) + \left(1 - PE_u \left(\frac{D}{V}\right) k_d\right)}{k_d \left(1 - (PE_u)\left(\frac{D}{V}\right) k_d\right)}$$

After separating the numerator into two distinct terms, we can eliminate the components of the right-hand term by canceling them with the denominator. This allows us to remove debt to value from the numerator:

$$\frac{E}{NI_{t+1}} = \frac{\left(PE_u k_d - 1\right)}{k_d \left(1 - (PE_u)\left(\frac{D}{V}\right) k_d\right)} + \frac{1}{k_d}$$

Next, we divide both the numerator and denominator of the first term by k_d:

$$\frac{E}{NI_{t+1}} = \frac{1}{k_d} + \frac{PE_u - \dfrac{1}{k_d}}{1 - (PE_u)\left(\frac{D}{V}\right) k_d}$$

Finally, we multiply the numerator and denominator of the second term by -1:

$$\frac{E}{NI_{t+1}} = \frac{1}{k_d} + \frac{\dfrac{1}{k_d} - PE_u}{\left(\frac{D}{V}\right) k_d (PE_u) - 1}$$

As seen in the above expression, a company's P/E ratio is a function of its unlevered P/E ratio, its cost of debt, and its debt-to-value ratio. When the unlevered P/E ratio equals the reciprocal of the cost of debt, the numerator of the fraction equals zero, and leverage has no effect on the P/E ratio. For companies with large unlevered P/Es, P/E systematically increases with leverage. Conversely, companies with small unlevered P/Es would exhibit a drop as leverage rises.

Index

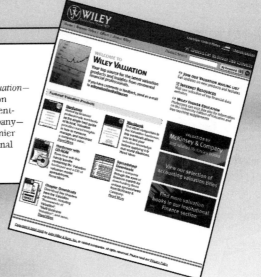

Cartridge Pen .